Plays

Volume One

Luigi Pirandello

ONEWORLD
CLASSICS

ONEWORLD CLASSICS LTD
London House
243-253 Lower Mortlake Road
Richmond
Surrey TW9 2LL
United Kingdom
www.oneworldclassics.com

The translations (now revised for the present edition) of *Six Characters in Search of an Author*, *As You Desire Me*, *Clothe the Naked*, *Think It Over, Giacomino!*, *Lazarus*, *Limes from Sicily* and *The Man with the Flower in His Mouth* first published in Pirandello's *Collected Plays* (Vols. 1–4) by John Calder (Publishers) Ltd, 1987–1996

All the translations contained in this volume © the relevant translators

Cover image: Peppe Aveni

ISBN: 978-1-84749-144-2

Printed in Great Britain by CPI Antony Rowe

Contents

Plays

Volume One

Introduction

Surprisingly little seems to be known in Britain about Luigi Pirandello, who died in 1946, and of whom *The Times* said: "It is largely to him that the theatre owes liberation, for good or ill, from what Desmond MacCarthy called 'the inevitable limitations of the modern drama, the falsifications which result from cramming scenes into acts and tying incidents down to times and places'." Only a few of his major works have been published in English to date, some of which are not direct translations, but the result of British or American writers who neither spoke nor understood Italian, who commissioned a literal translation, and then reconstructed the author's statements in the light in which they themselves saw them.

Pirandello was born at Caos in Sicily in 1867. He studied letters at Palermo University and later in Rome. For many years he taught at a girls' school, living in comparative poverty and growing steadily unhappier in his work. His marriage ended in disaster when his wife became mentally unbalanced and had to be sent to an institution. His literary efforts began with poems and short stories, and later he wrote novels. He did not start writing seriously for the theatre until 1915 at the age of forty-eight, after which he gave to the stage no fewer than forty-three plays in Italian and several in Sicilian.

For a number of years he was in charge of his own theatrical company which had as its leaders Ruggero Ruggeri and Marta Abba, and many of his plays were written as tailor-made articles for them and for the rest of his group. Despite the severe lack of finance, he never succumbed to writing plays which conformed to the style and idiom of the more successful dramatists of his time. He deliberately created anti-heroes. His protagonists are like "soldiers who have been beaten in their first battle and have no belief in the future"!

Having lost a considerable sum of money with his own company, and become greatly disillusioned because his native Italy considered him "too original for the box office" (often his plays were translated and performed abroad long before they saw the footlights in their own language) and already in his seventies, Pirandello suddenly announced that Europe had grown too old for him, that it could boast of only one other young brain (Bernard Shaw) and that he would take himself off to a country of new ideas – and then journeyed to America.

Pirandello was a fiery, passionate man who had reached his own particular outlook on life through adversity and years of tortured wondering at the true significance of reality. His primary concern was with the illusions and self-deceptions of mankind and the nature of identity. His works grew from his own torment, and through his genius they came to speak for all the tormented and potentially to all the tormented, that is to all men. He delighted in creating an unusual but logical situation – developing it seemingly illogically – and by continually tossing the coin until both sides had been clearly revealed, managing to convince his audience that his unconventional and not very credible treatment was in fact wholly logical and convincing.

Many of his plays were written in the style known to the Italians as "*grottesco*": comedies developed tragically or tragedies developed comically. Nearly all spring from intensely dramatic situations – situations in which passion, love and tragedy make their presence strongly felt.

In Britain theatre productions of his works have been few and far between, and this may be due partly to the fact that directors and "adaptors" sometimes assume "he is going to be far too difficult for the audience so it will be up to us to put that right"! By approaching the text with the preconceived notion that a particular interpretation must shine like a beacon between author and audience in order to elucidate matters, one often succeeds merely in confusing the issue further. There have been examples of this author's brilliantly cynical humour, behind whose mask we are meant to see our own selves, being deliberately distorted to the level of unacceptable farce in an attempt to "clarify".

If Pirandello's plays were approached more simply, were permitted to play themselves more and did not have the Latin sentiment and human compassion ironed out by their interpreters, perhaps the fear that one may not be able to follow him would be removed from the minds of many of our theatregoers. It would be found that his works, as Kenneth Tynan once wrote: "wear their fifty-odd years as if they were swaddling clothes", and might then find themselves a regular niche in our commercial theatre.

Robert Rietti

Six Characters in Search of an Author

Sei personaggi in cerca d'autore (1921)

Translated by Felicity Firth

Pirandello's Introduction

For a great many years now, though it seems no time at all, I have been assisted in my artistic labours by a sprightly young helpmate, whose work remains as fresh today as when she first entered my service.

Her name is Imagination.

There is something malicious and subversive about her, as her preference for dressing in black might suggest; indeed, her style is generally felt to be bizarre. What people are less ready to believe is that in everything she does there is a seriousness of purpose and an unvarying method. She delves into her pocket and brings out a jester's jingling cap, rams it onto her flaming coxcomb of a head and is gone. She is off to somewhere different every day. Her great delight is to search out the world's unhappiest people and to bring them home for me to turn into stories and novels and plays; men, women and children who have got themselves into every conceivable kind of fix, whose plans have miscarried and whose hopes have been betrayed; people, in fact, who are often very disturbing to deal with.

Well, some years ago, this assistant, this Imagination of mine, had the regrettable inspiration, or it could have been the ill-fated whim, to bring to my door an entire family; where or how she got hold of them I have no idea, but she reckoned that their story would furnish me with a subject for a magnificent novel.

I found myself confronted by a man of about fifty, wearing a dark jacket and light trousers, grim-visaged, with a look of irritability and humiliation in his eyes. With him was a poor woman in widow's weeds holding two children by the hand, a four-year-old girl on one side and a boy of not much more than ten on the other. Next came a rather loud and immodest young woman, also in black, which in her case contrived to look vulgarly dressy and suggestive. She was a-quiver with a brittle, biting anger, clearly directed against the mortified old man and against a youth of about twenty who stood detached from the others, wrapped up in himself, apparently contemptuous of the whole party. So here they were, the Six Characters, just as they appear on the stage at the beginning of the play. And they set about telling me the whole sad series of events, partly in turns, but often speaking all together, cutting in on each other, shouting each other down. They yelled their explanations at me, flung their unruly passions in my face, just as they do in the play with the luckless Producer.

Can any author ever explain how or why a character came to be born in his imagination? The mystery of artistic creation is the mystery of birth itself. A woman in love may desire to become a mother, but this desire by itself, however intense, will not make her one. One fine day she finds she is to be a mother, but she has no precise indication of when this came about. In the same way an artist, as he lives, takes into himself numerous germs of life, and he, too, is completely unable to say how or why at a given moment one of these vital germs gets lodged in his imagination to become in just the same way a living creature, though on a higher plane of life, above the vicissitudes of everyday existence.

I can only say that, having in no way searched them out, I found myself confronted by six living, palpable, audibly breathing human beings: the same six characters you now see upon the stage. They stood before me waiting, each one nursing his own particular torment, bound together by the mode of their birth and the intertwining of their fortunes, waiting for me to usher them into the world of art and make of their persons, their passions and their adventures a novel or drama, or at least a short story.

They had been born alive and they were asking to live.

Now I have to explain that for me as a writer it has never been enough to portray a man or a woman, however individual or exceptional, just for the sake of portraying them; happy or sad, I cannot just tell a story for the sake of telling it or describe a landscape simply as a creative exercise.

There are writers, quite a lot of writers, who like doing this. It satisfies them, and they ask no more. They are by nature what one might properly term historical writers.

But others go further. They feel a deep-seated inward urge to concern themselves only with persons, happenings or scenes which are permeated with what one might call a particular sense of life and so with some sort of universal significance. These, properly, are philosophical writers.

I have the misfortune to belong to this second category.

I detest the kind of symbolic art where all spontaneous movement is suppressed and where the representation is reduced to mechanistic allegory; it is self-defeating and misleading; once a work is given an allegorical slant you are as good as saying that it is only to be taken as a fairy tale; in itself it contains no factual or imaginative truth; it is simply there to demonstrate some sort of moral truth. This kind of allegorical symbolism will never answer the innermost need of the philosophical writer, apart from certain occasions where a fine irony is intended, as in Ariosto for instance. Allegorical symbolism springs from conceptual thought; it is concept, recreated as image, or striving to recreate itself as image. The philosophical writer, on the other hand, is looking for value and meaning in the image itself, while allowing the image to retain its independent validity and artistic wholeness.

Now, however hard I tried, I simply could not find this kind of meaning in the six characters. Consequently I decided there was no point in bringing them to life.

I kept thinking: I have given my readers enough trouble with all my hundreds of stories; why heap more trouble upon them with the sad story of this unhappy lot?

And so thinking I put them out of my mind. Or rather, I made every effort to do so.

But one does not give birth to a character for nothing.

Creatures of my mind, those six were already living a life which was their own and mine no longer, a life I was no longer in a position to refuse them.

And so it was that, while I went on grimly determined to expunge them from my consciousness, they, who by now had almost completely broken free of their narrative context, fictional characters magically transported outside the pages of a book, were carrying on with their own lives. They would pick on certain moments of my day to appear before me in the solitude of my study, and one by one, or two at a time, they would try to entice me, suggesting various scenes I might write or describe and how to get the best out of them, or pointing out unusual aspects of their story which people might find particularly novel or interesting, and so it went on.

Each time, for a moment, I would let myself be won over, and whenever I relented a little they would draw strength from my weakness and come back with fresh arguments and I would find myself near to being

LUIGI PIRANDELLO · PLAYS VOL I

convinced. And so, as it became increasingly difficult for me to get rid of them, their task of tempting me became increasingly easy. There came a point where they had become a positive obsession. Then suddenly I hit on a way out.

Why not write a play, I thought, based on the unprecedented case of an author who refuses to allow a certain set of characters to live, and the plight of these characters who, being fully alive in his imagination, cannot reconcile themselves to being excluded from the world of art? They have already detached themselves from me; they have their own life; they have acquired speech and movement; by their own efforts, by struggling against me for their lives, they have emerged as fully-fledged dramatic characters, autonomous and articulate. They already see themselves as such; they have learnt to defend themselves against me; they are capable of defending themselves against anyone. Well then, why not let them go where dramatic characters usually go to live: put them on a stage. And see what happens.

And that is what I did. And what came out of it was an inevitable hotchpotch of tragedy, comedy, fantasy and realism in a completely original, and extraordinarily complex humoristic situation: that of a drama willing itself to be staged, determined at all costs to find a means of expression in the autonomous, living, speaking characters who embody it and suffer it in their inmost selves, and of the comedy resulting from the abortive effort at improvised theatrical realization. The surprise, first of all, on the part of the wretched company of actors, engaged in a daytime rehearsal of a play on a stage stripped bare of flats and scenery; surprise and blank incredulity on being faced by the six who introduce themselves as characters in search of an author and then this instinctive quickening of interest when the Mother in her black veil suddenly collapses in a faint and they get a glimpse of the drama encompassed by her and the other members of this extraordinary family, a dark ambiguous drama which comes crashing unannounced onto an empty stage in no way prepared to receive it and then the gradual intensification of their interest as the conflicting passions explode in turn, the Father's, then the Stepdaughter's, the Son's and the poor Mother's; passions, as I say, which vie to do each other down with a tragic lacerating fury.

And here it is, the universal meaning previously sought in vain in my six characters. They have found it; by going onto the stage by themselves

they have uncovered it in themselves, in the frenzy of the desperate battle waged by each one against the others, and by all of them against the
Producer and actors who do not understand them.

Unintentionally, inadvertently, each one of them, defending himself
in a state of considerable mental agitation against the recriminations
of the others, shows himself to be tormented by the same fierce sources
of suffering that have racked my own spirit for years: the delusion of
reciprocal understanding hopelessly based on the hollow abstraction
of words; the multiple nature of every human personality, given all the
possible ways of being inherent in each one of us; and finally the tragic
built-in conflict between ever-moving, ever-changing life, and the im-
mutability of form which fixes it.

The six characters give the impression of being on different planes, as
if they were not all realized to the same degree. This is not just because
some have leading roles and others have supporting ones; that would be
a basic matter of the structural perspective proper to any narrative or
dramatic work. Nor, given their purpose, can they be said to be incom-
pletely formed. All six are at the same point of artistic realization; all
six are on the same plane of reality, the imaginative plane on which my
play is set. But the Father, the Stepdaughter and even the Son are realized
as Mind or Spirit; the Mother is realized as Nature; and the last two are
realized as "presences": the Boy who is an onlooker but for his single
gesture, and the completely static Little Girl. This places the characters
in a new perspective. An instinctive prompting had told me I must make
some of them appear to be more fully realized artistically and others
less so; others, again, were to be represented by the barest outline; there,
simply, as part of what happens in the story. The most alive, the most
fully realized, are the Father and the Stepdaughter; these two are the
natural leaders who dominate the play, dragging along behind them the
practically dead weight of the others: the demurring Son, the submissive,
suffering Mother, and on either side of her the two children who consist
of little more than their appearance and have to be led by the hand.

This was the point. They had to appear at the exact stage of development each had reached in the author's imagination at the moment when
he decided to be rid of them.

Thinking back on it now, it seems little short of a miracle that I intuitively sensed the necessity for this, blindly hit on the solution with my
new perspective, and actually made it work. And indeed the play was

conceived quite literally in one of those flashes of imaginative illumination when all the elements of the spirit are miraculously in tune and work together in God-given concert. It would be quite impossible for any human brain, coming at it cold, however strenuous its endeavours, to fathom and fulfil all the demands made by the form of this play. And this is why the following explanations of the play's sum and substance are not to be taken as an apologia for preconceived authorial intentions, dating from the outset of composition, but must be looked on as discoveries which I have been able to make since writing it, returning to it with a mind refreshed.

I wanted to show six characters who are looking for an author. The play cannot be performed because the author they are looking for is missing; so instead we have the comedy of their abortive search, with all the tragic overtones which stem from the fact of their having been rejected.

Can it be done? How do you represent a character you have rejected? Obviously you can only give him expression once he has taken shape in your imagination. And this is exactly how the six characters took shape. They were fully realized in my imagination as rejects: in search of another author.

I must make clear what it is that I have rejected: not the characters in themselves, obviously, but their drama, doubtless of paramount interest to them, but which did not interest me in the slightest, for the reasons I have already given.

But think what your drama means to you if you are a character.

If you are a creature of art or of the imagination, your drama is your means of existence. You exist as a character only in the context of, and by reason of, your drama. The drama is the character's *raison d'être*, his vital function; without it he would cease to be.

In dealing with the six characters, I accepted their being, while rejecting their reason for being. I isolated the organism and asked of it, not its original function but a different, more complex function, in which the original one was no more than one factor amongst others. This created a terrible and desperate situation, especially for the Father and the Stepdaughter, who crave life more intensely than the others, and have a fuller awareness of their status as characters, a status which gives them an absolute need of a drama, their own drama, of course, the only one they can imagine for themselves, but which they have seen rejected. It is an "impossible" situation, one which they feel they must escape from at all costs; their life or death depends on it. It is true that I provided them with another *raison d'être*, another function, the one offered by the "impossible" situation, the drama of being rejected characters in search of an author. But having had a life of their own already, the idea of this new *raison d'être* was way beyond their comprehension. Never could they imagine that this might now be their true essential function and the condition of their existence. If someone were to tell them this, they would simply not believe it. It is impossible to believe that our sole reason for living lies in a torment which we find both unjust and inexplicable.

In the light of all this I cannot imagine how my critics justify their objection to the character of the Father on the grounds that he oversteps the bounds of his function as a character and usurps, at times, the role of author. I have a gift for understanding those who do not understand me, and this tells me that the objection arises from the fact that the character expresses as his own a mental anguish which is recognizably mine. Which is a perfectly natural thing and of absolutely no significance. Quite apart from the fact that the Father's mental anguish springs from causes which are worlds away from the drama of my own personal circumstances, and is suffered and lived through for his reasons and not mine, a consideration which alone destroys the validity of the criticism, I would like to point out a distinction. There is a clear difference between my own inherent mental anguish which I can quite legitimately reflect in a character, as an organic part of him, and the activity engaged in by my mind in the creation of this work, the activity which has as its end product the drama of the six characters in search of an author. Now if the Father were collaborating in this activity, if he were actually helping to create this play about being an authorless character, then, and only then, would it be fair to say that he was usurping the author's role and open to criticism on those grounds. But the Father has not created his own status as "character in search of an author"; he suffers it. He suffers it as an inexplicable disaster and as a situation to be rebelled against and rectified with every resource he can muster. So this is what he is then, a "character in search of an author" purely and simply, even if he does claim my mental anguish as his own. If he were collaborating in the author's act of creation, he would have no problem in understanding the disaster which has befallen him; he would see himself as a viable character, conceived, certainly, as a rejected character, but the product of a poet's imagination like any other. He would then have no reason to agonize over his desperate search for someone to confirm and formulate his existence as a character. I mean, he would accept quite happily the reason for being his author has given him, and stop worrying about any he might give himself; he could snap his fingers at the Producer and his troupe instead of regarding them as a lifeline.

There is one character who is completely untroubled by this need simply to live, to live for the sake of living. It never occurs to her that she is not alive. It has never crossed her mind to wonder how she is alive, by what means or in what sense. She has no notion that she is a character because she is never, even momentarily, outside her "part". She does not know she has a "part".

Her unawareness is a natural part of her. Her role as Mother requires her to be close to nature; it does not demand any mental exertion; she does not exist as mind; she lives in a perpetual state of unresolved emotion which renders her incapable of realizing what she is, of knowing she is a character. But even so, she too is searching for an author in her own way and for her own reasons. At one point she seems glad to have been brought along to meet the Producer. Is it because she hopes he can give her life? No: it is because she hopes he will make her perform a scene with her son, into which she herself would put life, her own life, all that she can of it. But it is a scene which does not exist. It has never taken place and never could. Her hope of playing it shows how totally unaware she is that she is a character and of the limitations of the life available to her, fixed and predetermined in every moment, every gesture, every word.

She turns up on the stage with the other characters, but without any idea of what they are making her do. She obviously has her own view of the manic desire for life which possesses both her husband and her daughter and is the reason for her being here at all: as far as her tormenting and tormented spouse is concerned, this is just another of his unusual, weird and wonderful fixations; in her poor misguided daughter's case, she is filled with sheer horror at what she sees as fresh evidence of wantonness and rebellion. The Mother is completely passive. Everything about her circumstances, her life and what she thinks of it all is conveyed by the others; only once does she contradict them, and that is when her maternal instinct rises and rebels and she feels bound to explain that she never wanted to abandon either her son or her husband; her son was taken from her and her husband forced her to go. But she is simply setting the factual record straight; her knowledge and understanding are nil.

She is, in essence, Nature: Nature fixed and perceived as Mother.

This character did afford me one satisfaction which was new and must not be forgotten. Nearly all my critics, having in the past indiscriminately labelled my characters as peculiarly and irredeemably "inhuman", have had the goodness to say "with real pleasure" of this one, that here at last my imagination has produced a truly human figure. The reason for their compliment I think is this: that the poor old Mother, being all Nature, all Mother, and completely tied in her behaviour by her equation with this role, with no opportunity for the free exercise of the mind, emerges more or less as a chunk of flesh, fully alive in all her maternal functions: procreating; feeding, tending and loving her young, but with no need whatsoever to exercise her brain. And in this she is seen to be the realization of the true and perfect "human type". This must be so, since there appears to be no attribute of the human organism more superfluous than the mind.

But the critics, in spite of their nice compliment, have pretty well dismissed the Mother without exploring in any depth the complex of poetic values represented by this character in the play. I can grant that she is a very human figure because she is mindless and so is either quite unaware of being what she is or simply does not question it. But the fact that she does not know she is a character does not stop her being one. And in my play, this is her drama. And its most vital expression comes leaping out of her in her cry to the Producer when he is trying to make her realize that it has all happened already, and there is no cause now to shed any more tears, and she cries out: "No, it's happening now! It's happening all the time! My agony isn't made up! I am living my agony constantly, every moment; I am alive and it is alive and it keeps coming back, again and again, as fresh as the first time." She feels this, but she does not know that she feels it; it is experienced as something inexplicable, but felt in such a terrible way that it does not even occur to her that it is something that needs explaining, either to herself or to the others. She feels it, full stop. She feels it as pain and it comes straight out as pain in her cry. This is her way of giving utterance to the fixedness of life, which torments the Father and the Stepdaughter in quite a different way. These two are Mind where the Mother is Nature. Mind either rebels against fixity or seeks to exploit it; Nature, unless stirred up by sense, responds to it with tears.

The inherent conflict between the movement of life and the fixity of form is an inexorable condition not only of the spiritual order but of the physical order as well. Life can only come about by fixing itself in our corporeal form; it then proceeds to kill that form. Nature mourns this fixity in the irreversible and relentless process of the body's ageing. The Mother's mourning is similarly passive and perpetual. My device of giving this inherent human conflict three different faces in the play, of embodying it in three separate but simultaneous dramas, enables it to make its fullest impact. And what is more, the Mother's words are a declaration of the unparalleled power of artistic form – the only form which does not constrain or destroy life and which life does not destroy – in her cry to the Producer. If the Father and the Stepdaughter were to start all over again and re-enact their scene a hundred thousand times, her cry would still be uttered precisely at that point; it would ring out over and over again at the precise moment demanded by the life of the work of art: unchanging and unchangeable in its form, but not in any way a mechanical repetition or refrain, wrung from her by external pressure, but every time quite unexpected, bursting out afresh into new life, preserved for eternity in its imperishable living form. In just the same way, whenever we open the book, we shall always find the live Francesca confessing her sweet sin to Dante, and even if we go back again and again and read the passage a hundred thousand times, then, again and again, a hundred thousand times Francesca will speak her words, never in mechanical repetition, but every time as if for the first time, with such animated and unpremeditated passion that every time Dante will swoon in response. All living things, because they have life, have form, and for that reason must die: except the work of art, which lives in fact for ever, in that it is form itself.

The birth of a creature of the human imagination is the step across the threshold separating nothingness from eternity. This birth may sometimes be brought about quite suddenly, precipitated by necessity. While a play is gestating in the imagination, if a new character is needed to supply some necessary speech or action, he is born to order, exactly as required. This is the manner of Madame Pace's birth among the six characters, and it takes our breath away; it is like some convincing illusionist's trick. But it isn't a trick; it is a birth. The new character is alive, not because she was alive already, but because she has been successfully brought into being after the manner of her kind, as a "necessary" character. Theatrically the result is a break, a sudden change in the level of reality, because such a birth can only take place in the mind of a writer; it can't happen on the boards of a stage. Before anyone has realized what has happened, I have moved the scene: I have instantaneously shifted it back into my imagination without removing it from the spectators' gaze. I have set before them, not the stage now, but my own imagination in the guise of that stage, caught in the act of creation. This unforeseen and autonomous shifting of a given phenomenon from one plane of reality to another is a sort of miracle, rather like what happens when the statue of a saint starts to move; at that precise moment you cannot say that the statue is made of wood or stone. Mine of course is not an arbitrary miracle. The stage itself is fluid; in becoming the vehicle for the imaginative reality of the six characters it cannot exist as a fixed unalterable entity in its own right, just as, indeed, there is nothing established and preconceived anywhere in this play: everything here is in the making, shifting, experimental and unpremeditated. Even the place, the site of all this desperate transmutation backwards and forwards of formless, form-seeking life, has a shifting level of reality, and reaches a point where it changes organically.

When I first had the idea of making Madame Pace come into being before my eyes on the stage, I sensed that I could do it and I did it. If I had realized that her birth was going to have this effect of suddenly, silently, almost imperceptibly upsetting and recasting the scene's plane of reality, I surely would not have done it; the apparent illogicality of the idea would have restrained me. And the beauty of the work would have been lost. I was saved from delivering this deathblow by the sheer fervour of my inspiration, for contrary to all appearances and the misleading requirements of logic, the fantastic birth of Madame Pace is dictated by necessity and is intimately and mysteriously related to the whole life of the play.

The allegation that she does not quite come off because of the quasi-Romantic, unstructured and chaotic manner of her composition is to my mind absurd.

I understand what makes people say this. It is because the inner drama involving my six characters appears to be presented as a kind of free-for-all, without any co-ordinating pattern: there is no logical development, no sequential order to events. This is quite true. Had I searched until kingdom come I could not have found a method which was more harum-scarum, more weird, more arbitrary and complex, and indeed more Romantic, than the one I have used to present the inner drama of the six characters.

All this is true, but I have not in fact presented that drama: the one I have presented is an entirely different one – need I repeat it – in which among other delights available to the discerning spectator is to be found a modest satire on Romantic procedures. This can be seen in the heated struggle engaged in by my characters to eclipse each other as they act out their roles in one drama, while all the time I have cast them in quite a different one of which they are oblivious; their tempestuous emotionalism which might stamp them as Romantic is thereby deprived of any solid basis and is placed on a humoristic footing. And the characters' own drama emerges in my work in the only way it can, not in the form it would have taken had I accepted it as a play in its own right, but as a rejected play, a bare "situation", developed spasmodically, in hints, in sudden rushes, in violent foreshortenings, in chaos and confusion: it is constantly inter-rupted, deflected, made to contradict itself; it is not even lived by two of its characters and is repudiated by another.

There is one character in fact, the Son, who repudiates the drama which makes him a "character", and derives his whole dramatic weight and significance not from his role in the inner play – in this he hardly appears at all – but from his role in the play which I have made about it. Indeed he is the only one who exists exclusively as a "character in search of an author"; the author he is looking for is not a playwright. This too was something which could not have been done in any other way. The character's attitude is absolutely basic to my conception of him, just as it is absolutely logical that he should add to the disorder and confusion of the situation by introducing yet another note of Romantic conflict.

It was this natural organic chaos that I had to put on the stage, and the staging of chaos does not mean at all the same thing as chaotic staging in the Romantic manner. My presentation is perfectly clear, straightforward and orderly; it can hardly be called confused when all the audiences of the world have had no difficulty whatever in grasping the work's plot, characters and differing levels of fantasy and reality, drama and comedy, and when its finer subtleties are readily perceived by those who look more closely.

Great must be the confusion of tongues among men if this kind of criticism can find utterance. But if the confusion of tongues outside is great, equally great is the perfect inward law which, followed to the letter, makes of my play a classic model in forbidding the use of words at its catastrophe. Just at the point when all have finally understood that life cannot be created through artifice, and that the six characters' drama cannot be played without an author to quicken it with spirit, the Producer, full of vulgar curiosity about how the story ends, gets the Son to give a blow-by-blow account of the sequence of events; the catastrophe explodes brutally and uselessly – it makes no sense and needs no human words – with the detonation of a firearm on the stage, cutting into and dissolving the sterile experiment of characters and actors, apparently without the aid of the poet.

The poet meanwhile, without their knowledge, has been biding his time, looking on as if from a distance throughout their tentative struggles, and waiting to make of these the very substance of a work of his own.

Luigi Pirandello

THE CHARACTERS

THE FATHER
THE MOTHER
THE STEPDAUGHTER
THE SON
THE BOY (*non-speaking*)
THE LITTLE GIRL (*non-speaking*)
MADAME PACE (*conjured into being in the course of the play*)

THE COMPANY

THE PRODUCER AND DIRECTOR OF THE COMPANY
THE LEADING ACTRESS
THE LEADING ACTOR
THE SECOND ACTRESS
THE YOUNG ACTRESS
THE YOUNG ACTOR
OTHER ACTORS AND ACTRESSES
THE STAGE MANAGER
THE PROMPTER
THE PROPERTY MAN
THE CHIEF STAGEHAND
THE PRODUCER'S SECRETARY
THE COMMISSIONAIRE
STAGEHANDS AND THEATRE STAFF

Daytime: the stage of a theatre

N.B. The play is not divided into acts and scenes. It will be interrupted twice: once, though without a curtain, when the PRODUCER *and the* FATHER *withdraw to outline the scenario and the* ACTORS *leave the stage, and a second time when the* CHIEF STAGEHAND *lowers the curtain by mistake.*

The first sight that greets the audience on entering the theatre is the stage in its ordinary workaday guise. The curtain is up, the stage is empty, almost dark, and devoid of any items of scenery. This is to give us the impression, right from the start, that all we see is quite impromptu.

Two small flights of steps, one right and one left, link the stage to the auditorium.

On the stage the top of the prompter's box has been removed and lies shoved to one side.

On the other side, downstage, and facing away from the audience, are the working table and folding chair of the Producer-cum-Company Manager. Two other small tables of different sizes and various chairs are dotted about, available for the rehearsal if needed. There are chairs again right and left for the actors' use, and at the back somewhere, just visible, a piano.

As the house lights are lowered the CHIEF STAGEHAND *in blue overalls comes through a doorway onto the stage. He has a tool bag slung from his belt. He picks up some lengths of wood in a corner, brings them downstage and kneels to nail them together. The sound of his hammering brings the* STAGE MANAGER *running from the direction of the dressing rooms.*

STAGE MANAGER: What do you think you're doing?

CHIEF STAGEHAND: What does it look like? I'm banging this nail in.

STAGE MANAGER: Now? (*He looks at his watch*) It's gone half-past ten. The producer will be here in a minute to rehearse.

CHIEF STAGEHAND: Yes, well. I've got a job to do an' all!

STAGE MANAGER: Maybe you have, mate, but not now.

CHIEF STAGEHAND: And when might you suggest?

STAGE MANAGER: Well, not just at the moment; a rehearsal's about to start. Come on, clear up all this clobber and let me get the set ready for Act Two of *The Rules of the Game*.

The CHIEF STAGEHAND, *with much grumbling and muttering, collects up his wood and departs. In the meantime the members of the company,* ACTORS *and* ACTRESSES, *begin to assemble on the stage, wandering on in ones and twos. There are nine or ten of them, as required for today's rehearsal of Pirandello's* The Rules of the Game. *As they arrive they exchange "good mornings" with each other and with the* STAGE MANAGER. *Some go off to their dressing rooms: others, including the* PROMPTER, *with the rolled-up script tucked under his arm, stay chatting on the stage waiting for the* PRODUCER *to arrive and start the rehearsal. They sit or stand in groups, smoking, grumbling about their parts, reading out snippets from the odd theatre magazine.* ACTORS *as well as* ACTRESSES *should be dressed in cheerful clothes, light in tone, and this first improvised scene should be very lively and entirely natural. At one point one of them could sit at the piano and strum a dance tune to which the younger ones could dance.*

STAGE MANAGER (*clapping his hands to call them to order*): Right! That's enough now! Come on! The Producer's here!

Song and dance are immediately broken off. The ACTORS *turn to look into the auditorium as the* PRODUCER (*who is also the Director of the Company*) *enters from the back of the house and makes his way down the gangway. He wears a bowler hat, carries a stick under him arm, and has a fat cigar in his mouth. The actors acknowledge him as he advances down the auditorium and mounts the stage by way of one of the sets of steps. His* SECRETARY *hands him his post: the odd newspaper, a script.*

PRODUCER: No letters?

SECRETARY: No letters. That's all there is.

PRODUCER (*handing him back the script*): Put that in my office. (*He looks round and addresses the* STAGE MANAGER) I can hardly see what's going on. Get us a bit of light, will you?

STAGE MANAGER: Sure. (*He goes to see about it, and soon the right side of the stage where the* ACTORS *are is flooded with brilliant white light. Meanwhile, the* PROMPTER *has gone to his box, switched on his light and opened up his copy of the play.*)

PRODUCER (*clapping his hands together*): OK. Let's make a start. (*To the* STAGE MANAGER) Who's missing?

STAGE MANAGER: Our leading lady.

PRODUCER: I might have known. (*He looks at his watch*) We have lost ten minutes already. Put her name in the book, will you? She'll have to learn she can't be late for rehearsals. (*While he is speaking the* LEADING ACTRESS's *voice is heard from the back of the auditorium*)

LEADING ACTRESS: No need for that, my dears! Here I am! I'm here! (*She is all in white and wears an enormous dressy hat. She carries a small lapdog in her arms. She comes running down the aisle and hurries up the steps.*)

PRODUCER: You do it on purpose, don't you – keep people waiting?

LEADING ACTRESS: I'm sorry. I had a ghastly time getting a taxi. I really meant to be on time. But I see you haven't started yet. And I'm not on at the beginning. (*She calls the* STAGE MANAGER *by name and hands over her dog*) Be a dear, and pop him in my dressing room!

PRODUCER (*muttering under his breath*): Even the damned dog! As if the place wasn't a bloody zoo already! (*He claps his hands and turns to the* PROMPTER) Right. We're off. Act Two of *The Rules of the Game*. (*He sits down*) Are you with me, gentlemen? Who's on?

The ACTORS *and* ACTRESSES *clear the front of the stage and seat themselves on chairs at the side, except for the three who are on stage to rehearse the scene, and the* LEADING ACTRESS *who, ignoring the* PRODUCER'*s request, sits herself down at one of the two small tables.*

PRODUCER (*to* LEADING ACTRESS): Do I take it you're in this scene?

LEADING ACTRESS: Me? No... why?

PRODUCER (*irritated*): Then get off for God's sake!

The LEADING ACTRESS *gets up and goes and sits with the others who are now well out of the way.*

PROMPTER (*reading from the script*): "Leone Gala's house. An unusual room which doubles as dining room and study."

PRODUCER (*to* STAGE MANAGER): We can use the red set.

STAGE MANAGER (*jotting it down*): The red set. Right.

PROMPTER (*still reading*): "A table laid for a meal. Desk with books and papers. Bookcases and glass-fronted cabinets full of good china and silver. A door, back, leading to Leone's bedroom. Another door, left, leading to kitchen. The main entrance is on the right."

PRODUCER (*standing and pointing*): Right, let's sort this out. Main entrance over there. Kitchen, here. (*To the actor playing Socrates*) You will use this door here. (*To the* STAGE MANAGER) Perhaps you can organize an inner door at the back, there, and some curtains. (*He sits down again*)

STAGE MANAGER (*making a note of it*): Right.

PROMPTER (*still reading*): "Scene I. Leone Gala, Guido Venanzi and Filippo, otherwise known as Socrates." (*To the* PROMPTER) You want me to read the stage direction too?

PRODUCER: Yes, yes! That's what I said, isn't it?

PROMPTER (*reading*): "As the curtain rises, Leone Gala, in chef's hat and apron, is hard at work beating an egg in a bowl with a wooden spoon. Filippo, likewise dressed as a cook, is also beating an egg. Guido Venanzi is sitting listening to them."

LEADING ACTOR (*to the* PRODUCER): Look, do I really have to wear this thing on my head?

PRODUCER (*annoyed by this remark*): It would seem so! It's in the script! (*He makes a gesture to indicate the script*)

LEADING ACTOR: Well I'm sorry, but I think it's ridiculous!

PRODUCER (*rising in fury*): Ridiculous, is it? You find it ridiculous! And what do you suggest? Can I help it if we can't get hold of good French plays any more so that now we're reduced to putting on plays by Pirandello? Nice stuff if you can understand it, but designed it would seem to get up the noses of actors... and critics... and audiences! (*The* ACTORS *laugh. The* PRODUCER *stands up, moves over to the* LEADING ACTOR *and yells at him.*) So it's "yes" to the chef's hat! And beat those eggs! And there's more to beating eggs than you might think! You're supposed to convey a sense of the very eggshells that they come from – so mind you do! (*More sotto voce laughter and ironic comment from the* ACTORS) Quiet, please! I'd be obliged if you would listen! (*Again, addressing the* LEADING ACTOR) I mean it, the very eggshells! The shell being the empty form of reason, devoid of its content of blind instinct. You, Leone Gala, are reason. Your wife is instinct. It's known as role-playing, right? And your role is to be a man who deliberately sets out to be his own puppet. Get the idea?

LEADING ACTOR (*with a hopeless gesture*): Frankly, no.

PRODUCER (*returning to his place*): Nor do I! Well, come on! Let's get started. Wait till you see how it ends... you'll like it! (*Confidentially to the* LEADING ACTOR) Actually I think you should give us about three-quarters face. Otherwise, what with your mumbling and Piran-dello's bumbling nobody is going to understand a thing! (*Clapping his hands together*) Come on, then! Right, everybody? Let's start!

PROMPTER: Might I just ask – I'm so sorry – but may I put my lid back on? There's an awful draught!

PRODUCER: God, yes! Do what you like!

Meanwhile a uniformed COMMISSIONAIRE *has approached the stage via the central aisle of the auditorium to tell the* PRODUCER *of the arrival of the* SIX CHARACTERS, *who have followed him in and now stand a little way behind him in a bewildered group, looking about them with a lost and puzzled air. Any stage production of the play must make absolutely clear the fundamental distinction between the* SIX CHARACTERS *and the* ACTORS *of the Company. The physical separation of the two groups, recommended in the stage directions once both are on the stage, should certainly help to make the distinction clear. Different-coloured lighting could also be used to reinforce it. But the most effective and apposite means I can suggest would be the use of special masks for the* CHARAC-TERS *of some material solid enough not to go limp with sweat, but light enough for the* ACTORS *to wear them comfortably, and so designed that the eyes, nostrils and mouth are left free. This device will elucidate the play's essential message. The* CHARACTERS *must not, in fact, seem to be phantasms; they must appear as figures of created reality, immutable constructs of the imagination: more real and more consistent, because of this, than the natural and volatile* ACTORS. *The masks will help convey the idea that these figures are the products of art, their faces immutably fixed so that each one expresses its basic motivation: the* FATHER'S *face registering Remorse; the* STEPDAUGHTER'S, *Revenge; the* SON'S, *Contempt and the* MOTHER'S *Sorrow. The* MOTHER *will have fixed wax tears in the dark hollows of her eyes and down her cheeks, like those seen on ecclesiastical images of the Mater Dolorosa. Her dress, too, while simple, should be of some special material and of an unusual design, with stiff folds falling like those of a statue; it must not look like a shop dress or be of a familiar pattern.*

The FATHER *is about fifty, balding slightly, his reddish hair receding at the temples. A thick curly moustache fringes his still youthful lips, which tend to part in a meaningless, uncertain kind of smile. He has a wide forehead, outstandingly pale in a pallid face; oval blue eyes, very bright and piercing; light trousers and a dark jacket: his voice is sometimes mellifluous, sometimes jerky and harsh.*

The MOTHER *gives the impression of someone appalled and oppressed by an intolerable burden of shame and humiliation. She is quietly dressed, in widow's black. When she lifts her heavy crêpe veil she reveals a face which is more like wax than ailing flesh. She keeps her eyes permanently downcast.*

The STEPDAUGHTER *is eighteen, arrogant and brash to the point of insolence. Strikingly beautiful, she too is in mourning, but in her case the clothes have a flashy stylishness. She is clearly contemptuous of her shy, unhappy, bewildered younger brother, a scruffy* BOY *of fourteen, also in black. She is warmly affectionate, however, towards her little sister, a* LITTLE GIRL *of about four, who wears a white frock tied at the waist with a black silk sash.*

The SON *is a tall young man of twenty-two. He bears himself stiffly, as if grown rigid in the suppressed contempt he feels for his* FATHER *and the sullen indifference he shows his* MOTHER. *He wears a purple overcoat and has a long green scarf tied round his neck.*

COMMISSIONAIRE (*cap in hand*): Excuse me, sir.

PRODUCER (*snapping*): Well, what is it?

COMMISSIONAIRE (*hesitating*): There are some people here, sir, asking for you.

PRODUCER (*again, very angry*): For Heaven's sake, man, I'm rehearsing! It's your job to keep people out while rehearsals are in progress! (*Peering into the auditorium*) Who are you people? What do you want?

FATHER (*approaching the steps which lead up to the stage, followed by the others*): We are here in search of an author.

PRODUCER (*both angry and astonished*): An author? What author?

FATHER: Any author, sir.

PRODUCER: Well, there aren't any authors here. We're not rehearsing a new play.

STEPDAUGHTER (*rushing up the steps, with jubilant enthusiasm*): But that's even better! That's terrific! Have us! We can be your new play!

ONE OF THE ACTORS (*amid lively comment and laughter from the others*): Listen to her! How about that!

FATHER (*following the* STEPDAUGHTER *onto the stage*): Well, yes... but if there's no author... (*To the* PRODUCER) Unless... would you like to be our author?...

The MOTHER, *leading the* LITTLE GIRL *by the hand, starts up the steps. The* BOY *does so too, and halfway up they pause expectantly. The* SON *remains at the bottom, evidently sulking.*

PRODUCER: Is this some kind of a joke?

FATHER: It's very far from being a joke, sir. What we bring you is a grievous and painful drama.

STEPDAUGHTER: We could make your fortune!

PRODUCER: Well, perhaps you would be so good as to remove yourselves! We really haven't time for all this nonsense!

FATHER (*hurt, using his "mellifluous" voice*): But I don't need to tell you, sir, I'm sure, that life is like that; it's made up of absurdities, things which don't make sense – and which, like it or not, don't need to be credible, because they are true.

PRODUCER: What the hell are you on about?

FATHER: I'm saying that it is actually more nonsensical to do the opposite, to force things into the mould of credibility to give them the appearance of truth. And might I point out, that, mad as it is, this is exactly what your profession tries to do.

Indignant reaction from the ACTORS.

PRODUCER (*getting up and looking the* FATHER *squarely in the face*): I see. You think our profession mad, is that it?

FATHER: Well, all this making untrue things seem true... pointlessly, as a kind of game... Your job is to make fictional characters seem true to life, am I right?

PRODUCER (*quickly, voicing the growing indignation of his* ACTORS): I really must insist on defending the dignity of the actor's calling. Today's playwrights, I grant you, may be turning out some pretty dull plays with some pretty dumb characters in them, but you know, we can claim to have given life, here on these boards, to some immortal masterpieces.

The ACTORS, *mollified, give him a round of applause.*

FATHER (*interrupting and pressing his point home passionately*): Right! That's exactly what I mean! You have created living beings! As much alive, or more so, as the kind who breathe and wear clothes! Not as real, possibly, but more true! So you see, we agree!

The ACTORS, *impressed, exchange looks.*

STAGE MANAGER: I don't get... First you said...

FATHER (*to the* PRODUCER): No, I'm sorry, that was meant for you, sir, when you barked at us that you had no time to waste on nonsense. Actually, in fact, who better than you should know that Nature's highest instrument in the creative process is the human imagination!

PRODUCER: All right, that's fine. But where does it get us?

FATHER: Nowhere. I'm simply trying to show you that there are a great many ways, and guises, in which one can be born: it might be as a tree or a stone, or water, or a butterfly... or a woman. It's also possible to be born as a character!

PRODUCER (*with ironic feigned amazement*): You mean you and your friends here have all been born as characters?

FATHER: Exactly so. And alive, just as you see us.

The PRODUCER *and the* ACTORS *find this funny. They burst out laughing.*

FATHER (*hurt*): I'm sorry you find it funny, because, as I said, we carry within us a painful drama, which I imagine you are capable of deducing from the sight of this lady here in her black veil. (*As he speaks he offers his hand to the* MOTHER *to help her up the remaining steps. Still holding her by the hand, he leads her with an air of tragic solemnity to the far side of the stage, which is suddenly bathed in an unearthly light. The* LITTLE GIRL *and the* BOY *follow the* MOTHER. *Then the* SON *crosses over, holding himself aloof and retiring to the background. Lastly comes the* STEPDAUGHTER, *who moves away from the others downstage, and stands leaning against the proscenium arch. The astonished* ACTORS *are momentarily silenced by this development, then applaud to show their appreciation of the little show that has just been staged.*)

PRODUCER (*amazed and then annoyed*): Stop that! Keep quiet! (*He turns to the* CHARACTERS) I must ask you to leave! Will you kindly remove yourselves! (*To the* STAGE MANAGER) Get them out of here for God's sake!

STAGE MANAGER (*approaches them and then stops as if restrained by a strange sense of awe*): Clear the stage, then, please! Come along!

FATHER (*to the* PRODUCER): But we can't, you see, we…

PRODUCER (*raising his voice*): Some of us have a job of work to do!

LEADING ACTOR: It shouldn't be allowed! They're making fools of us…

FATHER (*moving resolutely over to them*): I am amazed by your scepticism! Surely as actors and actresses you're quite accustomed to seeing fictional characters suddenly take on life before your eyes, here on this stage? What's the difficulty? Is it because (*pointing towards the* PROMPTER's *box*) we're not in a script?

STEPDAUGHTER (*approaching the* PRODUCER *with an ingratiating smile*): You must believe we really are six characters, and fascinating ones at that!… Displaced, though… homeless.

FATHER (*edging her out of the way*): Displaced, yes, that is so… (*Quickly, to the* PRODUCER) In the sense that the author who created us, who gave us our life, found later that he didn't want, or perhaps technically wasn't able, to bring us to birth in art. And this was criminal of him because you see, if you're lucky enough to be born as a character, you have nothing to fear from death. You don't die! Your creator dies, the writer, the instrument of your being, but you, the creature, can't die! Nor do you have to be particularly brilliant to achieve this kind of immortality; there's no need for you to do anything extraordinary. Who, after all, was Sancho Panza? Who was Mr Micawber? But they, you see, will live for ever, because as living germs they each took root in a fertile medium, an imagination able to nourish and develop them and ultimately give them immortality!

PRODUCER: Well, all that sounds very nice! But what do you want with us?

FATHER: We want to live, sir!

PRODUCER (*ironically*): So, it's immortal life you're after, is it?

FATHER: No. We want to live just for a moment. In them.

AN ACTOR: Oh, no! Come on!

LEADING ACTRESS: They want to live in us!

YOUNG ACTOR (*eyeing the* STEPDAUGHTER): It's OK by me! Do I get her?

FATHER: It's like this, you see: the play has yet to be made (*to the* PRODUCER), but if you're willing and your actors are willing, we can sort something out between us now, straight away!

PRODUCER (*annoyed*): Sort something out? Our job isn't to sort something out! We put on proper plays here by professional dramatists!

FATHER: Well, that's what we want! That's what we came here for!

PRODUCER: And where's the script?

FATHER: It's in us. (*The* ACTORS *laugh*) The drama is in us; we are it! And we are desperate to get it out and put it on the stage. It's a compulsion, a passion!

STEPDAUGHTER (*with a sneer, and adopting a shameless attitude of mock seductiveness*): Passion, now! My passion! You don't know one half of it! My passion... for him! (*She is speaking of the* FATHER *and makes as if to embrace him, but instead bursts into strident laughter*)

FATHER (*snapping at her fiercely*): You keep your place, miss! And you can take that laugh off your face for a start!

STEPDAUGHTER: No? Well, perhaps I may be allowed to show you my other talents! Ladies and gentlemen, in spite of my recent bereavement, I have pleasure in presenting to you my latest song-and-dance number! (*Vindictively she embarks on her song-and-dance act, the first verse of* Chu-Chin-Chow, *lyric by Dave Stamper, music* (*in fox-trot or slow one-step rhythm*) *by Francis Salabert*)

In a fairy book a Chinese crook
Has won such wondrous fame
That nowadays he appears in plays
And Chu-Chin-Chow's his name.[*]

The ACTORS, *particularly the young ones, seem drawn towards her by some mysterious fascination. They crowd round as she performs, making as if to grab at her, but she eludes their clutches. Finally when they applaud her and the* PRODUCER *remonstrates with them, she stands looking abstracted as if lost in thought.*

ACTORS AND ACTRESSES (*laughing and clapping*): Bravo! Encore!

PRODUCER (*angry*): That's enough! This isn't a bloody nightclub! (*Confidentially and even anxiously to the* FATHER) Is she a bit touched or something?

FATHER: Touched? No, it's worse than that!

STEPDAUGHTER (*running to the* PRODUCER, *cutting in quickly*): Worse! I'll say it's worse! It's worse, all right! Listen! Please! Let's act it now, our drama, then you'll see how at a certain point, I... when this sweet baby (*she takes the* LITTLE GIRL's *hand and brings her from her* MOTHER's *side across to the* PRODUCER)... Have you ever seen such a pet? (*She picks her up and kisses her*) Oh, my little love! (*She sets her down and speaks in great agitation, as if hardly aware of her words*) Well, when this sweet baby here eventually gets taken from that poor Mother, and when this idiot here (*she roughly grabs the* BOY *by the sleeve and pushes him forward*) plays his rottenest trick of all, like the dumbhead he is (*shoving him back towards the* MOTHER), you won't see me for dust, I can tell you! I shall be off for good! And believe me, it can't come soon enough! Because after what... after what "took place" between him and me (*with a lurid wink in the* FATHER's *direction*), I can't stick the present company a moment longer; I can't bear to stand by and watch while this Mother eats her heart out over that poor sap. (*She indicates the* SON) Look at him! Just look at him! Really cool, uninvolved, because he's legitimate, see, the legitimate son, much too good for the likes of me, or him there (*pointing to the* BOY) or this little thing here. Because we are the bastards. Are you with me? Bastards. (*She goes up to the*

---

[*]   These are the original words of the Dave Stamper song written for Ziegfeld Follies of 1917. A modern or more familiar alternative could be substituted.

MOTHER *and puts her arms round her*) And this poor Mother, who is Mother to us all, he refuses to acknowledge as his own. He treats her like dirt. To him she's just the Mother of us three bastards. He is… vile! (*All this is said rapidly in a state of extreme agitation. She reaches a crescendo with her "three bastards" and then utters the last word "vile" in a whisper, almost spitting the word out.*)

MOTHER (*in a tone of total anguish*): Please, sir, for the sake of these two little ones, I beg you… (*She totters, unable to go on*) – oh my God…

FATHER (*rushing to support her; the astonished* ACTORS *in their consternation do so too*): Get a chair, someone! Quickly, a chair for this poor creature!

ACTORS (*coming forwards*): Is it real? Has she really fainted?

PRODUCER: Can we have a chair here, quickly!

One of the ACTORS *brings a chair; the others crowd round anxious to help. The* MOTHER *is now sitting. She tries to stop the* FATHER *from removing the veil that hides her face.*

FATHER: Take a look at her, sir! Just take a look at her!

MOTHER: Oh, don't! For God's sake, don't!

FATHER: Let them see you! (*He lifts up her veil*)

MOTHER (*getting up and covering her face with her hands in desperation*): Oh, sir, I beg you, stop this man from doing the dreadful thing he has in mind! It's too horrible!

PRODUCER (*taken aback, bemused*): Can someone tell me what the hell's happening round here! (*To the* FATHER) Is this lady your wife?

FATHER (*promptly*): Yes, she's my wife.

PRODUCER: Then how does she manage to be a widow, if you're still alive?

The ACTORS *release some of their tension in a noisy guffaw.*

FATHER (*cut to the quick, with acrimony*): Don't laugh! Don't laugh like that! For pity's sake! This is the point, this is her drama! She had another man. Another man who should be here!

MOTHER (*with a shriek*): No! No!

STEPDAUGHTER: He's dead, and well out of it. I told you, he died two months ago. You can see, we are still in mourning for him.

FATHER: He's not here… but that's not because he is dead. He's not here because… well, one look at her should tell you. Hers isn't the drama of a woman torn between two men; I don't think she felt anything for them. She wasn't capable. Beyond, perhaps, a little gratitude.

(Not for me! For him!) No, she isn't a woman; she's a mother! Her drama (and oh, yes, it's powerful stuff!) her whole drama is bound up in these four children, the children of the two men she had.

MOTHER: I had two men? You can stand there and say that I had two men, as if that was what I wanted? (*To the* PRODUCER) He wanted it! He gave me the other man, he forced him on me! He made me, yes, he made me run away with him!

STEPDAUGHTER (*cutting in bitterly*): That's not true!

MOTHER (*startled*): What's not true?

STEPDAUGHTER: It just isn't true!

MOTHER: What do you know about it?

STEPDAUGHTER: It isn't true! (*To the* PRODUCER) Don't you believe it! Do you know why she says that? She says it because of him! (*She points to the* SON) She's tearing herself apart over the coldness of the son she abandoned when he was two years old. She's desperate to convince him that she only left him because she had to, because he (*pointing to the* FATHER) forced her to.

MOTHER: He forced me, all right! God knows he forced me! (*To the* PRO-DUCER) Ask him if he didn't. Make him admit it! She (*she gestures towards the* STEPDAUGHTER) is not in a position to have an opinion.

STEPDAUGHTER: I just know that all the time you were with my father, as long as he was alive, you were perfectly happy and at peace. You can't deny it!

MOTHER: No, I don't deny it, I...

STEPDAUGHTER: He was so loving. He looked after you so sweetly! (*To the* BOY, *angrily*) Didn't he? Bear me out! Say something, you fool!

MOTHER: Leave the poor boy alone! Why do you want to make me out so ungrateful? I wouldn't dream of saying anything against your father. I was simply answering his insinuation. (*She is referring to the* FATHER) When I walked out of his house and left my son, it wasn't my fault! Nor was it for my pleasure!

FATHER: She is perfectly right. It was my idea. (*A pause*)

LEADING ACTOR (*to the others*): It wouldn't make a bad show!

LEADING ACTRESS: Nice to be the audience for once!

YOUNG ACTOR: It makes a change!

PRODUCER (*beginning to get really interested*): OK, let's listen! Sh! Let's listen! (*As he says this he goes down the steps into the auditorium where he stands facing the stage, as if to get an audience's impression of the scene)*

SON (*without moving and without raising his voice, which is cold and ironic*): If you want to know what's coming next, it's a slice of potted philosophy! He's about to tell you of his evil genius, his Daemon of Experiment!

FATHER: You think you're so damn clever, but you're stupid! That's typical! (*To the* PRODUCER) He despises me, you see, for this expression I have hit on to explain my behaviour.

SON (*scornfully*): Words!

FATHER: Well, yes! Words, words! As if we didn't all find them a source of comfort! When we are desperately perplexed or distressed, what do we do? We find some word which in itself means nothing, but which offers us peace of mind!

STEPDAUGHTER: Super remedy for remorse, for instance! Nothing like it!

FATHER: Remorse? That's not fair. I have used more than mere words to still my remorse.

STEPDAUGHTER: Oh... of course! What was it he wanted to offer me for my services? Oh yes, a hundred lire!

There is a horrified reaction from the ACTORS.

SON (*contemptuously to his stepsister*): That was vile!

STEPDAUGHTER: Vile? But there it was, in a nice little pale-blue envelope on the mahogany table, round the back at Madame Pace's. (*To the* PRODUCER) You know the kind of thing, sir! Smart boutique in the front, providing a cover for Madame's other little business, the "work rooms" at the back where she can employ girls from decent homes who need the cash.

SON: And now she's holding us all to ransom with the wretched hundred lire she was going to cost him. And bear in mind – as things turned out – he never had reason to pay it!

STEPDAUGHTER: Get it right, now! It was a very near thing! (*She bursts out laughing*)

MOTHER (*getting up*): Have you no shame!

STEPDAUGHTER (*quickly*): Shame? This is revenge! I am at this moment trembling, trembling in every nerve to get at that scene and to live it! The room, now. There's a glass case displaying clothes, over here! Over there a sofa, doubling as a bed. A long mirror, here, and a

33

screen. By the window we've got the famous mahogany table with the blue envelope on it with the money. I can see it! I could even pick it up! Perhaps you should all be looking the other way, as I've hardly got anything on! Not that it makes me blush. I can't blush any more. He's the one who is red in the face now. (*She indicates the* FATHER) However, at the time I'm speaking of I can tell you he was pale! Very, very pale! (*To the* PRODUCER) Of that I can assure you!

PRODUCER: I can't keep up with this!

FATHER: Of course you can't. Give the man a chance! (*To the* PRODUCER) Can't you organize this a bit, sir?… let me explain things? You shouldn't really listen to this savage piece of character assassination without hearing what I've got to say!

STEPDAUGHTER: But it's not a story! You can't tell it like a story!

FATHER: I'm not telling a story – I just want to explain!

STEPDAUGHTER: Oh, yes, lovely! Explain it your way, you mean!

The PRODUCER *climbs back onto the stage to try to restore order.*

FATHER: But isn't this the whole trouble! It all comes back to words! We all carry round inside us a world made up of things as we see them; each one of us a whole world of his own! How can we ever hope to understand each other if I put into the words I use the meaning and value that things have for me in my interior world, while the person I'm talking to is bound to receive them with the meaning and value those words have for him, in a world that exists only inside him? We think we understand each other. In fact we never do. Look! The pity I felt for this poor woman (*he indicates the* MOTHER) – all my pity for her she took as cruelty!

MOTHER: But you sent me away!

FATHER: There, you see? She thinks I sent her away!

MOTHER: You're good at talking; I'm not… (*To the* PRODUCER) But believe me, once he had married me… though goodness knows why he did!… I was a very simple person, no money or anything…

FATHER: But that's right! That's what I loved! You were simple, and I thought… (*She is clearly in disagreement, and he breaks off, shrugging desperately at the utter impossibility of making himself understood by her. He turns to the* PRODUCER.) It's no good, you see? She won't see it! It is terrifying! Her mental deafness is absolutely terrifying! (*He taps his forehead*) That's it, mental deafness! Plenty of heart, mind you, where her children are concerned. But in the head she's deaf! Dear sir, to the point of desperation!

STEPDAUGHTER (*to the* PRODUCER): You'd better get him to tell you just where all *his* intelligence has got us!

FATHER: If one only realized beforehand all the harm that can result from one's efforts to do good!

At this point the LEADING ACTRESS, *distraught at the* LEADING ACTOR's *attempts to flirt with the* STEPDAUGHTER, *comes up to speak to the* PRODUCER.

LEADING ACTRESS: Is there going to be a rehearsal this morning?

PRODUCER: Yes, yes! But let me just hear this!

YOUNG ACTOR: It's new. I mean, it's not been done before!

YOUNG ACTRESS: It's fascinating!

LEADING ACTRESS: If you find that sort of thing fascinating! (*She darts a glance at the* LEADING ACTOR)

PRODUCER (*to the* FATHER): Now, let's get this clear. (*He sits*)

FATHER: Right. Well, look. I had this secretary. He was my junior, a rather downtrodden kind of fellow, utterly devoted... And he had this extraordinary understanding with my wife. They thought the same way about everything. Absolutely innocent, of course. He was as good and simple as she was. Both quite incapable of doing anything wrong... or even of thinking of it.

STEPDAUGHTER: So he did the thinking for them – and the doing!

FATHER: That's not true! I meant to do what was best for them – and for myself, I admit! It had got to the point, you see, where I couldn't say a word to either of them without their exchanging understanding looks. Their eyes kept meeting, looking for clues as to how to react to what I had said, how to keep me sweet! Well, you can imagine, this was enough in itself to keep me permanently on the simmer; I was in an unbearable state of constant exasperation!

PRODUCER: But... why didn't you sack the secretary?

FATHER: Exactly what I did! I sacked him, and then was left with the spectacle of this poor woman drifting round the house like a lost soul. She seemed not to belong, like a stray animal you keep out of kindness.

MOTHER: Is it any wonder!

FATHER (*quickly, turning to her, as if to get in first*): Ah, yes... our boy.

MOTHER: He had already taken the child from my arms, you realize!

FATHER: But not from cruelty! I did it so that he would grow up strong and healthy, close to nature!

STEPDAUGHTER (*pointing to the* SON, *ironically*): As you see!

FATHER (*quickly*): Is it my fault that he turned out like this? (*To the* PRODUCER) I put him in the care of a foster mother, in the country, a peasant woman. My wife didn't seem strong enough, despite her humble origins. I was looking for the same kind of thing again, you see, that I looked for in marrying her. A fad, I suppose, but there you are. I have always been dogged by a hankering after a kind of sound moral wholesomeness. (*Here the* STEPDAUGHTER *again produces a guffaw of raucous laughter*) Can't you stop her doing that? It's insufferable.

PRODUCER (*to the* STEPDAUGHTER): Stop it, for God's sake! Let me hear what he's saying!

At this remonstrance from the PRODUCER *the* STEPDAUGHTER *immediately reassumes her lost far-away look as she is cut off in mid-laughter. The* PRODUCER *again takes up his position in the stalls to get the audience's view of the stage.*

FATHER: I could no longer bear to have this woman in the house. Not so much because her presence was oppressive, which it was, really oppressive, but more, quite honestly, because of the pain – well, the anguish she was going through.

MOTHER: And he sent me away!

FATHER: Yes I did, I provided for her properly and sent her to that man – I gave her her freedom!

MOTHER: Your own freedom, more like!

FATHER: Well, yes, mine too, I admit it! And it all went horribly wrong! I thought I was doing the right thing! More for her than for me, I swear to that! (*He lays his hand on his heart, then turning quickly to the* MOTHER) But I didn't lose sight of you, did I? I didn't lose sight of you... until the day when the damned fool carted you off to another town, overnight, without a word! He was idiot enough to resent the interest I took... which was perfectly innocent! There wasn't a thought in my head that wasn't entirely innocent! I got incredibly fond of this new little family that was growing up. I was interested. (*He points to the* STEPDAUGHTER) She'll bear me out!

STEPDAUGHTER: You were interested all right! I was, you know, a real little girl. With pigtails down to my shoulders and my little knickers showing! About so high! I used to see him as I came out of the school gate. He came to see how I was growing up…

FATHER: That is a vile thing to say! That is disgusting!

STEPDAUGHTER: Have I got it wrong?

FATHER: This is quite outrageous! (*His tone suddenly changes to one of desperate self-explanation*) The fact was, you see, once she had gone, my house seemed empty. She had filled it with the nightmare of her presence. Left on my own I almost went off my head. I used to wander blindly from room to room. He, you see (*indicating the* SON) had been in a foster home up till then. When he came home, somehow he didn't seem to be mine any more. With his mother no longer there to keep us together, he grew up in a world of his own. There was no relationship there, no feelings, no common interests. So then, it sounds odd, I know, but this is what happened – first I got curious, and then bit by bit I began to feel drawn towards her little family – I had created it in a way. The thought of it began to fill the emptiness of my life. I needed, I really needed to know she had found peace, to know she was completely taken up with the little tasks of daily life, safely and happily out of reach, where my complicated spiritual agonizings could no longer touch her. And to prove it to myself, I used to go and watch that little girl coming out of school.

STEPDAUGHTER: He did too! He used to follow me all the way home, smiling! And when we got there he used to wave, like this! And I'd glare at him, give him nasty looks. I didn't know who he was! I told my mum. She knew who it was all right. (*The* MOTHER *nods*) At first she wanted to keep me off school, and I stayed at home for several days. When I started back at school, there he was again, waiting at the gate – he looked ridiculous – holding a big paper parcel! He came up and patted me and unwrapped a lovely big, real-straw hat with little rosebuds round the brim – for me!

PRODUCER: But this is a story not a play!

SON (*scornfully*): Fiction! Romantic fiction!

FATHER: Fiction? This isn't fiction! This is life! This is passion!

PRODUCER: That's as may be. It will never do on the stage!

37

FATHER: Now there you're right! This all happens before the play starts. I'm not suggesting we act this bit. I mean, you can see for yourself, she's hardly a little girl with pigtails any more...

STEPDAUGHTER: Nor can you see her little knickers!

FATHER: The drama is what comes next! An extraordinary, complicated story!

STEPDAUGHTER (*coming forwards, proud and menacing*): Once my father had died...

FATHER (*quickly to stop her saying any more*): ...they were faced with destitution! They came back here. I didn't know. She (*he points to the* MOTHER) was too stupid to tell me. She can hardly write, but she could have got her daughter or that boy to let me know they were in trouble.

MOTHER (*to the* PRODUCER): But how could I have known he felt like this!

FATHER: That was the wrong you did me – never guessing anything of how I felt!

MOTHER: Well, after all those years away, and everything that had happened...

FATHER: How could I help it if your fancy man went and carted you off like that? (*To the* PRODUCER) I tell you, they disappeared overnight... He had got himself some kind of a job in another town. I never managed to trace them, and then, naturally over the years, my interest flagged. The drama erupted, unforeseen and cataclysmic, when they got back. Because I, Heaven help me, still suffering the misery of physical frustration... and misery is right! It is misery when a man lives alone, if he doesn't want some sordid affair, but he's not yet old enough to do without a woman nor young enough to go out and get one in a straightforward and acceptable fashion! Misery, did I say? Horror would be nearer the mark! Horror, because no woman can give him love any more... And once you've realized that, you should really do without... So! The fact is, we all clothe ourselves with a kind of outward dignity, for the benefit of other people. Inwardly, of course, one knows perfectly well the unconfessable intimate things that go on. One gives in, of course one does, to temptation, but one scrambles up again very smartly afterwards in a great rush to re-establish the old dignity, set it upright whole and solid like a tombstone over a grave. That way we don't have to look at our shame; we have hidden and buried all trace of it and can forget it. We all do it, you know! It's just that some things... well, one can't quite bring oneself to talk about them!

STEPDAUGHTER: Doing them's all right though, isn't it!

FATHER: Oh, people do these things! But in secret! That's why it takes more courage to talk about them. If you mention them, people say you are cynical. Which isn't true. You are only the same as everyone else – in fact a bit better, because you're not afraid to look rationally at the blushing face of human sexuality. There it is; it's part of our bestial nature, but we shut our eyes to it and refuse to see it. A woman... look... a woman... what does she do? She looks at us, all invitation, all enticement. So you grab her! And what happens? As soon as she's in your arms, she shuts her eyes – like that! It's her signal of surrender; she's saying: "Be blind, as I am blind."

STEPDAUGHTER: And what about when she gets past that stage? When she has grown out of the need to shut her eyes against her own blushes? When she can stare, quite unmoved, with wide dry eyes at the shame of the man in her arms, lying there, without love, his eyes closed against his lust! That's when it really makes you sick! That's when you can't stomach all this hair-splitting and high-flown philosophizing about man and his animal nature, all your excuses and justifications. I can't stand it, I tell you. Because if you are ever actually driven to live at that level, at the simple animal level, if you're ever forced to do without all the human "extras" like chastity, purity, idealism, duty, modesty, shame – you'll find nothing makes you more angry, nothing is more nauseating than bogus remorse: it's eyewash!

PRODUCER: Can we get to the point, do you think? All this is hardly relevant!

FATHER: Ah! Yes... well! A fact you see, on its own, is like an empty sack: it won't stand up! If you want it to stand up, you have to put something inside it, the motivation, the feelings that brought it about. I couldn't know, you see, that after the death of that chap when they all came back here without a bean, she tried to support her children by looking about for work as a seamstress... and in fact got taken on by Madame Pace!

STEPDAUGHTER: ...Who, I'd have you know, is a first-rate dressmaker. She serves a very distinguished clientele. It's a nice little arrangement. Her distinguished ladies come in very useful, as a cover for her other ladies, the not so distinguished ones!

39

MOTHER: And it goes without saying, I'm sure, that I hadn't the faintest suspicion that that monstrous creature gave me work because she had got her eye on my child…

STEPDAUGHTER: Poor Mum! And do you know what the old so-and-so did when I brought her the sewing my mother had done? She made me note down the amount of stuff she had ruined, and then she would deduct it, she'd deduct it from my pay! I was being made to pay, you see, while my poor old Mum thought she was making sacrifices on behalf of me and the other two. She used to sit up half the night doing Madame Pace's sewing!

The ACTORS *register indignation.*

PRODUCER (*anxious to get on*): And it was there that one day you met…

STEPDAUGHTER (*pointing to the* FATHER): Him! That's right! Him! Old-established client! You'll see what a good scene it makes! It's brilliant!

FATHER: When she bursts in in the middle, you see, the mother—

STEPDAUGHTER (*quickly, treacherously*): Almost in time!

FATHER (*shouting her down*): No! In time! In time! Because luckily, I recognize her in time! And then I take them all home with me! But just try and imagine how impossible things are between us now! She's, well, she's as you see her! But I can't even look her in the face!

STEPDAUGHTER: It's a laugh! There's no way – after that – that I can pass myself off as a nice well-brought-up young lady in keeping with his damnable notions of "sound moral wholesomeness".

FATHER: And this, for me, is the heart of the drama: I'm intensely aware, you see, that people are wrong to think of themselves as just one person. Each one of us is lots and lots of people. Any number, because of all the countless possibilities of being that exist within us. The person you are with me is quite different from the person you are with somebody else. But we go on thinking we're exactly the same person for everybody, the person we think we are in our own mind and in everything we do. But this isn't the case at all! It comes home to us best when by some ghastly mischance we are caught out in an untypical act. We suddenly find we are sort of dangling from a hook! I mean we can see that the act isn't "us", our whole self isn't in it. And it would be a savage injustice to judge us on that act alone, never to let us off the hook, to hold us to it, chain us up for life on the strength of it for all to see, as if that one action summed up our whole existence! So now do you see how treacherous this girl is being? She caught me out in an unrecognizable situation, in a place where for her I should never have been and doing something which in her eyes I should not have been able to do, and now she insists on seeing this undreamt-of contingency as my reality, identifying me with a single fleeting shaming moment of my life. This, sir, is what I feel most strongly of all. And you'll see that this is really what gives the play its power. And then of course there's the situation of the others. His, for instance (*he points to the* SON)...

SON (*with a contemptuous shrug*): You can leave me out of it! I don't come into it!

FATHER: What do you mean, you don't come into it?

SON: I don't come into it! I don't want to come into it! You know quite well I was never meant to be mixed up with you lot!

STEPDAUGHTER: He thinks we're dead common. He reckons he's got class. Though you'll notice perhaps that whenever I manage to wither him with a glance he always shifts his eyes away. He knows what he's done to me, all right.

SON (*hardly looking at her*): ...What I've done?

STEPDAUGHTER: Yes, you! You're the one who put me on the streets, matey! (*The* ACTORS *are shocked*) Did you, or didn't you, oh, by your whole manner, make sure we never felt at home in your house? You didn't even treat us as guests! We were intruders, weren't we, invading your legitimate territory! (*To the* PRODUCER) I'd like to show you certain little private scenes that took place between him and me! He says I took over the household. But can't you see? The way he was carrying on, I had to exploit my bit of advantage, my "cheap" advantage as he calls it, and make sure that when I walked into that house with my mother (who's his mother too!) I was going to be boss!

SON (*coming forwards slowly*): You see how it is. I'm fair game; they have an easy case against me. But try and see it my way. You are someone's son, quietly at home one day, and in marches a cheeky young woman who looks down her nose at you and says she has some sort of business with your father! Then back she comes, as if she owned the place, bringing that little girl with her, and proceeds to treat your father – God knows by what right – in a highly equivocal and offhand manner, asking him for money in a voice which suggests he has no choice but to give it her, that he's in no position to refuse.

FATHER: But that's right. I can't refuse. It's for your mother.

SON: Well, what do I know about that? When have I even seen my mother? When have I ever heard her mentioned? For me she just turns up one day, with her, and that boy, and that little girl. They tell me, "Oh, didn't you know? She is your mother, too!" And then I get it. I pick it up from her manner (*he indicates the* STEPDAUGHTER) how it was they were suddenly able to come and live with us just like that... (*To the* PRODUCER) What I feel, what I'm going through, I can't express and I don't want to. I can't even bring myself to think about it. So you see: no action can possibly be got out of me. Believe me, in dramatic terms, I'm an "unrealized" character. I'm just not one of them, I really don't belong! So leave me out, will you?

FATHER: How can we! Come on! Just because you're like that—

SON (*in violent exasperation*): How the hell do you know what I'm like! When have you ever bothered about me?

FATHER: I agree! I grant you that! But isn't this a dramatic situation in itself? This cutting yourself off is so cruel; I find it cruel and so does your mother. Think of her, coming home and meeting you for the first time, this fully grown stranger who she just knows is her son... (*He draws the* PRODUCER'*s attention to the* MOTHER) Look at her now, she's crying.

STEPDAUGHTER (*angrily, stamping her foot*): She's so wet!

FATHER (*to the* PRODUCER, *with a quick gesture towards the* STEPDAUGHTER): And she can't stand him, you see! (*He points to the* SON) He says he doesn't come into it, but in many ways he's the pivot of the action! Look at this young fellow clinging to his mother all the time. Do you see how abject and intimidated he is? Well, that's his fault! (*Indicating the* SON) Perhaps the poor little chap is in the most hurtful situation of all: more than any of them he feels he doesn't belong. He finds it painfully humiliating to have been taken in – well, out of charity... (*Confidentially*) He's exactly like his father. A dim sort of chap... never spoke.

PRODUCER: Can't really see it working, you know. Children are a damn nuisance on the stage.

FATHER: Don't worry, the nuisance removes itself pretty quickly! And so does the little girl. In fact she goes first...

PRODUCER: That's good. Well, then, yes! And I may say I am completely hooked, it is all deeply intriguing. Something tells me that we have the makings of a first-rate play here.

STEPDAUGHTER (*trying to butt in*): With a character like me you have!

FATHER (*pushing her out of the way in his anxiety to hear the* PRODUCER'*s decision*): Shut up, you!

PRODUCER (*not noticing the interruption*): It's certainly new…

FATHER: Oh yes, it's very new!

PRODUCER: I hand it to you for sheer nerve, though, coming in here and shoving the thing under my nose…

FATHER: You must understand, sir: born, as we are, for the stage…

PRODUCER: Are you an amateur company?

FATHER: Oh, no. I say "born for the stage" because…

PRODUCER: Come off it! You've had acting experience!

FATHER: None at all. Only the acting everybody does, in the parts we give ourselves in life or that other people give us. In my case I'd say the theatricality comes from passion itself. Strong feeling does that, gets a bit stagy, you know, when one gets worked up…

PRODUCER: Well, never mind! It doesn't matter. Now, look! You have to understand, I'm afraid, that without an author… I could put you in touch with someone…

FATHER: Oh, no! Don't do that! You be the author!

PRODUCER: Me? How could I?

FATHER: Yes, you! Why not?

PRODUCER: I've never written a play in my life!

FATHER: Well then, why not start now? There's nothing to it! Look at all the people who do! And your job is made that much easier for having us all here alive in front of you!

PRODUCER: There's more to it than that!

FATHER: Well, is there? I mean, seeing us actually live our play…

PRODUCER: OK! But you've still got to have somebody to write it!

FATHER: No, you haven't! All you need do is transcribe it, scene by scene, as it unfolds before you. All that's necessary at this point is to map out a very rough plan and then try it out!

PRODUCER (*climbing back onto the stage, tempted by the idea*): I'm almost tempted… ye-es, almost… for fun, maybe… Well, we could have a go…

FATHER: Oh yes, you must! You'll be amazed at the scenes which come out! I can give you a rough outline straight away!

PRODUCER: It's tempting... It's certainly tempting... OK. Let's give it a go. Come with me to my office. (*To the* ACTORS) Take a break but don't go away. Be back here in a quarter of an hour or twenty minutes. (*To the* FATHER) Come on then, let's see what we can do. You never know, it might result in something quite extraordinary...

FATHER: But it will! There's no doubt! They had better come too, don't you think? (*He refers to the other* CHARACTERS)

PRODUCER: Oh yes, they'd better come. Come on! (*He turns to the* ACTORS *again before leaving the stage*) Don't be late, then! A quarter of an hour! (*The* PRODUCER *and the six* CHARACTERS *cross the stage and disappear. The* ACTORS *remain on stage, exchanging baffled looks.*)

LEADING ACTOR: Can he be serious? What's he playing at?

YOUNG ACTOR: He's clean off his rocker!

A THIRD ACTOR: Does he expect us to improvise a whole play just on the spot?

YOUNG ACTOR: That's it! *Commedia dell'arte* type stuff!

LEADING ACTRESS: I hope he doesn't think I'm going to take part in such nonsense...

YOUNG ACTRESS: Well, I'm not going to!

A FOURTH ACTOR: I'd like to know just who those people are.

THE THIRD ACTOR: It's obvious! They're either loonies or crooks!

YOUNG ACTOR: I can't think what induced him to listen to them!

YOUNG ACTRESS: He fancies himself, perhaps. Sees himself as a playwright.

LEADING ACTOR: Well, it's preposterous! If this, my friends, is what the theatre's coming to...

A FIFTH ACTOR: I don't know, I think it's rather fun!

THE THIRD ACTOR: Oh, well! Let's see what comes of it!

Chatting amongst themselves, the ACTORS *leave the stage, some through the small door at the back, some in the direction of the dressing rooms. The curtain stays up. There is an interval in the play of twenty minutes or so.*

Bells throughout the theatre warn the audience that the performance is about to start again.

The ACTORS, STAGE MANAGER, CHIEF STAGEHAND, PROMPTER *and* PROPERTY MAN *return to the stage from the dressing rooms, from the outside door and from the auditorium. At the same time the* PRODUCER *re-emerges from his office with the six* CHARACTERS. *The house lights go down and the stage is lit as before.*

PRODUCER: All right, ladies and gentlemen! Are we all here? May I have your attention, please! Can we begin? (*He calls the* CHIEF STAGE-HAND *by name*)

CHIEF STAGEHAND: Yes! Here!

PRODUCER: Can you give us the small drawing room – three flats, one with a door, that's about it. As quick as you can!

The STAGEHAND *at once goes off to carry out his instructions, and while the* PRODUCER *is making necessary arrangements with the* STAGE MANAGER, *the* PROPERTY MAN *and the* ACTORS, *the* SCENE-SHIFTERS *have organized a set as requested, a small parlour with pink-and-gold-striped wallpaper.*

PRODUCER (*to the* PROPERTY MAN): Have a look and see if we've got a divan or a chaise longue.

PROPERTY MAN: Yes, we've got the green one.

STEPDAUGHTER: We can't have a green one! It was yellow plush with flowers on it. A great big thing, really comfortable.

PROPERTY MAN: We've got nothing like that!

PRODUCER: It doesn't matter! Give us the one we've got.

STEPDAUGHTER: How can you say it doesn't matter? Madame Pace's famous couch!

PRODUCER: It's only for a run-through! Please don't interfere. (*To the* STAGE MANAGER) See if there's a display case, preferably long and low.

STEPDAUGHTER: And the table! The small mahogany table for the blue envelope!

STAGE MANAGER (*to the* PRODUCER): There's the small gilt one.

PRODUCER: That'll do fine.

FATHER: And a long mirror.

STEPDAUGHTER: And the screen! There has to be a screen. I can't possibly manage without that.

STAGE MANAGER: That's all right, miss, don't worry. We've got lots of screens.

PRODUCER (*to the* STEPDAUGHTER): Then some hat stands, right?

STEPDAUGHTER: Yes, a lot of those!

PRODUCER (*to the* STAGE MANAGER): Get them to bring whatever we've got.

STAGE MANAGER: No trouble, sir! Leave it to me! (*The* STAGE MAN-AGER *hurries off to do as he is told, then returns and arranges as he thinks best the props brought on by the scene-shifters, while the* PRODUCER *carries on talking to the* PROMPTER, *the* CHARACTERS *and the* ACTORS)

PRODUCER (*to the* PROMPTER): You could be getting yourself ready. Look, here's an outline of the scenes divided up into acts. (*He hands him several sheets of paper*) You'll have your work cut out, you know.

PROMPTER: Do you want it in shorthand?

PRODUCER (*pleasantly surprised*): What? You can do shorthand?

PROMPTER: I may not be much of a prompter, but shorthand, now…

PRODUCER: Better and better. (*To a* STAGEHAND) Go and get some paper from my office – get plenty, as much as you can find! (*The* STAGE-HAND *hurries off and returns almost at once with a thick wad of paper which he hands to the* PROMPTER)

PRODUCER (*to the* PROMPTER): Just follow the scenes as we do them and try to get down the lines, well, the main ones anyway! (*To the* ACTORS) Right, clear the stage, please! Can you all come over onto this side (*he points to stage left*) and let's have your full attention!

LEADING ACTRESS: But, look here, we…

PRODUCER (*cutting in*): Keep calm, nobody's asking you to improvise!

LEADING ACTOR: What do we have to do, then?

PRODUCER: Nothing! Just keep your eyes and ears open for the present. Then later, you'll all have proper scripted parts. Right now we're going to have a rehearsal, of a sort. They (*he indicates the* CHARAC-TERS) are going to be doing it.

FATHER (*as if roused from a reverie, suddenly aware of the confusion all around him*): You mean us? But what do you mean, a rehearsal?

PRODUCER: You're going to rehearse, rehearse for my actors!

FATHER: But if we *are* the characters…

PRODUCER: OK. So you're the characters. But my dear good sir, we don't have characters acting here. The actors do the acting. The characters belong in the script (*he gestures towards the* PROMPTER)... when there is a script!

FATHER: Exactly! But since there isn't one and you good people are lucky enough to have the characters here in person...

PRODUCER: Bloody marvellous! You're proposing to do the whole thing on your own, then! Be your own actors, your own producers, everything!

FATHER: Of course, just as we are.

PRODUCER: Well, my word, that would be some show, I can tell you!

LEADING ACTOR: And what would that leave for us to do?

PRODUCER: You don't for one moment imagine you can act, do you? This has got to be a joke! (*The* ACTORS *are in fact laughing*) Look, there you are, they're laughing! (*Recollecting himself*) Anyway, where were we! Now, to cast this thing! Well, it's easy: the parts pretty well cast themselves. (*To the* SECOND ACTRESS) You will be the mother. (*To the* FATHER) We shall have to find a name for her.

FATHER: Her name's Amalia.

PRODUCER: No, that's your wife's name. We shan't want to use her real name.

FATHER: Why ever not? If that's her name... But of course, if this lady here has got to do it... (*He waves bleakly in the direction of the* SECOND ACTRESS) I see her (*referring to the* MOTHER) as Amalia. But it's up to you... (*He gets more and more confused*) I don't really know what to say... I'm beginning to feel... well, as if my own words are ringing false, and are no longer really mine, somehow.

PRODUCER: Don't let that worry you! Don't let that worry you at all! We'll see we get the tone right! As for the name, if you want Amalia, then Amalia it shall be, or whatever you like. For the moment let's not use names. Let's simply say that you (*to the* YOUNG ACTOR) are the Son; (*to the* LEADING ACTRESS) that you, of course, are the Stepdaughter...

STEPDAUGHTER (*galvanized*): What? What? That woman there? (*She bursts out laughing*)

PRODUCER (*angrily*): What's so funny?

LEADING ACTRESS (*indignantly*): I'm not having this! No one has ever laughed at me! If I can't be treated with respect, I'm off!

STEPDAUGHTER: Well, no, I'm sorry. It's not you I'm laughing at.

PRODUCER (*to the* STEPDAUGHTER): You should feel honoured at being played by...

LEADING ACTRESS (*promptly and furiously*): ..."That woman there"!

STEPDAUGHTER: It really wasn't you I was thinking of! It was me! I just don't see myself in you at all! That's it. I don't know, you're not... you're not in the least bit like me!

FATHER: That's just it. (*To the* PRODUCER) Look! What we want to express...

PRODUCER: What you want to express! Do you think, then, that you can provide your own means of expression? You couldn't begin!

FATHER: What? Are you saying we haven't got it in us to express ourselves?

PRODUCER: Of course you haven't! In this theatre anything you express becomes material for my actors to work on. They give it body and shape, voice and gesture. And they have usually tackled far more ambitious material than yours, which, let's face it, is pretty trivial stuff. If it works as a play, it will be entirely thanks to them, no doubt about it.

FATHER: Well, I daren't contradict you. But may I say that for us this is an extremely painful process. This is what we look like! You can see *these* are our bodies, *these* are our faces...

PRODUCER (*cutting him short, losing patience*): That's no problem! Faces are no problem! Make-up will fix all that!

FATHER: All right. But what about voices, gestures...

PRODUCER: Look, the fact is... There's no place here for you, as yourself. Here you just don't exist. An actor represents you, and that's it!

FATHER: I understand. And I think I'm beginning to get a glimmering of why our author decided not to write us into a play. He saw us as we are, alive... I'm not casting aspersions on your actions, I wouldn't dream of doing that! But the idea now of seeing myself acted by someone else, by some actor...

LEADING ACTOR (*pompously rising and coming over with his entourage of giggling young* ACTRESSES): By me, if you have no objection.

FATHER (*with honeyed deference*): I am deeply honoured. (*He bows*) (*To the* PRODUCER) The fact is, I think, that however hard our friend here tries, with all the will in the world and with all his professional skill, to absorb my being... (*He gets confused*)

LEADING ACTOR: Go on, go on. (*The* ACTRESSES *laugh*)

FATHER: Well, I mean, his rendering of me, even with the help of make-up... well, with his build... (*There is laughter from the* ACTORS) ...it will hardly be me, I'm thinking, as I really am. It will be more – quite apart from the face – it will be more of a personal interpretation of what I'm like, an impression of what I'm like – if indeed he has one. It won't be me, as I feel myself to be inside here. And this is something that needs to be taken into account by anybody forming an opinion of us.

PRODUCER: Is it the thought of the critics that's worrying you? Here was I, thinking you had something to say! The critics can say what they like. Our job is to get on with putting this play together, if we can! (*Breaking away and looking round*) Right! Now – is the set ready? (*To the* ACTORS *and* CHARACTERS) Out of the way, please, everyone! Let's have a look! (*He climbs down off the stage*) Don't let's waste any more time! (*To the* STEPDAUGHTER) Will the set do, do you think?

STEPDAUGHTER: Frankly, no! I don't recognize it at all!

PRODUCER: Oh, for Christ's sake! You can't expect us to reproduce for you *in toto* an exact replica of Madame Pace's back room as you knew it! (*To the* FATHER) A small parlour, you said, with flowered wallpaper?

FATHER: Yes. White flowered wallpaper.

PRODUCER: Well, it's not white. It's striped. So what! I think the furniture is just about OK. Can we have that small table forwards a few inches please! (*The* STAGEHANDS *move it*) (*To the* PROPERTY MAN) Bring an envelope, too, would you? Blue, if possible. And give it to the Father.

PROPERTY MAN: An ordinary envelope?

PRODUCER: ⎫
FATHER: ⎭ Yes, an ordinary envelope!

PROPERTY MAN: Ordinary envelope coming up! (*Exit*)

PRODUCER: Right! Let's get going! We want the young lady on first. (*The* LEADING ACTRESS *steps forwards*) Hold on a minute! Not you! This young lady! (*He indicates the* STEPDAUGHTER) You're supposed to watch...

STEPDAUGHTER (*chipping in quickly*): ...How I live it!

LEADING ACTRESS (*huffily*): Don't worry, I shall live it all right, once I get a look in!

PRODUCER (*with his hands to his head*): Ladies and gentlemen, can we please cut the cackle! Now: Scene I, the Young Lady and Madame Pace. Oh! (*He looks round momentarily flummoxed, then climbs back on stage*) What about Madame Pace?

FATHER: She isn't with us.

PRODUCER: So what do we do?

FATHER: But she is alive! She's just as alive as we are!

PRODUCER: Fine! Can you tell us where?

FATHER: Look, let me try something. (*To the* ACTRESSES) Would you ladies be good enough to let me have your hats a moment?

ACTRESSES (*surprised and amused, all speaking at once*): What? Our hats? What does he want? Whatever for? Whatever next!

PRODUCER: Whatever are you going to do with those? (*The* ACTORS *laugh*)

FATHER: Nothing much. Just hang them up here a moment on these pegs. Perhaps some of you would be good enough to let me have your coats as well...

ACTORS (*all at once, again surprised and amused*): Coats too? Now what happens? I reckon he's bonkers.

ACTRESSES: What do you want them for? Just our coats?

FATHER: I just want to hang them up here a moment... I'd be awfully grateful... I hope you don't mind...

ACTRESSES (*taking off their hats and some their coats, and hanging them up amid a good deal of laughter*): Well, why not? There we are, then! It's a laugh, but he really means it, I reckon! Is it a fashion show?

FATHER: That is exactly what it is! There! A fashion show!

PRODUCER: May one ask what all this is in aid of?

FATHER: Indeed you may! If we prepare the scene a little more authentically, who knows but what she may not be drawn towards the implements of her trade and appear among us! (*He invites them to look towards the door at the back of the set*) Now watch! Watch!

The door opens and MADAME PACE *emerges and advances a few paces onto the stage. She is a hideous old harridan, enormously fat, with a garish carrot-coloured woollen wig perched above her raddled face and a scarlet rose stuck over one ear, à l'espagnole. She wears a tasteless but modish gown of gaudy red silk, and carries a fan made of feathers in one hand while flourishing a lit cigarette between two fingers of the other.* At her appearance the ACTORS *and* PRODUCER *back away with horrified gasps and slip hastily down the steps into the auditorium as if making for the central aisle and main exit. The* STEPDAUGHTER, *however, runs up to* MADAME PACE *with all the deference befitting an employee.*

STEPDAUGHTER (*as she runs up to her*): Here she is! Here she is!

FATHER (*glowing with pleasure*): It's Madame Pace. Didn't I tell you! Here she is!

PRODUCER (*controlling his initial amazement, indignantly*): What the hell are you playing at?

LEADING ACTOR: Can someone tell me what's going on?

YOUNG ACTOR: Where has she sprung from?

YOUNG ACTRESS: She must have been there all the time!

LEADING ACTRESS: They do it with mirrors, darling!

FATHER (*raising his voice above theirs*): Let me speak! Why do you have to be so small-minded and pick everything to pieces! You're destroying the miracle, for that's what it is! Reality itself kindled into life, conjured up, brought into being by the scene itself and drawn towards it, with more right to life in this place than you have. She has more truth than you have! Which of you actresses is going to be Madame Pace? Well: here is Madame Pace! You've got to admit that whoever takes the part will be less true than she is, for she actually is Madame Pace in person! Look! My daughter recognized her and ran straight up to her! Now watch, just watch this scene!

With some hesitation, the PRODUCER *and* ACTORS *return to the stage. The* STEPDAUGHTER *and* MADAME PACE *have by now been engaged in their scene together for some time, throughout the* ACTORS' *protestations and the* FATHER's *reply. Their low whispered conversation is naturalistic, held at a pitch totally unsuited to the stage. So when the* ACTORS' *attention is drawn to the scene by the* FATHER *and they turn to watch it, they see* MADAME PACE, *her hand under the* STEPDAUGHTER's *chin, gabbling away unintelligibly into the girl's raised face. For a moment they strain to hear what is being said, but give up almost at once.*

PRODUCER: Well?

LEADING ACTOR: What's she saying?

LEADING ACTRESS: I can't hear a word!

YOUNG ACTOR: Speak up! Speak up!

STEPDAUGHTER (*leaving* MADAME PACE *smiling – an indescribable smile – while she comes towards the group of* ACTORS): Speak up? How can we speak up? These aren't things that can be said out loud! Oh, I could say them out loud to put *him* down! (*She is referring to the* FATHER) That was just revenge! But with Madame it's a very different matter. She could go to prison!

PRODUCER: Well, well, well. Is that so? My dear child, in the theatre you have to make yourself heard! Do you realize we can't hear you even up here on this stage? What the devil's it going to be like when there's an audience? And anyway you can perfectly well speak out loud to each other; we shan't be here when the time comes. You've got to imagine the two of you are on your own in that back room and there's no one to hear you.

The STEPDAUGHTER *with a winning gesture wags her finger several times to disagree. There is a touch of malice in her smile.*

PRODUCER: Why not?

STEPDAUGHTER (*in a knowing whisper*): Because there's someone who will hear us if she says it all out loud!

PRODUCER (*in consternation*): You haven't got somebody else about to jump out at us? (*The* ACTORS *make as if to leave the stage again*)

FATHER: Oh, no, no! She means me. I would be there you see, on the other side of that door, waiting. And Madame knows this. In fact, you must excuse me. I must go so as to be ready for my cue. (*He makes as if to go*)

PRODUCER (*stopping him*): No, wait a moment! This is theatre! You've got to consider the requirements of the medium! Look, before you're ready to come on...

STEPDAUGHTER (*interrupting*): Let's get on! Let's do it now! I'm dying to live that scene, I'm mad to live that scene! If he's ready to do it straight away, I'm ready too! More than ready!

PRODUCER (*shouting her down*): But first we've got to get that first scene straight, the one with you and Madame! Can you not take that in?

STEPDAUGHTER: For Heaven's sake, she has only told me what you already know: that once again my mother has done her sewing badly; that the stuff's ruined; and that I must be patient if I want her to go on helping us out of our financial difficulties.

MADAME PACE (*advancing with an air of great importance*): It is so, *señor; porque* never would I try to profit myself, to advantage myself...

PRODUCER (*flabbergasted*): Is that how she speaks?

The ACTORS *burst into fits of laughter.*

STEPDAUGHTER (*laughing too*): That's how she speaks! Half in Spanish, half in English; it's really funny!

MADAME PACE: It does not seem to me *buena crianza*, how you say – good manners, that you laugh of me. I try to *hablar* your language *como puedo, señor*!

PRODUCER: But it's terrific! Leave it in! Don't change it! This will get them! In fact it is just what it needs to lighten the crudity a bit. You speak exactly like that, dear! It will be great!

STEPDAUGHTER: It will be great all right! You bet it will! It will be great for me, too, won't it, listening to my special instructions in that language. It ought to be a right good laugh! Hilarious, wouldn't you say, hearing that there's a *viejo señor* who wants to amuse himself *con migo*! Wouldn't you agree, Madame?

MADAME PACE: Not "*viejo*", *linda*, "*viejito*", a little bit old! But *mejor para ti*, all the better! If you don't like him, at least he will have *prudencia*.

MOTHER (*She rises from her seat, to the astonishment and consternation of the* ACTORS, *who have taken no notice of her until now. They rush to hold her back and burst out laughing as she tears the wig from Madame Pace's head and flings it to the ground.*): You devil! You devil! You monster! Oh my child!

STEPDAUGHTER (*trying to hold her back*): No, Mum, no! No, please!

FATHER (*at the same time ditto*): Come on, just be calm. Sit down, now.

MOTHER: Get her out of my sight!

STEPDAUGHTER (*to the* PRODUCER *who has also hurried over*): We can't have my mother here, we just can't!

FATHER (*also to the* PRODUCER): They can't be in the same place! That's the reason why she wasn't with us when we first arrived. If you put them together it all happens too soon.

PRODUCER: Never mind! Don't let's worry! This is just a sort of rough sketch. It's all useful, even if it's a bit of a muddle. It gives me a chance to piece together the various strands. (*He turns to the* MOTHER *and takes her back to her chair*) There we are, take it easy, now. Sit yourself down.

Meanwhile the STEPDAUGHTER, *back on the stage, takes up her scene with* MADAME PACE *again.*

STEPDAUGHTER: Come on then, Madame.

MADAME PACE (*offended*): Oh, no! *Gracias*, no! I, here, do not do *nada* if there is your Mother.

STEPDAUGHTER: Come on, show in the *viejo señor*, who wants to amuse himself *con migo*. (*She turns to all assembled and announces in dictatorial tones*) This scene, now, it has to be done! So let's get going! (*To* MADAME PACE) You can go!

MADAME PACE: I go! I go! Most *seguramente* I go! (*She leaves in high dudgeon, picking up her wig on the way and glaring at the* ACTORS *who snigger and clap*)

STEPDAUGHTER (*to the* FATHER): Make your entrance! No, don't bother to go off again! Come here! Let's say you're on already! Right! Now I'm standing here, all modest, with my head down like this! OK then! Nice and loud. Sort of fresh-sounding, like someone coming in from outside: "Good afternoon, my dear…"

PRODUCER (*back in the auditorium*): Hold on! Who's directing this show, you or me? (*To the* FATHER, *who looks rather hesitant and perplexed*) Carry on, go right ahead! Go to the back. Don't exit. Just come forward again.

The FATHER *does this in something of a daze. He is very pale. Wholly engrossed now in the reality of his created life, he smiles as he moves downstage, as if not yet touched by the drama which is about to burst upon him. The* ACTORS *are suddenly attentive as the scene begins.*

PRODUCER (*in a hasty whisper to the* PROMPTER): Be sure to get all this down, won't you!

THE SCENE

FATHER (*as he approaches, a new note in his voice*): Good afternoon, my dear.

STEPDAUGHTER (*her head bowed, barely controlling her disgust*): Good afternoon.

FATHER (*he eyes her tentatively, peering under the hat which almost hides her face. When he sees how very young she is, he exclaims, as if to himself, half-delighted and half-fearful of landing himself in a risky situation*): Ah! Er... it won't be the first time, will it?... I mean, it won't be your first time here?

STEPDAUGHTER (*her head still bowed*): No.

FATHER: You've been here before? (*The* STEPDAUGHTER *nods*) More than once? (*He waits for her answer, peers again at her face, smiles and then speaks*) Well, then... you oughtn't to be so... Would you let me take your hat off?

STEPDAUGHTER (*quickly, to stop him, her disgust now all too evident*): No, no. I'll take it off myself. (*She quickly does so, trembling. The* MOTHER *watches all this in a state of extreme agitation. She sits with the* SON *and the younger children who cling to her closely all the time, on the opposite side of the stage from the* ACTORS. *As she follows the scene between the* FATHER *and the* STEPDAUGHTER *her face registers pain, outrage, anxiety and horror. From time to time she hides her face or utters a moan.*)

MOTHER: Oh God! Oh, my God!

FATHER (*he seems momentarily stunned by this sob from the* MOTHER; *after a pause he resumes his earlier tone*): Here, give it to me. I'll put it down. (*He takes the hat from her hands*) But a pretty little head like yours needs something a bit more special, I think. Why don't you come over here and help me choose you one of Madame Pace's confections?... No?

YOUNG ACTRESS: Hey! Those are our hats you've got there!

PRODUCER (*quickly and angrily*): Shut up, can't you! For God's sake don't try and be funny! This is the big scene! (*To the* STEPDAUGHTER) Carry on then, please!

STEPDAUGHTER (*to the* FATHER): No, really, I couldn't.

FATHER: Don't say you refuse! You must accept! I should be so disappointed... Look, they really are extremely pretty. Madame Pace would be so pleased. She puts them out specially, you know!

STEPDAUGHTER: Oh no, sir. You see... I shouldn't be able to wear it.

FATHER: What's the trouble? Are you worried about what they will think at home when you turn up in a new hat? Well! Shall I tell you? Shall I tell you what to say?

STEPDAUGHTER (*desperate, finding all this unbearable*): No, that's not it! I shouldn't be able to wear it, because I'm... well, look: you might have noticed! (*She shows him her black dress*)

FATHER: You're in mourning! My dear, I'm sorry. Of course, I see now. I really beg your pardon. Believe me, I'm most desperately sorry.

STEPDAUGHTER (*mustering all her strength in an effort to conquer her abhorrence and disgust*): All right, all right, it doesn't matter! I should be thanking you, really! There's absolutely no call for you to go apologizing and getting upset. Please don't think any more about what I told you. As for me, well, obviously (*she forces herself to smile*), I've really got to stop thinking about it, these clothes I mean.

PRODUCER (*breaking in, addressing the* PROMPTER *and coming back up onto the stage*): Hold on! Stop a minute! Don't write that down. Omit that last bit! (*To the* FATHER *and the* STEPDAUGHTER) You're doing fine! Absolutely fine! (*To the* FATHER) Go straight on with the next bit as we said! (*To the* ACTORS) That hat scene was ravishing, don't you think?

STEPDAUGHTER: But the best bit's just coming now! Can't we go on?

PRODUCER: Hold your horses a moment! (*To the* ACTORS) Obviously it has all got to be treated rather lightly…

LEADING ACTOR (*nodding in agreement*): Nice and zippy!

LEADING ACTRESS: It shouldn't present any problems. (*To the* LEADING ACTOR) We could try it now, couldn't we?

LEADING ACTOR: Fine by me!… I'll make my entrance! (*He goes off ready to come in again through the door at the back*)

PRODUCER (*to* LEADING ACTRESS): All right, then. Now, you've just finished your scene with Madame Pace. I'll take care of writing that up. You will be over here… Hey, where are you off to?

LEADING ACTRESS: Wait a sec, let me put my hat back on… (*She goes to get her own hat from the hat stand*)

PRODUCER: That's lovely. Right. You stand here, with your head bowed…

STEPDAUGHTER (*amused*): But she's not wearing black!

LEADING ACTRESS: I shall be, don't worry, and with more success than you, duckie!

PRODUCER (*to the* STEPDAUGHTER): Keep out of this, will you? Just watch! You might learn something. (*He claps his hands*) OK. Let's have your entrance!

He climbs down again to get the audience's view. The door at the back opens and the LEADING ACTOR *comes on. He has the breezy over-familiarity of a seasoned ladies' man. Performed by the* ACTORS, *the scene*

*comes over as completely different. In no way, however, must it smack
of parody. It is clearly supposed to be the new improved version, with
embellishments. When the* STEPDAUGHTER *and* FATHER *hear their own
words uttered by the* ACTOR *and* ACTRESS, *they obviously completely
fail to recognize themselves. During the scene which follows they express their surprise, amazement and distress in various ways, in gesture,
laughter and downright protest. The* PROMPTER's *voice can be clearly
heard throughout.*

LEADING ACTOR: "Good afternoon, my dear."

FATHER (*butting in, unable to restrain himself*): No!

The STEPDAUGHTER's *response to this entrance of the* LEADING ACTOR
is to burst out laughing.

PRODUCER (*furiously to them both*): Shut up! And stop laughing for
    Christ's sake! How the hell do you expect us to get anything done!

STEPDAUGHTER (*turning towards him*): I'm sorry! But how can I help
    it? Your actress manages to stand in her place without moving, but
    Heavens, if it were me and I heard someone say "good afternoon"
    to me in that voice, I'd burst out laughing, as in fact I did.

FATHER (*also approaching the* PRODUCER): She's quite right... it's the
    manner, and the tone of voice...

PRODUCER: Well, stuff the manner and the tone of voice! Just get out of
    the way, will you, and let me watch this rehearsal!

LEADING ACTOR (*coming downstage*): Look, I'm supposed to be an old
    bloke in a brothel, right?

PRODUCER: Yes, of course, take absolutely no notice. Start again! You're
    doing fine! Start again! (*He waits for the* ACTOR *to continue*) Right
    then...

LEADING ACTOR: "Good afternoon, my dear."

LEADING ACTRESS: "Good afternoon."

LEADING ACTOR (*going through the same motions as the* FATHER *peering
    under the girl's hat, but then expressing very distinctly satisfaction
    followed by apprehensiveness*): "Ah!... but, I say, this won't be the
    first time, I hope..."

FATHER (*who can't help correcting him*): Not "I hope". "Will it?" "Will
    it?"

PRODUCER: He says it should be "Will it?" – question.

LEADING ACTOR (*with reference to the* PROMPTER): I heard him say "I hope".

PRODUCER: Don't worry! It's the same thing! "Will it", "I hope" – nothing in it! Just carry on! Come on! A bit lighter, maybe. Look, let me show you. Look, like this! (*He mounts the stage and plays the scene through from the* FATHER's *entrance*) "Good afternoon, my dear."

LEADING ACTRESS: "Good afternoon."

PRODUCER: "Ah! but, I say…" (*He turns to the* LEADING ACTOR *to ensure that he has taken in his gesture of peering under the brim of the girl's hat*) See? Surprise, and anxiety, and satisfaction, all at once. (*Back in the role, to the* LEADING ACTRESS) "…it won't be the first time, will it? The first time you've been here?" (*Turning back to the* LEADING ACTOR) See what I mean? (*To the* LEADING ACTRESS) Then you say "No, sir." (*To the* ACTOR *again*) A little more… how shall I put it… *souplesse*! (*He returns to the stalls*)

LEADING ACTRESS: "No, sir."

LEADING ACTOR: "You've been here before? More than once?"

PRODUCER: No, hold on! Let her nod first. "You've been here before?" (*The* LEADING ACTRESS *raises her head, her eyes half-closed in a show of pained disgust. At a word from the* PRODUCER *she nods violently twice.*)

STEPDAUGHTER (*involuntarily*): Oh, my God! (*She claps a hand to her mouth to muffle her laughter*)

PRODUCER (*turning*): What now?

STEPDAUGHTER (*quickly*): Nothing, nothing!

PRODUCER (*to* LEADING ACTOR): Come on, it's you now!

LEADING ACTOR: "More than once? Well, then… you oughtn't to be so… Would you let me take your hat off?" (*The* LEADING ACTOR's *voice and gestures as he utters this last line cause the* STEPDAUGHTER, *whose hand is still held over her mouth, to burst out into a noisy guffaw through her fingers, in spite of her real effort to restrain herself*)

LEADING ACTRESS (*furious, returning to her chair*): I'm damned if I'm going to stay here to be laughed at by her!

LEADING ACTOR: I agree! I've had enough!

PRODUCER (*shouting at the* STEPDAUGHTER): Stop that noise! Don't you dare do that again!

STEPDAUGHTER: Yes, of course. I'm sorry. I'm sorry.

PRODUCER: Your behaviour is quite appalling! Appalling! I don't know how you dare!

FATHER (*trying to intervene*): Yes, sir, I know, you are perfectly right! But don't be too hard on her!

PRODUCER (*remounting the stage*): Why shouldn't I be hard on her! She's a disgrace!

FATHER: You're right of course, but you know it really is such a very strange sensation...

PRODUCER: What's a strange sensation? What's strange? What's strange about it?

FATHER: I admire your actors, I really admire them. This gentleman, and this lady here. But there's no doubt about it – they're not us!

PRODUCER: Well, of course they're not! How could they be? They are actors!

FATHER: That's it! Actors! And they both do a very nice job playing our parts. But you've got to see that to us it looks quite different. It's supposed to be the same, and it just isn't!

PRODUCER: How isn't it the same? What's different about it?

FATHER: It has turned into something... which belongs to them now; it's not ours any more.

PRODUCER: Well, that stands to reason! I've been over all this already!

FATHER: Yes, I do understand. I do.

PRODUCER: Well, then. That's it then, isn't it? (*He turns to the* ACTORS) This really means we'll have to do the rehearsing on our own in the normal way. I have always found it impossible to rehearse with authors present! Nothing is ever right! (*He turns again to the* FATHER *and the* STEPDAUGHTER) Come on, we'll give it another go with you two. If you can manage not to laugh.

STEPDAUGHTER: Oh, I shan't laugh now, I shan't laugh now. My good bit is coming now, don't you worry!

PRODUCER: All right, then! Now when she says "Please don't think any more about what I told you"... and then "I've obviously got to stop thinking about these clothes" and so on, well at that point (*turning to the* FATHER) you've got to come in quickly and say "Oh yes, I understand, I understand!" and then immediately afterwards you've got to ask her...

STEPDAUGHTER (*interrupting*): What! What does he ask?

PRODUCER: He's got to ask the reason why you're in mourning!

STEPDAUGHTER: But he didn't! You're so wrong! Look, when I said to him to take no notice of my dress, do you know what he said? He said, "Right! Well, let's take this little dress off, then, shall we, as quickly as we can!"

PRODUCER: Oh, that would go down a bomb! My dear girl, you'd bring the whole theatre about my ears!

STEPDAUGHTER: But it's true!

PRODUCER: But for Heaven's sake, truth doesn't come into it! This place is a theatre. Truth's all right, but only up to a point!

STEPDAUGHTER: How do you want to do it, then?

PRODUCER: You'll see! Just let me carry on for the moment!

STEPDAUGHTER: Oh, no, you don't! You want to use my feelings of disgust, you want to use all the cruel and humiliating stages by which I became the thing I am, to concoct a sentimental little romantic sob story; you want him to ask me why I'm in mourning and me to tell him that my daddy died two months ago. Well, we are not having it! Not on your life! He has got to say to me exactly what he did say! "Let's take this little dress off, then, shall we, as quickly as we can!" And I, still sick at heart and grieving for my father, I went over there, do you see?... behind that screen. And with fingers trembling with embarrassment and loathing, I unhooked the top half of my dress...

PRODUCER (*tearing his fingers through his hair*): Good God, girl! What are you saying!

STEPDAUGHTER (*her voice raised in frenzy*): The truth! Only the truth!

PRODUCER: Well, I don't deny this may well be the truth... and I understand, I understand how horrifying all this must have been for you, but I urge you to see that it's just not possible to put this stuff on the stage!

STEPDAUGHTER: Not possible? Well! In that case... thank you very much... you can count me out!

PRODUCER: No, wait... look!

STEPDAUGHTER: You can count me right out. You've decided between you what's possible on the stage; you've fixed it together in that room! Thanks a lot! I know exactly what's happened! I know what he's after! He wants a chance to flaunt his spiritual agonies. Well, I want to put on my drama! The drama of what has happened to me!

PRODUCER (*with a fierce shrug of annoyance*): Your drama, is it? I see! But it isn't just your drama, is it? What about everybody else's! What about his! (*He points to the* FATHER) What about your mother's! One character can't be allowed to go hogging the stage like that and upstaging all the others! They have all got to come together in an evenly balanced picture. We can only represent the representable. I know as well as anybody else that everyone's got a rich inner life they want to lay bare. But this is precisely the problem: how to expose just the right amount to keep a proper balance with the rest of the cast; just enough to give an indication of all that inner life you've got tucked away! I mean, can you imagine, if each character were given a full-scale monologue... why not a lecture?... in which he could stand up before the audience and dollop out publicly the rich mix that's stewing away inside him! (*In a kindly, conciliatory tone*) You'll have to exercise self-restraint, I'm afraid. In fact it will be in your own interest. Let me warn you, that it might not go down at all well, all these ferocious outbursts and protestations of disgust, when you yourself have admitted, if I may say so, that you had already been with other men before him, and more than once, in that establishment of Madame Pace's.

STEPDAUGHTER (*She pauses to recollect herself, then in a low voice, her head bowed*): That's true. But can't you see that for me, those other men are all him!

PRODUCER (*not understanding*): All him? What is that supposed to mean?

STEPDAUGHTER: When somebody goes wrong, isn't it always the responsibility of the person who set the whole thing going in the first place? All the blame goes back to him, before I was born even. I mean, look at him! You can see it's true!

PRODUCER: All right, then! That's quite a packet he's got on his conscience! Give him the chance to act it out!

STEPDAUGHTER: What? How can he? How can he present himself as a man of conscience, tormented by fine moral scruples, if you're going to let him off the other bit?... if you're going to skip the horror: the moment when he realizes that the woman in his arms, the prostitute, whom he's just asked if she will kindly remove her black dress – is the little girl... right?... the little girl he used to go and watch coming out of school? (*These last words have been spoken in a voice shaking with emotion. The* MOTHER, *hearing them, is overcome by an access of irrepressible anguish, which finds expression first in a kind of stifled moaning and then erupts in a paroxysm of tears. Her emotion silences everyone and there is a long pause.*)

STEPDAUGHTER (*as soon as her* MOTHER'*s sobs allow, in a sombre resolute tone*): So far this is all just between us. We haven't been seen by the public. And tomorrow you will make your own play out of us, and you'll put it all together in whatever way you fancy. But do you want to see it really, our drama? Shall we let it explode for you, as it really happened?

PRODUCER: What could be better? Then I can pick out whatever I can use.

STEPDAUGHTER: All right, then. Get that Mother on stage.

MOTHER (*her tears giving place to a high scream*): No, no! Don't let them do it! Don't let them do it!

PRODUCER: It's only to have a look, my dear!

MOTHER: I can't! I can't!

PRODUCER: But why not, if it has all happened already? Why should it matter now?

MOTHER: No, it's happening now! It's happening all the time! My agony isn't made up! I am living my agony constantly, every moment; I'm alive and it's alive and it keeps coming back again and again, as fresh as the first time. Those two children there, have you heard them speak? They can't speak, not now. Their business is to cling to me, all the time, to keep the pain alive. For themselves, they don't exist, they don't exist any more! And my elder girl here has run away; she had made off and left me, and now she's lost... lost... If I see her standing here before me now, it's the same thing, it's for the same reason, to keep the agony fresh, to keep it going, all the agony I have suffered through her as well!

FATHER (*solemnly*): The eternal moment! I told you about it. She's here to catch me, to string me up before the public, fixed, hooked, chained for ever to the pillory of that one shaming fleeting moment of my life. It is what she has to do. And you, sir, cannot really let me off it.

PRODUCER: Oh, I don't say I'm not going to show it: it will be the focal point of the whole first act, making a great climax when she (*he indicates the* MOTHER) discovers you...

FATHER: That's right. That's the moment that seals my fate; that final scream of hers that marks the culmination of all our suffering.

STEPDAUGHTER: I can still hear it now! That scream sent me out of my mind! Oh, you can do what you like with my part, I don't care! Have me in my clothes, if you like. As long as my arms are bare, just the arms. They have got to be bare because, you see, standing like this...

(*She goes up to the* FATHER *and places her head against his breast*)
…with my head here like this, and my arms like this round his neck,
I could see a vein throbbing, just here in my arm. And then, as if
that single palpitating vein filled me with revulsion, I screwed up my
eyes like this… like this… and buried my head in his chest! (*Turning towards the* MOTHER) Scream, Mum, scream! (*She buries her
head in the* FATHER's *breast again, and with her shoulders tensed as
if to protect herself from the scream, she adds in tones of muffled
anguish*) Scream like you screamed then!

MOTHER (*flinging herself upon them to separate them*): No! Oh my
child! My child! (*She tears the* STEPDAUGHTER *away*) Oh you brute,
you dirty brute! It's my daughter! Can't you see it's my daughter!

PRODUCER (*moving back, at the scream, to the edge of the stage, while
the* ACTORS *appear flabbergasted*): Splendid! Absolutely splendid!
And then curtain, curtain!

FATHER (*hurrying over, distraught*): That's it, you see! That's exactly
how it happened!

PRODUCER (*enthusiastically, entirely won over*): Yes, we'll cut it right
there! Curtain! Curtain!

At the PRODUCER's *repeated cries of "Curtain!" the* STAGE MANAGER *lowers the curtain, leaving only the* FATHER *and the* PRODUCER *in front of it.*

PRODUCER (*looking up and raising his hands*): Good God! When I say
"Curtain" I mean, "That's where we'll have a curtain", so they go
and lower the bloody thing! (*He lifts up the curtain to enable the two
of them to return to the stage*) But what a curtain! It's absolutely
stunning! Can't fail! I'd stake my shirt on that first act!

The PRODUCER *and the* FATHER *return through the curtain to the stage.*

*When the curtain goes up we find the first set dismantled and in its place
a small garden fountain.*

The ACTORS *are sitting on one side of the stage and the* CHARACTERS
on the other. The PRODUCER *is standing lost in thought, chin in hand,
in the centre of the stage.*

PRODUCER (*shaking himself out of his reverie, after a pause*): Well, then.
Let's move on to Act Two. Best to leave it all to me, I think, as we
agreed. Everything will be just fine!

STEPDAUGHTER: It's the bit where we go to live with *him* (*she indicates the* FATHER) much to his disgust over there! (*She is referring to the* SON)

PRODUCER (*out of patience*): All right. But leave it to me, will you?

STEPDAUGHTER: As long as you make it clear how much he loathed us coming!

MOTHER (*shaking her head in her corner*): Not that it did us any good!

STEPDAUGHTER (*turning on her, sharply*): That's not the point! The worse it was for us, the guiltier he felt about it!

PRODUCER (*still impatient*): I've got the picture, don't worry! I'll keep it all in mind. Specially at the beginning.

MOTHER (*in beseeching tones*): But please… make me easy in my mind… please make sure people realize that I tried every means I could think of—

STEPDAUGHTER (*interrupting bitterly*): …Of squaring me! Oh yes, of getting me to give up the fight! (*To the* PRODUCER) Go on, let her have her way! It's perfectly true. She did try. I get quite a kick out of it in fact because, well, you'll see: the more abject she gets, and the more she makes up to him – the more he holds himself aloof. He just… is… not… there. Serves her right!

PRODUCER: Are we going to get on with it then, this Act Two?

STEPDAUGHTER: I'll shut up! But your idea of putting the whole thing in the garden isn't going to work!

PRODUCER: Why not?

STEPDAUGHTER: Because of him! (*She points to the* SON) He spends the whole time shut up in his room, on his own! And anyway, my little brother's bit all happens in the house. I told you. Poor little soul!

PRODUCER: All right, then. But we can't keep switching about all the time changing scenes. You can't put up little signs saying "House", "Garden", "House" three or four times in one act!

LEADING ACTOR: They used to…

PRODUCER: Yes, in the days when audiences were about as sophisticated as that little girl!

LEADING ACTRESS: They were better at accepting the illusion!

FATHER (*jumping up suddenly*): Illusion? I would ask you not to speak of illusion! I would beg you not to use that word. For us it has a particularly cruel ring!

PRODUCER (*astonished*): For Heaven's sake, why?

FATHER: Oh, yes, cruel, cruel! You really ought to understand.

PRODUCER: What are we supposed to say? Illusion is our stock-in-trade... the illusion we have to create...

LEADING ACTOR: ...With our acting...

PRODUCER: ...To make the play live for the audience!

FATHER: I understand. But maybe you are incapable of understanding us. I'm sorry, but the fact is, you see, for you and your actors all this is – quite rightly – a kind of game...

LEADING ACTRESS (*taking offence and interrupting*): A game! This isn't kids' stuff! This is serious acting!

FATHER: I'm not saying it isn't. And let me say, I entirely understand how you play it! As artists – as your producer says – you have to create a perfect illusion of reality.

PRODUCER: That's right.

FATHER: But what if you stop to consider that we, the six of us (*he gestures briefly to indicate the six*) have no other reality; that we don't exist outside this illusion!

PRODUCER (*floored by this and looking round at the blank puzzled faces of his* ACTORS): How exactly do you mean?

FATHER (*he stands and looks at them a moment, then, with a bleak smile*): Can't you see? What other reality could we have? What for you is an illusion, that has got to be created, for us is our only reality. (*He pauses briefly, then walks over to the* PRODUCER *and continues*) And we're not the only ones, you see. Just you think about it! (*Looking him straight in the eyes*) Can you tell me who you are? (*He stands, pointing his finger at him*)

PRODUCER (*disturbed, with a half-smile*): Tell you who I am? I'm me!

FATHER: And if I suggested that you were not you, that you were me?

PRODUCER: I'd tell you you were mad! (*The* ACTORS *laugh*)

FATHER: You're quite right to laugh. Of course everything here is a game! (*To the* PRODUCER) That's how you can argue that your actor there, the man himself, will only be playing at being me, the person I am. Do you see I've caught you out?

PRODUCER (*annoyed*): But you have *said* this before! Have we got to have it all again?

FATHER: No, that wasn't in fact the point I was trying to make. I am actually asking you to set aside your game a moment (*he glances apprehensively at the* LEADING ACTRESS *and corrects himself*)... your art, the art you practise here with your actors, and consider my question, my serious question which I repeat: who are you?

PRODUCER (*in amazement and exasperation to the* ACTORS): My God, the man's got a nerve! Calls himself a "character" and has the gall actually to ask me who I am.

FATHER (*with quiet dignity*): A character, my dear sir, may always ask a man who he is. Because a character really does have a life of his own, stamped with his own characteristics which ensure that he is always who he is. While a man – I don't mean you in particular, but a man in general, can very easily be "no one".

PRODUCER: Right! Well, perhaps I'd better get it into your head that I'm the producer of this play and the director of this company!

FATHER (*continuing softly, his tone mellifluous and deferential*): I'm trying to find out, sir, how your present self sees your past self, how the man you are today sees the man you were once upon a time. Think of yourself as once you were, sir, and the illusions that you had, the way you saw the world around you and inside you! That was the world for you, in those days, sir! Now, thinking back on those lost illusions, on all that vanished-seeming world which once was the world for you, don't you feel something give way beneath your feet, not just these boards but the very ground of your existence? Knowing that in just the same way the "you" of today, which feels like reality here and now, is destined to seem an illusion tomorrow?

PRODUCER (*who has not really understood, but is dazed by the speciousness of the argument*): Well, where does that get you?

FATHER: Oh, nowhere, I just wanted to show you that if we (*he refers to himself and the other* CHARACTERS) have no reality outside illusion, then perhaps you ought not to place too much faith in your reality, either, the solid flesh and blood you have today – on the grounds that like yesterday's reality, today's too will surely turn out to be illusion by tomorrow.

PRODUCER (*determined to make light of all this*): That's good! Now tell me that you and this play of yours are more real and true than I am!

FATHER (*with the utmost seriousness*): Of that there can be no doubt at all.

PRODUCER: Is that so?

FATHER: I thought you had understood that all along.

PRODUCER: You are more real than me?

FATHER: If your reality can change from one day to the next...

PRODUCER: Of course it does! That's obvious! It's always changing. Everybody's is.

FATHER (*raising his voice to a shout*): But not ours! Not ours, do you see? That's the difference! It doesn't change, it can't change, it can never be any different, ever, because it's fixed, as it is, once and for all. We are stuck with it, sir, and therein lies the horror; stuck with an immutable reality. You should find our presence chilling.

PRODUCER (*suddenly facing him squarely, struck by an idea which has just occurred to him*): What I'd like to know, though, is: who has ever heard of a character stepping out of his part and holding forth about it like you do, expounding it and explaining it. Who has ever heard of such a thing? Tell me that! I'm sure I haven't!

FATHER: No, you've never heard of such a thing because on the whole authors keep quiet about the birth pangs they endure producing their creations. Once an author's characters come to life and stand before him as living beings, they decide what to say and do, and he simply follows their suggestions. If he doesn't like the way they are, that's just too bad! A character, once born, takes on such a degree of independence from his author that one can imagine all sorts of situations for him that have never occurred to the author. He can take on a completely new meaning sometimes that the author never dreamt of.

PRODUCER: Yes, well, I know that!

FATHER: Well, then, what's so amazing about us? If you can imagine the disaster it is for a character to go through what I've described, to be born in the imagination of an author who then turns round and refuses him life – can you then say that such a character, abandoned like that, alive but denied life, is wrong to go and do what we are doing? Aren't we right to come and beg of all of you the thing we begged of him, time and time again, beseeching him, urging him, appearing before him one after the other... I would go... or she would go (*indicating the* STEPDAUGHTER) or sometimes this poor Mother...

STEPDAUGHTER (*moving downstage in a kind of trance*): Yes, it's true, I did. I used to go, to tempt him, time after time... in that cheerless study where he did his writing, just as it was getting dark. He would be sitting there, sunk in his armchair, not even bothering to turn on the light. The room would get darker and darker and the darkness would be teeming with our presence. We went there to tempt him. (*She seems to be back in the study she is describing. The* ACTORS' *presence appears to irritate her*) Go away, can't you? Can't you leave us be? Mum's there, with that "son"... I'm there with the little one... that kid always on his own... and then, me with *him* (*she nods almost imperceptibly in the* FATHER'*s direction*)... and then me alone, alone in the dark again! (*She gives a sudden start as if anxious to grasp hold of the vision she has of herself, glowing with life in that darkness*) Oh, my life! What scenes, what scenes we used to suggest to him! And I was the one who tempted him most of all!

FATHER: You did. But maybe that was it! Perhaps it was your fault; you tried too hard, you overdid it!

STEPDAUGHTER: Rubbish! He made me like this, didn't he? (*She approaches the* PRODUCER *and adopts a confidential tone*) I think the real reason was discouragement with the theatre, or disgust with it – the way it lets itself be dictated to by public taste...

PRODUCER: Let's get on! Let's get on, for Heaven's sake! Let's get to what in fact happened!

STEPDAUGHTER: It seems to me you're going to have an awful lot to choose from, once we get inside that house! Especially as you said we couldn't keep changing the scene or putting up notices every five minutes.

PRODUCER: Too right! We have to take the facts, knock them into shape and compress them into a close-knit plot. It can't be done your way; you want to see your little brother coming home from school and wandering round the rooms like a lost soul, hiding behind doors and hatching his plot, the plot you spoke of as... what was it you said?

STEPDAUGHTER: It drained him, sir, it drained the life out of him!

PRODUCER: Yes... odd way of putting it... Still, we see the plot "looming larger and larger in his eyes", was that it?

STEPDAUGHTER: That's right, sir. You have only to look at him! (*She points to where he stands beside his* MOTHER)

PRODUCER: Fine! And then, at the same time, you want us to show the little girl playing away, all unawares, in the garden. One in the house, one in the garden... you really think we can do that?

STEPDAUGHTER: Oh yes, having a lovely time in the sunshine! That is my one compensation, to see her so happy, so thrilled with that garden; coming after the misery and squalor of that horrible bedroom where the four of us all slept together. She and I shared a bed – think of it! Me with my horrible contaminated body next to hers! She used to hold me ever so tight in her loving, innocent little arms! And whenever she saw me in the garden she used to come running up to me to hold my hand. She had no time for the big flowers; she was only interested in finding the "ickle baby ones", and how she used to love showing them to me! She'd get so excited! (*At this point she breaks off, overwhelmed by the memory, and gives way to a long and desperate fit of crying. She is sitting at a small table where she lets her head fall onto her arms. Her emotion silences every one. The* PRODUCER *approaches her in a fatherly manner, and says to comfort her:*)

PRODUCER: We'll have the garden, don't worry, we'll have the garden! We'll make it all right for you, you'll see! We'll put the whole action in the garden. (*He calls a* STAGEHAND *by name*) Send down a tree or two, will you? Couple of small cypresses here in front of the fountain! (*Two cypresses are lowered and hammered hastily in place by the* CHIEF STAGEHAND) That's roughly it for now, just to give us an idea. (*He calls out to the* STAGEHAND *again*) Hey! Can we have a sky-cloth?

STAGEHAND (*from the flies*): What?

PRODUCER: A sky-cloth! A backcloth! Here, behind the fountain! (*A white cloth is dropped from the flies*) Not white, you idiot! I said sky, didn't I? Never mind! Leave it now! I'll manage. (*He calls the* ELECTRICIAN) Lights! Switch off, will you, and let's have a bit of atmosphere. Moonlight, please! The blues in the batten and a blue spot on the cloth! Good! That's fine! (*A mysterious moonlit scene appears as ordered; the atmosphere of a garden at evening under the moon affects the way the* ACTORS *move and speak*)

PRODUCER (*to the* STEPDAUGHTER): How's this then? Instead of wandering about the house and hiding behind doors, the boy can do his wandering about here in the garden and hide behind the trees. But you realize it may be a bit tricky finding a child actress to do the little girl's scene with you, the bit where she shows you the flowers. (*To the* BOY) Anyway you come on out here! Let's see if we can work this one out! (*The* BOY *does not move*) Come on! Come on! (*He drags him forwards and tries to make him hold his head up. Each time the boy's head sags forwards.)* Good God, he's a total disaster! What's wrong with the lad? He has surely got to speak sometime! (*He puts a hand on his shoulder and guides him behind the trees*) Now, come on! Let's see what you can do! Just hide here... that's the idea... Try peering out a bit, sort of on the lookout... (*He stands back to see the effect. As the* BOY *follows his instructions the* ACTORS *show signs of disquiet. They are very much impressed.*) Ah, that's splendid... splendid... (*He turns again to the* STEPDAUGHTER) How would it be if the little girl were to come upon him peering out like that? Then she could run over to him and that would surely make him say something?

STEPDAUGHTER: It's no good hoping he will say anything as long as *he's* around! (*She indicates the* SON) You would have to get rid of him, first.

SON (*firmly making his way towards one of the sets of steps leading off the stage*): Only too ready to oblige! My pleasure! What could be better?

PRODUCER (*rushing to hold him back*): No! Where are you off to? Wait!

The MOTHER *gets up, horrified, deeply distressed at the thought of his going. She instinctively reaches out her arms to stop him, but without leaving her place.*

SON (*at the footlights, to the* PRODUCER *who is holding on to him*): I've really got nothing to do with all this. Will you please let me go! Let me go, will you?

PRODUCER: What do you mean, you've got nothing to do with it?

STEPDAUGHTER (*in a cool, unruffled tone, tinged with irony*): Don't stop him! He won't go away!

FATHER: He has to play the dreadful scene in the garden with his Mother.

SON (*quickly, with fierce resolution*): I'm not acting in any play! I have said that right from the start! (*To the* PRODUCER) Let me go!

STEPDAUGHTER (*running over to the* PRODUCER): Allow me, will you? (*She frees the* SON *from the* PRODUCER'S *grasp*) Let go of him! (*She turns to the* SON *as soon as he is freed*) All right then, off you go! (*The* SON *stands, his arms outstretched towards the steps, but he is held back as if by some mysterious force so that he cannot go down them. Then to the astonishment and perturbation of the* ACTORS, *he moves slowly across the footlights towards the other set of steps, where he stands at the top in the same attitude, posed for descent but unable to move. The* STEPDAUGHTER, *who has followed his movements as though challenging him to go, bursts out laughing.*) He can't, you see? He can't get away! He has got to stay here. He is tied and chained by a bond that's quite indissoluble. But if I'm still here – and I do get away in the end when everything happens as it must and at last I get out because I hate him so much and can't bear the sight of him – I say if I'm still here and can put up with seeing him and having him here, do you think he would stay here a moment if he could go? No, he can't budge! He has got to stay here with that marvellous father of his, and that mother, and be their only child again... (*Turning to the* MOTHER) Come on then, Mummy! Let's have it! (*Explaining the* MOTHER'*s movements to the* PRODUCER) Look, you see, she had got up already. She had got up to try and stop him going. (*To the* MOTHER, *as if exercising some kind of magic power*) Come along, that's the way... (*To the* PRODUCER) Imagine what it's costing her to show her feelings like this in front of your actors, but she's so desperate to get near him that – look! See? She's even willing to go through that scene again!

The MOTHER *has indeed crept up to the* SON, *and the moment her daughter finishes speaking she stretches out her arms towards him to indicate her readiness to play the scene.*

SON (*quickly*): Oh, no! Not me! Not me! If I can't leave, then I'll stay here, but, for the umpteenth time, I'm not acting in any play!

FATHER (*seething with fury, to the* PRODUCER): Make him, can't you?

SON: No one can make me!

FATHER: Well then I will!

STEPDAUGHTER: Wait a minute! Wait! First we've got to get the little one over to the fountain! (*She runs to get the* LITTLE GIRL, *falls to her knees in front of her, and takes her little face between her hands*) Oh, my poor darling, and such a lost look in those lovely big eyes; whatever do you make of this place! It's a stage, my pet! What's a stage? Well, look, it's a place where people play at being serious. They act plays there. And we're going to act a play. Yes, seriously, that's right! You, too... (*She puts her arms round her, hugging her close and rocking gently to and fro*) Oh, my little love, my little love, what a horrid play it's going to be for you! What a horrible thing they have thought up for you! The garden... the fountain... Yes, of course, it's a pretend fountain! That's the trouble, my pet, that everything here is pretend! And perhaps for you a pretend fountain is more fun than a real one, because you can play in it, can't you? But no... it's only for the others that it's a game; not for you, my poor pet, you're all too real! You are really playing in a real pond, a lovely big green one with reeds growing in it to make shade and reflections, and lots of baby ducks swimming about and making ripples in the shady surface. Then you want to catch one of the baby ducks... (*She gives a shriek which fills everyone with horror*) No, Rosetta my love, no! Your mummy's not looking after you, because of that swine of a son! I am half out of my mind with distress... and that boy there... (*She leaves the* LITTLE GIRL *and turns with her usual impatience to the* BOY) What do you think you're doing out here, skulking around like a little tramp? The way you carry on, it will be your fault too if that poor little thing gets drowned: you don't have to look like that – I have paid for you all to be here, haven't I? (*She seizes him by the arm to try and drag his hand out of his pocket*) What have you got there? What are you hiding? Let's see your hand, come on! (*She wrenches the hand out of the pocket and, to everyone's horror, reveals that he is grasping a revolver. She registers satisfaction as she looks at it and then adds darkly.*) Ah! And where did you get that gun? (*The* BOY, *his eyes vacantly staring, seems stunned and does not answer*) You stupid idiot! In your place I shouldn't have killed myself; I'd have killed one of those two, or both of them, father and son together! (*She pushes him back into his hiding place behind the cypress; then she takes the* LITTLE GIRL *and lifts her into the fountain and lays her gently down inside it out of sight. She then sinks wearily down beside the fountain, and leans against it, her face hidden in her arms.*)

PRODUCER: That's terrific! (*He turns to the* SON) Meanwhile...

SON (*peevishly*): Meanwhile nothing! It's a lie! There never was a scene between her and me! (*He is referring to the* MOTHER) Go on, get her to tell you! She'll tell you what happened! (*While he speaks the* SECOND ACTRESS *and the* YOUNG ACTOR *have detached themselves from the* ACTORS' *group and are now standing carefully observing the* MOTHER *and* SON *with a view to recreating their parts*)

MOTHER: Oh yes, it's true all right. I had gone to his room.

SON: To my room! Right? Not the garden at all!

PRODUCER: It doesn't matter where it was! We've got to rearrange the action. I explained that.

SON (*suddenly aware of the* YOUNG ACTOR'*s scrutiny*): What the hell do you want?

YOUNG ACTOR: Nothing. I'm just watching.

SON (*looking round and seeing the* SECOND ACTRESS): And here's another one! I suppose you're doing her part?

PRODUCER: Of course she is! Of course! And you should be damn grateful they're taking so much trouble!

SON: Yes, well! Thanks very much! But haven't you realized yet that you're not going to be able to do this play? You haven't got us inside you! Your actors can only look at us from the outside! How can you expect anybody to live their life in front of a kind of distorting mirror, which doesn't just freeze our expression in a reflected image, but twists it into a total travesty which we don't even recognize?

FATHER: He's right! He's quite right! He really is, you know!

PRODUCER (*to the* YOUNG ACTOR *and the* SECOND ACTRESS): All right, then, you two take yourselves off!

SON: It's all useless, anyway. I'm staying out of it.

PRODUCER: Just shut up a moment, will you? I want to hear what your Mother has to say! (*To the* MOTHER) So – you had gone in?

MOTHER: Yes, I had gone to his room. I couldn't bear it any longer. I was sick with anxiety. I had to get it off my chest. But as soon as he saw me come in…

SON: I didn't want a scene! I went out of the room. I went because I didn't want a scene. I never have gone in for scenes. Do you understand?

MOTHER: It's true. Everything he says is true!

PRODUCER: But all the same we've got to do it now, this scene between you two! It's the key to the whole thing.

MOTHER: I'm here. I'll do it. Oh, if only you could find some way for me to speak to him a moment! If only I could pour out my heart to him!

FATHER (*violently, coming threateningly close to the* SON): You're going to do this scene, son! You're going to do it for your mother's sake!

SON (*more determined than ever*): I'm not doing anything!

FATHER (*seizing hold of his coat and shaking him*): Oh, yes you are, by God! I'll see to that! Can't you hear what she's saying to you? Haven't you any natural feelings?

SON (*grabbing in turn at his* FATHER): I won't! I won't! That's all there is to it!

There is general agitation. The MOTHER, *horrified, tries to come between them and separate them.*

MOTHER: Don't fight! For pity's sake don't fight!

FATHER (*not letting go*): You'll do as you're told! You'll do as you're told!

SON (*struggling with him and finally throwing him to the ground near the steps, much to everybody's shock*): But what the hell's got into you? Aren't you ashamed to go flaunting your disgrace – our disgrace – in front of people? I'm keeping out of it! I'm keeping out! That's what *he* wanted, isn't it! Our author who wouldn't put us on a stage!

PRODUCER: But you came and found yourselves a stage.

SON (*indicating the* FATHER): He did! I didn't!

PRODUCER: Are you saying you're not here?

SON: He's the one who wanted to come. He dragged us along here! And he's the one who went in there with you to dream up not just what happened, but, for Heaven's sake, a whole lot of stuff that never happened at all!

PRODUCER: Go on then, you say what happened! Tell me! You left your room… did you say anything?

SON (*after a moment's hesitation*): Nothing. Because, I told you, I didn't want to make a scene!

PRODUCER (*egging him on*): Right, and then what? What did you do next?

SON (*everyone watches uneasily as he walks a few steps across the stage*): Nothing. I went across the garden… (*He breaks off, lost in dark thoughts*)

PRODUCER (*made uneasy by his reticence, urging him to say more*): Well? What happened when you went across the garden?

SON (*at the end of his endurance, holding up an arm to hide his face*): Why must you make me talk about it? It's horrible!

The MOTHER *is shaking all over. A stifled moaning sound comes from her as she looks towards the fountain.*

PRODUCER (*softly, taking in her look, and turning to the* SON *with rising apprehension*): The little girl?

SON (*staring straight in front of him, towards the audience*): There, in the fountain…

FATHER (*on the floor still, pointing towards the* MOTHER, *his voice full of pity*): She followed him out there, you see.

PRODUCER (*to the son, anxiously*): What did you do then?

74

SON (*slowly, still staring straight out in front*): I ran to the fountain. I rushed over to fish her out... but suddenly I stopped, because behind those trees I saw a sight which made my blood run cold: it was the boy. He was standing there stock still and staring like a mad thing at the drowned body of his little sister in the fountain. (*The* STEPDAUGHTER *is still huddled up against the fountain so that the child's body is hidden from view. Her uncontrollable sobs reach us like an echo from the depths. There is a pause.*) I went up to him, and then... (*A revolver shot rings out from behind the trees where the* BOY *has been hiding*)

MOTHER (*with a harrowing cry, as she comes running with the* SON *and all the* ACTORS *amid general confusion*): My son! my son! (*And then amid all the hubbub and shouting can be heard her cry*): Help! Help!

PRODUCER (*his voice distinguishable among the cries of the others as he cuts a path through them all, while the* BOY *is carried out, and taken behind the white cloth*): Is he hurt? Is he really hurt? (*All except the* PRODUCER *and the* FATHER, *who is still on the floor over by the steps, have disappeared behind the white sky-cloth and stay there awhile murmuring in subdued and anxious voices. Then the* ACTORS *return to the stage, emerging from either side of the cloth.*)

LEADING ACTRESS (*returning from the right, very upset*): He's dead! Poor boy! He's dead! Oh, how ghastly!

LEADING ACTOR (*returning from the left, laughing*): Some corpse! He's pretending! It's a fake! Don't you believe it!

OTHER ACTORS (*from the right*): It's not a fake! It's true! He's really dead!

OTHER ACTORS (*from the left*): Rubbish! It's a fake! He's pretending!

FATHER (*standing up and shouting them all down*): There's no pretence! It's the truth; it's real! That, ladies and gentleman, is reality! (*And he too disappears, in despair, behind the cloth*)

PRODUCER (*who can stand it no longer*): Pretence! Reality! What the hell! I've had enough! Lights! Lights! Lights! (*Suddenly the stage and auditorium are flooded with brilliant light. The* PRODUCER *heaves a great sigh as if released from a nightmare. Baffled and bemused looks are exchanged all round.*) Dear God! What a crazy set-up! They have made me lose a whole day's work! (*He looks at his watch*) You can go! You can go! There's not time to do anything now. It's too late to start rehearsing again. I'll see you all tonight! (*As soon as the* ACTORS *have said goodbye and left, he calls to the man on the lights*)

Hey! (*He calls his name*) Switch off, will you! (*The whole theatre is immediately plunged into total darkness*) Good God! You might have left me a light or two to get out by!

The next moment a green floodlight comes on behind the backcloth. It seems a mistake. Four enormous clear-cut shadows of the CHARACTERS *(less the* BOY *and the* LITTLE GIRL*) are projected against the cloth. The* PRODUCER *takes one look and rushes in terror from the stage. As he does so the green light at the back goes off and is replaced by the earlier blue moonlit effect on the front of the stage. Slowly the* CHARACTERS *emerge from behind the cloth. First the* SON *comes forwards, from the right side, followed by the* MOTHER*, her arms outstretched towards him. Then the* FATHER *advances from the left. They come to a halt halfway down the stage and stand there like figures in a trance. Lastly the* STEPDAUGHTER *emerges from the left and runs towards one of the stairways. She stops at the top step for a moment to look back at the other three. She lets out a piercing squeal of laughter and hurls herself down the steps. She runs up the central aisle to the back of the auditorium where she stops again, turns and gives another burst of laughter at the sight of the three left on the stage. She disappears from the auditorium and as she runs out through the foyer, her laughter is heard growing fainter and fainter. There is a short pause, and then the*

CURTAIN

As You Desire Me

Come tu mi vuoi (1930)

Translated by Robert Rietti

CHARACTERS

THE WOMAN
CARL SALTER, *a writer*
GRETA, *his daughter, known as* MOP
BRUNO PIERI
BOFFI
AUNT LENA CUCCHI
UNCLE SALESIO NOBILI
INES MASPERI, *wife of:*
SILVIO MASPERI, *a lawyer*
BARBARA, *Bruno's sister*
THE MADWOMAN
A DOCTOR
A NURSE
FOUR YOUNG MEN IN EVENING DRESS
A PORTER

The first Act takes place in Berlin, in the home of Carl Salter; Acts Two and Three take place in a villa near Udine. Ten years after the First World War.

ACT ONE

The living room of CARL SALTER's *flat in Berlin, furnished with bizarre magnificence. Through an archway on the right, part of the study is visible. It is night, and both living room and study are lamplit. The various coloured shades set off the strangeness of the furnishing and decoration, giving the whole a sense of mysterious "set-apartness".* SALTER's *daughter,* MOP, *is huddled in an armchair, her face hidden. She might be asleep, but in fact she is crying. Her hair is cut in a boyish fashion and her face bears a strange, disturbing expression which makes one think she must have suffered much.* CARL SALTER *comes in from the study. He is a man of fifty with a swollen whitish face and dark bags under his pale eyes. He is wearing a rich dressing gown and keeps his hands in the pockets.*

SALTER (*excited, upset*): She's back with them again. I've just seen her from the window. (*Almost involuntarily he draws one hand out of his pocket – it is clutching a small revolver*)

MOP (*seeing it at once*): What have you got in your pocket? It's a gun...

SALTER (*putting his hand back immediately – with irritation*): Nothing. Look, if she brings them up here, you're not to stay with them.

MOP: What are you going to do?

SALTER: I don't know. But I will not have these idiotic drunks from the nightclub following her here. It's got to be stopped somehow.

MOP: Somehow? Are you mad?

SALTER: Go and listen at the door. See if she's coming up alone. (MOP *moves towards the corridor*) Wait a moment. (*He holds her back, listening*) I can hear her shouting. (*Distant and confused voices are heard echoing on the stairs below*)

MOP: Perhaps she's getting rid of them...

SALTER: They're all drunk. And there was someone else following them.

MOP: Give me the gun.

79

SALTER: (*moving away, angrily*): Oh, don't be stupid – I'm not going to use it. It's just here – in my pocket – that's all.

MOP: Give it to me!

SALTER: Leave me alone! (*The voices are louder and nearer*)

SALTER: Listen!

MOP: They're quarrelling… Quick, we must let her in. She may need help.

The front door opens. THE WOMAN, *the* YOUTHS *and* BOFFI *surge in. The men are in evening dress and very drunk. They are swirling round* BOFFI *and* THE WOMAN. MOP *attempts to rescue her while her father,* SALTER, *endeavours to push the men out.*

One young man is fat with a ruddy complexion, another is bald, another is very effeminate and has dyed hair. They look to us like battered marionettes as they whirl their arms about meaninglessly. THE WOMAN *is in her thirties and very beautiful. She is also a little tipsy and cannot quite manage her usual dark frown which masks her contempt for everything and everyone, her despair and abandon in which – if she were to let herself go – she would lose complete control of herself after all she has been through. She wears a most elegant cloak beneath which she has a fanciful costume she dons when dancing at the Club.*

BOFFI *manages to look out of place wherever he is. He is convinced that life is one great gamble – he is intent on not losing a single trick. He tries hard to make an impression on others, but it is only a mask to hide a simple and naive nature. From a habit of jerking up his head as though he were suffocating, he has contracted a twitching in his neck muscles which causes him at times to stick out his chin and draw in the corners of his mouth. He often laughs at this habit, and mutters – more to himself – "Let's be serious!"*

THE WOMAN: Stop it! Shut up! I'm sick of you all! Go away! It's not a joke any more!

FIRST YOUTH: Won't you do just one last dance for us – the one with the broken glasses?

SECOND YOUTH: Give us a drink first, one for the road! Do the "Champagne Bubbles" dance!

THIRD YOUTH: We'll sing you the music. All together now…

FOURTH YOUTH (*singing drunkenly*): Cloo – dovee – o – (*He is singing the name "Clodoveo"*)

FIRST YOUTH: No! It should be sad! Sad as death!

THE WOMAN: Oh, leave me alone!

BOFFI: That's enough now! Off you go! (FOURTH YOUTH *breaks into song again*)

BOFFI: It sounds lovely, but can't you see she's had enough?

SALTER: Get out of my house!

FIRST YOUTH: A charming host, I must say! Give us a drink first!

SECOND YOUTH (*to* SALTER): She invited us in for one herself, so you can't refuse.

THIRD YOUTH (*confidentially*): And we're all going to get undressed!

THIRD YOUTH (*singing*): Clooo – dovee – o… (*Then as* SALTER *hits him*) Oh, you beast!

MOP: This is disgusting! It's an invasion! (*Then to* THE WOMAN, *embracing her protectively and at the same time pulling her into the living room*) Come away from them, Elma, darling!

THE WOMAN (*freeing herself and entering the living room*): Oh, for Heaven's sake. Mop, no – now you have to start mauling me – that's the last straw!

SALTER (*in the corridor with* BOFFI, *keeping the youths out*): I warn you, if you don't get out, I'll shoot!

BOFFI (*pushing them out*): Go on – get out! That's enough! Get out!

FIRST YOUTH (*before the door closes in his face*): Elma! Come and caress me! Just one little cuddle!

SECOND YOUTH: For you bow-wow!

MOP: They make me sick!

The FOUR YOUTHS *are out now and the door is closed. But they can still be heard making an uproar on the stairs. The* THIRD YOUTH *continues singing "Clooo – dovee – o…"*

SALTER: What did they want?

THE WOMAN: What do they always want? Bastards… And they made me drink so much…

SALTER: It's outrageous! And now the neighbours'll be complaining again.

THE WOMAN: All right, then, turn me out! I've always told you to!

MOP: Elma – no!

THE WOMAN: Well, listen to him – he says it's outrageous.

SALTER: It's quite simple – all you have to do is stop going with them.

THE WOMAN: I won't stop – I'll join them now. (*She makes a quick move towards the door*) I'll soon catch them up!

BOFFI (*stopping her*): Lucia!

THE WOMAN (*turning to him*): Who the hell *are* you?

SALTER (*to* BOFFI): Right! And what are you doing here?

BOFFI: I came to help her.

SALTER: He was following them – I saw him.

THE WOMAN: For so many evenings – like a sheepdog – he's always with me.

MOP: And you don't know who he is?

BOFFI: She knows perfectly well who I am. (*He twitches*) Let's be see-erious! (*Then, as though to tempt her into surrender he calls her again*) Lucia…

MOP (*worried*): Lucia?

THE WOMAN: That's right – just like that – in every tone of voice he calls me – "Lucia" – "Lucia" – following me everywhere…

BOFFI: And you always turn round.

THE WOMAN: Only because—

BOFFI (*interrupting*): Because you are Lucia…

THE WOMAN: No!

BOFFI: I say yes – every time I called her by her name, she started and went pale.

THE WOMAN: Well, of course – hearing someone call out like that…

BOFFI: Hearing your past call out, Lucia.

THE WOMAN (*to* MOP): At night, too, Mop – well, I mean – and then you turn and see that devil's face…

BOFFI: Oh, it's not really a devil's face – it's a trick of the light.

THE WOMAN: It's a trick of the trade!

BOFFI: All right, then – just as it's a trick of your trade to play God knows what part before these people – when you are Lucia.

MOP: What is all this about?

THE WOMAN: He really believes it, you see – he really believes it.

BOFFI: I'd stake my life on it.

THE WOMAN: That I am Lucia?

BOFFI: Lucia Pieri.

THE WOMAN: What?

BOFFI: Don't pretend you don't understand!

THE WOMAN: I didn't hear the name!

BOFFI (*turning to* SALTER – *a denunciation and a challenge*): I said Pieri. Her husband's name is Pieri.

THE WOMAN (*falling into a chair – worried*): My husband?

BOFFI: Your husband, Bruno. And he's here.

THE WOMAN: What do you mean? Here, where?

SALTER: This is crazy!

BOFFI: I called him here.

THE WOMAN: You really *are* mad!

BOFFI: He arrived this evening.

SALTER: Her husband has been dead for four years.

THE WOMAN (*turning on* SALTER, *spontaneously and involuntarily*): No...

SALTER (*stopped*): No?

BOFFI: I sent for him. He arrived this morning. He's at the Eden Hotel. Just round the corner.

THE WOMAN (*to* BOFFI, *very wrought up*): Stop this joke about a husband. I have no husband. Who did you send for?

BOFFI: Look how upset she gets.

SALTER (*to* THE WOMAN): So he's still alive?

BOFFI (*answering for her*): I tell you he's just round the corner. (*To* THE WOMAN) If you like... (*he looks round*) you can phone him. (THE WOMAN *breaks into hysterical laughter*)

SALTER: What is all this?

THE WOMAN: I've got a husband just round the corner. You hear? I can call him whenever I like.

SALTER (*to* BOFFI, *to cut the matter short*): Look, you – whatever your name is – we neither of us feel like going on with this idiotic game...

THE WOMAN (*to* SALTER – *jokingly, but at the same time as a challenge*): No – wait a moment, Salter. What if I really were?...

SALTER: If you really were?...

THE WOMAN: Lucia. The person he's so sure he can see in me. What would you say?

SALTER: I've already told you – I called it an idiotic game.

THE WOMAN: All right, then – an idiotic game. But if I'm not Lucia – who am I?

SALTER: Who are you?

THE WOMAN: That's what I said. Do you know me any better than he does?

SALTER: I know you better than you know yourself.

THE WOMAN: Oh, no, my darling. Do you imagine that if I wanted to know myself – if I wanted to be a real person even in my own eyes – (*turning to* SALTER) this gentleman's Lucia, for example – (*taking* BOFFI's *arm*) – I could bear to go on living here with you? (*She leaves* BOFFI *and turns to* MOP, *capricious now*) You tell them, Mop – what is my name?

MOP: Elma!

THE WOMAN: You see? It's an Arabic name. And you know what it means? Water… Water… (*And she stretches out her hands, rippling her fingers as though she were illustrating the deliberate inconsistency of her life now. Then with a sudden change of tone.*) Oh, God, they made me drink so much! Five cocktails and then champagne. (*To* MOP) Give me something to eat!

MOP: Yes, of course. What do you want?

THE WOMAN: I don't know… I don't know… I'm all burnt up inside!

MOP: I'll go and see…

THE WOMAN: Don't do anything complicated, darling.

MOP: Some sandwiches?

THE WOMAN: A piece of bread'll do – anything to stop my head spinning.

MOP: I'll get it right away. (*She runs off, right*)

SALTER (*to* BOFFI): Now, Herr what's your name… will you please admit you've made a mistake… and go.

THE WOMAN: Oh, leave him alone… he's a friend of mine…

BOFFI: She knows that I haven't made a mistake.

THE WOMAN: Providing you don't make me speak to my husband on the telephone – I draw the line at that.

BOFFI (*firmly*): Your husband has waited…

SALTER (*interrupting violently*): Shut up about this husband! (*Turning to* THE WOMAN) You told me he died four years ago.

BOFFI (*louder, determined*): She told you a lie.

84

THE WOMAN (*rises and goes to shake hands with* BOFFI): I did… and I'm delighted to hear you say so.

BOFFI: Thank God!

SALTER: You did lie?

THE WOMAN: Yes! (*Then to* BOFFI) But don't thank God too soon! I only said I was delighted because you – affirmed my right to lie – under these circumstances. (*To* SALTER) Shall I tell you all the lies I've told you, Salter, and you tell me yours?

SALTER: I've never lied!

THE WOMAN: No? But we never do anything but lie – all of us!

SALTER: I've never lied to you!

THE WOMAN: You even lie to yourself! With your own revolting sincerity, you lie – because you're not really as nasty as you make out. But don't worry – nobody really lies completely – we just tell tall stories – to other people and to ourselves. (*To* BOFFI) Four years ago someone did die for me – even if he wasn't my husband! But that doesn't mean that my husband's alive and here – not for me. (*Deliberately mysterious, as though she were making up a poem*) At the very most – he's the husband of someone – who no longer exists – a poor widower, which is like saying that… as a husband… he too is dead! But tell us your story just the same. It must be interesting if you've come all the way here. So we'll learn something at last about his Lucia – who you think I am.

BOFFI (*having made up his mind – moving to her*): May I speak to you alone for a moment?

THE WOMAN: Oh, no… not alone. Here in front of Salter – I want him to know. (*She lies down*) Besides, there are no secrets any longer today – there's no modesty. (*To* MOP, *who enters with a sandwich*) Ah, clever Mop, you've found me something. (*She draws herself up on one elbow*) Excuse me. (*She bites the sandwich*) Oh, God, I'm hungry.

MOP: Look – your sleeve…

THE WOMAN: Torn? It must have been those bastards…

MOP: No, I think it's just come unsewn.

THE WOMAN: D'you know I couldn't knock the bottle down this evening – perhaps I was too far away. (*She playfully kicks off her slippers and, with the grace of a dancer, runs over on her toes to* BOFFI, *and takes his opera hat from under his arm*) May I borrow that a moment? (*She snaps it open and places it on the floor in the centre of the stage; then she pulls her skirt up as far as her knees and, balancing on one foot, she lifts the other as if to knock over a bottle of champagne represented by the opera hat. She hums under her breath, accompanying the movement.*) Tairirari... tairirari... (*Twice she lifts her foot and gracefully kicks at the hat, missing it each time*) You see? I was too far off! (*She picks up the hat, closes it against her chest and gives it back to* BOFFI) Thanks. Did you know that Lucia – let's hope it won't offend her husband – Lucia dances in a nightclub. The "Lari-Fari"? Did you know that?

BOFFI: The more you go on like that, the more you convince me that you are she. Besides, how could I fail to recognize you? I've known you since you were a baby.

THE WOMAN: Really? Since I was a baby? Well, well... And have I changed much since then?

BOFFI: Everybody changes. But you've changed very little considering all you must have gone through!

THE WOMAN (*she looks at him for a moment*): You know you interest me? I've got all sorts of pasts. Even now – look at these two, father and daughter. (*She indicates* SALTER *and* MOP) Such things – if only you knew!

SALTER (*shaking – he can't stand much more*): Be quiet! Aren't you ashamed?

MOP (*rallying to* THE WOMAN *– moved*): No, poor girl, she's right... (*She makes to embrace her*)

THE WOMAN (*irritated, escaping from* MOP): Oh, Mop, for Heaven's sake!

SALTER (*taking advantage of* THE WOMAN's *irritation – to* MOP *furiously*): Leave her alone! And stop playing around in those ridiculous pyjamas! Go to bed!

MOP (*tragically, moving towards her father*): It's you who should be ashamed of yourself, Father – not she.

THE WOMAN (*holding her back, with weary exasperation*): Oh, for God's sake don't start again!

SALTER (*to* MOP): I told you to get out – go to bed!

THE WOMAN: Yes, darling, go, go, go – go and make me another sandwich, eh?

MOP: You'll come and eat it in the kitchen?

THE WOMAN: All right… on condition that you don't kiss me, you know I can't stand it when you kiss me. (SALTER *laughs ferociously*)

MOP: You pig!

THE WOMAN (*a sudden burst at* SALTER): Stop laughing! (*Then turning to* BOFFI) It's the sort of thing that only happens to me! They're jealous of each other!

MOP (*hurt – begging her*): Elma – no! Don't say that, darling!

THE WOMAN: There we are, "darling" – I only wish it weren't true, but just look at him. (*She indicates* SALTER)

SALTER (*fuming, his hands in his pockets*): I can't stand much more of this!

THE WOMAN (*deliberately provoking, cruel, turning to* BOFFI): His wife won't divorce him, you see. So she sends her daughter to get him away from me. And what happens? I get landed with the daughter as well. (*To* MOP) And she's worse than he! He may be old, but at least… (*She intends to say "he is a man"*)

MOP (*moving forward, looks first at her father, then at* THE WOMAN. *A clear denunciation*): I warn you – there's a revolver in his pocket – and it's intended for you.

THE WOMAN (*turning to look at* SALTER, *cold*): Is that so?

SALTER (*does not reply, sneers with tightly closed lips, takes the revolver out of his pocket and goes to put it on the table by* THE WOMAN): There you are – there it is – help yourself. (*He moves back*)

THE WOMAN (*smiling*): Thanks. Loaded?

SALTER: Loaded.

THE WOMAN (*picks it up*): For whom?

SALTER: Whoever you like.

BOFFI (*as she raises it*): Let's be see-e-rious! Put it down! Lucia, are you crazy?

THE WOMAN (*lowering the revolver, then putting it down – to* BOFFI): You see? Nothing but tragedies.

SALTER (*once more holding himself back with difficulty*): Stop talking to him all the time – he's an outsider. It's me you should be talking to. You've got to decide about us, this evening. Don't pretend you've forgotten that? I haven't.

THE WOMAN: All right, then – let's decide. With the gun? (*She looks at the revolver*)

SALTER: I'm ready.

THE WOMAN (*jumps up, pale, decided, picks up the gun and points it at him*): You really want me to kill you? I could do it, you know. (*She relaxes, lowers the gun*) Oh God, I'm so tired of it all. (*She moves to him*) Suppose instead of killing you – I give you – one kiss – here on your forehead. (*She kisses him*) You might say thank you... (*She gives him the revolver*) There's your pistol, sweetheart – go on – you kill me now, if you want.

MOP (*jumping up*): No! Look out – he'll do it!

THE WOMAN: Let him! After all, when you can't bear it any longer – I really do wish he had the courage... (*Going back to where she was before, to* BOFFI, *with desolate sincerity – it seems as though her own tiredness is talking*) It's true, you know, I simply can't bear it any longer... (*Then rallying*) I'm half-dead with hunger – I ask for a bit of bread and he gives me a revolver – you keep calling me "Lucia" – it really is a gorgeous evening...

SALTER (*jumping up – going to face* BOFFI): Look here, once and for all, this is my house – and I'm asking you to leave!

BOFFI: No. I'm here for the lady – not for you.

SALTER: The lady is in my house. She's my guest!

BOFFI: Are you in the habit of receiving guests with a revolver?

THE WOMAN: And can't I invite someone who says he knows me, if I want to?

SALTER: No, not at this moment, when an understanding must be reached between us. (*To* BOFFI) Now, will you go?

BOFFI: Yes – with the lady.

THE WOMAN (*rising unexpectedly, firm*): Very well! I'll come with you!

SALTER (*fierce, he springs over to her and grips her wrist*): You shan't move from here!

THE WOMAN (*unsuccessfully trying to free herself*): You can't stop me going out if I want!

SALTER: Oh yes, I can!

THE WOMAN: By force?

SALTER: If necessary – if you insist on taking up with anybody who comes...

BOFFI: Ah, but I'm not just anybody who comes.

SALTER: You're not wanted here – and she doesn't know you!

BOFFI: She doesn't want to know me. My name is Boffi.

THE WOMAN (*quickly*): The photographer?

BOFFI (*to* SALTER, *triumphant*): You see? She does know me!

SALTER: Boffi? (*Remembering*) Yes, course I've heard of you – you had an exhibition here...

MOP: We saw those pictures of his in the paper...

THE WOMAN (*determined, having taken a dramatic decision, gambling all in one throw*): I've been lying! I do know him! I do know him! He's a friend of my husband! (*Wrenching herself free*) Let me go!

SALTER: But you laughed at the idea!

THE WOMAN: Because I didn't want to let him see it was me!

BOFFI: At last! But how could you imagine your husband doesn't know everything that happened to you?

THE WOMAN: No – he can't know! He can't!

BOFFI: He knows everything. Why, they collected all the evidence there.

THE WOMAN (*bewildered, instinctively*): Where?

BOFFI: At the villa, where you lived...

SALTER (*seeing her bewilderment – a challenge*): Villa? What villa?

THE WOMAN (*immediately – proud*): My villa! (*Turning to* BOFFI) Tell Salter what it was – the evidence they collected! He took advantage of the position I was in – now throw that in his face!

BOFFI: She was heard screaming by the old gardener – Filippo – he died a little while ago.

THE WOMAN: That's right – Filippo!

BOFFI: How could she defend herself alone? When we came back, it was enough to see the ruin of the invaded countryside, to know how...

THE WOMAN (*as though struck by the sudden memory of something which had really happened*): The occupation! (*Triumphantly, to* SALTER) You see, Salter, I told you!

SALTER (*taken aback; he is forced to admit this*): Yes, you did say something about the occupation...

THE WOMAN: And I lived there – near Venice!

BOFFI: We all know what the enemy was like. (*To* SALTER, *with dignity, as though to blame him for the barbarity of the one-time enemy*) You see, Bruno Pieri, a gallant Italian officer, came back to the villa which had been reduced to rubble, he could find no trace of the young wife he had married just a year before...

THE WOMAN: Bruno...

BOFFI: He called you Cia...

THE WOMAN: That's right – he called me Cia... Cia...

BOFFI: He could only imagine what they had done to her... the officers who had seized the villa and he went mad. He was mad for more than a year! If you only knew how he searched for you at the beginning – he thought you'd been carried away by the flood of the retreating enemy.

THE WOMAN: I was! I was carried away on the flood!

SALTER (*to* BOFFI): Wait a moment... Wait a moment! (*Searching his memory*) I read that story somewhere...

BOFFI: In the newspapers.

SALTER: Of course... years ago...

BOFFI: Her husband had it printed.

THE WOMAN: I never read it!

SALTER (*to* THE WOMAN): You're a fake! (*To* BOFFI) I know exactly what she's doing, of course. It was a friend of mine, a psychiatrist in Vienna... (*Turning back to* THE WOMAN, *with contempt*) You're deliberately mixing up two stories – yours and the one in the papers – and you're trying to pass yours off as hers.

BOFFI: It's impossible – she is Lucia!

SALTER (*to* THE WOMAN, *with even greater contempt*): You!

THE WOMAN (*calm*): He says so – and he's known me since I was a child.

BOFFI: And I can't be wrong!

THE WOMAN (*to* SALTER): You've known me only a few months.

SALTER (*disturbed*): I've ruined my whole life because of you!

THE WOMAN: Not because of me – because you were crazy about me!

SALTER: And who made me crazy?

THE WOMAN: You think I did? You wanted me so badly... that's why you took me in!

SALTER: You tempted me!

THE WOMAN: Oh, temptation! That's a woman's trade, sweetheart. Besides, after what life has done to me – you heard what he said?

SALTER: Once and for all, will you stop hiding behind this ridiculous fraud!

BOFFI: This is no fraud!

THE WOMAN: And anyway, why shouldn't I hide behind it? (*To* BOFFI) You might have been sent by the gods to help me this evening, Boffi. My saviour, that's what you are. Tell me about when I was a child. I was so different then, that when I think about it, it seems like a dream…

BOFFI: Childhood seems like that to everybody, Cia.

THE WOMAN: Do you call me Cia, too? Does everybody call me Cia? Oh, what a pity – I thought it was only *he*.

SALTER (*unable to hold himself back*): Don't think you can get rid of me just like that – after the way you picked me up!

THE WOMAN: I – picked you up?

SALTER: Yes, you did.

THE WOMAN: Then why did you let yourself be picked up? You should have looked after yourself better. All right then, in a sense it's true. But you tricked me just the same.

SALTER: You've got no pity.

THE WOMAN: You've got the face to say that? I've shown you such pity – and your daughter will bear witness to it… (*To* BOFFI) Look at him, people take him for a famous writer, and he's really nothing but a clown!

SALTER: Oh, leave me out of this!

THE WOMAN: How can I when you go on about your poor, ruined life. Do you imagine it will frighten me?

SALTER: You're already afraid.

THE WOMAN: I've never been afraid of you.

SALTER: Then it's time you were now!

THE WOMAN: Because of your revolver? Look – I'm going out with this gentleman. I'm Cia, and he's taking me for a walk as he did when I was a child. Then you can pull the gun out of your pocket and kill me, as though it were a game. Shall we try?

SALTER: Don't tempt me!

THE WOMAN: It's all right by me. (*To* BOFFI, *taking his arm*) Come, Boffi, let's go. (SALTER *takes out the gun*)

BOFFI (*immediately putting himself between them*): No! Put that gun down!

THE WOMAN: Look – I've been through the war. Let me have myself killed if I feel like it. Besides, he'd have to kill himself afterwards, and he hasn't got the courage.

SALTER: I have – you know very well I have!

THE WOMAN: What a nerve he's got! (*To* MOP) Mop, isn't it true that he left your mother because she kept on complaining that he didn't behave as a famous writer ought to behave?

MOP: True enough. He had that nasty affectation of pretending not to believe in himself when visitors came to the house. "Excuse me, ladies, but I find it impossible to be serious in the presence of my wife who – as you can see – watches over my reputation like a sitting hen!"

SALTER (*exasperated*): I couldn't be serious! I just couldn't! (*To* BOFFI) It's terrifying how something like that – something quite stupid perhaps, you say for a joke, you see what I mean? How it can harden into an idea that sticks for ever – that's why she calls me an old clown!

THE WOMAN: Well, isn't that what you were – weren't you clowning in front of all those people when I first met you?

SALTER (*interrupting, wildly*): Because I was trying to hide the misery I felt inside me! My life was impossible!

THE WOMAN (*to* BOFFI): Did you see before how he chased away those poor young men who'd only had a drop too much to drink and wanted to have a little fun?! He was afraid their presence might compromise his precious reputation! He's become just like his wife! (*More furious than ever*) You wanted me to make life possible for you, didn't you? With your daughter who… oh, God! (*She covers her face in her hands – disgust, exasperation, desperation*)

MOP (*running to her, terrified*): No, Elma, no! Please!

THE WOMAN (*almost a scream, pushing her away*): Get away! I must say it!

MOP: Say what?

THE WOMAN: What you've done to me!

MOP: What have I done?

THE WOMAN (*almost beside herself*): You – all of you – I can't stand it any longer – this lunatic asylum – I'm drowning in it – my stomach's splitting open – drink, drink, drink – lunatics laughing. Hell let loose – mirrors, bottles, glasses – all whirling, crashing – they're screaming and dancing – twined together naked – all the vices under the sun mixed in together. And all because they can't find satisfaction any more! (*Grabbing* BOFFI *by one arm and pointing at* MOP) Look, look at Mop, and tell me if you can see an atom of humanity in that face! (*Pointing at* SALTER) And Salter over there – with a dead man's face – with all his vices crawling like worms in his eyes – and me dressed like this – and even you with a face like the Devil! Look at this house – and not only this house – this whole city – writhing, screaming mad! (*Pointing at* MOP *again*) She arrived – I knew nothing about her, it was evening and I was at the nightclub, I came back – drunk: well, obviously – I knock down champagne bottles and then I drink them – it's called "Champagne Bubbles". (*Showing her dress*) You see? It's my most famous dance – so obviously I'm drunk every evening – and that evening I came home to find her with her face covered in blood... a scratch from the forehead to her cheek! God knows what happened between them! (*She takes* MOP'*s face and turns it so that* BOFFI *can see*) Take a good look: she still has the scar!

SALTER: I didn't do it!

MOP: I did it myself... but you never believed me!

THE WOMAN: I was so drunk I didn't even see who took me up to bed that night.

MOP (*trembling, she almost throws herself on* THE WOMAN *to stop her going any further*): Elma, stop, I beg you!

THE WOMAN (*pushing her away*): No, I'm going to tell them everything! (*Indicating* SALTER) He'd gone out...

MOP (*clinging to her*): What are you saying? Are you mad?

THE WOMAN (*pulling away from her and throwing her into the armchair, where* MOP *huddles with her face hidden*): Oh, yes, I'm mad all right. Only the mad can shout these things from the rooftops in front of everybody! (*To* BOFFI, *pointing at* SALTER, *who is smiling*) Look at Salter, he's laughing – just as he laughed that morning when he found out what had happened the night before.

SALTER: Only because you...

THE WOMAN: Because I was disgusted and you didn't think it mattered. Nothing matters to you. But what about Mop, look at her!

SALTER: She's suffering from remorse now!

MOP (*jumping up and shouting wildly*): No! Because it's not fair!

THE WOMAN (*to* BOFFI): They're really proud of what they do, you see? It's their right, they say. But accuse them and they scream that it's not fair! I must get away from here – away from all of them – all of them – even from myself – get away – away – away! I can't stand it any longer!

BOFFI: Then come away, I'm offering you the chance to pick up your own life again.

THE WOMAN: My life? What life?

SALTER (*with fierce mockery*): Your life as Lucia... with your husband... or had you forgotten that?

THE WOMAN (*to* SALTER, *with pride*): No, I hadn't forgotten! (*Changing tone, to* BOFFI) This man you say... is he still looking for his wife after ten years?

SALTER: His Cia.

BOFFI: Yes, his Cia! In spite of all the opposition from people who wanted to think her dead after ten years...

THE WOMAN: But how can this husband still think she's alive, if she hasn't come back to him after all this time?

BOFFI: Because he believed that after all that happened to her... to you...

THE WOMAN: The woman he's searching for *is no more*!

BOFFI: That's not true. He was convinced you were alive but were too afraid to come back because after what happened to you... you feared you would never again be the same for him.

THE WOMAN: Does he really think she *could* be the same?

BOFFI: Why not, signora... if you choose to be.

THE WOMAN: After ten years? After all the things that must have happened to her? The same person? It's impossible – and the fact that she's never gone back to him proves it.

BOFFI: But I'm saying that now... if you want to, signora...

THE WOMAN: If I want? I want to escape from myself – that, yes – to have no more memories of anything – anything at all – to empty myself of all the life that's in me. Look at this body. You say it's *hers*? That I am like her? I no longer feel anything – I no longer want anything – I don't even know myself! My heart beats, and I don't know it – I breathe, and I don't know it. I no longer know I'm alive. I'm just a body without a name – waiting for somebody to take it over! All right, then... if he can recreate me... if, out of his memories, he can give back a soul to the body of his Cia... let him take it. Let him make a happy life... a new life... a beautiful life! I no longer want my own!

BOFFI (*resolutely*): I'm going to telephone him!

SALTER: You'll call nobody from my house!

THE WOMAN (*starting to run towards the study*): Then I'll call him!

SALTER (*immediately, stopping her*): No, wait. I'll go. I'll call him from the study. Then we shall see... (*He goes quickly into the study*)

THE WOMAN (*perplexed, stunned*): He's going to... But why is Salter going to... I thought he...

BOFFI: Signora... what do you want us to do?

MOP (*who has moved to the door to see what her father is doing – a scream of horror*): No! (*She starts to run into the study as the sound of a revolver shot is heard*) Father! Father!

BOFFI (*running into the study*): Good God, what has he done?

THE WOMAN (*also making for the study*): He's done what he always said he would do.

Their voices come from the study where they are now grouped round SALTER's *body. They examine him, later lift him from the ground to lay him on the sofa.*

MOP: He shot himself in the heart.

BOFFI: No – he's not dead. His heart's still beating.

MOP: There's blood coming out of his mouth.

BOFFI: The bullet must have pierced his lung!

THE WOMAN: Lift him up! Lift his head a little!

MOP: No – gently. Let me do it. Father! Father!

BOFFI: We'd better move him. Put him on the sofa there. Give me a hand!

MOP: Gently! Gently!

BOFFI: Come round this side – that's right...

MOP: It's Mop, Father – your Mop. Over here – that's right... easy... mind his head... give me that cushion, there.

THE WOMAN: We must get a doctor!

BOFFI: I'll go – I'll go... (SALTER *groans and tries to speak*)

MOP: What is it, Father? What are you trying to say? (*To* THE WOMAN) He's looking at you!

THE WOMAN: It's not serious – you'll see it's not serious – but we must get a doctor...

MOP (*to* BOFFI): Yes, a doctor: there's one living here in the block! Fetch him quickly, please, quickly! (*The doorbell rings*)

BOFFI (*moving back to the living room*): All right, I'll go...

THE WOMAN (*following him*): His flat's on the floor below. Doctor Schultz. I'll show you.

BOFFI *has opened the door and a huge, typically German house porter enters. He is furious, and is just finishing dressing.*

PORTER: What's going on here? I heard a gunshot. Are we ever going to have peace in this place?

THE WOMAN: Herr Salter has wounded himself. He's over there.

PORTER: Wounded *himself*? How?

BOFFI: Shot himself through the lung. It's serious.

THE WOMAN: You must call Doctor Schultz. Quickly!

PORTER: At this time of night? He'll be fast asleep.

THE WOMAN: Then wake him up. For God's sake!

PORTER: Not on your life! He'd have me sacked!

BOFFI: I'll call him.

PORTER (*holding him back*): You're not leaving this room – not while there's a wounded man here!

BOFFI (*wrenching his arm free*): You're mad!

PORTER: Not me, sir... it's these tenants here. They've turned this block into a madhouse. Anyway it's the rules of the place. Where's this man you say shot himself? Oh, I see him. Is it serious?

BOFFI: Of course it is, you fool. Why d'you think we need a doctor?

PORTER: Well, if it's that serious...

MOP (*enters from the other room*): I think we should take him to hospital – right away!

PORTER: Now you're talking. I'll call an ambulance.

MOP: Please! (She *returns to her father. The* PORTER *exits, mumbling to himself.*)

BOFFI: He wasn't very helpful.

THE WOMAN: That's how it is here. The Porter runs the place!

BOFFI: So, you're now free to come with me.

MOP (*calling from the study*): Elma, Elma, come quickly!

THE WOMAN: How can I come with you now?

BOFFI: But, Signora Lucia...

MOP (*appearing in the archway*): Elma!

THE WOMAN: She calls me Elma, you hear?

BOFFI: Then I'll fetch your husband.

MOP: Elma, you can't leave him now! You mustn't go!

BOFFI (*taking her arm*): After you've all been insulting her all evening? I'll bring him back here, signora – and I'm certain that as soon as you see him, you'll…

MOP (*takes her other arm*): Elma, he's asking for you. He wants you.

BOFFI *gives up. He shrugs and goes out determinedly.*

THE WOMAN: All right, Mop. You go to him. I'm coming.

MOP (*takes a step, then turns*): Promise you won't leave?

THE WOMAN: I told you I'd come to him. In a minute. I need a moment to myself.

MOP *exits to the other room. Left to herself,* THE WOMAN *presses her fingertips against her face, then suddenly takes them away and holds them against her temples, as though to support her head, raised in desperation. She closes her eyes. She murmurs.*

THE WOMAN: Just a body without a name! Without a name!

CURTAIN

ACT TWO

*A large, richly furnished ground-floor room of the Pieri villa, near Udine
in the north of Italy. Four months have passed and it is an afternoon in
April. At the back is a loggia with a marble balustrade and four slender columns supporting the glass roof. The sunny, green and peaceful
countryside, which can be seen from the loggia, is delightful and, like
the room itself, full of clear, light colours. Towards the end of the Act,
violet-coloured shadows settle over it. A staircase leads to the upper
floors of the villa and on one wall hangs a large portrait in oils of Lucia
Pieri as a young woman – as she was when she was newly married before
the First World War.*

AUNT LENA CUCCHI *is discovered talking to someone in the garden.
She is about sixty, sturdily built, with an unfeminine face and a mass
of grey curls. She has thick, dark eyebrows and tortoiseshell spectacles.
She is dressed in black with a stiff, starched collar. Her manner is direct
and efficient.*

LENA: Do come in. That is quite enough, for Heaven's sake! Well, really – look at that bunch! They're falling all over the place! No, no,
don't waste time picking them up! (*She turns away*) He'd strip the
garden bare if he got half a chance!

UNCLE SALESIO NOBILI *enters through the glass doors, carrying a huge
bunch of flowers he has just cut. He is a wizened, dried-up old man who
would still be energetic if it weren't for the fact he has a bad back and
has difficulty moving his neck. He is wearing his Sunday-best clothes
and his hair and little moustache are well "pomaded". The moustache
resembles a couple of dabs of soot under his large nose.* SALESIO *is always
concerned with looking smart – his most important aim and perhaps the
cross he has to bear! He wears a stiff high shirt collar which he assumes
gives him an air of elegance.*

SALESIO: Here we are then – here we are! Now let me explain why…

LENA: I don't want to hear any explanations. Put those flowers down!

SALESIO: No, nò, no, dear cousin, I wish to explain!

LENA: Give me the flowers. (*She starts to arrange them in various vases*)

SALESIO: I didn't pick them for the visitors, you know – I only meant to...

LENA: I don't care who you picked them for – you picked far too many!

SALESIO: Let me explain...

LENA: Explain! Explain! You spend half your life explaining!

SALESIO: And a lot of good it does me! No one ever tries to understand.

LENA: If you must explain... then tell me why I feel so fit today – while you're under the weather.

SALESIO: That's not true. I'm feeling *very* well.

LENA: Very *bad*!

SALESIO: Why should I feel bad?

LENA: If you need explanations for that, it just goes to show that you've no idea of what you've done.

SALESIO: What have I done?

LENA: Never mind that now. God willing, it's all over! Today they'll be agreeing on this blessed affi... affi... affidated...

SALESIO (*laughing*): Affidated? Oh, ha ha! That's good – that's very good! Affidated indeed! It's an affidavit.

LENA: Well, affi... whatever it is, that'll be the end of it. If I had my way... I'd pension you off! With Cia here, there's no room for both of you.

SALESIO: That's a fine thing! That's all the thanks I get after robbing myself of everything for my niece's sake!

LENA: Nonsense. When you gave Cia the villa and grounds as a dowry, you weren't robbing yourself of anything! You were rich then – and it hardly meant a thing to you.

SALESIO: And now that I'm poor, I'm to be thrown out like an old coat!

LENA: That's what you deserve for not sharing Bruno's faith that poor Cia was alive.

SALESIO: And just how much faith did you have, eh?

LENA: I never had anything to do with declaring her legally dead.

SALESIO: Only because nobody asked you to.

LENA: I wouldn't have done it even if they had asked. Trying to rob poor Bruno of the villa and the estate!

SALESIO: But, for Heaven's sake, they were never his! You keep forgetting that there was no evidence she was alive. Bruno just wasn't one of the family any longer.

LENA: It's you who are forgetting how much Bruno put into the place! Rebuilding the villa and increasing the value of it all. And now you would deny him the right to…

SALESIO: He had no right!

LENA: Oh yes, I know what you're getting at! That nasty little scheme Ines and you concocted to try and get the State to be responsible for all the repairs! I refused to have anything to do with that dirty affair!

SALESIO: But Ines was my only other niece – and when she got married I was too poor to do anything for her!

LENA: So you admit it was all on her account! The idea of getting back what you'd given Cia! It turns my stomach to think about it! That's why I could never face marrying one of your family.

SALESIO (rebelling after having swallowed so much): And they – let me tell you – they could never face marrying you!

LENA: I'm perfectly happy to admit it.

SALESIO: And you know why, Lena? You're ugly. And you've got an ugly character, too. You just won't admit that I'm poor because I've given away so much.

LENA: On the contrary – I've accepted your motives, as a poor man, for trying to get your property back. But as far as your other niece is concerned. I'm sure that even you must have felt sickened at her crocodile tears when her sister was declared dead!

SALESIO: She was upset over the unpleasantness with Bruno. It's strange that Bruno understood my predicament – but not you!

LENA: …Because I used my gumption and didn't take sides! I can understand Bruno's behaviour – and in a way I can even understand your own motives in trying to recover your gift to your niece once you'd become so poor – I can understand – even though I find it despicable, all the same! But as for that niece of yours… that Ines, who has the nerve to face her sister today… if I had my way I'd make sure the villa would never become hers! Never! I'd see her dead first! (She catches sight of THE WOMAN coming down the stairs) Ah, here she is – our dear Cia! (CIA's appearance seems to stun the two of them, for she has dressed herself to look like the large portrait hanging on the wall)

LENA: But… dear God – you've turned yourself into her!…

101

SALESIO: The very image of the portrait.

THE WOMAN: I was just coming down to check. The part, after all, has got to be played...

LENA: The part?

THE WOMAN: Well, aren't they all coming to see me playing it? And then, when one's been dead for ten years, you never know, do you? It's better to go back where one started... Except that I... (*She strikes her stomach as though it were independently in revolt against what she is doing*) No! Tell me, who's coming, apart from my sister Ines?

LENA: Her husband.

THE WOMAN: Livio?

LENA: Silvio... Silvio!

THE WOMAN: I don't know why, but I keep thinking of him as Livio.

SALESIO: He's a lawyer, so be careful.

LENA: Why should she be careful?

SALESIO: Well, after all, it was he who was responsible for...

LENA: Oh, for Heaven's sake, he won't be thinking about that any more. He's polite...

SALESIO: Oh, a gentleman in every sense of the word...

THE WOMAN: I shall be delighted to meet him.

LENA: But you've already met him. Oh, of course he wasn't your brother-in-law then... just a friend of Bruno's.

THE WOMAN: Yes, of course. Bruno must have had so many friends. I hope I shan't be expected to know them all if he brings them here... now that it's open house for everybody... Who else is coming?

LENA: Your cousin Barbara, that is, if Bruno thought to send for her.

SALESIO: She doesn't count.

LENA: What do you mean "doesn't count"? She's the worst of the bunch!

THE WOMAN: And Boffi? Will Boffi be here too?

SALESIO: I don't know if he's in town.

THE WOMAN: Oh, he is, he is! I told Bruno to make sure that he was here. I want Boffi... he must be here! (*She looks at the portrait, then at herself*) It's a perfect resemblance, isn't it?

SALESIO: You might have walked out of the frame!

LENA: True enough – but I must say I never thought that that portrait was really you.

THE WOMAN: No? And yet Bruno said that it was painted from a photograph.

SALESIO: Oh, indeed it was.

THE WOMAN: And that he'd given the painter all the details about me.

SALESIO: And now we can see for ourselves just how like you it is! Couldn't be more exact, for God's sake – what I've always said – there you are – you!

LENA: Yes, but it was – the eyes. May I... just a second... (*She takes* THE WOMAN'*s face and looks into her eyes*) That's it. Her eyes. Her eyes as I always knew them. These are her eyes... not those in the picture.

THE WOMAN: Cia's eyes?

LENA: Yes! Cia's eyes!

SALESIO: But aren't they the same as the ones in the portrait?

LENA: Of course not! These are her eyes – not those! Just a hint of green...

SALESIO: Green, rubbish! They're blue!

THE WOMAN (*to* LENA): For you, Lena, green. (*To* SALESIO) For Uncle Salesio, blue. And for Bruno, grey... under black eyelashes. You see? And then, of course, the painter must have had his say, too. What were Cia's eyes really like? Go and check for yourselves, the portrait's as good a test as any.

SALESIO: I don't need to check. I was your father's best friend, and you've got his eyes.

LENA: His eyes? Oh, no! Ines has got his eyes. They're not like these at all! Believe me, Cia, you've got your mother's eyes. We grew up together – two cousins with the same name, poor Lena and me, it's hardly likely that I shouldn't know.

(SALESIO *laughs*)

That's right, laugh!

THE WOMAN: Why are you laughing?

LENA: Because, since we were girls, boys used to tease us when they saw us together...

SALESIO: They would call out, "Pretty Lena and Ugly Lena!"

THE WOMAN: Oh no, not ugly Lena!

LENA: That's exactly how I used to reply, "I'm not ugly!" And that "ugly" one... when the "pretty" one died... became like a mother to you...

THE WOMAN (*disturbed*): Don't Lena... please.

LENA (*as though to keep a promise she had made*): All right dear, I won't. But I don't see why it should upset you.

SALESIO: Can't you see it does?!

LENA: But she was so tiny… she can't possibly remember. (*Changing the subject*) But you really are your mother all over again. She was just like you when she died.

SALESIO: Well, if you want to know, I see her completely differently.

LENA: Arrgh!

THE WOMAN: There we are, Uncle, that's the play I'm going to act in. It'll be about how you see me, and how Lena sees me. It'll be about how you recognize somebody, missing believed killed, after an army's trampled all over her. (*She sits and invites them, with a gesture, to sit, too*) But in the meantime I should like you both to explain to me exactly what is Bruno's position with regard to this villa and the estate.

SALESIO: You mean you don't know?

THE WOMAN (*drily*): No. I don't know.

SALESIO: But Bruno must have told you…

THE WOMAN: He told me – it wasn't very clear – something about having his rights denied him. He was so overwrought…

LENA: Oh, I know what you must have felt. When I tell you how it turned my stomach to hear…

THE WOMAN (*with the air of someone who suspects something which both saddens and disgusts her*): No, Lena, it's not what you think. It was something else that shook me. Bruno just shrugged his shoulders and said: "Oh, don't worry anyway. It doesn't matter if you don't know anything about it. Indeed it's just as well for them to realize that I haven't told you anything." But I want to be told. I want to be told everything!

SALESIO: But the situation could hardly be clearer now…

LENA: Now that you're back…

THE WOMAN: But the certificate of Cia's death hasn't been invalidated yet?

LENA: What does that matter? It will be invalidated with the affi… affidated they're making out now.

SALESIO: It would have been invalidated already if only you had… right from the start…

THE WOMAN (*with a contempt which she cuts off short*): From the start, I never wanted to have anything to do with all this…

LENA: Well, of course we know that. You should have been spared at least this bitterness about the death certificate.

THE WOMAN: If it was only bitterness!

LENA: But you see, there are financial interests involved.

THE WOMAN: Nobody told me anything about that!

LENA: Your interests, too.

THE WOMAN: I have no interests!

SALESIO: But of course you have interests…

THE WOMAN: No. Oh, no. I'm not having anything to do with interests. And if there's any question of that… I couldn't dress like this any longer. Like the portrait. That would be really horrible!

LENA: But of course it wouldn't! Why should you think that?

THE WOMAN: Because that's how it is. And you know something? The death certificate is right.

SALESIO (*stunned*): What do you mean – right?

THE WOMAN: Just what I said. Right. I told Boffi so in Germany, I even told Bruno. Ten years you waited for her to come back. And did she? No! Why didn't she come back all that while? It's not so difficult to see the reason, is it? She was dead. Dead. Or at any rate dead to every memory of a life that she didn't want any more – it's clear she couldn't have wanted it any more. Assuming she was alive at all.

LENA (*moved*): Of course, dear child, you're perfectly right. Don't think I don't understand you.

SALESIO: And I understand, too. Oh, yes, indeed. But you see, now that you've come back…

THE WOMAN: Quite ignorant of all these conflicting interests – not knowing that I should be forced to play a part that disgusts me. I came for Bruno's sake! I did it only for him! And I made it quite clear that nobody should expect to be recognized by me – no memories should be awakened. At first, I wouldn't even see you two, even though you were living here with him…

SALESIO: Didn't we keep away for more than a month?

THE WOMAN (*rising, furious*): He should have told me! He ought to have told me! I wouldn't have come!

LENA (*after a pause, timid*): Perhaps he didn't want to hurt you, because after all, it was your own sister...

SALESIO: After you'd disappeared, mind...

LENA: There you are, he's trying to excuse her again!

SALESIO: I'm not excusing anybody, I'm just explaining. Cia says exactly the same thing herself – after ten years...

THE WOMAN: ...My sister very rightly asked for a death certificate so that the estate and the villa could go to her. Isn't that right?

LENA (*correcting her*): No, no, not to her, to Salesio. He had given them to you as a dowry...

THE WOMAN (*to SALESIO, with joy*): So it's all come back to you? It isn't Bruno's any longer?

LENA: Oh no, it's Bruno's all right...

THE WOMAN: But what about the death certificate? I thought that had solved everything, and freed me from... I thought it had freed him, too... (*Sitting*) Explain it to me better... How can it all still be Bruno's?

LENA: Because Bruno quite rightly opposed...

SALESIO: No, that's the whole point! Not rightly! No!

LENA: He was absolutely right...

SALESIO: No, he wasn't!

THE WOMAN: But don't you see, Lena, I should be perfectly happy if it had all come back to Uncle Salesio, so that he could give it to Ines.

LENA: No, no!

SALESIO: No, indeed! What's Ines got to do with it? Your return cleared up everything. It's just that before you came down, Lena and I were discussing the motives behind the quarrel – quite academically. You can imagine for yourself what it was like here after the war – just a heap of rubble.

LENA: And while it remained like that nobody thought of having you declared dead! They started to get greedy only after Bruno began putting things right.

SALESIO: If you're going to do all the talking...

LENA: Can you deny that it's true?

THE WOMAN: Let him talk, Lena, I want to know what he thinks, too.

SALESIO: You always did have enough common sense for everybody, Cia. And now you want to know the whole truth.

THE WOMAN: That's exactly what I do want.

SALESIO: Well, then, I have your permission to continue, Lena? Thank you. (*To* THE WOMAN) This is the point. Who was responsible for repairing the damage after the war?

LENA: The government. Go on, tell him it was the government and make him happy. And so, you see, Cia, any claim Bruno might make for having rebuilt everything in the hope that you'd turn up at any moment was opposed by the others. "That's all very fine," they told him, "but the repairs don't give you any rights at all because the government would have got round to doing them anyway, sooner or later!"

SALESIO: And that was how things stood when...

LENA: When the news of your return from the grave exploded like a bomb. (*Pause.* THE WOMAN *is rapt in gloomy concentration.*)

THE WOMAN: So if there hadn't been this return from the grave as you call it, Bruno would have lost the villa and the estate, everything?

SALESIO: Of course he would, absolutely everything!

LENA: And when the death certificate was obtained...

THE WOMAN: Did Boffi know all this when he came to Berlin?

LENA: Indeed he did. It would have been hard for him not to know. It was all such a dreadful scandal.

SALESIO: All this while, nobody's been talking about anything else here...

LENA: Reasons of the heart on one side and reasons of the pocket on the other, serious ones, too, because the estate's so big, and it's worth so much after all Bruno's done to it. And the opposition had a strong hand to play because poor Bruno's reasons of the heart, well, there were nasty-minded people who sneered at them as though he'd invented them just to protect his own interests.

THE WOMAN: Ah, so they said that, too, did they? His heart was just an excuse for looking after his pocket?

LENA: Only nasty-minded people!

SALESIO: They'd all become so bitter, you see... (*Pause*)

THE WOMAN (*darkly, more and more shaken by a suspicion which has assailed her*): I see... I see...

LENA (*to distract her*): But come now, that's all over. We'll stop talking about it altogether. Of course it must upset you now... seeing it all again...

THE WOMAN (*a burst of contempt*): Oh, no, for God's sake... that doesn't bother me! (*Change of tone*) It's something else that upsets me... (*Then falling back into her black mood*) Because in Berlin, too...

LENA (*timidly*): What?

THE WOMAN: No, nothing.

LENA: You see, this is all just a formality. You're officially dead, and so you must be officially brought back to life.

THE WOMAN (*without listening to her*): Boffi told me that he'd called Bruno just as soon as he thought he'd recognized me.

LENA: So he did – and you can imagine how Bruno came running.

THE WOMAN: ...Because there was the problem of the death certificate and he stood to lose the case...

LENA: Good God, no! Whatever put that into your head?

THE WOMAN: I'm right, Lena. Believe me, I've hit on the truth!

LENA: You're wrong! He was the only one who never believed you were dead! He never gave up!

SALESIO: That's true.

LENA: He tore straight off to fetch you, trying to imagine all the reasons that you've described yourself to explain why you hadn't come back before.

THE WOMAN (*rising, very strained*): You know where I was when he found me? It was night-time, and I was going to hospital with a girl whose father had just tried to kill himself...

LENA: For you?

THE WOMAN: Yes...

LENA: Oh, how dreadful!

THE WOMAN: He didn't want to let me go – he still writes to me now. Then at the door, as I was following the stretcher-bearers, I saw him standing in front of me...

SALESIO: Bruno?

THE WOMAN: Yes, Bruno. Boffi had gone to fetch him at his hotel, and he didn't want me to go to the hospital. I told him he was raving – I told him to let me go – that I had no husband – that I'd never had one.

SALESIO: And Bruno? What did he do?

THE WOMAN: I went away with the man on the stretcher before he had a chance to say anything. When I came back two hours later, they were both still there. Obviously Boffi must have told him that I...

(*To* LENA) You see, Lena, trapped as I was… that lunatic had a gun in his pocket, and he'd already threatened me… to get away, to find some sort of escape… I had given way… I'd admitted something or other. Oh, I don't know – that I knew him – that I'd been alone in the villa… But then seeing them there again – knowing perfectly well that they'd been discussing these stupid admissions together – I denied everything – the whole story! I told them that I'd been forced before… I told them to get the hell out… to go… to stop the idiotic farce which Boffi insisted on sticking to, pretending he had recognized me.

SALESIO: But Bruno recognized you immediately, too!

THE WOMAN: No! That's a lie… he didn't!

SALESIO (*stupefied*): He didn't?

THE WOMAN: That's why I call it a farce. He didn't. I saw perfectly clearly that he didn't. When I saw him in front of me for the first time – he just didn't see the likeness that Boffi had told him he would. He was disappointed. I saw it! You know how it is… you spot a likeness and you tell somebody else about it. He looks, and it's just not the same as it was for you. (*Almost to herself*) That's what worries me… why? Why? If he didn't recognize me… (*Then to the others*) Oh, yes, some likeness there must have been. I admitted it – I could hardly do anything else. I admitted that I came from near Venice, too – but not from here – not here! I told them so much, I did so much, that in the end I managed to persuade them both that it really was just a likeness. Oh, a strong one, perhaps, a string of coincidences, too, but no more than that. In fact I persuaded them that it wasn't me. What more could I have done? But then… I don't know why… I…

LENA: You repented?

THE WOMAN: No! But in the state I was then… (*Almost to herself*) That shouldn't be an excuse for him now… he shouldn't be taking advantage of it. But if he has done…

LENA: Oh, no… why torment yourself like this? What are you trying to say?

THE WOMAN (*letting herself be overcome by misery*): Oh, Lena, I was so tired… and desperate in a way I'd never been before… Lost and finished… So sick with disgust at that life that I just couldn't go on any longer. And it was on that terrible night when my whole life seemed to be hanging over an abyss of pain…

LENA (*moved*): Oh, my poor child!

THE WOMAN: It was then that he began to talk about his Cia... what she was like... what she'd meant to him in that one year she'd been with him. He was so desolate, that listening to him, I began to cry and cry, not dreaming that he might see my tears... tears for my own misery... as a sign of repentance for having denied so much. And there was my body as a living proof that I was his Cia. I let him embrace it, pull it against his body so hard that I couldn't breathe. But I did it for no other reason... I... I came here with him only for that. I made him understand and promise that it was to be only that... that I should come as from the grave... for him only... only for him!

LENA: Oh, yes, I see... with your old life cut right off behind you... I could see it so clearly in your eyes as soon as you let us see you.

THE WOMAN: Did you recognize me, too... immediately?

LENA: No, my poor child, even I didn't recognize you immediately.

THE WOMAN: Even you?

SALESIO: Come to that, neither did I. But that's easy to understand... after all those years...

LENA: The years have got nothing to do with it – on the contrary... No, it was – I don't know, something about her, her bearing – even her voice a little...

THE WOMAN: Did you notice a difference in the voice?

LENA: Yes, I thought...

THE WOMAN: So did Boffi... he told me afterwards... it was the only difference he noticed! (*Pause*) It's odd that Bruno must have noticed it, too... but he didn't say anything. (*Rising, almost to herself*) So many impressions are beginning to make sense now...

LENA: But you were away for so long, talking a foreign language. And then – the change in your heart above all. "Lena," you said to me, just like that, in a dead voice – and I could hear – in your voice – that everything you'd been before was dead.

THE WOMAN (*completely rapt in herself, she hasn't listened to what* LENA *has been saying*): I wonder...

SALESIO: It's time that you stopped wondering now!

THE WOMAN (*still to herself*): Of course, that's it... that's how he tricked me at the beginning... he told me there was every reason in the world for me not to see her...

LENA: You mean Ines?

THE WOMAN: Oh, Ines doesn't concern me... I'm talking about this double game that he's been playing with me. At first I refused to come here because I knew...

LENA: You knew what Ines had done to you?

THE WOMAN: No, not that! I didn't know anything about that at the time. But then he used precisely that to get me to come here – he pretended that I wouldn't see her – that what she'd done was the reason I could give to everybody for not seeing her. And now he's doing just the opposite – he's using what Ines has done – this death certificate she's asked for – to force me into seeing her!

LENA: Remember, though, he never wanted this quarrel with your sister!

SALESIO: And after all you have been closed up here by yourself for four months.

THE WOMAN: Perhaps even that was a part of his plan.

LENA (*shocked*): Part of his plan?

THE WOMAN: I'd swear it was!

SALESIO: What do you mean?

THE WOMAN: What do I mean? (*She stops herself*) It's flawless, the whole scheme – even the way he's looking so strained and tense now!

SALESIO: No, no, no! You're being unfair, Cia! Believe me you are!

LENA: Yes, I think you are, too.

THE WOMAN: You think that only because you don't know everything!

SALESIO: Then let me tell you that you don't know everything either, or rather, forgive me, you don't wish to know; Bruno's got every reason in the world to feel strained and tense. After all, you must remember the curiosity which your reappearance gave rise to after ten years, and all the... the fermentation of that curiosity in the four months you've been closed up here – what people are thinking and saying...

THE WOMAN: Ah, yes – of course, the wagging tongues will be busy.

SALESIO: Naturally. What with the lawsuit – and your refusing to see your own sister... your husband's relatives have been saying...

THE WOMAN (*interrupting*): ...Every spiteful thing they can think up. Especially about my life, up there, that must give them a wonderful cause to gossip. They must know everything about me by now. And Boffi...

SALESIO: Oh no, Boffi would never—

LENA (*interrupting*): No... no... no... he has always taken your part. Believe me. I know!

THE WOMAN: But he must have told them where he found me: what sort of life I was leading. Even if he didn't tell them in so many words, with his eyes, his gestures – and that horrid little twitch of his – he doesn't need to hide anything! Goodness only knows what they must be thinking! Do they know I was a dancer?

LENA: Don't pay attention to them and their malicious slander.

THE WOMAN: But it's true. I was a dancer. And worse! Much worse! You can't imagine the things I've done. I used to make up my own dances to the music. Erotic movements which drove the men crazy. And the less I wore, the more they liked it.

LENA: Does... does *he* know?

THE WOMAN: Bruno? Of course he does! But what's worse – *they* know! They do, don't they, Uncle Salesio? What do they say about me?

SALESIO: They say so many things, but you shouldn't—

THE WOMAN (*interrupting*): Do they say he's decided to overlook all that because I can be useful to him now?

LENA: No... No!

THE WOMAN: I wasn't asking you.

LENA: Who do you suppose could have said such a thing? Or even thought it!

THE WOMAN: Tell me the truth, Uncle Salesio. Is that what they are saying?

SALESIO: Yes, it's true. They do say that.

THE WOMAN: You see?

LENA: Who says it?

SALESIO: Various people.

THE WOMAN: It's all so sordid! Who'd have thought that business interests would—

LENA (*interrupting*): It's not Bruno's fault!

THE WOMAN: All the same, if I thought... (*She stops as the sound of a car driving on gravel is heard outside*)

SALESIO (*shaking himself*): Ah, here they are – this must be them now!

THE WOMAN (*suddenly coming to herself, with a tone of challenge*): All right then – let's have it out!

LENA: Have they come so early?

SALESIO (*looking into the garden*): No, it's Bruno.

LENA: I thought they said six o'clock.

SALESIO: There's Boffi, too, you know… Boffi, too.

LENA: You see? Bruno did bring him. (*Long pause*)

THE WOMAN: What are they doing?

LENA: Bruno's reading a letter.

THE WOMAN: A letter?

SALESIO: The porter's just given it to him.

LENA: Whatever are they doing now? Boffi's going away with the letter.

THE WOMAN: No! Run and call him back, Uncle Salesio. I want him here!

SALESIO (*going into the garden*): Bruno! Boffi! Come here! Both of you! You, too, Boffi!

BRUNO *and* BOFFI *enter, followed by* UNCLE SALESIO.

BRUNO *is very upset and is in the throes of a nervous crisis which has drained his face of all colour and made him restless and impatient in every glance and gesture.*

BRUNO: Whatever do you want Boffi for? Let him go, please.

BOFFI (*to* THE WOMAN): Good evening to you. Yes indeed, it's better if I go at once.

BRUNO (*anxiously*): Yes, straight away. And at all costs stop…

THE WOMAN: Stop what?

BOFFI: Another letter's come.

THE WOMAN: From Salter? Another?

BOFFI: He's taking advantage of the fact that he isn't dead after all. And he's getting his own back.

THE WOMAN: What does he say?

BRUNO (*to* BOFFI, *impatiently*): Go on, please Boffi – don't waste time!

THE WOMAN (*to* BOFFI): No, wait a moment! (*Then to* BRUNO) Bruno, I want to know. Give me the letter.

BRUNO: Oh, for Heaven's sake, the letter's not important. If it were only a letter! (*Turning to* LENA *and* SALESIO) Lena, please – and you, too, Uncle – would you mind leaving us?

LENA: Yes, of course, immediately.

SALESIO: Come along then, let's go. Yes, yes, yes. (*They both exit up the stairs*)

THE WOMAN: Why? What's the matter?

BRUNO: It just would have to happen today... today of all days. This persecution's become outrageous.

THE WOMAN: What's he written this time?

BRUNO: Written! He's done a great deal more than write. He's coming here. He says that he's coming to prove you're a fraud.

THE WOMAN: A fraud? Is he bringing his daughter with him?

BOFFI: No. It's the same old line. You remember the threat he made...

THE WOMAN: What threat?

BOFFI: About some doctor friend of his in Vienna?

BRUNO: Well, he's gone to Vienna! He's written from Vienna! (*He shows her the letter without giving it to her*) There you are, look!

THE WOMAN: But – what's he gone there for?

BOFFI: He's playing his last card – and he's staking everything on it!

THE WOMAN: But what does he say in this letter, for God's sake?

BRUNO: I'm telling you, darling. He says that he's coming here this evening with some imbecile woman – and the doctor who looks after her. And he says that he's got proof...

THE WOMAN (*watching him closely*): Proof? Proof of what?

BRUNO: That she... that it's she... and not you!

BOFFI: And he's bringing her here.

BRUNO: Now do you understand?

THE WOMAN (*unmoved, still staring at* BRUNO): Here? But how can he bring her?

BRUNO: He wrote to us both several times – to you and to me – perhaps we were wrong not to answer him...

THE WOMAN: But he never said anything to me about this!

BRUNO: Well, he did to me. As a matter of fact he asked me to go to Vienna to see the woman...

THE WOMAN (*surprised but still watchful*): Oh, yes?

BRUNO (*irritated at being watched so closely*): Yes, I tell you! He wanted me to talk to the doctor at the hospital there – this friend of his who's arriving with him now!

THE WOMAN (*still staring at him, as though she were interested in nothing more than his reactions*): Why did you never tell me anything about this?

BRUNO: I was hardly likely to tell you that I'd been asked to go to Vienna to see another woman...

BOFFI: You should, you know, Bruno... you really should... have answered him at least – even if only to tell him he was mad!

BRUNO: When I knew that he was only doing it to revenge himself on Cia?

THE WOMAN (*very distinctly*): I should have advised you to go.

BOFFI: There you are, you see?

BRUNO (*more and more irritated*): What should I have gone there to do? To look at a poor idiot, giggling and senseless, with a face to...

THE WOMAN: How do you know?

BOFFI: He sent me a picture of her.

THE WOMAN: Have you got this picture?

BOFFI: Yes... not with me though... But believe me, it's nothing to worry about... there's not the slightest possibility... In fact, I was just going to answer him... but when the injunction came... (*Indicating* BRUNO)

THE WOMAN: What injunction?

BOFFI: The one he sent me...

THE WOMAN: I don't know anything about it... I'm learning everything for the first time now. And yet, I did have a right to know. Pictures... injunctions... what injunction is this?

BOFFI: Well, you see – when Salter got no answer to his letter he must have thought that it was in your husband's interests – having once recognized you – not to come out with another claimant. So he wrote to me. He sent me an injunction ordering me to show the photograph to other relatives – if there were any – to see if they could identify her. He even wanted them to go to Vienna!

BRUNO: It's become a mania with him!

BOFFI: Well, of course we just didn't know what to do. You see, the picture only came a few days ago. Should we show it to the relatives? Things were complicated enough as it was. Should we go to Vienna? Well, in fact, I was in favour of that idea. There, face to face, we could have cut it off short.

BRUNO: Just leave like that? It's easier said than done. But how? Secretly?

THE WOMAN: Why secretly?

BRUNO: Would you have liked them all to know about it? A hint's quite enough round here, and everybody knows everything! They do nothing but look at us and talk about us...

THE WOMAN: And so... you told me nothing, you didn't answer – you didn't make a single move.

BRUNO: I'm just telling you why.

THE WOMAN: An ostrich with your head in the sand...

BOFFI: It's true that if you'd gone there you might have stopped him...

BRUNO: Was I to know that they'd come here?

THE WOMAN: But I wonder how he managed to persuade the doctor?

BOFFI: He explains that in the letter. Apparently he's got money to throw away. And somehow he's just convinced this friend of his, the doctor. There are four of them making the journey... Salter, the doctor, the woman and a nurse. He's obviously persuaded the doctor that it's in all our interests here not to discover the truth – and then, perhaps, that the sight of all these places might awaken in that poor wreck of a woman – I don't know... but what proof can they possibly have?...

BRUNO: He's only out for revenge!

BOFFI: I was talking about the doctor! Of course, we know *his* motives! But what possible "proof" could he have? (*A pause. They all three stand there for a moment, hesitant, hovering, motionless.* THE WOMAN *studies* BRUNO, *then suddenly asks him:*)

THE WOMAN: What do you want, Bruno? (*He does not reply*)

THE WOMAN: You seem anxious. I'd even say afraid!

BRUNO: Nonsense. Why should I be afraid?

THE WOMAN: What are you hoping for?

BRUNO: I want, oh, darling, for God's sake, what can I possibly want now, with things as they are? You tell me! I was just sending Boffi to find out what train they might arrive on.

THE WOMAN: I see. And then?

BRUNO: Then do something at least to stop them coming in when the others are here.

THE WOMAN: Why? They've left Vienna – sooner or later they must arrive here. You look to me so...

BRUNO: How do you expect me to look? Naturally I'm concerned...

THE WOMAN: No, my darling, more. You look to me like someone who's expecting that at any minute the house will fall about his shoulders.

BRUNO: But, don't you understand, they're going to descend on us while the relatives are here, bringing some sort of proof with them? Proof that they must consider more or less valid, I imagine, if the doctor's come all this way with a sick woman?

THE WOMAN: Ah, I see... it's the proof that you're afraid of.

BOFFI: Of course it's not. Bruno's afraid that the others might try to trade on...

THE WOMAN: On what? On the proof?

BOFFI: Well, on any doubt they might feel faced with the proof that...

THE WOMAN: That she is really Cia... and I'm a fraud?

BRUNO: Not that they really believe that! But it would suit their ends!

THE WOMAN (*ironically*): I see. You're saying that they might wish to play on this doubt in their own interests?

BOFFI: Exactly. Doesn't that seem likely to you?

THE WOMAN: But if you stopped that happening today, you couldn't stop it tomorrow. That's a game they can always play, even if they do recognize me today. I have no proof.

BOFFI: But you don't need any.

THE WOMAN: I don't? Dearest Boffi, nothing could be easier than to doubt me. Listen, I could show you all the reasons I have to doubt myself... I... to doubt myself! Seeing Bruno like this... (*With a violent movement of contempt*) Just think that whichever way things fall out now, he can't lose.

BRUNO: I? What do you mean?

THE WOMAN: I mean you can't lose what's worrying you most at the moment.

BRUNO: What's worrying me at the moment is the scandal that's going to be created! There's already been enough gossip about our living here without seeing anybody for four months.

THE WOMAN: Are you complaining about that?

BRUNO: No! But now you can see for yourself the effect...

BOFFI: Bruno's right.

THE WOMAN: Well, if the worst comes to the worst, my darling, there's no need for you to worry. You will just have been tricked.

BRUNO: What do you mean – tricked?

THE WOMAN: Tricked into thinking that I was Cia. Like Boffi in Berlin... Like Lena and Uncle Salesio here. You're in good company, aren't you? And you wouldn't lose a thing over it because it'll be my imposture which will have tricked you! (*She laughs*)

BRUNO: Oh, rubbish! What trick are you talking about? That you are Cia?

THE WOMAN: That's right... Cia. Oh, we've settled that for sure. You don't have to worry about that. Look at the portrait! What more could you ask for? (*She laughs*) You'll bear me witness, Boffi, that I did everything I could to save him from being taken in by a possible – suspected imposture. Never mind, though – here I am! Ready to answer. But only for myself, mind! I'm not answering for you any more. Because I've been tricked, too – did you know that?

BRUNO: You? About what?

THE WOMAN: About you – if only you knew how much! (*Turning to* BOFFI) Go away then, Boffi – but don't go looking for easy ways out any longer – it's a waste of time. Indeed, I'd like you to try and see that they arrive while the others are here.

BRUNO: What are you going to do?

THE WOMAN: You'll see.

BRUNO: The family should be here at any minute now...

THE WOMAN: I've told you that I'm quite ready. I just want a few words with you first. Perhaps you won't be able to understand me, but that doesn't matter. Oh, and don't worry that the game's going to be all in their hands – it isn't. I'm going to do all the playing there is to do myself. I feel well in the spirit of it already! And it's going to be a hard-fought game for everybody – even for me. (*To* BOFFI) Go on, Boffi – go now!

BOFFI: So you really want me to bring them here?

THE WOMAN: Yes, bring them here.

BOFFI: All right. I'll be off then. (*After* BOFFI *has gone through the door into the garden, she continues in a burst of exasperation*)

THE WOMAN: It's a waste of time – hard facts must always win in the end. There's no getting away from this heavy earth of ours. Your soul may fly up for a moment – escape – soar beyond even the most appalling things that Fate may have made you suffer – go on, little soul, fly – create a new life for yourself! But when you're all full of that life, down you come again – there's no escaping it – down until you smash into the hard facts that begrime your sweet new life for you – down into the profit and loss, and the mean little family squabbles... You know very well that I know nothing of all that. But it doesn't matter. I just want to say this to you. I've been here with you for four months. (*She grips* BRUNO *by the arm and pulls him round to face her*) Look at me! Look in my eyes! Right into them. They haven't been seeing for me any longer – not even to see myself with! They've been like this – see – fixed in yours – all the time – so that the image of myself as you saw me might be born in them from your eyes – and with it the images of all things and of life itself as you saw it! I came here and I gave myself to you completely – I told you: "I'm here and I'm yours. Now make me – make me yourself just as you want me, as you desire me. You've been waiting for me for ten years? Pretend they don't exist! No – there's no memory of hers any longer in me. Give me your memories! And now they'll come alive again in me, alive with all your life, with your love, with the very first joys that she gave you!" How many times have I asked you: "Like this? Is it like this?" And I was blessed in the joy that was being reborn in you from my body – and my body shared the joy!

BRUNO (*almost drunkenly*): Oh, Cia – Cia!

THE WOMAN (*stopping him as he tries to embrace her. She seems almost drunk too, but with pride at having been able to create herself as she has.*): That's right – Cia! I... I am Cia! Only me! Me! Me! Not her! Not the portrait. She was! Don't you see that existence by itself is nothing? Existence means creating oneself. And I have created myself as her. And you have understood nothing!

BRUNO: Oh, yes, yes – I have understood!

THE WOMAN: Understood what? Haven't I felt – haven't I felt your hands searching my body here... (*She indicates vaguely a point on her body somewhere above her hip*) ...For... I don't know – some mark you knew you should find there. And because of a mark that isn't there – or for some other reason – I'm not Cia after all, am I? I can't be Cia, can I? Or maybe the mark's disappeared? I just didn't want it any more, and so I had it removed. Yes, that's it! Because I knew – I'd realized that you were searching me for it – and you were, weren't you?

BRUNO: Yes!

THE WOMAN: You see? But now you're terrified that Ines, with all the intimacy of a sister, or even Lena, might want to find this mark on me again – as a nice, legal proof, signed and sealed. And you're terrified they won't believe what I've told you. "Oh. Disappeared. That's serious! How can a mark like that disappear?" They'll want to call in doctors. All the more so as this poor imbecile creature who's coming now might perhaps really have the mark herself. If she had it and I didn't... that really would be the end! Poor, poor Bruno! So worried about all these documents and proofs that might be brought forwards! But you mustn't worry. I am Cia – a new Cia! You want so much. And I wanted nothing when I came here – absolutely nothing.

I gave you back alive the woman who I thought you'd waited for with love for ten years, so that I could live a pure life myself, too, after so much squalor and shame. And to show you just how true that is, I'm ready to shout in all their faces, in spite of all proof, and even against you – yes, you, if you're forced not to recognize me in order to save your own interests – I'll shout in their faces that I am Cia – I alone – because she up there on the wall – can no longer have that life, except in me! (*Once again the sound of a car on the gravel outside*)

BRUNO (*strained and shocked*): It's them! The family! They're here!

THE WOMAN: Leave everything to me! You just go and receive them. I can't show myself any longer dressed up like this! I'll be down straight away. (*She goes quickly towards the stairs and begins to climb them*)

BRUNO (*almost a plea*): Cia…

THE WOMAN (*stopping and turning; she is very calm and speaks with a voice that indicates that what she is saying is now unarguable*): Yes. Of course. Cia.

CURTAIN

ACT THREE

About twenty minutes have elapsed and it is now almost evening. The room is flooded with a violet aftermath of sunset which streams in from the open loggia. The landscape is more peaceful than ever. The tiny lights of another village twinkle in the distance.

BRUNO and UNCLE SALESIO, CIA's sister INES and her husband, MASPERI, are waiting impatiently. Although INES is younger than CIA, she looks older. She is elegantly dressed and has everything that a woman of her sort should have. She asked for the death certificate because it was right, not because she is greedy and certainly not in order to harm her sister, for whom she has sincerely grieved ever since it was believed that she had died. But UNCLE SALESIO didn't part with the villa and the estate to have them enjoyed by an outsider, and as CIA was presumed dead, it was only right that the property should come back to the family.

BARBARA is an unmarried woman in her forties. She has shiny black hair tinged with grey. She is full of complexes, stemming from a tortured sense of having been born ugly.

MASPERI has an odd face: his upper lip looks as though it has been thrust onto his face and pasted under his nose. He has protruding teeth and a pink complexion which looks almost artificial. He wears spectacles which he fidgets with and frequently adjusts on the bridge of his nose. He is a man of the world and knows just how things should be done. He likes to be polite but now he can hardly restrain his annoyance at the ill-mannered reception he and his wife are being given. After all, they have already waited four months for a confrontation which should have taken place immediately.

At last, LENA comes down the stairs.

BRUNO: What's she doing, for Heaven's sake? Did she say she was coming down?

LENA: Yes, she said, "I'm coming," but...

BRUNO: But what?

LENA: She was standing there surrounded by all her clothes – she'd opened all the trunks.

BRUNO (*dazed*): The trunks?

LENA: Perhaps to look for something... Or to put something back... I don't know... (*Pause*)

INES: She doesn't by any chance intend to – go away?

BRUNO: No, for Heaven's sake, why should she? I suppose you didn't ask her what she was doing, Lena? (*To the others*) She did say something about wanting to change...

LENA: In fact, she has changed. And she looked so nice as she was!

BRUNO: Why isn't she here then?

LENA: She's terribly nervy. She almost pushed me out of the room. "Go on down," she said, "go down and say that I'm coming."

SALESIO: Then she will come! (*A pause.* BARBARA *goes over to the loggia.*)

BARBARA: What a lovely view you get from here. The countryside is enchanting... and those lights...

MASPERI (*who has joined her*): Yes, it's a beautiful evening. (*Pause*)

BRUNO (*whispering to* LENA): How is she?

LENA: I'd swear she'd been crying.

SALESIO: She is indeed very upset. And after all that's most understandable – the idea of seeing...

MASPERI: Oh no, no, no! I'm sorry, Uncle Salesio, but it's nothing to do with seeing anybody. Unless by any chance she's got a grudge against her sister.

LENA: No, no, not against her sister! What makes you think her sister's got anything to do with it? I hope you haven't been listening to Salesio's explanations?

BRUNO (*stressing each word*): No, the grudge she bears is against me.

MASPERI: Oh well... if it's something between the two of you...

BARBARA: That's all very well, but we've been kept here waiting for a quarter of an hour. (*Pause*)

INES: She shouldn't bear grudges now...

LENA (*to* INES): But who's saying anything about grudges? She even told me that what you did was right, Ines. What more could you ask for? She said she'd be happy if everything here were to be given back to Uncle Salesio so that he would then be free to give it to you.

INES: Why should she want me to have it?

LENA: Well, it all goes to show how she really feels about things.

SALESIO: After ten years, she said, it was only right that you...

INES: I didn't do it for myself. You know I didn't, Uncle. It was for you. And then... yes, I admit it – because I have a daughter.

MASPERI: She must have understood that, Ines, and I didn't wish to do anything against her.

BRUNO (*very clearly*): What she won't understand, Masperi, is what you have all done against me.

MASPERI (*spreading out his hands*): Oh, please, I devoutly hope we haven't come all the way here to start discussing that again!

BRUNO: No, no, it's not that, that I...

MASPERI (*trying to continue*): We are all waiting here...

BRUNO (*cutting him off*): It's that I want to understand what she really feels... for myself as well as for you. I want to be able to see things straight myself! (*With an outburst of anger*) I tell you I'd rather be anywhere else than here at the moment... Lena, Salesio – she's talked to you – what is it that she's got against me? Has she started suspecting that I...

LENA: I think... she has.

SALESIO: She said that if she'd known she was going to find herself in the middle of a squabble about financial interests...

MASPERI: What squabble? As soon as she came back all squabbling was bound to be cut short!

SALESIO: Exactly, Masperi. Just what we told her!

INES: Oh, I would have rushed here immediately... if Bruno...

MASPERI: Precisely. If Bruno hadn't told us all...

INES: That she didn't want to see anybody. And least of all me! I could have shown her that I never, but never, oh, the idea! God alone knows how much I cried for her... (*Moved, she covers her eyes with a handkerchief*)

MASPERI: Oh, don't start that again, Ines. Besides it seems pretty clear that she's accepted your side of it – so you're all right. Here and now it seems that other factors are involved – haven't you gathered that?

BRUNO: I didn't say that she didn't *want* to see anybody, I said that she *couldn't*!

LENA: And that's absolutely true – she really couldn't! She couldn't! She couldn't even bring herself to see Salesio and me at the beginning. After all, we must remember that the poor girl has been through a terrible experience!

SALESIO: All the horror of the past – and then coming back here. She could only bring herself to do it because she loved Bruno so much. She didn't want to come…

LENA: She was forced to! (*As* BRUNO *looks at her angrily, she adds*) That's what she said – forced! (*Pause*)

MASPERI: And this… suspicion of hers that you mentioned?…

BRUNO (*unable to evade the question any longer*): All right, then… she suspects that I did just that… that I forced her, as you put it, to come here – because I needed her in my quarrel with you. It's true that she didn't want to come. And I think that she began to suspect, because I promised her there in Berlin that she wouldn't have to see anybody. I told her there was a perfect excuse for her not to see you – the family quarrel. And she came to think of it as no more than an excuse. I was sure that after a while, when she'd got over the first moment, when she'd calmed down a little and with the passing of time, she'd have been able to conquer this fear of you all.

INES: But I could have made her conquer it straight away simply by assuring her…

BRUNO: In a sense, it wasn't so much you that frightened her as herself – at least, that's how it seemed to me… (*With anger*) There you are, Lena! That's all the force I used, if you can call it force! I put no pressure on her whatsoever! (*Getting more irritated*) Then there had to be some way out of this situation, hadn't there? I had to try and convince her that we couldn't go on for ever like this – that the excuse would have to stop… (*Turning to* LENA *and* SALESIO) Particularly as she'd made it so plain to Lena and Salesio that (*turning towards* INES) she had nothing against you, Ines – I mean she put an end to the excuse herself. (*Sweating and agitated*) I just don't know! (*Little pause, then a fresh outburst*) And don't think I enjoy having to give the impression of justifying myself before you… (*Pacing the room*) And now she suspects me. As if I wasn't the only one here who consistently refused to believe she was dead! I was so sure that I didn't hesitate to spend all that I did spend to rebuild everything here. And why? I'd have been an idiot to do it just so that you could come along and take it from me, wouldn't I? All right – I admit that I took a pretty firm line with you about it, I may even have been spiteful. God knows it's natural enough. I've had to fight – I've had to defend my property as well as my feelings. That's not a crime… (*Angrily looking towards the staircase*) What's she doing, for Heaven's sake?

INES: Exactly. Because if she doesn't intend to come down there seems to be no point in our going on waiting for her.

LENA: Try and be patient. She's obviously trying to calm her nerves first.

BRUNO: But she must realize that at any minute now… (*He stops, then goes on immediately to* LENA) Lena, will you please go back up there and tell her from me to remember where Boffi has gone and why. She must be here when… And anyway we've been waiting for long enough already. There are limits.

LENA: All right. I'll go. (*She goes towards the staircase*)

INES: To see how she is, too.

LENA: Yes, of course. (*She exits up the stairs*)

INES: Because if she really doesn't feel up to it this evening we can just go! (*Pause*)

MASPERI: I'm only sorry that something which was all cleared up for us as soon as we heard she was coming back should be causing trouble now between you two…

BRUNO: Unfortunately, there's something else which… You see, not everything has been cleared up between all of you and me. There's something else…

MASPERI: Something else? What?

BRUNO (*with a gesture towards the floor above*): Cia knows very well what! And she shouldn't leave me like this now! (*Pacing again*) You'll have to excuse me – I really am a bit shaken… Oh, God, if I'd even dreamt that something like this… It's all very well to ignore facts. How can you ignore them when they happen? (LENA *comes back down the stairs*)

INES: Here's Lena…

BRUNO: Well, what did she say?

LENA: I hardly know... she said that what you said about Boffi was the very reason why she wasn't coming down yet...

BRUNO: What I said?

LENA: Yes.

BRUNO: So she intends to wait until...

LENA: Until Boffi comes back.

BRUNO: She said that? She really wants to drive me quite mad!

LENA (*shrugging her shoulders*): What can I do about it? I'm just telling you what she said.

BRUNO: I'll go and see her myself. (*He runs up the stairs*)

INES (*rising and going to* LENA): What exactly is going on, Lena? What's happened?

SALESIO: Must be something behind all this... something new!

LENA: It looks like it.

MASPERI: In fact Bruno himself hinted that...

INES: Yes, but what? He said that perhaps everything's not cleared up yet...

MASPERI: So he did! Between us and him. But I can't think what he was talking about.

LENA: I think it must have something to do with that letter...

INES: Letter?

SALESIO: That's right. I think so, too. You can be sure...

INES: But what letter?

LENA: A letter they got a little while ago... apparently it came from abroad.

SALESIO: They were talking about it together for a long time...

LENA: That's right... About somebody who... Oh, I don't know... in Austria or somewhere...

SALESIO: Threw 'em into a fine old how-d'you-do.

LENA: There was Boffi, too... then they sent him away immediately... I don't know where... to stop something...

Through the loggia comes the dazzling gleam of car headlights. We can hear a car horn and, once again, the sound of tyres on the gravel.

SALESIO: Ah! There we are! That must be Boffi now!

LENA: Good, good! Now she'll come down. She was just waiting for him... (*Looking through the French windows*) Yes, here he is... (*With a gesture and an expression of surprise*) But... he's not alone!

SALESIO (*also looking out*): There're several people...

MASPERI (*also looking*): Whoever are they?

INES: Who's that strange woman? What is going on?

SALESIO: They're getting her out of the car...

MASPERI: They're helping her out...

INES: Oh, God, what is it? What's happening?

SALESIO: They look like Germans.

LENA: Oh yes, they're foreigners all right...

MASPERI: Look at that... Look at that woman! She's...

INES (*going back*): Oh, how horrible!

The MADWOMAN *enters supported by the* NURSE *and the* DOCTOR, *and followed by* BOFFI *and* SALTER. *The* MADWOMAN *is fat, flaccid, with a wax-like face, hair in disorder, motionless, empty eyes. There is a perpetual idiot smile on her mouth – a wide, empty smile which never ceases even when she is making odd noises or babbling one or two words, clearly without any idea of their sense. The* DOCTOR *and the* NURSE *are typically German in appearance and manner. Even* SALTER *seems more German-looking than before.*

SALTER (*approaching*): Come along, come along, my dear. This way, now... In here, that's right... Come along...

MADWOMAN: Le – na... Le – na... (*These two syllables, which are no longer a name to her but rather a sound which has long since become automatic, are uttered by her large, breathy mouth almost in cadence*)

LENA (*shattered*): Oh God – but what?... Is she calling me?

INES: Who is she? For God's sake, what's happening?

BOFFI (*entering, distraught*): Where's Bruno? Where's Lucia?

MADWOMAN: Le – na...

LENA (*looking from face to face, bewildered*): She's speaking to me!

SALTER: Do you belong to the family? Is your name Lena?

LENA: Yes... I'm the aunt...

SALTER (*to the* DOCTOR): There now, Herr Doktor. D'you hear that? There is somebody in the family called Lena! That's another proof! Oh, it's absolutely certain now! We didn't know that!

MASPERI (*coming forwards*): What is absolutely certain?

BOFFI: Don't pay any attention, Masperi! She makes that sound all the time... she's been doing it all the way here.

MADWOMAN: Le – na...

MASPERI: But she really is saying Lena though.

BOFFI: Yes, but she's not saying it to anybody. And she laughs all the time like that... (*Then referring to* BRUNO *and* THE WOMAN) For Heaven's sake, where are they? Where are Bruno and Cia?

INES: Oh God, has everybody gone mad?

MASPERI: What is all this about? What have they brought this woman here for? Who are these people?

BOFFI (*still speaking about* BRUNO *and* THE WOMAN): How can they possibly stay upstairs now? Would somebody please call them?

SALTER (*to* BOFFI, *indicating the others*): Are these ladies and gentlemen also relatives?

BOFFI: Yes... (*Introducing* INES)... This is the sister, Signora Ines Masperi.

SALTER: Her sister? So there *is* a sister! Her sister? Right then, we'll soon know...

INES: Who is this gentleman?

BOFFI: His name is Carl Salter. He's a writer.

SALTER (*to* INES): Will you please look at her, Signora Masperi. Look... There she is.

INES: Me? (*To* BOFFI) Boffi, what is he talking about? Look at who?

BOFFI: He will insist on believing...

SALTER (*to* INES): Don't tell me that she doesn't remind you of somebody?

INES: No... who? Oh, God! Who should she remind me of?

BOFFI (*ironically*): Your sister!

MASPERI: What?

INES: Cia?

LENA: Where? What is he talking about?

SALTER: Yes! This woman! This woman!

SALESIO: Then he must be off his head, too!

SALTER: I've brought her all the way here...

MADWOMAN: Le – na...

SALTER (*at the sound of her voice, gesturing towards her*): There! Isn't that proof? You must accept that as proof! She's saying Lena! The doctor says that for years now she's kept calling for Lena!

LENA: Oh, no! It's impossible!

SALTER: Don't you recognize her? Look in her eyes! How can you fail to recognize her?

LENA: What... who can you expect me to recognize?

SALTER: My friend here, the doctor who's been studying her case for years, he's got documents, proof...

MASPERI: What proof? Let him show it then!

INES: Oh, but it's impossible!

MASPERI: Please, Ines, let him talk. We've been so taken by surprise that... What proof?

LENA: But our Cia's upstairs!

SALTER: I know the lady upstairs. Very well.

SALESIO: This really is the most extraordinary thing...

MASPERI: Please, Uncle Salesio, let him say what he has to say! (*To* SALTER) So you know?...

SALTER: The lady upstairs... only too well!

LENA: Do you think you know her better than I do? I who was a second mother to her?

SALTER (*gesturing towards the* MADWOMAN): No, to her! To this poor woman here.

LENA: Rubbish!

MASPERI: If you think that you really have proof...

SALESIO: But what are you talking about proof? Masperi, you don't seriously think?...

MASPERI: No, but I'm just saying that if they think they have this proof, the simplest thing is to...

BOFFI (*ironically*): Here we go!

SALESIO: This proof would only make us laugh, or weep with pity more likely!

MASPERI: ...The simplest thing is to go to the proper authorities...

BOFFI: Even when you know why all this is being done?

MASPERI: I have no idea why it's being done!

BOFFI: But I have... so have Bruno and Lucia! Where are they?

SALTER: Here's the motive you want... revenge!

BOFFI (*to* MASPERI): There you are!

SALTER: But I should add... punishment!

MASPERI: I don't know this gentleman... I can't possibly...

SALESIO: Oh ho! Anyway the gentleman's motives have no great importance. Out with them then! These documents and proofs if you've got any! Because we don't want anybody round here getting any funny ideas into their heads because of this... revenge... or punishment or whatever it is.

BOFFI (*to* MASPERI): I knew it, you know.

MASPERI: What d'you mean you knew it? Who could possibly have known a thing like this?

BOFFI: I mean I knew that you would start getting ideas.

SALESIO: But nobody is to start getting ideas!

INES (*contemptuous*): Of course not! (*To* SALTER) Now look, all of us... I... her sister... her aunt here, her uncle and Boffi, too... we are all of us looking at this poor creature you've brought here, and not one of us recognizes her.

SALTER: Perhaps because you have already recognized the lady upstairs?

INES: No! In my case, no!

SALTER: What? You mean you haven't recognized her?

INES: I haven't seen her since she arrived. I came here to see her today.

SALTER: You've had no desire to see her until today?

INES: No, it wasn't I... It was she who...

SALTER: Ah! So it was she. I see. Because she couldn't do it... not with a sister. With a sister – blood must tell – her cheek against yours – that touch would be unbearable even for her. She was terrified you'd know something was wrong. But try – try now, and you'll feel there... (*indicating the* MADWOMAN) that this woman's your sister.

INES (*horrified*): Oh no... for God's sake... stop!

SALTER: If you can only let your pity get the better of your horror – look! It *is* Cia! It's ten years, remember! All the havoc, the war, the hunger she's lived through – I know the woman upstairs who's pretending to be her – if she seemed to resemble the image in your minds, then look – look well here – if you look carefully at this woman, if you search for the reality, underneath all the distortions and changes, she's got – she has got that face...

INES: Oh, no!

LENA: But where can you see it?

SALESIO: The man's talking rubbish!

SALTER: Look at the eyes... if they weren't so dead...

BOFFI: They're completely different... an altogether different shape... perhaps just the colour a little.

SALTER: She's been mad for nine years. She was found with an old uniform coat of a hussar over her. It was torn to pieces, but there was still a flash on it!

INES: What flash?

SALESIO: Where was she found?

SALTER: At Lintz.

MASPERI: What's all this about flashes and coats?

SALTER: The flash was of the regiment to which that hussar belonged. And that regiment had been here – right here!

MASPERI: Here during the invasion, you mean?

BOFFI: What does that prove? She might have begged it in Lintz off a hussar who'd been here during the invasion.

MADWOMAN: Le – na...

SALTER: And she calls for Lena! You hear? Why? Why should she have only that name fixed in her mind? (*To* LENA) And you, who say you were a second mother to her?...

LENA (*with sudden resolve, overcoming her own horror and surrounded by the horror of the others*): Wait! Let me look – let me speak to her. (*Pause*) Cia! Cia! Cia!

The MADWOMAN *remains impassive with her silent, empty laugh. They all watch her. Meanwhile,* THE WOMAN *has come down the stairs, followed by* BRUNO. *Nobody is aware of them. They become aware of her as she moves in front of them towards the* MADWOMAN *as soon as* LENA, *having abandoned her attempt, breaks from the* MADWOMAN. *It is an odd thing, but after what has happened and simply because the* MADWOMAN *is there, even though nobody has been able to recognize her, everybody – even those like* LENA, SALESIO *and* BOFFI *himself who have hitherto believed implicitly in* THE WOMAN *– now looks at her with perplexity and doubt.*

THE WOMAN (*to* BRUNO, *in the silence which has fallen as they all look at her*): Well, Bruno, why don't you try and call her, too?

SALTER: Ah, here she is!

THE WOMAN (*quickly, proud*): Here I am!

INES (*perplexed, but feeling she must overcome it*): Cia…

THE WOMAN: Wait a moment. Let's have some light. You can't see anything here. (SALESIO *goes to the door and switches on the light*)

INES (*looking at her in the light, repeats after another moment of hesitation*): Cia…

SALTER (*faced with* THE WOMAN'*s arrogant certainty and the double "Cia" of* INES, *his reaction is exactly the opposite of the others' – he begins to doubt himself. He turns to* INES): D'you really believe?…

THE WOMAN (*to* SALTER, *indicating* BRUNO): Well, Salter, you see… I kept him upstairs, I stayed upstairs myself, deliberately to give you time to make your effect. I recognize your ruthlessness very clearly. Only you would be capable of doing something so abominable… bringing her here… Poor creature – I want to look at her. (*She goes up to the* MADWOMAN *and with a delicacy which is all compassion, she puts her finger under the* MADWOMAN'*s chin, so as to look closer into the laughing face*)

MADWOMAN (*as* THE WOMAN *studies her, chants her double note without altering her empty, soundless laugh*): Le – na…

THE WOMAN: Lena?… (*Overcoming a shudder, the* MADWOMAN *turns towards* LENA)

SALTER (*quickly*): There you are, you see! She turned to look at her.

LENA: It's not me she's calling.

BOFFI: It's just a sort of chant she sings all the time.

SALTER: As far as I'm concerned, it's sufficient that she turned her head.

THE WOMAN: And that proves it, doesn't it? I can't be Cia.

SALTER: Even you suggested that he should try and call her too!

THE WOMAN: I knew that you wouldn't believe me. But then I discovered all the rest of you just now, while Lena was bending over her like this, calling, "Cia! Cia!"

LENA (*guilty, trying to excuse herself*): It was only because… Don't you see?

SALESIO (*at the same time, indicating* SALTER): This gentleman insisted so much…

BOFFI (*at the same time*): She kept on calling, "Lena… Lena!"

THE WOMAN (*topping them all*): But of course. There's nothing wrong with it. It's quite natural. (*To* LENA) I can see how you look at me now, Lena.

LENA (*bewildered*): How I look at you?...

THE WOMAN (*to* SALESIO): And you, too, Uncle Salesio.

SALESIO: Me? Oh, no, no, no...

THE WOMAN: Even you, Boffi...

BOFFI: No, that's not true at all. Nobody has recognized her.

SALESIO: We were all so... (*He doesn't know how to go on... surprised? Overwhelmed? And anyway, they don't give him time.*)

BOFFI: Even your sister saw immediately that...

THE WOMAN: Yes, Ines called me Cia, didn't she? Twice.

BOFFI (*to* SALTER): You heard, Salter? (*Then to* MASPERI, *deliberately*) And you, Masperi, did you hear?

INES (*contemptuous*): I told you before that nobody here had any desire to take advantage of this situation.

BOFFI: I was making it clear because even Bruno might take advantage of this!

THE WOMAN (*in a burst*): Oh, no, he won't! He won't take advantage of anything. Besides, look at him... he's more bewildered than anyone else.

BRUNO (*shaking himself out of it*): Bewildered? No, dumbfounded at this man's impertinence... if anyone is taking advantage of things, it's he!

THE WOMAN: Don't worry. He won't be able to take any advantage either – neither of me, nor of this poor woman.

SALTER: I considered it my duty...

THE WOMAN: To bring her here...

SALTER: Yes, to punish you!

THE WOMAN (*going up to him*): Punish me?

SALTER: Precisely. I nearly died because of you, and while I was lying between life and death, you calmly came down here to start cheating other people!

THE WOMAN: I have cheated nobody!

SALTER: You've cheated and cheated!

BRUNO (*with a menacing move towards* SALTER): Don't you dare!

THE WOMAN (*stopping him immediately*): No, no, Bruno, keep calm.

BOFFI: He's being deliberately provocative!

THE WOMAN: I can manage him by myself. (*Turning to* SALTER) I take it you're talking about my famous imposture, eh? And have you proved it? How? Like this? By this ghastly thing you've done? Well, I assure you I'm delighted you've succeeded – doubt has been sewn.

LENA: No, no, it hasn't!

BOFFI (*at the same time*): When?

SALESIO (*at the same time*): Doubt? In whom? It's not true!

THE WOMAN (*almost yelling*): I say I'm delighted! (*With a change of tone*) You all deny it... and yet I caught you just now...

SALESIO: But we didn't recognize her!

THE WOMAN: That doesn't matter!

BOFFI: You don't need to worry, Cia. I'll bet that he doesn't even believe it himself.

THE WOMAN: And that doesn't matter either. Let's examine this imposture of mine. It must be an odd sort of imposture, mustn't it, if I drew your attention myself to the odd way you were all looking at me when I came down just now. And you, Boffi, when you began to doubt...

BOFFI: I swear that I never doubted for a moment...

THE WOMAN: Oh, yes you did. And to console yourself for that doubt you went out of your way to notice... and to point out to me... how Ines called me Cia twice...

BOFFI: I noticed it because it was the truth. Besides, what possible doubt could I have because of this poor wretched woman?

THE WOMAN: No, no... not because of her... because of me... even though you couldn't recognize her. It was a very natural doubt... as soon as I appeared unexpectedly... you were all so confused... (*She indicates* SALTER) And Salter had just the opposite doubt, when he heard someone who hadn't seen me until then call me Cia. Oh, it's all very natural... (*To* LENA, *who is crying quietly*) It's no good crying, Lena. There's no certainty on earth so firm that it can't be shaken as soon as even the smallest doubt arises... and then you can never again believe quite as you did before!

SALTER: So you admit yourself that you might not be Cia?

THE WOMAN: I admit a good deal more than that! I admit that this woman might be Cia! (*She points to the* MADWOMAN) If that is what they want to believe!

SALTER (*quickly, gesturing first towards* THE WOMAN *and then at the* MADWOMAN): Yes, because she looks like Cia while you don't.

THE WOMAN: Ah, no – that's not true! Not because I look like her! I was the very first to say that my likeness is no proof at all – the likeness that made you think you recognized me. You know, that could well be a proof that it's not me!

MASPERI (*struck by this, spontaneously*): That's true... I hadn't...

THE WOMAN (*turning to him quickly*): It is true, isn't it Signor Masperi? It proves that it can't be me. (*Back to* SALTER) You see, Salter? It's only just occurred to some people...

BRUNO: It seems to me that you're doing everything to...

THE WOMAN: But you recognized the strength of that argument, too!

BRUNO: I did?

THE WOMAN: Yes, you, Bruno!

BRUNO: When? What are you talking about?

THE WOMAN: When I pointed out to you there in Berlin. And you were shaken by it, too, Boffi. Understandable come to that. It's only when you believe in someone or perhaps when it suits you to believe in someone that you don't think of something as obvious as that, or maybe you don't want to think of it. Cia may well be this woman – precisely because she no longer looks anything like her.

BRUNO: You're taking a perverse pleasure in...

THE WOMAN: I told you I was going to explain my imposture to Salter.

BRUNO: Well, this is a fine way to do it – making everybody doubt you.

THE WOMAN: Exactly! That's just what I am doing. I want everybody to doubt me... just as he does... so that I can at least have the satisfaction of being alone in believing in myself! (*With a gesture towards the* MADWOMAN) You haven't recognized her. Because she's unrecognizable? Because they haven't brought you enough proof? No. For none of these reasons! It's only because you don't yet feel that you can believe. It's as simple as that. Hundreds of poor devils have come back as she's done after several years – unrecognizable – without any memory – and sisters and wives and mothers – even mothers – have argued over them. "He's mine!" "No, he's mine!" They wanted to believe! And nothing can prove you wrong if you want to believe! You say it's not he? But for that mother it is! She believes in the face of all proof! She believes without any proof! Didn't you believe in me without proof?

BOFFI: There wasn't any need of proof – you are you.

THE WOMAN: That's not true! (*Turning quickly to* BRUNO *who is about to protest*) Don't worry, Bruno, my darling, I'm not damaging your interests if I try to prove that Cia might really and truly be this woman. On the contrary. After all there has been so much suspicion. Uncle Salesio told me so. (*She indicates* SALESIO) Suspicion when I stayed shut up here for four months without seeing anybody…

BRUNO: But everybody understood why!

THE WOMAN (*smiling at* LENA): Except for the nasty-minded people, eh, Lena? (*Then to* BRUNO) The trouble is that you imply it yourself… (*To* MASPERI) And you're already thinking, too, aren't you, Signor Masperi? It's in your face.

MASPERI (*surprised*): No, no, I…

THE WOMAN: You can't deny it. It's written all over you – you're mulling over what I've been saying just now. On you go then. It's not going to be so very difficult to suspect – well, let's see now – that a person who wanted to ride on a likeness that other people found it useful to notice.

BRUNO (*spitting it out*): Useful to me… is that what you mean?

THE WOMAN: So somebody's already suspected it, have they?

BRUNO: You raised the suspicion.

THE WOMAN: Exactly! (*She crosses to* MASPERI) Well then, is it so very difficult to suspect that I've been here, taking my time comfortably… (*She enigmatically smiles at* SALESIO)… Four months – to get myself ready to turn myself into Cia – first of all saying that I couldn't bear to see anyone – and luckily, you see, there was a very good excuse… Very convenient for Bruno, too. (*She indicates* BRUNO)

BRUNO (*quickly, to the relatives*): There you are – didn't I tell you that's what she'd say?

THE WOMAN: You may have told them so – but now it's me they're listening to! (*To* SALTER) You see, Salter, there was a clash of interests between them! It's easy to pretend at the beginning that one just doesn't want to remember anything… You can even pretend that you really have forgotten everything… and then in the meantime, eh?… Slowly, slowly build up the memories… Bruno needed time, didn't he, to rebuild the ruined villa and put the estate to rights. Well, I needed time, too, to build myself again, stone by stone, just like the villa – and to transplant all the poignant little memories of poor Cia into my soil – time to nurse them and let them blossom into life again…

(*She crosses slowly to* INES *with her arms outstretched*) Until one day, I should reach the point when I could even receive my sister… (*she takes her hands*) and talk with her about – oh, when we were little girls together, and about the jokes that we had, even though we were both orphans, brought up by an aunt. (*To the others*) Do you know, I even went to the trouble to make myself a dress exactly like the one in the picture, so that when I came down I'd look as though I'd walked straight out of the portrait. Isn't that true, Lena? But then I changed my mind because I thought it was going a bit far!

(*The others seem embarrassed*)

You're really beginning to suspect, aren't you? If the suspicion's not already fully grown…

MASPERI (*almost horrified*): No, no… that never…

INES: Who could even think, even dream of such a thing?

THE WOMAN (*pointing to* BRUNO): Bruno could. He did… think… of such a thing.

BRUNO: I did?

THE WOMAN: You. And now you're terrified that this suspicion – which is quite feasible, after all – might turn out to be the truth.

BRUNO: Oh, rubbish. Could any of you ever believe it?

THE WOMAN: They do – they do! Because it really is true – it's the truth as the facts show it to be. It really is the imposture Salter believes it to be. (*She indicates* SALTER)

BOFFI: But what are you saying?

SALESIO: How could it be possible?

BRUNO: This is just your revenge – and it's even fiercer than his!

THE WOMAN: Not my revenge – no! It's the revenge of the facts, my darling – the facts! By asking them to come here, you wanted us to reach this point, didn't you? But their recognition doesn't mean anything! It was you who should have recognized me – alone and disinterestedly – I didn't come here to defend a dowry! That would have been the imposture that he talks about! So look – if it's going to help you – so that it shan't seem like revenge against you – why don't you believe it? Face the facts as they are and believe it!

BRUNO: Believe what?

THE WOMAN: Believe that I really have been cheating. What more can I say?

BRUNO (*exasperated, facing her*): You're doing this to test me – it's all to test me!

THE WOMAN: No, I swear it isn't.

BRUNO: It is – it must be!

THE WOMAN: And what if this is just a new move of yours, too?

BRUNO: What move?

THE WOMAN: To let them think that I'm really only doing it to test you.

BRUNO: No!

THE WOMAN: No? All right then – accept the fact that I've tricked you. In fact there's nothing to stop you all accepting it – go on, all of you – accept in full what Salter says! (*She indicates* SALTER) Accept that he is right about everything – even about this poor creature – that it may well be her – really Cia. Look at her! (*She goes up to the* MAD-WOMAN *and with the same gesture of delicacy and compassion as before she puts her finger under her chin*)

MADWOMAN (*as soon as she feels the touch*): Le – na...

THE WOMAN (*to* LENA): Lena – you hear? She's really calling you. Why won't you believe it?

MADWOMAN: Le – na...

THE WOMAN: There you are... it's you she wants – really you – I didn't even want to see you. But she called for Lena as soon as she came – she's always called for Lena, Lena – and you just won't believe in her? Because she didn't answer you? But how could she? Look at her. (*She studies the* MADWOMAN *with infinite sadness*) If she can call for Lena like that – with that laugh all the time – no human voice will ever be able to reach her again! (*To the* MADWOMAN) Where are you calling from? From what distant, happy moment in your life where you've remained fixed – shut off in the blessing of that laugh – you're safe – immune... (*To* LENA, *who, almost repenting her instant dismissal of the* MADWOMAN *and pulled by the emotional magnetism of the scene, has moved near her*) Ah... so you've come to her again?

LENA (*frightened, almost in a whisper*): Oh, no, no... I just...

THE WOMAN (*gently*): Stay here. Perhaps Ines, too. I've got something to say to Salter. (*She indicates* SALTER *and takes him aside, then continues, staring hard at him*) Apart from being an unpleasant man – you must be a very bad writer, too.

SALTER: Quite possibly.

THE WOMAN: It's all just a fake, isn't it?

SALTER: What?...

THE WOMAN: Your "literary works". You can't have ever put anything that's really yours into it... no heart or blood – no trembling of the nerves, of the senses...

SALTER: In fact, nothing?

THE WOMAN: Nothing. I don't think you've ever suffered real anguish or despair! The despair which makes you want to take revenge on life – the life others have forced you to lead – by creating another more beautiful life – the one that might have been... the one you would like to have lived! And because you're like that yourself – because you knew me for three months as I was with you – you think I'm the same sort of fake that you are?

SALTER: I suppose you put your heart and blood and nerves and all the rest of it into it?

THE WOMAN: Why else should I have done it?

SALTER: To get rid of me.

THE WOMAN: I could have got rid of you without tricking somebody else.

SALTER: But I thought you'd just been confessing that you were in fact tricking?

THE WOMAN: All right, then – so you think that I really have tricked them?

SALTER: And now you may well have had your own good reasons to confess, with the inducement of...

THE WOMAN: Of what?

SALTER: Some chance of making something out of it...

THE WOMAN: That too, eh? It's very clear that your writing really is just a game you play to make money. Would you like to see somebody playing free, gratis and for nothing? It's all a question of what a person can become as a result of disaster. Look – you might become like that poor wretch... (*She points at the* MADWOMAN) Having fallen into the hands of a savage enemy who rips you to pieces – beautiful as you were – and young – taken by surprise alone here in the villa, your body marauded, and your soul made havoc of, until you're hunted into madness, and reduced to what she is now, and all return is impossible. Or again, you might still crash, but with a difference, undergo all the shame and torment just the same, and be hunted just the same into madness – but with a difference – you might find in the very madness itself a sort of inspiration to revenge yourself on your own fate – and in the horror of what's been done to you, the feeling of being so completely filthied that you really do feel disgust and horror at the idea of going back to your old life…

SALTER (*calling her fiercely back to her terms of reference*): Remember, you said this was only a game!

THE WOMAN: Wait a moment! Let's say, for example, the old life here – in this villa – where – oh, God! Like a flower, and quite innocent, only eighteen… and close, close to a sister you love… (*She is referring to* INES, *without, however, turning to look at her, as though she were not there and she could only see her in the past when she got married at the villa given her in dowry by her uncle. Very slowly as she goes on speaking she moves backwards towards* INES, *so that the last lines of the speech are said with her head leaning on* INES's *breast.*) …hugging her so tightly, never wanting to leave her. Not because I didn't love him… but because – knowing nothing that first night – what she said to me – oh, as ignorant as I was and she crying her heart out… "You know what they say? Now he'll have to look at you…"

INES (*violently, excited, embracing her*): Cia! Cia!

THE WOMAN (*stopping her convulsively*): No! Wait! Wait a moment!

BRUNO (*with triumphant joy*): I never told you that!

THE WOMAN (*after looking at him, says coldly*): I could easily drive you mad, couldn't I, Bruno? No, nobody told me that. (*And she adds quickly as* BRUNO *turns almost involuntarily to look at* LENA) Not even Lena. How could she? Something as intimate as that… it wasn't by accident I brought it up just now – no one could have told me that except the person who said it at the time. (*To* INES) Could they, Ines?

INES: No, of course not!

THE WOMAN (*turning quickly to* BRUNO): You didn't search for your Cia well enough, you know! You rebuilt the villa immediately. But you didn't look – you never looked well enough among the rubble and the bricks to see if there was something of her still there, something of her soul left behind, some memory still really alive – but alive for her! Not for you! Fortunately I found it!

BRUNO: What do you mean?

THE WOMAN (*not answering him, turning to* SALTER): Are you following me, Salter? And so, too filthy ever to get clean again, off she went with the very stupidest of those officers – just exactly as I told you in Germany – off to Vienna first of all, for years there in all the chaos of a lost war. Then Berlin – that other lunatic asylum… and she learned to dance, and suddenly the madness grew bright, and there was applause, and there didn't seem to be any reason ever to strip off those coloured veils of madness – you could wear them to go down into the square, and walk through the streets with them – and in the all-night bars at three, four, five in the morning, with all the clowns in white tie and tails around you. Until one evening when you least expect it (*she goes towards* BOFFI), someone passes close to you, slipping by like a devil, and calls you "Lucia, Lucia, your husband's just round the corner. If you like I'll call him for you!" (*Moving away, with her face in her hands*) God help me, I thought he was searching for somebody who couldn't exist any longer – somebody he realized he could find alive only in me, to remake her, not as she wanted, because she no longer wanted anything for herself, but as he desired her! (*She makes a violent movement as though to liberate herself from a wild illusion, and goes towards* SALTER) Stop! That's enough of that! (*To* SALTER) So you came here to punish me for my imposture, did you? How right you were! D'you know how far this imposture of mine was going? To a point where I should have myself recognized by my sister and my brother-in-law… who I'm now seeing for the first time in my life!

INES (*shattered*): Cia, whatever are you saying?

THE WOMAN: Just as I'd never been here before until Bruno brought me!

BRUNO (*trembling – loud*): You know perfectly well that's not true!

THE WOMAN: It is! It is true!

BRUNO: You're trying to make us believe that it is. You're just saying it because…

THE WOMAN: Because I wanted you to go on believing that I was Cia! But now Cia's going! She's going back to dance again!

BRUNO: What?

THE WOMAN: I'm going away with him! With Salter! (*She indicates* SALTER) I'm going back to dance in Berlin!

BRUNO: You're not moving from this house!

THE WOMAN: I told you you didn't search well enough for Cia! D'you know, my darling, that up there in the attic, without even realizing it, you let them throw away a little sandalwood cabinet. It's all broken, but there are still one or two little silver insects stuck onto the doors. Lena reminded me about that cabinet which Cia had kept because it belonged to her mother. D'you know what I found in a little drawer of that cabinet? A notebook of Cia's with the very words that Ines spoke to her on the day of her marriage: "You know what they say? Now he'll have to look at you." It's my notebook and I'm taking it everywhere with me. Particularly because, it's very odd, you know, but even the handwriting looks like mine! (*She laughs, starts off, then stops to add*) Oh, by the way, there's something else. Don't forget to look on this poor woman's hip to see if there's...

SALTER: A birthmark – yes, there is.

THE WOMAN: Red? Slightly swollen? Is there really?

SALTER: Yes, it's slightly swollen, but not red – black. And it's not exactly on her hip...

THE WOMAN: In the notebook it says: "Red and slightly swollen... on the hip... like a ladybird." (*To* BRUNO) There you are, you see? It may have darkened in colour. It may have shifted slightly. But she's got the birthmark. Another proof that it's she! Believe in her... all of you... believe in her! All right, Salter, let's go! (*To* BOFFI) You'll send my things on, won't you, Boffi? (*To* SALTER) You've got the car outside? I'll come just as I am. (*She runs to the door*)

SALTER: Yes, just as you are! All right! Let's go! (*And they both almost rush out to the car in the garden*)

BOFFI: No, no, wait a moment.

BRUNO: Wait... Cia... wait!

MASPERI: Perhaps it would be best to let her go.

BRUNO (*like all the rest of them, stunned and bewildered*): Let her go? Just like that? I can't just let her go back... Cia... Cia... (*And he goes off into the garden, too, followed by the others. We can hear confused and agitated voices off. Only the* MADWOMAN *and* LENA *remain on stage.* LENA, *however, stays at some distance from her, uncertain and bewildered.*)

MADWOMAN: Le – na...

LENA (*almost voicelessly, not quite able to bring herself to believe*): Cia... Cia... Oh, no... Please God, not this, not Cia...

LENA buries her face in her hands as the

CURTAIN FALLS

A Woman in Search of Herself

Trovarsi (1932)

Translated by Susan Bassnett and David Hirst

CHARACTERS

DONATA GENZI, *an actress*
ELJ
COUNT GIANFRANCO MOLA
ELISA ARCURI
CARLO GIVIERO
MARCHESA BOVENO
NINA, *her granddaughter*
SALÒ
VOLPES
A DOCTOR
ENRICO, *Elisa's manservant*
A MAID IN THE HOTEL

*Time: the present. The First and Second Acts take place on the Riviera.
The Third Act takes place in an expensive hotel room in a large city.*

ACT ONE

*Entrance hall of the Villa Arcuri on the Riviera. To the left an open plain
wooden staircase with a handrail leading to the upper floors. Part of
the first floor can be seen, the landing onto which all the upstairs rooms
open. Below this landing, at the back in the centre of the stage is the
door leading into the dining room, panelled with stained glass. To the
right, set back, is a corner, lined with bookshelves, with a leather-covered
bench below the shelves. A small table in the centre with vases, cigarette
boxes, ashtrays etc. Rich modern entrance-hall furnishings. When the
curtain rises,* ENRICO *the manservant and the* MAID *are on stage standing by the entrance to receive the guests.* CARLO GIVIERO *is the first to
arrive, a young-looking man in the prime of life, fortyish, very elegant in
a dinner jacket, with the sort of pale face people today like to describe
as "interesting", thick glossy black hair well cut, with the odd silvery
streak, tall, slim, a slightly bored manner, rather ironic.* GIVIERO *is a
doctor of medicine, but being a rich one he does not have to practise,
and so studies and writes over-literary learned essays on psychology
as a hobby. As soon as he enters he takes off his light overcoat and hat
and, as though he already knew the answer, even going so far as to move
towards the staircase, asks:*

GIVIERO: Is the signora upstairs?

ENRICO: Yes, signore.

GIVIERO: Better now, I hope?

ENRICO: Indeed she is, signore. She'll be down to dinner tonight.

GIVIERO: Splendid, splendid. (*Going upstairs*) And the guest, La Genzi
— has she arrived yet?

ENRICO: Yes, signore, at four o'clock this afternoon.

GIVIERO: With that storm blowing…

Knocks on one of the doors on the landing, opens it and goes in.

ENRICO (*left alone with the* MAID): Though who the devil she is, I can't imagine!

MAID: La Genzi? Haven't you ever heard of her?

ENRICO: Me? No, never. Who is she, a singer?

MAID: No, she's not a singer, she's an actress.

ENRICO: Oh, I thought she must be some sort of singer.

MARCHESA BOVENO *and her granddaughter* NINA *come in. The* MARCHESA *is a massive, heavy woman but a real lady. Her granddaughter is a lively, sharp-featured tomboy, with inquisitive eyes and a small straight nose that sniffs and ferrets into everything.* NINA *is distressed and irritated by her doll-like shortness, which is inclined to spread into the curvaceousness of a woman rather than the sinuous line of a girl. They treat her like a child, as someone rather silly and this constantly annoys her.* NINA *would like to be a trendy young woman. Her grandmother, who is also rather comical with her antiquated pronouncements of wisdom, is open-minded but keeps her on a tight rein. Both women enter wrapped in shawls. The* MARCHESA *wears a hat,* NINA *is bareheaded. The older woman is out of breath.*

MARCHESA BOVENO: Good evening, Enrico. (*To* NINA) Come along, Nina, take off that shawl. (*To the* MAID) It's so dreadfully windy out. We simply had to wrap ourselves up like this.

NINA: I didn't need to, you did.

MARCHESA: And when we go out again you will put on your shawl and no buts about it! That's the end of the matter. I shall insist on it. (*To the* SERVANTS) There don't seem to be any seasons these days. We've had no summer at all. (*Hits* NINA)

NINA: So I'm forced to feel cold…

MARCHESA: Absolutely, if it *is* cold. You modern girls, you're perpetually over-heated. It's all that sport. Quite shameless! (*To the* SERVANTS) Why is no one here yet?

MAID: Oh they are, Marchesa, upstairs.

MARCHESA: Good Heavens, do I have to go up there? Stairs for me are…

MAID: Of course not, Marchesa, you may stay here if you prefer.

ENRICO: They will be down to dinner shortly.

MARCHESA: Good.

NINA: Is La Genzi here yet?

MAID: Yes, signorina, she is.

NINA: Fancy that. I didn't think she would be.

MAID: She arrived on the four o'clock train.

MARCHESA (*spitefully, to* NINA): I didn't think she would be! And why didn't you think she would be here?

NINA: I don't know… I just said that… I'll go up now.

MARCHESA: Stay here. You can't possibly go upstairs. You don't even know her.

NINA: No, I meant I was going up to see Signora Elisa.

MARCHESA: Oh, that's different. Tell Elisa… (*to the* MAID) I don't suppose she's still in bed, is she?

MAID: No, Marchesa, she's been up since noon.

ENRICO: She even went to the station.

MARCHESA: To meet her friend. I see. (*To* NINA) All right, go on up. (*To the* MAID) Who is here then?

MAID: Count Mola, Marchesa.

ENRICO: And Signor Giviero has just gone up.

MARCHESA: If Mola is here, that's splendid. Now, tell Elisa I shall wait here. Those stairs would absolutely kill me.

NINA *starts to go up the stairs and the* MARCHESA *goes to sit down, saying:*

MARCHESA: At this rate, one of these days I'll turn into a tortoise.

The door on the landing through which GIVIERO *entered opens and* COUNT MOLA *begins to come down, stopping* NINA *on her way up.* COUNT MOLA *is about fifty, dark-skinned, stocky, silver hair, small thick moustache, still black, probably through the help of some dye, very elegant, blessed with a refined, sensible, cheerful disposition.*

COUNT MOLA: No, Nina, back downstairs if you please. Everyone is waiting downstairs. (*To the* SERVANTS) Change of orders. Don't let anyone else go up now. (*This is said from the staircase, leaning over the banisters. The* SERVANTS *bow and exit stage rear into the dining room.*)

NINA (*still on the stairs with the* COUNT *but starting to come down*): But Giviero went up…

MARCHESA (*below, overhearing*): Stupid girl.

COUNT MOLA: As you see, I'm coming down myself…

NINA: Because Giviero went up?

MARCHESA: Stuuuuuupid girl.

COUNT MOLA (*downstairs now with* NINA): These girls are quite dreadful, aren't they, Marchesa?

MARCHESA (*to* NINA): I ask myself how you could possibly think that the Count had to come down just because Giviero went up.

NINA (*innocently*): No, I didn't think that at all, Granny. Giviero had gone upstairs, then the Count came down and said that nobody else could go up there...

MARCHESA: Well then?

NINA: Nothing, Granny. Giviero went up... the Count came down.

MARCHESA: She's still doing it.

NINA: Isn't that what happened?

COUNT MOLA: It may well be, but there's really no reason for you to say so, young lady.

Pause. The COUNT *crosses to the table, takes a cigarette and lights it.*

NINA (*still deep in thought, with large vacant eyes and her small inquisitive nose in the air*): Signora Elisa must be dreadfully worried tonight about Giviero meeting La Genzi.

COUNT MOLA: Now steady on there.

MARCHESA: For Heaven's sake, Nina.

NINA: Down on the beach everyone was saying that Giviero used to have his rooms covered with pictures of Miss Genzi...

COUNT MOLA: But nobody has ever said that he was...

NINA: ...Her lover. Go on, say it.

MARCHESA: Nina! Really!

NINA: Good Heavens, Granny, it's common knowledge.

COUNT MOLA: I would have said "friend"... But nobody knows anything of the sort, either about him or any other man for that matter.

MARCHESA: Come now, let's not go too far; after all, an actress, lovers...

COUNT MOLA: I'm sure she's had her share. But the fact is that nobody has ever been able to say precisely whom she was involved with.

MARCHESA: She knows how to handle things, Count, you can be sure of that. Let's not close our eyes to that fact. A woman's reputation these days is dressed up in...

COUNT MOLA (*gallantly*): Surely you wouldn't wear a reputation like a garment, Marchesa.

MARCHESA: But you shouldn't leave her undressed, my dear man, if you want her to defend herself. (*Glares at* NINA *who is standing stiffly as a dummy*) That's enough. Let's change the subject.

NINA (*after a pause, still standing like a dummy*): I'm afraid of… something else. I'm afraid of Elj meeting Donata Genzi.

MARCHESA: Elj? Where is Elj?

COUNT MOLA: My word. I was just thinking about him.

NINA (*strangely, as though she were somewhere else*): I know.

COUNT MOLA: How do you know?

NINA (*still in the same tone*): Because he isn't here and you want him to come.

COUNT MOLA: Quite! Just imagine, Marchesa, he took it into his head to go off sailing tonight, with the sea in that state.

MARCHESA: Quite mad! It's so dreadfully windy…

COUNT MOLA: And did you see those waves?

NINA: Oh, let him go. It's a thousand times better for him to go out to sea than to come here.

MARCHESA: The girl really is unhinged! She's raving. Can't you control your tongue at all tonight? Dear Lord, the way she talks!

NINA (*still somewhere else*): It's because I can see.

MARCHESA: What can you see? Do stop all this at once. Look at her eyes! Oh, I could shake you, I really could. (*Shakes her*)

NINA: That won't do any good. I can still see, I can see…

COUNT MOLA: That Elj is in danger?

NINA: Yes.

COUNT MOLA: If he goes out in the boat.

NINA: No, if he comes here.

COUNT MOLA (*shrugging his shoulders*): Oh, really. (*Looks through the door at the back, shouts*) Enrico! Hey there!

NINA: Oh God, he'll make him come, Granny, he'll make him come!

COUNT MOLA: Of course I'll make him come.

MARCHESA: Why should it matter to you whether he makes him come or not?

COUNT MOLA: But he gave me his word he would come. And Elisa has given me permission to send for him. (*To* ENRICO, *who is standing in the doorway*) Do me a favour, Enrico…

ENRICO: At your service, Signor Conte.

NINA: No, no...

MARCHESA: For Heaven's sake stop it, Nina...

COUNT MOLA (*continuing, to* ENRICO): Yes, it's my nephew. I think he's still at home. Or he may have gone to the Bar del Sole. Whichever, go and look for him and tell him from me not to delay any longer in coming here. Tell him to come just as he is, it doesn't matter... and say you are under orders not to come back without him. (ENRICO *nods, bows, goes out*)

NINA: I hope to goodness that such a silly order will just annoy him.

COUNT MOLA: Naturally it will. He's bound to feel offended, but he'll come so as not to displease me. Don't you think he would be even more offended if he knew why you don't want him to come?

NINA: You wouldn't be so unkind as to tell him, would you?

COUNT MOLA: I'll tell him. Oh yes, I'll tell him, all right.

NINA: If you tell him I'll...

MARCHESA (*menacingly, as though daring her to continue*): You'll what?

NINA (*on the verge of tears*): Nothing. I'll make him regret it. (*She runs out into the garden, upset*)

MARCHESA: Oh.

COUNT MOLA: Leave her be, my dear Marchesa. We must learn to respect the profound sorrows of our children. I feel deeply moved.

MARCHESA: It's quite incredible. I've never seen her like this before.

VOLPES *and* SALÒ *come in.* VOLPES *is about fifty, small with a moustache and spiky iron-grey hair which looks as though it has been blown back by a strong wind; dark-skinned, grubby-looking, he has the habit of stroking his fat, pendulous lower lip with two fingers.* SALÒ *is about the same height, possibly even shorter, with long rather wild grey hair and a clear, sharp, youthful expression. He has a straight, aquiline nose that gives an impression of not having been placed in quite the right position, thus compelling him to keep his head bent over backwards with his chin sticking out, as though he were trying to keep it from dropping.*

VOLPES (*greeting the others*): Good evening, Marchesa. My dear Gianfranco.

SALÒ (*to the* MARCHESA *only*): Marchesa...

MARCHESA: Oh! You two. What a pleasure to see you both together. The North Pole and the South Pole, I believe!

VOLPES: We have always been on the best of terms...

MARCHESA: Personally, I grant you that. But when you write...

VOLPES: Naturally, Marchesa. I, being the Southern Pole, am an old has-been, whereas he, being the North Pole, is the essence of youth. (*To* COUNT MOLA, *referring to* SALÒ) But you don't know one another, do you?

COUNT MOLA: I have not had the pleasure...

VOLPES (*introducing*): Count Gianfranco Mola... Salò.

They shake hands.

COUNT MOLA: Since art is eternal it really ought to be ageless.

SALÒ: But the problem is that art loves fashion, just like a woman. (*To the* MARCHESA) And La Genzi?

VOLPES: Ah, yes, Donata?

MARCHESA: She hasn't come down yet. (*To* VOLPES) I see, Volpes, you refer to her as "Donata"...

VOLPES: Well, one does... everyone...

MARCHESA: Tell me, what sort of woman is she?

COUNT MOLA: A very nice lady, they say.

MARCHESA: You aren't saying much.

VOLPES: Yes, possibly...

MARCHESA (*to* MOLA): You see, he says "possibly".

VOLPES: As a matter of fact, I've never been very close to her. She has only risen to favour fairly recently... And ever since I've been a little out of favour... but that is not the point. She is reputed to be...

MARCHESA: Flighty.

VOLPES (*immediately*): No, no... rather...

MARCHESA: Temperamental?

VOLPES: Not in the silly sense of the word, no. Dissatisfied. Uneasy. Yes, that's it... a difficult woman, I'd say... certainly not... very easy-going!

MARCHESA: I see. Haughty, touchy.

VOLPES: No, no. Touchy, perhaps. But not haughty, at least not by nature. It's her disposition. How can I put it?

SALÒ: Allow me. The Marchesa wants to know what she's like "as a woman". With respect, Marchesa, that is the problem.

MARCHESA: Oh, why?

SALÒ: Because it isn't possible to pin down an actress "as a woman".

MARCHESA: Are you trying to say that she acts in real life as well?

COUNT MOLA: Without actually wanting to, through some sort of occupational hazard.

SALÒ: No, not at all, I wasn't trying to say anything like that. Such a person could be perfectly described as "a woman who acts even when offstage". A ghastly sort of creature! What I am saying is that an actress, a true actress like Donata Genzi, "comes alive" on stage, not that she "acts" in real life.

MARCHESA: Well, no doubt she does in some way in life too, and I can tell you how! Unless you're suggesting that a "true" actress is no longer a woman at all.

SALÒ: Now there you are! Not one woman, no. Many women. And so far as she's concerned, no one at all.

ELISA ARCURI *comes down the stairs with* GIVIERO. *She is about thirty, thin, with bleached-blonde hair, an imposing nose, turquoise eyes and the general air of a woman who has lived a great deal. As she comes downstairs, she overhears the last words spoken by the* MARCHESA *and* SALÒ.

ELISA: Poor, dear Marchesa, are you getting to grips with that wicked Salò? Dear Volpes! And where's Nina?

COUNT MOLA: In the garden.

ELISA: Don't listen to a word Salò says, Marchesa. My dearest Donata is the sweetest, most straightforward creature in the world.

MARCHESA: Do tell me – if you have no objection, of course – how did you actually come to meet her?

ELISA: How? I've known her since childhood. We were at school together.

MARCHESA: Oh, in that case... I thought it was quite recent...

ELISA: Oh, yes, quite recent that we've become friends. One might say she was rediscovered. I had virtually forgotten everything about her. When she began to be the great Genzi in the eyes of the world, I suddenly remembered that I had had a schoolfriend when I was little called by the same name, Genzi, and she was Donata too. A timid, slender little girl who was always by herself... So that I simply couldn't believe at first that it could be her. I wrote to her. And it was her! She invited me to go and see her backstage one evening. She remembered me too, and not only that, but she reminded me of all sorts of things that I'd forgotten and which she had not... little, childhood things... simple, naive things... That's how it all came about.

MARCHESA: And she became fond of you?

ELISA: Instantly! But she's always travelling, you know… We write to each other. Now I've invited her to spend a few weeks with me and I've promised her that she won't have to see anyone, because she really does need to rest.

GIVIERO: It sounds like nostalgia?

ELISA (*irritated*): What has nostalgia got to do with it? Nostalgia for what?

GIVIERO: Well, her friendship with you, I mean… nostalgia for her childhood self… for girlish innocence…

SALÒ: Yes, that's possible… The pleasure of finding herself again, with you, in a distant memory of herself.

ELISA: For Heaven's sake, when? And where? Neither she nor I even think about our silly childish past…

NINA (*who has come back in from the garden without being noticed*): I can't believe she's sincere.

General astonishment.

SALÒ: Nina! Where have you sprung from?

MARCHESA: Nina's made a pronouncement! Nina makes official pronouncements. Nina has done nothing else all evening but make pronouncements.

SALÒ: You've got red eyes, Nina.

NINA: I don't care. I've been crying.

ELISA: Oh, poor Nina. Who's been making you cry?

NINA: Count Mola.

ELISA: Oh, you nasty man.

MARCHESA: That's not true! If anyone did, then it was me, and for good reason.

COUNT MOLA: No, with respect, Marchesa. If anyone did then it was La Genzi, who Nina claims to be afraid of.

MARCHESA: Quite.

ELISA: Afraid? You, Nina.

NINA: No, I'm not. I'm not afraid of anyone.

COUNT MOLA: She's afraid for Elj… who really does have me worried now, by the way.

SALÒ: Where is he?

COUNT MOLA: I don't know! He should have been here by now. He assured me he would come...

ELISA: Did you send anyone to fetch him?

COUNT MOLA: Yes, some time ago... And I still can't see anyone...

SALÒ: Oh, he'll turn up...

NINA: Let's hope not.

ELISA: Now how could you possibly be worried about Elj, Nina, on account of my poor Donata?

NINA (*rashly, turning to* GIVIERO): Look, you tell her why I'm worried, Giviero.

GIVIERO (*as astonished as everyone else*): Me? Oh, that's rich! How the devil should I know? Why ask me?

NINA: Because down on the beach this morning everyone was saying you knew her better than anybody else.

GIVIERO (*laughing at her*): Oh, I see, the portrait story, all my pictures. Some idiot saw them and tried to spread malicious rumours. What a good job I still have them all, so I can show them to you. There isn't a single one with any kind of dedication or even a signature. I bought every one in a shop.

NINA: But so many, for goodness' sake...

GIVIERO: So many... that's the point... a whole lot of them instead of just one... and all different. I used them for one of my investigations into the representation of emotion.

VOLPES: Really, I didn't know about that. Has it been published yet?

GIVIERO: No, I never finished it...

ELISA: Does Donata know about this?

GIVIERO: No, of course not, how could she? I'd never met her, never talked to her.

NINA: What can she be doing, why doesn't she come down?

ELISA: She said she was coming down, but I don't know... she was so tired when she arrived, and so... well, I thought... she seemed upset... She can't be feeling very well.

MARCHESA: Does she suffer from anything in particular?

SALÒ: Yes, something quite terrible for a woman of her age, an insidious, incurable sickness.

GIVIERO (*ironically*): Love?

SALÒ: No. Quite the opposite.

MARCHESA: What do you mean?

SALÒ: Quite simply, Marchesa, she suffers from a lack of intimacy.

NINA: Here he goes!

SALÒ: Who? Me?

NINA: Yes. Granny says I make pronouncements, but it seems to me that you're the one who's going to pronounce to us all now.

SALÒ: I am simply replying to your grandmother who was asking about illnesses.

Pause.

COUNT MOLA: Does she live alone?

VOLPES: So far as I know…

ELISA: Yes she does. Quite alone.

MARCHESA: Does she have no relatives?

VOLPES: Yes, I understand she has a mother who lives with a brother.

SALÒ: She talks about them occasionally, but nobody has ever seen them.

VOLPES: They say that her brother…

ELISA: Oh, yes but for Heaven's sake don't mention that in front of her.

VOLPES: I don't even know if it's true or not. Somebody told me about it.

ELISA: It's quite true. Absolutely true. And you can't imagine how much she suffered over it all.

COUNT MOLA: Why… What about her brother?

VOLPES: Well, it seems that he was the first to imply…

MARCHESA (*continuing the sentence*): …That when someone chooses the career of an actress… yes, of course, we quite understand.

ELISA (*angrily, then modifying her tone through politeness*): We quite understand what? On the contrary, we don't understand anything, believe me, Marchesa; anything at all.

COUNT MOLA: I told you so, didn't I?

ELISA (*to* VOLPES, *continuing*): Since you mentioned her brother, you had better go on and tell the rest of the story, Volpes.

VOLPES: But I really don't know all the details.

ELISA: Well, I do! And I can't really blame her brother, after all, the silly man, he should have known how easy it would be to gossip when talking about an actress… well, to defend his own stupid male pride, he implied that… yes, that all actresses… "and my sister too, why ever not?" – all so casually just like that, with a group of his cronies, laughing and shrugging his shoulders! When Donata found out about it, she was… Oh! Wounded to the very depths of her being. She couldn't even bear to look at him. And she has never seen her mother again either since then.

MARCHESA: I do admire her, but… you have to agree, it is such an anomaly, isn't it?

COUNT MOLA: Quite… and then… her own mother… I must say…

ELISA: When her mother was faced with making a choice, she preferred to go on living with her son.

SALÒ: So there's your "normal", Marchesa. In a "normal" household a mother might say "You'd be an embarrassment, dear"… or "You certainly do need your own independence". Which would be perfectly in order, of course. Nothing wrong in that. But one has to realize that what constitutes "normal behaviour" for chickens is irrelevant when talking about the headlong flight of cranes.

MARCHESA: We appreciate those chickens, Salò.

SALÒ: No, Marchesa, as God is my witness, I wasn't trying to get at you. The chicken represents ordinary bourgeois morality with all its preconceptions and prejudices. You have to judge people by what they do – and she's an actress!

MARCHESA: No, my dear man, she has to be judged in all conscience by what can be seen and by what everybody knows.

SALÒ: Exactly! Well done! And when nobody knows anything, what then? You go on believing it all the same because an actress usually… There! The preconceived idea and the prejudice for you.

MARCHESA: There may well be the rare exception…

SALÒ: But believe me, Marchesa, a true actress is always a rare exception. When she becomes a woman like any other and creates a life for herself and tries to enjoy it in the way she chooses, then she stops being an actress.

MARCHESA: As if the two were incompatible!

SALÒ: But they are! And we call it "denial" in the truest sense of the word: "to deny oneself, one's own life, one's own being, to give all of oneself and put that self into the characters one plays". Yet people generally tend to believe that being an actress is just an excuse for loose living.

VOLPES: May I butt in here? I'd like to ask you how an actress can give life to her characters if she retains nothing for herself and doesn't even know what real life is. Like loving, for example. What if she has never been in love? What then?

SALÒ: Oh yes, you're the man who believes in experience, I was forgetting that. The man who has to feel everything before he can really understand it. Now I, on the other hand, know that I've only ever had true feelings for things that I had previously imagined.

MARCHESA: Oh that's ridiculous. So you've never felt disappointment then, I suppose?

VOLPES: Now there's an experience for you.

SALÒ: Disappointment? Oh, thank you. That would constitute experience for you, would it?

VOLPES: Facts would, yes... not imagination.

SALÒ: But my dear fellow, when something unexpected has happened concerning a person or a feeling... it didn't constitute an experience... Quite the reverse!

MARCHESA: So what did it constitute?

SALÒ: I found myself unable to understand anything at all.

Everyone bursts out laughing, as though he had made a joke. But SALÒ *has answered in all seriousness and goes on to sustain his argument.*

SALÒ: Yes, Marchesa. Precisely because the facts did not correspond to the idea I had formed for myself. I was unable to understand anything at all. (*To* VOLPES) At best, you can formulate another idea which will inevitably be different, until you come to that special moment when you can exclaim "So there it is, that's love", because you will have to recognize love as the confirmation of your previous image! And that's a real experience for you, while anything else must be the opposite, the failed test, disenchantment. But I ask you, do you really believe that in order to love you have to understand love?

MARCHESA: Good Heavens, understanding it must be different from not understanding.

VOLPES: And women all want to understand, by God they do.

SALÒ: I agree. Who wouldn't? But when does an actress learn that? We're still there: either it's disappointment or precisely what you had imagined it would be like. There's no need for her to "know" love herself. She just has to be able to perceive intuitively how the character she is playing would feel. As for her, if she does feel it then she will never see it. Feeling is blind. People who love close their eyes.

157

NINA: Oh look, here she comes.

Silence falls. DONATA GENZI *appears on the staircase, in evening dress and begins to descend. She is pale, anxious-looking, and her strange, tragic mouth is drawn in a pained line. Her large eyes with their very long lashes have a dark, lost look. Everyone turns to look at her, standing as they do so.* ELISA *goes to meet her and to make the introductions.*

ELISA: Darling, let me introduce you to Marchesa Boveno – Count Mola – (you know Salò and Volpes already, don't you.)

SALÒ: Dear Donata...

VOLPES: A pleasure to have you with us...

ELISA: Carlo Giviero, your "learned" admirer...

MARCHESA: Yes, quite. Very "learned", as you put it. Apparently he has filled his rooms with portraits of you, did you know that?

DONATA: Really? There isn't a single one I actually like...

NINA: He has them all!

GIVIERO: Not quite all. Nearly all. The most expressive ones.

There is a sudden embarrassed pause.

ELISA (*concluding the introductions in this moment of embarrassment*): ...And Nina, the Marchesa's granddaughter.

SALÒ (*to break the silence*): ...The dreadful Nina!

NINA (*angrily, red-faced*): Listen, Salò, don't start or I'll go home.

MARCHESA (*sharply restraining her*): Nina!

NINA: No, I'm sorry, Granny. I don't want to be the scapegoat just because you can't talk in front of her like you have been doing.

ELISA (*in slightly reproachful tone*): What on earth is the matter?

SALÒ: Can't we go on talking now? Who told you that? On the contrary, we can continue...

ELISA (*to* DONATA): Naturally we were talking about you... Donata.

VOLPES: Or rather, about actresses in general.

COUNT MOLA: And we were saying good things, of course.

NINA: About you, yes. Not about actresses in general.

SALÒ: That's not true. Perhaps, shall we say, we were talking about the ones that, in my opinion, cannot be considered true actresses. But on the other hand, since you have the effrontery to wave the truth in our faces, why don't you admit that you were passing moral judgements and saying that Donata couldn't possibly be sincere?

MARCHESA: Well said, Salò.

DONATA (*to* NINA, *amused*): Now don't be shy. This is marvellous! Do answer, please.

NINA: I'm not shy! I'm not shy at all. It's just that Granny... (*Looks at her, bewildered*) Don't you mind? You were saying...

MARCHESA: What was I saying? I'm quite ready to repeat anything I may have said... (*To* DONATA) I only know you as an actress, Signorina Genzi, not as a person, and I wanted to know...

DONATA (*simply, smiling*): ...Whether I'm sincere?

NINA (*immediately*): No. I was the one who said you couldn't be. And do you know why? Because I've seen you play all sorts of contra-dictory parts and every one with the utmost sincerity. So I thought that you...

DONATA: Couldn't be equally honest with all those contradictory parts? Why ever not? I don't come into it. Every time I am what the part demands of me, and I am as honest as possible.

GIVIERO: Salò was saying something very interesting: that an actress doesn't need to have experienced life directly; it's enough for her to be able to understand the experiences of the character intuitively.

DONATA: That seems right.

NINA: Actually, Salò said "love" not "life".

GIVIERO: It's the same thing.

DONATA: "People who love close their eyes" is what I heard. Very serious for me if that's the case, because I don't close...

SALÒ: You don't ever close your eyes? Perfectly natural! That's why you're an actress.

DONATA: No, I mean in life...

SALÒ: Yes, darling. Because you have something more than the rest of us: you can live in front of a mirror.

DONATA: What do you mean, in front of a mirror?

SALÒ: Look here. If one of us happens to surprise himself fleetingly in a mirror whilst crying over some excruciating pain or laughing at some joyful experience, those tears and that laughter will be cut off short by the image reflected back from that mirror.

GIVIERO: That's quite true. We can all testify to that. You just have to catch sight of yourself and you can no longer laugh or cry at all. The image stops you.

SALÒ (*to* DONATA): Well then, you have this great gift: you can live on stage, knowing that everybody is looking at you, with all those eyes in the audience reflecting back like mirrors.

DONATA: But I never even see the audience, when I'm acting I don't even realize they are there.

SALÒ: Precisely! You can live in front of them as though they weren't there. And you don't really believe that you close your eyes too, instinctively in love scenes when you let yourself go.

DONATA: Really? I don't know... Without realizing or without intending to, you close your eyes.

GIVIERO: I have a picture of you like that...

DONATA: With my eyes closed?

GIVIERO: Yes. A group photo taken at the end of an act.

SALÒ: So then if one day in your real life, and I sincerely hope for your sake this happens, you really do close your eyes yourself, my dear friend, you'll actually be copying yourself. That's all. (*To* VOLPES) So you see, experience doesn't come into it.

MARCHESA: Pardon me, but doesn't it seem dreadful, to make love in public in front of everybody without knowing anything about it oneself.

DONATA (*smiling, while the others laugh*): But it's still the only way to live so many lives...

MARCHESA: Well on stage, quite! Pretending!

DONATA: Why see it as pretending! No, it's actually life for us. Life that we discover for ourselves, life that finds its own means of expression. We aren't pretending when we take over the means of expression and make it throb in our veins... so that it brings tears to our eyes or a smile to our lips... Just compare the many lives that an actress can live with the actual life that you each live out every day and that is so often either tedious or oppressive... We may not notice, but we all lose part of ourselves every day... or else we cut off the vital energy of goodness knows how many seeds of life... how many possibilities that we have within us... because we are forced to give things up, or to lie or be hypocritical... Let's avoid that! Let's transform ourselves! Let's become someone else!

MARCHESA: But, good Lord, then we wouldn't ever be anything for ourselves in our own "secret" life, would we?

GIVIERO: Well, naturally an actress can't keep secrets from anyone.

DONATA (*becoming more depressed*): Why not?

GIVIERO: But, look here, you said that on stage you reveal all sorts of inner possibilities, so what secrets are you left with? We know you, not just you as you are, but also you as you might be.

DONATA: No! Only as I might be, if at all. Because on stage I am never myself. I mean, how on earth can you know how I really am if I don't know myself?

GIVIERO: Oh but I can.

NINA: He has your photographs.

GIVIERO: No, I have your eyes. (*To* DONATA) You can't see yourself, whereas we spectators have all seen you.

DONATA: Not me! Please take on trust the way in which I might love. You see the way in which a given character played by me makes love.

GIVIERO: But you let that character use your body, use your own lips to kiss with, your own arms to embrace with, your own voice to speak loving words... we know how you reject someone or how you give in... all the different nuances you use... the expressions of your mouth and eyes... your smile... the way... this is something I've noticed, for example – the way you stroke or ruffle the hair of the man you're in love with.

DONATA: I tell you, in those moments I'm living the life of my character. It is not me.

GIVIERO: But you can't be any different. Forgive me for insisting, because you yourself are in the character. An actress belongs to everyone. So much so... and you must be aware of this... the audience falls in love with you, not with the character.

SALÒ: The most serious thing, my dear, is this: that when the time comes for you to live out your own drama, you won't be able to see yourself any longer.

DONATA: I shall always see. And perhaps that's my problem.

GIVIERO: Not being able to close your eyes?

DONATA: In the face of danger, perhaps... who knows?

VOLPES: Yes, go ahead and commit yourself, and you've had it!

DONATA: Commit myself... but that's just it; the ghastliness of... So long as you stay like this, outside it, allowing your mind freedom of movement, to respond to every feeling and impression that's conjured up – all the images that a moment of desire can arouse or a memory evoke, allowing these vague impressions, not of deeds, maybe, not even real issues to flow through us – but precisely those desires that have almost vanished before they come to light... things you think about without wanting to, things that are hidden from yourself... dreams... the fear of not being... like flowers that have never been able to open, so long as you'd stay like that, it's true that you'd have nothing... but you have at least complete liberty to let your mind wander, to imagine yourself constantly in a different light... But when you finally fulfil an action it isn't your entire being – all the life within you – which performs it; merely what you are at that precise moment, and yet that momentary action (in the very moment of performing it) imprisons us, binds us there fast... with obligations and responsibilities which spring from that specific moment and no other... Think of the many seeds that have created a forest. Only one seed falls in a particular spot, a tree grows there and it's fixed in that place, it will remain there for ever. This monstrous situation, you see, is what I live through with my eyes wide open every night in front of a mirror, as soon as the show is over and I go backstage and shut myself in my dressing room and take off my make-up.

SALÒ: That must be the saddest moment of all for you: going back to being yourself.

DONATA: And not finding myself.

MARCHESA: But what do you mean not finding yourself? Why ever not? In front of that mirror, good Heavens, you're bound to find yourself, still young, so attractive... Friends must go round to see you.

DONATA: Yes, some do... They take me back to my hotel... we have a coffee or a chat... But I never really feel like it. I'm often so very tired... Fortunately there's so much to do and so little time to think about myself... But that moment (*turns to* ELISA) ...you know, darling... is so very squalid... The theatre is empty... you can't imagine the awfulness of the place... everyone has gone home with something of me alive in their minds... yes... and I go into my dressing room, still excited by the warmth of the crowd that has been standing there giving me a final round of applause. And then I am alone, empty-handed in that terrible silence in front of the huge mirror on the dressing table that reflects my image back at me, surrounded by all the useless costumes hanging there motionless with me sitting in the midst of them shoulders hunched, hands in my lap, and my eyes wide open staring into the void... I'll never close my eyes... never!

Everyone is silent for a moment, disturbed. DONATA, *who is more upset than anyone, sees this: she can no longer restrain herself; she stands up, trying to smile and says to* ELISA:

DONATA: Listen, darling Elisa, if you don't mind... it's because I'm so tired – do please... forgive me. I simply don't feel in the right frame of mind to stay with you all tonight. Please forgive me, all of you, I'll go to my room.

They have all gradually stood up. DONATA *crosses to the staircase and starts to go up.*

ELISA: Would you like me to have something sent up to you?

DONATA: No, thank you. I couldn't. Goodnight everyone.

She goes up the stairs, opens her bedroom door and goes in. Everyone stands for a moment in profound embarrassment.

ELISA: I did warn you all not to talk that way in front of her...

SALÒ (*joking*): It's all Nina's fault.

NINA: Mine? Why me?

MARCHESA: Yes, your fault. Because you let her know we'd all been talking....

GIVIERO: ...About things she finds very painful right now, seeing herself perceived as...

MARCHESA: ...A woman. Of course. (*To* SALÒ) My dear Salò, you talk about "the actress", "many lives" and all that so nicely. When she doesn't have any sort of life for herself.

VOLPES: But it's she who doesn't want one...

COUNT MOLA: It hurts her though. It's so obvious that it hurts her.

VOLPES (*shrugging his shoulders*): It hurts her... all that suffering... all she has to do is make her mind up to behave like everyone else.

ELISA: Can't you see that is precisely what holds her back? Knowing what opinions everyone has formed of her... her own brother to begin with?

VOLPES: But good Lord, we're not talking about "being like everybody else", we're talking about natural behaviour. Does she act like this out of pure whim?

SALÒ: Yes, if you want to reduce it to that level. It could be a different way of responding to oneself, compared with other people.

ELISA: That's exactly what it is!

SALÒ: So that it wouldn't be possible for her to "be like other people". She might even despise a basic need just because it is considered to be ordinary and natural.

COUNT MOLA: Ah, so we've stopped talking about love, have we?

SALÒ: I'm sorry, I was under the impression that up to now that was all we had been talking about – "trial", "experience", "lips for kissing"…

GIVIERO: That's exactly why I'm convinced that is the point at issue. Dignity and intelligence don't cancel out fever in the blood. Even her flesh is flesh, for God's sake. She's beautiful, she's young…

NINA (*in a strange new voice*): Why doesn't she get married?

SALÒ: There you are, Nina has solved her problem.

ELISA: That's the same question I asked her in a letter a few months ago.

VOLPES: But there's no need for her to get married. Besides, it wouldn't be so easy if she wanted to go on being an actress. As a husband, I certainly wouldn't agree to that. And I don't suppose she would be willing to give up and just become somebody's wife.

SALÒ: She couldn't.

VOLPES: Agreed!

COUNT MOLA: What if she married a fellow actor, for instance?

VOLPES: With her experience in the theatre of what actors' marriages are like? We all know how they turn out. Someone like Donata Genzi would never do that. In my view, we should bide our time; all right, she isn't like "ordinary people", but she is a woman after all…

GIVIERO: That business about her eyes, did you observe that? She either can't or won't close her eyes.

NINA: Oh here's Elj at last. Thank goodness.

ELJ *comes in, followed by* ENRICO, *who crosses the stage and goes out through the rear exit.* ELJ *is twenty-six, very blond, suntanned, light eyes, exotic-looking, wearing casual beach clothes. He does not stand on ceremony. Direct, though something of a romantic.*

COUNT MOLA (*immediately*): Aha. So we really did have to send someone out to look for you.

ELJ (*to* ELISA): Good evening, Elisa. Good evening everyone. (*To* GIAN-FRANCO) I told you, I think, that I was going over to see the man who was repairing my sail.

MARCHESA: Well, I really hope he didn't manage to repair it.

ELJ: Sorry to disappoint you, Marchesa, it's perfectly in order and already rigged.

COUNT MOLA: Yes, but you will leave it here tonight, won't you? At least do me that favour.

ELJ: Of course. Why else do you think I'm here? I've come and I'm staying. What more do you want?

ELISA: It's not very nice of you to put it like that, Elj... nor very polite to all my friends here...

ELJ: I'm sorry. It's not your fault nor your friends'. I said I would come later and spend some time with you all, so there was no need to send anyone out to look for me. That's all. As for dinner, I've had mine already.

ENRICO *comes in to announce:*

ENRICO: Dinner is served.

ELISA: Splendid, let's all go in. (*To* ELJ) Do you want to stay in here? Or are you going to come and sit with us?

ELJ: If you don't mind, I'll stay and browse through a few books.

COUNT MOLA: No, don't do that. Come in to dinner with us.

ELJ: Are you afraid I'll run off?

ELISA: That would be priceless. But do as you like... we shall be through there, when you feel like joining us... After you, Marchesa...

They all go out through the rear door. ENRICO *turns off the lights in the hall, which is in shadow. Only the book corner where* ELJ *is standing is lit. He shrugs, shaking his head as if to say "Damn it all, I'm not even able to do what I feel like doing". Turns to cast his eyes over the books on the shelves, finally takes one down, an illustrated art book, and throws himself down on the bench to look at it. Shortly afterwards,* NINA *comes in cautiously, to peep at him.*

NINA (*softly*): Elj...

ELJ: Is that you? What do you want? Have you come to check that I'm still here? I'm here all right! Tell him he can eat his meal in...

NINA: No, I was just going to ask if you wanted the butler to bring you a drink.

ELJ: Oh... a drink... (*Thinks for a minute*) Yes.

NINA: If you really have had dinner...

ELJ: Of course I have! I'd like a brandy. Tell Enrico to bring me the bottle. At least then I can get my own back by getting drunk.

NINA: Good. Do it right away. Do get drunk, but just make sure you do it thoroughly. If you get yourself drunk it will solve everything.

She runs out silently.

ELJ: Solve what? (*Turns, can't see her*) Oh, she's gone. (*Goes back to leafing through his book*) She's mad... (*Still leafing through the book*) Sooner or later I'll end up grabbing her by the scruff of the neck and shoving her against the wall like a she-cat... (*Still turning pages*) Well, look at that... it looks like her... that little dancer...

Puts the open book down on the table; sees a portable gramophone on the bench with the record already in place. Turns it on. Sits down again and leafs through the book while a jazz record plays. At a certain point ELJ *gets up, irritated, and switches it off.* ENRICO *comes in with a bottle of brandy and a glass on a tray.*

ELJ (*pointing to the table*): Splendid! Put it down there.

ENRICO: I apologize for the delay. I was serving at table.

ELJ: I trust you aren't going to tell them that you helped me rig the sail and take the boat down to the jetty?

ENRICO: Certainly not! Rest assured! But do remember, Master Elj, that I don't want to be held responsible for you. As you might have noticed, the sea is getting even rougher now.

ELJ: Don't keep going on about the sea. What possible responsibility could you have if nobody knows you helped me?

ENRICO: I was thinking about my conscience.

ELJ: Go away, don't make me laugh!

ENRICO: I don't want to feel guilty. I followed your orders. But I ask you not to risk you own neck as soon as your uncle has gone to bed. (*With a snigger*) I know that's what you're going to do... And just keeping the secret is a huge responsibility for me.

ELJ: You don't know anything. The rest is my business. That's all.

ENRICO: Well, Master Elj, at least don't have much to drink.

ELJ: You can take the bottle away.

ENRICO: Really? Then I certainly will.

Goes out with the tray and the bottle.

ELJ: Well, the cunning old devil.

DONATA *comes back downstairs. She looks like a different person, such is her ability to transform herself. She wears a pretty, green mackintosh and waterproof hat in the same colour, a blue silk scarf round her neck and little boots. The hall is still in shadow. The book corner stands out, she goes towards it.* ELJ *does not move; he does not even raise his head to look at her.* DONATA *stands for a minute staring in surprise, then irritated by his indifference. Finally she asks:*

DONATA: Are they still in there?

ELJ: Yes, having dinner.

Pause.

DONATA: And... are you waiting for them?

ELJ: For them to finish... I hope they won't stay long talking after dinner, seeing that the person they expected didn't turn up.

DONATA: Oh, how do you know she didn't turn up?

ELJ: I assumed it, I saw them all creeping off in there... I don't know anything. I'm not interested.

DONATA: Don't you even know what her name is?

ELJ: Oh, I don't know... some actress I think... I've never been able to stand the theatre... They're keeping me prisoner here, did you know that? Because my uncle, yes sir, has taken his role as guardian rather too seriously. The sea is pretty rough tonight... Yes, laugh, go on, do... it's funny... He's afraid I'll go out in my boat.

DONATA: And he doesn't want you to? Sorry, I'm laughing because the idea of a man your age having a guardian is...

ELJ: Well, not really a guardian. I'm overage of course. It's just that I'm fond of him. He sent someone out to look for me and he wants me to stay here. Every so often he sends a girl with snake eyes to check up on me... Oh, maybe he's sent *you* this time?

DONATA: No, don't worry, I haven't come in from there.

ELJ: I'm sorry, it's just that this is so ridiculous and so infuriating...

DONATA: Perhaps it really is dangerous.

ELJ: Well of course it is. But that's what is so wonderful. What's the alternative? Regattas on a lake with a gentle breeze blowing across the prow? Thanks a lot! That's not why I bought a boat! I have my father's blood in my veins. He was a Swedish sailor who died at sea when he was twenty-six.

DONATA: You can hardly have known him.

ELJ: I never knew him at all. I was born two months after the wreck. And my mother waited just long enough to bring me into the world and not a moment longer before she went to join him. I think that is everything. If only my uncle could understand.

DONATA: Your mother's brother?

ELJ: He brought me up, here in Italy. He's all I have. But I'm Swedish: Elj Nielsen. Now that's enough. I'm angry with myself, believe me, not him. And with my own stupidity that makes me put up with this nonsense out of respect for him.

DONATA: Doesn't your uncle like sport?

ELJ: I don't like sport myself. I detest it, the way it is – all the trickery, the gambling, the way people become obsessed with it. I like to keep seeing things in a new perspective. Do you understand that? And I love nature. I keep away from close relationships like the plague. I don't like disappointments. I want other people to stay fresh and new for me too. Always fresh and new. The great thing to me is the unexpected… anything hard to believe, whatever takes me by surprise… If I think about something too long, in too much detail, that's the end of it. Live in society? Go round asking why somebody did this or said that? It would kill me off. I want to be an outsider, be a stranger. And no, thank you, I don't want to stay around here half-baked and choking in the steam, stewing away…

DONATA: …When it could be so wonderful to face the dangers of a storm at sea… Let's go! Take me out in your boat!

ELJ (*taken aback*): What?

DONATA: Don't you want to now?

ELJ: I'm sorry, but who are you?

DONATA: Do you really have to know who I am? Do you have to ask questions like everybody else? And you want to be an outsider? I'm an outsider too… Now let's go.

ELJ: I'll bet you're this actress they were expecting?

DONATA: He doesn't even know my name! So much the better. I dare you to take me out with you in your boat.

ELJ: No, steady on, signora.

DONATA: Not signora. I'm not married.

ELJ: Signorina…

DONATA: Don't imagine that word can upset me... You can say it louder if you like... Signorina!

ELJ: Signorina...

DONATA: That's it.

ELJ: But you're a guest here.

DONATA: Yes, I'm staying with my friend.

ELJ: It wouldn't be right...

DONATA: I am my own mistress.

ELJ: But at least let them know...

DONATA: Are you frightened?

ELJ: I can be brave enough for myself. But concerned for you...

DONATA: I will absolve you from any concern about me. I'm the one who wants to do this. I'm just testing what you said. If you really do love the unexpected, something hard to believe: then here I am, let's go!

Door: at this point NINA *comes in and overhears* DONATA's *last words.*

NINA: Elj! You're not going, are you?

ELJ: Don't get on my nerves!

NINA (*to* DONATA): With you? You came down again?

DONATA: Yes, I had gone upstairs to rest. But I couldn't. I need to go out. I'm going down to the sea...

NINA: No... Elj. She's looking for danger... she said so.

DONATA: Danger! Exactly!

NINA: So you can close your eyes?

DONATA (*to* ELJ): Make her shut up!

ELJ: Right! You go ahead. I'll shut her up. Wait for me outside. I'll be there right away.

DONATA *goes out.* ELJ *grabs* NINA *by the hair, pulls her back, kisses her violently, runs out.* NINA *stands quite still, as though stunned by the kiss. Her legs give way, she falls onto the bench, overwhelmed, excited, happy, unable to utter a word; then she groans, like someone coming back up to the surface.*

NINA: Oh God... Oh God...

And she struggles to regain her composure, breathing heavily; she tries to stand up but cannot; finally she lets out a great cry; she stands up and runs to the rear exit:

NINA: Help! Help! Come quickly! Run! They've got away! Both of them!

And she falls into the arms of the first to arrive, as they come in stunned, shocked, asking her all kinds of questions in total confusion.

Piano music.

CURTAIN

ACT TWO

Three weeks later. A room in one of GIANFRANCO MOLA's *villa on the Riviera that has been converted into a studio for* ELJ NIELSEN. *The room is on the ground floor and at the rear is a large window that opens onto the beach. An exit to the right; another, to the left, leads into a changing room. Decorated in a bizarre manner and very untidy. Canvases, drawings, an easel, a dummy that can be moved into all kinds of positions with a moth-eaten cardboard head that cannot say a word. A bed-settee with a velvet cover and a lot of cushions. Models of sailing boats. A small bar, a writing table, armchairs, ordinary chairs. A large mirror on the left-hand wall that* DONATA *has hidden from view with a Venetian shawl. Three weeks have gone by since Act One.* DONATA *has been brought here half-dead by* ELJ *on the night of the shipwreck and has stayed here ever since.*

When the curtain rises DONATA *is in a nightgown with a towelling bath-robe over it on doctor's orders and is sitting in the middle of the room, head down, back to the window. The* DOCTOR *has just finished changing the dressing on the wound at the back of her neck.* ELJ *is holding a small basin into which the* DOCTOR *has tossed the last pieces of lint dressing.*

DOCTOR: There we are. Just ease your neck back slowly. That's right. Do you want to have a look before I put back the bandage?

DONATA (*immediately horrified*): Certainly not.

ELJ: Besides, where could she look? Donata has done away with all the mirrors here. See, she's even covered that one with a shawl.

DOCTOR: Goodness, for a woman, that's...

DONATA (*immediately, to change the subject*): Do you think the scar will be very visible?

DOCTOR: I'm afraid we still haven't come to the scarring stage.

ELJ: After three weeks!

DONATA: Darling, it's a miracle to me that you didn't bite right through my neck.

DOCTOR: Of course… with a low neckline, it's bound to be seen.

DONATA: And… will they see it was a bite?

ELJ (*finishing the sentence*): …By a mad dog?

DOCTOR (*to* ELJ, *showing him*): Well, look… there's the sign of teeth marks…

DONATA: Sunk right in!

ELJ: I was on the point of sparing you two of them and then the rudder hit me across the face. You would have at least missed those two marks – that would have been two cuts less.

DONATA: I'm glad I didn't.

DOCTOR: Now, shall we put the bandages on again?

Begins to do so.

DONATA: I seem to recall that in order not to lose cattle they used to brand them on their haunches.

ELJ: What a comparison!

DONATA: Luckily you branded me on my neck.

DOCTOR: Just as well that instinct led him to do that! Otherwise you'd both have drowned. Only I don't understand why you bit her there…

ELJ: Where else?

DONATA: Well, it would have been worse in the throat.

DOCTOR: It certainly would! And much more dangerous.

ELJ: Sorry, I could only manage it there. She was hanging so tightly round my neck that…

DOCTOR: Was this before or after the boat capsized?

DONATA: I wanted to die.

ELJ: Well, thanks, I certainly didn't. Die when? You see? I couldn't get a grip anywhere except the back of her neck… and life bit through death until it made her let go and she fainted. I had her there in my power.

DONATA: Your life…

ELJ: No, ours! Yours and mine. We would both have died. This way we've both been saved.

DONATA: But just in that instant when you bit me, weren't you perhaps… go on, you can be honest with me…trying to get rid of me? Like an animal…

ELJ: No! How could you say such a thing!

172

DONATA: Instinct…

ELJ: Instinct be damned! It wasn't instinct at all. I did it on purpose. I suppose I could have let you go down to the bottom and saved myself. But I risked drowning a second time to hold you up. I swam with just one arm, even I don't know how I did it. Thank God the other boats came by… I couldn't have kept going much longer.

DOCTOR (*to* DONATA): But I tell you everybody gets their strength back once they're on dry land. He picked you up in his arms like a little girl and fended off the rest of the world.

ELJ: Who all wanted to take you back to your friend's house, I ask you!

DOCTOR: He threw everyone else out – like a lunatic he was, I tell you – and only let me in to offer first aid.

DONATA: But it was entirely justified…

ELJ: …To take you back there?

DONATA: They should have…

ELJ: But you were in my arms!

DONATA: Then you should have…

ELJ: Nothing of the sort! First of all, it was a long way off. The jetty is right here.

DONATA: Only a few yards further down…

ELJ: Besides, to hell with what I should have done! Hadn't you risked your life along with me? I was the one who saved you. And as for dying together, thanks a lot! We didn't die. So you had to stay with me. That seems fair, doesn't it, doctor?

DOCTOR: By the rules of life.

DONATA: Sealed with a bite, and I'll carry the mark until the day I drop.

DOCTOR (*finishing off the bandage*): Let's hope for the best.

ELJ: Oh no, doctor.

DOCTOR: I mean the scar. The scar.

ELJ: I don't intend to let go.

DOCTOR: But at least right now you aren't holding on with your teeth, thank Heaven. Now that's enough. I must be going, I'll see you both tomorrow. Goodbye.

DONATA: Goodbye, doctor.

ELJ: I'll see you out.

Goes out with the DOCTOR. DONATA, *left alone, tries to bend her head backwards with her eyes closed, and lets out a moan that is possibly due to some other pain than just the wound.* ELJ *comes back and surprises her like this.*

ELJ (*solicitous*): Does it hurt?

DONATA: No, it's the bandage.

ELJ: Too tight.

DONATA: No, it feels like a collar. I've never been able to stand anything round my neck. But didn't you... want to go out?

ELJ: Me? No. Where to?

DONATA: I had the impression you wanted to go with the doctor... yes, why don't you go out for a while?

ELJ: No, you can't mean that. Do you really want to be left alone?

DONATA: You see? You're staying for my sake so I won't be on my own.

ELJ: No, I'm staying here because I want to. I can't bear to be away from you.

DONATA: Shut up in here for three weeks, you who...

ELJ: I hadn't even realized...

DONATA: – you said you avoided close contacts like the plague...

ELJ: Because I still hadn't made contact with you. Contact with other people, yes, I avoided that all right, for the reason I told you: because I don't like being disappointed. But there's no danger of that with you.

DONATA: It's early days yet... and we're still in the situation that according to another of your principles you'd like to remain in...

ELJ: Would I? What's that?

DONATA: Well, we're still strangers—

ELJ: Still strangers? Us? Nothing of the sort. We already know everything we need to. It's all straightforward.

DONATA: Oh, no, darling, it's not straightforward. Quite the reverse. It's far more complicated.

ELJ: Yes we do, believe me. I meant strangers in the sense of experiencing a new situation, you see, and of continually discovering one another.

DONATA: And do you think that's possible?

ELJ: Yes I do. Listen, loving each other so much that we never imagine we could hurt one another, not you me, nor I you. And then constantly experiencing each other, so that you'd never know what to expect from me, things I do or think, ways I surprise you, I don't know. Things that wouldn't seem quite real coming from someone like me.

And if at first they seemed unwelcome or strange, then you'd only need to exclude all possibility that I'd tried to hurt you and you'd be able to enjoy it all. And that would always be better than never having any doubts at all – which would be the case if you knew me completely or I knew you completely. I tell you frankly, I hardly know what I'm like myself… (*With sudden doubt that throws him off balance*) If I have any sense… which maybe I haven't and it takes a lot to deal with you…

DONATA (*laughing*): Good Heavens… what has sense to do with it?

ELJ: I've never tried to find out what I'm like… never had a clear idea of myself…

DONATA: Oh Heavens, but at least you know what you like and what you don't like…

ELJ: I like you! And I like living!

DONATA: Living… but there's more than one way…

ELJ: Yes. Without really knowing how: living not with other people, that's for sure. You see, what is certain is that when I'm alone at sea or out in the country with my paints, out in the open, to put it simply – even if I'm struggling with something or facing up to some risk – I don't lose myself, I face up to the challenge and I'm happy. But when I'm with other people, it's not like that. I'm always bad tempered, I don't appreciate anything. I can't stand normal, commonplace things.

Takes a picture he has painted down from the easel.

I paint badly – OK, I know that – but that's because it's not easy to paint the way I'd like to – to paint things as they appear at certain crucial moments… the destruction, the blurring of all those everyday features that tend to reduce life or nature – my God, they do – to something like an old penny that no longer has any value. I don't understand, it's a feeling of humiliation… of having to endure something. The same sky, with the same stars squinting at you, the same houses with the same windows yawning at you, you walking down the same pavement in the same streets… it's suffocating.

Then just sometimes it happens… and you don't know how or why… that you see life and everything with fresh eyes… everything quivers and seems to breathe light… and you feel uplifted at moments like that, your soul bursts right open with an extraordinary power… I live like that! In that special state! And I don't ever want to know anything else. You gave me that kind of feeling too, when you first appeared to me, when I saved you, now when you're mine right here... all this is that special feeling... your beauty... your eyes... the way they look at me...

Takes her head in his hands.

DONATA: I'll close my eyes... yes, I'll really close my eyes... if you hold me... I can't see anything else... I'll die for an instant in this joy that you can take from me and give back to me... we have to lose ourselves.

ELJ: Yes, in love. Heaven help either of us if we try to hold on to something. That's why instinctively at a certain point we close our eyes. We can't look at each other, at ourselves... You're not crying, are you?

DONATA: No... take no notice. It's nothing.

ELJ: What do you mean nothing? If I'm causing you pain without wanting to, then I must know... what is it?

DONATA: Nothing... I've discovered... in myself... I don't know.

ELJ: Something that's causing you pain? Was it because of me?

DONATA: No. Perhaps you've been... (*she does not know how to go on*)

ELJ: How have I been?

DONATA *hesitates.*

Tell me, go on... it's not a bad thing, you know, at the beginning to feel some kind of hurt...

DONATA: Really? Why?

ELJ: Because, my darling, in love we have to guard against ideal relationships. A little pain at the beginning is... well... helpful. But tell me... what did I do?

DONATA (*softly*): Do you really want to know? (*She still hesitates slightly. Then without altering the softness but lowering her eyes:*) You thought about yourself... too much...

ELJ: Myself? You think so?

DONATA (*smiling again*): Perhaps that's the way men are.

ELJ: Won't you say how exactly? Look, I'd like to understand this.

DONATA: Leave it be, please, darling. It doesn't matter... I doubt I know how to explain...

ELJ: You said I'd hurt you...

DONATA: No... not any more.

ELJ: Tell me! It isn't right that you should keep something hidden that... I ought to know about.

DONATA: Maybe it's really my fault...

ELJ: Don't you like the way I love you? You must tell me because I... I don't understand anything now... I'm on fire the instant I touch you.

DONATA: Yes, that's how you are. It's only natural. Don't think about it any more. I mustn't dwell on it either... I should just go on living, have a life of my own, be like you. Yes, because up to now... you perhaps don't realize it... I've never really belonged to myself, in one sense, even though... in another way... I've belonged too much to myself... always on my own – without ever wanting to think about certain things – that is, about some of the things you have suddenly made me aware of... but don't you see? In such a way... I don't know... that now I wish they were still hidden, because you...

ELJ: Because I?...

DONATA: Because you could search them out in me again, though in a different way...

ELJ: How?

DONATA: Oh, it's so difficult to explain. But that's all in the past now, all in the past. And perhaps that's how it should be. Life is like that. And I only want to see and feel my own life in you. To touch it in you, like this... the light in your eyes (*and she passes her hands lovingly over his eyes*) the taste of your lips. (*And she passes her fingers lightly across his mouth, then caresses and ruffles his hair*) Now it's really *me* who's alive... really *me* who's in love...

Suddenly she recognizes the action of ruffling and stroking hair that GIVIERO *had mentioned in the previous act and pulls back in horror.*

No!

ELJ (*dumbfounded by the sudden movement, but not understanding and still wanting to be caressed*): What's the matter? Do that again.

DONATA: No! No!

ELJ: I like it so much when you stroke my hair or ruffle it like that...

DONATA: Your hair? Me? Have I done it before?

ELJ: Yes. What's the matter?

DONATA: Nothing. I just hadn't realized it.

ELJ: You clench your hands... I see you make certain gestures...

DONATA: Gestures? No. What gestures!

ELJ: Oh, I can't copy them for you... the way you stand up... and yes, the way you're looking at me now...

DONATA: Oh, God no! No! For pity's sake, don't say another word!

ELJ (*more dumbfounded than ever, but also a bit entertained by it all*): Why? What is it?

DONATA: Don't make me think what I'm like, how I move, how I look at you. The gestures I make... I don't want to see myself.

ELJ: Is that why you've hidden all the mirrors?

DONATA: Yes. I know my own face too well. I've always made it up, made it up too often. Now I've had enough! Now what I want is "my" face as it is, without having to look at it.

She is still feeling in her fingertips the horror of her realization about the caress.

DONATA: You know, it's... it's perhaps... because I've always been honest, always honest... but not on my own account... I've always lived as though I were somewhere outside myself... and now I want to be really here – me, my real self, have a real life of my own, for myself – I have to "find myself". (*She becomes increasingly depressed, then angry*) See? I said "find myself". It's so horrible. If I say anything... I ought not to speak at all... I can hear myself speaking... I don't want to go on recognizing my own voice. I've used it too much. I'd like to speak with a new voice, but that's impossible because I've never had a real voice of my own. And that never mattered before. I've always spoken with this voice. Now I can't have any other, can I? Well, can I? This is mine.

ELJ: Of course, it's yours. Who else could it belong to? Though many times, you know, not just your voice but all the rest of you is quite unrecognizable... you seem like some other person. Yes, even your voice changes.

DONATA: Even my voice?

ELJ: Yes. Sometimes when you're thinking... maybe about things that are still unformed... and it's as though someone inside you were calling to someone else and then you wander off... Then suddenly – while I'm here looking at your body which is the last thing you're thinking about at that moment – you suddenly turn and stare at me as though you were a stranger.

DONATA: Well, if you're looking at my body...

ELJ: Where else should I be looking?

DONATA: Exactly... don't you see? That really is outside me then. And you really believe that in such moments you can be an outsider. I'm outside my body so much of the time.

ELJ: Where are you then?

DONATA: How do you know where you are when you're thinking? We can't see ourselves when we speak... I'm fully alive... in the things I feel... that are stirring inside me... in everything I can see outside – houses, streets, the sky – the whole world... Until the moment when I suddenly catch sight of myself fixated by the gaze of people looking at my body and I find I'm a woman... Oh God, I don't mean to say I don't enjoy it... but it seems like such a hateful necessity at times like that and I want to rebel against it, I tell you. I don't see the reason why I have to recognize my body as being more mine than anything else, the object by which other people define me. You know, sometimes I actually feel that my body is... unpleasant! I've wanted another, different one so many times!

ELJ: But I don't. I want this one. I love this one. And you're ungrateful if you can't be satisfied with it.

DONATA: Elj, you have to understand that it isn't just my body... if your life and mine are going to be bound together, don't you think we ought to start talking to each other about things?

ELJ: Of course I do. Anything you like.

DONATA: We're just going along with whatever happens day by day...

ELJ: Yes, and we'll find so many things to do, just wait. We'll devise all kinds of things – hundreds every day – leave it to me.

DONATA: I mean now – the desperate need for... things we have to do or say... There comes a point when... like this morning, when I came back from my swim... we need that too... and this... caring for each other... but there comes a time when the kissing has to stop. It was so light, I was blinded by it – I stayed there quite still, thinking... the sea... I didn't just swim. I threw myself into the sea like a blind woman.

ELJ (*opening his arms*): You threw yourself here into my arms and they'll never let go. What else do you want to think about?

DONATA: About you too... lots of things... our life – what it will be like.

ELJ: Plans? Rules? No. None of that. It will just happen. One way or another. In lots of ways.

DONATA: But... in lots of ways... darling, that's how it's been up to now. And you say you can't stand the theatre? That's odd.

ELJ: No, it's the place. That gloom – boxes, rows of seats – shutting yourself up in there – and then the kind of people who go – all those people trying to concentrate – God knows, on things they know aren't even real...

DONATA: But are possible! – created – as you can create in your own way.

ELJ: Why can't we go on living like this?... It's like being on holiday... without having to create anything. Just letting things happen at random... with their own truth and logic, just like yours or mine... So we might suddenly decide to run away and leave everything behind us – and that couldn't ever happen in the theatre.

DONATA: Why ever not?... Of course it could – cut short a scene and run off unexpectedly... I've done it lots of times.

ELJ: Well, it doesn't matter. Let's go out. Let's go out for a while.

DONATA: What? In a dressing gown?

ELJ: Don't worry about that. We're at the seaside. You know, you're thinking too much: you've been shut up in here too long. Let's go out. Come on. Just onto the veranda so we can breathe a little.

DONATA: Oh, Elj, no... we have to think, darling, we have to decide things... Oh, all right, if you insist, I'll come. This is all very well for us now... but what sort of life would it be if we just let things happen like this, at random?

ELJ: What sort of life? Life – as it happens – any way you like – with no excess baggage...

DONATA: Excess baggage? If you only knew how much baggage I carry.

ELJ: From now on I suggest you carry a small shoulder bag and nothing else. People will see us going by arm in arm, and say: "There's a man with intelligence and a woman with a heart!"

DONATA: Oh, I see... like beggars... you mean?

ELJ: Does that worry you?

DONATA: No, why should it? I tell you, that's the way I've lived up to now. But it isn't life. Living like that, do you know what I've had to do to really find life? I've had to look for it and try to feel it in other beings all created – in one way or another – by my imagination, and make them real with my body and my voice. In a hundred different cases – and they've all been given me to live out – I've lived them all.

There on stage. You can't imagine how many situations I've found myself in...

ELJ: None of which were real...

DONATA: Exactly! Now it's my real self who's involved – and I need to see things as they are, dear Lord, and how I feel inside – I, myself in this existence that finally has to be part of me alone... how I really am – I've leapt into this like a blind woman... but otherwise I wouldn't have done it at all... Now, listen. You brought me here yourself, you took me. I don't reproach you with anything, nor am I pretending that I didn't want it as much as you did – I was virtually the one responsible...

ELJ: No. In what way?

DONATA: You didn't want to – I dared you – but afterwards, yes, you did bring me back here. Right then. Now I'm here in your life, as you are in mine. We can't stay together like two passing strangers. You have to pick up your life again.

ELJ: But with you.

DONATA: Yes, with me, of course. Maybe it will be easy for you, if you're like that, wanting everything just to happen with no rules... but it won't be easy for me. It'll be very hard for me.

ELJ: Why?

DONATA: Because I have... I have... my own life... and I want it for myself – and I don't know what it will be like, with you like a child who might get frightened – children do get frightened when they see masks.

ELJ: Do you want to go back to the theatre?

DONATA: Of course...

ELJ: No. Not back to the theatre!

DONATA: Darling, I have to. My month's holiday ends in just ten days' time.

ELJ: No. I won't let you go back. No more theatre. They can go on waiting for you in ten days' time.

DONATA: I have my commitments.

ELJ: Tell them to go to the Devil.

DONATA: Now how do I do that?

ELJ: Any way you can! I don't want to know! You're mine, and you're staying with me. You must be joking if you think I'm going to let you go back to the theatre and let those puppets of yours take over your life. I'm the one giving life to you now, if you've never really been alive before. As you do to me.

DONATA: I'm glad you said that. But surely you can see that there's even more reason why we have to talk and see…

ELJ: Yes, of course… first you have to get out of your commitments…

DONATA: That isn't easy.

ELJ: It isn't impossible.

DONATA: Not impossible, no. But it's a serious matter. There are commitments to other actors – to a whole company – commitments to theatres…

ELJ: Will you have to pay them anything?

DONATA: We'll have to come to some agreement…

ELJ: Right… we can do that straight away…

DONATA: Yes, we should do that straight away. We really can't wait – ten days.

ELJ: Straight away. Fine. You tell me what has to be done because I don't know.

DONATA: First of all, send a cable to my manager and tell him to come here right away.

ELJ: Right, I'll do that… I'll do it now – I'll send it straight off – come on, we mustn't waste any time.

DONATA: No, Elj, wait. You can't rush things like this.

ELJ: Why not? You took the decision to throw yourself into life without reflecting on it, so let's get on with this – now. You've got to swim, you know, and keep on swimming!

DONATA: But don't you realize I didn't know what I was doing? I clung on to you with my eyes closed.

ELJ: And that's where you'll stay, clinging on to me with your eyes closed if you really want to live! You want to find yourself. We're forced to do that again and again without having to search. Because in the end, if you go on searching, you may manage to find yourself, but you know what will happen? You won't find anything left and you won't be able to go on living. You'll be as good as dead, with your eyes wide open.

DONATA: So what then… give up everything?

ELJ: Yes, everything. All those suitcases filled with other people's clothes.

DONATA: But that's where my life was – in all those clothes.

ELJ: Yes, so they could have an existence while you didn't.

DONATA: That's not true. I lived my life too, in those clothes.

ELJ: Yes, outside yourself, you said. Now you're yourself, here...

DONATA: And where am I?

ELJ: With me.

DONATA: And who are you?

ELJ: What do you mean, who am I?

DONATA: Nothing seems real to me yet, can't you see that?

ELJ: That's what's so marvellous.

DONATA: Don't you even want to find out how we can live together?

ELJ: You'll be my wife.

DONATA: Yes, but...

ELJ: Listen. One flick of a tail like a fish, and we can change direction. The sea is boundless...

DONATA: No... what are you saying?

ELJ: I'm saying something that's absolutely true. No one, my darling, ever really pauses to consider the fact that the planet Earth is as small as this pebble... as tiny as that in the spaces of the heavens. And it isn't the grain of sand some people talk about, you know. Nothing of the sort. It's a drop of water.

DONATA: And what about it?

ELJ: Water! Water! What about it, you ask? What this means is that you have to think again about who this planet really belongs to. Its true owners are the fish. Yes, it's fish we should be guided by. I'm serious, you know... I believe that the main reason why human beings and all the other so-called animals of the earth are unhappy is because of this: we are all an accursed, degenerate species which at some point in the distant past was left trapped on dry land.

DONATA *laughs*.

It's true, believe me. It came to me once in a moment of inspiration in an aquarium, when I kept recognizing in different fish the features and expressions of many of the human beings that I know. The Marchesa Boveno belongs to the cod family, my uncle belongs to the shark family...

DONATA (*still laughing*): Oh for goodness' sake... stop it!... What on earth are you saying?

ELJ: See? You're laughing… This is life… See what I mean? One flick of your tail and you can head off somewhere else… Little bubbles… Nothing but a trail of little bubbles… And just think that the fish's main attribute is silence. Silence! But we have lost that great gift and all we can do is go round shouting out in every conceivable manner how wretched we are being out of our true element…

Look at the seal, for example, whose voice has in it everything that is worst in human beings and animals, or look at woman! Women are all water. Their bodies move like waves. They bend and ripple just like the sea. Since woman is more a sea creature than a land creature, she should never find herself out of place in this drop of water we inhabit. (*With sudden decision*) Let's go back in. I'm going round to my uncle's to tell him everything. He's a wild old shark, my uncle is, and when it comes to working things out, he's invaluable. I'll tell him what we've decided.

DONATA: But we still haven't decided anything…

ELJ: What do you mean, we haven't decided anything? We've decided everything. We've decided to throw commitments overboard and get married!

DONATA: Getting married is fine. But first we have to consider all sorts of things, Elj, not go on like this. We can't just brush aside my commitments… goodness knows how much I shall have to pay.

ELJ: Uncle will take care of all that.

DONATA: Yes, I think it's best for you to go and see your uncle now…

ELJ: I threw him out of his own house, poor old soul. Slammed the door in his face. He's been in a hotel for the past three weeks. As soon as he sees me, the old shark'll give one flick of his tail and be off in a different direction.

DONATA: I can't imagine what he must think about me. He must have the most dreadful impression of me.

ELJ: Don't worry about that; he'll soon get over it. I'm all the family he has, he's just like a father to me. I'll go and bring him back here. We'll talk everything through, and it will all be sorted out, you'll see. If you want to talk to your friend too…

DONATA: Yes, I do now…

ELJ: Wonderful! Let's throw open the doors then. She keeps asking about you every day. She's right opposite. I'll call her for you.

DONATA: Yes, thanks.

ELJ: Right, goodbye, darling, I'm off. I shan't be long.

ELJ *goes out. She suddenly tears down the shawl covering a large mirror.*

DONATA: I can't, I can't, I mustn't. Myself... Donata Genzi... I'd almost forgotten what she looked like... my hair... my face... My God, every move I make, every gesture looks contrived... I've brushed my hair back like that a thousand times on stage... Now... closer... those eyes... what do my eyes really say to anyone... to me... I can see...

She breaks off abruptly, as though she were afraid. ELISA *comes in and catches her in this attitude.*

ELISA: Donata.

DONATA: Oh, darling.

She throws herself into ELISA's *arms, trembling, and lets the shawl fall to the ground.*

ELISA (*surprised, with feeling*): Donata darling... what's the matter?... you're trembling...

DONATA (*not letting her go, holding her even closer*): I've been so frightened... so frightened...

ELISA: Of me?

DONATA: No. I saw myself.

ELISA: Saw yourself? Whatever do you mean?

DONATA: Yes, I did, lost in that mirror over there. I hadn't seen myself for three weeks.

ELISA (*astonished*): Really? Why not?

DONATA: See?

She bends down and picks up the shawl, throws it onto the sofa.

I'd hidden the mirror with this... and I hid all the others too.

ELISA: But what a thing to do? Why on earth did you do that?

DONATA: I didn't want to have to see myself again.

ELISA: You poor dear. Well, now you have seen yourself. You're more attractive than ever.

DONATA: I don't understand anything now. I don't recognize myself! I can't find myself at all!

ELISA: You can't find yourself? With him do you mean?

DONATA: No, it's nothing to do with him... He's so easy-going, so casual, so full of curiosity.

ELISA: That's certainly true.

DONATA: But he's such a dear. Such a darling!

ELISA: So?...

DONATA: It's me. I can't recognize myself... in myself. I thought I wouldn't even recognize myself in that – (*points to mirror*) – but I saw myself as I was before, exactly the same... exactly.

ELISA: Of course.

DONATA: Then when I went closer to look myself in the eyes, I was afraid of being... like... I don't know... I don't know what.

ELISA: That's because all this has happened so unexpectedly, my dear. That's why! In a way that nobody could have foreseen. Now you'll see, gradually...

DONATA: Yes, that's why...

ELISA: Of course that's why. You'll see...

DONATA (*changing her tone, slightly ashamed*): Have you forgiven me?

ELISA: Me? Whatever for? You don't and never did have to explain yourself to anyone. Your own life was in danger. In the state you were in...

DONATA: No, it was a kind of madness that just came over me...

ELISA: It had to happen, I could see that so clearly. You couldn't have stayed any longer in that state. Well, you did it. You threw yourself into something new, and you have my full support. But do tell me, aren't you happy?...

He's such a lovely young man... strong... handsome... rather wild... a bit unusual... but everybody envies you, you know. All the ladies down on the beach and all the local girls, they all do... So you won't be surprised to hear what a scandal you've caused.

DONATA: A scandal? Well, yes, of course...

ELISA: Because nobody could ever prove anything about you before, so now they are all making up for it with a vengeance. It's as though you had done something absolutely outrageous, utterly beyond the pale compared with what other women do, and they are all terribly indignant about it. It's quite ridiculous! I've stood up for you against everybody. But, you see, it's as though you don't have the right to behave like this now because you've always refused to do it before. But you shouldn't worry about such silly things.

DONATA: I can't think why it's such a scandal if we're going to get married...

ELISA: Really? You're going to get married? And you've waited all this time to tell me? Oh, that's wonderful! Look, I simply must rush off and make everyone wild with the news. I'm so happy for you, I really am. What a frightfully normal thing to do! Have you both agreed on this already?

DONATA: He proposed to me. He's gone to talk to his uncle about us.

ELISA: But surely you aren't going to leave the theatre, are you? That would be such a shame.

DONATA: It looks like it. He doesn't like the idea. He's totally against it.

ELISA: You simply couldn't do it.

DONATA: I don't know yet. I still have all my commitments and it won't be easy to get out of them. But it isn't only commitments...

ELISA: I understand. If it's a question of...

DONATA: I wasn't ready for this. He only told me a little while ago. I hadn't so much as even hinted at it. You see, I only did it because I wanted to... free myself from... maybe even from this life of mine. You can't imagine what the past few days have been like. It's incredible!... I can only say that whether we're alone with our private feelings or with other people we're quite mad. I've had a kind of almost arrogant satisfaction at having finally gone through with something. Yes, a sense of satisfaction at having overcome some inherent weakness both as an actress and a woman. And faced with those other women (the ones you tell me are the most outraged) I've been trying to let them see... don't laugh... the challenge in my look and expression, that mark which I will always bear... that says I am a woman who stands on her own feet and accepts what she is... a woman who has loved outside convention and who rejects the stupid assumption that since she has done this once, she will do it again, like other women... And believe me, this is in spite of knowing that they think I have given in to what was expected of me... and been diminished by that... No, it wasn't inevitable, as you say it was...

And I swear, far from feeling any pleasure... if I were honest I'd have to say I was suffering; perhaps... yes... with the one satisfaction of experiencing it as something that a woman has to go through in order to come to terms with accepting a man... and afterwards, feeling as I did that extraordinary sense of peace just for a second, without giving it any thought, or worrying about what it might have cost me, consoling myself with the gentle, almost embarrassed gratitude that he showed me. This, I suppose, is the one thing that will really hold the relationship together... This caring... I just shut my eyes to everything and only open them when I sense that caring. That's the way to hang on to it all.

ELISA: Yes, but men today expect women to be grateful to them for the pleasure they give.

DONATA: Do they? Because women have been stupid enough to let them see that... yes, they have... and now they believe it utterly. They even make women come to them.

DONATA: That's not true.

ELISA: It certainly is true! But I do understand that you have to wait for real love to develop.

DONATA: But I do love him.

ELISA: Yes, but you still don't love "with him". When you love with him, at the same time and in the same way that he does, then everything will be different, you'll see...

DONATA (*getting up, agitated*): All I know is that there are times when I see him in front of me, standing there... so self-assured and so good-looking (yes, he's handsome, but that's not what matters...) and at times like that, if he comes near me... I don't know... I really hate him.

ELISA (*smiling*): What a thing to say!

DONATA: Yes, I do. I can't bear the idea of being there in his arms, being something which exclusively belongs to him, just a body, nothing else, something he takes possession of... I feel overwhelmed by it... I disgust myself... If that's all the life I can look forward to... Would you really want me to live like that?

ELISA: Of course not. That's why I say you shouldn't leave the theatre.

DONATA: No, I'm not thinking about the theatre now. If I could only see how it would turn out...

ELISA: It's too soon.

DONATA: Yes, of course. It's too soon...

ELISA: You still have to get to know him...

DONATA: He can't be pinned down... he won't stop to think for a moment... and I... (*She breaks off, because she is thinking about what* ELISA *said before*) Yes, perhaps you're right. What I would like to feel at moments like that is the exact opposite... not to be defined as his possession, but to have him... as mine... It isn't, it isn't because I cease to exist, I don't cease to exist at times like that with him, but I experience a feeling of distrust that mortifies me and depresses me utterly. As if I were being egged on by a curiosity, forcing me to suppress myself, or by the need to feel that even I...

ELISA: Don't worry about it... believe me. I understand... but just wait a little. You hadn't been expecting anything like this, you weren't prepared for it... And you still don't know him well enough to be able to defend yourself.

DONATA: How do you mean, defend myself?

ELISA: You'll learn. It's always like this at the beginning. You'll manage to make him slow down... of course, you will... and see your point of view... without running away... you'll find a way of living together that makes you happy. He's so good-hearted really, just like a little boy.

DONATA: Yes, he's so impulsive...

ELISA: And if he really loves you and wants to marry you...

DONATA: Yes, perhaps it's just me... what can I say? But I did believe that as soon as I began a life of my own, everything would have become perfectly clear and I would have escaped from all that uncertainty. How wrong I was! It hasn't happened! This is even worse! And he contributes to this feeling of unease by telling me this is how things ought to be... random, unplanned, a matter of taking each day at a time...

ELISA: Life as it happens...

DONATA: You say that too? Then it is true!

ELISA: What is?

DONATA: My sense of disorientation must be natural, like this sense of anxiety... Nothing is certain nor ever can be... Oh, there's the will to try and create an existence, the need to make it as solid as possible... if that's feasible, because it doesn't depend on us, there are all the other people too, the other situations, the other circumstances and there's the person who is closest to us... all of which can get in our way and frustrate us... You're not alone in the midst of all that potential life that is struggling to take shape and can't manage it... you aren't free any more! And when it comes down to it, the one place where life is created spontaneously is the theatre. That's why I have always instinctively felt safe there. And the sense of something vague and uncertain that I felt before was not due to my not having a life of my own. No, it's much worse actually to have one! You cease to understand if you recklessly give in to such a life. You open your eyes again, and if you don't want to go along with all that's commonplace, habitual, dull, monotonous, tasteless and colourless, then you are faced with uncertainty and instability again.

Though with one difference: you aren't the same as you were before, you're tied down and compromised by what you have done and it's impossibly difficult to go back feeling safe and complete. I understood this before, but now I know it through experience. But tell me something about him... so that at least I can learn something I don't know already.

ELISA: You know he doesn't have any relations except one uncle...

DONATA: Yes, I know that. What about his uncle?

ELISA: You met him at my house.

DONATA: Yes, Count Mola.

ELISA: Such a nice man... a perfect gentleman...

DONATA: Is Elj financially dependent on him?

ELISA: They've always lived together, like father and son.

DONATA: Elj's mother was the Count's sister, she died very young, I gather.

ELISA: Yes, she did. But I simply wouldn't know precisely what their arrangements are. I rather think that Elj has an income of his own from his mother's side. They are... well, they're reputed to be... rather well-off.

DONATA: I wanted to know, because... you see... if Elj does depend on him financially...

ELISA: Oh, but he always does exactly what his nephew tells him.

DONATA: Have you seen him since?

ELISA: Yes, we actually had an argument. He is very cross, as you can imagine.

DONATA: With me?

ELISA: Not with you exactly; with him; after all he asked him to move out... and then there's the scandal... A man like that... such a proper person... a stickler for good behaviour... He was offended by the way it was done... But I'm sure that where you're concerned...

DONATA: Do you happen to know if he had made any plans for his nephew?

ELISA: Oh, I think so... Which reminds me. You'll never guess what Elj did to Nina that night, you know that girl who...

DONATA: Who didn't think I could be sincere?

ELISA: Yes, her. It was so typical of him. But dreadfully cruel.

DONATA: I don't know anything about it. What did he do?

ELISA: Well... it seems that to make her keep quiet he said or did... I'm not quite sure what... she was talking about a "seal" or a "sealed pact"... and she put her hand over her mouth... We found her there, gasping, calling for help and choking...

DONATA: Really?

ELISA: You can just imagine, poor child, she follows him round like a puppy. She's absolutely wild about him... still is...

DONATA: And you think his uncle would have approved?

ELISA: I suppose so... along with her grandmother... you know, the old lady, Marchesa Boveno... Oh, she's furious. The Marchesa is absolutely furious.

DONATA: She must have gone straight to his uncle clamouring for revenge.

ELISA: What do you think?

DONATA: And now that girl will be involved too... since his uncle...

ELISA: No, why bother about that? It's completely insignificant. Childish nonsense. The Count is angry because of the implications of it all... the way in which that poor girl was so upset...

The voice of COUNT MOLA *is heard.*

COUNT MOLA: May I come in?

ELISA: Oh, here he is. Would you like me to go?

DONATA: Wait a little – come in.

COUNT MOLA (*coming in, forcing himself to overcome his embarrassment*): Good morning, Donata... Elisa, my dear...

DONATA: Good morning...

ELISA: Dear Count Mola...

DONATA: Do sit down...

COUNT MOLA: Thank you.

DONATA: And Elj?

COUNT MOLA: Elj?... If you'll allow me, this time I got my own back on him. I left him outside so that we could have a serious talk...

ELISA (*standing up*): I'll leave you then, Donata...

COUNT MOLA (*standing up swiftly too*): No, Elisa, it would be a great help to me if you stayed...

ELISA: But if you have things to say...

DONATA: If the Count says he would like you to stay...

COUNT MOLA: Yes, I would like you to. I knew you were here, Elj told me. So I hurried round to catch you while you were still here...

ELISA: Well... then... all right... (*To* DONATA) If you want me to...

DONATA: Yes, of course, do stay. But I really have to say that all this...

She stands up agitatedly, runs her hand over her face.

Oh, God, no... (*bursts out laughing*) You can't imagine how theatrical all this seems to me...

ELISA: That's so absurd!

DONATA (*laughing bitterly, choking*): Oh yes... a well-rehearsed scene for three with Elj left out of it... Should I sit here?... Or there? What pose should I strike? I'll start acting... probably rather better than either of you, if you'll forgive me...

COUNT MOLA (*very embarrassed*): No... why... why does it strike you like that?

ELISA (*looking at the* COUNT *and catching* DONATA's *contagious laughter*): Yes... how curious... like you said, Donata... it's having the same effect on me now... What an idea!... Perhaps because life itself is theatrical, darling.

DONATA: Oh, no! The theatre! At least there one can be sure that everything which is meant to happen will happen, right up to the finale... No, Count, I'm sorry. It's serious for me, it really is. My life is involved. I'm here now living in a condition you can imagine only too well. I know what I've done... look... I have no illusions. If I have upset you, if you had other plans for your nephew and you don't approve... well, please don't try to be tactful or polite. I can't cope with much more... what I need to know is where I stand. Have you any objections? Then tell me what they are.

COUNT MOLA: But I... well...

DONATA: You are against it. All right. Now answer me: does Elj need your consent?

COUNT MOLA: Well… I…

DONATA: Go on, answer me… yes or no… for Heaven's sake.

ELISA: No, wait, Donata, you can't go on like this.

COUNT MOLA: I wouldn't have any objections at all if…

DONATA: If what?… Tell me, please. I insist, I need to know.

COUNT MOLA: But you don't give me a chance…

ELISA: Calm down, darling, come and sit here with me… Now then, Count…

COUNT MOLA: I'm really sorry now that I left Elj outside…

At this point ELJ *puts his head around the door, but the* COUNT *does not see him and goes on.*

…if this has given the impression that…

ELISA (*seeing him*): There's Elj! Speak of the devil!

ELJ (*leaping into the room*): What devil? I'm a guardian angel! (*To his uncle*) See? Didn't I tell you? Uncle?

COUNT MOLA (*getting up angrily*): Well, I can still speak my mind with you here, you know.

ELJ: Then go ahead. Say what you have to. Throw anything you like at me.

COUNT MOLA: I wanted to spare her (*pointing to* DONATA) from having to hear my feelings of indignation and outrage at your behaviour.

DONATA: But whatever Elj did was what I wanted too.

ELJ: No, wait, Donata. He said he didn't want you to know. (*To his uncle*) Well, what have you let her know now?

COUNT MOLA: I'm angry with him, not with you.

ELJ: Because I brought you back here. You could hardly have wanted that; you were barely even alive. And he's angry with me because I shut the door on him, aren't you? Uncle?

DONATA: But I was the one who dared him to go out in the boat. He didn't want to.

COUNT MOLA: No, I'm sorry, Donata, but that's just it. He had no right to accept that challenge and take advantage of the state you were in.

DONATA: But Elj couldn't have known anything of how I was feeling…

ELJ (*in a rush*): It was so beautiful! So brave! So stupendous! You haven't regretted it! You can't have regretted it!

DONATA: No, Elj, no.

ELJ: Don't go back on it now! Don't let me down!

DONATA: No, of course not... but we have to think...

ELJ: No, we don't. We're going to get married. You're mine. And he's angry about what I did just before that.

COUNT MOLA: Oh yes, what you did was quite despicable.

DONATA: Oh, that... that adds another dimension...

ELJ: No, it doesn't. (*To his uncle*) Stop going on about what I did, Uncle. I gave that silly girl what she was asking for to get rid of her. Now let's forget about it. Good God, are you trying to condemn me for kissing some silly girl who wouldn't get out of the way?

ELISA (*unable to stop herself laughing*): Oh, it was a kiss, was it?

COUNT MOLA: Now don't you start laughing too, Elisa, please...

ELJ (*to* DONATA): It was just on impulse. You see, I couldn't think of any other way... she was getting on my nerves... it was just a kiss... anyway, it's over and done with.

COUNT MOLA (*furious*): No it is not! I forbid you to add insult to injury.

DONATA (*to* ELJ, *trying to explain why his uncle is so angry*): Elj! Count Mola is a friend of the Marchesa...

COUNT MOLA: And so I have been for many years, a very good friend, Donata. One doesn't do things like that! Life isn't a joke, you know, and still less is it something to mock at. I am seriously worried about you, too. Dear Donata, if you'll allow me to call you by name...

DONATA: Yes, of course. I'm delighted you want to.

ELJ (*trying to embrace his uncle*): He's a good old sort, like I told you...

COUNT MOLA (*pushing him off angrily*): Leave me alone, Elj. I have no intention of continuing to be made a fool of. (*To* DONATA) Donata, please... I can't talk while he's here...

ELJ: All right, keep your hair on. Feel free to say what you like. I'll go out again... there you are... I'm off right now. Don't get in such a state, for God's sake. And above all, don't try to make me feel small, don't try it...

ELJ *goes out.*

COUNT MOLA: He's quite mad, you know, quite mad.

ELISA: How right you were... (*To* DONATA) What did you call him? "Impulsive" didn't you...

COUNT MOLA: Quite mad.

ELISA: Now, please!

DONATA: Oh really... if that's all... In fact, if he's like that...

COUNT MOLA: I'm not saying for one moment that you might not like him as he is. But believe me, living with him… Up to now I've let him be…

ELISA: Then you're rather to blame…

COUNT MOLA: There's absolutely no way on this earth of prevailing on him by reason alone… you can see that. The way to get through to him is with a little tenderness, if he responds to it… yes, I do say that, because he carefully inhibits his feelings so as not to worry or frighten the person he cares about.

ELISA: Now that really is absurd.

COUNT MOLA: Yes, I'll give him that, he's affectionate by nature.

ELISA: So, you see…

COUNT MOLA: Well, what I say is… (*Hesitates, to* DONATA) May I continue?

DONATA: Of course, please do.

COUNT MOLA: Now then, what I say is that to give him his due, the life he's been living so far has been that of a young man of leisure… without problems and consequently, I'm afraid, unfortunately rather out of the ordinary… all excitement… (believe me, it can't last…) one whim after another… no bills to pay, no accounts to settle… and no sense of responsibility whatsoever (he's completely ignorant, he has no idea of what he owns, though I have to say that he is perfectly upright, very honest, he's never spent beyond his means)… (his whims are dangerous simply because he leads a charmed life)… Well, living like that… and believing so readily (and he's wrong! quite wrong!) that he has suddenly found his ideal companion in you, by which I mean a companion for all his foolish schemes, all his mad pranks, you must understand (perhaps I'm not succeeding in expressing how very concerned I am)…

DONATA: I do understand what you're trying to say: you don't feel that I should entrust my life to him blindly, do you?

COUNT MOLA: No, precisely. Your own life is another matter, Donata, your own life is precious… it can never have been easy for you…

DONATA (*sharply, with feeling*): No… never!

And she gets up, as though she can no longer contain the impulses within her.

COUNT MOLA: I well believe that. Who knows what price you must have paid… all kinds of unimaginable difficulties, struggles, disappointments to get where you are now.

DONATA: Yes... quite... to get where I am now. But who can say exactly where that is, Count. I had reached the point of throwing it all away... back there... if he hadn't saved me...

ELISA (*troubled by the sudden change in* DONATA): My dear, what on earth are you saying?

DONATA: Yes... that's how it was, if you really want to know. I don't know exactly what was happening to me that one moment of terror with the sea raging around me... with death howling and shrieking in my ears – all I know is that I shut my eyes ready to die... That's the point I had arrived at, Count.

COUNT MOLA: Yes, and if I remember correctly, you had said something to the effect that night. Perhaps when you said... there was nothing to worry about... But you still have to consider, I think, that despite it all... yes... you're the winner.

DONATA: Despite it all. Yes, but you know, that's what it means to win the way I wanted to win. The price of my winning – to me as a woman – do you know what it felt like when I had it in my grasp? What my feelings as a woman were? I felt insulted... yes, I did. Because the woman in me could so easily have let the actress win – and make my life easier too – All I needed to soil that victory even just a little was praise for the actress that was really due to the woman. I've never been able to stand that confusion of identity between actress and woman, I wanted to save the self-respect of the actress who wanted to win on her own account, convinced that what was new and alive in my work was all I would need to win... I won, yes, I won on my own... as much on my own as if I had been on top of a mountain – in the ice... I wake up, I open my eyes to find myself in a silence and a light that are unfamiliar to me, amongst things that have no meaning for me... What sort of woman am I then? Who am I? What do I feel? Where am I? What do I have within my grasp which I am quite unable to relish? The pride in winning? That's nothing but a dead weight, about as useful as a lump of concrete tied round my neck to pull me to the bottom. That's what it feels like when you can't cope any longer. I assure you in the end you come to ask yourself if it was worthwhile. Life makes demands on you all the time, heavy, insistent demands... I've given my whole being... always... without ever stopping to think about myself treated as though I had no right to feel anything, as though I were made of stone... people have little respect for me... or else they tie my insides in knots... and all those nights of painful crying, unable to see why I have to lose the best years of my life like that... with no comfort and no pleasure... I've won, oh yes, I've won... but take a look at me... I can't stand it any more, I can't stand it...

ELISA (*moved, going over to hug her*): Dear Donata! Can't you see, can't you see what your life is really worth?

COUNT MOLA: All your work... all it has cost you... your tears... your noble feelings... he doesn't know anything about any of that.

DONATA (*deciding*): Yes, that's true. He must know.

ELISA (*getting worked up*): He doesn't know you. He's never really seen you.

COUNT MOLA (*pressing the point home*): Exactly... who you really are... what a life like yours is really worth... That's what I was trying to say. That's it! He has to know the true value of the gift you are prepared to give him.

ELISA (*continuing*): Yes, for his sake too, Donata. You can't just make a gift of it to him like this, as though it had cost you nothing.

DONATA (*stiffly, staring into space*): For my sake too. Yes. This has to be a test for me too. I need it. Now I really can see that I need it.

ELISA: A test? What do you mean?

DONATA: Yes. Of whether I... I... can have a life of my own at last.

CURTAIN

ACT THREE

A room in an expensive hotel in a big Italian city. An alcove at the back, where the bed is hidden behind a damask curtain. Several steps lead up to it. In front of the alcove is a kind of sitting room, with a large sofa in the centre, small tables, armchairs... On the table is an ornate lamp with a lavender shade. The main exit is on the left-hand side. On the right is the door leading to the adjoining room, which is ELJ's. This setting must be heavy and in complete contrast with the two preceding acts: it must be as gloomy, heavy and oppressive as the previous acts were bright, airy and light.

When the curtain goes up the stage is dark and empty. Shortly afterwards, the left-hand door is heard to open. ELJ comes in, pushes a button near the door. It is the wrong button. Only the lavender-coloured table lamp lights up, illuminating the room with a gloomy light. ELJ is in evening dress, wearing a hat and still has his black overcoat on; he crosses the stage looking pale and irritated, very edgy, goes to open the door in front of his room which is right in front of him. Goes in, leaving the door open. A light is turned on in his room which shines brightly out across the stage through the open door. Short pause. Knocking is heard at the left-hand door. Still wearing his hat and coat, ELJ comes to the door of his room and shouts:

ELJ: Come in!

To the HOTEL MAID *who appears:*

ELJ: What is it?

MAID: Has the signora come back yet, signore?

ELJ: No. You can see perfectly well that she hasn't.

MAID: I'm sorry. I thought the performance was over.

ELJ: No, it isn't.

MAID: Very well then. I'll come back and lay the table later.

On her way out, she bumps into COUNT MOLA, *also in evening dress, looking very agitated and distressed on his way in. The* MAID *steps aside, turns the light on in the room and leaves, shutting the door behind her.*

ELJ: For God's sake, don't say a word!

COUNT MOLA: What a way to leave a theatre!

ELJ: I couldn't stand it any longer.

COUNT MOLA: You might have waited until at least the end of the second act, until the curtain came down.

ELJ: I tell you I couldn't stand it.

COUNT MOLA: For a member of the audience to walk out at that point in the performance... The whole theatre froze. I could feel shivers running down my spine.

ELJ: Shivers, eh?

COUNT MOLA: When you walked out, I mean. You might at least have gone out quietly. The Lord only knows what people must have thought...

ELJ: Who the devil knew I had left?

COUNT MOLA: Everyone did! You don't realize what incidents like that mean in a theatre... the slightest rustle, the least sound can destroy everything. And what about her? The third act will have just ended. She'll be waiting...

ELJ: I sent her a note.

COUNT MOLA: What kind of note?

ELJ: Saying I couldn't stand it any longer and I would wait for her back here at the hotel. But I can't even bear to wait. I don't want to see her again. I'm leaving. You can tell her I've gone.

COUNT MOLA: What? You're leaving?

ELJ: Right now. I'm going back to the coast. In the car.

COUNT MOLA: Oh no you're not! I won't let you take the car for a start.

ELJ: All right, I'll go by train!

COUNT MOLA: For Heaven's sake, pull yourself together and stop this.

ELJ: I just can't stand the thought of seeing her again, can't you get that through your head? I'm leaving so she won't find me here. If there's a night train, I'll take it. If not, I'll take the first one in the morning.

COUNT MOLA: You're determined to leave like this without even talking to her?

ELJ: You can tell her I'll be waiting down there – when she's come back to her senses – when she's stopped showing herself off to everyone…

COUNT MOLA: Good Lord, what now? You must be mad. Didn't you realize what happened to her?

ELJ: She must have felt ashamed of herself…

COUNT MOLA: It was a disaster. A total disaster!

ELJ: God, how could she? How could she do such a thing? Exposing herself in such an intimate way… just like she has always been with me… with all those people watching… I could recognize every movement she made.

COUNT MOLA: Oh no you couldn't. You didn't recognize anything. Quite the reverse!

ELJ: Quite the reverse? What the hell do you know about it?

COUNT MOLA: I've seen her play that part before. I've seen her play that love scene many times.

ELJ: Are you trying to tell me how she looks when she says certain things? How she smiles when she… It isn't even a smile, it's sort of a gentle, pleading look.

COUNT MOLA: And couldn't you see that she could hardly get the words out? Or smile, or even look convincing? It was absolutely pitiful.

ELJ: Because I was there, that's why. And I knew… only I could have known.

COUNT MOLA: Only you be damned! Everybody knew!

ELJ: Really? The way she looks away, almost to hide what she's saying?

COUNT MOLA: Yes, exactly.

ELJ: And the way she smiles, like a little girl gazing into the water, holding out her hands, just like she did when I wanted to take her in my arms?

COUNT MOLA: But my dear boy, this play has been her greatest success of the year.

ELJ: So everybody knows that's how she is? That's how she behaves? But if I could prove – for certain – that she wasn't aware – you see? – wasn't aware of anything? Was it all an act before? Or afterwards, with me?… No. She was aware tonight and because she was aware she was like that, holding back what she said and did… What was so shameful was that I was there watching her… up on the stage revealing to everybody what only I have a right to know, what she felt like when she was with me… and what the devil does she want?

Does she want me to accept that? Accept her parading herself like that? As though she were common property? No thanks...

I'm ashamed for her sake, whether she's ashamed or not. I can't accept this pretending. And it's even worse if it seems real to her. I'm leaving! I have to leave! Otherwise it would seem like taking her back after she's been with other men. No thanks! Tell her how I feel, what I'm going through – tell her I can't take it. Let her stay here and be everybody's property.

He starts to go.

COUNT MOLA (*restraining him*): Wait! For God's sake, wait! Maybe she'll be convinced now that she finds it equally intolerable. She had to test you both in this way – she told you that.

ELJ: Yes – on your advice! To show me her true value. What the hell can the true value of that woman you see up there be, compared to what she was like when she was mine... when I believed she was like that for me alone, with the face God gave her, so beautiful and pure, with her vulnerable, laughing eyes... The woman I've just seen was a painted mask... with false eyelashes and all that make-up... looking like a...

He shudders.

Oh! And you think she's talented, do you? Really talented? I thought she was a feeble wisp of a thing that didn't know how to walk properly or speak a true word. And there you all were, applauding what you thought was her amazing acting ability. I thought she was ridiculous – a grimacing puppet, that's all! Not worth anything. Talented? Oh yes, you really have put me through a fine ordeal.

COUNT MOLA: I'm telling you she wasn't there. She wasn't there for the whole two acts in front of the audience. Nobody could recognize her, it came as a shock to all of us to see her there on stage as though she hadn't learnt the part, precisely because she knew you were there.

ELJ: Trying not to look at her.

COUNT MOLA: Unless you could become all the public she needs... and you know what that would mean for you?

ELJ: Me? Her public? There's only one of me.

COUNT MOLA: But you want her to be able to find in you alone all the vitality, all the emotion, all the satisfaction that up to now has been provided by the love her public has for her. What can you be for her? Think of that.

ELJ: Me? What can I be? Didn't you tell me yourself? If she wasn't there tonight for her public – then that's what I am to her. Fine. Let her choose! Either the love of her public with all she's had from them so far, or my love for all I've given her.

COUNT MOLA: Don't you understand that anybody can give her what you've given her if you let her down now and go?

ELJ: Of course... anybody... if that's what she wants. But apparently she doesn't share your view... if she's tested us both and if, as you say, she isn't up to it.

COUNT MOLA: Then why go... if you've won? Wait until she comes back to tell you... that since she loves you so much she can't go on acting.

ELJ: No. I want her... on her own... here... to take the decision to give it up. I want her to come to me... on her own... and I'll be waiting. I don't want her to find me here humiliated by what she put me through, and by what she's made me watch, seeing her up there on the stage humiliated by the feelings she had for me and by having – dear God – to express them just as she did when she was with me, using the same tone of voice and the same gestures... I was appalled by her. My suitcases are through there. Have them sent on to me. I don't need anything else. All this dressing up. If she won't come, tell her I'm going to put out to sea and never set foot on dry land again.

He leaves by the left-hand exit. COUNT MOLA *runs after him.*

COUNT MOLA (*shouting through the door*): Elj!

He steps back as the MAID *comes in.*

MAID: I'm sorry, signore, but there are people asleep...

COUNT MOLA: I do beg your pardon. It's just that... I can't stay here... This is her room.

MAID: Yes, signore. But if you prefer, you can wait in there.

She indicates the adjoining room.

COUNT MOLA (*who cannot calm down*): He's even left the light on... and the suitcases...

MAID: Has the gentleman left?

COUNT MOLA: Yes. That is... I'm not sure... possibly, for the time being...

MAID: Shall I take the suitcases down?

COUNT MOLA: Not just yet... Wait until Signora Genzi comes back.

MAID: Then please make yourself comfortable.

COUNT MOLA: Not in here, no... I can't let myself be found here in her room... I shall wait for her downstairs in the lobby...

MAID: Here she is now.

DONATA *comes in in a hurry, flustered. In order to get back to the hotel as fast as possible, she has not even taken off her make-up and under her cloak she is wearing her costume.*

DONATA: Oh, it's you, Count... Is Elj through there?

She starts to go towards ELJ's *room. The* MAID *goes out.*

COUNT MOLA: No, Donata. Didn't you see him just now?

DONATA: No. Was he downstairs?

COUNT MOLA: He went downstairs a moment ago.

DONATA: Downstairs where? I was in such a hurry. I didn't even take off my make-up...

COUNT MOLA: Allow me... where can he have gone? Perhaps he still hasn't left the hotel... he may be at the desk...

DONATA: At the desk? Why?

COUNT MOLA: Well, I suppose... I could try... (*he starts to leave*)

DONATA: No. Wait. Is he leaving the hotel? Is he going away?

COUNT MOLA: Yes.

DONATA: Ah, so he actually told you he was leaving?

COUNT MOLA: He said he was going back to the coast... and would wait for you there...

DONATA: Me?

COUNT MOLA: He said he couldn't bear it...

DONATA: I know that.

COUNT MOLA: He ran out of the theatre... I met up with him here...

DONATA: And he ran away from here too... so he wouldn't have to see me like this, right?

COUNT MOLA: He finds it impossible to...

DONATA: And so I should go and join him, should I? Stupid man.

She sees ELISA *coming in, followed by* GIVIERO.

Elisa, my dear, come along in. Do come in, Giviero. I was just about to ask Count Mola to go downstairs and invite you both to come up.

ELISA (*agitated, trying to explain why she has come up without being invited*): Down in the lobby we met...

DONATA: Oh, so he really was still down there...

ELISA: Yes, in quite a state...

COUNT MOLA (*to* DONATA, *to break the deadlock*): If you like, I can...

DONATA (*emphatically*): No! (*Then softening a little*) I'm sorry, would you like me to call him back? (*Almost to herself, very upset but trying to overcome it with dignity*) The stupid man... (*To* ELISA) He's gone away...

GIVIERO: Yes, he told us that as he pushed past us and went out.

DONATA: Because watching me act made him suffer too much... he suffered. Can you imagine? After all that... No, that's enough. He's a silly man... tell Count Mola here, go on, tell him what happened in the third act. You see, I rushed away like this, still in costume. I wanted to be the first to tell him, I was so happy...

ELISA: A phenomenal success, it was extraordinary.

GIVIERO: Oh yes. She's never been so magnificent.

COUNT MOLA: Really? You recovered for your last act?

ELISA: An extraordinary performance. If only you'd stayed... The whole theatre went wild, they gave her a standing ovation.

GIVIERO: It was the most amazing success.

DONATA: No, I am not talking about what happened to me on stage. I'm talking about my own personal triumph, my victory over myself... what it meant to me finally...

ELISA: An absolute triumph.

DONATA (*swiftly irritated that* ELISA *does not understand*): No, I'm talking about my freedom. When I went back to my dressing room everything inside me was throbbing – it was like wild laughter – but it was triumph, yes, it was! I caught a glimpse of myself in a mirror, my head was high, my hands were raised and I felt I had a grip on my whole life. Then I thought about him, I thought it would make him happy too, you see, so I ran here to shout out the news that I had finally found myself. You saw me, Count, didn't you? I was lost, everything had collapsed, I could feel myself being dragged down because the audience weren't with me. That dreadful silence! That emptiness! I was sweating blood – it was agony! Absolute agony! Then suddenly, I don't know how, something snapped inside me and I was free. I forgot everything. I felt myself taken over and lifted up… I regained all my senses, the ability to hear which I had lost; everything was so clear and so absolutely right. My whole life was restored to me, and it felt complete and utterly straightforward. I felt such contentment I was drunk with happiness. I could feel a sense of illumination, of rebirth, of complete control.

COUNT MOLA: I'm so happy for you, Donata. I'm really glad to hear this.

ELISA: You can't imagine what she was like.

GIVIERO: The audience joined in and were carried away with her; everyone could sense that freedom and recognize their own actress again.

DONATA: No! Why do you all keep talking about the actress? It isn't that. I felt happy as a woman! A woman! Happy I could still love like that. That was what I felt I'd won. I was happy I could run back here to tell him, even though he had been hurt – though not nearly as much as I was, because out there I'd been in torment through two whole acts, while all he did was to write me a note saying "I can't stand it any longer" and run out of the theatre. What I suffered during those two acts, knowing he was out there watching me for the first time and recognizing my every gesture, separating me from my character, holding me back and preventing me from entering into the part! I had to free myself, to distance myself from that unformed, uncreated ghastly thing that was his and not mine… it was so painful to be stripped naked out there, exposed by his feelings, and I would never have been able to live on a stage again, nor in life either. But then I found the strength to free myself… and I did! And what I felt in that instant of freedom in the deepest part of myself was this: that I was able to love, that I was able to open myself fully and completely to receive love too… I hadn't expected that in the brief moment of triumph over all those terrors when my entire being seemed to be fully illuminated, I would regain not only as an actress my passion for art, but as a woman my passion for life. I wanted to make him understand that too, wanted to tell him here and now if he hadn't already understood that much, that he didn't need to go to the theatre any more. And that was all. He wouldn't need to put himself at risk ever again, nor cause me to run the risk of not finding myself when I was acting. Oh God, the risk of losing sight of myself, of feeling lost when I was acting, something that had never ever happened to me before! I looked into the utter depths! I felt so much self-hatred… no, worse, such wretchedness, that it suddenly seemed clear to me that if life and the love I felt for him were going to reduce me to that and make me feel so debased, then no! I couldn't be worth anything myself, not even for him. Whereas now... you see, I was coming here to share this joy and pride and give the love derived from so many to just one man... to him... Yes, I was... And where is he?... The stupid, stupid man... he's gone.

COUNT MOLA: Yes, he is stupid. He hasn't understood anything. He didn't try. He felt disgusted. He will never understand the actress in you, Donata. It will never mean anything to him... he told me as much.

DONATA: But the woman means something to him... the one who was ashamed... yes, I know that. He wants the woman all right, Giviero, the one who was actually ashamed of stroking his hair (you know, the gesture you noticed before). I felt appalled at myself... at being real, as I had always been on stage... at being myself... me, the person I am, almost as though as an actress I'd ceased to be a woman... True to myself in that way, just as I am... in my life and in my work... Don't I seem real now?

GIVIERO: Of course you are, Donata.

DONATA: Well then? If I can't find myself... in life... can't be as I am... like this!... That means I shall never find my true self in life... never... because it isn't possible to find yourself outside the feeling that gives you certainty... security... in yourself.

GIVIERO: Yes, that's right. And so be very careful not to put yourself down, not even in the slightest degree!

COUNT MOLA (*decisively*): No!... The actress can never be with him... never!

ELISA: Then that's his loss.

COUNT MOLA: Indeed it is. His loss.

DONATA: And mine too.

GIVIERO: No, hardly yours. What about your huge success tonight then? Haven't you finally passed your own test?

DONATA: Passed the test... yes... I've won again... and I'm alone... again... But this time I will always be. This time it's for ever. And now I'm afraid for two reasons – for my work and for myself – afraid of going back to real life. I've had enough... (*She breaks off, tired and sickened*) Yes, I've had enough, for God's sake. Leave me alone now please. I need to be left alone... to stay here alone... to sort myself out... Yes, that's it. Ultimately we all find ourselves alone...

Thank Heavens we still have our imaginative lives that are often more real and more true than any real and true things in life itself. At least they can be relied upon, and since we create those imaginative lives they never let us down. (*With abrupt uncontrollable irritation*) Oh God, the light is still on through there!

COUNT MOLA: Would you like me to switch it off? I'll go and…

DONATA: Yes, do me the favour…

COUNT MOLA *does so.*

ELISA: You know you can always call me, whenever you like, if you need…

DONATA: Yes, thank you, dear Elisa, I know. Goodnight. Goodnight, Giviero. Thank you for everything, Count, goodnight.

COUNT MOLA (*very embarrassed*): He left his suitcases there too…

DONATA: He'll be expecting us to take them down to him in his car…

COUNT MOLA (*taken aback*): What?

DONATA: No, you can come by and collect them tomorrow. I was joking…

COUNT MOLA: He said that if you didn't come he'd put out to sea and never set foot on land again…

DONATA: The sea…

The other three leave, bewildered and upset. DONATA *stays quite still in the middle of the room, her head bent over backwards, her eyes closed. She remains like this for some time. Then she raises her head again, and frowns, still with her eyes closed, as though willing herself to come to terms with her fate. She crosses to the door, turns on the violet table lamp, turns off the ceiling light. Then she goes over to the big mirror on her left and switches on the two lamps on either side. She sits down to take off her make-up, but first she looks at herself. As she raises her hand to take off her false eyelashes, she remembers a line from the play that had signalled the start of her feeling of freedom back in the theatre.*

DONATA: "One cannot show any mercy to people who are weak. So throw her out! Throw her out of here!"

To herself, as though dissatisfied with her delivery of the second phrase.

DONATA: No.

Repeats the lines in a more commanding, contemptuous voice.

DONATA: "Throw her out! Throw her out! Don't you realize that she is the one who has made me so cruel? How could you think that he

208

would have hesitated in choosing between us? Yes signora, I know all about your nobility, your elevated good taste that you"…

Her memory fails.

DONATA: No, how did it go?

Running through the part, with no expression.

DONATA: "that underpins everything you do and every little thing about you, that may seem simple but is actually carefully calculated"… no, not calculated, "controlled", that's it, "controlled" – calculated would be better – "controlled by your excessive pride".

She runs through this in her memory without acting it. Now she begins to act, and without thinking takes a photograph from the mirror frame because the role requires her to fan herself and she does not have a fan:

DONATA: "Do you still want to stay?"

She stops fanning herself abruptly, because she realizes she is holding a photo of ELJ. She looks at it, slightly upset, then sticks it back face downwards into the mirror frame; she flings herself back in her chair, leans her head backwards, laughs challengingly and shouts at her imaginary companion:

DONATA: "All right then! Go on! Take me!"

During this last sequence, from the moment when DONATA sat down in front of the mirror and began to go over her lines, the stage behind her has gradually been changing and becoming larger. The alcove with the bed has opened out in the centre and split into two halves, leaving a space in the middle that is in semi-darkness like an auditorium. The enlarged arch of the former alcove now looks like the proscenium of an imaginary stage, the very stage on which she is performing, lit by a strange hallucinatory light – for DONATA is in the grip of just such an illusion, when she leans back in her chair and shouts:

DONATA: "All right, then, go on, take me."

The other characters from the play begin to appear, over behind the sofa; a young man and woman. He is tall, handsome, dark-haired, in evening dress; she is aristocratic, slightly faded, very blonde, in elegant clothes. They both stand motionless and detached, like apparitions. At DONATA's cry, he runs over to stand on her right and she puts her right arm round his waist. Then she reconsiders this, saying to herself:

DONATA: "No. She was over there."

And as though the next move had been thought out by DONATA, *the woman who had stayed behind the sofa now crosses from stage left to stage right. At the same time* DONATA *moves the man round the back of her chair so she can embrace him with her left hand.*

DONATA: "That's it"…

She turns to the woman:

DONATA: "Do you still want to stay?"

She stands up, and cries:

DONATA: "Take me in your arms."

But as he does so, the woman hides her face in her hands and DONATA *bursts out laughing.*

DONATA: Oh, look… just look… she can't bear to watch.

Disentangling herself:

DONATA: Leave me be, you fool. Can't you see that I'm not causing the trouble here? She's the one, and if she doesn't get out of here I won't be responsible for what happens. (*To the woman*) Well? Isn't that enough for you? I'm the one who doesn't want him. He is quite capable of making love to me in front of your very eyes. I assure you, signora, that everything that has happened can be blamed on your excessive sense of self-sacrifice! I didn't choose your husband. He chose me. I may have been flattered for a second or two. Yes, I was, I admit it. But you have to take the circumstances into account. He was the only one to arouse any kind of interest amongst us women. There were far too many of us and we were so bored, and we had so few men and he was so charming. When he singled me out from all the others, naturally I was pleased. But that was it! Beyond that he would have seemed importunate, to put it mildly! An intelligent man would have understood that. I promise you, I never felt anything serious for him at all. It was your doing, it was you with your sense of superiority and your concern that made him seem interesting to me. You certainly were jealous, weren't you? Jealous of me who was "quite outside" your social circles… So then I made a point – out of spite – and even though I knew he wasn't worth the trouble – of proving to you that you were right to be frightened of me. And you fell for it completely, right away, like any "common woman". I wouldn't have behaved like that, but you went on telling me, I could see it in everyone's eyes, especially in yours and so what did you expect? You managed to make me believe that I really was "capable of anything". I was completely trapped in that opinion which you all had of me, as a woman "capable of anything". There was no way out. I was even capable of stealing, why not? I would have been a fool not to take advantage. Well, not exactly stealing... let's say taking pleasure in the game... you know I even used to let them examine my cards right in front of me? "Well, one never knows with you..." they'd say... and I would smile... Yes, I was capable of cheating... It's dreadful because – you see – doing something or not doing it is all the same... And then one derives a certain sense of pride from all this... oh yes, a diabolical pride... that brings a certain smile of collusion to the lips of other women, and a certain shamelessness creeps in. That's it, shamelessness! There we are! Look at me. Why don't you leave? All right then, stay. Here we are, two women together. What have you got to offer this man? Go on, tell me. Do something. Show me. I'm quite capable of tearing your clothes to shreds. I'm so certain of him that I can treat you with the utmost contempt here in front of him. You're a poor, miserable, made-up creature... I'm the winner now. Look at me! I can have all the love I want and I can give love too – I can give all my love! And have the love of anybody I want. Anybody!

The imaginary scene disappears with DONATA's *last cry. She instantly recognizes the irony in what she has said. The set abruptly closes in again, all the lights go out except the violet lamp and the two lamps on either side of the mirror. As this happens, a distant sound of wild applause can be heard.* DONATA *slumps in an armchair near the table lamp, with her arms limp and her hand empty, but with her head up as though she were trying to smile in response to that distant applause. She gets up abruptly, and says, opening her arms:*

DONATA: Yes... this is real... no, nothing is real... the only truth is that we have to go on creating... And then perhaps, somehow, we will find ourselves.

CURTAIN

Caps and Bells

Il berretto a sonagli (1917)

Translated by Carlo Ardito

CHARACTERS

CIAMPA, *a clerk*
BEATRICE FIORÌCA
ASSUNTA LA BELLA, *her mother*
FIFÌ LA BELLA, *her brother*
SPANÒ, *a police officer*
LA SARACENA, *old clothes dealer*
FANA, *Beatrice's old retainer*
NINA CIAMPA, *Ciampa's young wife*

A small inland town in Sicily

NOTE ON THE TEXT

Caps and Bells *was first performed in 1917 in Sicilian dialect. An Italian version was published in 1918, but was not staged in that language until 1928.*

Ciampa the clerk is a wronged husband, who will only tolerate his wife's infidelity as long as he is not forced to admit that others believe he is aware of it. Once that line is crossed, he is honour-bound to kill his wife – and her lover, if caught in the act.

The role of Ciampa requires an exceptionally able actor. Many distinguished leading men essayed the part over the years, but it is generally agreed that the finest performances were given by actor and playwright Eduardo de Filippo in his own translation into Neapolitan from 1936 onwards. Pirandello himself, after watching Eduardo in the role, is quoted as having said to him: "Ciampa has waited twenty years to point at you as his true interpreter."

Carlo Ardito

ACT ONE

Living room in the Fiorìca household, lavishly furnished in a provincial style. Main door upstage centre; two doors stage right and left, draped with curtains.

When the curtain rises, BEATRICE *is sitting on the sofa, sobbing.* LA SARACENA *is sitting opposite her, looking cross.* FANA *is standing by.*

FANA (*pointing at her weeping mistress*): Happy now? Aren't you ashamed of the damage you've done? Is this the way to upset the family?

LA SARACENA (*a thick-set, formidable woman, about forty; showy, with a large yellow silk scarf, and a pale-blue silk shawl with long fringes, tight at the waist. She rises and rounds on* FANA): What the devil do you think you're saying? Me? Ashamed? Don't talk rubbish!

BEATRICE (*about thirty, pale, hysterical, blowing hot and cold and continuing to sob*): Pay no attention to her... let her say what she likes.

LA SARACENA: Excuse me: tell her rather that all I did was to carry out a specific order you gave me, no more and no less.

BEATRICE: I don't need to justify myself to her.

FANA: You certainly don't! I'm only a servant here. I know that. But you are required to justify yourself to God – we all have to!

BEATRICE (*angrily*): Out! Back to the kitchen! And mind your own business!

LA SARACENA (*seizing* FANA *by the arm*): Oh no. Not so fast. Wait, please, madam. And you too. We all have souls in the eyes of God, masters and servants. I'll allow no reflections on my character. What about *your* conscience? How can you bear to see your mistress shed tears of blood, suffer the tortures of the damned and say: "It's nothing. It is the will of God. Offer it up to him!" You call that right?

FANA: It is. For those who fear God.

215

BEATRICE: I see! So when a man hurts you, treats you like dirt, that's God's will too, is it?

FANA: No. I say we should offer it up to God, ma'am. You can't grab a man by the scruff of the neck and face him head on! You can't use force with someone stronger than we are! Gently, gently does it. Tact and good manners will bring a man back to his hearth again!

LA SARACENA: Nonsense! If women carried on like that, men would turn us all into doormats!

FANA: That could never apply to my mistress. That master is ever so gentle… and respects her. Gives her everything she asks for. He treats her like a queen.

BEATRICE: Do keep quiet! Gentle, you say. Respectful. And generous. But what does he get up to when he's not at home? What about *my* heart, *my* peace of mind? You're judging his behaviour when he's at home, and are blind to the way he carries on when he's out!

LA SARACENA: Is that what you call conscience? Where I come from it's called hypocrisy. In a nutshell: did you or did you not fetch me from home and bring me here?

FANA: I did as I was told.

LA SARACENA: So did I. "Saracena…" – your mistress's words – "…help me! My husband… and so-and-so… I suspect them… Find out if it's true. It's hell at home. I've got to leave at all costs!" (*To* BEATRICE) Isn't that what you said?

BEATRICE: Yes, yes, and I'm leaving. Immediately. Once and for all!

FANA: Holy Mother of God!

LA SARACENA: Leave the Mother of God alone! A house where jealousy prevails is finished, done for! It's a constant earthquake, you listen to me! And if there were children around…

FANA: That's the real trouble: there are no children.

LA SARACENA: So? Do you want her to die, the poor woman? She wants to get out!

FANA: That's what she says, but look at her crying!

BEATRICE: Because I'm furious, that's why I'm crying! If he were here I'd murder him! Tell me, Saracena, is there a chance of catching them together… tomorrow?

LA SARACENA: Like two birds in their nest. What time is he expected back?

BEATRICE: At ten.

LA SARACENA: Then rest assured that by ten thirty you'll catch them both together, alive and cooing. Lodge a complaint with the Police Inspector. I'll do the rest. Tell me something: is it true that your husband is passing through Palermo on his way to Catania?

BEATRICE: Yes. Why?

LA SARACENA: Well... because... I heard – no. It's nothing...

BEATRICE: Tell me, tell me... What have you heard?

LA SARACENA: A little matter of a present he promised to bring her from Palermo.

BEATRICE: A present? For her?

LA SARACENA: A beautiful necklace, yes. With pendants.

FANA: You're not a woman! You're a witch!

LA SARACENA (*to* BEATRICE): Write out the complaint.

BEATRICE (*consumed with uncertainty*): No... no. It's better if I... oh God, I'm going mad! It's better if we get Inspector Spanò over here. He's a family friend. Owes everything to my father, may he rest in peace. He'll tell me what to do. In fact, you go and fetch him, Saracena, tell him to come and see me.

FANA: Think it over, madam, please! Think of the scandal!

BEATRICE: I don't care.

FANA: I warn you you're courting disaster!

BEATRICE: I'll be rid of him! Rid of him! I'm leaving him! Please go, Saracena, don't let's waste any more time.

FANA (*holding* LA SARACENA *back*): Just a moment. Just a moment. (*To* BEATRICE) Think carefully, please. Have you given any thought to the woman's husband... to Ciampa?

BEATRICE: I've thought of everything, don't you worry, him included. Don't interfere. I know where to send him.

LA SARACENA: Send him... where? There's no need. They'll take care of that, don't you worry. The moment your husband gets back to the office, Ciampa'll turn round and leave of his own accord.

FANA: Who? Ciampa? Are you mad? Are you trying to tell my mistress that Ciampa knows everything and is keeping quiet?

LA SARACENA: You be quiet! You know nothing!

FANA: You're wrong. You're making a big mistake!

217

LA SARACENA: Oh yes? You think it's all like a fireworks display. Bang! Bang! Then it's over? Don't be taken in! He's seen his wife with the finest earrings, four rings on her fingers... tomorrow she'll show off the necklace with pendants. What'll he think? That she paid for them out of her savings? A likely story! When your master's at his desk in the office, where is Ciampa? Out in the street with his head in the air, walking around with nothing to do.

FANA: He follows orders, the poor man. He's sent out on errands, and does as he's told. But everyone knows that whenever he leaves the office, he bolts and bars the door leading to his living quarters.

LA SARACENA: Yes. And the master unlocks it.

FANA: Ciampa's got a great big padlock!

LA SARACENA: The master's got a key to it, too.

BEATRICE (to FANA): Stop it! I told you to get out and stop interfering! (To LA SARACENA) I know how to get rid of Ciampa. I'll send him off this very evening. As a matter of fact... Fana... come here... But for goodness' sake don't let on to him... Can I trust you?

FANA: Can you trust me? I held you in my arms when you were a baby! (Bursts into tears)

BEATRICE: Come, come, stop crying.

FANA: Look: there's your brother... your mother. Let them advise you, they're your own flesh and blood. They won't let you down.

BEATRICE: Stop it, I said. I don't need anybody's advice. Go and fetch Ciampa, this minute! And you, Saracena, get me Inspector Spanò. Tell him I want to see him. Immediately.

LA SARACENA: No. Let's do it the other way round.

BEATRICE: What do you mean?

LA SARACENA: Send her (points at FANA) to get the Inspector. I'll get Ciampa.

BEATRICE (to FANA): Do you know the way to the police station?

FANA: If that's really what you want me to do, I'll find it.

LA SARACENA: Come, come, both of you. There's not going to be a tragedy, believe me. Not a bit of it! (To BEATRICE) All you're going to do is teach him a lesson, that's all. It'll be quite enough. My husband... now my husband... four years ago I kicked him out of the house. Result? He follows me round like a poodle, and daren't leave my side unless I give him my special look – like this! – guaranteed to terrify him out of his wits. Shakes like an aspen leaf, he does! So there – a little lesson, that's all. You'll see. Men! It's a pleasure to watch them with their tail between their legs. I'm off. We're all agreed, then. You've made up your mind.

BEATRICE: Yes, I have. Absolutely.

LA SARACENA: Tomorrow's the day?

BEATRICE: Tomorrow.

LA SARACENA: Then I kiss your hands and I'll go and call Ciampa. (*Begins to make for the upstage door when the doorbell rings loudly*) Someone at the door!

BEATRICE (*to FANA, who goes to answer the door*): Wait. It's probably my brother. If it's him, not a word! (*Makes a sign enjoining silence*)

FANA: I won't say a thing, don't worry. (*Goes out of the room by the upstage door to answer the front door*)

BEATRICE: I've asked him to come specially, so we can arrange Ciampa's departure.

LA SARACENA (*visibly annoyed*): There was no need! When it comes to these things, the fewer people involved the better. Even Fana we could have done without.

BEATRICE: Fana can be trusted, have no fear. As for my brother, let me deal with him. I've got an idea.

FIFÌ LA BELLA *enters upstage centre. He is about twenty-four, elegant, good-looking.*

LA SARACENA (*bowing*): Your servant, sir.

FIFÌ (*regarding her with contempt*): You... here?

LA SARACENA: I was about to leave...

BEATRICE: Yes, you'd better. We're agreed, then. I'll be expecting Ciampa.

LA SARACENA: He'll be here directly. Your servant... (*Goes*)

FIFÌ: Are you having dealings with that hag?

BEATRICE: Me? Well, she's doing something for me.

FIFÌ: Don't you know a lady can't possibly receive that creature without damaging her reputation?

BEATRICE: Oh? Because she knows all about the shameful tricks you men get up to, and you're afraid she'll let on to your wives and mothers?

FIFÌ: Bull's-eye! Go on thinking that and I know where you'll end!

BEATRICE: I know exactly where I'll end. Don't you worry. As far as you are all concerned I'm supposed to sit here quietly, I'm to be kept in the dark about everything that goes on.

FIFÌ: We are on edge today!

BEATRICE: Did you bring the money?

FIFÌ: I have.

BEATRICE: No wonder you're so scathing with me. Remember what you said when you needed the money? "Please, little sister… help me! You're always so good and kind – please save me. I've been gambling. I've lost. Think of the dishonour!" You know perfectly well I was forced to resort to this "hag" no lady can receive without damaging her reputation. I did it for you, since I sent her to Palermo to pawn earrings and a bracelet behind my husband's back.

FIFÌ: I see. You got her here over that business.

BEATRICE: Give me that money. Is that all of it?

FIFÌ (*reaching for his pocketbook*): Not quite.

BEATRICE: I knew it. How much?

FIFÌ: If only you could have waited… not that long… say a fortnight… I can't make out why you're in so much of a hurry.

BEATRICE: It's vital that both earrings and bracelet should be back here tomorrow. I've sent for Ciampa for this very reason: I'm sending him to redeem them right now.

FIFÌ: Did your husband suspect anything? He isn't due till tomorrow.

BEATRICE: That's right. That's the reason.

FIFÌ: I don't get it. Is it absolutely necessary that you display all your finery your husband's return tomorrow?

BEATRICE: Yes it is. You can't imagine the welcome I've in mind for him. You'll see. It'll be quite a party! (*The doorbell rings*) That'll be Ciampa. Give me the money. Is there much missing?

FIFÌ (*taking the money out of his pocketbook*): Here you are. You count it. I'm not sure. I think there's three one-hundred lire notes.

BEATRICE (*counting*): …And one fifty note. One hundred and fifty is missing.

FIFÌ: As I said, if only you'd waited.

BEATRICE: Never mind. I'll make up the difference. You may go now.

FANA (*enters upstage centre*): Ciampa's here. Can he come in?

BEATRICE: Show him in. But wait… come here first. (*Takes her to one side and whispers*) You go straight where I told you.

FANA (*equally soft*): To the Inspector's?

BEATRICE: Tell him I'd like him to come here. If he comes straight away, make him wait in the study. Take the key and go. Be quick.

FANA: Yes, madam. I'll get my wrap and go. (*Goes*)

FIFÌ: Will you tell me what you're up to? What's all this mystery?

BEATRICE: Be quiet. Here's Ciampa.

CIAMPA *enters upstage centre. He is about forty-five, with long, thick hair brushed backwards, somewhat untidily. He has no moustache, but sports broad brush-like sideboards which overrun his cheeks up to his eyes, which sparkle harshly and cruelly, with a hint of insanity. A pen is stuck behind his ear. He wears an old frock coat.*

CIAMPA: I kiss your hands, madam. Sir. Madam, I'm yours to command.

BEATRICE: Always mine to command, dear Ciampa! Always on parade.

CIAMPA: As you say, always on parade… often like Christ on the cross. But in this case "yours to command" means, unless I'm mistaken, that I'm your humble servant.

BEATRICE: You? A servant? We're all masters here, my dear Ciampa. No distinctions between us: you, Fifì here, my husband, *me*, *your wife*… we're all equal. In fact I'm not even sure whether I'm not a little beneath you all.

CIAMPA: What? That's heresy, madam! What are you saying?

FIFÌ: Let her have her say. All women, according to her—

BEATRICE: Not all women, only *certain* women. There are others who know how to sweet-talk you men, how to flatter you… like this. (*Strokes her brother's cheek*) …Now they stand above all others, even if they come from the streets.

CIAMPA: Excuse me, madam. You happened to mention my wife.

BEATRICE: I was generalizing, that's all: Fana, my mother, *me*, *your wife*…

FIFÌ: All women… all equal.

CIAMPA (*to* BEATRICE): Forgive me. (*Turns to* FIFÌ) And you too, sir. But I feel that my wife… even if you're having a general discussion, shouldn't really be brought into it. She's as out of context as Pilate is in the Creed. I am at your service, that's understood, but my wife is perfectly looked after and in her own home. It's my duty to see that she's not talked about, either for or against.

BEATRICE: Are you so jealous you can't even bear to have her mentioned? That's rather overdoing it!

221

CIAMPA: It's a matter of principle with me, where wives, sardines and anchovies are concerned. Sardines and anchovies under glass; wives under lock and key. And here's the key. (*Takes a key out of his pocket and displays it*)

FIFÌ: A splendid principle for my sister.

CIAMPA (*places his hands on* FIFÌ's *chest*): Each to his own, sir.

BEATRICE (*to* FIFÌ): There's always the risk you bolt the door and leave the window open.

CIAMPA: Still, it's the husband's duty to shut the door.

BEATRICE: I never suspected you'd be such a tyrant.

CIAMPA: Me? A tyrant? Never. I like things to be arranged neatly. There is the window. The door I've already shut, of course. Lean out of the window, by all means. But mind no one comes up to me and says: "Ciampa, your wife is about to break her neck trying to jump out of it!" Does this make me a tyrant? Man realizes that a woman needs to take a little air at the window. And a woman recognizes that a man has the duty to lock the door. That's all. You wanted me for some service, madam?

BEATRICE: Fifì, I'm sorry… I've something to discuss with Ciampa.

FIFÌ: You want me to leave just to tell him to…

BEATRICE: I'd sooner not go into it in front of you.

FIFÌ: Why not? You may speak freely. I've paid off my loan.

BEATRICE: I suppose so. Well… listen, Ciampa: I need you. I know I can trust you. You're more than a member of the family. I am grateful.

CIAMPA: I am very devoted to you all.

BEATRICE: I know you are. And I am very grateful for that… and *everything else*.

CIAMPA: I must warn you that I'm not that slow.

BEATRICE: I beg your pardon?

CIAMPA: I've a feeling… the way you're talking this morning… you sound as if you've been eating lemons.

BEATRICE: Lemons? Why, never. Honey. I've had honey for breakfast. Anyway, you were saying?

CIAMPA: Dear God, it's not words I'm talking about. We're not children! You're trying to tell me something the words aren't saying.

BEATRICE: What? What do you mean? If you've got a guilty conscience…

CIAMPA (*turns to* FIFÌ): I appeal to you, sir. What does she mean by saying that I'm more than a member of the family? I tell her I'm devoted to the family, and she adds: "…and I'm grateful for *everything else*". What am I to make of that *everything else*? What does she mean by saying that we're all masters here, without any distinction, my wife included? I haven't got a guilty conscience. But she's trying to get at me. Why?

FIFÌ: She's not trying to get at you. She's against everyone. It's a serious business.

BEATRICE: Will someone tell me what I'm supposed to have said that's so terrible? Can't one open one's mouth any more?

CIAMPA: That's not it. Would you like me to explain what the matter is? The instrument's out of tune.

BEATRICE: Instrument? What instrument?

CIAMPA: What I call the social spring. I must point out that we all possess three watch springs, as it were, in our heads. (*His right hand clenched, with his thumb and forefinger close together as if they were holding a watch key or winder, he mimes a watch-winding gesture first on his right temple, then in the middle of his forehead, and finally on his left temple*) They have separate functions: one serious, one social, one insane. We need the social spring above all, as we are social animals – that's why it's placed right in the centre of our forehead. Without it, dear lady, we'd all devour one another like so many savage dogs. That wouldn't do. (*Turns to* FIFÌ) I'd eat you up, for example. And that's not allowed. So what do I do? I give the winder a little turn, walk up to you all smiles and put out my outstretched hand: "I am delighted to see you, my dear fellow!" (*To* BEATRICE) You see what I mean? But at some point the waters might look troubled, in need of the proverbial oil. Therefore I first wind up the serious spring, then set about clearing matters up, give my reasons, state things plainly, without frills, as is my duty. If that produces no results, then I give the insane spring a good turn… but then I lose my head… and God help us all!

FIFÌ: Excellent! Splendid! Bravo, Ciampa!

CIAMPA (*to* BEATRICE): I think that you, madam, begging your pardon, must have given several turns, for reasons best known to yourself – which are none of my business – to either the serious or the insane springs, which are causing your head to buzz like a swarm of hornets! Meanwhile, you'd like to talk to me by means of the social spring. Result? The words you utter flow from the social spring, but they're out of tune. Am I making myself clear? Be advised by me, stop using it. Ask your brother to leave... (*Approaches* FIFÌ) I beg you, sir, you'd better leave...

BEATRICE: Why? Let him stay.

FIFÌ (*to* CIAMPA): You want to deny me the pleasure of listening to you?

CIAMPA (*pointedly, to* BEATRICE): Because you should now, right there – will you allow me? – on your right temple... wind up the serious spring and have a private talk with me, a serious talk, for your own good and mine.

BEATRICE: I'm being serious, too. I'd like a serious talk.

CIAMPA: Very well, then. Here I am. But let me say this though, I must warn you that unless you wind up the serious spring in time, you might well wind up the insane one, or cause others to do so.

FIFÌ: I've a feeling it's you, Ciampa, who is off key at the moment.

BEATRICE: I think so too. I've felt it for some time. I don't understand...

CIAMPA: Please forgive me. (*With a sudden outburst, to* FIFÌ) My father's forehead was often split open.

FIFÌ: How does your father come into this?

CIAMPA: When he was a youngster, my father, rather foolishly, instead of protecting his head, when he stumbled and fell... preferred to save his hands. So when he tripped and as he fell, do you know what he did? He instinctively put his hands behind his back and fell flat on his face. No wonder he split his forehead. But I, sir, fall down with my hands well forwards. Why? Because I'd sooner my forehead were unharmed, free of all marks or encumbrances.

FIFÌ: That's all very well, but if you don't know the reason why my sister sent for you, why put your hands forwards, so to speak?

CIAMPA: I take your point. Very well: I'll disable the serious spring and call into service the social. (*To* BEATRICE, *bowing*) I'm yours to command.

BEATRICE: I'd like you to leave tonight for Palermo.

CIAMPA (*starting*): For Palermo? How?... The master returns tomorrow.

BEATRICE: Do you think he'll need your services the moment he's back?

CIAMPA: Naturally. Otherwise why should he employ me in the office?

BEATRICE: I know he pays you to guard the safe, and consequently gives you living accommodation in the rooms next to the office.

CIAMPA: That's not the only reason. You mustn't belittle my services. I am his clerk. I write.

FIFÌ (*to his sister*): Note, my dear, the pen behind his ear.

CIAMPA: Just so. It's my badge of office. Just as the innkeeper displays a vine leaf and a jug – that's his sign. I'm a clerk: I carry a pen.

FIFÌ: A clerk and a journalist, no less!

CIAMPA: Don't mention journalism! That's just a hobby of mine, something I dabble in at night, in my spare time. I write on behalf of my employer: I keep his ledgers, I look after the business. You don't imagine we just pass the time of day at the office, telling each other stories? I'm not just an onlooker. Has your husband ever complained about me?

BEATRICE: What? My husband? Complained about you? Never! He won't hear a word against you.

CIAMPA: So. You'd like me to go to Palermo. Tonight.

FIFÌ: Why not? I see no harm in it.

BEATRICE: I'll tell my husband I've sent you. Am I not allowed to send you on a special errand?

CIAMPA: On an errand? But of course you are. You are the mistress here. (*To* FIFÌ) Can you imagine how I feel at the prospect of taking a breath of fresh air in a big city like Palermo? Why, that'll be heaven on earth! I am choking out here. I can hardly breathe! But the moment I step out into the avenues of a big city... why, I'm in paradise! Ideas flow freely within me! The blood courses blissfully through my veins! Ah, if only I'd been born in a city, somewhere on the mainland... God knows what I might have become!

FIFÌ: An academic... a member of parliament... a minister... a...

CIAMPA: King! Let's not fantasize, though. (*To* FIFÌ) After all, we're puppets, aren't we? The divine spark enters into us and pulls the strings. I'm a puppet, you're a puppet... we're all puppets. It should be enough for us all to be puppets as instruments of God's will. No, sir! Each one of us turns himself into a puppet of his own accord, into the puppet he could be or believes himself to be. That's when the rows begin. (*Turns to* BEATRICE) Because you see, dear lady, every puppet demands respect, not so much for what he really believes himself to be, but for the part he plays in public. Let's be honest with ourselves: no one is happy with the role he plays. If each of us were faced with the image of the puppet he really is, he'd spit in its face. But from others... ah, from others he asks for, nay demands respect. For example (*addressing* BEATRICE), within these walls, madam, you are a wife, true?

BEATRICE: A wife... well, yes... at least...

CIAMPA: One can tell immediately you're not happy with your lot. Nevertheless, as the wife you evidently are, you wish to be respected.

BEATRICE: Naturally. And how! I demand it – God help those who refuse it!

CIAMPA: You see? Just as I said. And everyone's the same. As far as you are concerned, if you knew my respected employer the Cavaliere Fiorìca only as a friend, you might get on with him in perfect amity. The actual war is waged between the two puppets: the husband-puppet and the wife-puppet. Within they tear out each other's hair. But outside, in the public glare they walk hand in hand: both of them having activated the social spring, also employed by us bystanders: we raise our hats, smile, make way for the happy pair. And the two puppets glow with pride and satisfaction.

FIFÌ (*laughing*): You're a character, my dear Ciampa, you really are!

CIAMPA: This is life, my dear sir! Madam: it's vital to keep the respect of others. We should hold our puppet high – whatever its nature – so that everyone reverently raises his hat. Have I made myself clear? But let's get down to business. What do you want me to do in Palermo?

BEATRICE (*shaken, with an abstracted look*): In Palermo, did you say?...

FIFÌ (*drawing her attention to the matter being discussed*): Wake up, Beatrice.

BEATRICE: What? Oh... I thought I heard Fana come in...

CIAMPA: Have you changed your mind?

BEATRICE: Certainly not. (*To* FIFÌ) Where is the money?

FIFÌ: Over there, on that table.

BEATRICE: Here it is. Now, Ciampa, here's three hundred and fifty lire. (*Hands the money to Ciampa*)

CIAMPA: What do you want me to do with it?

BEATRICE: Wait. I'll get another hundred and fifty from the other room... and two tickets.

CIAMPA (*looking at* FIFÌ *with some severity*): Pawn tickets?

FIFÌ: That's right. And don't look at me like that!

CIAMPA: Me? I was not, sir! I'm waiting for instructions.

BEATRICE: It's a question of redeeming the items. A pair of earrings and a bracelet, in two cases. I'll get the tickets. (*Goes right out*)

FIFÌ: My sister pawned the stuff to do me a favour. Her husband doesn't know.

CIAMPA: Bear in mind, sir, that he's my employer.

FIFÌ: I can be quite open about it. I've repaid the loan to my sister. And she wants the jewels back by tomorrow.

CIAMPA: Tomorrow? By tomorrow? And what excuse will she give her husband for sending me out of town on the eve of his return?

FIFÌ: Have no fear. Women are never short of excuses.

CIAMPA: Surely he's been away a number of days… she could have sent me earlier, so he wouldn't hear of it at all.

FIFÌ: As a matter of fact I've only just returned the money.

CIAMPA: I smell a rat. I suspect your sister is up to something.

FIFÌ: I tend to agree with you. She's acting a little strangely. What can it be? Maybe it's the old old story – jealousy.

CIAMPA: Is that why she's sending me to Palermo?

BEATRICE *enters, looking flustered, as if emerging from a disquieting argument.*

BEATRICE: Right. Here I am. Here I am.

FIFÌ: What's the matter now?

BEATRICE (*attempting to compose herself*): Why… nothing's the matter.

FIFÌ: You look to me… a bit…

BEATRICE (*now at ease*): It's nothing, don't worry. I couldn't find the tickets at first and I was worried. (*Hands* CIAMPA *the tickets*) Here are the tickets. And the rest of the money.

CIAMPA: Very well. But how are you going to justify my absence to your husband? Have you thought of that?

BEATRICE: I've thought of everything! (*Shows a roll of banknotes she has been holding in her other hand*) You see? This is for your fare, and another hundred and fifty lire.

FIFÌ: Well, well, look at those banknotes!

CIAMPA: As long as we have banknotes…

BEATRICE: So? What do you mean? Out with it! (*To her brother*) It's my own money. Part of my savings. (*Turning to* CIAMPA) You were saying… as long as we have banknotes?…

CIAMPA: All I meant was that the money enables you to pull strings and send another puppet all the way to Palermo.

BEATRICE: I take no pleasure in doing that, I assure you. You know perfectly well why I'm sending you. Now then, with the extra one hundred and fifty lire I want you to buy me a necklace, Ciampa – and that will give me pleasure! Shall I tell you what kind of necklace it is I want? One with pendants.

CIAMPA: I see.

BEATRICE: With pendants. I'll tell my husband that I've seen a friend of mine wear the same necklace and I liked it so much that... well, it's just a whim of mine. My husband will understand.

CIAMPA: Frankly I don't know whether I'm competent enough to select...

BEATRICE: Don't worry. If you can't manage it, just say you couldn't find one when you get back.

CIAMPA: But then why give me the money at all?

BEATRICE: Because I'd really be very glad if you'd get me the necklace. I'd like one that's *exactly the same* and *bought by you*.

CIAMPA: I don't get it. Bought by me? What do you want from me? Exactly the same as what? I've no idea what it looks like.

BEATRICE: I'll tell you. Go to our jewellers, Mercurio. I know my friend's necklace was definitely bought at their shop. Go there and you'll find it. I'd like you to leave as soon as possible.

CIAMPA: I'm stunned. Stunned? I'm petrified, I tell you.

FIFÌ: Admit though, it's a marvellous excuse she's thought of.

BEATRICE: It is, even if I say so myself. Can you think of a nicer surprise for my husband? When he sees me tomorrow, wearing the necklace, why... There's a train leaving at six. You haven't much time.

FIFÌ (*consulting his watch*): He's got an hour.

CIAMPA: A couple of minutes is all I need. I'll lock up the office, secure the door to my rooms with lock and bolt, and go to the station. (*Addressing* BEATRICE) However, I'd like you to make use of the hour that's left before the train is due to leave.

BEATRICE: How?

CIAMPA: You might like to pause and think things over.

BEATRICE: What is there to think about?

FIFÌ: Let's make a move, Ciampa. I'll come with you. Au revoir, Beatrice.

BEATRICE: Goodbye.

CIAMPA (*to* BEATRICE): Let me remind you once again of the case of my father, who failed to use his hands for protection.

BEATRICE: Not again!

CIAMPA: I'm on my way. Good day. (*Having reached the door, he retraces his steps*) Madam, would you like me to bring you my wife?

BEATRICE: Your wife? Here? (*Laughs scornfully*) That's all we need! That really is a good one! Why?

CIAMPA: For my own peace of mind.

BEATRICE: Really! Are you mad? What would I do here, with your wife?

CIAMPA: Naturally, a lady like you would have little in common with... still, just as I said, for my own peace of mind.

BEATRICE: But you'll have her under lock and key, in accordance with your principles! Isn't there a steel bar as well?

CIAMPA: And a padlock, madam. I'll bring you the keys.

BEATRICE: There's no need for that. Keep your keys.

CIAMPA: Sorry, but no. If you refuse to have me bring my wife here, allow me at least to leave the keys with you. I'm not going to budge.

BEATRICE: Oh, very well. But don't waste any more time.

CIAMPA (*to* FIFÌ): Let's go, then. (*Begins to leave. At the door, turns again.*) You were saying... with pendants?

BEATRICE (*impatiently*): Not again! Yes! With pendants.

CIAMPA: I kiss your hands. (*Goes with* FIFÌ)

BEATRICE *rushes to the door on the right.*

BEATRICE: Inspector... come in... come in... at last!

Inspector SPANÒ *enters. He is about forty, the typical comic country policeman, bearded and generally hirsute. He gives himself heroic airs, and now and then, as he talks, shows the depth of his bigotry.*

SPANÒ: I am astonished. As if struck by lightning. You know the kind of lightning I'm referring to... followed by a deafening clap of thunder right at my feet!

BEATRICE: We've little time for small talk, Inspector. We must agree on a plan. Imagine: he wanted to bring his wife here and leave her with me!

SPANÒ: His wife? He... Here?

BEATRICE: What better proof do we need? What have we come to?

SPANÒ: Calm yourself. Yes. Absolute calm is of the essence.

BEATRICE: How can I? I want to give him a lesson he'll never forget. In front of witnesses.

SPANÒ: Of course. Of course. But the consequences... have you thought of the consequences?

BEATRICE: You mean... I'll have to seek a separation. I am ready for that. But not on an amicable basis, as they say. No. First I'll revile him in front of everyone, then we'll split up. It must never be said that I was in the wrong. I want a scandal – a big scandal. The whole community must be made aware of the kind of man the Cavaliere Fiorìca is... this man they all cherish and respect! I'll lodge the complaint with you officially. You're an officer of the law and can't object.

SPANÒ: Yes, madam... of course... if you lodge a complaint...

BEATRICE: I'll draw it up now. Tell me how to do it and I'll get down to it.

SPANÒ: No, no. That's not possible. You want me to tell you how to write it out?

BEATRICE (*coquettishly and with a hint of irritability*): Won't you help me? Inspector... won't you help me?

SPANÒ: Naturally I want to help you. But bear in mind I'm a friend of the family as well.

BEATRICE: Aren't you on the side of justice?

SPANÒ: Yes... well... I'm on the side of the law. It is my sworn duty to be impartial. And I go forwards with my head held high, even in the presence of God Almighty. But as you know I honour the memory of your late sainted father, who was a father to me too. You know he loved me, madam. The things he taught me! On the other hand here's this... the question of these little sins of the flesh... hardly mortal sins...

BEATRICE: Little sins? Is that what you call them?

SPANÒ: Let's call them... diversions, if you like. I speak as a friend.

BEATRICE: As *his* friend?

SPANÒ: Yes. I mean: no! I'm your friend as well...

BEATRICE: I like that: diversions. Sweet, charming, harmless diversions! You call yourself a man of justice? Is that the way you give a helping hand to a weak, wronged woman who cannot defend herself? I want to lodge a complaint. Now. This instant. How do I set about it?

SPANÒ: The complaint itself is pretty standard. It's the investigation that follows that's the problem. Not at all simple. It's all most delicate and fraught with difficulties. I shall have to carry out inquiries unnoticed... study the lie of the land. You've no idea... Clues... proof...

BEATRICE: There'll be no need for any of that, Inspector. You know Saracena?

SPANÒ: She's one of our informants.

BEATRICE: Better still. Send for her. She'll give you chapter and verse.

SPANÒ: Madam, I've already talked to her. We are always one step ahead, believe me. Two doors are involved: one into the office, the other, on the opposite side, leading to the two rooms next to the office, that is to say Ciampa's living quarters. Now then, is there a door in between, yes or no? Between the office and Ciampa's two rooms? Of course there is. And Ciampa usually locks it up from the office, with bar and bolts and padlock, right? What next? I raid the place with a couple of officers, both sides at the same time. Result? They won't open the door till they have secured the middle door, and by the time we gain access, one'll be in the office, the other in the private section.

BEATRICE: Can nothing be done?

SPANÒ: Ah, there comes into play the art of successful policing, madam. Something can and will be done! Supposing, madam, you had the key to the office—

BEATRICE (*cutting in*): I have! That is, Ciampa is going to let me have it right now, before he leaves. I'm waiting for him.

SPANÒ (*stunned*): What? Ciampa's going to let you have the key?

BEATRICE: Yes. I didn't even have to ask him for it. He insisted... he forced me to accept. As a matter of fact I didn't want it at first.

SPANÒ: I don't understand. No. It must mean that... you can be sure that Ciampa hasn't the least suspicion. None!

BEATRICE: What are you saying? Why then did he want to bring his wife here?

SPANÒ: Because... dear me... because the whole village knows... if you'll allow me...

BEATRICE: That I'm jealous? Is that it? And using the fact I'm jealous, my husband's always done as he pleased... I'm going to show them all whether or not my jealousy is justified! You say that once we have the key we're home and dry? You get into the office before he's had time to secure the middle door and...

SPANÒ (*smiles commiseratingly*): Me? Open the office door? Yes, then what happens? Do you think your husband is so careless as to pay the lady a visit having taken the naive precaution of locking the office door? He'll have barred it as well. So where am I now? How do I open a door barred from the inside? First I utter my warning: "Open up, in the name of the law!"… followed by various prescribed cautions… Then I proceed to break the door down… While all this is going on, the Cavaliere will have had ample time to lock and bolt the central door. Madam, if that's all there was to policing, I'd be the happiest inspector in the force.

BEATRICE: Oh my God! What are we going to do?

SPANÒ: What indeed… Now… Your husband gets in at ten tomorrow. Very well. I'll tell you what we do. One of my men will be in hiding in the office… in the cubbyhole where the Cavaliere stores the duplicator… let's say half an hour before his arrival… that is to say… (*with the air of a conjurer producing a rabbit out of a hat*)… at half-past nine! That's it. Caught on the wing!

BEATRICE (*triumphantly*): Well done, Inspector! Bravo! And now, please help me with the written complaint. (*The doorbell rings*)

SPANÒ (*with a knowing air*): There's someone at the door, unless I'm mistaken.

BEATRICE: Right again! It'll be Ciampa, with the key. You'd better disappear, in there. (*Points to the door on the right*)

SPANÒ: We'll catch them in full flight! (*Goes out right*)

CIAMPA (*behind the curtain of the upstage door, carrying an overnight case*): May I come in?

BEATRICE: Come in, come in, Ciampa. (*Registers surprise and indignation as* CIAMPA *enters together with his wife*) What's this?

CIAMPA: I've brought my wife.

BEATRICE (*enraged*): Take her back, take her back this minute!

CIAMPA: Let me explain…

BEATRICE: I'm not going to listen! Off with her, now! I won't have her here!

CIAMPA: But madam… my wife is clean… modest…

BEATRICE: I'm sure she's perfectly clean… and modest, naturally! But I won't have her here. (*Turns to* CIAMPA'*s wife*) I am surprised at you, daring to come here with your husband… you don't belong here!

NINA (*she is about thirty, more fastidious than modest. She dresses neatly, aiming at a ladylike effect: elegant shoes, silk shawl, earrings, rings.*

She answers softly but clearly, her eyes downturned): It was my husband who ordered me to come.

CIAMPA (*jubilant*): Just so!

BEATRICE: You could have saved yourself the journey. I specifically told your husband he was not to bring you.

NINA (*her eyes still lowered, answers in a clear voice*): I was not to know that, madam.

CIAMPA: Indeed she did not.

BEATRICE: You've trained her well, haven't you?

CIAMPA: No, madam. She's telling you the truth, quietly and in all modesty – as she should. I alone am responsible for bringing her here. You won't have her?

BEATRICE: I thought I'd made it abundantly clear!

CIAMPA: You could keep her in the kitchen. Or in the coal cellar. She could sleep under the kitchen range, with the cat.

BEATRICE: Are you set on provoking me? Don't make me say what should be left unsaid.

CIAMPA: Say it, say it! Out with it. I wish you would!

BEATRICE: Go. Just go. That's all!

CIAMPA: Very well. You won't have her. That's established. I've brought her here and you refuse to keep her. That's also established. Therefore, here are the keys. I'm on my way. Remember that now I am in your hands. (*Hands over the keys. Then he approaches his wife and pretends to wind up an imaginary spring on her forehead.*) Wait, Nina: social spring activated. A little curtsy, eyes suitably averted and straight home!

NINA (*bowing slightly*): Your servant.

CIAMPA: Excellent! (*Follows his wife up to the door. By the door he turns her round and addresses* BEATRICE, *pretending to wind up the serious spring on his right temple.*) If you'd care to open…

BEATRICE: I'm opening nothing!

CIAMPA: Then keep everything shut tight!

CURTAIN

ACT TWO

The next day.

BEATRICE (*angrily, her hair dishevelled, is standing by the door on the left, yelling at* FANA *somewhere off left*): It doesn't matter! Bring it here, now! I've got to be out of the house by this evening! Away from this wretched place!

The doorbell rings.

FANA (*enters left, laden with clothes*): Holy Mother of God, who could that be?

BEATRICE: Go and answer it. If it's the Inspector, show him in and tell him to wait and be patient. I can't receive him like this.

BEATRICE *goes out right.* FANA, *still carrying the heap of clothes and puffing, goes out through the upstage centre door to answer the door. Shortly after we hear voices off.* ASSUNTA LA BELLA *enters, followed by* FIFÌ LA BELLA, *who has seized* FANA's *arm and is shaking her vigorously. Mother and son are clearly agitated.*

ASSUNTA (*rushes out towards the right door, then crosses the stage to the left, shouting*): Beatrice! Beatrice! Where is she? Where is she? Beatrice! (*Goes out left, still shouting*)

FANA (*attempting to disengage herself from* FIFÌ): Why are you cross with me?

FIFÌ (*still shaking her angrily*): Because it was your duty to come to me and warn me!

ASSUNTA (*enters left*): Where is my daughter? Tell me where she is! Beatrice! Beatrice!

BEATRICE (*enters right at the summons and falls into her mother's arms*): Mother! Mother! (*She bursts into tears*)

ASSUNTA: Beatrice, what have you done? You're ruined!

235

FANA (*still trying to shake off* FIFÌ): It was entirely her own idea. She won't listen to anyone. I said it to her many times – haven't I, madam? I said: "Talk to your brother. He's a man. But first seek your mother's advice!"

ASSUNTA: How could you keep it all from me, your own mother! How could you go to such lengths without telling a soul!

FIFÌ (*seizing his sister by the arm away from her mother*): What's the use of tears now? Are you aware the whole town is seething with rumours?

ASSUNTA: They've arrested him, did you know? They've arrested him!

FANA: The master? Mother of God!

ASSUNTA: And they've arrested *her*.

FANA: Ciampa's wife as well?

BEATRICE: Both of them? Hurrah! I'm delighted! Good! Exactly as I planned.

ASSUNTA: What are you saying, Beatrice…

FIFÌ: The shame of it all. The scandal.

BEATRICE: Yes, yes! The scandal. The shame: his shame!

FIFÌ: Your shame, too! What do you think you're going to get out of this fine mess?

BEATRICE: I will tell you, since you ask. This: (*takes a deep breath of relief and exhales*) I can breathe again now. I've taught him the lesson he deserved. And I'm free now! Free!

FIFÌ: Free? You're mad, that's what you are! You're free to hide in my house, and never show your face in public again. You call that free? You'll have no status…

BEATRICE: I don't care. As long as I don't have to set eyes on him again. I was getting ready to leave. I've been packing since last night.

FIFÌ: Don't forget I was here yesterday. Was it that witch I found you plotting with yesterday?

FANA: Yes, yes – she was the one. The very person.

ASSUNTA: Who are you talking about?

FANA: Saracena.

ASSUNTA: My God! How could you, Beatrice? How could you have dealings with a… creature like that? (*To* FIFÌ) Didn't you suspect anything?

FIFÌ: I certainly never suspected she'd go that far.

FANA: They sent me to fetch Inspector Spanò...

FIFÌ: Spanò?

ASSUNTA: Inspector Spanò? How could you?

FIFÌ (*to* FANA): Did I hear you say Inspector Spanò?...

ASSUNTA (*to* BEATRICE): You mean to tell me that Inspector Spanò – who owes everything to your father – allowed you to go through with it, without advising you against it?

FIFÌ: You're such an innocent, Mother. He can't have believed his luck when he saw the chance to put one over his betters! Don't you understand?

ASSUNTA: To think I've lived to see such shame heaped upon the women of our family!

FANA (*to* ASSUNTA): You've always been known as a paragon of prudence by one and all... Never a word out of place.

ASSUNTA: And yet I could tell you things, Fana, you know that.

FANA: The world is not what it was, madam.

ASSUNTA (*to* BEATRICE): Why didn't you think of me, daughter? I am an old woman. I can't take these blows. I'll probably be dead by tomorrow... Only God knows how I'm feeling just now...

FIFÌ: Calm down, Mother. Calm down, or I don't know what I'll do! She wanted to get herself into a mess – let her get out of it!

ASSUNTA: Oh yes? Have you forgotten she's my daughter? Your sister? What a thing to say!

FIFÌ: Now she thinks she's my sister. I was here, with her, yesterday. What can we do? All we can do is take her home with us, because she clearly can't stay here with her husband!

BEATRICE: Who wants to stay here?

The doorbell rings. They all start in anticipation.

ASSUNTA (*dismayed*): Who could that be?

BEATRICE: I'm not afraid of anyone!

FIFÌ (*to* FANA): Go and answer it. Don't worry: I'm here.

FANA (*to* FIFÌ): Come with me, sir, please. I'm scared.

FIFÌ (*to his mother and sister*): Go into the other room, both of you. (*To* FANA) Don't make a fuss. Answer the door.

ASSUNTA: Come, come with me, Beatrice... (*Goes out right with* BEATRICE)

237

FIFÌ (*now alone, faces the door upstage centre.* FANA *opens it, followed by* INSPECTOR SPANÒ): Ah, it's you, Inspector.

SPANÒ: Always at your service, sir.

FIFÌ: And a fine service you've done us, Inspector. The whole family has reason to be grateful to you.

SPANÒ: You're being unfair, sir.

FIFÌ: Am I? Was that the way to treat a family who – let's not mince words – did so much for you?

SPANÒ: That's exactly why I'm telling you you're being unfair. I am deeply hurt! Surely you realize I am a public servant!

FIFÌ: Thank you very much. Don't I know it! Is it a friend I am talking to? You came here—

SPANÒ (*cutting in*): ...At your wife's request!

FIFÌ: ...Be that as it may... and accepted a written complaint?

SPANÒ: Accepted? Wait... I'm cut to the quick, sir. In the first place I did all I could to dissuade her. But she – where is she? She could tell you... I did all I could to stop her.

FIFÌ: You might have checked with me first.

SPANÒ: She'd put her signature to the complaint already. What could I do?

FIFÌ: You could have made her withdraw it.

SPANÒ: All I can say then is that you don't know your own sister. Dear God, she threatened that unless I cooperated she'd take it straight to the Commissioner and tell him that I refused to... ah, here she is... (ASSUNTA *and* BEATRICE *enter right.* SPANÒ *rushes to kiss* ASSUNTA's *hand, who refuses the advance.*) Please, please let me kiss your hand... (*Turns to* BEATRICE) And you, madam, please tell your brother—

ASSUNTA (*interrupting*): It's no use, my dear Inspector... (*Turns to* FIFÌ) It's no use at all to go on pretending...

BEATRICE: Frankly, I think the Inspector is right.

SPANÒ (*to* FIFÌ): You see?

BEATRICE: I alone was responsible. No one else.

SPANÒ (*to* FIFÌ): What did I tell you? That was gospel truth you've just heard. How can you hold me responsible, sir, or (*addressing* ASSUNTA) you, dear lady. I worship you as if you were my own mother. You see? You see what you've reduced me to? I'm crying, sir, yes, crying because if I'm at fault at all it's due to... an excess of friendship!

You can't imagine how difficult it is for me to carry out my filthy duties – excuse the expression, madam – in this town of ours. Forgive me, but how could I possibly dare apprehend the Cavaliere myself? Do you know what I did? I made matters even worse. Blame me for that, sir, if you like. You'd be quite justified.

FIFÌ: I've no idea what it is you did. What else have you done? Tell me.

SPANÒ: The fact is... as I couldn't possibly... bring myself to make the arrest myself... I entrusted the task to someone else... my fellow officer Logatto. He's a stranger... (*with a hint of contempt*) from Calabria. And what did he do, the blockhead?

FIFÌ: Don't tell me: he arrested them both, my brother-in-law and the lady.

BEATRICE: He did his duty, you mean. He acted as he was meant to.

ASSUNTA: Do be quiet, Beatrice. You don't know what you're saying!

FIFÌ: Were they caught together? Go on, out with it!

SPANÒ: Well... yes and no... together and yet not together... That is... not quite in the act... Now, you'll admit that's some consolation. In fact I'd go so far as to say that with the evidence so far available, nothing conclusive can be proved. Nothing at all!

FIFÌ: In that case... why were they arrested?

SPANÒ: Why? Because I wasn't there, that's why! Because that jackass from... Calabria... was in charge! I admit that that was entirely my fault, and I shall live to regret it. But have no fear, sir, the Cavaliere will be released immediately, tonight! I promise and swear it to you! Or my name is not Alfio Spanò!

FIFÌ: You'd better tell me the whole story, from beginning to end.

SPANÒ: Very well. This is what happened. My wretched colleague, using the key obtained from Mrs Beatrice, let himself into the office and hid in the cubbyhole next to the office. Now, when the other officers knocked at the front door of Ciampa's rooms, and asked to be let in in the name of the law etc... the Cavaliere – as soon as the lady opened up – the Cavaliere made as if to open the connecting door with the office—.

BEATRICE (*triumphantly*): There you are! You see? So he was in Ciampa's rooms. He's opened the connecting door!

SPANÒ (*baffled*): Yes... but...

BEATRICE: How could he have opened it, if Ciampa had locked it and brought me the key? That's your proof.

SPANÒ (*recovering*): No. I'm afraid that's no proof at all.

BEATRICE: Why not?

SPANÒ: Let me explain. It's an English lock. Two keys are always provided.

BEATRICE: Two keys, fine! One with Ciampa, the other in my husband's pocket.

SPANÒ: May I proceed? According to the verbal disposition, Cavaliere Fiorìca stated that having just detrained from Catania, and unable to make out why Ciampa was not at his desk, and furthermore needing to freshen up after the journey – I sympathize with the poor gentleman – and in addition wishing to take sight of the correspondence received in his absence – let me remind you: these are the very words of the deposition – he says he knocked at the door to ask Ciampa's wife whether he could possibly wash his hands.

BEATRICE (*laughing stridently*): His hands... Wash his hands indeed! Just fancy that!

SPANÒ: Yes, his hands. The poor gentleman wanted to open his correspondence.

FIFÌ: Pay no attention to my sister, Inspector. Go on.

SPANÒ: That's when she... Ciampa's wife that is... when she slipped him the other key under the door.

BEATRICE: Fancy that! Under the door, really? How convenient.

SPANÒ (*continuing*): It was in fact proved conclusively, madam, that there is sufficient clearance between the door and the floor for the key to be slipped under the door from one side to the other. Moreover the Cavaliere was found to be in his shirtsleeves, in other words decently clad.

BEATRICE: Oh yes? What about her? How was she... dressed?

SPANÒ: Well now... well... she was...

BEATRICE: Say it! Say it! After all it's all in the deposition, isn't it?

SPANÒ: I can definitely tell you that she was not wearing a blouse.

BEATRICE: She must have been naked. Was she naked?

SPANÒ: Of course not! What are you implying? What I meant was that she was wearing more than just a blouse... A skirt *and* a blouse: you know the kind of clothes women wear about the house... women of the people, I mean... at this time of year. What with the heat... I swear to you I'm slightly perspiring myself... She was properly dressed, I assure you! A slightly plunging neckline, granted... short sleeves... a summer blouse that is...

BEATRICE: So as long as you didn't find them completely naked—

ASSUNTA (*interrupting*): I forbid you to talk like this! Is that my daughter speaking?

FIFÌ: Shame on you! And in front of a man! (*Points to* SPANÒ)

BEATRICE: You call that a man?

ASSUNTA: Beatrice!!

BEATRICE: Let's all pretend then! Let's pretend it never happened. Let's sweep it all under the carpet. The shame is in talking about it, not in the actual act.

FIFÌ: I'm not quite clear about one thing, Inspector. Why were they both arrested if the accusations proved groundless?

SPANÒ: I was coming to that. The woman was arrested owing to her... *excessively* plunging neckline, you understand... that amounts to disturbing the peace. As for the Cavaliere... Well, picture the scene: the moment they set about arresting him he lost his control. He was furious. Had I been present I'd have understood and overlooked his outburst. He could have slapped me about and I'd have put up with it, out of friendship. But my colleague from that benighted province of Calabria... put his foot down and apprehended him for resisting arrest. Have no fear, sir: he'll be released. Tonight! And God help my colleague if he doesn't shut up. I'll fix him, I promise you! I'll fix him!

FIFÌ: In other words, you're telling me no offence was committed.

SPANÒ: None. A thorough search was made, including the suitcase and the jacket the Cavaliere had taken off.

BEATRICE: His jacket, too? What about his briefcase? Tell me, didn't they find by any chance a necklace – with pendants – which he had promised her as a gift from Palermo?

FIFÌ: Would that be why you wanted Ciampa to get you an identical necklace?

BEATRICE: Yes. (*To* SPANÒ) Was such a necklace found during your search?

SPANÒ: Forgive me, madam, but who mentioned such a necklace to you? Saracena?

FANA: That's it! She's the culprit.

SPANÒ: I know all about it, of course. She mentioned it to me. It's all nonsense, and this is how it started: Ciampa's wife is forever bickering with her neighbours, who make fun of her because of all the rings she wears. Well, she bragged that one of these days she'd surprise them all by appearing on her balcony looking like Our Lady and wearing a huge necklace – with pendants! That's all there is to the story. Would you really like to know what was found in the Cavaliere's suitcase? A prayer book. A small, beautiful prayer book, bound in ivory-tinted leather, with gilt pages.

ASSUNTA: You see, Beatrice? It was meant for you.

SPANÒ: Wait. That is not all. We also found a box of candied almonds.

ASSUNTA (*to* BEATRICE): Your favourites!

FANA: Haven't I always said he treats you like a queen?

FIFÌ: Ungrateful wretch!

BEATRICE *falls tearfully into her mother's arms, repentant and highly emotional.*

SPANÒ (*evidently pleased with the effect he has produced, nods and winks at* FIFÌ): I think it would be prudent, sir, if your sister were not at home when her husband returns. I am hoping to release him before the evening is out.

ASSUNTA: An excellent idea.

FIFÌ: We'll take her home with us.

SPANÒ: For a few days, at least. We must sympathize with him. The poor man is furious and is threatening all kinds of mischief.

FIFÌ: He's right. Absolutely right. I don't know what I'd do in his place!

SPANÒ: It'll all blow over. You'll see. Give him a few days, he'll be back to normal. He'll be himself again. Isn't domestic peace a wonderful thing?

A long pause, as if the status quo had been restored. Suddenly, a persistent ring at the door breaks the hush.

FANA (*starting with fear*): Help us, dear Lord! It's him! Ciampa!

FIFÌ: I'd forgotten all about Ciampa.

SPANÒ: Of course! Ciampa! And his wife in prison!

ASSUNTA: What do we do now? What can we do for the poor man?

SPANÒ: It might be better not to let him in.

FIFÌ: No. I think we should receive him. And give him chapter and verse, sensibly.

SPANÒ: I'm not sure about that. The man might react... irrationally.

FIFÌ: Let him! As long as in the end...

FANA (*cutting in*): I'm shaking with fear!

BEATRICE (*meekly*): Mama and I should leave the room perhaps...

FIFÌ (*glaring at her and shouting*): I should think so too!

ASSUNTA: Come, come, Beatrice. Let's leave the men to their own devices... (*Goes out right with* BEATRICE)

FIFÌ (*to* FANA, *who is following the women out of the room*): Where do you think you're going? Answer the door! (FANA *exits upstage centre*)

FANA (*enters immediately, backwards*): Mother of God! He's dead! He tripped and fell!

FIFÌ and SPANÒ: What? What's happened?

They rush towards the upstage door to help. CIAMPA *enters, cadaverous, his clothes soiled with mud, his forehead bruised, his collar and tie undone. He is holding his spectacles.* FIFÌ *and* SPANÒ *go to his help and brush his clothes with their hands.*

FIFÌ: What on earth... My dear Ciampa, what's happened?

SPANÒ: Did you have an accident?

CIAMPA: That's it: an accident. It was nothing. But my glasses are broken.

FIFÌ (*runs to get him a chair, while* SPANÒ *gets another;* FANA *does the same*): Here, sit down... sit down here.

SPANÒ: Here's a chair.

CIAMPA: Thank you. I prefer to stand.

FIFÌ: But why?

CIAMPA: I'd sooner not.

SPANÒ: But you can hardly stand up!

CIAPMA: Have no fear. I have nine lives, like a cat. I'll be better presently. Never mind. I'll be leaving soon. (*To* FIFÌ) Where is your sister?

SPANÒ: She's in the room next door.

FIFÌ: You'll understand, Ciampa, that right now she can't talk to you.

CIAMPA: Talk? There's no need to talk any more. The deed is done.

FIFÌ: The deed, as you call it my dear Ciampa, is not perhaps what you think it—

SPANÒ (*cutting in, officiously*): The verbal deposition is totally negative!

FIFÌ: There! Straight from the horse's mouth. And if the Inspector tells you, you can believe him. No reason for you to be upset.

CIAMPA: I have your assurance?

SPANÒ: My assurance? It's the legal document itself that provides the assurance, do you understand, Ciampa?

CIAMPA: Ah well, if the document—

FIFÌ: That's it! There was no foundation to any of the accusations...

SPANÒ: ...And the document carries legal authority!

FIFÌ: Will you accept the Inspector's word?

CIAMPA: Very well. I have something here to deliver to your sister.

FIFÌ: The items you collected in Palermo? You may hand them over to me.

CIAMPA: Very well. Might it not be better, since the Inspector is here, if I leave the items with him?

FIFÌ: Leave them with him or with me, as you please. (*To* SPANÒ) A few articles Ciampa redeemed from...

SPANÒ: Fine, fine.

FIFÌ (*to* CIAMPA): You could even leave them on that table. (*Points with patrician disdain at the small table next to the sofa*)

CIAMPA: Why do you attach so much weight to a verbal declaration?

FIFÌ: A verbal deposition is a statement of fact, as the Inspector explained.

SPANÒ: Precisely. It's legally binding.

CIAMPA: Very well. I'd like the following declaration to carry legal weight as well: that I hereby deliver to the Inspector, having been sent by the mistress—

SPANÒ (*interrupting*): I know all that!

CIAMPA: You do, do you? I was sent away on this particular errand, and I require you to take note of the fact that I, a humble servant, went and returned, having discharged the errand and turned over to you these two items. (*Takes two jewel cases out of his pocket*) One... two. That's all. (*Begins to leave*)

FIFÌ: What are you doing now?

CIAMPA: Nothing. I'm going.

FIFÌ: Just like that?

CIAMPA: There's nothing further for me to do here. I wanted to speak to your sister. It seems I can't. Therefore I'm going.

FIFÌ: What have you got to say to my sister?

FANA, *behind* CIAMPA, *shakes her head at* FIFÌ *hoping he'll drop the subject, a hand under her chin.*

CIAMPA (*suddenly turns round and surprises* FANA *in mid-gesture. He replicates her gesture*): Have you a sore throat? Breathing problems maybe? For your information I've got eyes at the back of my head, and they don't require glasses! (*To* FIFÌ) Are you afraid that if I talk to your sister—

FIFÌ (*interrupting*): Why should I be afraid? The fact is that my sister, at this particular moment, is not in a position to talk to anyone. The Inspector here, my mother, who's in the other room with her, and I myself have made her see the folly of her ways. And now she's sorry she acted as she did… she's most contrite. Isn't that so?

SPANÒ: Too true. Floods of tears…

CIAMPA: Floods of tears, you say…

FIFÌ: Yes. Frankly she's also been crying because I've given her a piece of my mind. I've been blunt in the extreme.

SPANÒ: Too true. A veritable avenging angel…

FIFÌ: Let me assure you, Ciampa, that you couldn't possibly add to the string of home truths I subjected her to.

CIAMPA: Come now, what do you think I'd say to the lady? All your sister did was to take my name – my puppet that is… you remember yesterday I talked about puppets – my own puppet. She threw it to the ground and stamped on it… like this. (*Throws his hat on the floor and stamps on it*) Why? Because she – the poor puppet! – felt herself trodden under as well. Our positions, mine and hers, are on the whole identical. What could I say to her? I wanted to put only one question to her. Not to the lady herself, but to her conscience.

FIFÌ: And what would that question be?

CIAMPA: My question would be addressed to her conscience. (*Turns to SPANÒ and opens his frock coat wide*) Inspector – search me!

FIFÌ (*pushing him away*): Don't be absurd!

SPANÒ: We know you're a gentleman, Ciampa.

CIAMPA: Inspector. I'm glad, very glad you're here, looking at me as my heart bleeds, and I weep tears of blood: yes, blood, because I've been assassinated! (*He bursts into sudden and uncontrollable sobs*)

FIFÌ and SPANÒ: Come… come. There's no need for that. Please, please, Ciampa! Control yourself!

CIAMPA: I'll control myself. But… may I put this one question to the lady?

FIFÌ: Of course! I'll call her right now. (*Calls out in the direction of the door on the right*) Beatrice! Mama! Come, Beatrice! (BEATRICE *enters with* ASSUNTA) I want you to listen to Ciampa. He wants to ask you a question.

ASSUNTA: The poor man! Are you hurt?

245

CIAMPA: It's nothing. The trouble is… it's just my glasses… they're broken. My vision is a trifle blurred. In any case there's nothing left for me to see. (*To* BEATRICE) One question only. Do you believe… and let's leave aside everything that happened this morning… everything… do you believe in all conscience you were right in acting as you did, despite the fact that yesterday I, in your brother's presence—

ASSUNTA (*attempting to interrupt him*): Yes yes, we know everything, my good man!

FIFÌ: You even brought your wife here!

CIAMPA: Please allow her – allow her to answer the question. It's just possible that your sister intended to injure me as well, in the belief she had every reason to do so. Answer me… truthfully.

BEATRICE (*hesitantly*): No… I… with you…

SPANÒ: She meant no harm towards you, Ciampa. In fact she took care to keep you out of it by sending you to Palermo.

BEATRICE: Quite so. As the Inspector says… I…

CIAMPA: No, madam! It isn't possible you didn't include me. Yesterday, in this very room for over two hours I put my hands well forwards…

BEATRICE: Yes. That's exactly why I sent you to Palermo. In order to have a free hand here, to deal with your wife and my husband.

CIAMPA: Without considering me?

BEATRICE: Without considering you.

CIAMPA: I see. Then what was I? A nonentity? Some dirt? Something you picked up between thumb and forefinger and flung away again, into any old corner, as if I didn't count at all? But I want to let it all out now, madam, and look into the very depths of your conscience, and declare that you did intend to injure me! And why? Because according to you I knew *everything* and kept quiet! Am I right? Answer me. Am I right?

BEATRICE: Since you say it yourself… yes. That's the way it was.

CIAMPA: I see. So if someone, let's assume, is blind, you stick a notice on his back saying: "Look everyone – he's blind!"

BEATRICE: No. That's beside the point.

CIAMPA: Let's ignore the blind man, then, after all everyone knows his condition without any need for a notice on his back. You must prove to me that one solitary person – one only – in the whole town could suspect me of knowing what you suspected I knew, and come up

246

to me and say to my face: "Ciampa, you're a cuckold and are well aware of the fact!"

FIFÌ (*cutting in*): Impossible. Never. Not a soul!

SPANÒ (*chiming in*): Who could ever even think such a thing?

ASSUNTA (*chiming in*): No one, no one!

FANA (*chiming in*): What a thing to say!

CIAMPA (*out-shouting the others*): But she could always say that even if the others didn't know... *I knew*, and that'd be enough! Is it true? Don't deny it! Never mind the verbal declaration – I need to know what you think deep down! Is it true? The truth!

BEATRICE: Yes. It is true.

A sudden stir of surprise and consternation among the others. Silence.

CIAMPA (*wounded, shaking his head*): Ah, at last. It's my turn to speak now... Not about myself. In general terms. (*Addressing* BEATRICE) How could you know why someone steals, or kills... Because, you see, that someone – who might be ugly, old, poor – might love a woman who holds his heart in a tight grip, as in a vice – yet he won't yell with pain. No. She can quickly put an end to his suffering with a kiss, and the old man is suddenly intoxicated with joy! How could you know how much suffering the poor man experiences, how cruel his torture really is, to the point that he'll even agree to share the woman's love with another man, someone rich, young, handsome, especially if the woman gives him to understand that he is still the master, and that no one will be aware of the arrangement? I'm generalizing, madam, naturally. I'm not speaking of myself. This is a festering wound I'm talking about, full of shame and cleverly concealed. And what do you do: stretch out your hand and uncover it for all to see? Let's change tack and come to ourselves. Madam, I know you suspected my wife and your husband. Ah, jealousy. Who hasn't experienced it who truly loves someone? I can feel sympathy for crimes. How could I not feel for you if you're jealous? I came here to see you yesterday so you could talk about it, unburden yourself! If you had your suspicions, I was not the one to relieve you of them. I know only too well that with suspicions of this kind, the more you try to root them out, the sturdier they grow. If you'd only opened your heart to me, I'd have gone straight home and said to my wife: "Pack up – we're leaving." Today I'd have said to your husband: "Cavaliere, I kiss your hands and here's my resignation." "But why, my dear Ciampa?" "Because I can't stay with you any longer. I've other things to attend to." That's the way it's done, madam. Why else do you think I brought my wife here with me yesterday? So you'd explode, so you'd let out all the anger that's been building up inside you! I begged you: "Speak out! Speak out!" But you said nothing. You pushed me aside and... murdered me as it were... What do you want me to do now? Tell me what to do. Shall I wear my disfigurement with pride? Shall I buy myself a cap with two antlers and display myself to the entire neighbourhood? So that the children can follow me mocking and yelling, "Boo! Boo!"? And there I am, all smiles, bowing and thanking them right and left?

FIFÌ: Why? Disfigurement? Where? A cap... children? Nothing's happened, I tell you!

SPANÒ: Absolutely nothing!

CIAMPA: Of course, that's what the deposition states. And who's going to believe any of that after all the scandal? Policemen, dawn raids, arrests...

SPANÒ: Even so: everything's been explained. Therefore—

CIAMPA (*interrupting*): Inspector, this is a great deal of mud we're talking about! A lot of it will stick. They'll say: "He's an important man. They've fixed it all up among themselves." Where does that leave me? I agree that you, madam, could have indulged in the luxury of teaching your husband a lesson if you thought he was having an affair with a girl... a girl without brothers or a father to breathe down her neck and cry vengeance. Everything could have been arranged neatly and without any bother. But someone else was involved. I was involved, and you ignored that completely. I repeat: am I a nonentity? Well, you've had your little joke, your little diversion. The whole community has had a good laugh and tomorrow you'll kiss and make up with your husband. What about me? As far as you are concerned everything's back to normal. But... what about me? I'm left with a verbal deposition that states nothing out of the ordinary has taken place. From tomorrow onwards I'll have to put up with everyone coming up to me looking suitably concerned: "Nothing's happened at all, Ciampa. Mrs Fiorìca was joking!" (*Turns to* SPANÒ *with a sudden movement*) Inspector... feel my pulse! (*Stretches out his wrist*)

SPANÒ: Why?

CIAMPA: Feel my pulse. You'll find it's normal. I am calm and relaxed, you're all witnesses to this, and I'm telling you that either tonight or tomorrow, as soon as my wife is home again, I'll split her head open with an axe. (*A very short pause*) But she'll not be the only one to be done away with. If that was all, the dear lady here would be only too pleased. I'll mete out the same treatment to the Cavaliere. It's only fair.

FIFÌ and SPANÒ (*seizing* CIAMPA, *while the women weep and cry*): What's that? What are you saying? You're mad! You're not going to kill anybody!

CIAMPA (*pale, convulsed, with a hint of a smile*): Both of them! I've no choice. I didn't start all this.

FIFÌ: You're not going to kill anyone. You've no reason and no right to do so, and you know it. And if you try we'll be there to stop you!

SPANÒ: I for one!

CIAMPA: Inspector, you may be able to stop me today—

SPANÒ: …And tomorrow!

CIAMPA: …But the day after tomorrow I'll kill them! You know what we say here in Sicily: "Woe betide the man who is dead in another's heart!" I am not in any way excited, Inspector. As you are my witness, I never wanted any of this to happen. But I've been forced into a corner! I can't walk about disfigured as I am for all to see! Bear in mind that I won't rest until—

BEATRICE (*cutting in*): What if I tell you now, Ciampa, that you have no reason, no reason at all to—

CIAMPA: Now you tell me? Now you recognize you shouldn't have put a man through this ordeal? It's too late.

FIFÌ: Forgive me, but if she herself admits that nothing has happened, surely…

CIAMPA: You call that nothing, sir? You ought not to say that to me.

FIFÌ: What you call a scandal was due to a moment of madness, I tell you.

ASSUNTA (*chiming in*): Sheer madness!

SPANÒ: While the balance of her mind was disturbed – the lady admits it!

FIFÌ: She has admitted it. We confirm it, all of us. A moment of madness.

THE ASSEMBLED COMPANY: Madness! Madness! That's all!

CIAMPA (*while everyone is busy shouting "Madness! Madness!" his gloom gives way to joy, as if struck by a welcome idea*): Thank you, dear God! This is wonderful. Wonderful! Yes, ladies and gentlemen! All can be solved peacefully! What a relief! I could dance... leap about with joy! What a weight off my chest! I needn't soil my hands with crime... they can stay clean... and I kiss them! Look at me: I'm kissing my own hands! (*To* BEATRICE) You go and get ready. Right now!

BEATRICE (*dumbfounded*): Me? Why?

CIAMPA: Do as I tell you, please, go and get ready. Let's not waste any time. (*Consults his watch*) You'll make it. You'll make it in time.

BEATRICE: What? Where am I going?

FIFÌ: What is it now?

SPANÒ: Where is she supposed to go?

CIAMPA: She'll make it, I tell you. Fana! And you (*to* ASSUNTA), madam... go help her pack. Put a few things in a suitcase. But hurry up, please. We've no time to lose!

BEATRICE: Where am I going? Why must I hurry? Are you quite mad?

CIAMPA: I most decidedly am not. But you are. Everybody here is agreed. Your brother, your mother, the Inspector – we all agree that you are mad. If we all say so it must be true. You're mad and you're off to the madhouse. It's all perfectly simple.

FIFÌ: What? Who?...

ASSUNTA: My daughter? To the... What are you saying?

BEATRICE: The madhouse? Me?

CIAMPA: Let's not call it that. Let's call it a nursing home. Three months. An extended holiday.

BEATRICE (*indignantly*): If anyone's for the madhouse, that's you! Get out of my house! This instant!

CIAMPA: Why send me away? I've your best interests at heart.

SPANÒ: Is that the way to talk to the lady?

FIFÌ: This is intolerable!

CIAMPA (*to* FIFÌ): Intolerable? Intolerable? Don't you see this is the only remedy at hand? It's for her sake! For her husband's sake! For everybody's sake! Can't you see your sister has made her husband ridiculous, and owes him an apology before the whole community? On the other hand if we say: "She's insane!" – that settles everything. "She's insane, let's lock her up and that's that." In this case I shall be fully vindicated. Disarmed. I say to myself: "The woman's mad,

250

nothing I can do about it!" That's all. And my employer will no longer feel any embarrassment among friends. And you, madam, enjoy a splendid three-month vacation! Come, admit it: there's no better solution. But she's to leave right now.

FIFÌ: What a brilliant idea! That's it! (*To* BEATRICE) Don't you see? It's all a game of make-believe!

BEATRICE: What? Me? To the madhouse? Did you hear that, Mother – I'm to go to a madhouse...

ASSUNTA: A nursing home, dear. It's all for the best, you know...

SPANÒ (*ponderously, to* BEATRICE): It's the perfect solution. Bound to satisfy the judicious *and* the judicial. Think of the Cavaliere, too...

BEATRICE: Are you all out of your minds? You want them all to think I'm mad?

CIAMPA: One moment. It was you who branded three people with the mark of infamy before the whole town. The first as an adulterer, the second as a whore, the third as a cuckold. Perhaps you merely want to *say* it was a moment of madness. That's not enough, dear lady. You must *show* them you're really mad – mad enough to be committed to an institution.

BEATRICE: You're the one who should be locked up!

CIAMPA: No. Definitely not me. You're the one. For your own good. All of us here know you're mad. Now the whole town must be made aware of it. Don't be alarmed, it'll be quite painless. It's no hardship to appear insane. I'll tell you how you set about it: tell everyone the truth. Nobody'll believe you. They'll all think you're insane.

BEATRICE (*convulsed with rage*): So you do know I am right, that I had to act as I did!

CIAMPA: No. Certainly not. Turn over the page, madam. If you turn the page you'll see that there's no clearer sign of insanity than the belief that one is right. Go on – give yourself the treat of being really insane for three whole months. Do you think that's nothing? If only I could allow myself that luxury! (*Points to his left temple*) Oh, how wonderful it would be to wind up the spring of insanity to its limit, pull down over my ears the cap and bells of madness and parade myself in the town square, spitting out the truth at them all! Man's maximum lifespan might turn out to be not one hundred, but two hundred years! It's injustice, cruelty, brutality, all the bitter pills we're made to swallow that shorten our lives and poison our systems...

the fact that we can't let off steam… that we can't open the valve of insanity! But you can. Yes! Give thanks to God you can open it, madam! You'll live for another hundred years. Make a start: yell to your heart's content!

BEATRICE: Me? Yell?

CIAMPA: Yes. Right here. In front of your brother! (*Pushes* FIFÌ *forwards*) Go on! In front of the Inspector! (*Pushes* SPANÒ *forwards*) Go on! In front of me, too! And bear in mind that only the insane are allowed to shout: "Boo!" to my face.

BEATRICE: Very well. Boo! You see, I'm doing it. Boo! Boo!

FIFÌ (*attempting to restrain her*): Beatrice, really!

SPANÒ: Madam, please!

ASSUNTA: Stop it!

BEATRICE (*with fury*): No! Am I not insane? Very well, I'll have to make it clear to him: Boo! Boo! Boooo!

CIAMPA (*the others endeavour to take* BEATRICE *away, as she continues to yell as if really unhinged*): She's mad. Do you hear that? She's stark raving mad! Isn't it wonderful? She'll have to be locked up! Locked up! (*Dances with delight, clapping his hands. There is a great deal of confusion, and uninvited neighbours suddenly appear, attracted by the noise, enquiring more through gestures than words as to the cause of the mayhem.* CIAMPA *continues to clap his hands, exhilarated, answering questions.*) She's mad! Mad! They're about to take her to the loony bin! She's mad, I tell you!

FIFÌ *and the* INSPECTOR *gently clear the assembled neighbours from the room, who exit murmuring sadly among themselves.* CIAMPA *collapses on a chair, centre stage, and bursts into a heart-rending laugh, full of rancour, savage relish and despair, as…*

THE CURTAIN FALLS

Honest as Can Be

Il piacere dell'onestà (1917)

Translated by Donald Watson

CHARACTERS

ANGELO BALDOVINO

AGATA RENNI

SIGNORA MADDALENA, *her mother*

THE MARCHESE FABIO COLLI

MAURIZIO SETTI, *his cousin*

THE PARISH PRIEST OF SANTA MARIA

MARCHETTO FONGI, *stockbroker*

FOUR DIRECTORS

A MAID

A SERVANT

A NURSE (*non-speaking*)

The action takes place in a city in central Italy, about 1920.

ANGELO BALDOVINO. *About forty, serious, tawny unkempt hair, short reddish rather bristly beard, penetrating eyes, a deep voice with a somewhat slow delivery. He is wearing a heavy brown suit. Fingers almost always holding pince-nez. His general slovenly appearance and his way of speaking and smiling denote a broken man whose life has taught him to keep well hidden the bitterest and most tempestuous memories, from which he has derived a strange philosophy combining irony and self-indulgence. All this specially in the first act and partly in the third. In the second he appears, superficially at least, transformed: soberly elegant, self-possessed but dignified, a gentleman, with well-kept hair and beard and no longer clutching his pince-nez.*

AGATA RENNI. *Twenty-seven. Proud, almost severe with the effort it takes to overcome the risk to her reputation. Desperate and rebellious in the first act, she then presses proudly and compliantly on to fulfil her destiny.*

LA SIGNORA MADDALENA. *Fifty-two. Elegant, still beautiful, but accepting her age. Passionate for her daughter, she can only see though the latter's eyes.*

THE MARCHESE FABIO COLLI. *About forty, upright and well-mannered, with that touch of awkwardness which predisposes some men to be unlucky in love.*

MAURIZIO SETTI. *Thirty-eight. Smart and free-and-easy, a good talker, a man of the world.*

MARCHETTO FONGI. *Fifty, an old fox, a shady little character, misshapen and listing to one side. Shrewd all the same, not lacking in wit and with a certain gentlemanly air.*

ACT ONE

An elegant drawing room in the Renni household. Main entrance to the rear. A door to the right, a window to the left. The stage is empty when the curtain rises – the main door opens, the maid comes in and ushers in MAURIZIO SETTI.

MAID: Please take a seat. I'll go and say you're here, signore. (*She goes out on the right. After a while* SIGNORA MADDALENA *enters through the same door, anxious and upset.*)

MADDALENA: Good morning, Setti. Well?

MAURIZIO: He's here. Arrived with me this morning.

MADDALENA: And it's... all arranged?

MAURIZIO: Everything.

MADDALENA: You made it all clear to him?

MAURIZIO: I explained everything. Don't upset yourself.

MADDALENA (*hesitantly*): But quite clear? How did you put it to him?

MAURIZIO: Oh Lord! Well... I told him... exactly how things stand.

MADDALENA (*shaking her head, bitterly*): And what things!... Oh yes!

MAURIZIO: Signora, I had to tell him straight out.

MADDALENA: Why yes, of course... but...

MAURIZIO: Circumstances change the way it looks. Rest assured it all depends on the sort of people involved, the whole situation.

MADDALENA: Why yes of course, you're right.

MAURIZIO: And don't doubt I put him completely in the picture.

MADDALENA: What kind of people we are? Who my daughter is. And he agreed? No problem at all?

MAURIZIO: None. Stop worrying.

MADDALENA: Worrying?... Oh, my dear friend, how can I help it? But what's he like? At least tell me what he's like.

MAURIZIO: Well... nice-looking. Lord, I don't mean an Adonis, but pleasant, you'll see. He presents well. A sort of dignity about him, but without affectation. Aristocratic family in fact. He's a Baldovino.

MADDALENA: But his opinions? His attitude?

MAURIZIO: Of the very best, believe me.

MADDALENA: And he knows how to talk... express himself, I mean?

MAURIZIO: Oh, signora, he's from Macerata! They're good talkers, you know, in those parts.

MADDALENA: No, you see... I wonder how discreet he will be. You understand, that's what really matters. One word out of place... without a certain... (*she hardly whispers her words, as if it hurts her even to utter them*) a bare minimum of... Oh dear, I just don't seem to know how to put it. (*She takes out a handkerchief and starts crying*)

MAURIZIO: Look on the bright side, signora.

MADDALENA: It could be so distressing for my poor Agata.

MAURIZIO: No risk of that, signora. Not an unseemly word, I promise you. He's extremely reserved. Restrained. A perfect gentleman, I tell you. Quick on the uptake, too. Nothing to fear on that score. Promise you.

MADDALENA: My dear Setti, believe me, I don't know where I am in the world today... I feel helpless... Suddenly have to face such a crisis. It's like one of those nightmares... you know?... When the door gets left open for any Tom, Dick or Harry to walk in and spy on you.

MAURIZIO: Well in life, you know...

MADDALENA: And that poor daughter of mine! Such a sensitive soul. If you knew what she's going through! It's too dreadful.

MAURIZIO: I can imagine. You know, dear lady, that I've done my very best to—

MADDALENA (*interrupting and grasping his hand*): Oh, I know! Of course I do! You see the way I trust you? You're one of the family. More than a cousin, more like a brother to our dear Fabio.

MAURIZIO: Is he here?

MADDALENA: Yes, he's in there now. He probably can't leave her on her own yet. He has to keep a close eye on her. As soon as she heard you'd arrived, she dashed to the window.

MAURIZIO: Good God! Because of me?

MADDALENA: No, not for *you*! Because she knows why you went to Macerata and who'd be coming back with you.

MAURIZIO: But all this... I'm sorry, but I thought she...

MADDALENA: No! Just imagine! She's in turmoil, in a desperate state. She frightens me.

MAURIZIO: Forgive me, but... wasn't it all settled? Didn't she agree to it herself?

MADDALENA: Of course she did. But that's just the point.

MAURIZIO (*in consternation*): She's changed her mind?

MADDALENA: No! But could she really *want* this to happen? There was no choice. She *had* to agree.

MAURIZIO: Of course. And make the best of it.

MADDALENA: Oh, Setti! She'll never survive it!

MAURIZIO: She will, signora, you'll see that...

MADDALENA: It will kill her! If she doesn't do something dreadful first. I know I've been too indulgent. But I trusted Fabio... I was sure he'd be more responsible. You shrug your shoulders? You're right. What else can we do? But close our eyes and let shame take over?

MAURIZIO: Now don't talk like that, signora. When we're doing our best to...

MADDALENA (*hiding her face in her hands*): No, please! Don't remind me, it makes it worse – at first I was only conscious of my own weakness. Now, I promise you, all I feel is remorse.

MAURIZIO: I'm aware of that, dear lady.

MADDALENA: But you'll never understand! You, you're a man. And not even a father. How can you ever understand the torment it is for a mother to watch her daughter getting older and losing the first bloom of youth. You no longer have the strength to be as strict as prudence would advise or honour would dictate. Oh! Respectability, my dear Setti, makes a laughing stock of us all. When your daughter gazes at you with eyes begging for pity, what can her mother say, a mother who for good or ill knows the ways of the world and has been in love herself? So as not to give the game away, we pretend not to notice. And this pretence, together with our silence, make us accomplices... until we come... to this! But I really did hope, as I said, that Fabio would be more sensible.

MAURIZIO: Yes, dear lady... but good sense is not always...

MADDALENA: I know! I know!

MAURIZIO: If he could have…

MADDALENA: I know… I can see, it's as if he's quite distraught too, the poor thing. Had he not been an upright man of integrity, how else would we have reached this point?

MAURIZIO: Fabio is a gentleman.

MADDALENA: And we knew he was unhappy. Separated from that worthless wife of his. And this very fact, which should have altered us, is precisely what led us into this mess. You are sure aren't you, in all honesty, that if Fabio had been free he would have married my little girl?

MAURIZIO: No doubt about it.

MADDALENA: Please be perfectly frank with me.

MAURIZIO: Can't you see for yourself, signora, from the state he's in now, that he's hopelessly in love?

MADDALENA: It is true, isn't it? You'll never know what a consolation it is, to have even the slightest reassurance at a moment like this.

MAURIZIO: But what can be in your mind, signora? You know how much I respect you both, how sincerely devoted I am to you and Signorina Agata!

MADDALENA: Oh thank you! Thank you!

MAURIZIO: Please, you must believe me. Or I'd never have become so involved.

MADDALENA: Thank you, Setti. A woman, you see, a poor young girl, who has honourably waited so many years for a partner with whom she could spend her life, at last meets a man worthy of her love. And she finds him hurt and embittered by the unfair treatment he has suffered at the hands of another woman. Believe me, she is sorely, irresistibly tempted to prove to him that all women are not the same. That there exists at least one who can match love for love and appreciate the good fortune his wife has stamped on.

MAURIZIO: Oh yes! You're right, dear lady. Stamped on, poor Fabio never deserved that.

MADDALENA: Sound sense tells us all in our hearts: "No, you can't, you shouldn't do it." She knows it and, if he's an upright man, he knows it as well. So does her mother, who watches anxiously from the wings. For a time you keep silent, you try to do the right thing and you stifle your doubts…

MAURIZIO: …And in the end, the moment comes…

MADDALENA: It comes all right! It creeps up on you… One perfect evening in May. Her mother was leaning out of the window. Outside, the flowers and stars. Inside, heartbreak and torment. And she murmured to herself: "Doesn't my daughter, for once in her life have a right to them too? Those flowers and those stars?"… And so I stayed there in the shadows, mounting guard over a misdemeanour that the whole of Nature connived at, while still knowing that the next day society and our own conscience will condemn it. But at the time one is glad to let it happen, strangely content emotionally, and proud to face the abuse whatever the cost tomorrow… That's how it was, my dear Setti… I ask for no excuse, only compassion. One ought to die afterwards. But one doesn't. Life goes on and needs the support of all the conventions we cast aside in one single moment of madness.

MAURIZIO: Yes, I know. And that's why we need to keep our heads. You acknowledge that up to now the three of you, you in one way, Fabio and Agata in another, have all let your feelings run away with you.

MADDALENA: Of course we have!

MAURIZIO: Well then, now is the time to control and restrain them. And then listen to the voice of common sense?

MADDALENA: Indeed it is.

MAURIZIO: We have to move forward. There's no time to lose… Ah! Here's Fabio.

FABIO *comes in from the door on the right, desperately anxious and upset. He makes straight for* MADDALENA.

FABIO: Please go to her at once. Don't leave her alone!

MADDALENA: Yes, of course… But I thought…

FABIO: Go, please go!

MADDALENA: Yes, of course… (*To* MAURIZIO) Forgive me! (*She goes off to the right*)

MAURIZIO: What's this? You in a bad way too?

FABIO: For God's sake, Maurizio, not another word! You think you've found the answer, do you? You know what you've done? I'll tell you! Offered a sick man a placebo.

MAURIZIO: I have?

FABIO: Yes, you. A palliative. The illusion of a cure.

MAURIZIO: But it's what you asked for! Let's get this straight. I never wanted to be your guardian angel.

FABIO: I'm in pain, Maurizio. Going through hell for that poor young girl. And all because of that solution you proposed. I'm sure it's the right one, but that only makes it worse. Do you see? It's cosmetic, a cover-up, that can do no more than save appearances.

MAURIZIO: And they don't matter any more? Four days ago that's what you were desperate to do, save appearances. And now it's possible you can…

FABIO: I only know how wretched I feel. Isn't that natural?

MAURIZIO: Maybe. But that way you lose everything. Appearances do matter. So you have to create them for yourselves. *You* can't be objective about it. I can. And I must bully you, give you a good shake… make you take the placebo, as you put it – he's here with me now. We came together. As we have to move fast…

FABIO: Yes, you're right…Tell me about it… But it's no good! Did you make it clear I won't let him handle any finance? Not one penny.

MAURIZIO: I did.

FABIO: And he agrees?

MAURIZIO: He's here, isn't he?… However, he does ask – and it seems fair enough to me – in order to fulfil all the terms of your mutual agreement and in view of the conditions, that you wipe out his past life and pay off a few debts.

FABIO: How many? A lot? I bet there are!

MAURIZIO: No. Only a few. My God, Fabio, a man with no debts, did you expect that too? He doesn't have many. But he insisted I told you that if he hasn't acquired more it's not because he wasn't ready to. His creditors no longer trusted him.

FABIO: Oh, that's rich!

MAURIZIO: At least it's honest! You do realize that if he'd still had any credit left, he wouldn't have had to…

FABIO (*his head in his hands*): For pity's sake, that's enough! Tell me how you put it to him… What's he like? Shabbily dressed? In bad shape?

MAURIZIO: He's a bit run down since I saw him last. But we can put that right. I've done something already. Morale is important, you know, for a man like that. The bad things he's felt compelled to do…

FABIO: Gambling? Stealing? Cheating at cards?…

MAURIZIO: He used to gamble. For a while now he's been banned. He was so bitter I felt sorry for him. We spent a whole night walking round, outside the walls of the town. Ever been to Macerata?

FABIO: No.

MAURIZIO: For me, I tell you, it was a fantastic night. Walking round that avenue in the flashing of thousands of fireflies with that man beside me. He was alarmingly frank: startling thoughts from the depths of his being darting into your mind like fireflies before our eyes. I don't know how but I seemed to be out of this world, in a strangely mournful mysterious dreamland. He was master of it. Where the weirdest and most improbable things could happen and yet appear familiar and everyday. He knew what I was feeling. He doesn't miss much. And he smiled. Then started talking about Descartes.

FABIO: Who?

MAURIZIO: Descartes, the philosopher... Oh yes, as you'll see, he's a highly cultured man too. Above all, philosophical. He said that Descartes...

FABIO: But in God's name, now of all times, what do I care about Descartes?

MAURIZIO: Listen and you'll find out. When Descartes, he told me, was investigating our notion of reality, he had one of the most terrible thoughts any human has had to face. If our dreams came to us with any regularity, we'd be hard pressed to distinguish our waking life from our sleep. Have you ever noticed how strange it is when the same dream crops up time and time again? It hardly seems possible that it's not real, because our whole grasp of the reality of our world hangs on a most tenuous thread: the re-gu-lar-ity of our experiences. We whose lives are governed by repetition can't divine what may seem real or believable to a man like Baldovino, who has no rules to live by... So you can see how eventually it was easy for me to put our proposal to him. He mentioned some of his own projects. Highly plausible to him. To me so bizarre and unattainable that my scheme suddenly looked so blatantly simple and obvious, you couldn't think of anything more straightforward. Anyone would have accepted it... And surprise, surprise! I wasn't the first to mention money. It was he who at once indignantly protested there'd be no question of payment. He wouldn't dream of it... And do you know why?

FABIO: Why?

MAURIZIO: Because, according to him, it's easier to be a hero than a gentleman. You can be a hero for once in your life, but a gentleman must remain one all the time. Which is far from easy.

FABIO: I see. (*Anxious, gloomy and disturbed, he starts pacing the room*) So... it seems he's quite a character?

MAURIZIO: A man of many talents!

FABIO: Who's made little use of them... apparently!

MAURIZIO: Far too little. Even as a boy. We were at school together as I told you. Gifted as he was, if he'd wanted he could have gone far. But always he studied only what suited him, things of no use to him at all. Education, he says, is the enemy of wisdom. Because you need to learn so many things which, if you were wise, you'd be wiser to ignore. He was brought up a member of the upper class: tastes, habits, ambitions – and then vices too... But chance stepped in. His father went bankrupt and... After that, it's no wonder!

FABIO (*resuming his pacing*): And... and you say he's a fine-looking man.

MAURIZIO: Yes, very presentable... What's wrong? (*He laughs*) Come on now, confess you're beginning to feel a trifle nervous I might have chosen too well!

FABIO: Oh please! It's just... he's too much of a good thing. A highly cultured intellectual...

MAURIZIO: A philosopher too! Not inappropriate, I think, given the circumstances.

FABIO: Don't take it so lightly, Maurizio! Can't you see I'm on edge? I'd rather have someone less... unusual, that's all, more modest, ordinary...

MAURIZIO: Who'd give the game away at once? Who wouldn't have looked the part? Think about it. We had to consider the kind of house he was coming to... A middle-aged nonentity would have seemed very odd. We needed a man of distinction to inspire respect and consideration. It had to be possible for people to believe that our signorina would agree to marry him... And I'm sure that...

FABIO: Then what?

MAURIZIO: That she will... And what's more that she at least will be more grateful to me than you are!

FABIO: Oh yes! She'll be grateful all right! If you could hear her now!... Did you tell him it all has to be settled as soon as possible?

MAURIZIO: Of course! You'll see how quickly he fits into the family.

FABIO: Meaning what exactly?

MAURIZIO: Oh, good Lord, only so much as you want him to!

Enter the MAID, *and then* MADDALENA.

MAID (*from the door on the right*): Signor Marchese, madam would like to see you for a moment.

FABIO: I can't just now. I have to go out with my cousin. (*To* MAURIZIO) I must see him. And talk to him. (*To the* MAID) Ask madam to wait a little. I can't come now.

MAID: Very well, signore. (*She goes*)

MAURIZIO: It's only a few doors from here. The nearest hotel. But in the state you're in...

FABIO: I'm out of my mind... This is driving me crazy. What with her in there in floods of tears and you out here bullying me...

MAURIZIO: Remember we're not committed yet. And if you really don't want...

FABIO: I want to see him, I tell you, and talk to him first.

MAURIZIO: Well, let's go then. He's only round the corner.

MADDALENA (*bursting in, alarmed*): Fabio! Fabio, please come at once! Don't leave me alone with her!

FABIO: Oh God!

MADDALENA: She's hysterical! Please, I beg you!

FABIO: But I've simply got to...

MAURIZIO: No, Fabio... Go to her now!

MADDALENA: Yes, Fabio, *please*!

MAURIZIO: Shall I bring him here? With no commitment. It might be better for you to talk to him here. For Agata as well.

FABIO: Yes, go and fetch him. Without obligation, mind! Not before he's had his talk with me. (*He goes out through the door on the right*)

MAURIZIO (*shouting after him*): A few minutes! I'll come straight back. (*He exits through the main door*)

MADDALENA (*after him*): You're bringing him here? (*She is making for the door on the right when Agata and Fabio rush in*)

AGATA (*dishevelled, and struggling wildly to break away from* FABIO): Let me go! No! Let me go! I must get away, away from here!

MADDALENA: But darling, where do you want to go?

AGATA: I don't know. Just away.

FABIO: Agata, for God's sake!

MADDALENA: This is madness.

AGATA: Leave me alone! I will go mad or I'll die! There's no other way out. I can't bear it! (*She collapses into a chair*)

MADDALENA: Wait at least until Fabio's seen him and talked to him. Till you've seen him too.

AGATA: Me? No, not me! Can't you both see how awful it is, what you want me to do? It's monstrous.

MADDALENA: But, my darling, it was you yourself...

AGATA: No! I won't do it! I won't!

FABIO (*desperately, resolutely*): Well then, you shan't! If you don't want to, neither do I. Yes, it *is* monstrous. It's horrible for me too. But in that case are you ready for us to face it together?

MADDALENA: What are you thinking, Fabio? You're a man! Can't you see that *you* can shrug the scandal off? We're just two poor women on our own. All the shame will be ours to bear. It's a choice between two evils. Either public disgrace for us all...

AGATA (*quickly*): ...Or a private one! That's it, isn't it? I'm the only one who will be utterly shamed. To have to live with this man and see him every day. A man who must be absolutely vile and loathsome to agree to such an arrangement. (*Springing to her feet and trying to reach the main door before being pulled back*) No! No! I won't! I won't see him! Let me go away!

MADDALENA: But where? What will you do?... Face the scandal alone? If that's what you want, I don't know what I...

AGATA (*throwing her arms round her and sobbing helplessly*): No it's for your sake, Mamma... no, for your sake...

MADDALENA: For my sake? Oh no, darling. Why for my sake? Don't worry about *me*. We can spare each other the pain. Or run away from it. We have to stay and endure it, all three of us, try and help each other, because we all have our share of the blame.

AGATA: No, not you, Mamma... Not you!

MADDALENA: I'm more to blame, my darling. And I swear I'm suffering even more than you!

AGATA: No, Mamma. I suffer for you too.

MADDALENA: And I above all for you. It's even worse for me. I can't share my pain because, darling, you are everything to me. Hold tight... wait... we must wait and see...

AGATA: It's dreadful, so awful!

MADDALENA: I know... but let's meet him first.

AGATA: I can't, Mamma! I can't!

MADDALENA: But if we're here with you!... None of us will be taken in, we're not hiding anything. We'll stay here with you, Fabio and I, right beside you.

AGATA: But he'll come and live here! Imagine! Always here with us, Fabio... Someone who knows our secret.

FABIO: But it will be in his interest to hide it too, to keep our secret for all our sakes. And he'll stick to our arrangement. If not, all the better for us! As soon as he shows signs of breaking it, I'll have an excuse to send him packing. After a time we won't need him.

MADDALENA: You see? Why think it's for ever? Only for a while.

FABIO: Just a short while. It'll be up to us to see it's not for long.

AGATA: No, no! He'll always be with us.

MADDALENA: Let's meet him first... Setti has made quite sure...

FABIO: We'll find a way to make it work.

MADDALENA: He's a very intelligent man and he... (*A knock at the front door to the rear. A pause for alarm and then:*) Oh, that's it! It must be him now...

AGATA (*jumping up and clutching her mother*): We can't stay! Let's go, Mamma! Oh God! (*She drags her mother to the door on the right*)

MADDALENA: Yes, all right. Fabio can talk to him... We can both go in here. (*They both leave on the right*)

FABIO: Don't worry!... Come in!

The MAID *appears through the front door.*

MAID: Signor Setti and another gentleman.

Exit MAID. *Enter* MAURIZIO *and* BALDOVINO.

MAURIZIO: Ah, here we are... Fabio, this is my friend Angelo Baldovino. (*Fabio bows to* BALDOVINO) The Marchese Fabio Colli, my cousin. (BALDOVINO *bows*)

FABIO: Please sit down.

MAURIZIO: You have things to discuss, so I'll leave you. (*To* BALDOVINO, *shaking his hand*) See you later back at the hotel. All right? Bye, Fabio. (*Exit* MAURIZIO *through the main door*)

BALDOVINO (*sitting, his pince-nez on the tip of his nose, his head tilted back*): First, I'd like to ask you a favour.

FABIO: Please go ahead.

BALDOVINO: Signor Marchese, I'd like you to be quite open with me.

FABIO: Why, naturally... There's nothing I want more.

BALDOVINO: Thank you. But maybe what *you* understand by "open" is not exactly what I mean.

FABIO: But... I don't know... "open"... frank and sincere... (*and as* BALDOVINO *waves his finger at him*) so what do *you* mean by it?

BALDOVINO: Something more than that. You see, Marchese, inevitably we reinvent ourselves. Let me explain. I arrive here, and immediately in your presence I become what I'm meant to be, what I'm able to become... I construct myself... that is, I adopt a new self to suit the relationship I'm meant to establish with you. And of course you do the same thing with me. But basically, behind the façade we present to each other, behind our shutters and our blinds, our true selves lie hidden inside, with our most secret thoughts, our most intimate feelings – what we know ourselves to be, quite separate from the two of us who both wish to reach agreement... Do I make myself clear?

FABIO: Yes, admirably... very clear. My cousin told me how intelligent you are.

BALDOVINO: I see. So you probably think I just wanted to show off.

FABIO: No, no... all I meant was... you expressed yourself very clearly and I agree with you.

BALDOVINO: So, if you allow me, I'll start with some plain speaking. For some time, Marchese, I've been deeply, unspeakably disgusted by the deplorable picture of myself I've had to invent in my relations with... if I can say it without offence... my peers.

FABIO: No... please go on...

BALDOVINO: I see myself doing it, continually watching myself, Marchese. And I think: "Look at what you're doing now! It's shabby, revolting!"

FABIO (*disconcerted, embarrassed*): No, but for God's sake why?

BALDOVINO: I'm sorry, but it is. So, you may ask me why I go on doing it? Why indeed? Partly the fault is mine, partly of others, and this time through force of circumstances. I cannot help myself. It's easy to want to live this way or that. It's hard to be what you really want to be. We are not quite alone, you see. There's us... and then the beast we rise on. You can strike him, but you'll never teach him to think... try to train a donkey to keep off the edge of a cliff. You can try, beat or whip him, but go there he must. And when you've finished kicking or thumping him, just look at his sorrowful eyes. Can you help feeling sorry for him? Pity doesn't excuse him... Excuse brutishness and it brutalizes the mind. But compassion's not the same thing at all. Is it?

FABIO: No, of course not... But can we now talk about us?

BALDOVINO: Marchese, we are. I've told you all this so you realize that, feeling as I do about our arrangement, I need to keep my self-respect too. Which means being honest and open... Pretence would be odious, not to say demeaning, even vulgar. The truth!

FABIO: Definitely, quite right... Now let's try and reach an understanding...

BALDOVINO: So I have a few things to ask you, if you don't mind.

FABIO: What now?

BALDOVINO: A few questions please.

FABIO: All right then. Ask away!

BALDOVINO: Here goes. (*He takes his pocketbook out*) The situation in a nutshell. I've made some notes. It's best for us both to treat it seriously. (*He opens it, leafs through it and begins his questioning, rather like a judge but without severity*) You, Marchese, are the young lady's lover...

FABIO (*jumping in to cut him short and avoid further use of the pocketbook*): No, no! I'm sorry but is this...

BALDOVINO (*smiling calmly*): You see? You jib at the very first fence!

FABIO: Of course I do! Because...

BALDOVINO (*suddenly severe*): ...It's not true? Is that what you're saying?... Well then (*rising*) I'm sorry, Signor Marchese, I told you, I'm a proud man. I could never lend myself to a dreary humiliating farce.

FABIO: What do you mean? It's your attitude that seems to me...

BALDOVINO: Mistaken? I can only maintain my self-respect – for what it's worth – so long as you deal with me as you address your own conscience... Either that, signore, or we'll get nowhere. I will not involve myself in unseemly fictions... Nothing but the truth ... Will you answer me?

FABIO: Well… it's yes. But no more notebook, for God's sake! You mean Agata Renni?

BALDOVINO (*goes on searching regardless, finds the entry and repeats*): Agata Renni, that's right… aged twenty-seven?

FABIO: Twenty-six.

BALDOVINO (*consulting the notebook*): On the ninth of last month. So she's in her twenty-seventh year. And… (*another look in his notebook*) there's a mother?

FABIO: Oh really!

BALDOVINO: Just being conscientious, you know. That's all. It makes it easier for you to trust me. Always meticulous, as you'll find.

FABIO: Well, yes. Her mother is here.

BALDOVINO: And… forgive me, how old is she?

FABIO: Oh… I'm not sure… about fifty-one or two…

BALDOVINO: Is that all?… It's just that… Frankly, it would be easier without one. A mother's an inconvenient complication… But I knew about her… So shall we stretch a point and say fifty-three? You, sir, will be roughly my age… I'm a bit worse for wear. I look older, but I'm forty-one.

FABIO: So I'm a bit more. I'm forty-three.

BALDOVINO: Bravo! You don't look it. Perhaps if I took more care… Forty-three then… Now I'm afraid I have to bring up another very sensitive matter.

FABIO: My wife?

BALDOVINO: You're separated. I know you're not at fault. You're a perfect gentleman. Incapable of wrongdoing. So it's tempting to wrong *you*. The fault must be your wife's. And here you found consolation. But life is a hard taskmaster. For every joy it brings, we pay a hundredfold in trouble and strife.

FABIO: Too true!

BALDOVINO: I should know! Now, Marchese, it's your turn to pay up. The threatening shadow of the creditor looms over you. Settlement without delay. And I come to stand surety and offer a guarantee that your debt will be honoured. You won't believe, sir, the joy it gives me to wage a vendetta against society when it distrusts my signature. I long to validate it and say: here stands a man who has taken from life what he has no right to, and now I am paying his debt for him because if I didn't, decency would be jeopardized and a family's honour made bankrupt. For me it's a source of great satisfaction, signore, I'm getting my own back! Believe me, that's my only motive. You doubt my word? You've every right to. Because I'm like… do you mind if I make an analogy?

FABIO: Why no, of course, go on.

BALDOVINO (*continuing*): …I'm like a man come to spend gold coin in a land where the currency is banknotes. At first no one trusts gold, it's only natural. I'm sure you're inclined to refuse it, aren't you? But rest assured. It's real gold, Marchese. I never could squander it, because it weighs heavy in my soul, not in my pocket. Otherwise…

FABIO: Fine! Well done! Excellent! I couldn't ask for more, Signor Baldovino. Honesty and kindness of heart.

BALDOVINO: I have memories of my own family too. Dishonesty can cost me so much: endless bitterness, disgust, abhorrence and the sacrifice of my self-respect. How could honesty cost me as much? You're inviting me… yes, I mean it… to a double wedding. Apparently I'm taking a wife. But my true bride will be honesty.

FABIO: Yes, exactly, that's fine by me. Enough said!

BALDOVINO: Enough? You think that's enough? I'm sorry, Marchese, but what does all this entail?

FABIO: Entail? I don't follow.

BALDOVINO: Consequences, sir… I can see you feel awkward in my presence, when you're struggling so hard to come to terms with this painful situation and find a way out… but you seem to take it all very lightly.

FABIO: No, on the contrary! Why do you say lightly?

BALDOVINO: Let me put it to you, sir. Do you wish me to be honest or not?

FABIO: Of course I do! It's the one condition I insist on.

BALDOVINO: Excellent. Because I am honest. I feel it in my bones. I wish it, I intend to act accordingly, and I shall prove it to you. So what do you say?

FABIO: Exactly what I said before. That's fine by me.

BALDOVINO: But, I'm sorry, sir, what are the consequences? Listen. What is it, the sort of honesty you want from me? Think about it – it's nothing. An abstraction. Pure form… may we call it an absolute? Now if I'm to be scrupulously honest, I shall simply have, in a way, to breathe life into an abstraction, to embody a concept, to experience this pure, absolute honesty within myself. And what will that lead to? First of all, now listen, that I must act as a tyrant.

FABIO: A tyrant?

BALDOVINO: Inevitably! But not because I want to! Only as pure form dictates, of course – nothing else concerns me – but for form's sake, to be honest in the way you wish and I desire, I warn you I must become tyrannical. I shall want appearances meticulously observed. And that is bound to occasion great sacrifice on your part, you, the signora and her mother: a most distressing curtailment of freedom and respect for all the abstract conventions of good form in society. And if only to prove how seriously I take all this, may I point out bluntly, signore, the way people will react at once? How what happens between us will look in other people's eyes? Have no illusions that in your dealings with me – honest as I'll be – any wrongdoing will be laid at your door, not mine. Only one thing matters to me in this whole unhappy affair: the chance you all give me – and which I accept – to be an honest man.

FABIO: Yes, but you can understand, my dear signore – you've already said it yourself – that I'm not in the mood just now to grasp all this. You're extremely eloquent, but do let's come down to earth!

BALDOVINIO: Down to earth! Me? Impossible.

FABIO: I'm sorry, but why not? What do you mean?

BALDOVINO: I can't, just because of the position you put me in – I'm compelled to dwell in the abstract. If I become earthborne, I'm done for. Reality is not my element, that's your preserve. You can keep your feet on the ground. You talk and I'll listen. I'll be the intelligence that finds no excuse but feels compassion for…

FABIO (*suddenly, pointing to himself*): …The donkey?…

BALDOVINO: I'm sorry. It has to be.

FABIO: Why yes, you're right. Of course you are. So let me talk now. It's the beast talking. You know, down to earth, straight out? And you can listen and be compassionate. That way we'll reach an understanding…

BALDOVINO: With me, you mean?

FABIO: Of course, who else?

BALDOVINO: No, signore. An understanding with yourself! I know all about it already. I've done so much talking – I don't usually talk so much, you know – because I want to be sure you're quite able to carry it through.

FABIO: Me?

BALDOVINO: Yes, you. I am already, it's easy for me. What do I have to do? Nothing but incarnate form. The active part – and not an agreeable one – is your prerogative. It's something you've started already and it's up to me to repair the damage. You keep on with it. It'll be the cover-up. But to make this work, in your interest and above all the signorina's, you must respect me. And the role you've chosen to play yourself won't be easy for you. The respect is not for me, but for the form I embody: the honest husband of a respectable woman. That is what you expect, isn't it?

FABIO: Naturally.

BALDOVINO: And you do realize, don't you, that the more honest you want me to be, the more strict and tyrannical this form must be? That's why I warned you of the outcome. Not for my sake but yours! My philosophy, you see, improves my vision. And to justify my conduct in this case, all I need is to look on the wife who will be mine in name only... as a mother-to-be.

FABIO: That's exactly right.

BALDOVINO: And to see that my relations with her are always governed by the thought of that little baby to come. The function I'm called on to fulfil – a decent noble function – is dictated by the innocence of a child. Is that all right?

FABIO: Oh yes! That's excellent.

BALDOVINO: Careful now! All right for me. But for you, Marchese, the more you agree, the harder you make it for yourself.

FABIO: I'm sorry, I don't... but why... I don't see what problems there are.

BALDOVINO: It's my duty, I believe, to point them out. You are a gentleman. Force of circumstances has led you to behave dishonestly. But for you, honesty is essential. So unable to be honest yourself, you ask me to stand in for you: which means playing the honest husband of a lady who can never be your wife, the honest father of a child you can never acknowledge as yours. That's true, isn't it?

FABIO: Yes, yes, that's true.

BALDOVINO: But if the lady is yours and not mine... If the child is yours and not mine, don't you see that it's not enough that I alone should be honest? You, signore, must be honest with me too… If I'm to be honest, so must we all. There's no alternative.

FABIO: How's that? I don't see why. Wait a minute…

BALDOVINO: Now you can feel the ground shake under your feet.

FABIO: No, but I mean… if our ways have to change…

BALDOVINO: Of course they must! It's you who are changing them. The appearances you wish to save don't only concern other people. There'll be one that concerns you too… One that you yourselves have demanded and wanted me to represent. Your own honesty. Have you thought about that? It won't be easy, you know.

FABIO: But if you know how things stand.

BALDOVINO: Precisely. It's because I *do* know!… It won't make things easier for me, but what else can I do? I advise you, Marchese, to give it careful thought.

A pause. FABIO *stands up and starts pacing about excitedly, in consternation.* BALDOVINO *stands up and waits.*

FABIO (*still pacing*): It's true that if… you realize… that if I…

BALDOVINO: Yes, believe me, you'd better think a bit more about what I've said. And discuss it, if you think it wise, with the signorina too. (*With a brief glance at the door on the right*) That may not be necessary, because…

FABIO (*suddenly turning to him, angrily*): What? Do you imagine…

BALDOVINO (*sadly, with great calm*): Oh, after all, why shouldn't she know? I'll leave you – you'll inform me or send word to the hotel, what you've decided. (*He makes to leave, then turns round*) Meanwhile, Marchese, you can count on my complete discretion.

FABIO: I do.

BALDOVINO (*slowly, seriously*): I too have many things weighing on my conscience. I don't think anyone's to blame for what's happened here. It's just unfortunate. Whatever you decide, please know how grateful I shall always be – in private – to my old school friend for trusting enough in my honesty to let me involve myself in this troublesome affair. (*He bows*) Signor Marchese…

CURTAIN

ACT TWO

Grand parlour in what has become the BALDOVINO *household. Several pieces of furniture seen before are now in this different room. Main entrance at the rear, side doors left and right.*

When the curtain rises MARCHESE FONGI, *hat and stick in one hand, with the other is holding open the door on the left and addressing* BALDOVINO *offstage.* FABIO *appears to be waiting as if unwilling to be seen or heard.*

FONGI (*into the next room*): Thank you, Baldovino, thank you… you don't imagine I'd miss such a splendid meeting. I'll be back with the other members of the board in half an hour. See you then.

FABIO (*in an anxious whisper*): Yes? You think he really will?

FONGI (*still winking, he answers first with a nod*): He's fallen for it all right!

FABIO: It looks like it. It's taken almost a week!

FONGI (*waving three fingers of one hand*): Three… three hundred… 300,000 lire! What did I say? It couldn't fail! (*Taking* FABIO *by the arm and moving towards the main entrance*) It'll be quite a show-down. Just you leave it to me. We'll catch him red-handed!

They both leave. The stage is empty for a moment, the door on the left opens. BALDOVINO *and* MAURIZIO *enter.*

MAURIZIO (*looking around*): You're well set up here, aren't you?

BALDOVINO (*vaguely*): I know. (*With an ambiguous smile*) All quite above board. (*Pause*) So tell me… where have you been?

MAURIZIO: A little trip. To get away from it all.

BALDOVINO: Really?

MAURIZIO: Why not? You don't believe me?

BALDOVINO: How far away? You mean you didn't go to Paris or Nice or Cairo – so where did you go?

MAURIZIO: A land of rubber and bananas.

BALDOVINO: The Congo?

MAURIZIO: Yes. The jungle. The real thing, you know.

BALDOVINO: Aha! Did you see any wild things?

MAURIZIO: A few poor tribal natives...

BALDOVINO: Wild beasts, I mean, leopards or tigers?

MAURIZIO: Good Lord no! But they put a sparkle in *your* eyes!

BALDOVINO (*with a bitter smile, cupping his hand to show his nails to* MAURIZIO): You see what we've come to? But we don't cut our nails to appear less aggressive. Just the opposite. Grooming our hands makes us look more civilized: better fitted for a struggle far fiercer than the one our brutal forebears fought, poor wretches, with nothing but their bare nails. That's why I've always envied animals in the wild. And you've been in the jungle, you rogue, and you never even saw a wolf!

MAURIZIO: Forget that! Let's talk about you – well, how's it going?

BALDOVINO: What?

MAURIZIO: With your wife of course... or should I say your good lady?

BALDOVINO: How do you think? It's fine.

MAURIZIO: And... er... you get along all right?

BALDOVINO (*staring at him a moment, then getting up*): What did you expect?

MAURIZIO (*changing his tone, regaining assurance*): I find you in great shape.

BALDOVINO: Yes, I keep busy.

MAURIZIO: I'm sure you do! I hear Fabio has launched a joint stock company.

BALDOVINO: Yes, to give me a finger in the pie. It's doing very well.

MAURIZIO: And you're the managing director?

BALDOVINO: That's why it's so successful.

MAURIZIO: Indeed. That's what I heard. I'd like to get in on it myself, but... they say you're terribly strict.

BALDOVINO: To be sure! And I don't cheat!... (*He goes up to* MAURIZIO *and clasps both his arms*) Just think! To handle hundreds and thousands of banknotes, see them as so much waste paper and no longer feel any need for them.

MAURIZIO: That must really please you...

BALDOVINO: Divine! And not a single deal that's gone wrong! But it's hard work, you know, very hard. And they all have to follow my example!

MAURIZIO: Yes, I know… that's just it…

BALDOVINO: They're moaning, are they? Tell me. They're squealing? Champing at the bit?

MAURIZIO: They're saying… they say you don't have to be quite so… punctilious, that's all.

BALDOVINO: Don't I know it! I suffocate them all. Anyone who comes near me – but you understand: what alternative do I have? For ten months now I've not been myself, not my own man at all.

MAURIZIO: No?… Who are you then?

BALDOVINO: As I told you – almost a godhead! You should be able to see that! Even physically I only appear to exist. I'm immersed in figures and financial speculation, though only for other people. Not a penny, not a fraction of it for me. And that's the way I want it. Here I am in this beautiful home and it's as if I neither hear nor see not touch anything here. At times I'm astonished even by the sound of my own voice or my own echoing footsteps; by the knowledge that I too need a glass of water or the time to rest – it's a delightful way to live, you know… in the perfect detachment of pure form!

MAURIZIO: You ought to feel some pity for us poor mortals!

BALDOVINO: I do. But I can't behave any other way. I told your cousin the Marchese, I warned him well in advance – I'm only sticking to our agreement.

MAURIZIO: But you get a kick out of it too. A devilish kick.

BALDOVINO: Devilish? Oh no! It's the pleasure enjoyed by the saints in the church frescos, floating in the air, reclining on a cloud.

MAURIZIO: You realize, though, that it can't go on for ever like this.

BALDOVINO (*gloomily, after a pause*): I know all right! It must come to an end soon perhaps… But watch out, it all depends how. (*Staring into his eyes*) I say this for their sake. Open your cousin's eyes! He's too keen to be rid of me as soon as he can… You're worried? You've heard something?

MAURIZIO: No, nothing, Truly.

BALDOVINO: Come on now, be honest. I'm sorry for them, it's quite natural.

MAURIZIO: I've heard nothing, promise you. I've spoken to Signora Maddalena, but I haven't seen Fabio yet.

BALDOVINO: Oh, I understand. They must both have thought, her mother and your cousin: "We'll marry her off for form's sake. Then after a while on some pretext or other, we'll send him packing." It was the best solution for them. But they can't really expect it! Here too their attitude has been appallingly casual.

MAURIZIO: You suspect this but how do you know?

BALDOVINO: Isn't it true that they made my honesty the whole basis of our agreement?

MAURIZIO: Well, there you are! How can they hope...

BALDOVINO: You're so naive. Reason is one thing, feeling is another. It's easy to work out a logical course of action and hope in one's heart for a different outcome. I could please them both, believe me, and provide a pretext to let them dispose of me. But they can't rely on that. Because, although I could do it, I won't – in their own interest. I won't because I just don't believe they can genuinely want me to do it.

MAURIZIO: God! What a frightful man you are! You even refuse them the hope they might be able to put you in the wrong.

BALDOVINO: Now look. Supposing I did. At first they'd breathe again. They'd be free of the crushing burden of my presence. They'd appear to retain at least some of the honesty found wanting in me. Agata would still be a married woman separated from a disreputable husband. His disgrace would allow her, young as she is, to seek consolation with an old friend of the family. What was forbidden to a single young woman is excused in a wife no longer bound to fidelity in marriage. All right? Why shouldn't I, the husband, then be dishonest and make myself scarce? Because it wasn't only as a husband I let myself in for this. If that had been all, I would never have done it. There'd have been no real need of *me*. I was needed in so far as this husband was soon to become a father. By soon I mean... at the normal time. What was needed here was a father. And this father – well, it was in Fabio's interest too – simply had to be an honest man! Because, though I as her husband can walk out without wounding my wife – as she can revert to her own maiden name – as a father my dishonest departure couldn't help harming the child, who by law can have no name but mine. And the further I fall, the more the boy will suffer for it... Fabio couldn't possibly wish for that.

MAURIZIO: No, you're right there!

BALDOVINO: So, you see? And you know me. If I did it, I'd sink into iniquity. To take revenge on them for driving me away in disgrace, I'd want the little boy with me. He is legally mine. I'd leave him with them for two or three years to give them time to get attached to him, then I'd prove my wife was living with her lover in adultery. I'd take him away and drag him down with me... right down. You know the horrible beast there is inside me. How I've tried to control him by chaining him to the terms of this agreement. It's in their interest above all that I should observe them. And I fully intend to. Because if I felt no longer bound by them, God knows where I'd end up. (*Suddenly changing his tone*) Enough of this!... Just tell me: did they want you to see me as soon as you got back? Out with it! What were you meant to ask me? Tell me quickly please! (*He looks at his watch*) I've given you more time than I should. You know the boy's to be christened this morning? The members of the Board have been invited and I have to fit in a meeting with them before luncheon... Was it your cousin or her mother who sent you?

MAURIZIO: It's true. It's about the baby's baptism – the name you want to inflict on him...

BALDOVINO: I know!

MAURIZIO: I'm sorry... but isn't it...

BALDOVINO: I know, poor little lad. It's such a ponderous name! Enough to squash the life out of him.

MAURIZIO: Si-gis-mon-do!

BALDOVINO: It's a tradition in my family... my father's name and his father's too...

MAURIZIO: Not a reason that appeals to them, you must see!

BALDOVINO: I wouldn't have chosen it either, you know. So it's hardly my fault, is it? It's an ugly, clumsy name, especially for a child... and I confess (*very softly*) that if he had been my own son, really mine, I doubt if I'd have called him that...

MAURIZIO: There you are, you see!

BALDOVINO: What do I see? That it should be clear to you now why I can't give this name up. It's the same old story: it's not for my sake. It's for the façade, on account of the form. You realize that, since he has to have a name, I can give him no other. It's no good, you know, no good at all their persisting. I'm sorry, but you can tell them I won't give way! Why the hell don't they let me get on with my work? All this is a waste of time. I'm sorry, dear friend, to welcome you back like this. Until later then? See you later. (*He hurriedly shakes his hand and goes off left*)

MAURIZIO *is left standing, like someone wrong-footed. A moment after,* SIGNORA MADDALENA *and* FABIO *come in sheepishly from the right, one after another, anxious to hear the news.* MAURIZIO *looks at them and scratches his neck. First* MADDALENA, *then* FABIO, *look questioningly at him, without a word, she piteously and he with a frown.* MAURIZIO *responds with a negative shake of his head, half-closing his eyes and spreading out his arms.* MADDALENA *collapses on a chair and sits there helplessly.* FABIO *sits too but is very tense, clenching his fists on his knees.* MAURIZIO *also sits, shaking his head and sighing deeply. None of them has the courage to break the crushing silence.* MAURIZIO's *nasal sighs are answered by* FABIO's *open-mouthed snorting.* MADDALENA *can neither snort nor sigh, but every time the others do she shakes her head disconsolately and the corners of her mouth turn down a little more. The actors must not be afraid of prolonging this dumb show. All at once* FABIO *leaps to his feet and starts pacing fretfully up and down, clenching and unclenching his fists. Shortly after,* MAURIZIO *stands up too, goes to* MADDALENA *and bows, proffering his hand to take her leave.*

MADDALENA (*quietly and mournfully taking it*): You're going?

FABIO (*instantly turning on them*): Let him go then! I don't know how he had the cheek to show himself. (*To* MAURIZIO) Don't you dare look me in the face again. (*He resumes his pacing*)

MAURIZIO (*not daring to protest, hardly turning to look at him and speaking softly to* MADDALENA *whose hand he is still holding*): Agata?

MADDALENA (*quietly and plaintively*): In there with the baby.

MAURIZIO (*softly, still holding her hand*): Say goodbye for me. (*He kisses her hand, then turns and spreads out his arms*) Ask her… to forgive me.

MADDALENA: Oh, she at least… she has her baby boy now.

FABIO (*still pacing up and down*): Oh yes! And a fine time she'll have with him once he falls under the influence of this monster!

MADDALENA: That's my nightmare!

FABIO (*still pacing*): He's made a good start with that name!

MADDALENA (*to* MAURIZIO): For ten months now, believe me, we hardly dare say a word.

FABIO (*still pacing*): Imagine the way he'll want to bring him up!

MADDALENA: It's awful... he won't even let us see the daily papers.

MAURIZIO: You can't? Why not?

MADDALENA: He's got a thing about the press, you see.

MAURIZIO: But in the house, how is he? Strict? Bad-tempered?

MADDALENA: Not a bit of it! Worse... extremely well-mannered! He says the most painful things to us in such a way... using arguments that are so outlandish, and so unanswerable, that we always feel we must do exactly what he wants. He's a frightful man, Setti, terrifying! I'm almost afraid to breathe.

MAURIZIO: My dear signora, what can I say? I'm quite devastated. I'd never have thought...

FABIO (*exploding again*): Oh, give it a rest! I can't leave here just now because of the christening, but if I could, I would. Nothing's stopping you! Get out! Can't you see I won't hear another word? I can't stand the sight of you!

MAURIZIO: You're right. Yes, I'll go, I'll go...

Enter a SERVANT.

SERVANT (*opening the rear door, announcing*): From Santa Marta. The parish priest.

MADDALENA: Ah! Show him in.

Exit the SERVANT.

MAURIZIO: Goodbye, signora.

MADDALENA: You really feel you must go? You won't stay for the christening? Agata would love you to be here. Please come. I'm counting on you.

MAURIZIO *spreads out his arms again, bows, glances at* FABIO *without daring to address him and goes out at the rear with a nod to the* PRIEST, *who has just entered, introduced by the* SERVANT *who closes the door as he leaves.*

MADDALENA: Come in, Father. Please sit down.

PRIEST: I hope you're well, signora.

FABIO: Reverend Father!

PRIEST: My dear Marchese! Signora, I've come to discuss our arrangements.

MADDALENA: Thank you, Father. The altar boy you sent is here already.

PRIEST: Excellent!

MADDALENA: Yes, and we've prepared everything in there, including the ornaments he brought from the church. Oh, and there's a cherub, you know? It looks really lovely! Now I'll take you in to see...

PRIEST: And Signora Baldovino?

MADDALENA (*somewhat embarrassed*): Well yes, I'll send for her.

PRIEST: Not if she's busy. I just wanted to know how she was.

MADDALENA: Oh yes, she's fine now, thank you. As you'll understand, she's much taken up with the baby.

PRIEST: So I imagine.

MADDALENA: She can't tear herself away.

PRIEST: And it's you, Signor Marchese, who'll be the godfather?

FABIO: Why... yes...

MADDALENA: And I'm the godmother.

PRIEST: That goes without saying... And... er... the name? Still the one you gave me?

MADDALENA: I'm afraid so... (*With a deep sigh*)

FABIO (*furiously*): Horribly afraid!

PRIEST: Yet, you know... after all... Sigismondo was a great saint... a king! I'm a humble servant of hagiography...

MADDALENA: Oh, we know what a scholar you are!

PRIEST: No, no... please... don't exaggerate! An enthusiastic amateur perhaps... yes... Saint Sigismondo was a king of Burgundy, whose wife was Amalberga, Theodoric's daughter... But when she died, the widower unfortunately married one of her ladies-in-waiting... a treacherous woman who infamously plotted to make him commit... the most... yes, the most atrocious of crimes... against his own son...

MADDALENA: Heavens above! His own son? What did he do?

PRIEST: Well, he... (*A gesture with both hands*) He strangled him!

MADDALENA (*to* FABIO, *in a shocked cry*): Did you hear that?

PRIEST (*quickly*): Ah, but he repented of course. Immediately. And in atonement he submitted to the strictest penitence. He withdrew to a monastery and put on sackcloth. His virtuous conduct there, and the punishment he endured with saintly resignation, led to his being honoured as a martyr.

MADDALENA: He was tortured too?

PRIEST (*with half-closed eyes, extending his neck and bowing his head, with one finger indicating decapitation*): In the year 524 if I'm not mistaken.

FABIO: That's choice! A splendid saint! He strangled his own son... and had his head cut off...

PRIEST: The worst sinners, Marchese, often turn into the most respected saints! And believe me, he was a truly learned man. It's to him we owe the famous Lex Gombetta, the Burgundian Codex!... That's only a theory. Strongly contested. But Savigny maintains... and I support him... oh yes... I trust Savigny.

MADDALENA: The only comfort I see, Father, is that I can call him by the shortest form of his name – Dino!

PRIEST: Yes, indeed... Sigismondo... that's wonderful! Dino! A very good name for a child. Suits him perfectly, doesn't it, Marchese?

MADDALENA: Yes, but will he let us use it?

FABIO: That's it, precisely.

PRIEST: Well, after all, if Signor Baldovino is so keen on his father's name... we'll have to be content – so now what time have we fixed on?

MADDALENA: We'll have to let him decide that too, Father... Excuse me. (*She presses a bell on the wall*) We'll ask him to come at once. If you don't mind waiting a moment. (*The* SERVANT *enters from the rear door*) Tell Signor Baldovino that the priest is here and ask him to come in... He's in there (*she points to the door on the left. The* SERVANT *bows, crosses the stage, knocks on the door and goes in.*)

BALDOVINO (*entering hurriedly from the left*): Oh, most Reverend Father, I'm highly honoured. Please don't get up.

PRIEST: The honour is mine. Thank you, signore. We've disturbed you.

BALDOVINO: Oh no! Not at all! I'm delighted to see you here. How can I help you?

PRIEST: I wonder if you'd mind... you see... we wanted to agree a time for the baptism.

BALDOVINO: At your disposal, Father. Whatever suits you. Both the godparents are here, the nurse is in there, I think, I'm ready... and the church is just down the road.

MADDALENA (*amazed*): The church?

FABIO (*barely controlling his anger*): The church?

BALDOVINO (*turning to them in astonishment*): Why, what's wrong?

PRIEST (*quickly*): Well, Signor Baldovino... it was all arranged... don't tell me you didn't know?

MADDALENA: It's all ready in the other room.

BALDOVINO: Ready? What for?

PRIEST: For the baptism. So you can have the ceremony here to make it more meaningful.

FABIO: We've even been sent a few sacred objects from the church.

BALDOVINO: More meaningful? Forgive me, Father, but I never thought I'd hear you say a thing like that.

PRIEST: No, but... what I mean is... it's the custom, you see, for all the best families to have this celebration in their home.

BALDOVINO (*simply, with a smile*): And wouldn't you prefer, Father, that people like us set an example of that Christian humility that in God's eyes sees no distinction between rich and poor?

MADDALENA: No one means to offend God when a christening is kept to the family!

FABIO: Of course not! I'm sorry, but you seem to enjoy spoiling everything. You always object to what others propose. It seems odd to me that you of all people would interfere and preach to us.

BALDOVINO: My dear Marchese, please don't tempt me to raise my voice. Perhaps you'd like to hear the principles I believe in?

FABIO: Oh no! Not that! I won't hear a thing from you!

BALDOVINO: If you take me for a hypocrite...

FABIO: I never said that! Stubborn and prejudiced, that's all!

BALDOVINO: You think you can read my mind? What do you know about it? I can see why you imagine, being aware of my sentiments, that I shouldn't care how you conduct this christening which you have all set your minds on. Well, it goes beyond that. What if it's not for my benefit, but the child's? Like you, I'm totally in favour of this ceremony, but I intend it should be carried out correctly. The boy must be taken to church and baptized at the font. Why should he enjoy a privilege that betrays the whole spirit of this sacrament? I find it strange that you oblige me to say all this in front of the parish priest. He can't fail to acknowledge that a baptism celebrated with great simplicity in the place intended for it is an occasion far more solemn, more devout. Isn't that the case?

PRIEST: Indeed it is, no doubt about it.

BALDOVINO: What's more, I'm not the only interested party. Since it concerns the child, who depends first and foremost on his mother, let us hear what she has to say. (*He rings the bell on the wall twice*) We'll let our priest do the talking. We won't say a word. (*The* MAID *comes in from the right*) Ask the signora if she can spare a moment. (*The* MAID *nods and goes*)

PRIEST: Well, really you know... I'd rather you talked to her, signore, you're so persuasive...

BALDOVINO: Oh dear no! I'd better not be here. You can tell her what I think. (*To* MADDALENA *and* FABIO) Then you can both give your views. That way the boy's mother is free to choose for herself. And we'll accept her decision. Here she is. (AGATA *enters the room from the right. She is wearing an elegant housecoat. She is pale and tense.* FABIO *and the* PRIEST *stand up.* BALDOVINO *is already standing.*)

AGATA: Oh, good morning, Father.

PRIEST: My congratulations, signora.

FABIO (*bowing*): Signora...

BALDOVINO (*to* AGATA): It's about the baptism. (*To the* PRIEST) Reverend Father.

PRIEST: My respects, signore. (BALDOVINO *exits left*)

AGATA: I thought it was all settled. I don't quite know...

MADDALENA: Yes, it's all ready in there... it looks splendid!

FABIO: Now there's a new problem!

PRIEST: Yes, you see... Signor Baldovino...

MADDALENA: He doesn't want the baptism at home!

AGATA: Why's that?

MADDALENA: Why, because he says...

PRIEST: Allow me, signora? He didn't exactly say no. He wants you to decide, signora, because after all... it's up to the mother. So if you want to hold the baptism here...

MADDALENA: Of course! As we agreed!

PRIEST: I really see no harm in it.

FABIO: It's been done in so many homes.

PRIEST: I said that, didn't I? I pointed it out to him myself.

AGATA: So what's left for me to decide?

PRIEST: Ah well, you see… Signor Baldovino maintained – and quite rightly one must admit – with a moral rectitude that does him honour, that a baptism held in a church is bound to be more solemn and devout. Ah! And he put it so beautifully – "without enjoying a privilege," he said, "that betrays the whole spirit of the sacrament." A matter of principle, you see. Of principle.

AGATA: Well, if you would rather…

PRIEST: In principle, dear lady, how can I not agree?

AGATA: Then we'll do as he wants.

MADDALENA: Oh no, Agata! You too?

AGATA: Why, yes, Mamma.

PRIEST: In principle, I said, signora. But on the other hand…

FABIO: You wouldn't mind holding it here?

PRIEST: By no means, why should I?

FABIO: He enjoys upsetting us all!

PRIEST: But if that's what the signora wants…

AGATA: Yes, Father, I do. In church.

PRIEST: That's settled then. It's near at hand. Just let me know when. My respects, signora. (*To* MADDALENA) Signora…

MADDALENA: I'll see you out.

PRIEST: Please don't bother… Signor Marchese…

FABIO: My respects, Father.

PRIEST: There's no need, signora.

MADDALENA: But of course… this way please…

They both leave by the main door. Looking extremely wan, AGATA *is about to leave on the right.* FABIO, *in a fury, goes up to her and speaks in a low agitated voice.*

FABIO: Agata, for God's sake, don't push my patience too far!

AGATA (*gravely indicating, more with her head than her hand, the door on the left*): Not here, please, Fabio!

FABIO: Always… it's what he wants, again!

AGATA: If what he wants is right…

FABIO: To you he's always been right, everything he's said since he was first sent to try us.

AGATA: Not that again! We all agreed, didn't we?

FABIO: But now it's just you. All you needed was to get over the first shock. Then listening to him behind the door was enough to overcome your reluctance – now look at you! You're only too happy to abide by the terms I only first accepted to set your mind at rest. Now it's you, it's because of you... that he knows...

AGATA (*all at once, stiffly*): ...What does he know?

FABIO: You see? You see? You're on his side! He knows there's been nothing between us since then.

AGATA: It's for my sake!

FABIO: No, for his sake, for him!

AGATA: It's for me. I can't bear the idea he'd think anything else.

FABIO: Yes, that's it! You want him to respect you! As if he'd had nothing to do with our agreement.

AGATA: Listening to you just reminds me of one thing only: that the shame, if shame there is, is as much ours as his. You want it to be his alone. That makes me ashamed and I won't have it!

FABIO: But I want what belongs to me and ought to be mine again! You, Agata! You, you, you! (*He grabs hold of her frenetically and tries to pull her to him*)

AGATA (*struggling, with no sign of yielding*): No... no... stop it! Let me go! I told you! Never, never again, till you manage to get rid of him!...

FABIO (*without releasing her, his ardour increasing*): I will! I'll do it today! I'll turn him out like the swindler he is. And I'll do it today!

AGATA (*stunned, no longer able to resist*): A swindler?

FABIO: Yes, yes... a swindler! A criminal! He's done it now! He's been cooking the books!

AGATA: Are you sure?

FABIO: Of course I'm sure. Already he's pocketed more than 300,000 lire. Now we'll send him packing... today... and you'll be mine again, mine, mine, mine...

The door on the left opens and BALDOVINO *appears, wearing a top hat. Finding the couple embracing, he at once stands still in surprise.*

BALDOVINO: Oh, I beg your pardon... (*Then with a severity tempered by a shrewdly amused smile*) Well, well! It's only me of course, so it doesn't matter. But it could have been a servant. I suggest you should at least lock the door.

AGATA (*highly indignant*): There was no need for that!

BALDOVINO: Not on my account, signora. I'm reminding the Marchese. For your sake.

AGATA: That's what I was trying to tell him. But now… (*severely*) he has something to say to you.

BALDOVINO: To me? By all means. What about?

AGATA (*scornfully*): You should know!

BALDOVINO: Do I? (*Turning to* FABIO) What is it?

AGATA (*imperiously to* FABIO): Tell him!

FABIO: No, not now…

AGATA: I want you to tell him now, while I'm still here…

FABIO: It would be better to wait…

BALDOVINO (*quickly, sarcastically*): Perhaps you need witnesses?

FABIO: I don't need anyone. You have embezzled 300,000 lire.

BALDOVINO (*very calmly, with a smile*): No. More, Signor Marchese. Much more! Not three, but five hundred and sixty-three thousand… Wait! (*From his inside pocket he takes out his wallet from which he removes five small cards listing the figures of an officially stamped statement of accounts and from the last one reads out the total sum:*) 563 thousand 728 hundred lire and 60 centimes. More than half a million. Signor Marchese – you greatly underestimate me!

FABIO: The amount is neither here nor there. I don't give a damn. You can keep the lot and get out!

BALDOVINO: Hold on, Marchese… not so fast! You think you have every reason to fly off the handle. Not so. You must realize first that it's all far worse than you think.

FABIO: Not again, Mr Know-all.

BALDOVINO: Know-all? Oh no! (*Turning to* AGATA) Please come over here and listen carefully. (*Then, when she has moved forwards, frowning coldly*) If it pleases you both to take me for a thief, we can even agree about that. And the sooner the better. But I beg you above all to consider how unfair you are to me. You see these? (*He holds up accounts spread out fan-wise*) These entries – you see, Marchese – show that your company is in credit to the tune of more than 500,000 lire from savings and excess profits. But forget that, Agata. We can sort that out. All I had to do was slip them into my pocket… according to them (*pointing to* FABIO *and meaning to include all the members of the Board*), had I fallen into the trap they set for me. That same misshapen individual Marchetto Fongi, who was here again this morning, was meant to trip me up. (*To* FABIO) Oh I don't deny it was quite skilfully planned! (*To* AGATA) You don't know about these things, Agata. But they'd concocted a suspense account for me, showing this surplus profit which I could have quietly laid hands on, sure that no one would be any the wiser. If I *had* been taken in and stolen the money, the inventors of this phoney account would have caught me red-handed. (*To* FABIO) Wasn't that the idea?

AGATA (*hardly mastering her indignation, staring at* FABIO *who never answers her*): And you did this?

BALDOVINO (*quickly*): No, Agata. You mustn't let it upset you. Scornful as you are when you ask him that question, bear in mind that it is I and not Fabio who would suffer the most – if he is placed in an intolerable situation, mine becomes intolerable too.

AGATA: Why yours?

BALDOVINO (*gazing at her with great intensity, then quickly looking down, disturbed and seemingly bewildered*): Why? Because... if you actually began to look on me as a man, a real human being, I... I could never... oh, Agata... it would have a terrible effect on me: I could never look anyone in the face again. (*He puts his hand to his brow and covers his eyes to control his emotion*) No... enough of this! It's really time we decide what to do. (*Bitterly*) I thought I'd enjoy myself today, cutting Marchetto Fongi and the board members down to size. You too, Marchese, who kidded yourself you could catch me out like this, a man like me. But now I come to think of it... you were able to sink so low as to label me a swindler in order to hang on to you (*indicating* AGATA). And you never gave a thought for the shame that would shadow your newborn child when I'd been booted out like a thief in front of five witnesses – I believe the pleasure I take in being honest should have a better outcome. (*He hands* FABIO *the accounts he had shown before*) These are for you, Marchese.

FABIO: What am I supposed to do with them?

BALDOVINO: Tear them up. They're the only proof of my innocence. The money's all in the safe, down to the last centime. (*He looks him steadily in the eye, then harshly and scornfully:*) But now *you* have to steal it.

FABIO (*as if lashed in the face*): I do?

BALDOVINO: Yes, you. You.

FABIO: Are you mad?

BALDOVINO: You don't want half measures, do you? I told you what would be bound to happen if you agreed to me being honest – that you would be responsible if anything went wrong. You steal the money and I'll play the thief. Then I'll leave, because I really can't stay here any more.

FABIO: But this is madness.

BALDOVINO: No, it's not. I'm using my head. For you and for us all. I don't say you should send me to jail. You couldn't anyway. You'll be stealing the money, but on my behalf. That's all.

FABIO (*confronting him angrily*): What are you saying?

BALDOVINO: Now don't take offence. That's just one way of putting it. You'll come out with clean hands. You'll remove the money from the safe just long enough to prove that I took it. Then you return it naturally, so your associates don't suffer in any way for the trust they had in me out of respect for you. I'll still pass for the thief.

AGATA (*rebelling*): No, no! You can't do it! (*Confrontation of the two men. Then, correcting without contradicting the impression her protest has made:*) And what about the child?

BALDOVINO: It's unavoidable, signora…

AGATA: No, I can't, I won't allow it!

A SERVANT *appears at the main door to announce:*

SERVANT: The Board of Directors and Signor Fongi. (*He leaves*)

FABIO (*quickly, in great consternation*): We'll put all this off till tomorrow.

BALDOVINO (*without hesitation, firmly and defiantly*): I've made up my mind. I'm ready now.

AGATA: I won't have it, I tell you! You understand? I won't let you do it!

BALDOVINO (*utterly resolved*): All the more reason why I should…

FONGI (*entering with the four directors*): May we come in?…

At the same moment, from the door on the right, enter MADDALENA *in a hat and the* NURSE *in her very best clothes with ribbons and bows, carrying the baby in an elaborate cradle draped in a blue veil. Everyone crowds round with various congratulations, exclamations and compliments, while* MADDALENA *cautiously raises the veil to reveal the baby.*

CURTAIN

ACT THREE

BALDOVINO's *study. Richly furnished with sober elegance. Door at the rear, side door on the right.* BALDOVINO, *in the same suit he was wearing in Act One, is seated, elbows on knees and his head in his hands, gazing sternly and gloomily at the floor.* MADDALENA *is close to him, talking anxiously.*

MADDALENA: But you must realize you have no right to do this. It's not you that matters now. Or Fabio or even Agata. It's for the baby's sake! For the child!

BALDOVINO (*raising his head and glaring fiercely at her*): And why should I care about the child?

MADDALENA (*alarmed, then quickly recovering*): My God! I suppose not – but remember what you yourself said: about the harm the child would suffer. Precious words that went straight to my daughter's heart. You must realize that now she is a mother, simply a mother, this thought is tearing her apart.

BALDOVINO: Signora, I don't know a thing any more.

MADDALENA: That's not true. After what you said to Fabio yesterday.

BALDOVINO: What was that?

MADDALENA: That he shouldn't have done all this because of the child.

BALDOVINO: I said that?… Oh no, dear lady. I don't care what he's done. I knew he'd do something like this. (*He looks at her with more annoyance than contempt*) And so, signora, did you.

MADDALENA: No, I swear I didn't!

BALDOVINO: You're right there. To get me out of the house. I'm sure that was the main reason. He hoped, while I was busy elsewhere, to have a free hand here for himself and your daughter…

MADDALENA (*suddenly interrupting him*): Oh no, not Agata. That may well have been Fabio's idea… but I assure you that Agata…

289

BALDOVINO (*in an outburst, waving his arms*): Good God! Are you really so blind? How can you say that to me of all people?

MADDALENA: It's the truth.

BALDOVINO: And that doesn't alarm you? (*Pause*) Don't you realize the implications? That it forces me to leave? Instead of coming to see me, you should be trying to persuade your daughter that it's best for me to go.

MADDALENA: But how to do it? That's the problem.

BALDOVINO: How's not important. All that matters is that I go.

MADDALENA: No... She'll stop you!

BALDOVINO: Please signora, let me at least keep my wits about me. Don't rob me of what strength I have left to foresee the consequences of what others do so blindly. Blindly, mind, not because they're stupid, but because when you live, when you're really alive, you can't watch yourself living. If my vision is clear, it's because I came here in order *not* to live. Do you insist on bringing me back to life? Be warned that if life reclaims me I go blind too... (*Interrupting himself, he strives to control the human feelings which, whenever they threaten to emerge, make him seem almost fierce. Then he resumes, calmly if not coldly:*) Now look... listen... I simply wanted to make the Marchese aware of the result of his actions, that by trying to make out an honest man was a thief – not my real self, you understand, but the man whose honesty he needed and I consented to represent in order to demonstrate his own blindness to him – the only way to achieve it would be to steal the money himself.

MADDALENA: But how can you think he would do that?

BALDOVINO: To pass me off as a criminal.

MADDALENA: But he can't do that! He musn't!

BALDOVINO: He will steal it, I tell you! He'll pretend to. But if he doesn't, I will – do you really want me to take it?

MAURIZIO *comes in from the right in great consternation. As soon as he sees him* BALDOVINO *bursts out laughing.*

BALDOVINO: I suppose you've come to beg me as well "not to commit this crazy act"?

MADDALENA (*suddenly to* MAURIZIO): Yes, yes, for God's sake, Setti, persuade him not to!

MAURIZIO: Don't worry, he won't! He knows quite well it's lunacy, not so much for him as for Fabio.

BALDOVINO: Did he urge you to come to the rescue?

MAURIZIO: No, he didn't. It's because you wrote and asked me to come.

BALDOVINO: I know! And of course you've brought me the hundred lire I asked you to lend me?

MAURIZIO: I've brought nothing.

BALDOVINO: Because, being a bright spark, you realized it was all a charade! Bravo! (*He takes hold of the jacket he is wearing*) However, as you see, I'm dressed for departure – as I told you in my note – in the same suit I came in. All he needs, isn't it, an honest man dressed like this, is the hundred lire I asked the proverbial old school friend to lend me, in order to make a decent exit? (*On a sudden impulse, grasping the others arms with both hands*) You know how important this charade is to me!

MAURIZIO (*bemused*): What the hell do you mean?

BALDOVINO (*turning to look at* MADDALENA *and laughing again*): This poor lady is staring at me in amazement… (*Friendly and equivocally*) Now I'll explain, signora… Well, you see, the mistake the Marchese made – a most excusable one, mind, that I understand perfectly – lay simply in believing that I could really fall into a trap. It can all be put right. He will finally realize that as I came here to play a charade I started to enjoy, it has to be played out to the bitter end – oh yes, until the theft takes place. But not a real one, you see? Would I really pocket 300,000 lire as he believed – actually, signora, more than five hundred? Even for this simulated theft, essential as it is, my sole reward is the enjoyment it all brings me. Above all don't worry about the threat I made, merely to impress the Marchese, that I'd come and claim his child in three or four years time. Rubbish. What would I do with a child? Or were you expecting blackmail?

MAURIZIO: Oh, come off it! No one here thinks that!

BALDOVINO: And what if I had considered it?

MAURIZIO: Stop it, I tell you.

BALDOVINO: Blackmail, no. But I meant to keep the game going till I could relish the exquisite pleasure of seeing you all beg me *not* to take the money you'd tried so hard to make me steal.

MAURIZIO: But you haven't taken it!

BALDOVINO: Exactly! Because I want him to take it with his own fair hands! (*As he sees* FABIO *appear at the doorway on the right, very pale, out of breath and in great turmoil*) And I promise you, he will steal it!

FABIO (*deathly pale and anxious as he goes to* BALDOVINO): I'll steal it?... Me?... But then... Oh my God! Did you leave the safe keys with anyone else?

BALDOVINO: No, why?

FABIO: My God! My God!... But then... Could someone have found out? Could Fongi have told someone?

MAURIZIO: Is the money missing from the safe?

MADDALENA: Heaven forbid!

BALDOVINO: No, Marchese, don't worry. (*He taps his jacket to indicate his inside pocket*) I have it here.

FABIO: Ah! So you *did* take it?

BALDOVINO: I warned you. No half measures with me.

FABIO: But what are you really after?

BALDOVINO: Never fear. I knew a gentleman like you would be horrified at the thought of removing that money from the safe for a single minute, even as a joke. So last night I went and took it myself.

FABIO: You did, did you? And why was that?

BALDOVINO: Why? To allow you, signore, to make a magnificent gesture... and put it back.

FABIO: You still persist in this madness?

BALDOVINO: I really did steal it, you see. And now, if you don't do as I say, what should still be a charade will become what you first wanted it to be.

FABIO: I did... Don't you realize I've changed my mind now?

BALDOVINO: But *I* haven't.

FABIO: What *do* you want?

BALDOVINO: Precisely the same thing as you. Didn't you tell Agata yesterday that I had money in my pocket? Well, now I have.

FABIO: But you don't have me in your pocket, by God!

BALDOVINO: Yes, I do. You as well. Now I'm off to the board meeting to make my report. You can't stop me. Of course I won't mention the surplus profits Marchetto Fongi so cleverly conjured up for me. And I'll give him the satisfaction of showing me up. Oh, have no fear. I'll give a superb performance as an embarrassed thief caught in the act. Then we'll sort it all out back here.

FABIO: You won't do it!

BALDOVINO: Oh yes, signore, I will.

MAURIZIO: But you can't deliberately pretend to be a thief when you're not one.

BALDOVINO (*firmly, threateningly*): I told you, if you persist in opposing me, I'm determined to walk off with the money.

FABIO: But why? For God's sake why? If I myself ask you to stay?

BALDOVINO (*with sombre, slow gravity, turning to gaze at him*): And how could you really expect me to stay here now?

FABIO: I told you how sorry I was, most sincerely sorry...

BALDOVINO: What for?

FABIO: For what I've done.

BALDOVINO: But it's not what you've done, my dear sir – that was quite natural – but what you haven't done!

FABIO: And what should I have done?

BALDOVINO: What should you have done? After a few months you should have told me that if we both stuck to our agreement – it cost me nothing and it was natural for you – there was someone here more important than either of us, whose integrity and noble spirit – as I often predicted to you – would have prevented her keeping to it. Then at once I would have shown you the absurdity of your proposition: that an honest man could be brought here and persuaded to accept such a role.

FABIO: Yes, you're right. In fact I was cross with him (*indicating* MAURIZIO) for involving someone like you.

BALDOVINO: No, he was absolutely right to choose me. Believe me! Did you really want to take on an honest mediocrity? How could any ordinary man have agreed to such an arrangement, unless he was a scoundrel? I alone could do so, because, as you see, I'm also willing to pass as a thief.

MAURIZIO: But how can you? Why?

FABIO (*at the same time*): What for? You enjoy it?

MAURIZIO: Who's forcing you to do it? No one wants you to!

MADDALENA: No one! We all beg you not to!

BALDOVINO (*to* MAURIZIO): You, as a friend. (*To* MADDALENA) You, for the child's sake. (*To* FABIO) And you, why you?

FABIO: The same reason as hers.

BALDOVINO (*looking him straight in the eye*): No reason apart from the child? (FABIO *is silent*) I'll tell you the true reason. Because now you see what your actions have led to. (*To* MADDALENA) Do you think, dear lady, that he really cares about the child's good name? Illusion. (*Indicating* MAURIZIO) He knows only too well... the sort of life I used to lead... Yes, and my present life... spotless since this baby came into the world... could perhaps wipe out the memory of so much... in my sad and murky past. But he, signora (*indicating* FABIO), had other things on his mind just now than the child. (*Addressing the others too*) But what about me? Don't I exist? You seem to think I can stay here for ever to lighten your darkness. And that's all? I'm a poor sick human being too! I have blood in my veins, black blood, made bitter by my poisonous past, and I'm afraid it might boil over. Yesterday, in there, this gentleman (*indicating* FABIO), in front of your fine daughter, accused me to my face of this presumed crime. Then, blinder than he is, than all the rest of you, I fell into another still more fearful trap than I did ten months ago. Living here, cheek by jowl with a woman I hardly dared glance at, my feelings were imperceptibly engaged. Your latest childish trick, Marchese, was all I needed to open my eyes to the abyss at my feet. I had intended to keep quiet, you see? Swallow your insult in front of her and confess I was a thief. Then get you on your own, prove to you it wasn't true and compel you privately to hold to our agreement to the end. But I couldn't keep quiet. My senses rebelled. Is any one of you prepared to stop me doing what I have to do? I tell you that to chasten this yearning of my old flesh, as I must, what else can I do but walk off with this memory?

They all stare at him in bewildered silence. A pause. AGATA *comes in from the right, pale and determined. After a few steps, she stops.* BALDOVINO *looks at her. He would like to force himself to stay calm and composed, but in his eyes one can almost glimpse a flash of fear.*

AGATA (*to her mother,* FABIO *and* MAURIZIO): Leave me to talk to him alone.

BALDOVINO (*almost stammering, with lowered eyes*): No. No, please... You see... I...

AGATA: I must talk to you.

BALDOVINO: It's... it's no good Agata... I've told them... all I had to say...

AGATA: And now you'll hear what I have to say.

BALDOVINO: No, no... for God's sake... it's no good, I tell you... Enough is enough.

AGATA: I insist. (*To the others*) Leave us alone please. (*The other three go off to the right*) I didn't come to tell you not to go. I came to say I'll go with you.

BALDOVINO (*another moment of bewilderment. He can hardly stand and speaks in a low tone*): I understand. You don't want to bring up the welfare of the child. A woman like you doesn't accept sacrifices – she makes one herself.

AGATA: I wouldn't call it a sacrifice. It's what I have to do.

BALDOVINO: No, no Agata, you don't. For the baby's sake or yours. I must prevent you at any cost.

AGATA: You can't. I'm your wife. You want to leave? Fair enough. I approve and I'll follow you.

BALDOVINO: Where? What on earth are you saying? Spare yourself and take pity on me... don't make me tell you why... work it out for yourself, because I... face to face... I can't... I don't know how to...

AGATA: No more need for words. What you said the very first day was enough for me. I should have come in at once and offered you my hand.

BALDOVINO: Oh, if only you had! I promise you I hoped... I hoped for a moment that you might... might have come in, I mean... I would never have dared even touch your hand... But it would all have ended there!

AGATA: You would have drawn back?

BALDOVINO: No, Agata. But I was ashamed... just as I am now in front of you.

AGATA: Of what? Of having spoken honestly?

BALDOVINO: That's easy, Agata. It's easy to be honest, you see, when it's just to save appearances. If you'd come in to say that the deception was more than you could bear, I couldn't have stayed a moment longer. Any more than I can now.

AGATA: So you thought I agreed...

BALDOVINO: No, Agata. But I waited when you didn't appear, I spoke as I did to show him that I couldn't *pretend* to be honest – not for my own sake but for yours, all of you. So you must realize that now… now you've changed the conditions, it becomes impossible for me to go on. Not because I don't or won't want to, but because of the sort of man I am, for what I've made of my life till now. Think only of the part I agreed to play…

AGATA: We asked you to do it!

BALDOVINO: Yes, and I accepted.

AGATA: But you warned Fabio in advance what it might lead to, to make him change his mind. And I accepted too.

BALDOVINO: You shouldn't have, should you, Agata? That was your mistake. You never heard my voice here, not my real voice. I only spoke through a grotesque mask – and why was that? Here you were all three of you, poor creatures suffering and relishing the ups and downs of life. A poor unfortunate mother who overcame her scruples and allowed her daughter to engage in an illicit love affair. And you were able to forget that the man you were in love with was regrettably committed to another woman. You all realized you were guilty, didn't you? And at once you tried to find a solution by calling me in. And I came in with my stultifying concept of unnatural fictitious honesty. So in the end you courageously rebelled against it. I was sure that in the long run your mother and the Marchese would never be able to live with the consequences. Their natural feelings were bound to revolt. I was aware they were huffing and puffing. And believe me, I enjoyed watching him hatch this last plot to avert the most serious of the dangers I had warned him about. You, Agata, were the one at risk. If you stuck with it all to the last. And you did. And you could – because becoming a mother, sadly the young girl in love had to die. Now you are a mother. And nothing else. But I, Agata, am not the father of your child – do you know what this means?

AGATA: Ah! It's all on account of the child? You want to leave because you're not the father?

BALDOVINO: No, no! Listen! That's not what I'm saying. The mere fact that you should want to come with me shows that you feel the child is yours and belongs to you alone. And this makes the boy still more precious to me than if he were really mine – a token of your sacrifice and your esteem for me.

AGATA: Well, then?

BALDOVINO: But what I've said is meant to remind you that this is not the real me. Because you can think of nothing but your child. I am only a mask, the mask of a father.

AGATA: Oh no!... I'm talking to the real you, the man behind the mask.

BALDOVINO: And what do you know about the real me? Who am I?

AGATA: This is you. Here and now. (*And as* BALDOVINO, *overwhelmed, bows his head*) If I dare to look at you, you can raise your eyes to me. Because here we should all bow our heads, as you alone have been ashamed of the faults in your life.

BALDOVINO: I never dreamt Fate would let me hear words like that... (*Violently, as if emerging from a spell*) No, no, Agata! Enough! Believe me, I don't deserve this. Do you know what I have here... in my pocket? More than 500,000 lire.

AGATA: You'll give that money back and we'll go away.

BALDOVINO: What? I'd be mad! No, Agata! I'll not return it. I-will-not-give-it-back!

AGATA: In that case the baby and I will follow you just the same...

BALDOVINO: You would come with me... even a thief? (*He collapses into a chair, bursts into tears and hides his face in his hands*)

AGATA (*after staring at him for a moment, she goes to the door on the right and calls out*): Mother!

As MADDALENA *comes in, she sees* BALDOVINO *crying and stops, dumbfounded.*

AGATA: You can tell those gentlemen there's nothing more for them to do here.

BALDOVINO (*suddenly on his feet*): No, wait!... The money! (*He takes a large wallet from his pocket*) Not her... it's up to me! (*Trying to hold back his tears and control himself, he searches vainly for his handkerchief.* AGATA *suddenly offers him hers. He interprets this gesture as something that associates them in grief for the first time. He kisses the handkerchief and dabs his eyes, as he holds one hand out to her. With a deep sigh of joy he masters his emotions and says:*) Now I know what I have to tell them.

CURTAIN

Clothe the Naked

Vestire gli ignudi (1922)

Translated by Diane Cilento

CHARACTERS

ERSILIA DREI
LUDOVICO NOTA, *a celebrated novelist*
SIGNORA ONORIA, *Ludovico's landlady*
FRANCO LASPIGA, *ex-lieutenant of the navy*
ALFREDO CANTAVALLE, *a reporter*
GROTTI, *Italian Consul at Smyrna*
EMMA, *a charwoman*

The scene throughout is Ludovico's lodgings in Rome

ACT ONE

We are in the study of the novelist, LUDOVICO NOTA. *It is an ample, rented room, filled with mixed furniture, some modern and vulgar, owned by the landlady. The rest of the pieces* NOTA *has brought in himself – they are all shabby, but tasteful.*

Against the back wall is a large bookcase. Stage right are two large windows with old yellowing curtains; a high desk (where one could stand and write) with several dictionaries on it. An old chintz-covered divan is pushed back against the wall, probably hiding rubbish. There are some stuffed chairs and a card table.

One wall is covered by an old and discoloured tapestry. At the back of the room is the door which leads into NOTA's *bedroom.*

In the middle of the room is an oval table, covered with books, reviews, newspapers, vases, a cigarette box and several little statues. In front of this table is a lounge chair, with many cushions.

On the back wall there are lots of little pictures, of little artistic value, gifts from painter friends. In spite of the two large windows, the room is rather gloomy, because of the narrowness of the street, and the height of the buildings opposite. The street below is very noisy, and the noises one should hear in the pauses indicated in the script are those of carts, vespas, whistles, car horns, the confused sound of voices, cries of newspaper boys and sudden shouts of laughter.

The two windows are high and face the audience. They are shuttered and the stage is divided by a corridor. We can always see people before they enter the corridor.

When the curtain rises the stage is empty. Both windows are open, and one listens to the street noises for a moment or two. The door opens and ERSILIA DREI *comes in as though she doesn't know where she is. She is dressed in a neat, well-worn, blue schoolmistress dress. She is beautiful but her cheeks are hollow and she is very pale. She looks as though she is recovering from an illness. She stands looking around the room, waiting for someone else to come in, smiling slightly at the disorder she sees. She becomes aware of the sounds of the street.* LUDOVICO NOTA *enters, putting away his wallet. He is a fine-looking man, although past fifty. He has acute lucid eyes, and when he smiles he seems younger than his years. Cold and thoughtful, he finds it difficult to make a real "contact" with anyone. Instead, he tries always to be at least affable. Sometimes this affability, in its desire to be spontaneous, only disconcerts.*

LUDOVICO: Here I am. Sit down. Sit down. My God, these windows are a real curse! (*He hurries to shut them*) But if I don't leave them open for a little while there's such a musty smell in here. Ugh. Old houses. Take off your hat. Take off your hat. (ERSILIA *does so*)

Through the bedroom door we see SIGNORA ONORIA, *the landlady. She disappears again, having seen* ERSILIA *and* NOTA, *only to reappear again, carrying a bundle of dirty linen. She is forty years old, stumpy, rather thick in the head, hennaed and gossipy. Pretending not to have noticed* ERSILIA, ONORIA *enters.*

ONORIA: Excuse me!

LUDOVICO (*who didn't expect to see her*): Oh! Were you in there?

ONORIA (*chewing over her words*): I've changed the sheets like you said in the note you left on the table this morning.

LUDOVICO (*embarrassed*): Oh… yes.

ONORIA (*pretending to see* ERSILIA *for the first time*): Oh… I see… Well, if you meant me to change the sheets for that… (*She stops herself*) I think we'd better have a little chat. Wait a moment, while I get rid of this stuff.

LUDOVICO: Yes. It's quite filthy…

ONORIA (*snapping*): You're the one to talk – filthy is it?

LUDOVICO (*trying to laugh it off*): Well, it looks it, so if you feel you must get rid of it…

ONORIA: *Yes!* And that's not all I want to get rid of.

LUDOVICO (*furious*): What do you mean? Speak up! Speak up!

ONORIA: I mean, *her*! Signor Nota, I don't want any stray cats in my house!

LUDOVICO: My God! You watch what you're saying or…

ONORIA: Or what will you do? Let's get things straight, Signor Nota. (*Goes towards the door*) I'll be back – as soon as I dump this! (*Exit*)

LUDOVICO (*shouting after her*): Dirty-minded old bitch!

ERSILIA: No! No! For goodness' sake, let me go!

LUDOVICO: It's nothing. It's nothing. This is my home, and you'll stay here.

ONORIA (*shouting through the door, where she has been listening*): Yours? What do you mean yours? Bed and breakfast, that's all you get. Just you remember that I keep a clean house.

LUDOVICO: Clean! Who, you? (*He goes out to her*)

ONORIA: Yes, me. Me!

LUDOVICO: You'd have difficulty in proving that!

ONORIA: Oh, would I? One thing I know, I don't have my lodgers bring women to sleep here!

LUDOVICO (*furious*): You are an insolent bitch!

ONORIA: Look who's talking!

LUDOVICO: And a stupid bitch! Can't you see this young girl isn't well!

ERSILIA: I'm sorry. I just got out of hospital.

LUDOVICO: There's no need for you to explain to *her*!

ONORIA: Oh well, if she's sick… (*The noise of a heavy truck makes the windows rattle*)

LUDOVICO: That's enough I tell you! Anyway you can't prevent me lending my rooms to her for a couple of days.

ONORIA: Oh yes, I can. I've let the rooms to *you*, not to her.

LUDOVICO: And if she were my sister, or a relation?

ONORIA: She could go to a hotel.

LUDOVICO: Do you mean to say I couldn't even put anyone up for the night?

ONORIA: But this girl is no relation of yours, is she, Signor Nota? I wasn't born yesterday, you know.

LUDOVICO: How do you know she's not? What if *I* go and sleep in a hotel?

ONORIA: You'll still have to ask my permission, and politely.

LUDOVICO: Your permission!

ONORIA: Yes! And politely. And if you don't like the musty smell in here – if you find it too much for you – why don't you go? I'd like to have these rooms free for a while. Who knows, perhaps the smell would go too?

LUDOVICO (*furious*): I shall be leaving here very, very shortly. In the meantime, would you mind getting out?

ONORIA: So you're vacating?

LUDOVICO: Yes, in a couple of days. At the end of the month.

ONORIA: Well then, there's nothing more to say, is there?

LUDOVICO: Get out!

ONORIA: I understand. I'm going. I'm going. Well, there's nothing more to say, is there? (*Exit*)

LUDOVICO: What a hateful creature! I'm so sorry. The moment you come in, this dreadful scene.

ERSILIA: Please don't! I'm the one who should say sorry. It wouldn't have happened if I…

LUDOVICO: Oh no; I've been fighting pitched battles with that old dragon for a year now. But somehow I'm tied to this foul place – caught in a nightmare, when one finds oneself transfixed. Perhaps you saw yourself in some fabulous apartment? But you see, my dear, I haven't written anything popular for several years now, and…

ERSILIA: Oh no, I didn't see myself anywhere. But it is sad that such a famous writer as you should—

LUDOVICO (*interrupting*): By the end of the month we shall have found a quiet little apartment on the Macao. In the Via Sommacampagna, between the gardens. We'll go and look tomorrow, and we can choose some new furniture together, too, if you like. Then you'll be able to set up house just as you want it.

ERSILIA: All that for me?

LUDOVICO: Oh, I needed it, too. No – I needed to get myself out of this place! You know, I'm… I'm like a man who has never really got started. That's why I'm so happy that I had that sudden inspiration to write to you and ask you to start a new life – with me. Stench, flies, oppressive heat. One has a breath of fresh air – aah! What is it? Nothing. The wind has come up – that's all. My life is like that.

ERSILIA: I don't know how to thank you, Signor Nota.

LUDOVICO: Oh, my dear. You can start by calling me Ludovico. In any case, it's I who should thank you for accepting the little I can offer.

ERSILIA: But it's so much. To me it's so much.

LUDOVICO: Yes, my dear, to you. I mean – that little which I offer becomes so inflated to you.

ERSILIA: Not inflated, Signor Nota.

LUDOVICO (*smiling*): Ludovico.

ERSILIA: I'll have to get used to it… If you knew how ashamed I feel.

LUDOVICO: Ashamed of what?

ERSILIA: I don't deserve this great good fortune.

LUDOVICO: Nonsense! What do you mean?

ERSILIA: I never thought that the story of my stupid misfortunes, printed in a newspaper, could arouse the pity…

LUDOVICO: The interest, the selfish interest…

ERSILIA: …Of a man like you, Signor Nota. (*She corrects herself*) I mean, Ludovico.

LUDOVICO: Yes. I must say I felt fascinated reading that paper, jolted by a sudden feeling of great sympathy, as though I had found, without even looking, the embryo of a marvellous story…

ERSILIA: And perhaps you felt, that is, you thought – you might write it as a novel?

LUDOVICO: Oh no! Don't misunderstand me. Don't think it was just professional curiosity. I only chose that comparison to make you understand my sudden interest.

ERSILIA: But if the story of my life – if all this pointless suffering could at least have *some* meaning…

LUDOVICO: You mean I should make it into a novel?

ERSILIA: Why not? I'd be so proud and happy if you did. (*She has become quite animated*) Truly.

LUDOVICO (*he looks up at her for a moment*): Ah! I give up!

ERSILIA: Why?

LUDOVICO: Because, without meaning to, you're telling me that I am old.

ERSILIA (*immediately confused*): No, I only said…

LUDOVICO: I don't want to *write* your story, my dear. I want to *live* it with you. I stretch out my arms to you, but instead of offering me, how shall I put it – your lips – you stick a pen in my hand and tell me to sit down and write.

ERSILIA: But it's too soon…

LUDOVICO: The lips – I know – or too late?

ERSILIA (*pause*): ...No...

LUDOVICO (*realizing her embarrassment*): You see how differently we both react to the same situation? I felt rather upset that you should think my interest in you was purely professional. On the other hand, you were offended – well, perhaps offended is too strong a word – that I might want you, not as the protagonist of a novel, but as a person to share my life with. If I had just wanted a live subject, there was no need for me to offer you my home – collect you from the hospital. Nothing. The facts of your case I knew from the newspaper – the rest is not difficult for such an – no, we won't say old – experienced writer as myself to imagine.

ERSILIA: Ah... How did you imagine it?

LUDOVICO: I can visualize everything so clearly, right to the last detail... Greece – that villa by the sea with the flat roof where you took the child on cool afternoons – you, the governess, waking suddenly in siesta time, finding the child gone – and then the sickening realization that she had fallen... your dismissal... the journey back to Rome... arriving here – then the final blow... You see, I imagined everything, everything, without knowing you, without ever seeing you.

ERSILIA: You imagined me... What was I like? Like I am, like this? (LU-DOVICO *smiles, shaking his finger*) How then? Tell me. Please tell me, Signor... (*She corrects herself*) Ludovico.

LUDOVICO: Why do you want to know?

ERSILIA: Because I would like to be just like the girl you imagined.

LUDOVICO: No! No! I like you much, *much* better as you are – for myself, that is – not for the novel.

ERSILIA: Then you saw the whole story with another girl in mind?

LUDOVICO: Naturally – I had never met you.

ERSILIA: Is she very different from me?

LUDOVICO: Altogether. Altogether. (*Smiling*)

ERSILIA: But then, I don't understand... I don't understand any more...

LUDOVICO: What don't you understand, my dear?

ERSILIA: How you could possibly be interested in me.

LUDOVICO: Who else?

ERSILIA: But if what interested you, reading that paper, was the story of that other girl, if it was she who captured your imagination, then I... (*She stops, rather lost*) I...

LUDOVICO: What?

306

ERSILIA: Then I'd better go.

LUDOVICO (*laughing, and trying to make a joke out of it*): Not at all, my dear. You, no! We'll send *her* away, not you.

ERSILIA (*mistrustfully*): But if she's *not* me, then you don't believe my story.

LUDOVICO: Of course I do! Of course I do! But now I want you to imagine yourself in a new life. One which will be, which *could* be, perhaps, shared with me. I want you also to imagine yourself in this new life, with no memory of all the awful things that have happened to you.

ERSILIA (*beginning to smile*): Then I shan't be her, or me, but a completely new person?

LUDOVICO: Exactly! A new person!

ERSILIA (*wonderingly*): Do you really think so? (*She opens her hands, which were holding her knees*) But I've never been able to be anybody.

LUDOVICO: Come now. What do you mean, anybody?

ERSILIA: Nobody, ever!

LUDOVICO: But you are somebody...

ERSILIA: Who am I?

LUDOVICO: First of all, a beautiful girl.

ERSILIA (*shrugs her shoulders*): What? Beautiful? No! Anyway, I never knew how to take advantage of it. What good did it do me?

LUDOVICO: Mm... And when one doesn't know. Yes, very true... And when a girl doesn't know, it might occur to her, out of desperation, just to let herself go – go on the street. As a last resort before the final decision.

ERSILIA (*she turns and looks at him*): Oh, God! What did you say?

LUDOVICO: No! No! It was just something I imagined, about the girl in the novel. Towards evening she's sitting, looking at herself in the mirror, in that squalid little hotel room. She knows she can't pay the bill. She sees – herself. And suddenly decides that's the only thing she has left to sell – her body.

ERSILIA (*terrified*): But was all that written in the paper?

LUDOVICO: No, I just imag— (*stopping himself, leaning towards her excited*) Then, perhaps it's true? (ERSILIA *hides her face, shuddering. He is almost beside himself with pleasure, agitated.*) Ah! You see! You see how right my intuition was? (*Taking a new tone, commiseratingly*) That evening you went down into the street?

ERSILIA: Yes… yes…

LUDOVICO: You picked up some man? Any man – the first who came along?

ERSILIA (*still hiding her face*): And afterwards I… I didn't know how to… afterwards…

LUDOVICO (*quickly*): How to ask for the money? (ERSILIA *doesn't reply*) Not a penny, eh? How true! How true! And then the self-disgust, the nausea. This awful abortive attempt to be a whore – perfect! Perfect! (ERSILIA *is sobbing*) Are you crying? No. But why, my dear? (*He takes her in his arms to comfort her*)

ERSILIA (*trying to free herself*): Please let me go – now. Let me go away!

LUDOVICO: What are you saying? Why?

ERSILIA: Now that you know this…

LUDOVICO: But I knew it already. I knew!

ERSILIA: How did you know?

LUDOVICO: I knew instinctively. Don't you see? Intuition. How could I be wrong?

ERSILIA: …But I'm so guilty.

At this moment there is a great crash from the street outside. There has been a collision, followed by shouts, whistles, cries of abuse and horror, car horns, etc.

LUDOVICO: You weren't guilty… (*He breaks off and goes towards the windows*) What the devil's going on?

ERSILIA: They're shouting. Maybe it's an accident.

The noise increases from the street. Someone is shouting "Help! Help!" SIGNORA ONORIA *bursts into the room.*

ONORIA: They've knocked down a poor old man. Squashed him flat against the wall right under this window.

ONORIA *runs and opens one of the windows.* ERSILIA *and* LUDOVICO *go to the other window. As soon as the windows open a terrific noise invades the scene for a few minutes.*

We hear confused cries: "He's dead." "Hold his head up!" "He's not." "Give him some air." "Get back!" "Poor old man!" "Here's his hat!" "Give him some air!" "Give him air!" "Where's the driver of the truck?" "It's you, isn't it?" "He's trying to get away." "Catch him!" "Catch him." "Get hold of the bastard!" "Get an ambulance." "Where are the police?"

ONORIA (*hanging out of the window*): He's dead! Oh, the poor old man – that's the one who did it! He's trying to get away. Hold him! Hold him! What a face! Didn't give him a chance, just squashed him flat.

ERSILIA (*trying not to vomit, backs away from the window*): Oh, God! How horrible!

LUDOVICO (*closing his window*): Looks like some poor old civil servant. Shut the window! Shut the window, for God's sake!

ONORIA: Look! They're carrying him away. He must be dead by now.

LUDOVICO: He will be by the time they reach hospital.

ONORIA: I'm going downstairs to find out. What a terrible accident! What a terrible accident! (*She rushes out*)

LUDOVICO: In this filthy slum – when it rains you can't even walk in the street – they have the audacity to set up a market! Barrows, trucks, push carts, all fighting for a place! It's incredible!

ERSILIA (*after a pause, her eyes fixed*): The street... how horrible.

LUDOVICO: What a school for writers! The street... The marvellous hubbub of noise that distracts, interrupts and entangles us in its own life. Here we were quietly talking about this new life we may have together. Suppose that I had been that old man in the street – what would you have done then? That's just the kind of thing that can change the whole course of one's life. Just as your life changed, when that baby fell off the roof...

ERSILIA (*pause*): Just to serve, to obey. Not able to be anything. A uniform, a threadbare uniform, that every night you hang on a peg, against the wall. God, what a horrifying thing to know that nobody ever thinks of you. In the street I saw my whole life as if I didn't exist any more – as if I was dreaming those few people who passed by in that garden, at midday. The trees, those deckchairs. And I refused to go on being nothing any more.

LUDOVICO: But surely that can't be true?

ERSILIA: What do you mean, not true? I wanted to kill myself!

LUDOVICO: Surely, but also you wanted to create some lasting impression.

ERSILIA: Create? Do you think I made up the story?

LUDOVICO: No! No! Unconsciously, by telling your story, you created a lasting impression, in me. How can you say that you're nothing? When I tell you that your story, printed in the paper, has created a wave of sympathy throughout the whole city? Everyone is interested in you. I am the living proof of it.

309

ERSILIA: Have you still got it?

LUDOVICO: What?

ERSILIA: The newspaper. I want to read it! I want to read it!

LUDO: I think so. Yes, I must have kept it.

ERSILIA: Find it! Find it! I want to see it!

LUDOVICO: No, no, my dear. Why do you want to upset yourself all over again?

ERSILIA: Show it to me, please! I want to read what they said about me.

LUDOVICO: Just what *you* said, I suppose.

ERSILIA: But I don't remember what I said any more. At that moment, you understand? Let me see it. Please look for it!

LUDOVICO: Who knows where I've put it in all this mess. Let's leave it for the moment. We can look for it together later on.

ERSILIA: Did it tell everything? How long was it?

LUDOVICO: More than three columns – front page. In the summer when they haven't got much to write about, to get hold of a story like yours – it's a real scoop. They fill the papers with it. It's manna from heaven. They fill the papers with it!

ERSILIA: And him. What did they say about him?

LUDOVICO: That he was going to marry somebody else.

ERSILIA: No! No! I mean the other one!

LUDOVICO: The consul?

ERSILIA (*very upset*): Did they say the consul?

LUDOVICO: Yes. Our consul in Smyrna.

ERSILIA: But they promised they wouldn't print the name of the city!

LUDOVICO: Oh yes – journalists…

ERSILIA: There was no need to print that he was a consul, or that it was Smyrna. It makes no difference to the facts. What else did they say?

LUDOVICO: That after the little girl fell…

ERSILIA (*covering her face again*): My poor darling – oh, my…

LUDOVICO: …He was extremely harsh with you.

ERSILIA: Not him! His wife, the wife!

LUDOVICO: They said *he* was, too.

ERSILIA: No, no! His wife… Oh, my God!

LUDOVICO: Because she was jealous of you. Oh, I can just see her – a great policewoman.

ERSILIA: Her? No! She's a little shrivelled-up woman, with a complexion like an old lemon.

LUDOVICO: Not at all! I... You know, I was certain she was a tall woman, with eyebrows meeting at the centre. I could almost have painted her...

ERSILIA: She's just the opposite. Who knows how you saw me, then. No, no. She's just as I said.

LUDOVICO: There, you see: for my book I really needed a large woman. On the other hand, I see the child as a delicate-boned little girl – a waif.

ERSILIA: Delicate! My Mimmetta!

LUDOVICO: I called her Didi, in fact.

ERSILIA: Didi? No, her name was Mimmetta... Mimmetta. And she was a lovely round little cherub, with plump cheeks and golden ringlets. She loved *me* better than anyone else.

LUDOVICO: That made her mother even more jealous of you naturally.

ERSILIA: Of course. *That* more than anything. You know it was she – she who arranged my whole evening with him – with the other one...

LUDOVICO: The young naval lieutenant?

ERSILIA: Yes – she made me go with him, alone, that night, knowing that I would lose myself, carried away by the fragrance of the flowers, murmuring palm leaves... Alone with him in the dark fragrant night.

LUDOVICO: Ah... It's beautiful, beautiful. What a splendid setting for a story – the tropical night, sun, sea, the humidity...

ERSILIA: If I hadn't had so much to go through...

LUDOVICO (*finishing it for her*): With that bitch! I can imagine it. It's just the sort of thing a woman who'd never had any real pleasure in life would do. Insidiously arrange your seduction, and then sit back and wait for the inevitable disillusionment – it's magnificent!

ERSILIA: If you could have seen her – so motherly towards me, because he had formally requested my hand from them; they were my guardians. She threw us together. Then, the moment he'd gone – as though we saw the other side of the moon – she changed completely. If she wasn't reviling me, she was complaining of some imaginary ache or pain. And then finally she blamed me for the accident.

LUDOVICO: Knowing that she'd sent you on some errand when it actually happened.

311

ERSILIA (*standing up, frightened and worried*): Who told you that?

LUDOVICO: It was written in the paper.

ERSILIA: That too?

LUDOVICO: You must have told them…

ERSILIA: No… No!… I don't remember… I can't think…

LUDOVICO: Could I have imagined that too? Or perhaps the journalist invented it to colour the story of your dismissal. They sent you off without even the money for your return trip, didn't they? That's so, isn't it?

ERSILIA: Yes, yes! That's true.

LUDOVICO: Almost as if they wanted you to pay for the death of the little girl.

ERSILIA: But she *did* threaten me with that. She would have had me accused like a criminal, if she hadn't been too frightened that certain things would come to light…

LUDOVICO: About how she treated you – ah… Then I was right. What things would come to light?

ERSILIA (*becoming apprehensive*): No! I can't say. I can't tell you. I'm only sorry that they printed as much as they did. Anyway, I don't want to think about what happened out there any more. It's strange, but when I was coming back on the boat I had the most vivid impression that she was there – the little girl. She was with me. She left me that night… when I went onto the street.

LUDOVICO: But, excuse me – didn't you try to find your young lieutenant, the moment you arrived here in Rome?

ERSILIA: Where? I didn't know his address. I had always written to him "To Await Arrival, c/o the Admiralty". I went there, but they said he'd left the service and was getting married.

LUDOVICO: But you must trace him. He's committed "breach of promise" against you…

ERSILIA: I've never known how to assert myself.

LUDOVICO: He promised to marry you!

ERSILIA: When they told me he was about to marry into a wealthy family, I felt so forsaken, so impossibly alone – as though everyone had suddenly forgotten me. I couldn't go and throw myself on his mercy with no money, like some unwanted pauper. (*She starts to cry*) In the park that day I thought about Mimmetta… she came back to me and gave me courage, while I held those tablets in my hand. She was the only one who wanted me, and I wanted to be with her.

LUDOVICO (*embarrassed*): Come come, my dear! Pull yourself together. You don't need to think about those things any more.

ERSILIA: Yes but please at least – at least let *me* be *her*.

LUDOVICO: Her! Which "her" do you mean?

ERSILIA: The girl you imagined in my story. If only I could – might be – someone of importance, just once, like you said. Let me be the girl you imagined. *Me* as I am, like this. Somehow you seem to betray me by always seeing *her* instead of me.

LUDOVICO (*laughing*): An embezzlement, you mean?

ERSILIA: Exactly – of my life. *I* was the one who didn't want to go on living. The one who suffered all the misfortunes. *I* think I have the right to be the girl in the novel you will write. Oh, it will be tremendous; like the other book of yours I read: that was so good. What was it called, now? The… oh yes, *The Outsider*. That was it, *The Outsider*.

LUDOVICO: *The Outsider*. Oh no, my dear, you're wrong. *The Outsider* is no book of mine.

ERSILIA: Not yours?

LUDOVICO: No.

ERSILIA: Oh, but I was sure…

LUDOVICO (*astringent*): Actually it's by a writer whom I happen to find particularly insufferable.

ERSILIA (*mortified, lowering face*): Oh, Lord…

LUDOVICO: There there! Not to worry, my dear. You were just a little mixed up, that's all. (ERSILIA *starts to cry again*) What? Goodness me, you're not crying again? Come now, what does it matter to me that you were a bit mixed up, and credited me with some frightful book I didn't write?

ERSILIA: No… it's just that… it's always like this for me… nothing ever comes out right… (*Knock at the door*)

LUDOVICO: Who is it? Come in.

Enter SIGNORA ONORIA, *a completely different woman, honey-tongued and tenderness itself.*

ONORIA: May I? (*Looking for* ERSILIA) Where is she? (*Seeing that she is drying her eyes*) Oh, is she crying, then?

LUDOVICO (*not understanding the sudden change*): What is it?

ONORIA: You could have told me the young lady was the one in the newspaper, for Heaven's sake! You're Ersilia Drei, aren't you? Oh, you poor thing, you poor little girl! I want you to know that I'm really happy that you've come to stay here, and that you're so much better.

LUDOVICO: Just a moment! How did you know?

ONORIA: Don't you think I can read?

LUDOVICO: No. I mean – how did you know that this young lady was the one in the paper?

ONORIA: Oh, because the reporter who wrote the story is downstairs now.

LUDOVICO: Here?

ERSILIA (*worried*): The reporter?

LUDOVICO: What does he want?

ONORIA: He says he wants to ask the young lady some more questions, urgently.

ERSILIA: Questions?

LUDOVICO: Good God! She's had enough!

ERSILIA: What questions?

LUDOVICO: And how did he know he could find her here, may I ask?

ONORIA: I don't know.

ERSILIA: Nor do I! I had no idea I'd be coming here when I talked to him.

LUDOVICO (*very angry, beside himself*): Oh... I know, I know – it must have been that old windbag... (*To* ERSILIA) Well, what do you want me to do? Do you want to see him?

ERSILIA: I... I don't know. What questions does he want to ask me?

LUDOVICO: I'll go and find out. (*Exit door*)

ONORIA: Oh, you poor little thing. You know I really cried my eyes out when I read all those dreadful things that happened to you.

ERSILIA (*not listening to her and looking towards the door*): What do they want now?...

ONORIA: Well perhaps... Who knows?

ERSILIA: God, I can't stand it any more...

ONORIA: Do you feel sick, you poor little love?

ERSILIA: Yes! Yes, I do. I can't breathe. Here (*touching her stomach*)... something still... very wrong. I feel so sick, and then I get these sharp spasms of pain in my back. (*Pulling at her belt*)

From the street an organ starts to grind out some well-known tune in double time.

ONORIA: Undo your belt! Undo your belt!

ERSILIA: No! No! (*Suddenly irritated beyond control*) For God's sake make him go away!

ONORIA: Yes! Yes, at once! (*She looks for her purse in her apron, runs to the window, opens it, starts waving the organ-grinder off. The music persists. She throws down some coins, shouting out:*) Go on, off you go! Off you go! Someone is ill in here – do you hear me? Sick. Ill! (*She makes more signs. The music stops abruptly. She comes back to* ERSILIA.) There we are. Now listen to me. Undo that belt, it's too tight!

ERSILIA: No! What do you mean? (*To herself*) I must keep my head. I'm so frightened that even *this* won't last—

ONORIA: What won't last?

ERSILIA: It's so hopeless. If only you knew how hopeless I feel. I can't endure it any more… This belt… (*She starts to pull at it, but hears the voice of* LUDOVICO)

LUDOVICO: No, go ahead. After you.

Enter ALFREDO CANTAVALLE, *followed by* LUDOVICO.

CANTAVALLE: May I come in? Good evening, my dear young lady. Do you remember me?

LUDOVICO (*presenting him*): Alfredo Cantavalle.

ERSILIA: Yes, I do. Yes.

CANTAVALLE: You see, she recognizes me! (*Noticing* SIGNORA ONORIA) And this good lady would be… er… er… mm a relation? Your aunt?

LUDOVICO: No. Landlady.

CANTAVALLE: Oh, I'm sorry. Pleased to meet you. Of course, I remember now, the young lady hasn't got any relations. Had a bad accident downstairs, I hear?

LUDOVICO: Yes, yes. Some poor old man…

ONORIA: Right under this window! Right under this very window! Oh, it was dreadful!

CANTAVALLE: Well, he's dead, poor chap.

ONORIA: Oh, he died, did he? I thought he would.

CANTAVALLE: Yes, even before they got him to the hospital.

ONORIA: And who was he? Who was he?

CANTAVALLE: He hasn't been identified yet. (*Turning to* ERSILIA) Dear signorina, first let me congratulate you on your wonderful recovery. And then allow me to congratulate myself on my great good fortune in finding such a story! Which, I see, has, luckily, overflowed in your direction. I am honoured to have moved such a talented and illustrious writer as yourself, maestro, with my poor prose. What was all that cra— I mean nonsense your friend was talking about. You've never done anything that suited you better, maestro. (*Turning to* ERSILIA) You can't imagine, signorina, how pleased I am for you.

ERSILIA: Yes, I have certainly been very lucky.

LUDOVICO: Let's forget about it! Let's forget about it!

CANTAVALLE: No, maestro! You see, I would particularly like to hear the opinion of an unbiased witness such as yourself, in view of the new developments. Let me tell you... Oh, can I speak freely, in front of this lady? (*Indicating* ONORIA)

ONORIA: I'm just going. I'm just going... but as the young lady wasn't feeling...

LUDOVICO: Are you feeling ill, my dear?

ONORIA: She's feeling very ill.

LUDOVICO: Tell us what you feel!

ERSILIA: I don't know. I don't know – it's a stabbing pain, here... and I'm so cold.

ONORIA: Now listen to me! You come along with me, in here, into the bedroom. (*Indicating the bedroom door*)

ERSILIA: No! No!

ONORIA: Yes, yes, you must get to bed.

LUDOVICO: Yes, go, my dear, if you feel so ill.

ONORIA: Off with your clothes, and into bed.

ERSILIA: No, thank you. Let me stay. I'm quite all right for the moment.

CANTAVALLE (*aside to* LUDOVICO): The after-effects of the poison, no doubt! But, you'll see, with a little care...

LUDOVICO: ...And peace and quiet...

ONORIA: If you want anything at all, just call me – any time at all. Poor little thing. Any time at all I'll be waiting – I won't mind.

ERSILIA: Yes – thank you.

ONORIA: Well then, I'd better be going. I'd better leave you alone, to talk.

CANTAVALLE: Yes, thank you, signora.

ONORIA (*quietly and venomously to* LUDOVICO): Don't you get her all upset again. Can't you see how pale she is, poor little thing? (*Exit through door.* LUDOVICO *closes door after her.*)

CANTAVALLE: I'm sorry to be a nuisance, but...

LUDOVICO (*shortly, angry*): Let's make it quick, Cantavalle, if you please.

CANTAVALLE: Two minutes. Just two minutes is all I need.

LUDOVICO: Briefly, now. Just what the devil is that consul up to?

ERSILIA (*amazed and terrified*): The consul?!

LUDOVICO: Yes, him! (*To* CANTAVALLE) He's done quite enough harm already.

ERSILIA: Is he here, then?

CANTAVALLE: Yes, he is. He arrived yesterday, and he's been raising hell with my editor ever since.

ERSILIA: God... God... Oh God... Oh God.

LUDOVICO: What part of the story does he refute?

CANTAVALLE: All of it, he says.

ERSILIA (*suddenly vehement; to* CANTAVALLE): You see what you've done? I knew this would happen. That's why I made you promise not to do it—

CANTAVALLE: I? What did I do?

ERSILIA: You promised you wouldn't print that it was Smyrna, or that he was the consul.

LUDOVICO: You mean he actually wants a retraction? How can he?

CANTAVALLE: Excuse me a moment – let me answer the young lady first. My dear Signorina Drei, his name, his actual name, I never printed...

LUDOVICO: But you didn't exactly hide his identity, did you?

CANTAVALLE: Ah well... no. All I said was "our consul in Smyrna". Do you think anyone knows who our consul in Smyrna is? I don't know, even now. The last thing I expected was to see him thundering into my editor's office like a guided missile.

ERSILIA: Oh God... Oh God.

LUDOVICO: Did he come all the way to Rome just for that?

CANTAVALLE: Well, not just for that – his wife seems to have gone mad with grief, so he didn't think it was wise to stay out there, where the accident happened. You understand?

ERSILIA: Yes, they told me that, too.

CANTAVALLE: In short, he came back to arrange a transfer. Does that explain it to you? He read my story – "pow" – chain reaction.

LUDOVICO: But why?

CANTAVALLE: Why? Good God, he's in a very delicate position, diplomatically. He represents the country. Above reproach, you know. So he's threatened to sue us for defamation of character.

LUDOVICO: Bring an action; what did your paper actually print about him?

CANTAVALLE: A bunch of lies according to him.

LUDOVICO: Good Lord!

ERSILIA: I still don't know what you wrote about him, or his wife, or the accident.

CANTAVALLE: I can swear to you that I faithfully wrote down exactly what you told me – more or less. Certainly I expressed myself strongly, but then, I found your story very moving. But I never altered one point of your story, neither facts nor dates! You can see for yourself when you read the paper.

LUDOVICO (*ruffling through the papers on his desk*): It must be here! I must have it here, somewhere!

CANTAVALLE: Don't worry about it, maestro, I'll send you another copy. (*To* ERSILIA) You must realize, Signorina Drei, how concerned I am on your account. I came here today, to find out from you what line to take against this man's complaints and threats.

ERSILIA (*jumping to her feet in an outburst of indignation*): He's got no right to threaten… anybody! And nothing to complain about, that man!

CANTAVALLE: Just what I thought. Jolly good. So much the better.

ERSILIA (*collapsing onto the sofa*): Oh God! I feel so sick! So sick! (*She starts to cry: long racking sobs, which turn into hysterical laughter*)

LUDOVICO (*running to her, trying to comfort her*): Ersilia! No! No!

CANTAVALLE: Oh well, oh… It's all right! It's all right!

LUDOVICO: Don't cry like that. Don't cry!

CANTAVALLE: There's no need, signorina. There's no need.

LUDOVICO: Oh God! She's fainted. Call the landlady – quickly!

CANTAVALLE (*rushing to the door*): Signora! Signora!

LUDOVICO: Signora Onoria!

CANTAVALLE: Signora Onoria! Signora Onoria! (*Rushing out*)

LUDOVICO: My God! No! No! Ersilia – that's a good girl. It's nothing, nothing. Come along, now.

CANTAVALLE *enters with* ONORIA, *who is carrying smelling salts.*

ONORIA: Here we are! Here we are! Oh, the poor little thing! Hold her head up! That's right. That's right. That's the way. Oh, the poor little thing. I knew this would happen. I told them not to get her all fussed up.

CANTAVALLE: There, look. She's coming round.

LUDOVICO: Carry her into the bedroom! Carry her into the bedroom!

ONORIA: Wait! Wait! Wait!

LUDOVICO: Ersilia!

ONORIA: That's right. Poor little thing. It's all over now, isn't it? Come along.

LUDOVICO: Yes, come along. You must have courage, Ersilia.

CANTAVALLE: It was nothing, was it? You're all right now, aren't you?

ERSILIA (*almost childishly happy*): Did I fall?

LUDO: No, my dear, you just gave us all rather a fright.

ERSILIA: Are you sure I didn't fall?

LUDOVICO (*slightly amused*): No, my dear, you didn't.

ONORIA: Now let's see if you can stand up.

LUDOVICO: There we are. Gently, gently.

ERSILIA: How strange – I seem to be falling, just as if suddenly my whole body had become huge and leaden. (*She looks at* CANTAVALLE, *remembering suddenly why he is there*) No! No! (*She is about to fall, but* LUDOVICO *and* ONORIA *catch her*)

LUDOVICO: No, no. Really, my dear! What's the matter now?

ERSILIA (*she seems to try to hide her face from* CANTAVALLE): Go away! Go away! Go away!

ONORIA: Yes, we're going. We're going, right now. (*She and* LUDOVICO *guide her towards the bedroom door*)

LUDOVICO: Into bed, that's a good girl. We'll take care of you. Just lean on us.

ONORIA: Careful now. Careful. I'm going to sit with you. You can just stretch right out.

LUDOVICO: A good sleep is what you need.

ERSILIA: I can't see properly... I can't feel anything any more...

ONORIA (*in front of the door, to* LUDOVICO): Now you stay here, do you hear? I'll take care of her. (*She goes into the bedroom with* ERSILIA)

LUDOVICO (*to* CANTAVALLE): It's about time you all stopped tormenting that wretched girl.

CANTAVALLE: Don't tell me. I'm only too upset about it. That's nothing. There's something else, another little calamity she knows nothing about.

LUDOVICO: Calamity! As bad as that?

CANTAVALLE: Yes! I'd better come straight to the point. Actually, the consul told us.

LUDOVICO: Oh! I'm fed up with him!

CANTAVALLE: Wait a second! I don't want to harp on it, but the effect of my "piece" has been absolutely fantastic! Colossal! Really colossal! It seems the other girl, the one the young lieutenant got himself engaged to, was so incensed by his behaviour towards Ersilia Drei, that she's broken off their engagement completely.

LUDOVICO: Ah…

CANTAVALLE: Chain reaction – that's what it is! I tell you – colossal! Next thing, what happens? The young lieutenant suddenly sees the light, sees what a bastard he's been, and decides to do the right thing by this one. General uproar! And all because of an article I wrote about a poor creature who tried to commit suicide in a public park.

LUDOVICO: You mean, the young man who promised to marry her?

CANTAVALLE: That's right. He's called… let me see now. Yes, he's called Laspiga! He's evidently lost his head completely, or so says the consul.

LUDOVICO: And how does *he* know?

CANTAVALLE: Because he happens to know the father of that very irate young lady – Laspiga's ex-fiancée, who happens to be the Minister of Foreign Affairs.

LUDOVICO: God. What a grisly mess!

CANTAVALLE: Yes, and there *you* are right in the middle of it.

LUDOVICO: Me? What!

CANTAVALLE: Yes, *you*. Of course, I suppose I'm in it too – threatened with a criminal action, etc.

LUDOVICO: But this father – the Minister of Foreign Affairs—

CANTAVALLE: He's raving mad! Evidently, although his darling daughter was so outraged, and swore she'd never see her fiancé again, when she looked at her trousseau, all white and shining, it was quite another story. Tears, wailing, gnashing of teeth, absolute hysterics, you understand? So naturally, the loving father, knowing that the consul had met his future son-in-law at Smyrna, where Signorina Drei had been governess to the child...

LUDOVICO: ...Goes to see him to find out all about it.

CANTAVALLE: Right!

LUDOVICO: God! Imagine what a story they gave him! You know, they blame her for everything, even the death of the child.

FRANCO LASPIGA, *a tall, well-dressed young man, hurries in. He is in a highly excited state, and has obviously not slept for several nights.*

FRANCO: Is she here? Oh excuse me – I mean Ersilia Drei. Where is she? Where is she?

LUDOVICO: What! Who are you?

FRANCO: Franco Laspiga. I was hoping—

LUDOVICO: What! Who are you?

FRANCO: Franco Laspiga. I was hoping—

CANTAVALLE: Ah, Franco Laspiga! So you're here already.

LUDOVICO: Oh Lord, you've come too.

FRANCO: I was at the hospital, but she'd gone, so I rushed down to the newspaper office, and they told me that she... (*Interrupts himself, and to* CANTAVALLE) Oh, I beg your pardon, you must be Signor Nota...

CANTAVALLE (*laughing*): Not me. No! *This* is Nota.

FRANCO (*pleased*): Oh, it's you?

LUDOVICO (*very annoyed*): Good God! Does everyone know, then?

CANTAVALLE (*placating*): But maestro, you're forgetting who you are!

LUDOVICO (*irritable to boiling point*): Just do me the kindness to be quiet, will you!

CANTAVALLE: But you must realize what a sensation you've created.

FRANCO: Could someone just tell me – is she here or not?

LUDOVICO (*taking no notice, still to* CANTAVALLE): I have not the slightest intention of exhibiting myself or Signorina Drei to that "great reading public" of yours, like a couple of sideshow freaks! Understand?

CANTAVALLE: Come now – what do you mean?

LUDOVICO: I mean I'm absolutely fed up with the whole affair! (*Turns to* FRANCO) I want you to know that the young lady has been here less than an hour.

FRANCO: Ah, she is here! Where? Can I see her?

LUDOVICO (*taking no notice, stating facts*): I went to collect her when she came out of hospital. She had nowhere to go, so I offered her refuge here, in my flat. Of course, I shall move into a hotel myself early this evening.

FRANCO: Then I must thank you with—

LUDOVICO (*exploding; this is the last straw*): Why must you thank me? Because I'm not a *young* man any more, that's why you want to thank me, isn't it? Oh, this is quite ludicrous! What are you doing here, anyway?

FRANCO: I've got to make up for all the suffering I've caused her – try to make her forgive me.

CANTAVALLE: Great! Perfect! Spoken like a true gentleman!

LUDOVICO: It seems to me you should have thought of all that a little earlier...

FRANCO: You're right. I should have thought, but I didn't – I didn't want to think. I've spent weeks trying to forget her. Is she in there? Just let me see her, please!

LUDOVICO: I don't think that's at all wise, at the moment...

FRANCO: Please let me say a few words to her, for Christ's sake!

CANTAVALLE: It might be better to prepare her first, because...

LUDOVICO: She's in bed.

CANTAVALLE: ...Because she's in a very nervous condition and the sudden shock of pleasure might...

FRANCO: You mean, she's still not well? What is it? Is she very ill?

LUDOVICO: She fainted just before you arrived.

CANTAVALLE: It was all this brouhaha...

FRANCO: Oh, Jesus! I never imagined – I never thought that marvellous time we had together could end like this. The whole thing has blown up in my face. All those newspaper boys bawling out in the streets – I wanted to smash their faces in. Then my fiancée, her father and mother – all of them, hurling abuse, screaming and crying – people whispering on the stairs where I live. I'm being crushed under a huge weight of accusation and reproof. I've got to make up for it. It's all my fault. Maybe she will forgive me if I spend the rest of my life making up for all the misery I've caused her.

CANTAVALLE: Yes, that's it! That's the way. It's much the best solution, don't you think so, Nota? I feel very happy about the way it's all working out! Very happy!

ONORIA *comes out of the bedroom, making frantic shushing signs, and shuts the door behind her.*

ONORIA (*in a great stage whisper*): For goodness' sake, can't you be a little more quiet! She can hear everything you're saying!

FRANCO: Does she know I'm here?

ONORIA: Of course she does, and she's trembling all over, the poor little thing. She says she'll throw herself out of the window if you go in there!

FRANCO: But why? Does she hate me too?

CANTAVALLE (*moderating*): Hate you? (*Laughing*) I expect she's...

ONORIA: No, no, she's an angel. She says you mustn't do it.

LUDOVICO: Mustn't do what?

ONORIA (*to* FRANCO): She says you must go back and make it up with your fiancée.

FRANCO: No! It's over, I tell you! It's all finished with her.

ONORIA: She says you mustn't make your fiancée suffer for her sake.

FRANCO: She's not my fiancée any more, I tell you! Ersilia is!

ONORIA: She says she doesn't want to know anything more about it.

FRANCO: But I came here determined to make amends to her for all the pain I've caused her.

ONORIA: Keep your voice down, will you? Don't let her hear you say that!

FRANCO (*to* LUDOVICO): You go and explain to her, then. Please. Persuade her to listen to me!

LUDOVICO: Well, I suppose it *is* the solution to the problem. Yes, I'll do it.

FRANCO: Tell her not to worry about anything any more, because I'm here, and from now on my first duty will be towards her. And tell her please not to do anything that will prevent me being able to fulfil my obligation to her! Go on! Please go in and tell her! (LUDOVICO *goes into the bedroom*)

ONORIA (*obstinately*): She won't see you, because of that other girl.

FRANCO (*jerkily*): But I've told you already I've broken off with her! Finally! Utterly! Completely! Can't you understand that?

ONORIA: Well, she doesn't want you to break it off.

FRANCO: What do you mean, doesn't want me to? I've done it already and I can't go back now. Anyway, I can't for my own sake. It's all come back to me now, you see, and I'm not going to let go again.

CANTAVALLE: Ah, yes, "Remembrance of Things Past".

FRANCO: It seemed so far away, like some fantastic dream I'd dreamt. So much so that I could hardly believe that night actually happened – all those promises I made – because you always make promises on a night like that, and...

CANTAVALLE: And then they all fade away...

FRANCO: Can you believe that I had no scruples whatsoever? I actually tore up all her letters as though they were old bills. It's incredible – incredible – that I could have lied like that to myself – done all the things that I've done, and all this time it was *real* for her. *So* real that when she arrived here and found out what I'd done, it destroyed her. Now I'm beginning to understand how she felt. (LUDOVICO *comes back serious and determined*)

LUDOVICO: Nothing. No. It's not possible at the moment.

FRANCO: Not possible? What did she say? What did she say?

LUDOVICO: She promised me she'd see you tomorrow.

FRANCO: But I can't leave here without seeing her. No! I can't!

LUDOVICO: You can't see her, I tell you! It's not possible at the moment!

FRANCO: Listen, I haven't slept. Just let me see her for one second, I promise that's all!

LUDOVICO (*hard and firm*): It's pointless to insist. Believe me, it would be bad for her.

FRANCO: But why?

LUDOVICO: Let her think it over tonight. I spoke to her, told her what you proposed.

FRANCO: But why won't she see me? She knows it's all over with that other girl! She tried to kill herself because of me, didn't she? Why doesn't she want to see me?

LUDOVICO (*losing his patience*): She *will* see you! My God, just calm down for a moment, will you!

CANTAVALLE (*to* LUDOVICO): And you too, dear Nota.

FRANCO: I can't! I can't!

LUDOVICO (*gentler*): Now listen to me. I'm quite confident that tomorrow she will be perfectly ready to listen to your proposal. (*To* SIGNORA ONORIA) Go in and attend to her! Don't leave her alone.

ONORIA (*running*): Yes, I'm going. I am going, but put the light on, I can't see a thing! (*Goes into bedroom*)

LUDOVICO *switches on the light.*

LUDOVICO: In the meantime, we'd better be going.

FRANCO: So I'm not allowed even to see her.

LUDOVICO: Tomorrow morning, first thing, you'll see her and talk to her, and I shall be there too. Until then... (*He indicates the door*)

CANTAVALLE: You'll see – she's bound to realize that it's the best solution.

LUDOVICO (*starting towards the door*): We must leave her alone tonight – let her think it out in peace. Come along, come along.

FRANCO: But I thought that if I came to see her, she'd...

LUDOVICO (*pushing them through the door*): Come along, out you go. (CANTAVALLE *murmurs,* "Thank you") Thought that if you came to see her, she'd what? (*They leave*)

The stage is empty for a moment or two. We hear the noise of the street, once more. The lights dim. Suddenly the bedroom door opens, and ERSILIA appears, still buttoning up her dress. She is followed by ONORIA.

This scene is played in semi-darkness. Both women are very agitated but almost whispering.

ERSILIA: No! No! I want to go away! I want to go away!

ONORIA: But where will you go? Where?

ERSILIA: I don't know, but I'm going.

ONORIA: It's madness!

ERSILIA: Disappear – just get swallowed up down there in the street! I don't know! (*Takes her hat to put it on*)

ONORIA (*holding on to her*): No! No! I'm not going to let you do it!

ERSILIA: Let me go! Let me go! I don't want to stay here!

ONORIA: Why not?

ERSILIA: Because I don't want to see or hear any of them again.

ONORIA: Do you want me to say that you won't see *him* tomorrow morning?

ERSILIA: None of them! None! Oh, let me go away, for pity's sake.

ONORIA: All right. All right. Nobody. I'll tell Signora Nota, don't worry!

ERSILIA: Is it my fault that they saved my life?

ONORIA: Your fault? What are you talking about? What fault?

ERSILIA: They're blaming me! They all blame me!

ONORIA: No! Who's blaming you?

ERSILIA: All of them! All of them! Didn't you hear?

ONORIA: Not at all. That poor boy came here to beg you to forgive him.

ERSILIA: I've had enough, you hear? I've had enough!

ONORIA: Yes, of course you have, you poor little thing. And tomorrow I'll tell Signor Nota…

ERSILIA: …That I want to stay here in peace…

ONORIA: And why shouldn't you stay if you want to?

ERSILIA: Because – oh, you'll see – they'll wear him out, he'll get tired of me!

ONORIA: Signor Nota?

ERSILIA: He said he was fed up with the whole business.

ONORIA: No, I can't believe it. His head's in the clouds, but his heart's in the right place – is old Signor Nota's.

ERSILIA: But what about the other one, the other one…

ONORIA: Who?

ERSILIA: That other one. I don't even want to say his name. He's already threatening to sue the newspaper.

ONORIA: The consul?

ERSILIA: Yes, him! He'll never leave me in peace… Oh God. Let me go! Let me go!

ONORIA: Calm down, calm down. Signor Nota will know how to put that fine fellow in his place, don't you worry! Besides, what more can he do after the way he treated you? Poor little thing! (ERSILIA *sways*) You see, you can't even stand on your feet…

ERSILIA: I know. I know. But what am I to do? God…

ONORIA: Go back to bed and be good. I'll bring you a hot drink, and you'll have a good night's rest.

ERSILIA (*turning to her rather shyly, for one of those intimate confidences that one woman makes to another*): But you understand, I am just… just as you see me, and…

ONORIA: And?

ERSILIA: Well, I've got nothing... nothing with me... I had a small suit-case at the hotel, but I don't know where it is any more. They con-fiscated it...

ONORIA: We'll get it back tomorrow, don't fret yourself about it. I'll send someone or go myself.

ERSILIA: Yes, but at the moment... just now... I'm naked...

ONORIA (*as to a rather backward lovely child*): I'll take care of that! I'll take care of everything! Now off to bed like a good girl. I'll be here! Go on, go on. I'll be back in a minute or two. It won't take me a second. (*She exits*)

ERSILIA *stays seated, then leans back on the couch desperately tired. She is breathing heavily, and wipes her forehead. She gets up and opens the window, and stands silhouetted half behind the shutter.*

The noises of the street are muted and sporadic now the market is over. A GANG OF BOYS *is going past. They start to sing 'How wonderful to know you really love me' (The English words to 'Anima e Cuore') and some of the* VOICES *crack on the high notes. The singing turns into laughing, jokes and more laughter.*

ERSILIA *watches from behind the shutter: the* VOICES *die away...*

ERSILIA (*whispers*): The street... the street...

CURTAIN

ACT TWO

The next morning. Same scene. FRANCO LASPIGA *and* LUDOVICO NOTA *arrive, followed by* EMMA, *the char, who is very old and wrinkled.*

LUDOVICO (*to* EMMA): Where is Signora Onoria?

EMMA (*indicating bedroom*): She's with the young lady.

LUDOVICO: Do you know if the young lady had a good night?

EMMA: Oh no, sir! Terrible! The signora was up with her all night. Something awful, she says!

FRANCO: You see? If only I could have talked to her last night!

LUDOVICO (*to* EMMA): Go in very, very quietly, and tell Signora Onoria that we're here.

EMMA: Yes, sir. (*She starts towards the bedroom*)

LUDOVICO: Oh, by the way, has the post come?

EMMA (*turning back*): Yes, sir. It's on the desk, there. (*Goes laboriously into the bedroom with a great show of quietness*)

LUDOVICO (*going to get the post*): Well, sit down, sit down. Make yourself at home, Laspiga…

FRANCO: No thanks. I couldn't.

LUDOVICO (*sniffing the air*): Ugh! I'd better open the windows for a moment or two. (*He opens the windows, and then starts sorting the mail, mostly newspapers. The noises of the morning market mix with the familiar street sounds, and after a short time* LUDOVICO *shuts the window. He scans the newspaper, stopping abruptly at something of interest in it. He reads avidly… Going to* FRANCO *with the newspaper.*) Look at this – here – read it! Read it! (*Giving him the paper*)

FRANCO (*after reading it*): A retraction?

LUDOVICO: They say they'll publish it in full tomorrow.

ONORIA *enters from the bedroom, followed by* EMMA, *who crosses and exits.*

FRANCO (*anxious*): Ah, here you are!

ONORIA: Oh, what a night! What a dreadful night…

FRANCO: What's happening? Isn't she coming?

ONORIA: If she can. She guessed it was you. But you mustn't disturb her at the moment – she only dozed off early this morning.

LUDOVICO: It's all this din from the street.

ONORIA: No! She woke up when Emma came in to say that you were here. I was frightened that she would still refuse to see you…

FRANCO: No! No!

ONORIA: No, in fact, she said she *did* want to speak to you.

FRANCO: Thank God! She'll certainly see reason now.

LUDOVICO: Quite! If she hasn't already seen the light, surely both of us can convince her.

ONORIA: Well, I have my doubts about that. Last night, as soon as you'd all gone, she tried to run away.

LUDOVICO: Run away? What!

FRANCO: Run where?

ONORIA: Who knows? Away – I had to wrestle with her to keep her here. I just don't know how they let her out of the hospital. She's in no fit state.

LUDOVICO (*dignified*): Really? She was perfectly all right with me.

ONORIA: She went through hell so you wouldn't see how bad she was. She's so frightened you'll get bored with her.

LUDOVICO: Me? Not at all. Anyway, now it's much more up to… (*indicating* FRANCO)

FRANCO: Of course, I'll look after her. You'll see, I'll make her better. I'll make her better.

ONORIA: Well, I'll just go and lie down for a moment. I can't go on any more. I'm dropping with tiredness. Oh, but if you need me…

LUDOVICO: Yes, you go!

ONORIA: You'll call me, won't you? (*She goes towards the door, turns back to* LUDOVICO) Do you realize that poor little thing hasn't got anything with her at all? They confiscated her suitcase at the hotel, or maybe it was the police – I can't remember. I trust you to go and get it back – somebody ought to go and get it back!

LUDOVICO: Yes, yes. We'll see to it.

ONORIA: Yes, but soon. Today! She's stark… (*She is about to say "naked" but stops herself*) Good Lord, she's got to be presentable. (*To* LU-DOVICO) You will take care of it?

FRANCO: I'll see about it. I'll take care of it.

ONORIA: I think it would be better if you did, Signor Nota.

LUDOVICO (*fed up again*): All right! All right! (*Then, in a different tone*) We'll have to wait till she (*indicating* ERSILIA) tells us to.

ONORIA: Well, all I ask is that you treat her very gently, poor little thing.

LUDOVICO (*bitingly*): You're the one to talk! Oh, that's marvellous! You're full of all the protective instincts now, but only yesterday…

ONORIA: But I didn't *know* yesterday! She's like some poor little animal that's been set upon by a pack of mad dogs – the more timid she is, the more anxious they are to tear her apart. And she's so frightened and downtrodden, poor little love.

LUDOVICO: Well you must understand that, for me, things also look very different today.

ONORIA: You mean you don't want her… here.

LUDOVICO: I imagined that the whole story was finished – instead, it couldn't be turning out worse! First that newspaper man with his "chain reactions" – then this gentleman (*indicates* FRANCO). And now that consul Grotti publicly protesting. (*To* FRANCO) You saw the paper!

FRANCO: But is Grotti here in Rome?

LUDOVICO: He's here. *You're* here. They're here. And it seems that the… er… Minister of Foreign Affairs has been to see Signor Grotti.

FRANCO: …The father of my… (*Stops*) What for?

LUDOVICO: I don't know. Perhaps to make a few enquiries.

FRANCO (*indignant*): Why are they still pretending? They've already slammed the door in my face! So then this bastard Grotti has turned *him* against my poor Ersilia too.

ONORIA: They're all against her.

LUDOVICO: It seems so. In fact, it's certain they are. Now you understand, I live here absorbed in my writing…

FRANCO (*carried away, not listening*): I want to know why Grotti is doing this.

331

LUDOVICO: Then I suggest you ask him! As I was saying, as far as I'm concerned, I got interested in a real-life story – places, people – fascinating! Everything, of course, exactly as my own imagination recreated it. Now, this incoherent sequel – this awful muddle, I must admit, has spoilt everything. In fact, it's ruined the whole story for me! Fortunately, you're here now, so…

FRANCO: That's right! I'm here now.

ONORIA: Now you be careful with her! (*Exits through door*)

FRANCO (*resolutely*): I think I'll take her away – a long, long way away – I can do it, I have the means, with my connections. A long way away…

LUDOVICO: Don't get too "carried away". Surely you see what can happen.

FRANCO: Of course. But I was only thinking of what would be *best* for *her*.

LUDOVICO: Well, I should say she's the most terrible warning against getting "carried away". The victim of it, in fact.

FRANCO: Yes, she is – and why? Because there came a moment when I stopped myself being "carried away" as you call it, and in doing so I betrayed both myself and her. I actually left the sea. I left the sea to start to decompose in this rubbish tip of "ordinary life".

LUDOVICO: Oh, a time comes for all of us to settle down, unfortunately…

FRANCO: No! No! We just let ourselves be persuaded that it's difficult to live as we want to. We're taught that our dreams are unattainable "castles in the air", and yet *inside* we know that if we really wanted to make the effort, we could reach out and take hold of them.

LUDOVICO: Only in those rare moments when one's spirit frees itself from all the mundane banalities and soars above the petty obstacles of convention. It is no longer aware of the shabby little needs that surviving involves. It shakes off all the ridiculous duties of mediocrity, doesn't it?

FRANCO: Yes, that's exactly how I feel! I am free – I can breathe real air again. I can break the world in two!

LUDOVICO: Ah yes, everything becomes fluid and manageable, doesn't it? One's in a state of divine intoxication. But don't you see, dear boy, these moments are *rare – very*, very rare, indeed.

FRANCO (*immediate and convinced*): Only because we give in – we aren't strong enough to resist the drag of gravity! That's why they're rare.

LUDOVICO (*laughing*): No! No! You've no idea what tricks are being played on you – all this breathing and breaking the world in two – don't you see? It's a great delusion. Gravity's bound to catch up with you one fine day, and then…

FRANCO: Yes, I know all that! That's the whole point – it's happened to me once already! But there's no need to give in. There's no need to be dragged down like I was! That's why I want to take her away; perhaps back to the Greek Islands, near where she felt that same freedom of spirit that carried us both away. Where she waited for me confident and carefree, and where – above all – she *trusted* me. Don't you see that I betrayed her when I let myself be dragged down? My spirit, my conscience, everything became dulled and sluggish. I thought of my meeting with her, and of our brief happiness together, as an attack of madness – and in that awful complacent state, I considered that to forget her as soon as possible would not be a betrayal, but clever self-possession.

LUDOVICO: Well, all I can say is, please don't get too elated. You'll see, she's on the verge of a breakdown.

FRANCO: I'll cure her! (ERSILIA *appears at the door*) Ah! At last! Here she is! (*He sees how she looks. His voice muffled.*) Oh God! My God!

ERSILIA *comes in, having made no sign of having seen* FRANCO. *She hasn't done her hair, is deathly pale, and frantically determined. She goes straight to* LUDOVICO.

ERSILIA: I give up, Signor Nota! I give up the whole thing! I can't accept your offer – it's not possible, so I give up everything!

LUDOVICO: What do you mean? Don't you see who's here?

FRANCO: Ersilia! Ersilia!

ERSILIA: You – who are you talking to? Don't you see who I am? What I've become?

FRANCO: I can see that you've suffered, that you've been miserable. But you're still my Ersilia. (*Starts to embrace her*) It will be just the same as when we saw each other last, you'll see.

ERSILIA (*pushing him away in horror*): Don't touch me! Leave me alone, Signor Laspiga! Don't touch me!

FRANCO: What? Signor Laspiga! But you're mine, Ersilia. You've already been mine, and you can't forget that!

ERSILIA: This is really intolerable! Don't you understand? What do I have to say to make you see that for me everything must be finished.

FRANCO: But it's not finished! How can it be when I'm back again with you?

ERSILIA: Signor Laspiga, you can never mean the same to me – ever again – as you did before.

FRANCO: But I *can*, of course I can, because I *am* the same! I'm the same man!

ERSILIA: No! There's another reason, too. You should be able to see it. I tell you truthfully. I can *never* be the same woman again!

FRANCO: That's just not true, Ersilia. You wanted to kill yourself because of me! Well, then…

ERSILIA: …Well then – it's not true.

FRANCO: Not true?

ERSILIA: It's *not* true! Not true! Not for you. I didn't even try to find you when I came back. I was lying.

FRANCO: Lying? You lied?

ERSILIA: Yes. I had to justify my death. And somehow at that moment it seemed true to me – but not any more.

FRANCO: Why no more, my Ersilia?…

ERSILIA: Because, unfortunately for me, I'm still alive.

FRANCO: Unfortunately for you? It was a miracle!

ERSILIA: Thank you. Then I'd rather do without miracles. Look, do you want to condemn me to be the girl I tried to kill for ever? Or will you let her alone, she, and the reason she tried to kill herself? *She* was your Ersilia, but what she said doesn't count any more, neither for you, nor for me. That's all.

LUDOVICO: Why doesn't it count for either of you? Tell me, my dear. Oh, forgive me…

FRANCO: But if you wanted to die for that reason…

ERSILIA: Exactly! Die! Exit! Finish! I am not dead. It doesn't count.

FRANCO: You talk as if I couldn't put things right again, but I can!

ERSILIA: No! No!

FRANCO: I know I can! You must decide, my darling, to make the reason you wanted to die the reason you want to live. It seems so clear to me.

LUDOVICO: Yes, he's right.

FRANCO: Ersilia, that's why I'm here.

ERSILIA (*in another voice, suddenly she seems to be reciting, beating out each syllable*): But I find it hard even to recognize you. Who are you?

334

FRANCO (*completely bewildered*): Who am I?

ERSILIA *sits down*. LUDOVICO *and* FRANCO *stare at her in amazement, as though she's some new and unexpected arrival whom they've never met. After a pause, she speaks.*

ERSILIA: Don't make me go mad. (*Another pause, then using the same voice as before*) Maybe you find it hard to recognize me too?

FRANCO (*quietly, anguished*): No! No! What makes you think that?

ERSILIA: Oh, lots of things. Do you know, if I'd met you again before I went to that park, I couldn't have said it...

FRANCO: Couldn't have said what?

ERSILIA: That I was killing myself for your sake. It's not true – not even the voice... those eyes... Did you even speak to me with that voice, or look at me with those eyes? I remembered you... I imagined you – oh, what does it matter how it was!

FRANCO (*icily*): You're trying to drive me away, Ersilia... You make me doubt both myself and you...

ERSILIA: Because *you* – you can't comprehend what a horrible shock it is for me to have my life thrust before my eyes like this. I have no remembrance of you inside me, just an unexpected recollection of what *some* man was to *some* woman. I don't know how to find myself in that recollection, because I am changed completely, and I can't recapture any feeling that I had at that time. Yes, I'm sure that this *was* my life. That this was maybe how I looked, moved and spoke – but not for myself, *now*. Don't you see? I see myself in that memory as a stranger, someone who is not me.

FRANCO: But I am *me*, Ersilia – I'm the same. I've come back to you, the same man, and I want to be the same man that you loved out there!

ERSILIA: You can't! Oh, my God, can't you understand? When I look at you now, I become more and more sure that you were never that man...

FRANCO: What?

ERSILIA: Why are you so surprised? I am quite aware that even while you've been listening to me talk, you've had exactly the same impression...

FRANCO: Yes, it's true, but only because the things you are saying...

ERSILIA: ...Are true! Then why don't you take advantage of it? Everyone can take advantage of things, except me... (*She stops*) ...I don't know how to... It's not your fault.

FRANCO: What's not my fault, for God's sake?

ERSILIA: What you did to me?

FRANCO: Well, what do you think I'm doing here, if it's not my fault?

ERSILIA: Oh, in life, my friend; in life people do things – they can do things to other people...

FRANCO: And then they're conscience-stricken, just as I am. It's true remorse I feel, you understand? Not just a case of doing my duty towards you.

ERSILIA: Ah, but if you find out that I'm not what you thought me to be? If you find out that I'm not what you imagined?

FRANCO (*in despair*): Oh, Ersilia, stop talking like this!

ERSILIA (*changing completely*): You too, Signor Nota, you imagined someone else, didn't you? But I swear to you that I would do everything, anything to be her. Yes, yes. I could do it for you! I could, believe me! Because you live in a world of falsehoods – fiction – not real life. No, this is real life. This is what I tried to get rid of, but it refuses to let me go. (*She becomes hysterical*) It's sunk its teeth into me and it won't let me go. How can I get away? Where can I go?

LUDOVICO (*quietly, to* FRANCO): You see what I mean? She's on the verge of a nervous breakdown. With proper care she'll be herself again, in no time at all, and...

ERSILIA: *Be myself!* So now you want to torment me too?

LUDOVICO: On the contrary, my dear. I... oh...

ERSILIA: *You* know why the whole thing is quite impossible!

LUDOVICO: Why, my dear?

ERSILIA: Oh, it was nothing to you, except proof of your own intuition. In fact, it gave you such pleasure to know that your intuition was right that you forgot that it was *me*. You didn't even think that it was this body that suffered that shame. You forgot that it was *me* standing there before you, overwhelmed with self-disgust.

LUDOVICO: Oh, is that the reason?

ERSILIA: Then tell him! Tell him what I did! Then he'll go away.

LUDOVICO: I shall do nothing of the sort! Nobody can blame you for what happened at that time.

ERSILIA: Very well, then. I shall tell him myself. Did you know that I went into the street, and offered myself to the first man who came along?

LUDOVICO (*immediately, with vehemence, to* FRANCO, *who covers his face with his hands*): Out of sheer desperation, the night before she tried to kill herself! You understand, of course?

FRANCO: Yes, yes! Oh, Ersilia!

LUDOVICO: And the morning afterwards she poisoned herself in that public park, because she didn't even have enough money to pay her bill at the hotel. You understand, don't you?

FRANCO: Of course I do! This only makes me more determined to make up for all the wrong I've done you.

ERSILIA (*exasperated*): Not you! Not you!

FRANCO: Yes, me! Who else, then?

ERSILIA (*almost hysterically*): Do you want me to tell you everything? All the sordid details, things one doesn't even admit to oneself? (*She stops for a moment to pull herself together. She begins again, firmly, almost as though she is reciting a lesson, looking straight ahead of her, her eyes fixed on nothing.*) I measured quite coldly the disgust that I would feel, to see whether or not I could live with it. I put a lot of make-up on my face before I left the hotel. I had the poison in a small glass tube in my handbag. I had three of these tubes in my suitcase. I used it in the nursery as *disinfectant*. I made up my eyes as I'd seen in magazines. Then I looked at myself in the mirror, just as you imagined it – there *was* an old swivel mirror on the chest of drawers in my room. But that wasn't the only time I made myself up like a whore. I did it again, before I went out that morning. Yes, even when I was sitting on that bench, in the park, I didn't know, I didn't want to know what I was going to do right up until the last moment. I could perfectly easily have tried the same thing again, if things had turned out that way – if some man had gone past who liked the look of me, or who I'd felt attracted to, who knows, I might not have tried to kill myself? Don't forget I'd covered my face with make-up, I'd painted my mouth with care, and I put on this blue dress, it's my best… (*She jumps up*) But if I'm here now, tell me yourself, what does that mean? It means I've conquered my disgust, now that I've compared it with death. Isn't that so? Otherwise, what would I be doing here with this man, a complete stranger, who wrote, without knowing me, and offered me his protection?

FRANCO (*with sudden resolution*): Listen! I know why you're talking like this! Why you have this urge to tear yourself to pieces…

ERSILIA (*suddenly violent*): It's not me! It's all of *you*!

FRANCO: Very well, then. If you feel it's the result of other people's cruelty, then can't you allow one, one person at least, who feels a great obligation towards you, to try to make amends to you for all that you have suffered?

ERSILIA: How? By inflicting still more on me?

FRANCO: No, but don't you see…

ERSILIA (*hammering out every word*): Once and for all, I tell you I was lying! I invented the whole thing! It's not true! I lied, do you hear? It wasn't because of what the others did to me, nor you. It's just life, this life that persists in me. This life that I've never, never been able to give any shape or coherence to. Leave me alone! What more must I tell you to make you go away? (*Someone knocks at the door*)

LUDOVICO: Who is it? Come in. (EMMA *comes in*) What do you want?

EMMA: Sir, it's Consul Grotti.

ERSILIA (*with a cry*): Ah, he's come here! I knew he would! I knew it!

LUDOVICO: Does he wish to speak to me?

FRANCO: I'm here too, don't forget!

EMMA: No, he asked to speak to the young lady.

ERSILIA: Yes, yes, let me speak to him! I must talk to him – please! (*To* EMMA) Ask him to come in. (EMMA *goes out*) I want to speak to him now, the sooner the better.

CONSUL GROTTI *enters. He is dark, thickset and in his early thirties. He is dressed in black. He is a diplomat, but underneath his smooth exterior one feels he suppresses a passionate but slightly sadistic nature.*

ERSILIA (*to* LUDOVICO): Signor Grotti, our Consul in Smyrna. (*Then to* GROTTI) You know Signor Ludovico Nota?

GROTTI (*inclining his head*): Only by reputation.

ERSILIA (*continuing*): I am staying here with him. (*Indicates* FRANCO) You've met Signor Laspiga already.

FRANCO: We met under much happier circumstances than this. At this time I am here because— (ERSILIA *interrupts immediately*)

ERSILIA: For God's sake stop talking!

FRANCO: No! (*To* GROTTI) Look at her! Just look at this creature, the girl I asked you for permission to marry.

ERSILIA (*trembling with rage*): I told you there's nothing more for you to say!

FRANCO: You're quite right. (*He turns to* GROTTI) It should be enough to see the condition she's in, and this uncontrollable anger, to explain why I'm here.

ERSILIA (*exasperated with him*): My condition has nothing to do with you! I told you there was no reason for you to stay here. I shall be pleased to repeat it in front of Signor Grotti, so that he'll know my uncontrollable anger has been aroused solely because you so stubbornly refuse to understand me.

FRANCO: Ah yes, you are pleased to repeat it because you know that he and my ex-future father-in-law have been conniving together, discussing the whole situation, meddling and prying.

ERSILIA (*stopping*): No, I didn't know that. (*At first bewildered, she turns to* GROTTI *with great apprehension*) Ah, did you – and did you talk to him about *me*?

GROTTI (*cool and composed*): No, signorina, he just asked me to come and have a talk with you.

FRANCO: (*jumping in again*): It's useless! I tell you it's useless!

ERSILIA (*becoming at once commanding and disdainful towards* FRANCO): I should like to speak to Signor Grotti alone. (*In a completely different voice, to* LUDOVICO) If *you* don't mind, Signor Nota?

LUDOVICO: Oh, it's all the same to me. (*He moves towards the door;* FRANCO *stops him*)

FRANCO: No! No! Wait! (*Turns to* ERSILIA, *stiffly*) I shall go in one minute, but first (*he turns to* GROTTI) I should like a few words with this gentleman. You can tell whoever you like that it's useless to discuss her future with anyone but me. I shall be making all her decisions from now on. (*Turning to* ERSILIA *again*) I wanted you to hear that, so that you'd know that you haven't been able to drive me away yet. Oh, I've begged and supplicated and resigned myself to hearing you tearing yourself to pieces, but that's enough now! Now I shall do a little plain speaking myself. We both know that you can prevent me from seeing you ever again, but that doesn't mean to say that I should ever return to *her*. (*He turns back to* GROTTI) She made her decision when she read that story in the paper, when she threw me out of the house because of my disgraceful behaviour towards Ersilia. She can't just suddenly repent now and send you as her ambassador.

GROTTI: No, no, that's not the reason I came.

339

ERSILIA: How many times do I have to tell you that I didn't try to kill myself because of you?

FRANCO: Not true!

ERSILIA: What? Signor Nota here heard me tell you.

FRANCO: Yes – tell me, yes! (*To* GROTTI) She told me so many horrible things about herself; things that "one doesn't even admit to oneself" that I began to doubt my own existence. But I know my own conscience and everything she told me only made me more determined and more certain that I must not rest until I have made full reparation to her. Nothing will change that, neither you nor anyone whose interests you represent. There, that's it, I've said what I wanted to say. (*To* NOTA) Now we can go. I know that you approve of my decision. Goodbye, Signor Grotti. (*He goes towards the door*)

GROTTI (*nodding his head*): Goodbye.

LUDOVICO *goes over to* ERSILIA; *his tone is encouraging and almost loving.*

LUDOVICO: In the mean time I'll go and see about your suitcase. Don't worry, I shall bring it back as soon as possible.

ERSILIA (*she is moved*): Oh thank you, thank you, Signor Nota. And please excuse me for causing you all this trouble.

LUDOVICO: Not at all… Signor Grotti. (*Exit* FRANCO *and* LUDOVICO)

The moment the door is shut ERSILIA *loses her composure completely. She seems to shrink away, trembling and watching* GROTTI *fearfully. He surveys her with a look of cold furious scorn, and seems about to strike her. She cannot meet this look and covers her face with her hands. She hunches her shoulders as if to protect herself from the expected blow.* GROTTI *is moving nearer to her, even more threateningly, though his voice is quiet and hissing. He is always aware that they may be overheard.*

GROTTI: You stupid, stupid, stupid little fool. You silly lying slut!

ERSILIA (*genuinely terrified, she raises her arm to ward off the imaginary blow*): But I really tried to kill myself! I really wanted to die.

GROTTI (*reviling her*): Then why did you lie afterwards – to make yourself even more guilty?

ERSILIA (*quick to defend herself*): No, no! I didn't do it to get him back. Believe me I didn't do it for myself, and I screamed it in his face that I lied when I told them that I tried to kill myself for his sake.

GROTTI (*sneering*): But he doesn't believe you. Don't you see that he doesn't believe you?

ERSILIA: Is that my fault? It's not *me* he doesn't believe, it's his own conscience.

GROTTI (*contemptuously*): You're not exactly in a position to talk about other people's consciences.

ERSILIA: Do you think I'm more responsible for what's happened than the rest of you? No – less, much less (GROTTI *reacts*) – yes, yes, at least I have the courage to kill myself, which you could never have, though you'd never admit it.

GROTTI: Who me, kill myself?

ERSILIA: You can stay calm because you aren't crushed by guilt. You have things to do, your family to support. You have your place in the world... but there I was in the middle of the street... naked... I had nothing... I was going nowhere... no one knew me... like that it's harder, you know; it's almost impossible... and always there was the face of your child... and then the smug face of that man when I didn't know how to ask him for the money... What else could I do?

GROTTI: But you couldn't help lying even then.

ERSILIA: It wasn't because I meant to lie, you see he really did promise to marry me out there.

GROTTI: Yes, as a joke!

ERSILIA: That's not true! And even if it were it would make him twice as low. He came straight back here and proposed to that other girl and was about to marry her, even without knowing what had happened between you and me.

GROTTI: Let's get back to you: *you* knew what had happened between us and still you lied.

ERSILIA: And wasn't what he was doing worse – calmly arranging to marry someone else?

GROTTI: Doesn't that prove that his proposal to you was a joke?

ERSILIA: No! You've seen for yourself the state he's in. He wouldn't be like that if it had all been a joke. You're trying to ease your own conscience because of what you did behind his back the moment he left.

GROTTI: And you, you've caused all this scandal just to stop him from marrying another woman.

ERSILIA: I never even thought of that. I said it only when I thought I was dying. I didn't want to prevent anything. I still don't want to! I still don't want to!

GROTTI: So you say, but supposing, when you came back here, you had found him free, and ready to marry you?

ERSILIA (*with horror in her voice*): No! No! I would never have deceived him! I swear it! I swear it by the soul of your dead child. I didn't even try to find him. Ask him yourself. It was because of betrayal and on his part it was real treachery, that I could tell the lie I did. That I was killing myself for his sake!

GROTTI: And you made no attempt to see him?

ERSILIA: No!

GROTTI: Then how did you know about his engagement?

ERSILIA: I went, I went to... the Admiralty.

GROTTI: I see... But you made no attempt to find out where he was, did you?

ERSILIA (*trying to control her fury*): You ought to thank me!

GROTTI: For what? For trying to find out where *he* was?

ERSILIA: No! For suddenly losing all idea of revenging myself on you, when they told me he'd left the navy, and was getting married. Do you think my motives were dishonest as I climbed those steps of the Admiralty? You can't imagine how lost I felt when I arrived, having been thrown out by your wife, after she surprised us in that terrible moment... with the cries of the people who'd picked up the body of your dead baby... the baby who'd fallen off the roof. I was desperate, like a pauper who sees no escape but death or madness. I just wanted to find him and tell him everything. Everything!

GROTTI: About us as well?

ERSILIA: No! About you – how as soon as he left you took advantage...

GROTTI: I did. Was I the only one?

ERSILIA: Yes! About how you treated me! Take care, I can tell everything now, everything. Things that no one has ever dared to say. I know the truth that only mad people know. I can cry out the ugliest, filthiest things, because I feel I'll never get to my feet again. You caught me when I was still burning with the passion he had aroused, when the slightest touch made me lose all control. Deny it if you dare! Deny that I tried to stop you, scratched your neck, arms, hands – fought you off in every way I knew.

GROTTI: You bitch, you led me on.

ERSILIA: That's not true! That's not true! It was you!

GROTTI: At first, yes, but – after…

ERSILIA: No! Never! Never!

GROTTI: You used to clutch at me whenever you thought no one was looking.

ERSILIA: I didn't!

GROTTI: Liar! Once you even jabbed me with a needle.

ERSILIA: Only because you wouldn't leave me alone, Signor Grotti!

GROTTI: Oh! Listen to her now. Signor Grotti!

ERSILIA: I was a servant in your house.

GROTTI: Did that mean you had to obey?

ERSILIA: My body, my body obeyed! My heart never! I felt hate.

GROTTI: Pleasure, pleasure, is what you felt.

ERSILIA: No, hate! Hate – even when you gave me most pleasure! And afterwards I could have torn you apart, just like my own shame. I would look at my bare arms and bite them in my torment. I gave in to you, yes. I yielded, but in my heart of hearts I felt that I hadn't. Oh! You bastard! You took away from me the only joy I've ever known – of being in love, and about to marry the man I loved.

GROTTI: Meanwhile he was back here about to marry someone else.

ERSILIA: So you see? You're all *swine*. And you come here and accuse me? Accuse me, because I never had the strength to be anything. My God, not even a thing – something you could make with your hands out of clay, and if you dropped it, it would shatter, but there it would be, broken on the ground, and even then you could say: "That was something, and now it is nothing." But my life – one day dragging after the other, and no one I could ever call my own – just letting things happen to me – pulled this way and that, and never the power to rise and say: "Here *I* am." (*Changing her tone suddenly and turning on him like a hunted animal*) But what do you want now? Why have you come here like this?

GROTTI: Because you couldn't keep away – that's why. Because of the things you've said and done. You tried to kill yourself, remember?

ERSILIA: I should have kept my mouth shut, I know. That's it, a stone on top, and goodbye.

GROTTI: But instead you took that stone and you threw it into the gutter, and you splashed onto everybody. We're all of us covered with your filth. You've made a cesspool all around yourself…

ERSILIA: And you want me to be the only one who drowns in it, don't you? He finds out about us and goes back to his fiancée, while you go calmly back to your consulate in Athens.

GROTTI: Yes, and to all my life there, that you almost destroyed. Do you think I'd throw away all that for a few hours of pleasure with you? They've cost me enough already! They cost me my child!

ERSILIA: It was you! It was you! Always before me I can see that chair, that chair you wouldn't give me time to bring down from the roof, where I'd left the baby playing.

GROTTI: What were you doing up there anyway? Your place was in the room where my sick wife was sleeping, ready to look after her if she awoke and called you. What were you doing on the roof?

ERSILIA: I was watching the baby while she played.

GROTTI: Oh no! You went there on purpose because you knew I'd come looking for you!

ERSILIA: Liar! You would have come looking for me even in your wife's sickroom.

GROTTI: No! That's not true.

ERSILIA: You dare deny it? As if you hadn't done it many times before. And since I didn't feel safe even there...

GROTTI: But you wanted it too – you know you wanted me.

ERSILIA: No! But I know that after all your insistence, after all the temptations you put in my way, I *would* have wanted you. There! That's what you wanted me to say – so that your wife wouldn't hear us, that's why I went up to the roof. I'm certain now that a voice spoke to me, warning me not to leave the chair there. Because the baby, playing so innocently on the roof, might climb up and fall from the railing. But I didn't listen to that voice, because you, you remember, came at me in the doorway like a wild animal, and forced me to go with you. You forced me! And now I dream about it, and I see it, that chair, near the railing, and I can never move it in time. (*She bursts into tears. There is a pause.* GROTTI *absorbed in himself, cutting himself off into his own world.* ERSILIA *is still crying softly.*)

GROTTI: I was always working: I was – I was like someone cut off from everything except my work, and to fill the emptiness I felt in my life, I used to dream of the home I could never have. The woman I had married... she was always miserable or sick and irritable. And then you came – how did I treat you when you first came? Tell me, how did I treat you?

ERSILIA: (*tenderly, through her tears*): You were very kind to me.

GROTTI: Yes, because the more hopeless I felt in my own life, the easier I tried to make things for other people. It was only doing things for others that gave me any pleasure at all; I who could never be really happy. And how I sang your praises to Laspiga! I wanted him to love you. I wanted your lives to be as beautiful as mine could never be. And I was kinder to my wife at that time so that she too could share in the little plan I'd made for you both, made only for the pleasure of knowing that it was I who had designed and accomplished it, when I saw the two of you so much in love. No. No. It wasn't because I knew you'd gone too far and made love to him. That shocked my wife and made her lose all respect for you, but not me.

ERSILIA (*dreaming*): But he was the first. I was a virgin. And he was going away. It was the night before he left.

GROTTI: I know, I felt for you, I never thought of blaming you. And I would never have taken advantage of it, if you hadn't wanted me.

ERSILIA: Me?

GROTTI (*quickly*): You wanted me. I remember how you looked at me one evening as we were getting up from dinner. I knew at that moment that you didn't believe I had done what I did only for your happiness. And by not believing in me you spoilt everything, that's all. I needed your belief more than anything to keep myself going, and to overcome the terrible desire I had.

ERSILIA: But not my desire, not mine!

GROTTI (*slowly*): No, my own. But if only you could have believed I was being unselfish, the animal in me might have slept on, not sprung into life with such an all-devouring hunger. And even now that I look at you again, even after you've caused the last breach between me and the loss of our child. (*He goes to her, threatening, with hate*) No! You understand me? No!

ERSILIA (*looking away frightened*): What do you want of me?

GROTTI: I want you to cry. I want you to suffer with me for all the evil that we caused.

ERSILIA: More than I've suffered already?

GROTTI: I am not going to be the only one who feels that torment of guilt for the death of my child. You've shaken it off already, as if that terrible thing had never happened.

ERSILIA: No! No! I'll never be able to do that, I swear. Never! I shall stay here with Nota…

GROTTI: But you won't be able to. Because he already agrees with Laspiga, didn't you see them go off together? He's fed up with you already, and he'll think you're mad if you don't accept Laspiga's change of heart, and his obvious wish to make amends by marrying you.

ERSILIA: But I told him I didn't want him!

GROTTI: Yes, but you said it like a stubborn, unreasonable woman. Do you think either of them could accept that as your last word? You did not tell him the real reason.

ERSILIA: Very well. If I have to I will tell him the real reason.

GROTTI: And how ugly it will seem to him, all that you've done. The lies you told; the chaos you've brought with you; the marriage you've broken up; the scandal; the cloying compassion you've aroused, the public sympathy.

ERSILIA: But I never wanted all that. I told him just as I told you, that I only lied because I thought it was finished. There are things that one can't say, they're too ugly, too disgusting. We can speak like this now because we share a common guilt. How can you wish – why do you wish to uncover everything?

GROTTI: Because I was so disgusted by your lies when that girl's father came to see me and told me all the upheaval it had caused: her anger; Laspiga's terrible remorse: his anxiety to do the right thing – and marry you. I don't know how I controlled myself. I rushed to the newspaper office to make them retract the story! You don't know how furious my wife was when she read that story! She wanted to go straight to his fiancée and tell her how she'd caught us and thrown you out of the house. I had to promise her, swear to her, that your deception would be found out, or, at least, the consequences would not disrupt the life of that innocent family! You understand now?

ERSILIA: I do. I do. (*Dully*) Yes, I understand. (*Pauses, and adds*) Go away. I shall do it.

GROTTI: What will you do? What will you do?

ERSILIA: What you tell me I must.

GROTTI (*pauses, watching her*): You're more desperate than I am. How ghastly you look. (*Goes to her as if to embrace her*) Ersilia! Ersilia!

ERSILIA (*furious, pushing him away*): Ah! No! God! Leave me alone!

GROTTI: No! No! Listen! Listen! Ersilia, we must cling together. (*He caresses her, she tries to resist, but cannot help responding*)

ERSILIA: Let me go, I tell you! The baby, think of the baby. *You killed her!*

GROTTI: I'm going mad! But I need you, I need you! We're both wretched!

ERSILIA: Get out! Get out! I'll call out.

GROTTI: No! No! Listen!

ERSILIA: There… (*Running to open the window*) I'll call out! Go!

GROTTI *leaves as the*

CURTAIN FALLS

ACT THREE

The same scene, the same day, but towards evening.

The windows are open and noise from the street drifts in, but the market is over and the tempo and the noise are much diminished. SIGNORA ONORIA *is leaning out of one of the windows, having her evening gossip with the lady who lives opposite.* EMMA *is finishing the dusting and putting the room in order. There is a continual mumbling and grumbling from her.*

ONORIA: Yes, yes, well I'll tell you— (*She is obviously interrupted by her friend. Pause.*) Till midday, but you know how it is; it's never the sleep you get at night. (*She is interrupted again. Pause.*) What did you say? I can't hear... (*Pause*) Yes, ah yes, she's gone out with Signor Nota to get her bag, they wouldn't give it to him...

EMMA (*her mumble becomes audible*): And you'll see, they won't give it to her either!

ONORIA (*still talking to her friend*): Eh? No, she couldn't go before.

EMMA: It won't be like this every day, I hope. (*Various other mumblings we don't catch*)

ONORIA (*to* EMMA): Grumble, grumble, grumble, I can't understand a word you're saying.

EMMA: I said this is a fine time to have to do the room. It's getting dark already.

ONORIA (*who has turned back to her neighbour*): Eh? Oh, Signor Nota will be one— (*Interrupted again. Pause.*) What do you mean? (*She starts to laugh – the neighbour has obviously said that she saw* LUDOVICO *trying to embrace* ERSILIA) Well, he seems to think he can keep her here with him. (*Pause. The* WOMAN *probably says: "I saw that young naval lieutenant trying to kiss her too."*) No! No! She doesn't want to know about *him*. You say you saw him kissing her too? (*Pause. Gets very annoyed – touchily she says:*) No, no, you couldn't have. You're making it up. I tell you it's impossible!

349

(*She nods her head and waves her hand*) Yes, well goodbye for now. I'll see you soon. (*She shuts the window*) The old gossip! She says she saw three men in here and they all kissed her.

EMMA: That diplomat too?

ONORIA: Don't be silly. She made it up. She's just trying to stir up trouble.

EMMA: Well, I heard the two of them screaming at each other the moment they were left alone.

ONORIA: Oh... ah... You didn't... Did you happen to hear what they said?

EMMA: I wasn't trying to eavesdrop, you know – I was just going through to the sitting room when I heard them shouting, and that's all. She was shouting the loudest.

ONORIA: I'd be curious to know what more he's trying to get out of that wretched girl. What do you think he came here for, after all that fuss he's caused – protesting to the paper, threatening lawsuits. I wonder why?

EMMA: He probably doesn't want her to make it up with that sailor.

ONORIA: He's got no right to stick his nose into *that* affair. It's she who doesn't want to make it up, more's the pity. Such a lovely boy.

EMMA: Fancy her wanting to stay here with that dried-up old thing...

ONORIA (*finishing the sentence*): ...Who's fed up with her already – sick and tired of the whole thing, he is. He wants her out. I think he's already made that *quite* clear to her.

EMMA: Perhaps that would be the best thing for her, then she'll have to make it up with her sailor.

ONORIA: Well perhaps, who knows? She doesn't trust that boy any more, you know; although it seems to me he's really sorry for what he did to her.

EMMA: Oh yes, I'm sure he is.

ONORIA: I think she's got qualms about the other girl. You see, he's jilting her just the same way he jilted our poor little love.

EMMA: You wouldn't catch me having any qualms; not after drinking disinfectant.

ONORIA (*she hasn't heard what* EMMA *said*): She knows too well what it feels like to be jilted – left high and dry – oh, they put it so well in the paper. She's bound to be full of hate, and she must know by now that Signor Nota... (*makes a grimace of disgust*) well... You know, I saw her when she went out with him just now – she looked right through me, she didn't say a word, and she walked to the door like a zombie. When I asked her how she felt, she just smiled; it made me come over all gooseflesh. And her hand was so cold... so cold... (*She stops and listens... then, in a completely different tone*) Oh listen! That's the little man who sells clothes pegs. Yes. Quick, run and get some for me, two dozen will be enough. I'll call down to him from here.

EMMA *shuffles out.* ONORIA *goes to the window and opens it. She shouts down to the* MAN *to stop. In the meantime,* FRANCO LASPIGA *comes through the door. He has a strange, constricted look.*

FRANCO (*trying to make himself heard above the noise of* ONORIA *and the street*): May I come in? May I come in?

ONORIA (*turns and sees him; she shuts the window*): Oh, it's you, Signor Laspiga. Yes. Come in and sit down, won't you? Signor Nota will be back any moment with our young lady. (*Ingratiatingly and quietly*) Persevere, my boy, insist. She'll come round.

FRANCO (*looks at her as though he doesn't understand what she's talking about; in a sarcastic rage*): Yes, yes, you'll see! You'll certainly see just how I can persevere!

ONORIA (*confidentially*): He's straightened it all out, you know. He made her see reason. That consul, I mean!

FRANCO (*between his teeth*): Miserable... bastard!

ONORIA (*changing completely, rather bewildered*): You're right. Oh. You're right. What she hasn't had to put up with from him, poor young lady.

FRANCO: Lady? Don't say lady. Whore! Trollop! (*He is so angry, he can't stay still. He walks around the room, muttering, "bitch," etc., and hitting things.*)

ONORIA (*she cannot speak, but follows him round with her eyes, as though he had just slapped her*): Oh! Oh! My God! No! What are you talking about?

LUDOVICO NOTA *comes in at this moment and sees* FRANCO.

LUDOVICO: Ah, you're here already. (*Turns to* ONORIA) Hasn't she come back yet? (*He means* ERSILIA)

ONORIA (*she is flabbergasted; she looks at* NOTA, *and then without replying to him, turns back to* FRANCO): You can't mean it?

LUDOVICO (*doesn't understand*): Mean what?

FRANCO (*furious and venomous*): This morning, Grotti's wife found out that he'd been here visiting his mistress.

LUDOVICO (*startled*): Who? (*Looking at* ONORIA)

ONORIA: Here. You mean, she's his...

FRANCO: His mistress, slut, whore – what you want! This morning, Grotti's wife went to see my fiancée and her parents and told them about the whole cheap little affair!

LUDOVICO: Do you mean Signorina Drei is the consul's mistress?

ONORIA: Is she having an affair with him?

FRANCO: What I want to know is whether she was having an affair with him before or after I asked her to be my wife. That's why I'm here.

ONORIA: Oh... but how? Then... she... Oh, my God, I think I'm going out of my mind.

FRANCO: And do you know when his wife found out? She discovered the two of them in bed together just after the little girl had fallen from the roof...

ONORIA (*with a cry*): Oh, it's disgusting!

FRANCO: She caught them together and drove her out of the house like a murderess.

ONORIA: Yes, murderess – it's the same as if she'd pushed her off!

FRANCO: They left the little girl on the roof all by herself. And if our friend Grotti hadn't been compromised as well, she'd be in prison today! In prison! I tell you! And after all that...

ONORIA: ...She had the nerve...

FRANCO: ...To come here and upset my whole life!

ONORIA: All our lives! We *all* took pity on her!

FRANCO: But mine worst of all!

LUDOVICO: It seems incredible.

ONORIA: With that air of saintly persecution, the little faker!

FRANCO: I've been disgraced in public: I've had abuse heaped on my head by my fiancée; my whole life's been disrupted. I thought I was going mad: in fact, I don't know how I didn't go mad!

ONORIA: So... So that's why she wanted to run away. She guessed that the whole pack of lies would be uncovered as soon as she saw you again, and she knew that the consul's wife wouldn't let her get away with it. (*Her tone changes*) I'll make her pay for the pity I've wasted on her. (*She turns to* LUDOVICO) Out! Out! Out! I'm not having her in my house! Did you hear what I said? I am not having that slut under my roof another night!

LUDOVICO (*impatiently*): Wait! Wait!

ONORIA: No! No! No! No! Wait for what? I don't want her! I don't want her!

LUDOVICO: Be quiet for a moment, will you? I still haven't quite grasped all this. (*To* FRANCO) Just a moment – why did the consul – (*interrupting himself*) why should the consul be the first to protest against the newspaper story?

FRANCO: It's obvious why.

LUDOVICO: I don't see it. They must have had some sort of agreement, if they were lovers.

FRANCO (*as though he's talking to a child*): ...Because he was here with his wife! His *wife*! And don't forget his wife has been severely libelled by Ersilia in the newspaper.

LUDOVICO: Oh yes, of course. Yes, yes – ah... mm... That's why Ersilia was so disturbed when she didn't know what they'd written in the paper.

ONORIA: She said she'd been sent on an errand when the accident happened... the little liar!

FRANCO: I'm quite sure that it was his wife who forced him to deny the whole story.

LUDOVICO: Then it was all a lie...

FRANCO: The cheapest sort!

LUDOVICO (*continuing*): ...That she tried to kill herself for you?

ONORIA: How could anyone lie so shamelessly? I don't know...

LUDOVICO (*thinking to himself*): Mm... I see... yes... That must be why she refused to let you *do* anything for her.

FRANCO: I'd like to have seen her allow me to!

ONORIA: Oh. You poor boy! You were really taken in, just like me.

LUDOVICO *is extremely irritated by* ONORIA's *attitude and he turns with even more vehemence on* FRANCO.

LUDOVICO: I disagree! You must admit – at least she recognized her mistake.

FRANCO: And when? When she saw me standing there ready to make up for everything I thought was my fault.

LUDOVICO: I know, I know all that, but...

FRANCO: That's if we give her the benefit of the doubt. That's if she only became his mistress *after* I'd left. If they were lovers before we met – well, you can see it for yourself – I am the victim of one of the most infamous deceptions that ever happened.

LUDOVICO: No, this—

FRANCO (*interrupts him again*): I tell you, I've got to make sure! That's the only reason I'm here.

LUDOVICO: And what are you going to do about it? Excuse me, but you can't deny that when you came here she was violently opposed to seeing you again.

FRANCO: But I mean beforehand... the trick they played on me before.

LUDOVICO (*stopping him*): Excuse me again, but you've not been the victim of any trick or deception for that matter.

FRANCO: What do you mean? I...

LUDOVICO (*firmly*): No deception, not even beforehand. You forget, my friend, you were about to marry someone else, right here in Rome.

FRANCO: Ah. No! Wait a moment—

LUDOVICO: Let me finish, please! It seems to me you had already changed your mind and decided on marriage into an influential family long before you knew about her deception.

FRANCO: So I suppose the wrong I did excuses their treachery?

LUDOVICO: No! Certainly not, but it stops you having the right to call anyone to account!

FRANCO (*forcefully*): I say I have every right, every right in the world. They consummated their treachery. They completed it, whilst I threw up my marriage, and ran here like a penitent to try and make amends.

LUDOVICO: But only when you found out that she had tried to kill herself—

FRANCO (*breaking in*): But not for my sake! You heard her say so herself. Oh, it's marvellous. You reproach me with my so-called betrayal almost as if you thought I were more guilty than she.

LUDOVICO: No! No! Look here – I'm not reproaching anyone with anything. I'm simply trying to show you that you have only one bone of contention to pick with her – that she lied when she said she tried to kill herself for you, when she had no right to say that any longer. And for the life of me I can't understand why she told that particular lie right at the point of death. Some lies can be useful when one is living, but hardly when one is dying. And it's quite obvious that she realized that if she were to live, that lie would be completely useless to her.

FRANCO: Useless? Do you really think so?

ONORIA: You just don't want to face the facts!

LUDOVICO: Quite right! That's absolutely true. Yes. That's my greatest defect. I've never been able to face facts.

ONORIA: Well, it's a good job you admit it yourself. And what are the facts? Number one: she didn't die.

FRANCO: And her lie *did* prove useful. Yes. Useful… Oh, I don't mean she used it to get me back – that would have been too much – no – useful, because it helped her to find someone like you.

ONORIA (*with great disdain*): Let's face it – a writer.

LUDOVICO: Quite! An imbecile!

FRANCO (*immediately*): I didn't say that!

LUDOVICO: Well then, say it! Say it! That's what you meant, isn't it?

ONORIA: Well, if you know it, there's no reason for him to tell you so again.

FRANCO: She must have been really flattered to find her lies accepted, and herself taken under the wing of a famous literary gentleman; to have the romantic fable of her suicide – for love – written down by a famous writer, not just spattered all over the daily papers…

LUDOVICO: Yes, you're right. In fact, she did want me to write it.

FRANCO: You see?

LUDOVICO: She was very upset, too, when she knew that I had imagined another girl quite different from her for my novel.

ONORIA: What a pretty couple! Her babbling them all out – the lies – and him scribbling them down.

LUDOVICO: Lies. Quite – pretence. But what *are* stories but pretence? This story isn't less good because it's not true. What does the actual truth matter if it's a marvellous story? Probably it would have turned out badly for her and worse for me *if* we *had* written it down. But I'll tell you something else. The more we uncover her story, the better it gets. It's much more beautiful and exciting as it is. In fact, I couldn't be happier about these new disclosures. (*He indicates* ONORIA) For instance, take the good lady here; to begin with, she's disdainful, furious – then honey, pure honey. Now, she's gall – unadulterated venom.

ONORIA (*up in arms*): And I have good reason to be!

LUDOVICO (*placating her*): But of course! Of course, you're right! Still, you can't deny it's rather beautiful! (*Turning to* FRANCO) And you – you came here yesterday like some fervid knight, carried away with your plans and full of glorious endeavour.

FRANCO: But I had to talk to someone!

LUDOVICO: Yes. Yes, of course you did… I'm not blaming you. Yesterday it was true. It was the truest thing in the world for you! That's why I say it's beautiful! You both think that I have the part of the clown in this play – the imbecile who has been deceived by the charms of the fair young maid. Not at all! I am the chorus! I am the man who amuses himself explaining to the audience the beauty of the uncovered lie.

FRANCO (*sarcastically, but with suffering*): Beautiful, you call it?

LUDOVICO: Precisely! Because it has caused all this suffering and misunderstanding. Don't think I don't understand what a painful experience it has been for all of you. I have lived the whole thing vicariously – through all the joys, doubts and agony. I am more sure of my ability to bring it to life as a novel or a play than I have ever been of anything. As a matter of fact, it would make rather a good play, I think.

ONORIA: And I suppose you'll have me in it too?

LUDOVICO: If I make it a comedy – yes.

ONORIA: Oh! You wouldn't risk putting me on the stage, I'm sure.

LUDOVICO: What risk do you mean? That you might start shrieking out that it was all lies.

ONORIA: I'd say more than that! I'd say it's lies from beginning to end and that you're just as big a fraud as Ersilia Drei.

LUDOVICO: Don't worry, my dear lady, the critics would probably say it for you. (*Suddenly*) Why isn't she back yet? She ought to be here by now… I gave her some money to…

ONORIA (*shouting*): Money! To her! Oh, well done! Fancy that!

LUDOVICO: …To pay her hotel bill and recover her suitcase – just a small amount.

ONORIA: Well, if you gave her money, we've seen the back of her. That's that! Goodbye money! Goodbye play! Now I can really stop worrying about being in your comedy.

LUDOVICO: No. No, you see, one can always dream up a satisfactory ending to a play – even if there is never a true ending in life… except death.

FRANCO: Do you really believe she'll never come back?

LUDOVICO: I believe... that it depends... if the purpose of all her lying was in the world of "facts", as you both say... I'm afraid she'll never come back. But – and this is what I believe: if her aim – the object of her story – was in the world of fiction – a fantasy she made up for reasons outside "facts", then she will come back. And I will write my play. Of course, I'll write it either way.

FRANCO: Without paying any attention to the real facts!

LUDOVICO: Facts! Facts! My dear sir, facts are pieces of information that we take for granted. Once they are assumed into the mind, they are facts no longer. They are life! They sway our opinions this way and that! But actual facts are the past. Factum! Something finished and done for, when life has ebbed away. Things that life has abandoned. That's why I don't believe in facts.

EMMA *enters.*

EMMA: Signor Grotti is here. He's asking for the young lady, or for you, Signor Nota.

LUDOVICO: Ah! *He* has arrived instead. Perhaps he'll provide us with a nice conclusion.

FRANCO *gets up and moves to the door so as to be ready when* GROTTI *appears. He is fierce and threatening.*

FRANCO: If *he* doesn't, *I* have a very satisfactory finish to your story.

LUDOVICO (*calmly but firmly, stepping in front of* FRANCO): You will do me the courtesy of behaving yourself properly in my house, please. And let me remind you – you have no right to call anyone to account.

FRANCO: Then I had better go!

LUDOVICO: No! You will stay here and I will go and speak to Grotti myself.

At this moment, GROTTI *appears at the door. He is no longer the diplomat, but a very anxious and excited man.*

EMMA, *agog, is shushed out by* SIGNORA ONORIA.

GROTTI: Excuse me! Signorina Drei?

ONORIA (*she is both excited and rather alarmed*): Not here! She's gone away!

FRANCO: And she'll probably never be back!

GROTTI: Oh my God! But do you know that... Signor Nota, I had better explain to you...

LUDOVICO: My dear sir, you have forced your way into my house without so much as a by-your-leave...

GROTTI: And I apologize. But I must find out whether Signorina Drei is aware that my wife... has been to see the Minister of Foreign Affairs.

FRANCO (*breaking in and finishing for him*): Went to see the parents of my fiancée and informed them of—

GROTTI (*shouting*): OF HER OWN MADNESS!

FRANCO: Ah! Then you deny the whole thing.

GROTTI (*furious and contemptuous*): I don't have to deny or confirm anything. Especially not to you!

FRANCO: Oh yes, you do! Make no mistake! You *must* answer me.

GROTTI: For what? For the vindictiveness of a madwoman? I am ready to answer for that whenever you like.

FRANCO: Thanks. (*Sarcastically*)

GROTTI (*to* LUDOVICO): All I am anxious to find out, Signor Nota, is whether or not Signorina Drei knows what has happened?

LUDOVICO: No, I don't think so.

GROTTI: Thank God for that.

LUDOVICO: She was with me all afternoon. Then I left her because she didn't want me to accompany her into the hotel.

GROTTI: Then you didn't know either?

LUDOVICO: No. I learnt the story from Signor Laspiga, who was here when I got back.

GROTTI: Oh, good... good... good! You see, in the state she's in, another shock would be disastrous.

LUDOVICO: Well, the fact is, we've been waiting for her, but she hasn't come back yet.

FRANCO: Even if she doesn't know, she must be expecting it. And *since* Signor Nota gave her some money, she ran away.

GROTTI: I hope to God she has! But I'm afraid she may get to hear what my wife has done.

FRANCO (*breaking in*): Now you admit she should expect to be exposed?

GROTTI: I admit nothing!

FRANCO: Oh yes! I forgot you were a diplomat.

GROTTI: Can't you understand that I don't give a damn what you believe or don't believe! You can think what you like! Anything that makes you feel most comfortable!

FRANCO (*even more incensed*): *Comfortable!* I want to get at the truth.

GROTTI: And then what? I have told you already that my wife has been deranged by the death of our child. You just don't want to face the truth, which is that you – yes, you – have driven her to desperation!

FRANCO: *Me?*

GROTTI: *Yes! You!*

FRANCO: Listen! Even if she was innocent when your wife drove her out of the house – innocent even of the accident, if she wasn't there when the little girl fell—

GROTTI (*cutting in quickly*): She was there.

FRANCO: So that was a lie? That your wife sent her on an errand?

GROTTI: Yes! That is why I went to the newspaper office – to protest against that particular lie—

FRANCO: And then you came straight here to work out a common story with her.

GROTTI (*angrily, turning to* NOTA): Forgive me, Signor Nota. (*He turns back to* FRANCO) I came here because my superior, the Minister of Foreign Affairs, happens to be the father of one of the girls whom you promised to marry. He begged me to talk to Signorina Drei. I found her – and you can all bear witness to this, because you were all here – in a state of complete desperation because you— (*turning to* FRANCO)

FRANCO (*breaking in with steely force*): ...Because I wanted to make up for the wrong I'd done her? Then why was she in such despair, I'd like to know, if the harm I'd done her was real? And there I was ready to make reparation.

GROTTI: Because she doesn't want it! She doesn't want you! She doesn't want you! She said so herself! She repeated it again and again. God – how can you be so incredibly obstinate?

FRANCO: Surely you can't think then that I am here to make myself comfortable. She wants to get rid of me so that she can play the part of the betrayed girl more easily. So that this gentleman (*indicating* LUDOVICO) will feel it his duty to protect her from any more such events! But I assure you I'm not here for my own pleasure. I

359

am simply here because she herself stated that she had attempted suicide for my sake.

GROTTI: And hasn't she admitted already that that was a lie?

FRANCO (*even more steely*): Another lie! That makes two! (*Ironically*) Perhaps I compelled her to lie?

GROTTI: Perhaps she said that only to get rid of you?

FRANCO (*insistently*): Then that would make it true – that she did try to kill herself for me?

GROTTI: I don't know! I don't know why she did it.

FRANCO (*insistently*): It must have been because of me – because I was marrying another girl. There's no other reason I can see she would have done it.

LUDOVICO: Unless of course it was because... well... um... she was telling me...

FRANCO (*snaps, turning on him*): No! Excuse me. Just a moment ago you said you had no idea.

LUDOVICO: No... er... no. But... well, she did go down into the street that night. She said she felt so filled with self-disgust—

FRANCO (*breaking in, again ironically*): Oh yes. When she offered herself in the dark night to the first man who came along.

GROTTI: Did she tell you that as well?

FRANCO: That too! That too! Yes! And I am to blame for that too! Knowing that, do you think my conscience would ever let me rest if I thought that I'd done nothing to make amends? I'm ready to do anything – even now – on one condition – that you give me your word of honour that your wife was lying when she denounced Ersilia as your mistress!

At this moment, we hear EMMA *screaming – frightened. She comes shuffling and panting along the passage and through the door.*

EMMA (*agitated and out of breath*): Signora! Oh mercy! Oh my God! Signora! Oh signora! (*They all stop and stare at* EMMA)

ONORIA: What's the matter?

LUDOVICO: Is it—

EMMA: Yes, sir. She's come back!

GROTTI: Well, where is she?

ONORIA: Where is she?

EMMA (*puffing, etc.*): I just opened the... she fell in... she had that suit-case... she's ill.

LUDOVICO: The suitcase... God! That's where she had the rest of the poison...

They all start for the door, but at that moment ERSILIA *appears, and although she is obviously in great pain, she seems calm, and is almost smiling.*

ONORIA: Oh... look...

GROTTI (*bursting out*): Ersilia! Ersilia! What have you done?

FRANCO: You see! You see! He's given himself away!

LUDOVICO (*going to her to support her*): Signorina! Signorina Drei!

ONORIA: Oh, my God!... Not again... (*Surreptitiously, she moves to close the shutters in case of prying neighbours*)

ERSILIA (*putting her finger to her lips*): Nothing... this time it's nothing...

GROTTI (*with a great cry*): No! No! Oh God, we must get help quickly! We must get her to a doctor at once.

ONORIA (*frightened out of her wits*): Yes! Yes! Immediately!

LUDOVICO (*attempting to take her towards the door*): Come along... come along...

ERSILIA (*trying to ward them off*): No... I don't want to! Please don't.

GROTTI (*trying to lift her*): Yes... yes... come with me... I'll take you myself...

ONORIA: I'll send for an ambulance!

ERSILIA: For pity's sake, that's enough... it's useless anyway.

GROTTI: How do you know it's useless... we mustn't waste time arguing.

ERSILIA: It's no use!... Just leave me in peace...

ONORIA: Yes, sit down.

GROTTI (*once more bursting out*): What have you done! What have you done!

LUDOVICO: You should have remembered me, signorina. You could have stayed here with me, you know.

ERSILIA *sits with their help.*

ERSILIA: If I hadn't done this, nobody would have believed me again.

FRANCO (*very moved, but anxiously*): What – what do you want us to believe?

ERSILIA (*almost placid*): That I didn't lie to live... just that...

361

FRANCO: Why then?

ERSILIA: To die. That's all. Do you see now? I shouted it at you over and over – I told that lie to finish my life… to finish… you're right; yes, I didn't think of you… I thought of nothing… nothingness. You're right. I didn't think it would break up your life too… but I had no feeling left to care about anything…

FRANCO: But you accused me…

ERSILIA: No…

FRANCO: But you did!

ERSILIA: No… no… It's so difficult to explain… let alone for you to believe me. But now I'll tell you. I thought myself so little worth considering, that I forgot about the harm it might cause you… you can believe me now. You see – now I have the right to be believed. Oh, I have upset your whole lives… yours… your fiancée's and I knew… I knew I shouldn't be doing it… that I had no right to do it any longer because… (*She looks towards* GROTTI *and then turns slowly back to* FRANCO) You know, don't you? From his wife?

FRANCO (*almost inaudible*): Yes.

ERSILIA: I knew she would tell you. And then he came here to deny her story, didn't he?

FRANCO: Yes.

ERSILIA: There. You see? (*She looks at him and makes a small gesture with her hands that shows, without words, the reason why all tormented humanity must lie, then she adds, very softly and sweetly*) And you too…

FRANCO (*understanding her gesture, he is deeply moved and sincere*): Yes… I lied too… I lied.

ERSILIA (*smiling, but remote*): You told your dream… that's all… lovely things… true for a moment… and then you ran here to cover up for yourself – yes, just as he had to cover up – by denying his wife's story. (GROTTI *bursts into uncontrollable sobs. This is the first time* ERSILIA'*s composure is disturbed.*) Don't. Please don't cry! It's just that each one of us… everyone wants to be beautiful… the more we realize that we are… (*She is going to say "ugly", but the thought fills her with such disgust and then pity that she cannot bring herself to say it*)… The more we want to appear beautiful. That's it. (*She smiles*) Oh God, yes, to cover our nakedness with "decency"… the decent dress for all occasions, that's it – but I had nothing to wear when I had to face you again. And I knew that you too – you had thrown off your lovely white uniform. And then I saw myself in the street, with nothing on... and... (*Her face reflects the agony of the remembrance of that night outside the hotel*)... yes, then another handful of filth hit me, so I am covered with that and nothing else... God, what disgust!... What nausea! The only thing I wanted was to die... at least to die covered by a decent dress – not filth... That's why I lied! Just to cover myself... I swear it! I never had a dress for my life... a dress that would somehow show *me* clearly... one that would not be torn off me by all those dogs – those dogs that always jump up on me – they come at me from all directions and foul my clothes and leave me with nothing but a few stinking rags... So, you see, I wanted to make myself a beautiful dress... for my death... the most beautiful... the one I had worn for such a short time there in Smyrna... that had been ripped off me like all the others... a bridal gown. But only to die in it... to die in it... that's all... Just a little regret from all of you, that would have been enough... Well then! No! I couldn't even have that! Strip it off! Take it away from her! No! She must die naked! Uncovered... disgraced... despised. So here I am! Are you happy now? Go away! Now go away! Let me die in silence. Go away! I can say it now... I never want to see or hear any human being ever again. Go away and tell them... you – your wife... you – your fiancée... that this shell – this one could not cover her nakedness.

There is the sound of an ambulance and people hurrying up the stairs as the

CURTAIN FALLS

Think It Over, Giacomino!

Pensaci, Giacomino! (1916)

Translated by Victor and Robert Rietti

CHARACTERS

AGOSTINO TOTI, *a professor of natural history*
GIACOMINO DELISI
ROSARIA DELISI, *Giacomino's sister*
CINQUEMANI, *an old janitor of the school*
MARIANNA, *his wife*
LILLINA, *their daughter, and the wife of Professor Toti*
SIGNOR DIANA, *headmaster of the school*
DON LANDOLINA
ROSA, *a maid in Toti's house*
FILOMENA, *an old servant of Signorina Delisi*

The action takes place in a provincial town in Italy.

ACT ONE

The hall of a provincial high school in Italy. Facing the audience, at equal distance from each other, are three doors with the inscriptions: Class One – Class Two – Class Three. Downstage right, the Science and Natural History Laboratory. Facing it, downstage left, the headmaster's study. The school bell hangs on the back wall.

The only articles of furniture are a table and chair for the janitor.

CINQUEMANI *is discovered, wearing his janitor's uniform, a cap with the school badge, an old grey woollen scarf round his shoulders and a pair of woollen mittens. He paces up and down the hall with an air of "great importance". The voices of rather unruly students come from the laboratory where the lesson is about to end.* CINQUEMANI *raises his hands as if to say: "Heavens, what a noise!" The headmaster suddenly bursts out of his study.*

DIANA: I must put a stop to this scandal once and for all. (*He crosses to the laboratory – opens the door, and the noise ceases abruptly*) Professor Toti, is this the way you keep discipline in your class? You – boy – what are you doing over there by the window? And you? Yes you. Why aren't you at your desk? Leave the room, both of you. Pack up your books and go home! Professor Toti, take the names of those two students! I'll teach you how to behave properly in my school. You are suspended for three days. I'll inform your parents at once. Go! Professor Toti, please come here for a moment. (*The sound of a scuffle and of someone running is heard in the classroom*) Hold that boy! Hold him – don't let him get out of the window. (*To the janitor*) Cinquemani, quick – a student has jumped out of the window. Run and catch him! (CINQUEMANI *exits in haste*)

TOTI *comes into the hall. He is an old man in his seventies. He wears a pair of canvas slippers, a black velvet cap and a green scarf with tassels round his neck.*

TOTI: I assure you, Signor Diana, that young man doesn't belong to my class.

DIANA: Then who was he? How did he happen to be there? (*The sound of boys giggling*) Silence! (*Furiously, to* TOTI) Explain, Professor. (TOTI, *embarrassed, hesitates to answer*) Well? I am waiting.

TOTI (*quietly and good-naturedly*): What can I say Signor Diana? I... don't know! I had my back to the class, writing on the blackboard – look, you can see it from here – I was drawing the species and sub-species of monkeys... (*There is a burst of laughter from the class.* TOTI *turns to them, with an almost comical display of anger.*) Silence when I'm talking to the headmaster – you bad boys!

DIANA (*impatiently*): Come, come! How did that boy get into your classroom?

TOTI (*shrugging his shoulders*): Through the window, I suppose, as he went out that way. (*There is another burst of laughter from the class*)

DIANA: Silence, I say! Or I'll have the whole class suspended for two weeks! (*To* TOTI) You allow strange boys to enter your classroom "through the window" while the lesson is in progress?

TOTI: No, not exactly, Signor Diana. You see, it's partly the janitor's fault. He often falls asleep by the school gate and he doesn't notice if strange boys climb over the wall and get into the yard. Once they're there... as you know the window of my room is practically on ground level... they've only to lift one leg – and they're in.

DIANA: And you allow that to happen?

TOTI: *Santa pazienza!* Let's be reasonable. How can I be writing on the blackboard – and at the same time see what happens behind me? I don't have eyes at the back of my head now, do I?

DIANA: Oh!

TOTI: But you know, Signor Diana, it may be that that boy is a great lover of animals... (*he smiles good-naturedly and adds almost in parenthesis, as if to show that he can make such feeble excuses even in Greek*)... a "Zoophyte", in fact: that's it, a Zoophyte! He was so attentive and so very quiet that I didn't even notice him.

DIANA (*impatiently*): I see! Well... we'll speak of this later. Meanwhile...

CINQUEMANI (*enters panting*): No sign of him, Signor Diana. He must have run like the Devil!

DIANA: Ring the school bell, Cinquemani.

TOTI: I give you my word of honour, Signor Diana...

DIANA: That will do, Professor. I told you we'll discuss it later – after you've dismissed the students. (CINQUEMANI *rings the school bell. Professor* TOTI *talks to his class from the door.*)

TOTI: Now boys, you'd better get out of here through the other door. Make no noise or the headmaster will start thundering again. When you're home, have a good dinner and then get on with your homework... but don't work too hard, boys! Sh... sh... Quietly, please.

The headmaster has returned from his study during the above, and now approaches TOTI. *While the scene continues,* CINQUEMANI *takes off his cap, his woollen mittens and his scarf and from a drawer in his table takes out a blue tunic and a large red handkerchief. He puts on the tunic and with the handkerchief he fashions a kind of head-wear to keep the dust off his hair.* MARIANNA *and* LILLINA *enter later with brooms, dustpans etc. to start cleaning up and express impatience at finding the headmaster and* TOTI *still there.*

DIANA: Now, tell me, Professor Toti... Do you imagine it is possible to continue in this manner? That I should be compelled to leave my work, in order to enforce discipline in your class?

TOTI: Really, Signor Diana!

DIANA: Let me finish! It seems that my presence is necessary to prevent a revolution breaking out in my school through your inability to control the behaviour of your pupils. Take this morning for example. Why, the noise and laughter could even be heard in the gymnasium.

TOTI: They were happy, the dear boys. You know, Signor Diana, I like sometimes to crack a joke with them to keep their interest alive: I was describing the funny ways of monkeys...

CINQUEMANI (*shaking his head "knowingly" and sighing*): There are monkeys – and monkeys!

TOTI: You, dear Cinquemani, keep quiet please, while I'm talking to the headmaster. They're only boys after all, Signor Diana. They heard me talk of the prehensile tail of monkeys: of the fact that they use their tail and their feet in the same way they use their hands... which is as good as saying that monkeys have five hands. That reminded them that here in school we have a janitor (*looking at* CINQUEMANI) whom we call Cinquemani or "Five Hands" – and boys as they are – that made them laugh. (CINQUEMANI *looks none too pleased at this*)

DIANA: Stop making excuses for them. It only annoys me.

CINQUEMANI: That's right! It annoys me too!

DIANA: Cinquemani!

CINQUEMANI: Forgive my saying so, Signor Diana, but the noise they make in his class makes my head buzz!

DIANA: That will do, Cinquemani! Remember your place!

TOTI: That's right, Cinquemani, remember your place! Signor Diana, I admit that my pupils have been a little noisy this morning, but boys will always be boys, and after all, no harm has been done.

DIANA: No harm? And what about discipline? The dignity of my school?

TOTI (*resolutely*): Signor Diana, let's be serious for a moment...

DIANA: Serious? Did you imagine I was joking?

TOTI: Of course not, but I must tell you frankly that the cause of this "lack of discipline" as you call it...

DIANA: Yes!...

TOTI: ...Is the timetable. The time for my class is badly chosen! It's the last hour of the day. The boys come to me already tired and anxious to get home. How can you expect them to be attentive and quiet? (*Suddenly*) Have you a penknife?

DIANA (*taken by surprise*): What on earth do you want a penknife for?

TOTI: If you will make a tiny cut in your finger, or if you prefer it, in mine, it will soon become clear to you, Signor Diana, that at our age the blood is like water. But, *Santo Dio*, these boys have quicksilver in their veins. I get angry with them sometimes, I assure you... Yet I can swear to you that when I see them putting on that air of innocent saints, while I know they are planning some mischief... (*He laughs*)

DIANA: It's little wonder you cannot command respect if you let them see you are amused.

TOTI: No, no! I can be very severe with them, and they know it. I have only to look at them! Believe me, Signor Diana, they don't lack respect for *me*; it's the "Professor" they laugh at!

DIANA: Nonsense! (*Peremptorily*) Tell me! How many years have you been teaching?

TOTI (*warily*): I've never really worked it out.

DIANA: Answer me please.

TOTI: Well… Thirty-four years.

DIANA: And you have no family, have you?

TOTI: No. No family of my own. I only have a wife – when I go out for a walk in the sun.

DIANA: What do you mean?

TOTI: My shadow, Signor Diana: it walks, by my side. In my home there's no sun – therefore, no wife.

MARIANNA *appears in the corridor.* CINQUEMANI *nods to her to keep out of the way. Every now and then, she pokes her head round the door to listen to the conversation.*

DIANA: Pardon my asking, but how old are you?

TOTI (*smiling*): How old do you think?

DIANA: Sixty-six – sixty-seven?

TOTI (*pleased at this "underestimate"*): If you say so.

DIANA: Well – shall we say seventy?

TOTI (*shrugs his shoulders*): If you insist.

DIANA: Very well. Seventy years old: no family, and you've spent thirty-four years teaching. It surely can't be very pleasant for you to continue teaching at your age?

TOTI: Pleasant? The very thought of it weighs on my shoulders like thirty-four mountains!

DIANA: Then why don't you retire? You could live on your pension. By now you're entitled almost to the maximum, and…

TOTI: Retire? You're joking! After more than a third of a century I've carried this cross on my back, the government would pay me my miserable four-penny-worth of a pension for a few years – and then what? Does their responsibility to me end with that?

DIANA: But what more can you want? To retire: no work and plenty of rest…

TOTI: Rest? Be idle you mean! With nothing to do all day but feel old, miserable and alone. Take it from me, the government…

DIANA: Come now, the government is hardly to blame if you haven't a family!

TOTI: Isn't it? So the government is not responsible for my having been forced to live most of my life in a sixth-floor garret? The government is not responsible for my having had to do my own cooking, darn my own socks, scrub the floors. The joy of a family has never been mine. Indeed how could I have kept one with the miserable pittance the government has been paying me? Why, it couldn't feed me, a wife and eight or ten children...

DIANA: Ten children?!

TOTI: Naturally. You understand... when I was young! No, it would have been madness! I thank God I never married before, but *now* it's different. Now I mean to get married.

DIANA: Oh, surely not!

TOTI: Yes, Signor Diana. The government is not going to get away with it so lightly! I reckon that I may live another five or six years, and I intend to take a wife – to compel the government to pay my pension, not only to me while I am alive, but to my wife when I am gone.

DIANA: That's preposterous! You want to get married... at your age?

TOTI: Bother my age! What has my age got to do with it?

DIANA (*laughing*): But... but my dear Professor Toti, a wife... will expect more than a pension from... a husband. Why, people will laugh at you!

TOTI (*slowly*): I know what that look in your eye means, Signor Diana.

DIANA: But...

TOTI: It means that you are exactly like all the others; they see the Professor and they miss the man! They hear of my getting married and they laugh, thinking that at my age a wife will... well, you know what I mean. (*He makes the sign of a cuckold's horns over his head*) Or they lose patience with me – as you did just now – believing that my pupils play pranks on *me* when they are only poking fun at "the Professor". The Professor and the man are different beings. Outside, the boys respect me, they raise their hats to me. In here, they too follow their profession: that of a student, and they naturally have to play tricks on whoever is their teacher, even if it be this squeezed-out old lemon. But I don't mind their good-natured laughter, just as I'm not affected by the mockery of evil-minded grown-ups. (DIANA *coughs, a little ill at ease*) Yes, Signor Diana, I shall take a wife. She can be poor but she must be pretty and full of fun.

DIANA: Oh come now, Professor!

TOTI: Yes siree! Very pretty and fun-loving! I've had enough solitude and sadness in my life. I don't want any more! So I shall take a wife and the marriage will be legalized by both the Church and the State so that the government can't get out of paying her my pension. But she'll be my wife and I her husband for this and *no other* reason, do you understand?

DIANA: But surely, my dear Professor...

TOTI: Oh I know, I know only too well the limitations imposed on me by my years.

DIANA: Quite!

TOTI: But for a while I will enjoy the comfort of a little gratitude for the good I will have done at the government's expense – and "*après moi – le deluge!*"

DIANA: I beg your pardon?

TOTI: Amen!

DIANA (*laughs*): You are quite a character, my dear Professor. I admire your sense of humour: believe me – you'll need it!

TOTI: Ah, you already begin to see me with horns on my head, eh? (*He again makes the sign of "the cuckold" over his head*) The old cuckold!

DIANA (*remonstrating*): What are you saying, my dear Professor!

TOTI: But I assure you, Signor Diana, that I don't worry much on that score! I thought of that too and I know what to expect! Do you see: I know I cannot be, nor do I wish to be a husband in the true sense of the word. My marriage will purely be a gesture of charity... Therefore, that "badge of ridicule" will not be placed on me; it will decorate only the head of the husband. But as this is a part I will play in name only, if all the fools of the country want to laugh their head off, it won't matter a scrap to me!

DIANA (*ironically*): Well, yes, Professor, looking at it *your* way, I see your point. Let us hope this marriage will take place soon.

TOTI: As soon as I have found the right girl. And, to tell the truth, I already have someone in mind.

DIANA: Good. I hope you will ask me to the wedding?

TOTI: But of course. You'll be the first to be invited.

DIANA: Thank you. (*He turns to* CINQUEMANI) Cinquemani, fetch my hat and cane, please. (CINQUEMANI *nods and goes into the head-master's study. He returns shortly with a hat and a cane in one hand and a clothes brush in the other.*)

TOTI: You are no longer angry with me, I hope, Signor Diana?

DIANA: To be frank with you: as a man, no… but in my capacity as headmaster…

TOTI: Of course, as a headmaster you admonish me, but as a man – you won't refuse to shake my hand.

DIANA (*laughs and extends his hand*): There!

TOTI (*smiling*): Looking at it *my* way! (*He moves towards the laboratory. At that moment* LILLINA *and* MARIANNA *appear. He glances at* LILLINA *and slowly returns to the headmaster.*)

TOTI: And you know, the girl I choose will be *very* young – and that will compel the government to go on paying her my pension for at least fifty years after I die. They won't get away with it, I assure you!

DIANA (*smiling*): Goodbye, Professor. Take care of yourself.

TOTI: I will, I will – don't worry about that. (*He exits into the laboratory.* CINQUEMANI *starts to brush the headmaster's jacket.*)

CINQUEMANI: Ah, what a character! He's quite capable of doing it, you know? He's never cared a fig for what people say about him. You may be sure, if he says he'll take a wife – he'll take a wife!

DIANA: Well, we shall see. (*He takes his cane and hat*) Good day.

CINQUEMANI: Good day, Signor Diana. (*As soon as the headmaster has gone, he turns to his wife and daughter who have been standing there, waiting*) Come on – get on with your work!

MARIANNA: Listen to him! As if it was our fault we couldn't get on with it before! I'd have finished down here ages ago if it hadn't been for them making me waste my time with all that disgusting talk!

CINQUEMANI: Ssh! (*Pointing to the laboratory*) The Professor's in there.

MARIANNA: Let him hear me: it'll do him good! Why he nearly turned my hair red with shame! (*She goes into Class Three with her broom and things*)

CINQUEMANI (*shouting after her*): Shut up! Get on with your work and don't waste any more time. (*He turns to* LILLINA) And you go and clean Class Four.

LILLINA: Why? I usually do the lab.

CINQUEMANI: Do as you're told! Upstairs in the house your mother's mistress, but down here I give the orders, d'you understand?

MARIANNA (*re-entering from Class Three*): Listen to him! "He gives the orders now!"… "You go into Three! You go into Four! You go into

Five!" He thinks that because he wears that blue "nightshirt" he can boss everyone around while he does nothing himself!

CINQUEMANI: Nothing?

MARIANNA: Yes, nothing! (LILLINA *laughs*)

CINQUEMANI: So – you'd stand there laughing at me, would you? I'll teach you and your mother to show some respect for me. (*To* MARIANNA *as she returns to the classroom*) Shut that door while you sweep the floor… and open the window, or the dust'll blow out into the corridor and I'll have to sweep it up again! (*To* LILLINA) I told you to do Class Four.

LILLINA: I don't want to. It's so stuffy: I always feel I'm going to suffocate in there. (*Wheedling*) You do it for me, please, Papa. I'll do the lab.

CINQUEMANI: But can't you see… Professor Toti's still there.

LILLINA: Well, tell him to go. We can't wait all day for him.

CINQUEMANI: That's true. (*He calls to Professor* TOTI *from the doorway of the laboratory*) Are you still here, Professor? For Heaven's sake go home and let us clean up the lab. We've wasted enough time as it is.

TOTI (*offstage*): Come here, Cinquemani. I want a word with you.

CINQUEMANI: He wants to talk to me? (*He glances enquiringly at* LILLINA *and goes into the room.* LILLINA, *annoyed at being delayed from carrying on with her work in the laboratory, sighs angrily, looks at her wristwatch and stamps her foot. She sighs again and suddenly puts her hand over her eyes as though she were very worried.* MARIANNA *comes out of Class Three with her cleaning things. Her face is dirty.*)

MARIANNA: Thank God – that's done. (*Aggressively*) What are you doing here?

LILLINA: I'm waiting for the Professor to come out of the lab.

MARIANNA: Is he still there? And where's your father?

LILLINA: He's in there too, talking to the Professor.

MARIANNA: What's he got to talk about?

LILLINA: How should I know? Father asked *him* to come out, and he asked *Father* to go in. He said he had something to say to him.

MARIANNA: Is that so?! And of course you waste your time out here, listening at the keyhole.

LILLINA: I couldn't care less what they say. I'm only waiting for them to finish.

MARIANNA: That's fine! You wait; your father talks – and I do all the work.

LILLINA: How you love to grumble about nothing! You never do more than two classrooms any day: well, finish your two and go upstairs. I'll see to the rest.

MARIANNA: I like that! Me clean two classrooms and then get on with all my own work upstairs while you hang around here for hours – like you do every day – doing nothing!

LILLINA: Doing nothing!

MARIANNA: Yes – nothing! When I call you from upstairs, you don't answer, and you always have an excuse handy to stay behind when I've already finished down here. (*Mimicking her*) "I'll just fill the inkpots in the desks, Mother!" or "There's no chalk by the blackboard – I must go and find some!" You waste three solid hours every day that way. What on earth do you do with yourself?

LILLINA: Well you know what Father is like! With the excuse that he's been shut in here all day, the moment you go upstairs, he hops out to "get some fresh air"... out of a bottle... leaving me to do three classrooms, the headmaster's study, the laboratory and the whole corridor – on my own! And then you grumble at me! That's all the thanks I get!

MARIANNA: Oh, it's no use talking to you. Get on with your work. If the headmaster comes back he'll complain that the place hasn't been cleaned. Oh why did I ever have such a daughter! (*She goes off to the left*)

LILLINA (*getting more and more impatient, looks at her watch*): What the devil are they doing there? (*She peeps through the keyhole of* TOTI's *door. The door opens suddenly and* CINQUEMANI *comes out. There is a look of wonder mixed with joy on his face; as though he'd been pleasantly stunned by his talk with* TOTI. *He is so absorbed in thought that he hardly notices his daughter.*)

LILLINA: Well? Isn't the Professor coming out?

CINQUEMANI: Eh? Oh no... he's waiting for you. Go to him, dear. (*He chucks her under the chin and smiles sweetly at her. She hesitates.*) Go – go in there... Lil – li – na.

LILLINA: But... but what does he want with me?

CINQUEMANI: He'll tell you himself. He'll tell you, my little Lilly. (*He chucks her under the chin again*)

LILLINA (*puzzled and anxious, not knowing yet whether or not to be pleased*): Has he told you… something about me?

CINQUEMANI: Precisely! "Something" about you.

LILLINA: And… and what did you say?

CINQUEMANI (*who doesn't want anybody – least of all his wife to hear*): Where's your mother?

LILLINA: Doing Class Five… but tell me, are you… glad about it?

CINQUEMANI: My child, I'm happy if you are. But there's your mother! And one never knows how she'll take it! Now go… the Professor's waiting: go and hear what he has to say. He's not exactly in his prime – but he's got good sound common sense! (LILLINA *looks puzzled*) I know he's a bit eccentric – but he's got a heart of gold.

LILLINA (*suddenly happy*): So then?… Oh, I was sure he'd talk to you.

CINQUEMANI: Why, did he tell you?

LILLINA: No, I just thought he would.

CINQUEMANI: Well, my child… (TOTI *appears in his doorway with his hat on*) Oh, he's here. (*He picks up his watering can, broom etc. and exits to the left, pretending to be busy with his cleaning*)

LILLINA: Professor, I'm so grateful to you. Oh, what a relief! I couldn't find the courage to tell Father myself. Thank you with all my heart. You are so good to me. (*She kisses his cheek*)

TOTI (*moved*): Child… child. What are you saying? What good can I do you? Only the good… a father can do for his daughter. Nothing more.

LILLINA: Oh no – what you've done… is much more… (*very sweetly*) my dear, kind Professor.

TOTI: I am not and can never be your dear one. Oh, if I were thirty – even twenty years younger, it would be different… but at my age… no, you must think of me only as a father.

LILLINA (*smiling*): Very well then – we'll think of you as a father, and we'll take good care of you, you'll see. I promise you you'll never have reason to regret what you've done for me.

TOTI (*profoundly moved*): Don't say that, my child, don't. You've suddenly filled my heart with joy. This is so much more than I expected. What is the little good I do to you compared with the good you'll be doing for me, just to see you laughing happily by my side.

LILLINA: Not only me, Professor: you've made it possible for us both to be happy. (*With a sigh of relief*) Oh, and we'll really be able to laugh at last.

TOTI: Yes, we'll laugh a lot together – you and I.

LILLINA: And Giacomino!

TOTI: Eh? (*He is startled*) Giacomino? Who's Giacomino?

LILLINA (*laughing*): Did you expect him not to be happy too?

TOTI: I don't understand! Giacomino?

LILLINA: Of course. Didn't he ask you to speak to my father on our behalf?

TOTI: No, no, child – you're making a mistake.

LILLINA: What do you mean?

TOTI (*taking his head between his hands*): I mean, I mean... Oh, I don't know what I mean.

LILLINA: What's the matter, Professor, don't you feel well?

TOTI: I'm all right. Only it's a bit of a blow! Now, let me get things straight. I told you I wanted you to think of me only as a father, didn't I?

LILLINA: Yes, that's what you said.

TOTI (*with a touch of anger and as if he is forcing himself to accept a sudden reality imposed on him*): Father, yes, just a father. Now, don't lose your head, Agostino! Take a hold on yourself. (*He shakes himself as though he were freeing himself from an illusion, and swallows hard*) Tell me, my child. Who is this Giacomino who you imagine asked me to talk to your father on your behalf?

LILLINA: Giacomino didn't ask you? But then – what did you say to my father about me?

TOTI: I simply told him that I am... an old man... who wants to make your future secure, by taking you... with me... as a daughter. That's all.

LILLINA: And do you want only me?

TOTI: Did you want me to take Giacomino as well? There are too many wicked tongues about as it is. What would people say to *that*?

LILLINA (*very simply*): But – didn't you say you wanted me – only as a daughter?

TOTI: Yes, but you must understand that if people are not to get the wrong impression, it's not enough for you just to come and live in my house; we must… we must "legalize" your position.

LILLINA (*naively*): Without Giacomino?

TOTI: Well – I don't say that Giacomino wouldn't be there, but you see, he can't leave my pension to you. In the eyes of the law, only I can do that.

LILLINA: Pension? But then… I don't understand! My father told me that if I was happy about… what you had said to him… then he'd be happy too.

TOTI: Yes, my dear, but now there's a complication. I never expected a Giacomino to spring up like a jack-in-the-box. I knew nothing about him. Nobody ever mentioned him to me before.

LILLINA: But you know him well, Professor. Giacomino Delisi.

TOTI: Delisi? (*Pleased*) Well, well, well… of course I know him. Nice boy, nice boy. He was a pupil of mine, some years ago.

LILLINA: That's when I met him.

TOTI: And you've been courting since then?

LILLINA: Yes.

TOTI: Oh!

LILLINA: What's the matter? Don't you like him? You said you did.

TOTI: Very much. He often comes to see me.

LILLINA: I know, and that's why I thought he'd asked you to speak to my father about us. But now… Oh my God, what are we going to do? We're as badly off as before. And we must do something soon because I… I can't hide it much longer. (*She buries her face in her hands*)

TOTI: You can't hide what much lon— (*The truth dawns on him*) Lillina! (*He suddenly feels a little weak at the knees at the realization and puts his hand on her shoulder to steady himself*) Oh, poor child!

LILLINA (*sobbing*): For God's sake, Professor, help me. Help me.

TOTI (*gently*): How can I help you? What do you want me to do?

LILLINA: Talk to my father, tell him that you know Giacomino… that you know he's a good boy, and that you'll help to find him a job.

TOTI: Me?

LILLINA: Yes – so that he can earn enough for us to live on... And make my father understand that... that it has to be done at once, or else... Oh, help me, Professor. I beg of you.

TOTI: Well, yes – if it will help, my child. I will talk to your father. But will he listen to me?

LILLINA: Oh yes, he'll listen to you. You're a professor. The best professor here.

TOTI: What difference does that make? You've seen for yourself, that doesn't make him respect me. Besides, do you really imagine he'll seriously believe that I would be able to find a job for Giacomino?

LILLINA: Oh, please try all the same. I'm sure he'd listen to you.

TOTI (*shaking his head*): Money is all that matters to your father – and he thinks that I am rich. Besides, let's be reasonable; Giacomino is a good boy – I don't say he isn't – but he is very young; he hasn't got a position yet. How can he keep a wife? Love? (*He shakes his head*) Even love needs to eat! And moreover there is a child on the way. The problem was difficult enough with this blessed Giacomino!... But now there is a Giacominino, and that makes two Giacominos! Do you want me to become a father and grandfather all at once?

LILLINA: Oh, we should never have done it. I am so ashamed of myself. And he too – poor Giacomino – he's so upset. But we neither of us know what to do, and there isn't much time. (*Breaking down*) Oh please, please help us, Professor. Now that you know everything you must help us.

TOTI: Oh very well then. I'll do what I can. (*Ruminating*) If Fate has decreed that I should be a grandfather instead of a husband – well, that's what I'll have to be.

LILLINA: No... No...

TOTI: And yet, perhaps it's all for the best; (*almost to himself*) for now I can really say to my conscience that I am doing it only as a good gesture. Besides, I'll have a little grandchild, a Giacomin*ino*. I'll take him for walks... I'll play with him in the park... I'll tell him all about the earth, the sun, the stars, all the good things on this earth. No, I don't think I'd mind it at all. (LILLINA *stares at him with an expression which is a mixture of gratitude and wonder*) Now, don't cry any more, and don't be ashamed. Just think you've been confiding a secret in your father.

LILLINA: But Giacomino, Professor? What about Giacomino?

TOTI: Well, as for your Giacomino… (*He makes a gesture with his hand as if to say "We'll hide him"*) He'll be there, of course – but I mustn't know. I mean to say, of course I'll know – but it must seem as if I didn't. Do you understand? And I'll love him too – as if he were my son. Why not? Can't I love an old pupil of mine?

LILLINA: Oh no, Professor – not like that: Giacomino would never agree. It's very good of you to suggest it, and don't think I'm not grateful – but it would never work! No, there is only one way to help us: you must talk to my father and persuade him to let me marry Giacomino *now*. He'll find a job soon, you'll see; he'll earn enough to look after me. Please, Professor. (TOTI *shakes his head dubiously*) Now listen, I'm going into your lab with the excuse that I must clean it – and presently Giacomino will be joining me.

TOTI: What? Giacomino? In there?

LILLINA: Yes. He comes almost every day at this time, through the window.

TOTI: Through the window?!

LILLINA: Meanwhile you go and talk to my father. Please, please, Professor… if you have any pity on me. (*She runs into the laboratory and closes the door*)

TOTI *remains as if stunned, considering the heavy load* LILLINA *has burdened him with. He doesn't say a word, but his thoughts are clearly expressed in his face and gestures: will he succeed in persuading* CINQUEMANI? *How wonderful it would have been for him to have a little "Giacominino" to play with and to love. He sees himself walking in the park, hand in hand with the boy, and he is happy; then he recalls that there is the other "the older" Giacomino to be included in the "entourage". Himself, Lillina, Giacomino, the baby… four mouths to be fed on the government pension! Too many, far too many! He scratches his head, wondering. Then he glances at the door of the laboratory and thinks that Giacomino is probably there at this moment with Lillina. For an instant he is cross; then he makes a gesture implying "what on earth can be done? Why should I be mixed up in all this?" At this very moment,* CINQUEMANI *returns, cautiously and curiously, from the left, and surprises him gesticulating.*

CINQUEMANI: Are you talking to yourself, Professor? Where's Lillina?

TOTI: She's gone.

CINQUEMANI: Gone?

TOTI: I'm going too!

CINQUEMANI: Wait a minute. Have you spoken to her?

TOTI: Yes, I've spoken to her.

CINQUEMANI: And what did she say? (*Noting his expression*) No? She refused? But why? She seemed so pleased.

TOTI (*resolutely*): Cinquemani, listen to me: the matter is not as easy as we thought.

CINQUEMANI: What do you mean?

TOTI: Well, there is an obstacle... (*He puts his hat over his belly*)... a bump.

CINQUEMANI: A bump? What on earth are you talking about?

TOTI: Oh, *Santo Dio* – is it so difficult for you to understand? How shall I explain? Well, look... (*He removes his hat, pulls in his stomach and draws himself erect*) Now – do you see that my tummy is perfectly flat... (CINQUEMANI *looks at it, unconvinced.* TOTI *also glances down.*) Well – reasonably flat! Now, just imagine this is a straight road from here to here. Easy to walk on.

CINQUEMANI: To walk on?

TOTI: Yes. But if I put my hat on it (*he holds it against his belly again*) – it makes a hump... a mountain... and if you have to climb it, it isn't so easy. (CINQUEMANI *scratches his head and looks at* TOTI *as if to say "The man's gone mad!"*) Don't you see, the road was straight – but it isn't any longer.

CINQUEMANI (*nods his head, then shakes it, trying to follow the story*): Eh?

TOTI: How the devil can I make him understand? Now look, when I speak of a woman, what can such a hump – such a mountain – mean? Surely, you see what I'm getting at.

CINQUEMANI (*it has suddenly hit him*): Do you mean... Are you trying to tell me that my daughter... (*He grasps* TOTI *by the lapels of his jacket, menacingly*) Mind what you say!

TOTI: Take it easy, Cinquemani. Take it easy.

CINQUEMANI (*letting go of his jacket*): Who told you? Lillina? Answer me!

TOTI: Who else could have told me, God bless you!

CINQUEMANI: My daughter – dishonoured!

TOTI: Well, not exact—

CINQUEMANI: Yes – dishonoured! Who's the man? I want to know! I'll murder him!

TOTI: Come now: don't take it like that! You'll let her marry him... and everything will be all right.

CINQUEMANI: Let her marry him? When I don't even know who he is?

TOTI: He's a decent young man – I can assure you.

CINQUEMANI: Decent, you call him – after what he's done! And as for her... disgracing the family name! Where is she?

TOTI: Come now, Cinquemani – don't upset yourself so! You'll turn your blood sour!

CINQUEMANI: Tell me where she's gone or I'll... I tell you I won't be responsible for what I'll do. Oh, the shame of it!

At this moment, like an echo, from the laboratory comes MARIANNA's *shrill cry: "Shameful!" followed by the voices of* LILLINA *and* GIACO-MINO DELISI. *They have been surprised by* MARIANNA *who has seen them through the window on the other side of* TOTI's *room. Almost immediately the door is flung open and* GIACOMINO *and* LILLINA *are practically thrown out by* MARIANNA *– her clothes still disarrayed from having climbed through the window.* GIACOMINO *tries to bolt through the corridor, but* CINQUEMANI *catches him by the scruff of his neck.* MARIANNA *takes hold of* LILLINA *who falls to her knees. Professor* TOTI *is "buffeted" from one couple to the other, trying to protect the youngsters and calm down the parents. The scene must go very rapidly, the dialogue overlapping, all talking and shouting at once in great confusion and excitement.*

CINQUEMANI (*shaking* GIACOMINO *violently*): Ah, it's you, is it. You're the hero, eh? You filthy swine!

GIACOMINO: Forgive me. Forgive me.

CINQUEMANI: Forgive you? After what you've done to my daughter? Dragging our good name into the mud?

GIACOMINO: But I'm ready to make up for it. I want to marry her.

CINQUEMANI: Marry her? You expect me to give her to a starving good-for-nothing like you? (*Professor* TOTI *succeeds in freeing* GIACOMINO *from* CINQUEMANI's *hands*)

CINQUEMANI: Get out of here! Get out before I murder you!

GIACOMINO (*to* TOTI *who is now between them*): Professor, you tell him. I'm ready to marry Lillina. I'll find a job and work hard to support her.

MARIANNA (*simultaneously with the dialogue between* CINQUEMANI *and* GIACOMINO): So that's the way you clean the lab every day, is it? I caught you at it this time, you shameless hussy! (*Hitting her*) There! There! There!

LILLINA (*on her knees, trying to shield her face*): Don't hit me! Forgive me, Mother. Forgive me.

TOTI: Don't hurt her, poor girl.

MARIANNA (*to* TOTI): Mind your own business! (*To* LILLINA) Carrying on under my very nose!

LILLINA: Please, Mother, please...

MARIANNA: How far have you gone? What have the two of you been up to, eh?

LILLINA: He wants to marry me, Mother – can't you hear? He wants to marry me.

At this moment, the parents "change over" as it were. MARIANNA *goes for* GIACOMINO *and* CINQUEMANI *for* LILLINA. *Poor* TOTI *is again "buffeted" from one couple to the other, trying to keep the peace.*

MARIANNA: Marry? You think I'd give my daughter to you? You waster... you lout you! You've ruined my daughter, that's what you've done! Climbing through the window like a thief, to seduce my daughter!

CINQUEMANI (*simultaneously, to* LILLINA): Do you think I'd let him marry you? Look at him: he hasn't a penny to buy bread, and he wants to get married! I'll teach him he can't meddle with my daughter! (*He picks up a chair and goes for* GIACOMINO. TOTI *holds him back.*) Get out! Get out, or I'll murder you! (*With a violent jerk he frees himself from* TOTI, *but* GIACOMINO *escapes down the corridor.* CINQUEMANI *tries to follow, but* TOTI *bars the way. He turns to* LILLINA.) And you too! Never put your foot in my house again! Get out. Get out, I say.

TOTI (*powerfully, dominating them*): Where do you want her to go, you old fool? You take it out on her – when you've only yourselves to blame for what's happened. You who have let her grow up here among all these boys. What else could you expect would happen to a pretty girl in the midst of young rascals all the time? Boys are like young bulls, idiots that you are: don't you know that?

CINQUEMANI (*to* LILLINA): Get out, I said. We don't want you any more!

MARIANNA (*crying*): You're no longer our daughter!

TOTI: No longer your daughter? Very well then – from now on, she'll be my daughter. I'll take her away with me. Come, come, Lillina. Leave these two hard-hearted fools. (*He takes her head on his shoulder and caresses her hair tenderly as they walk out together to the right*)

MARIANNA (*attacking her husband*): It's all your fault!

CINQUEMANI: Mine?

MARIANNA (*softening as her tears overcome her*): Oh… Cinquemani.

CINQUEMANI: Marianna… (*They fall into each other's arms, weeping and consoling each other*)

CURTAIN

ACT TWO

The drawing room in Professor TOTI'*s house. The main entrance is in the centre of the back wall. There is another door to the left. There are some toys of Nini's on the settee. At the rise of the curtain,* SIGNOR DIANA *is discovered, standing, hat in hand. After a moment,* ROSA *enters from the left.*

ROSA: The Professor won't be a moment. Please sit down, Signor Diana. I'll take these toys out of the way.

DIANA: Don't worry, thanks. I can sit here. (*He indicates an armchair*)

ROSA (*removing the toys from the settee*): Oh, the child's toys are all over the place. Do please sit here.

DIANA: Thank you. (*About to sit on the settee, he takes a Pierrot, half-hidden under a cushion, and gives it to Rosa*)

ROSA: Oh, thank you. I'm glad it's turned up. They really spoil him. Not a day goes by without him buying a new toy for the little one. Oh, here is the Professor.

TOTI (*enters in his dressing gown; he looks worried*): Ah, my dear Signor Diana. (DIANA *rises*) Please don't get up. Excuse me just a moment. (*He talks swiftly and quietly to Rosa*) Rosa, I want you to run to my father-in-law's...

ROSA: Now?

TOTI: Yes, immediately.

ROSA: And who'll look after the child?

TOTI: He's with his mother now. (*To* DIANA) Please, Signor Diana, do sit down. (*To* ROSA) Well, didn't you hear me?

ROSA: What do you want me to tell your in-laws?

TOTI: Tell them to come here at once – both of them. But don't frighten them: just say that their daughter doesn't feel well and that she wants to see them. Now, run along – quickly. (ROSA *exits centre*)

Please forgive me, Signor Diana. Let me take your hat. (*He puts it on a chair by the settee*)

DIANA: I hope I haven't come at an inopportune moment?

TOTI: Oh no, not at all. It's just that my wife is a little... indisposed.

DIANA: Oh, I'm sorry to hear that. (*Rising as if to go*) But perhaps you'd prefer to be with her...

TOTI: Oh no – that isn't necessary. Please, do sit down. I sent for her mother because – well, you know, women understand each other better. My wife won't tell me what's the matter with her – but I know what it is!

DIANA: Oh? (*Smiling*) Another happy event, perhaps?

TOTI: No, no! God forbid! One child is enough. (*Smiling*) I expect it's merely that just as April needs rain, young people need to shed tears every now and then. Ah, youth! Youth! (*Suddenly*) Have you any instructions, any orders for me, Signor Diana?

DIANA: Orders? Goodness me, you mustn't use that word... (*He smiles*) Between us...

TOTI: Why not? It's true that my financial position has improved, and that I've been able to move from my garret to this comfortable flat, but you are still my headmaster.

DIANA: I have not come to talk to you as one of my teachers, but as a friend.

TOTI (*politely*): Your friendship greatly honours me.

DIANA: I am here to ask a favour... not for myself – although perhaps in a way it is for me too – however, a favour which I am sure will not be difficult for you to grant, in view of your recent good fortune (*sweetening the kill*), which was so well deserved, if I may say so.

TOTI: For Heaven's sake, Signor Diana, don't say it was well-deserved. Merit had nothing to do with it. My brother was living in Romania, and for years, neither of us knew whether the other was dead or alive. So I can't honestly say that he meant to leave his money to me. He left it simply because he couldn't take it with him, and it came to me simply because I was his only relative.

DIANA: And you don't call that a stroke of luck?

TOTI: I don't say it wasn't. (*Thinking*) Perhaps, in a way it was... But now the rumour has spread that I have goodness knows how much money hidden away in the house. Hidden indeed! Not a song! The entire inheritance – 140,000 lire – went straight into the bank the moment it arrived.

DIANA: Quite a sum!

TOTI (*smiling*): It is. And, as you probably know, I agreed to become the largest shareholder in the bank, on condition that someone I trust is employed there to "look after it".

DIANA (*a little uneasy*): You mean Giacomino Delisi.

TOTI (*unperturbed*): Exactly! Giacomino Delisi. But believe me, Signor Diana, I was happier when I was poor. Then people just thought of me as a nobody and took hardly any notice of me – but since my brother left me his money, little old Toti has become the man of the moment. Everybody wants to know what I do and what I don't, if I help one or befriend another, and whatever I say and whatever I do is discussed and criticized by everybody. But what do they all want from me? Aren't I entitled to do as I please, as long as I don't harm anyone? It makes me really angry, Signor Diana, and believe me if it weren't for that little child there who will soon begin to toddle about the house, I wouldn't hesitate to withdraw those 140,000 pieces of paper from the bank and start a bonfire that would make history!

DIANA: I am sorry; I seem to have touched on a sore point. But will you allow an old friend to make an observation?

TOTI: Please, please do.

DIANA: In view of the malicious tongues of many people in our town, it seems to me that you are not doing as much as you could to protect yourself from the harm their gossip can do you.

TOTI: Signor Diana, gossip is a congenital disease of the wicked-minded – women especially are affected – and there is no cure for it. I have done nothing wrong. My life has been spent between my home and your school. School and home, home and school: that's my simple routine.

DIANA: Ah, my dear Professor, now we've come to the very reason for my visit: the school.

TOTI: Oh!

DIANA: Do you remember that some months ago, when you had just completed thirty-four years of teaching, I advised you to retire?

TOTI: Of course I remember.

DIANA: You were not rich then, but now that you have been blessed with this substantial inheritance…

TOTI: Blessed my foot! I know what you're going to say, but you can continue to sing that song as often as you like and the government can whistle it: I am not going to retire!

DIANA: Please; please, Professor – listen to reason.

TOTI: Reason? I have every reason for not retiring. Only God knows the price I pay for my determination. I love that little child; the hours I spend in your school which keep me away from him seem like centuries to me. My heart thumps for joy when the school bell rings at the end of the day, and I can run home to play with him, as if I were a child myself. And in spite of that, I am determined not to retire!

DIANA: Oh, you are obstinate! And illogical! You make your work seem a martyrdom, and yet… when you're asked to leave…

TOTI: It is a martyrdom! And for that very reason I intend to carry my cross to the very day when my wife and the child will be entitled to the maximum pension.

DIANA: But now your inheritance has altered the position. You're no longer in need of your pension.

TOTI: That's what you say. My pension may be hardly enough to buy a dozen handkerchiefs, but I have earned it honestly, with hard work. It has far greater moral value than the riches that have suddenly fallen on me from the skies – money which you've only to do this to – (*he blows on his open palm*) and it blows away like the wind. Besides there are other reasons for my not wishing to retire.

DIANA: Oh?

TOTI: In confidence: if I didn't have the school, I'd be at home too much, playing with the child. I'm not exactly a youngster (*smiling a little sadly*), and – if you understand me – I'd be in everyone's way.

DIANA: But surely…

TOTI: That's enough, Signor Diana, let's not talk about my resignation any more!

DIANA (*standing on his dignity*): I'm sorry, Professor, but we'll have to thrash this out once and for all!

TOTI (*with a twinkle in his eye*): Are you trying to force me to resign?

DIANA: Be patient, Professor, and try also to see my point of view. For the past few months – at school, in my home, even in the street, I have had no peace! The fathers, mothers, brothers, sisters of our pupils – even complete strangers – have come to me to protest against your remaining a teacher in my school.

TOTI: Oh, really?

DIANA: Yes. It's most unfortunate, but there it is! It has grown into an organized protest from the citizens of the town. They say your private life and your conduct are scandalous.

TOTI: Scandalous? And what do you say to that, Signor Diana?

DIANA: I don't wish to enter into a discussion as to whether they are right or wrong. I only say that as a private individual, if your conscience is clear, you may ignore the censure of others, but as a schoolteacher – you cannot! You are entrusted with a public position, and you, no less than I in my capacity as headmaster, are obliged to take public opinion into account. That is why I have come to advise you once again to resign.

TOTI: And bow my head to a grave injustice?

DIANA: You must not put it like that.

TOTI: How else should I put it? As you are not prepared to, I must wait for someone else to come and discuss things with me, not as they *appear* but as they actually *are*. They will find my conscience clear. (*He rises*) Yes, Signor Diana, I accept the challenge of public opinion. I want to see who will have the courage to come and tell me to my face that I am not an honest man, and that what I am doing is not done for the best.

DIANA (*rises after a moment's pause*): Then there's nothing more I can say. I hope you will appreciate that I came here to advise you as a friend.

TOTI (*taking DIANA's hand in both his and shaking it warmly*): I do... I do... it was kind of you.

DIANA: I must warn you that they threaten to take their protest to higher authorities...

TOTI: Let them if they want to.

DIANA (*ill at ease*): ...And that if the Minister of Education were to demand a report from me...

TOTI: You will tell him that you have requested my resignation but that I refuse to give it. (*He smiles*) But don't worry, Signor Diana – we shall see what we shall see!

DIANA (*with a sigh of resignation*): My compliments to the signora, and I hope she will soon be well again.

TOTI: Thank you. She'll appreciate your thought, I know.

DIANA (*goes to the door, then turns to him*): One last word – as an old friend: think over what I have told you... and take my advice: resign.

TOTI: I'll see you to the door, Signor Diana.

DIANA *goes out, followed by* TOTI. *After a few moments,* LILLINA *enters left carrying Nini in her arms. She looks dejected, her hair is untidy and her eyes are red from crying.*

LILLINA (*calling*): Rosa... Rosa...

TOTI (*returning*): I sent her on an errand. She'll soon be back. You look tired, Lillina. Take a little rest and I'll look after Nini. Come Nini... (*He takes the child in his arms*) Let's leave Mammina alone. She isn't well, poor little Mammina, and she's in a bad mood.

LILLINA: Nini's been very restless.

TOTI: No wonder when he sees you like that. Isn't that true, Nini? We can't bear to see Mammina in such a state. (*To* LILLINA) For the last three days we can hardly recognize you.

LILLINA: That's because I'm not feeling well.

TOTI: I can see that. Come Nini! I'll take Nini to the other woman till Rosa comes back. (*He goes out with Nini. He comes back a moment later and he finds* LILLINA *much distressed. Suddenly realizing his presence,* LILLINA *addresses him anxiously.*)

LILLINA: Where's Nini?

TOTI: I handed him over to the other maid. (*Whimsically*) Really Lillina, the little rascal must be taught good manners... He must be taught to ask permission when he wants to be excused! But don't worry; now he is sucking his thumb and he is as quiet as a lamb... You instead seem to be more restless than before. (LILLINA *turns her head away*) Come now, Lillina: won't you tell me what's the matter with you?...

LILLINA: It's nothing really: just a headache. I can hardly keep my eyes open...

TOTI: ...Shall I send for the doctor?

LILLINA: No.

TOTI: Very well, now listen...

LILLINA: Please! Please leave me alone! Don't worry about me; just be patient for a day or so. I'll be all right. It'll soon be... it'll soon be... (*She bursts into unrestrained sobs*)

TOTI: Yes, yes – it'll soon be over! (*A pause. Then, very sweetly.*) Come my child: confide in me. Has anything happened between you and Giacomino?

LILLINA: No.

TOTI: Then why are you so unhappy? You still won't tell me? Then I will tell you. (*Firmly*) You are worrying yourself to death, and it's no use telling me that it's only a headache... that your eyes hurt. (LILLINA *shakes her head, trying to deny it*) Yes, Yes! You're worried by what people say about us. Don't deny it; don't shake your head. It's true that people talk, laugh and even threaten. They went so far as to send my headmaster here, a few minutes ago, you know! But you and I know that we do nothing wrong, and that's all that matters! The important thing now is for us all to keep together. We must have faith in ourselves until time will prove me right. After I am gone, you'll be completely free to marry Giacomino. Then the three of you will have a secure future, secure from financial worries. Do you understand? (LILLINA *nods her head*) Well, that's enough from me. Now you can speak. What has happened between you two? Have you quarrelled?

LILLINA: I haven't quarrelled with anyone.

TOTI: Then why hasn't Giacomino been here for the last three days?

LILLINA: I don't know.

TOTI: He hasn't even been to the bank. The cashier told me yesterday. Perhaps he's got "a headache" too! Ah, youth! Youth! You don't realize that time is on your side, but for me every day I am unhappy because of you two is a precious day lost. I haven't heard you sing or seen you smile for three days now! (LILLINA *bursts into tears again*) There, you see? And you say there's nothing wrong. Something really serious must have happened. (*The doorbell rings*) Ah, that'll be your parents. If you won't tell me what it is, you'll surely tell your mother.

LILLINA (*jumps to her feet; between sobs*): You sent for my mother? But I've nothing to tell her... I don't want... Oh, don't torment me! Leave me in peace!

LILLINA *rushes out through the door on the left.* TOTI, *downhearted, shakes his head as he gazes at the door through which she went out. He waits a moment, then, as no one enters, he goes to the centre door and calls.*

TOTI: Who is it? (*A pause*) Rosa!

ROSA: Yes, it's me. (*She enters*)

TOTI: "Yes it's me!" I know it's you... But have you seen my wife's parents? Are they coming?

ROSA: Yes. I expect they're on their way now. At first they wouldn't listen to me. They said they didn't want to be mixed up in your affairs.

TOTI: And who asked them to poke their noses into my affairs?

ROSA (*crossly*): I'm only telling you what they said!

TOTI: Did you tell them that their daughter isn't feeling well?

ROSA: Yes. And they didn't seem surprised.

TOTI: And then you had a nice gossip between you, *I* wouldn't be surprised! (*He looks at her searchingly*) I have a kind of feeling that you
know what's wrong with your mistress, and don't want to tell me.

ROSA (*snappily*): I know nothing. I'm only a servant here: I'm not a spy!

TOTI: Well there's no need to flare up like that!

ROSA: I have every reason to flare up! I'm a respectable girl I'd have you
know – and I don't approve of what goes on in this house. I feel sorry
for the signora, and I'm fond of the child... but as for you – I'm not
afraid to tell you to your face. I don't like what people are saying
about you. You should be ashamed of yourself! A man of your age!
And if you're not pleased with my services, then you can tell me to
go – so there! (*The doorbell rings again.* ROSA *makes a mock curtsy,
holding up her apron with both hands.*) So there! (*She goes out*)

TOTI: Wicked tongue! Wicked tongue!

After a moment, CINQUEMANI *and* MARIANNA *enter haughtily, without
greeting* TOTI. CINQUEMANI *is wearing an old grey top hat (of the English
Ascot type) and is carrying a thick walking stick with a horn handle.*
MARIANNA *has a large veil over her face, and is wearing a pleated skirt
with a pattern of green and black squares which shrieks of naphthalene
from miles away.*

TOTI: My dear father and mother-in-law. Come sit down and make yourselves at home.

CINQUEMANI: (*gravely and with an ill-fitting air of "Grand Seigneur"*):
This is hardly the place for us to make ourselves at home!

TOTI: At least take your hat off.

CINQUEMANI: I'll take nothing off.

TOTI: Well, you, Signora Marianna – won't you remove your veil?

MARIANNA: Why should I? I like it!

CINQUEMANI: I only take off my hat in my own home – and as this is
not my house, it stays where it is! (*He sits down*)

TOTI: This is your daughter's house. I can't help it if you never wanted
to look on it as yours too!

CINQUEMANI (*rising*): Marianna... Pst! (MARIANNA *rises*)

TOTI: One moment! Sit down there! I want to talk to you.

MARIANNA: Oh, do you? Well, you can just listen to what we have to say first! (*To* CINQUEMANI) Come on! You tell him!

TOTI (*resigned*): Very well, let's hear what you've got to say. But make it short.

CINQUEMANI (*in his most imposing manner*): Both me and my wife: *me* (*he points at himself*)... and *my wife*... (*He points at her, stressing each word*) Understand?

TOTI: Yes, well?

CINQUEMANI: I repeat that because I want to make it quite clear that...

MARIANNA (*finishing his sentence for him*): ...That we really are married!

CINQUEMANI: Marianna – leave this to me! As I was saying; me and my wife have set foot in this house only once – the day you got married.

MARIANNA (*unable to keep still on the settee*): And only God knows what that cost us!

TOTI: Cost you? Why? I don't remember any present?

MARIANNA (*on the attack*): I meant the way people stared at us when they saw us coming here!

TOTI: Well, they stared at you... What then?

MARIANNA: It's the shame...

CINQUEMANI: Marianna! I'm doing the talking!

TOTI: Just a moment, Cinquemani: I want to ask you something. Haven't I told you many times at school to bring your wife here to see your daughter?

CINQUEMANI: Yes, you have.

TOTI: Then why didn't you come? What prevented you?

MARIANNA (*starting to her feet*): What prevented us, he asks!

CINQUEMANI (*also jumping up*): Marianna, shut up! I'm dealing with this. Professor, as you've brought up the school, I'd like you to know that when the other teachers and your pupils are there, I say "good morning" and "good evening" to you just out of politeness, and nothing more! You don't know the filthy things the boys scribble about you and my daughter on the lavatory walls...

MARIANNA (*shocked at his mentioning the word*): Oh, Cinquemani!

CINQUEMANI (*raising his hat*): Sorry my love – but a spade's a spade, isn't it? (*To* TOTI) I have to scrub them off, because they're enough to make me blush with shame!

MARIANNA: And he asks us what stopped us coming here! Why, the whole town is talking about you!

CINQUEMANI: Yes, and I want you to know that my wife and I agree with what everyone says about you!

MARIANNA: Because we are decent people, and we can still blush! D'you understand?

CINQUEMANI: We have a sense of decency… even if *some people* haven't!

TOTI (*getting impatient*): Come, come… I think you've said enough. Do you want to know what you are? A couple of asses!

CINQUEMANI: Now look here: you'd better use more respect when you talk to me! Remember I'm your father-in-law!

TOTI: Father-in-law indeed! You know very well how and why I married your daughter.

MARIANNA: You took her because you wanted her.

TOTI: Yes, I did. With all my heart.

MARIANNA: Heart? Don't make me laugh! It certainly wasn't for our sake! As far as we were concerned she could have stayed at home – and it would have been far better. At least we could have hushed up the affair.

CINQUEMANI: Yes, but by doing what you've done, you've ruined her reputation – and ours!

MARIANNA: We feel so ashamed that we hardly dare show our faces in public.

TOTI: Well, they're not worth looking at anyway!

MARIANNA: Well! Of all the… There's no need for rudeness…

TOTI: Have you quite finished?

CINQUEMANI: No, we haven't finished! You'll have to stomach a bit more yet. You even had the cheek to put that… that blasted Giacomino Delisi…

MARIANNA (*clapping her hands to her ears*): Don't you dare mention his name to me!

CINQUEMANI (*raising his hat*): Sorry my love. (*To* TOTI) You've put him in a good position in the bank. What for? To make sure your money's safe?

TOTI: Ah – I see: so that's why you're so furious.

MARIANNA: No – that's only one of the reasons!

CINQUEMANI: Marianna, let me talk! Wasn't it enough that you let him come here to your house – in spite of the scandal it caused...

MARIANNA: And what a scandal!

CINQUEMANI (*to his wife*): Shut up! (*To* TOTI) Did you have to let him look after your money as well? Couldn't you have left your pension and this fortune you've inherited to my daughter *without* all this fuss, and let her be free to live as she pleased with her baby? Why did you have to marry her? Hasn't she a father and mother who could have looked after her? (*His emotion gets the better of him and he takes a large coloured handkerchief from his pocket and starts to cry.* MARIANNA *follows suit.* TOTI *allows them to weep freely and comfort each other for a few moments before taking up the cudgel.*)

TOTI: Good! The crocodile is crying – now's my chance to speak. Now tell me, how could your daughter inherit my meagre pension unless she was my wife? Tell me that? And as for the money my brother left me – who could have expected that? If it had come sooner, things might have been different. But in any case I would certainly have expected that Lillina... would have had the decency to wait patiently for my death before doing what she pleased with my money.

CINQUEMANI: Oh, we didn't come here to listen to all this stuff and nonsense! We only came because we knew that Giacomino had gone. It's all finished now.

TOTI: What do you mean?

CINQUEMANI: Just what I said. Giacomino's left her. It's all over – for good.

MARIANNA (*crossing herself*): Thank God.

TOTI: Giacomino's left Lillina? (*Almost to himself*) Oh no! It can't be!

MARIANNA: Everybody says so.

CINQUEMANI: Why are you so upset? I thought you'd be pleased?

TOTI (*confused*): How is it possible that everybody but me should know about it? (CINQUEMANI *and* MARIANNA *look at each other in surprise*)

TOTI (*almost to himself*): Oh – so that's why the poor girl's been crying her eyes out for three days now. (*He turns on them fiercely, his eyes blazing*) What are people saying about it in the town? (MARIANNA *crosses herself*)

TOTI: Oh stop crossing yourself: I'm still alive, you know – and I've plenty of fight left in me!

MARIANNA: Yes, but so has our Blessed Minister, thank God!

TOTI: "Our Blessed Minister"?

MARIANNA: Yes. Didn't you know that *his* sister…

TOTI: Whose sister, Giacomino's?

MARIANNA: Yes. Rosaria Delisi – has got the Church to take up the matter now.

CINQUEMANI: Yes, and Don Landolina is coming here himself, to talk to you today.

TOTI: Don Landolina? Who's he? Another nosey-parker?

MARIANNA (*shocked, crossing herself again*): A sainted man!

CINQUEMANI: He's the priest of St Michael's…

MARIANNA: …And her Father Confessor… that's who he is!

TOTI: I see! And you say he's coming to talk to me?

CINQUEMANI: Yes. He called at our house last night to find out if we approve of what goes on here between you three…

MARIANNA: And when we told him we did not…

TOTI: …He said he would come to talk to me! (*He rubs his hands as though he were glad of this*) Splendid. Splendid. Let him come! I'll give him a piece of my mind. You'll see! (*He turns to* MARIANNA) But in the mean time, please go and speak to your daughter. She's in her room. (*He indicates the door on the left*)

MARIANNA (*jumping up again*): No! I never want to see her again.

TOTI: Don't be silly. Try and find out as tactfully as you can what's happened between her and Giacomino.

MARIANNA: Have you gone mad? You expect me to talk about such things with my daughter? What do you take me for?

TOTI: For a good mother – whatever else you may be! I tell you it's a very serious matter. Please go in and talk to her.

MARIANNA (*to* CINQUEMANI): Shall I go?

CINQUEMANI (*after a moment's reflection, gravely*): Yes.

MARIANNA: Very well; I'll go in – but I warn you I won't speak to her. If she cares to talk to me…

TOTI: All right, but you'll see, as soon as she sees you, she'll throw herself into your arms, and tell you everything.

MARIANNA: Huh!

TOTI (*gently pushing her into the other room*): For Heaven's sake – be tactful. (MARIANNA *exits left*) Now, you, Cinquemani, you'll do something for me. I'll reward you for it.

CINQUEMANI: I will not be bribed, I'd have you know! Remember I am a civil servant! I've only a humble position, I know – still, I'm a servant of the State, and I haven't forgotten that!

TOTI: No, you haven't – but you seem to have forgotten something else.

CINQUEMANI: Oh – what's that?

TOTI: That you're also a father...

CINQUEMANI: I'd like to know how many of us are fathers in this house!

TOTI: You least of all, I can assure you! But now, stop this bickering, and listen carefully to me. (*He pauses and puts his ear to* LILLINA's *door a moment to hear whether she is confiding to her mother*) Come over here. I must talk quietly. I want you to go down to the Piazza...

CINQUEMANI: Yes?

TOTI: ...And call at the bank. (*He tries to listen at the door again*)

CINQUEMANI (*on his guard*): What for?

TOTI: Good Heavens, what a face! Is that how you look when I ask you to do me a favour?

CINQUEMANI: Well, you haven't told me what you want me to do at the bank?

TOTI: Just see if Giacomino Delisi is there.

CINQUEMANI: What? That son of a...

TOTI: Now, now, Cinquemani... (TOTI *puts his hand over* CINQUEMANI's *mouth*)

CINQUEMANI (*pulling* TOTI's *hand away*): If I see that scoundrel...

TOTI: You'll do like the hare before the hounds, you'll run for your life! But don't worry about that... It's more than likely that you'll not find him there. Instead you'll have a word with the cashier... You don't mind that, do you...

CINQUEMANI: No, I don't mind that...

TOTI (*jesting*): But don't pinch any money from him, eh?

CINQUEMANI: Oh, look here, Professor: I am an honest man, I'll have you know...

TOTI: I know, I know... I was only joking! You will only ask the cashier if he has any news of Giacomino, and then come back here as quickly as you can... (*The doorbell rings*)

CINQUEMANI: Oh Lord – if that's him, I'll… I'll… (*He is in a great panic and looks around for somewhere to hide*) I don't want to see him, d'you understand? I just don't want… (*He stops as* ROSA *appears in the centre doorway*)

TOTI: Yes, Rosa?

ROSA: It's Father Landolina. He says he'd like to speak to you.

CINQUEMANI (*relieved*): You see? I told you he was coming.

TOTI (*to* ROSA): Show him in. (ROSA *goes out centre*)

CINQUEMANI: I'll be off. Thank Heaven some decent people are visiting this house at last. (DON LANDOLINA *enters.* CINQUEMANI, *centre, greets him reverently.*) Your Reverence. (*He goes out centre*)

LANDOLINA (*unctuously*): My dear Professor Toti.

TOTI: Come in, Father. Do sit down please.

LANDOLINA: Thank you. You are very kind.

TOTI: To what do I owe the honour of your visit, Father?

LANDOLINA: First I must ask you to forgive my interfering in a very delicate matter, which concerns me in as much as I am a servant of God. I must call on your kindness and goodness – which are well known to everybody. I… (*He hesitates, trying to feel his "ground"*)

TOTI (*smiling*): Are you "calling on my kindness and goodness" in order to make me swallow a bitter pill, Father?

LANDOLINA: Not exactly, I… it is a little difficult to explain.

TOTI: Well, if it will help you, Father – you may have just as much of my "kindness and goodness" as is necessary to help you say what you have to say… (*changing his tone*) but no more!

LANDOLINA: I will come straight to the point. It is a question of conscience, Professor.

TOTI: Your conscience, or mine?

LANDOLINA: The conscience of a poor Christian soul. I will not dispute whether the person in question is right or wrong…

TOTI: You won't? Not even you?

LANDOLINA (*taken aback*): I beg your pardon?

TOTI: I should have thought that you of all people would have decided on that point before coming here.

LANDOLINA: I don't quite follow?

TOTI: Never mind. I was only thinking aloud. Please continue.

LANDOLINA: I was only saying that (I don't know whether rightly or wrongly) – that poor soul feels mortified, humiliated, insulted, by the rumours which have spread all over our town about... her brother.

TOTI: I understand. So you have come to me – on behalf of Giacomino Delisi's sister.

LANDOLINA (*not wishing to admit it*): I didn't say so! I...

TOTI: One moment, Father: if you wish to talk about Giacomino and my family, I think it's best that you take your gloves off first.

LANDOLINA (*showing his ungloved, white hands, with the faintest of smiles on his lips*): But really – I am not wearing...

TOTI: Come Father – I think you understand me. I may be blunt in my way of saying things, but that is because I have nothing to hide. I would prefer it if you too would be frank and honest.

LANDOLINA (*offended*): I must ask you to have more respect for my calling, Professor.

TOTI: Why – does your visit concern a secret told in confession?

LANDOLINA: No, no: it concerns – as I told you – the mortification... the sorrow of a poor penitent who comes to ask advice and help from her confessor.

TOTI (*nods his head*): Go on, Father.

LANDOLINA: I will be frank – as you have asked me to. Signorina Delisi is – as you know – very much older than her brother. Since he lost his parents as a child, she has been like a mother to him. Thanks be to God, under her guidance, he has grown up into a God-fearing, respectful and obedient young man.

TOTI: You have no need to tell me that, Father. Do you think I don't know Giacomino? I know him better than you or his sister, I can assure you.

LANDOLINA: I merely wanted to point out that in my estimation, all these good points in his character are due to that excellent woman and the good education she has given him.

TOTI: Oh – how exciting to end up like a candle on the altar!

LANDOLINA (*missing the irony*): I don't understand?

TOTI: She burns and melts, Father! Oh yes, an excellent woman, Signorina Delisi! But I agree, she has brought up her "little brother" beautifully.

LANDOLINA: I'm glad you agree, and for that reason, one must look elsewhere for the cause of so much injurious gossip in the town. It is clear to me that it comes from the fact that he frequents your house too much. People find it... improper, that your wife – so young and so charming, if I may say so...

TOTI (*impatiently*): In short, Signorina Delisi has sent you to ask me to persuade Giacomino not to come here any more – in order to stop people talking! Is that what you want?

LANDOLINA (*with sad humility which has a spiteful sting to it*): No, Professor – not exactly.

TOTI: Then what else *could* you want from me?

LANDOLINA: Till now I have spoken only of Signorina Delisi, and of the suffering brought upon her by these malicious rumours which, I must point out, are harmful not only to the young man, but also to... (*He hesitates*)

TOTI: If you mean me, Father, don't be afraid to say so.

LANDOLINA: Of course I know that *you* are above such shallow gossip – but not so a poor woman; an elder sister who we must look on al-most as a mother. She suffers, weeps, cries out for comfort and help. She is but a woman after all, and... well I'm sure you understand...

TOTI: Stop beating about the bush, Father, and tell me exactly what you want from me?

LANDOLINA: I will come to the point. I admit that Signorina Delisi did send me here, but it was only to implore you to have the goodness to – to let her have a few words in writing... a little "statement" shall we call it... (oh, solely for her comfort and peace of mind, you understand) that there is and can be no truth whatsoever in all these ugly rumours.

TOTI (*after a moment's pause*): Is that all she wants? Nothing more?

LANDOLINA: Oh nothing more – I assure you!

TOTI: I see. (*Very sweetly*) And of course, Signorina Delisi feels certain that Giacomino will never again set foot in this house; because she – as a good sister – has persuaded her "little brother" that it's for his own good if he stays away. Isn't that so, Father?

LANDOLINA: Yes, Professor: I believe she has convinced him of that.

TOTI: And now she wants a little "statement" from me? But certainly, certainly. I'll write one out for her.

LANDOLINA (*believing he has won his battle*): Oh thank you, thank you.

TOTI: Don't mention it. After all, what does it cost me? It's easily done: only a few words: "I, Professor Agostino Toti, in consideration of the ugly rumours etc., etc., etc..."

LANDOLINA: That's it... That's it!

TOTI: "Do hereby declare and testify, etc., etc., etc..."

LANDOLINA: Wonderful!... Wonderful!...

TOTI: Is that the idea?

LANDOLINA: Oh that would be fine.

TOTI (*sweetly*): Yes, it would, wouldn't it? (*Abruptly*) Well, you may go now, Father. I'll write it out and send it.

LANDOLINA: Thank you, thank you, my dear Professor. I am truly moved by your generosity and your true Christian spirit. (*He rises*) But – forgive me, could you not write it out now? Then I could take it straight to Signorina Delisi.

TOTI: No, I haven't time now. I have something rather urgent to do. But you may rest assured that I will see to it.

LANDOLINA: You'll send it to me, will you?

TOTI: No – why to you? I'll send it directly to Signorina Delisi.

LANDOLINA (*offering his hand*): Very well. Once again, my grateful thanks.

TOTI: Don't mention it. One moment, Father. Tell me, did you know that Giacomino, that God-fearing, respectful, obedient – and I must add – idle young man, is at last working at the bank, where I found him a job?

LANDOLINA: Oh, do you imagine I was not aware of that, Professor? I know it only too well, and you must believe me when I say that his sister is full of gratitude to you.

TOTI: Is she? Really?

LANDOLINA: Of course, of course.

TOTI: Well, well... that's nice to know.

LANDOLINA: And now I must be going, Professor. (*Shaking* TOTI's *hand*) And once again – many, many thanks.

TOTI: Goodbye, Father. (LANDOLINA *is about to go, when* TOTI *recalls him*)

TOTI: Oh, by the way, Father, I wanted to ask you something else: only a little thing which flashed through my mind just now. Tell me, what would you think of a young man who, after having seduced a girl and made a mother of her, suddenly declined all responsibility for her? And what would you say if that poor young woman accepted the help and protection of an old man who… (LANDOLINA, *having understood* TOTI'*s allusion right from the first, has begun to cough in order to cover his embarrassment.* TOTI *pauses in the middle of his sentence, stares at* LANDOLINA *for a moment, then smiles.*) You know, you have a very bad cough, Father. You must get rid of it. You really must. A good hot poultice, with plenty of mustard! That's what you need.

DON LANDOLINA *exists precipitously, holding a handkerchief to his mouth and coughing.*

TOTI (*goes to the other door on the left and calls*): Signora Marianna! Signora Marianna! (*After a moment,* MARIANNA *enters*)

MARIANNA: It's no use. She won't talk. She's lying on her bed and won't move.

TOTI (*resolutely and in haste*): Never mind… never mind. Please do me a favour and dress the child for me.

MARIANNA: Dress him? How would I know where his things are kept?

TOTI: Yes, that's true. Well, I'll do it myself. (*He goes off to the left*)

MARIANNA *stares at him as he goes, wondering.* CINQUEMANI *enters centre. He notices his wife staring at the door through which* TOTI *left.*

CINQUEMANI: What's the matter? Anything happened?

MARIANNA: Anything happened? This seems to be a madhouse!

CINQUEMANI: You're telling me. I've just bumped into Don Landolina on the stairs, tiptoeing as if he didn't want to be heard, and with his eyes starting out of his head. But what about Lillina? Did she tell you anything?

MARIANNA: Not a word, not a word.

CINQUEMANI: Oh well – let's be off.

MARIANNA: No, wait a minute. I don't think we ought to go just yet.

TOTI *comes in, still in his dressing gown, with his hat on his head, and his jacket over his arm. He is carrying the baby in a little basket which he places on the table while he removes his dressing gown and dons his jacket.*

TOTI: Now our little treasure is going out for a walk with his grandpa. Oh I'm longing to hear him call me grandpa. (*He places the basket on a table for a moment and the other two – despite themselves – crowd round and beam at the child*) Did you go to the bank, Cinquemani?

CINQUEMANI: Yes, but they'd no news of Giacomino.

TOTI: Well, never mind. We'll go out and find Giami, shall we, Nini? (*To* MARIANNA) That's what we call his father – "Giami"... (*He picks up the basket and makes for the door*)

CINQUEMANI (*stepping in front of them*): You're going to Giacomino's? You don't mean it!

TOTI (*pushing him aside*): Of course I mean it.

CINQUEMANI: For Heaven's sake think what you're doing!

MARIANNA: What will people say?

TOTI: To hell with what they'll say.

CINQUEMANI: You'll only bring more shame on yourselves!

TOTI: You! Out of my way. (*He pushes them both aside and goes out, talking to Nini*) Come along, Nini. A little walk'll do us good... and we'll see Giami.

CINQUEMANI: He's out of his mind!... Going to Giacomino's! (*He goes to the door and calls after him*) Professor! Professor!

MARIANNA (*sinking into a chair*): God, what a man! What a man! what a man!

CURTAIN

ACT THREE

The drawing room in Signorina Delisi's house. There are two doors in the back wall, overhung with curtains. Between them is a large painting of the "Madonna del Rosario" with a lit lamp hanging beneath it. A door in each side wall is also covered by curtains. The furniture is old and the room has a severe, almost monastic atmosphere.

DON LANDOLINA *is seated on a sofa, sipping chocolate.* ROSARIA DELISI *is in a small easy chair just by him. As the curtain rises, they are both laughing.*

LANDOLINA: Everything went well, believe me: exactly as I had hoped. I left him believing he had understood the motive of my visit. This chocolate is delicious.

ROSARIA: Is there enough sugar?

LANDELINA: Yes, thank you. An excellent sufficiency. (*Resuming*) "Let us come to the point," he said… "You've been sent by Signorina Delisi to ask me never to allow Giacomino to come to my house again. Isn't that so?" And I replied (*assuming his favourite expression and tone of humility and patient suffering*), "No, Professor – not exactly that!"

ROSARIA (*laughing*): I can just see his face when you said that.

LANDOLINA: He was dumbfounded! He never expected that. (*He rises to put his empty cup down.* ROSARIA *rises quickly and takes it from him.*) Thank you.

ROSARIA: Some more?

LANDOLINA (*he'd love it, but he must be polite*): N – no thank you.

ROSARIA: Sure?

LANDOLINA (*meaning yes please*): W – ell…

ROSARIA *puts the cup on the tray and sits down, obviously not intending to pour out a second cup.* DON LANDOLINA's *expression sours a moment, then he continues.*

LANDOLINA: But when I told him that you and I had already persuaded Giacomino not to go there again, he hardly knew what to say. (*Imitating* TOTI) "What! How's that? But then?..." (*He chuckles*)

ROSARIA (*laughing*): Yes, yes: I can just imagine it! But, Father, it would have been better if you had got him to write out the declaration we want – in your presence.

LANDOLINA: I asked him to. But he said he hadn't time then, and I didn't think it prudent to insist further. It was wiser, having hinted what we wanted (and I flatter myself I found the best way of doing that) – to let him feel that such a document was required solely to put your mind at rest, and had no urgent or practical value, if you understand me?

ROSARIA: I do understand. But you know very well that I don't want it for myself: it's his young lady who insists on having that statement. Now I'm afraid the Professor may change his mind.

LANDOLINA: Oh I think there's no fear of that. He assured me several times that he would do it. In fact – let us admit, it must have seemed to him a rather ingenuous request – I had the impression that he was even pleased to be able to rid himself of so much trouble so easily.

At this moment, FILOMENA *– Rosaria's old servant – bursts into the room and announces almost in trepidation.*

FILOMENA: The Professor, signorina! The Professor!

LANDOLINA (*rising – startled*): What?

ROSARIA: Here?

FILOMENA: Yes. I heard the bell ring and I was going to open the door, but luckily I looked through the window first to see who it was – and it's *him*! The Professor! With the baby!

ROSARIA: With the child? Oh, my goodness!

LANDOLINA: The impudence! This is really going too far!

ROSARIA: Do you see? He agrees not to let Giacomino go to his house any more – and immediately he comes here himself!

FILOMENA: What shall I do? What do you want me to tell him?

ROSARIA: Don't let him in. Send him away.

FILOMENA: Very well, signorina.

ROSARIA: Tell him Giacomino isn't in. You can talk to him through the window; don't even open the door.

FILOMENA: Very well, signorina, I'll do as you say. (*She goes out*)

ROSARIA: You see, Father? And you were only saying...

LANDOLINA: Believe me, signorina, I am astonished at the man's impudence. Absolutely astonished.

ROSARIA: But what are we going to do?

LANDOLINA: Let us not be hasty. I am wondering – as we have to deal with such an obstinate man – whether it wouldn't be wiser to see him after all and to challenge him openly, rather than keep up this pretence...

ROSARIA: But who is to "challenge" him? You?

LANDOLINA: Oh, no... not I. That would not be wise. Not that I'm afraid of him – please don't misunderstand me, but under the circumstances I think it best if a member of the family... yourself, signorina...

ROSARIA (*gasps*): Me?

LANDOLINA: Why not? You are Giacomino's sister. And if you don't wish to, then Giacomino himself.

ROSARIA: Oh no... not Giacomino!

LANDOLINA: But don't you see: if Giacomino had the courage to tell him to his face that everything is over and that he must never dare to show himself here again... (FILOMENA *bustles in again*)

ROSARIA: Ah, Filomena. Has he gone?

FILOMENA: No. He refuses to go.

ROSARIA: But didn't you tell him that Giacomino was not at home?

FILOMENA: I told him at least twenty times.

ROSARIA: And what did he say?

FILOMENA: He just laughed.

LANDOLINA: Laughed?

FILOMENA: Yes. He didn't seem to believe me. Now he wants to speak to you, signorina.

ROSARIA (*nervous*): To me?

FILOMENA: I took the liberty of saying you weren't in, either.

ROSARIA: Good. And what did he say to that?

FILOMENA: He just laughed again, and said: "Let me come in – I'll wait for her." I even told him that the door was locked and you had taken the key with you, but he simply sat down on the doorstep and said he would wait for you there. Nothing will make him go.

LANDOLINA: Signorina, I advise you to receive him. (ROSARIA *is about to remonstrate*) Believe me, it is for the best. Ask him in and try to keep as calm as possible. Be firm, but patient; you are the soul of patience, I know. (*As she still hesitates*) Be advised by me, signorina. Filomena, you may let him in.

FILOMENA: Very well, Father. (*She goes out*)

LANDOLINA: I will leave you now, signorina – if you will excuse me. (*He goes towards the door on the right*)

ROSARIA: You may go to Giacomino's room if you like, Father. He is there now.

LANDOLINA (*in his confusion, making for the wrong door*): Yes, yes, I'll do that.

ROSARIA: No, this way, Father.

LANDOLINA: Oh yes, yes of course, how stupid of me. (*He turns to the doorway*) Remember, be firm but patient… (*correcting himself*) be firm but calm… oh dear, oh dear, you do understand… (*And he goes*)

ROSARIA *looks round the room, worried, and decides to take out the tray of chocolate before the Professor comes. As soon as she has gone,* TOTI *enters slowly and proudly, carrying the basket, which he deposits on an occasional table by the sofa.* ROSARIA *comes back and he bows politely. She takes no notice but crosses to her chair and sits.*

TOTI: Good day, signorina. (ROSARIA *does not reply – a pause*) I am glad to see you, signorina.

ROSARIA (*cold and reserved*): Are you? May I ask what is the meaning of your visit, Professor? And why do you bring that child here?

TOTI: Well, it's such a beautiful day, and the poor little mite hasn't been out of the house for a few days now. He was crying so much, I said, "Come Nini, let's go out for a little walk together." As soon as he breathed the fresh air, he stopped crying. You see, children are like birds; one minute they are cross, with their feathers all ruffled, and the next minute, the sun comes out – and they are lively and happy again.

ROSARIA: Couldn't you have taken him for a walk somewhere else? Why just here?

TOTI: And why not here? We haven't seen Giacomino for a long time. I know he no longer goes to the bank, and I don't even meet him in the street these days. Nini began to miss him. I thought perhaps he wasn't well and we came to ask after him.

ROSARIA (*curtly*): He is perfectly well, thank you, but he's not at home. Filomena must have told you.

TOTI: Forgive me, signorina, you seem to be angry. Have I offended you or Giacomino by coming here? I'd be sorry if I had.

ROSARIA: As if you need to ask! Anyway I'm not angry... but I tell you again Giacomino is not in.

TOTI: Really?

ROSARIA: Yes, and I must ask you to save yourself the trouble of coming here again. If you have anything to say to my brother, he will meet you at your school or any other place you may care to suggest – but not here... and certainly not at your home. I hope that is well understood.

TOTI (*shaking his head*): Such a harsh tone – yet you say you are not angry? I think I had best give you time to cool down a little. Perhaps there has been some misunderstanding?

ROSARIA (*scornfully*): Mis – under – standing!

TOTI: And if there has, it's as well to clear it up – frankly and openly... and *calmly*.

ROSARIA: I agree, Professor. Let us have it out once and for all.

TOTI: Good. Now we're getting somewhere. But first, let me sit down – and you go and call Giacomino.

ROSARIA: How many more times must I tell you he's not in?

TOTI: Forgive my asking, but is some – "Reverend" in the habit of conversing with furniture in your house?

ROSARIA (*taken aback*): Reverend? What do you mean?

TOTI (*picking up Don Landolina's hat, which he had left on a chair*): Your religious fervour is much talked of in the town. Perhaps you've been having a visit from your "Spiritual Adviser"?

ROSARIA (*confused and irritated, snatching the hat out of his hands*): Give me that. It belongs to Father Landolina.

TOTI: And where is our dear Father? Busy giving "Spiritual Advice" to Giacomino, no doubt.

ROSARIA: Nothing of the kind. He was here with me: now he's... in the other room with Filomena. (*She indicates one door. At this moment* FILOMENA *enters from the opposite side and quietly crosses the stage at the back to exit the other way.*)

TOTI: Really?

ROSARIA (*continues*): Anyway you have no business to pry into my private affairs.

TOTI: I don't pry: that is not one of my vices, signorina! I leave that to others... to certain people who are forever prying into my private affairs. (*A pause*) So, Giacomino is not in?

ROSARIA: No.

TOTI (*about to go*): Then you force me to return later.

ROSARIA: I told you that was not necessary. Giacomino will call on you at your school.

TOTI: You would trouble him to come all that way, when – as I am here and he is just upstairs – it would be so easy for us to talk and settle everything now.

ROSARIA (*at the end of her patience*): Very well: I see there is nothing for it but to call Giacomino and let him put an end himself to this monstrous and immoral situation for good!

TOTI: Take it calmly, signorina. You may frighten the child.

ROSARIA: Oh! You are the Devil himself!

TOTI: See now – you've woken him up.

ROSARIA: Oh! (*She flounces out – to the left – slamming the door*)

TOTI: My poor Nini. The naughty woman has really disturbed your sleep. But you needn't worry – the old witch has gone. What? You want me to pick you up? But of course, of course, darling. (*He takes Nini out of the basket*) Perhaps if I rock him a little he'll go to sleep again. (*He sits down and begins to chant to him*) Ah, ah... baby... Ah, ah, baby... (*He glances at the child*) No, that won't do. (*He thinks it over a moment, then decides to try another way. He turns Nini over face downwards on his lap.*) I hope this is the right way to do it. (*He taps him gently on the back and resumes his chant*) Ah, ah, baby... (*He then gently picks the baby up again*) Ah, that's done the trick. (*He rises with Nini, and moves with him towards the corner. GIACOMINO enters and TOTI turns round to look at him. For a while they stare at each other.*)

GIACOMINO (*his clothes and hair are untidy; he is distressed, but tries not to show it*): You wanted to speak to me, Professor?

TOTI (*sweetly and persuasively*): Yes, Giacomino. Oh, but let's have a smile first. Why, you would frighten Nini, with a face like that! Look at him... see how beautiful he is! (GIACOMINO *avoids looking at*

Nini) Don't you want to look at him? Your child!… But what's the matter with you?

GIACOMINO (*bends down and pats Nini's head*): I don't feel well, Professor. I was lying down in my room; I have a splitting headache… A touch of flu perhaps… it wouldn't be fair to the child!

TOTI (*looks doubtfully at* GIACOMINO – *a pause*): Your sister said you weren't in…

GIACOMINO: Never mind what my sister said! I am here now. What do you want from me, Professor?

TOTI: Just a moment. (*He puts Nini back in his carrier*) Now you lie there quietly, like a good little boy. I felt somehow that you weren't well. And one can see it in your face.

GIACOMINO (*impatiently*): Professor, I…

TOTI: First of all, let's sit down on the settee, Giacomino. We'll be able to talk more comfortably then. (*They both sit down on the settee*) There. I wanted to know whether the manager of the bank had spoken to you.

GIACOMINO: No. I haven't seen him lately.

TOTI: You haven't been to the bank for the last three days.

GIACOMINO: I know. That was because…

TOTI: I don't want to know why. I met him on the street by chance yesterday. He mentioned something about your salary. I told him I didn't think you were getting enough, and we agreed that he would raise your wages.

GIACOMINO (*uneasy*): I'm much obliged to you, Professor… but I'd rather you didn't worry about me any more.

TOTI: Oh? Quite independent are we? We no longer need help from anyone, is that it?

GIACOMINO: It isn't that, Professor, but… Oh, I wish you would understand…

TOTI: What am I to understand? You surely won't stop me from taking an interest in you?

GIACOMINO: But I don't want you to…

TOTI: You may not, but I do!… Huh! Would you believe it! He tells me not to worry about him! But who am I to worry about if not you?

GIACOMINO: Now listen, Professor… (TOTI *stops him with a gesture*)

413

TOTI: Let me finish and then you will talk! But without anger, please! (*A slight pause*) You must know, my son, that my greatest desire is to see you and Lillina getting on well. And if I can help to make things easier for you, all the better... You know, don't you, that I took to you from the first day you came to my school, just as if you were my son... (TOTI *interrupts himself for a moment to look closely at* GIACOMINO) What's the matter? Are you crying? (GIACOMINO *is in fact trying to hold back the tears*) Why? Why? (*He puts his hand on* GIACOMINO'*s shoulder*)

GIACOMINO (*jumping up; his face bears a strange expression*): Leave me alone. Please!

TOTI: You look as though you're suffering, my boy.

GIACOMINO: Can't you see what you're doing? You're smothering me with all your kindness and goodness!

TOTI: I?

GIACOMINO: Yes, you! I don't want your affection! For God's sake leave me alone. Go away and forget that I ever existed!

TOTI (*stunned, quietly*): But why? Why? Giacomino – look at me.

GIACOMINO (*defiantly*): Well, if you must know, it's because... I must break off with Lillina. I... have become engaged to another girl, you understand? Another girl!

TOTI: En – ga – ged?

GIACOMINO: Yes, it's all over, with Lillina! Over for good! So there's no point in discussing it any more. Now, Professor, I must ask you to go!

TOTI (*almost without voice*): You... you are throwing me out?

GIACOMINO: Oh no, Professor – but believe me, it's best for you to go. (TOTI *slowly picks up the carrier and starts to go*) No... don't...

TOTI: You told me to go...

GIACOMINO: But... Nini...

TOTI: Nini, eh? You didn't think of him when you decided to desert his mother, did you? (GIACOMINO *buries his face in his hands.* TOTI *puts down the carrier again.*) I can see what torments you... It's a terrifying conflict between your heart and your mind... But tell me: you said you have become engaged to another girl. When did that happen?

GIACOMINO: A month ago.

TOTI: And yet you kept coming to my house...

GIACOMINO: Only for a few days... It wasn't easy for me to do otherwise...

TOTI: Who is the girl?

GIACOMINO: A friend of my sister…

TOTI: I see! And so you simply made up your mind to forget your past and with a shrug of your shoulders to leave it all behind you; Lillina, your responsibilities… everything…

GIACOMINO: What else could I do?… Oh, can't you see that you made me the slave of an impossible situation?

TOTI: I made you a slave? I who made you master in my home!… How can you say such a thing?… This is sheer ingratitude!

GIACOMINO: But…

TOTI: No, no, my boy! It's you who made the situation impossible! Don't you see? It's immaterial whether you are legally or illegally married to Lillina; by taking her you've made her your wife, and of course you are the father of her child!… What I did for you and Lillina was not for my benefit. Indeed, what have I derived from it? Nothing but mockery and insults, for no one, not even you, seems to appreciate the feeling of an honest man who only wanted to provide a comfortable living for Lillina and yourself… You blame me for what you've only to blame yourself! My conscience is clear! What about yours? (*For a moment* GIACOMINO *seems to be crushed by the logic of* TOTI's *argument –* TOTI's *mood suddenly changes*) No… I cannot believe you're responsible for such an abominable action! I am sure that it's your sister and her Spiritual Adviser who have turned your mind…

GIACOMINO (*fighting his own feeling*): Nobody has turned my mind! Oh, you don't want to understand! I know you mean well, Professor, but we can't possibly carry on as we have been doing… Don't you realize, Professor, that… certain… certain situations can only exist if nobody knows about them. They have to be hidden; you can't do things openly for everyone to laugh at.

TOTI: So! It's because people laugh! But my boy, it's not you: it's me they're laughing at… me! And only because they don't understand. The truth is they envy you because they see you in a good position, with a secure future, and because they know that you will inherit my money!

GIACOMINO: Money!!! If that's the case, then for Heaven's sake don't concern yourself about me any more, Professor. There are scores of other young men who'd be only too glad of your help.

TOTI (*deeply wounded, takes hold of him by the lapels of his jacket and shakes him violently*): What did you say? Lillina is young, but she is honest, by God! And she has always been loyal to you. And you dare to insult her? What do you take her for? Do you imagine she is the sort of girl who can be thrown from one man to another?... Oh! (*He pushes him away with disgust*) And to think that I am the cause of all this. I who protected you; I who took you into my home, spoke up for you; I who took from her every doubt, every scruple, so that she could love you wholly and without fear. And when at last she felt secure in your love, you... the father of her son... you want to... (*With great determination*) But you'd better think it over, Giacomino! Mind what you're doing, for now – I am capable of anything! Think it over, Giacomino! I'll have you thrown out of the bank! And let you starve!

GIACOMINO: It won't make any difference!

TOTI: I'll go to your fiancée – right now... and I'll take Nini with me!

GIACOMINO (*afraid*): My God, you wouldn't do that!

TOTI: Oh, wouldn't I?! Who's to stop me? (*He takes Nini out of the carrier*)

GIACOMINO: You've no right to...

TOTI: No right? I have every right to protect the family I have helped to create!... I'll go to your fiancée and to her people, and show them this child who you find it so easy to abandon. Your son, Giacomino! Look at him! Have you the heart to leave him? (*He holds Nini out towards* GIACOMINO. GIACOMINO *can no longer keep up his pretence of indifference and clasps Nini tightly to him.* TOTI *laughing and crying at the same time.*) I knew – I knew you were not really bad at heart... Thank God! You've listened to the voice of your heart. (*A short pause*)

ROSARIA's *and* LANDOLINA's *voices are heard from offstage.*

TOTI: Let's leave this house quickly, before these wicked people turn your head again. They pretend to have left us alone. It's my bet they're listening at the keyhole – come, we'll go back to Lillina... all three together. (*He leads them towards the door, when the other door on the right flies open and* ROSARIA, LANDOLINA *and* FILOMENA *rush into the room and try to hold* GIACOMINO. *They all talk at once.*)

LANDOLINA: We heard what he said, Giacomino, don't go...

ROSARIA: Did you hear, Giacomino: don't go...

GIACOMINO: I must go, Rosaria; I must…

LANDOLINA: It's a mortal sin… a mortal sin, Giacomino…

TOTI (*placing himself between* LANDOLINA *and* GIACOMINO): Mortal sin!!? You with your hypocritical morals would have broken up a family!… I with the principles which you call immoral have kept it together and saved it!… Get thee behind me, Satan!

TOTI *goes out after* GIACOMINO *and Nini, leaving* ROSARIA *and* LANDOLINA *at the door, shouting:* "Giacomino… Giacomino… don't go!"

CURTAIN

Lazarus

Lazzaro (1927)

Translated by Frederick May

CHARACTERS

DIEGO SPINA
SARA, *his wife, but now no longer living with him*
LUCIO *and* LIA, *their children*
ARCADIPANE, *a farm bailiff*
DEODATA, *Lia's governess*
GIONNI, *a doctor of medicine engaged in research*
MONSIGNOR LELLI
CICO, *God's rent-collector*
MARRA, *a notary*
THE TWO NATURAL CHILDREN *of Sara and Arcadipane (they do not speak)*
A DOCTOR
A POLICEMAN
PEOPLE WHO COME IN FROM THE STREET
TWO PEASANTS

The time is the present (i.e. 1929)

ACT ONE: *The hanging garden of* DIEGO SPINA'*s house*
ACT TWO: *The rustic porch of* DIEGO SPINA'*s farmhouse*
ACT THREE: *The same as* ACT TWO, *a few minutes later*

ACT ONE

The scene is the hanging garden at the house of DIEGO SPINA. *The house, an old and unpretentious building, is on the left (the actor's left, that is.) The front wall is seen in profile; there is a small drooping rustic porch, supported by pillars, beneath which one can see the doors that lead into the rooms on the ground floor. Along the back of the stage there runs a wall between three and four feet high, roughly constructed, whitewashed and topped off with a crest of broken glass. Halfway along this wall, and sharply outlined against the background of the strange blue sky – it's almost as if it were enamelled – there is a huge black cross bearing a depressing, painted, bleeding figure of Christ. Beside the cross there rises the trunk of a very tall cypress tree, which grows up from the road that lies below the wall. This wall, which bounds the house, continues round the right-hand side of the stage; it is broken into midway along by the upper landing of the flight of steps leading down to the road. At ground level there are one of two flower beds, with flowering plants here and there, intersected by gravel paths on which stand some seats painted green.*

When the curtain rises DEODATA *and* LIA *are on stage.* LIA *is fifteen, but looks a mere child. Her hair falls loosely over her shoulders, and is set off by a lovely bow of sky-blue ribbon. Her legs are paralysed, and she is confined to an invalid chair which she wheels about herself with a speed and dexterity that have become second nature to her. Her legs are covered by a shawl.* DEODATA *is about forty. Tall and strongly built, she is dressed in black and is wearing a black cap on her head. She is seated on an iron stool and is making lace on a pillow. It is an April afternoon.*

LIA (*absorbedly*): He hasn't written for more than a month.

DEODATA (*after a pause*): Lucio?

LIA: And his last letter… Well, Daddy couldn't make head or tail of it. He wouldn't let me read it.

DEODATA: He's probably all worked up about his exams. Your father is always getting such ideas into his head.

LIA: Maybe. But I'm just as bad, you know, I get ideas like that too.

DEODATA: Good girl! You're just as bad. You've infected me too with this *disease* of yours...

LIA: Ugh! No, you mustn't call it a disease...

DEODATA: Yes, it's a *disease*! A disease! Because... Oh, time and time again you... Look! You start imagining that somebody's thinking something. You make that person aware of what you're imagining. And the thought that didn't in the first place exist at all, now really does come into his head. And who has made that thought come into his head? *You*... by imagining what you did.

LIA: Forgive me for asking, but aren't *you* busy doing a little imagining at the moment? Suggesting that Lucio doesn't write because he's worried about his exams?

DEODATA: I'm just trying to find some sort of an explanation for his silence. Like many another explanation, it might quite well be the probable one. And it's got the virtue too of being one that, while I'm busy imagining it, doesn't harm him and doesn't cause me to grieve... At least, not till I have to. (*There is a pause*)

LIA: Oh, if only he hadn't been so obstinate about going up to the university!

DEODATA: Ah, as for that... You see, I didn't approve of him going there either. When he came out of the seminary he could have settled down quietly and contentedly and followed his sacred calling as a priest, without going off to learn all that devilry they teach you up there at the university!

LIA: But if he'd done that he'd have had to go off immediately and do his military service...

LIA: Oh yes, I know that! That was his excuse for doing what he did. As if he wasn't going to have to do it just the same when he was twenty-six! If you want my opinion, he'd have found it much less of a burden at twenty-one! But there, what's the use of talking about it? Your father too... The thought of seeing him turn up at any minute without his cassock, and in a soldier's uniform... Well, for *him*, it would have been like seeing the Devil himself!

LIA: It was because Lucio was so run down. He couldn't bear the thought of his having to face all the rough and tumble of life in the army...

DEODATA: It's no use! In this house I shall just have to keep my mouth shut quite tight! I reason things out. I've got into the nasty, vicious habit of reasoning things out, living here among you people...

LIA: Who don't reason anything out at all...

DEODATA: There you go! There's no happy medium about this family! Either you're mad or you're saints. Your father's probably a saint... No, he certainly *is* a saint! But sometimes, you know, if I forget myself and really start paying attention to what he's doing and saying, well... God forgive me!... but... with those glaring eyes of his... he really and truly seems to me to be stark staring mad!

LIA (*she smiles her amusement*): Why don't you tell him so?

DEODATA: I shall, don't you worry! I'll tell him all right! I've been bottling it up inside me for a long time now! I'll tell him this very day, in front of everybody! It'll help to get it off my conscience too! You make me laugh, you and your "run down"! Why is he run down? Because of the life he led in the seminary! Too shut up! Too much hard studying! If you want my opinion, the remedy for all his troubles was a complete change. A life in the open air! But, oh no! Not on your life! On with his studies! Heaven only knows how long he's going to go on cramming things into that head of his! He'll end up by ruining his health completely! But when you've told him all this and *shown* him what it all adds up to... it means absolutely nothing as far as he's concerned. He bothers about people's health as little as he bothers about anything else! He spreads out his hands and raises his eyes to heaven. Or if you do think that he's been listening to what you've been saying, and that he's picked up some suggestion that you've let fall, quite suddenly you're brought up against the realization that what you suggested... well, he's simply made use of it to commit some fresh piece of lunacy. Like what he's up to now...

LIA: You mean handing over the farm?

DEODATA: Yes. A fine way of giving you country air! Which is what Doctor Gionni next door suggested to him!

LIA: But what does he mean to do?

DEODATA: With the farm? D'you mean to say you still haven't realized? He's turning it into a hospice for the indigent poor.

LIA: And what does that mean?

DEODATA: It means that all the beggars in town, and for miles around, will get their board and lodging, here on the farm, at his expense!

And that the two of you, he and you, will be living there with them! *Yes!* You'll thrive on the country air! You mark my words! After it's been thoroughly polluted by all their wretched filthy rags and tatters!

CICO's *voice is heard coming from the foot of the steps right.*

CICO'S VOICE: May I come up? Any objections?

DEODATA: Oh, it's you, Cico? Come on up! Come on!

CICO *comes up the steps. He is a queer little wisp of an old man. His eyes are small and blue – almost glassy – sharp, merry, eloquent. On his scalp, which gleams with a high polish, he is wearing a small red convict's cap. Twisted round his neck is a long blue scarf, which hangs down before and behind. He speaks in spasmodic outbursts: every now and again he breaks off short, and looks at you with those small, merry, eloquent eyes of his, accompanying his gaze with a mute smile. He is both shrewd and cunning.*

CICO: Ruined, Deodata, ruined. (*He sees* LIA *and immediately whips off his cap*) Ah, so you're here too, dear little lady? Your humble servant! (*Then once more to* DEODATA) Ruined.

DEODATA: Who's ruined you, you stupid old donkey?

LIA: Daddy, I'll bet!

CICO: *And the Devil!* Daddy and the Devil! The pair of them. That's how things happen, little lady. The more a man's a saint, the closer the Devil creeps up to his elbow. (*Sneezes*) Do you mind? (*He puts his cap on again*) Once I start sneezing… I'm quite capable of letting rip with a hundred blasts, one straight after the other! And it's goodbye to what I was saying! I can't get another word out!

LIA: What have Daddy and the Devil done to you?

CICO: I've told you… *Ruined me!* I'd got a wonderful idea! Oh, it was a wonderful idea! I was raking the money in in sackfuls. I'd discovered a profession for myself. I'd taken out my licence.

DEODATA: You mean you'd given up begging?

CICO: Begging my foot! *I* am a rent-collector. Licensed.

DEODATA: You, a rent-collector?

LIA: For whom?

CICO: For God, little lady. God's rent-collector. I'd composed a bit of patter, and as soon as I began to recite it… Oh, you can't imagine the huge crowds I had gathering all round me!

Men and women, of every class, age

and profession –
sailors, countryfolk, townsfolk –
we are all tenants
of the Lord.
Tenants of the Lord,
Who is the owner of the two houses.
Two houses...
Yes...
Two houses.
One of them... Look, we can see it... Look, look at it... All around us.
And the Lord would be a good and kindly Landlord to all of us alike,
if it weren't for the fact that so many, so many of us,
avid in greed and haughty in their pride,
had taken it as their own private property,
when it
ought instead to be a house common to us all.
There's some that've got granaries, barns and store lofts,
and there's some that haven't got a yard of rope
nor enough wall to stick a nail in,
so as to be able to hang themselves,
and it's most of us that're like this, and that're like me.
But meanwhile the others had better be thinking
that God's the Landlord
of the other house as well... The one up there,
the one He makes us pay the rent for
...Each and every one of us...
In advance, whilst we're still down here.
The poor, like me,
we pay it every day with the suffering
and the toil we know, punctually, at every hour of the night and day.
As far as the rich are concerned, on the other hand, all that's asked of them by way of payment
is to do the odd good turn every now and again.
And so it comes about,
ladies and gentlemen, that I'm really and truly

here in the Lord's Name
to claim (*he holds out his hand*)
the little something that's due
from you.
God's rent-collector – that's me!
The money came raining in, little lady. Like hailstones. But now, with
all this devilry of a hospice that your father's thinking of founding...
Well, you can imagine just how much rent in advance for the house
up there I'm likely to collect from now on! They'll say to me, "You've
now got a house yourself down here... Go and live in it!"

DEODATA: Good for you, Cico! So you too think this idea of the hospice
is the suggestion of the Devil? Eh?

CICO: Of course it is! And I've got the proof of it tucked away inside me!
D'you know what I've got inside me?

LIA: Yes, I do. Yes. It's the Devil that says "No".

CICO: You're right... I swear he does too! He's always doing it! Without
me wanting him to! I say "Yes", and he says "No". And he says it in
my own voice. In a whisper... Right down low... While I'm speaking.
Look, here's what I mean... Yesterday, I was standing in front of a
mirror stuck in a shop window. I said to myself, "Why, God, *why*?
You've given us teeth, and one by one You take them away from us.
You've given us sight, and You take it away from us. You've given
us strength, and You take it away from us. Now look at me, Lord,
look at the state You've left me in! Just look at me! So, of all the
lovely things You've given us, we aren't supposed to bring any of
them back to You when we come? I must say You'll enjoy Yourself
a hundred years from now, when You see a bunch of scarecrows like
me popping up in front of You!"

DEODATA: That was the Devil talking! It couldn't possibly have been you!

CICO: Oh, it wasn't! *Possibly* it wasn't! It was the Devil. And I was ever so
glad that Monsignor Lelli, who happened to be passing at the time,
gave him the reply he was asking for! "Oh, you stupid stupid donkey,
God has brought you to this condition that it shall not trouble you
greatly to die!"

DEODATA: And quite right too! Good for Monsignor Lelli!

CICO: As you say! But do you know what that stinking Devil actually
dared to fling back at him in a whisper? Right down low he whispered
it! "Then when He takes away our teeth He ought to take away our

desire to chew as well... And He *doesn't*!" Oh, they all burst out laughing – Monsignor Lelli along with the rest of them. And I was left there, looking a proper muggins, I can tell you! It wasn't right... It wasn't fair of them to laugh! Leaving me like that, without a word to say for myself by way of reply! It's not the sort of thing people *ought* to find funny! This what-I've-said about the hospice... this charity home... that was one of the things he's been telling me... deep down inside me.

DEODATA: The Devil, you mean?

CICO: The Devil. Every time I got to the end of my bit of patter he'd say, "But, in the meantime, what about if the poor had a house of their own down here as well?" D'you understand? And now the master's really and truly gone and given them one! (*The voice of* DR GIONNI *is heard as he climbs the steps*)

DR GIONNI'S VOICE: She's alive again! She's alive again!

DR GIONNI *comes into sight. He is carrying a small white doe rabbit in his hands. He hurries over to* LIA's *chair. He's a handsome, yet unattractive man, with a full fair beard, gold-rimmed spectacles... About forty years of age. He is wearing a long white linen operating-theatre gown, belted in the middle.*

GIONNI: Here you are! Here's your dear little rabbit for you again! She's come back to life.

LIA (*quivering all over with a joy which is almost dismay, she takes the rabbit*): Alive? Oh, dear! Yes! Yes! Look!

DEODATA: Is it possible?

GIONNI: Since last night, as a matter of fact. Yes, soon after I took her home with me...

LIA: Oh, so very soon?

GIONNI: I didn't say a word to you about it this morning, because I wanted to be quite sure first...

LIA: But what have you done to her? How did you do it?

GIONNI: Nothing. Just a little prick with a needle.

LIA: Oh, my poor little Riri! Where?

GIONNI: In her heart.

LIA (*utterly astonished*): In her heart? And she came back to life again?

GIONNI: She's not the first case.

427

DEODATA: Get along with you! Who are you trying to fool? It's a different rabbit!

GIONNI (*to* LIA): Do you think it's a different rabbit?

LIA: Why, of course I don't! It's Riri! (*To* DEODATA) Do you really think I don't know her? Look, she knows me too!

CICO: Oh, no! No! This just can't be! She was dead... And you've brought her back to life?

DEODATA: It's a different rabbit, I tell you! Or if it's the same one... Well, that means it wasn't dead in the first place!

LIA: She was as dead as could be!

GIONNI: Adrenalin.

LIA: And now she's alive!

CICO: Oh, I'm going barmy!

DIEGO SPINA *and* MONSIGNOR LELLI *enter from the steps.* DIEGO SPINA *is a little over forty. Tall and lean, with an intensely pale and cadaverous face, the whole force and expression of which are concentrated in the fierce glow of his hard, ever mobile eyes. They are the eyes, you might almost say, of an infuriated madman. His beard and moustache are sparse, straggling and unkempt. His hair is parted in the middle and piled up on either side of the parting, as a consequence of the habit he has of pushing the masses of hair up like this when he passes his hands over his head.* MONSIGNOR LELLI, *outwardly sweet and gentle, is not always successful in concealing beneath his smile and his friendly gaze all the bitterness that lurks in his heart. He is very old.*

DIEGO (*coming forwards*): What's happening?

LIA (*immediately; exultant*): Oh, it's you, Daddy? Look! Look at my Riri! She's come back to life again!

DIEGO: What on earth are you talking about?

LIA: Look at her! Just look at her! Here she is... alive!

DIEGO: It's not possible!

CICO (*to* MONSIGNOR LELLI): Dead, and he's brought her back to life again!

MONSIGNOR LELLI (*with the smile of a man who doesn't believe what he's saying*): A miracle?

CICO (*quivering with rage*): Tell him at once that it's nothing of the sort! Don't laugh! It's not right, Monsignore, it's not proper!

MONSIGNOR LELLI: I'm not laughing, Cico! But, forgive me, if the rabbit has contrived to come back to life...

DIEGO (*promptly, harshly*): It's a sure sign that it can't possibly have been dead in the first place!

MONSIGNOR LELLI: Obviously! All quite simple!

DEODATA: There, just what I said myself!

LIA: No, Daddy! She *was* dead! She was really and truly dead! Wasn't she, Doctor?

DIEGO (*peremptory, stern, clipping his words incisively, without giving the* DOCTOR *a chance to reply*): It cannot possibly be true! (*Then, turning once more to the* DOCTOR, *with an air of nervous irritation*) Really, Doctor, you oughtn't to... You ought not to...

CICO (*as though unable to understand why all this fuss is being made about something which, to him, is the most natural thing in the world*): What oughtn't I to do?

DIEGO: You oughtn't to tell my daughter such abominable stories!

GIONNI: Why do you call them abominable?

DIEGO: Oh, so you think it's quite normal for us to be able to...

GIONNI: If you'd only taken the trouble to keep up with...

DIEGO: I have done so! We can read it about them in the newspapers, unfortunately, these triumphs of science – and all the other things like them! And I know all about the disgraceful way you torture those wretched little animals you keep in your laboratory! It appals me, *utterly*.

GIONNI: But I've brought this one back to life...

MONSIGNOR LELLI (*instantly*): ...From what was *apparently* death.

GIONNI (*promptly and firmly*): There was no *apparently* about it at all. She *was* dead.

DIEGO: Do you mind telling me how you can be so dogmatic about it?

GIONNI: Good Lord, do you really suppose that a doctor doesn't know when—

DIEGO (*severely, cutting him off short*): I know this... God alone can recall the dead to life by performing one of His miracles!

CICO: There you are! Good for you!

MONSIGNOR LELLI: Precisely!

CICO: That, Monsignore, is my belief too. God alone. I do not for one moment presume to have wrought the miracle myself. I can, you see, conceive of science as another instrument from the Hand of God. Everything depends upon our being able to comprehend one another.

MONSIGNOR LELLI: Are you really serious? I mean... About the way *you* interpret what's happened.

GIONNI: As serious as I'm convinced of the truth of our faith... Yours and mine.

DIEGO (*angrily, contemptuously, he snatches the rabbit out of* LIA's *hand and gives it to* GIONNI): Here, take it! Take it back to your laboratory!

LIA (*impulsively*): No, not my Riri!

DIEGO: That will do, Lia!

GIONNI: My intention, Signor Spina, was to bring a little joy to your daughter. Is this how you thank me?

MONSIGNOR LELLI: There is one faith, and one faith only!

GIONNI: And that bids me take this rabbit back to my laboratory?

LIA: No, Daddy!

MONSIGNOR LELLI (*to* LIA): If God took her from you...

GIONNI: God is giving her back to her again!

DIEGO (*at the end of his tether*): Doctor, I beg you, will you please?... Really!

GIONNI: Very well, then! I'll take her back with me! I'll take her! (*He goes off towards the steps. Just before he begins his descent he turns to* LIA.) Don't worry, my dear! I'll keep her alive for you!

DIEGO (*lovingly he bends over his weeping daughter*): I don't like to see you crying... I don't want you to cry, Lia... You know what it is we have to do... We offer up to God...

LIA: Yes, Daddy... Yes! Yes!... I'm going in now! I'm going in... (*She goes off towards the house in her wheelchair and disappears through one of the doors under the portico. They all follow her with their eyes.*)

MONSIGNOR LELLI: You might perhaps have let her keep it.

DEODATA (*angry and upset*): I should just think you might have! An innocent pleasure like that!...

MONSIGNOR LELLI: Ah, no! That's the precise point at issue! *Not* innocent! Not when it was regained by such means!

DIEGO (*a touch repentant*): You heard her say, all of you, didn't you, that as far as she was concerned the creature *was* dead?

DEODATA: And to get it back again... alive...

DIEGO (*turning upon her angrily*): Do you realize the full implications of what you're saying?

CICO: Dead and then back to life again!

DIEGO: That we should believe such a thing possible... Do you realize that? And that she should have the proof there on her knees? Oh, I felt so angry deep down inside me...

DEODATA: What? Who made you feel angry? The child?

DIEGO: No, listening to that man and what he had to say!

DEODATA: And what had that got to do with the child anyway? Snatching the rabbit out of her hands like that... like a brute...

DIEGO: And aren't I confessing that I regret my harshness? It seems to me that I am.

DEODATA: It never entered my head for a single instant to think of any of the horrible things you saw in the affair! Now, you listen to me! I've kept it bottled up long enough! And now I'm going to tell you, here and now, in front of Monsignor Lelli. The trials that God sends us... let's accept them with resignation... all the sacrifices, all of them... If He commands you to make them... well, make them... and be happy to do so... but it's got to be Him... or His Vicar down here on earth! Look here, Monsignor Lelli'll do just as well... if it's in His Name that he orders me to do something. But not you! *You*, if you like, *you* can sacrifice *yourself*...

DIEGO: I...

DEODATA: Yes, you've been sacrificing yourself, your whole life long! But when you start insisting that other people ought to sacrifice themselves as well... oh no, that's going too far!

DIEGO: I? I start insisting?... Against their will?

DEODATA: That's how I see it anyway! Will... What sort of will do you think your daughter's got, when it comes to facing up to you? Yes, I tell you! *Yes!* You sacrifice everyone else along with yourself! Perhaps you don't even notice you're doing it. But look here... at this very moment... what you're planning to do now...

DIEGO: What I'm planning to do?

DEODATA: Oh, that hospice of yours!

DIEGO: Oh, so it's the hospice again, is it?

DEODATA: Forgive me for asking... but have you thought about me?... Have you ever given a thought to all the love I've always bestowed on

431

your poor afflicted daughter? All the loving care… *my* loving care… that now she'll have to go without?

DIEGO: Why will she have to go without it?

DEODATA: You ask me that? You surely don't expect me to come and live in that hospice of yours? Along with all the retired beggars you're pensioning off? I've even heard a rumour that you're going to invite that Scoma slut to join you!

CICO: Yes, yes! That Scoma woman… she goes around telling everybody!

DEODATA: And, of course, we all know why! It's a reward for her virtue!

MONSIGNOR LELLI: That will do, Deodata!

DEODATA (*as though unable to rest in peace, revealing all the resentment of an ancient rivalry*): That witch! She goes about begging, with her own picture in a frame, slung round her neck like a scapula! And it's not in God's Name that she begs for alms! Oh, no! Not on your life! It's because of what she *was*… it's in honour of *that*! And we all know what *she* was, don't we? Her picture tells you *that* anyway. You just try not giving her anything! She'll spit the most foul language after you! Curse you up hill and down dale!

MONSIGNOR LELLI: I've already told you, Deodata… *that will do!*

DEODATA: Yes, Monsignor, but you do realize, don't you?…

MONSIGNOR LELLI (*his meaning clear, if subtly veiled*): It would be rather more to the point if you tried to do a little *realizing* yourself!

DEODATA: But I do realize! I do understand! And since you say that… will you allow me to?… No, it's not really me. Will you allow my *conscience* to say a word or two? Don't worry… I'll keep quite calm! Calm as calm! It's the voice of conscience. Look deep down inside yourselves. I may be mistaken. But I must speak out frankly. And say all I've got to say. (*To* DIEGO) It's an excuse… nothing more or less… an excuse for your own weakness, this idea of yours for founding a hospice up there on the farm!

DIEGO: My *weakness*?

DEODATA: Yes! Your weakness in never having plucked up enough courage to chuck them off the farm…

MONSIGNOR LELLI (*with the utmost severity*): Hold your tongue, Deodata!

DIEGO: No! No! Let her say what she has to say!

DEODATA: *Your wife.* Who's been living there for years and years in mortal sin with a man… your servant… by whom she's had two children.

DIEGO (*with a sorrowing simplicity*): Why do you call it weakness?

DEODATA: "Why" he says! *Why?* Why, because you've never had the courage to...

DIEGO (*promptly, cutting her short*): I have had the courage to... to resist myself! The more I've been humiliated in the eyes of other people by what she's done, the greater has been the courage I have shown! You're one of those other people yourself! And you call it weakness! Just like the rest of them!

DEODATA: Forgive me for asking, but this is *your* daughter that's here, or isn't it? And tell me... did the doctors prescribe country air for her, or did they not? Even if there wasn't anything else, your daughter... and no one else... your daughter ought to be able to give you the strength you need, to do what you should have done years ago. Instead of which you keep her shut up here in this house, just so that her mother... that worthless creature... can go on enjoying all the country air herself!

DIEGO (*loudly, so as to cut short what she is saying*): You're not to talk like that! You don't know what you're saying!

DEODATA (*after a short pause in a low voice, almost as if she can't help herself, but must say what she has to say – to herself at least*): So you'll even go so far as to *defend* her!

DIEGO (*promptly, at once*): No. It's you who's defending her... yes, you!... without knowing that you're doing it.

DEODATA: I am?

DIEGO: Yes, *you* are. Because it was she who wanted her daughter to have precisely what you have been demanding for her... just now.

DEODATA: Country air?

DIEGO: Country air. (*A pause. Then he says:*) Why do you think she left me? We were never able to reach any agreement on how we were to bring up our children. That came first... then we disagreed about their education too.

DEODATA: Oh, so that was why she left you?

DIEGO: That was why... that was why she left me. (*Another short pause*) Monsignore, she loved them with a love that was... I don't know... too... in my opinion, too *carnal*. The same as so many other mothers. Neither more nor less.

CICO: Oh, a mother... (*And immediately he claps his hand over his mouth*)

DIEGO: And it was on her account, as a matter of fact... the little girl's... when she fell ill... *she* firmly believed that it was all my fault... because I'd insisted on sending her away to school too young... I'd sent her to board with the Sisters... It was on account of the little girl that she hated me... She couldn't bear the sight of me any longer... she cursed my house and went away to live on the farm...

DEODATA: With that man?

DIEGO (*angrily*): What do you mean, "with that man"? That happened two years later. She went to live on the farm... waiting for me to take the child out there to her... the child who by this time had lost the use of her legs.

DEODATA: Ah!... And you?...

DIEGO: I refused.

DEODATA: That was wrong of you!

DIEGO (*to* MONSIGNOR LELLI): She made it a condition of our reconciliation that I fetch the other child back home as well.

DEODATA: Lucio?

DIEGO: Lucio. She wanted me to remove him from the seminary to which I'd sent him. Monsignore, I might... perhaps... have done even that. But to admit that it was all my fault...

MONSIGNOR LELLI: You mean, what happened to the little girl?

DIEGO: In all conscience I couldn't bring myself to believe that it was my fault! And if I'd withdrawn Lucio... prevented him from following his career in the Church... as if by way of making amends for something for which I refuse to accept the blame. If I'd done that it would have led to my giving way to her, to doing exactly as she wanted with my children.

MONSIGNOR LELLI: Inevitably.

DIEGO: It would have meant being false to myself, to what I felt to be true, to my principles...

MONSIGNOR LELLI: And you say that you might even have done all this?

DIEGO: Yes. I was on the point of doing it... more than once.

MONSIGNOR LELLI: It grieves me to hear you say so!

DIEGO: By the Grace of God, I was able to realize... each time... that I should have been doing it only because I still loved and... *wanted* that woman...

MONSIGNOR LELLI: I see.

DIEGO: And that it was only because of this vile lust of the flesh...

MONSIGNOR LELLI: I understand!

DIEGO: I won the battle with myself. And nobody ever knew the tears I shed as I refused to surrender! And nobody ever knew of my secret hope that *she* might give way instead... out of compassion for her crippled child.

DEODATA: She certainly ought to have felt compassion!

DIEGO: The hatred she felt for me was stronger, and she didn't yield.

DEODATA (*with an outburst of diabolical glee*): You're still in love with her! You're still in love with her!

DIEGO: Of course I'm not! What on earth are you talking about?

DEODATA: It's as plain as the nose on your face! You're still in love with her! You can see it a mile off!

CICO (*trembling all over with excitement*): There you are, you see! It's the Devil again! Mine was just about to say the same thing... and hers got his spoke in first!

DIEGO (*with a sad smile*): Yes, Cico... you're quite right... it was the Devil. What harm do you think there can possibly be now in this love which I must feel... Yes, even for her? I'm right, aren't I, Monsignore? (*To* DEODATA, *after a pause*) As you can see very clearly, it would be unjust of me... it would be a double injustice on my part... if I were now to take advantage of the fact that Lia needs the country air on account of her health... that's to say, of the very remedy which she herself proposed at that time for the child... and on account of which... since I refused to give in... she is now living in sin.

DEODATA: You don't mean to say, do you now, that you believe that *that's* your fault?

DIEGO: If I had only taken the children up there to her...

MONSIGNOR LELLI: No! No! The wrong which you committed was something quite different... quite, quite different. You did wrong in not throwing her out in time... I mean, the moment you saw that she'd taken up with that man...

DIEGO: Yes, but...

MONSIGNOR LELLI: You ought not to have tolerated it. You ought not to have allowed her to go on living her adulterous life in your house... if the farm was yours... I was under the impression that it belonged to her...

DIEGO: No, it's mine. It belongs to me...

MONSIGNOR LELLI: It really has been most shocking… absolutely outrageous! But since you didn't do it at the proper time… when you had every right to do it… well, you certainly can't do it now. (*To* DEODATA) He can't plead the excuse of his daughter's health… not now. That would put him in the wrong and her in the right.

DIEGO: No… you see, Monsignore, you don't know what a terrible effect it had on me when first I heard of it! I forced myself to keep in check. To do nothing… to… live out the life of my torment… letting it go on and on… without affording it the slightest relief… quite the reverse in fact… I chose rather to be the scorn of all my neighbours… the button which is radiant in the fire that moulds it… That was my victory… *martyrdom*. A long, long martyrdom. It was long because my wound kept opening afresh… and the blood… black, *bitter* blood… welled out again and again. They told me that she'd given up everything… that she'd cast off all her lovely clothes…

DEODATA: Ah, but that's because she knows that… well, dressing the way she does now…

DIEGO: Like a peasant, you mean?

DEODATA: Yes… she's an absolute joy to look at… so lovely… everybody says the same thing… an absolute delight…

CICO: Oh yes, she's lovely… lovely! She still looks like a girl of twenty! When she passes by everybody turns to look at her. It's just as if the sun were passing by! She's a *miracle*!

DEODATA (*she is alluding to* SARA's *bailiff lover*): I suppose she looks so lovely, because that's how he wants her!

DIEGO (*with a sudden, violent access of rage, which dismays and chills them all*): That is enough of that! I can't bear to stand here and listen to… Not from you!

DEODATA (*dully, insensitively, after a pause*): It was you who brought the subject up in the first place…

DIEGO: It wasn't out of wickedness that she gave herself to that man. Neither is he the sort of man that you suppose. You know, Monsignore, don't you, that he's always sent the profits on the farm to the hospital? And always in my name. Ever since I first refused to accept them. And those profits have gone on steadily increasing, year by year. That farm has become the richest and best-cultivated in the whole neighbourhood.

CICO: Oh, it's Paradise itself! An earthly Paradise! I go out there, so I know! And those two little boys… they're more handsome even than their mother! And they're already working on the land. Oh, you should just see them! Hoeing away, with two little hoes… so big!… working away beside their father… and simply bursting with health!

DIEGO: It would certainly be a very great pity to turn them out… a pity for the hospital, I mean.

DEODATA: Well, I'm… He's thinking of the hospital now!

DIEGO: What I'm thinking is that they live there as poor people… doing good to others. If I turn them out now, they'll have to provide for themselves…

DEODATA: It'll be their punishment!

DIEGO: That's as may be! But the good that they've been doing all this time mustn't just be allowed to go to waste. I shall have to carry on the good work they've been doing myself…

DEODATA: By setting up your hospice on the farm? You'll ruin the farm! And as for the amount of good you'll be able to do… that'll be precious little! And what's more, you've done as much good as you need to already! It's high time you stopped! You've stripped yourself of everything! As a matter of fact, it was about this point that I wanted to talk to you, Monsignore… Has he got the right to carry on the way he does? When he's got a daughter who's a cripple?

DIEGO: My daughter wants for nothing… save only to attain in heaven… when it shall please God to call her unto Him… all that she could not have here on earth. It's not enough to *talk* about poverty… we must *experience* it. And since that's the case, we must strip ourselves of all that we possess. My daughter will live in the country, but she will see there… a poor man among other poor men… her own father. And she will be happy, because she will see that I am happy! Yes, when all's said and done, that is the only way! Otherwise I couldn't possibly bear to think of those two, driven off the land, wanderers on the face of the earth, in search of work. (*Turning abruptly to* DEODATA) Don't stand there staring at me like that! I pray every night to God that He will call me back to Himself! Not that I may have relief from the trials which He has been pleased to visit upon me, but that I may raise *them* up from that life of sin which is now theirs. Because I know that she has found a man… she has found a man.

437

During his speech the sun has been setting, and now the sky is all aflame with the full splendour of sunset. A bell is heard ringing at the foot of the steps.

DEODATA: Somebody's ringing. Wonder who it can be? The gate ought to be open, unless *you* shut it when you came in. (*To* CICO) Go and see who it is, will you? Go on! (CICO *goes over to the steps. He starts back in utter astonishment, almost in dismay. He comes back over.*)

CICO: Ooooh! It's *her*! *Her*! The Missis!

DIEGO: She's… *here*?

CICO: Yes… all dressed in red… with a black cloak.

DEODATA: She must have got to hear about the… And perhaps she's come to…

MONSIGNOR LELLI: About the farm?

DIEGO: But how does she dare to…

MONSIGNOR LELLI (*catches sight of her as she appears on the steps and halts on the landing*): Here she is!

DIEGO (*in a low voice*): Go indoors, all of you! Leave me alone with her. (*To* DEODATA) Mind that Lia doesn't find out she's here.

MONSIGNOR LELLI, DEODATA *and* CICO *withdraw. They go out through one of the doors under the portico. Set against the background of the blazing sky* SARA, *dressed all in red under a black cloak, seems like an unreal apparition of ineffable beauty: she radiates freshness, health and power.*

SARA (*absorbed by what she sees, she looks around her, comparing her memory of things with how they appear to her now – less ample, meaner, shabbier*): The garden… The house…

DIEGO: You actually dare to come and see me again? In front of the whole world?

SARA (*the same absorbed, appraising look*): And you too… My God, what a face!

DIEGO: Leave my face out of this! Tell me why you've come!

SARA: Oh, don't worry! As soon as people get to know why I've come, they'll realize that *I had* to come… and they won't be at all surprised. There will be a great deal more for them to be surprised about… but not my coming here.

DIEGO: Have you come because you heard…

SARA: About the hospice? No. (*She laughs*) Oh, you were afraid that I'd come to intercede, to beg you to leave us on the farm?

DIEGO: *Isn't* that what you've come for?

SARA: No, no, of course not! It's not your farm that's keeping us alive…

DIEGO (*swiftly, trying to cut her short*): I know! I know!

SARA: Well, then? We live by the work that we do upon it. If necessary we can do that somewhere else. It's something that, so far as we're concerned, isn't of the slightest importance. It might, at most… yes, at most… it might be of some importance to the poor, sick people at the hospital.

DIEGO: That's the very thing I was saying myself, only a moment or so ago…

SARA: There you are, you see? And since you've brought up the subject…

DIEGO: No! Tell me first the reason why you've come…

SARA: Wait a minute… If you're trying to find some excuse for turning us out…

DIEGO: It's not an excuse!

SARA: What on earth do you think they want with a farm?… These old town beggars, who are used to spending their lives in wandering from door to door. Used to being with lots of people. If you shut them up there, they'll feel as if they were in prison… It would be like punishing them – not doing them a kindness. In a year's time the farm will have died on their hands.

DIEGO: I shall be up there myself, living among them.

SARA: You? And what could you possibly do with those arms of yours? You make me laugh! You've not seen the farm… Not since… And you've got no idea what it's like now, no conception of what we've done to it. There's not one square foot of land that's not growing something…

DIEGO: I know that…

SARA: The kitchen garden… the vineyard… the orchard… Oh, we've got every kind of fruit you could possibly want! And you know, we've found water! That spring which you said… do you remember?… said you could sometimes hear running under the bank alongside the path that leads down into the valley… Well, that's the one… We've found it! There's masses and masses of water! It's brought new life and freshness to everything! Three great cisterns always full… And it flows along the ditches… everywhere… joyously! And it makes you heave a deep sigh of contentment when you hear its noisy rush on those hot summer evenings… So… if this hospice of yours is only an excuse… don't give it another thought.

DIEGO: I've already told you… it's not an excuse.

SARA: We'll leave the farm. We'll go away of our own accord. Tomorrow, if you like. We won't even put you to the trouble of turning us out. Put in another bailiff, though… choose an honest one. And a man who knows the meaning of work. That's what you must do. And do it… now, listen to me… do it for the sake of your own flesh and blood! Have you given a thought to how you're going to provide for these children of yours?

DIEGO: The children… Do you mean to tell me that you're interested in them… *still*?

SARA: "*Still*", you say *still*? To *me*? *You*? Who was it that denied me the right to think of them *always*? *Always!* Of them and of them alone?

DIEGO (*his face darkening*): Let's drop the subject!

SARA: You no longer wanted me to be a mother to my children, even though it meant that you would lose me as a wife!

DIEGO: Yes, because I intended my wife to be the mother of my children, bringing them up according to my principles.

SARA: Oh, no! No! Not that! Never!

DIEGO: Yes!

SARA: Do you know what? The fact that things are as they are now proves to me… more decisively than ever… that I was in the right! Not you!

DIEGO: Let's change the subject! Let's change the subject!

SARA (*pointing to the crucifix*): You never see anything but *that*… And even that you see only in the way *you* want to see it.

DIEGO: Don't blaspheme!

SARA: I, *blaspheme*? I'm the first to go down on my knees before it! But, you know, that cross is there to give people life… not death!

DIEGO: Will you be silent? What right have *you* to talk of life and death? You have forgotten that the true life is the one which lies in the world beyond. When we have cast off this flesh.

SARA: I know that God gave us this life as well as that other… in order that we might live it out, here below, in health and happiness! And no one can know this better than a mother! I wanted joy… yes, I wanted joy and health for my children! And I looked for wealth too…

yes! For their sakes… not for my own! I've lived as a peasant myself. I still live as a peasant. And if you leave the farm to your children, then let me tell you… I shall be glad I've toiled with these arms… yes, you know, really and truly *toiled*!… to make it as prosperous as it now is… for their sakes!

DIEGO: They've done without it so far, with the help of God, and they can go on doing without it.

SARA: How can you possibly know that?

DIEGO: *I do* know.

SARA: So many things may happen which are far beyond your dreams.

DIEGO: Well anyway, I've provided for one of the children. And as for Lucio…

SARA (*as if she had been expecting this*): As for Lucio?…

DIEGO: He has his vocation.

SARA: And if that is no longer sufficient for him?

DIEGO: What do you mean… "If that is no longer sufficient for him"? It must be sufficient for him!

SARA: Lucio came to see me yesterday.

DIEGO (*utterly taken aback*): Lucio? What on earth are you saying? He's come back?…

SARA: Yes, he's come back. And he came to *me*. That's why I said that the fact that things are as they are proves… now more decisively than ever… that I was right.

DIEGO (*still almost incredulous*): Lucio came to *you*?

SARA: That is why you see me here. Your son came to me.

DIEGO: But… what do you mean… *came*? Did you write to him? You sent for him, didn't you?

SARA: How on earth could I possibly have sent for him? No. And why should I have done? (*Scornfully*) Oh, you're still thinking about the farm! I told you, I'm ready to hand it over to you tomorrow!

DIEGO: Then… it was of his own accord? But… why? (*In dismay and bewilderment*) He came without showing his face here… He's stopped writing… What's happened to him?

SARA: I don't know. I was in the vegetable garden. I saw him standing before me. I didn't recognize him at first. How on earth *should* I have recognized him?

DIEGO: But… he came out to you? With what object? What did he say?

SARA: I couldn't repeat it... not the way he put it... You must hear him yourself! What he had to say was not for me alone... for the whole wide world!

DIEGO: He must have gone mad!

SARA: He's a changed man!

DIEGO: *A changed man?* What do you mean? He must at least have given you some reason for coming.

SARA: Yes, he did. It was to recognize me.

DIEGO (*in bewildered astonishment*): To *recognize* you?

SARA: Yes. And to be born again. *He*, to be born again of me. To be born again of me, his mother. He said so! I looked at him, in dismay. How white his face has grown, just like wax! And his eyes! I saw him stretch out his arms... Tears welled up within those terrible eyes of his... "Mamma," he said... I felt myself... I felt myself purified by it... A blessed mother once again! He took me in his arms... He wept on my breast... for a long time... a very long time... in my arms... trembling all over. I've never felt anyone tremble the way he did then!

DIEGO (*almost to himself*): Oh, God! O God, help me! O God! God, God, what is it You want of me? (*To* SARA) But... how?... without giving a moment's thought to the fact that... up there, where he went to look for you... you were living with a man who's not his father... and that he... (*Suddenly, as though a doubt has entered his mind, leaving him thunderstruck*) But perhaps... Oh, God!... perhaps he's no longer wearing his cassock?

SARA: No.

DIEGO (*as if in terror*): He's taken off his cassock? He's thrown away his cassock?

SARA: But you should hear how lovingly he still speaks of God!

DIEGO (*frantic*): Where is he? Where is he? Tell me where he is! Is he up at the farm?

SARA: No, he came with me. To talk to you.

DIEGO: He wants to talk to me?

SARA: He wants to explain things to you...

DIEGO: Where is he?

SARA: He stayed at my sister's... down by Town Gate...

DIEGO: I'm going to see him! I'm going to see him! I'm going to see him...

And, as if quite insane, he hurls himself down the stairs. SARA *remains perplexed and a touch dismayed by his flight. She looks around her and perceives* CICO, *who is standing peering at her from behind one of the little columns, red cap on head. She waves him over. Quite suddenly the sky, which up till now has been red, becomes violet, and the stage is as if chilled all at once by this livid, sinister light.*

SARA: Come over here! You must run after him! I can't. Lucio's come home... without his cassock!

CICO: Oh, has he?...

SARA: Yes! He dashed off like a madman. Go and tell them in the house. Go and tell them in the house. *I'm going now. You must look after him!*

And she hurries away down the steps. DEODATA *comes out of one of the doors of the portico to see what's going on.* CICO *immediately calls out to her.* DEODATA *hastens over.*

DEODATA: What did she say to you? And why did he run away?

CICO: It's Lucio... Lucio... It's all the Devil's fault... He's thrown away his cassock!

DEODATA: Lucio? Did she tell you that?

CICO: She did! She did! It's all the Devil's fault!

DEODATA: O God, help us!

CICO: He tore off, dashed down the stairs! I'm going after him! (*Exit furiously down the stairs*)

DEODATA: Yes, you go! Run after him! But where will he have gone? Oh, Lord God in heaven! All dressed in scarlet she was! Like a flame from hell! And to bring such news too! (*She goes over to the porch*) Oh, Monsignore! Monsignore!

MONSIGNOR LELLI (*coming out, in consternation*): What's the matter? What's happened?

DEODATA: Lucio's stopped being a priest! He's thrown away his cassock!

MONSIGNOR LELLI: No! What on earth are you saying?

DEODATA: *She* came here... To break the news to him! And *he's* gone tearing off!

MONSIGNOR LELLI: Where to?

DEODATA: I don't know! He just dashed off! (*A confused sound of shouting, anxious voices is heard near at hand, and coming even nearer*)

MONSIGNOR LELLI: Do you hear that? What can have happened? Why are they shouting?

SHOUTS: Gently, now, gently!… Up there!… Up those steps!

But how did it happen?

Oh, it's Signor Spina!

Not so loud! Not so loud! Remember his daughter!

But is he… *dead*? How did it happen? Oh, poor soul!

Careful now! Careful as you go up the steps!

Turn round now! Head first! The steps are pretty steep!

DEODATA (*rushing over to the steps*): Oh, my God! It's the master! What's happened?

CICO (*coming back up the steps*): He's been run over! Run over!

MONSIGNOR LELLI: Run along, Deodata! Don't let the child come out!

DEODATA: But he can't be dead!

MONSIGNOR LELLI: No, no! Let's hope not! Now run along! Run along!

A group of men come up the steps, panting. They were men who were passing along the street when the accident occurred. They are supporting the limp body of DIEGO SPINA, *some at the head, others at the feet. Some people are carrying small lit lanterns. Laboriously the men carry the body over and set it down on one of the benches, so that it is in full view of the audience.* DEODATA *rushes over towards the house. When the knot of bearers has passed the head of the steps… that's to say, before they've got to the point of putting the body down… another group of curious, anxious people comes into sight. Their way is barred by* CICO.

VOICES OF THE BEARERS: Up a bit! Gently – gently! Over here! Over here!

Put him down on that seat there!

That's it! Gently now! Over here!

MONSIGNOR LELLI: But there's no sign of any injury!

ONE OF THE BEARERS: No, not a sign!

MONSIGNOR LELLI: How did it happen?

ANOTHER OF THE BEARERS: He threw himself under a motor car!

MONSIGNOR LELLI: What… *deliberately*? Impossible!

FIRST BEARER: Well, it certainly seemed like it!

THIRD BEARER: He was running like somebody who'd gone stark staring mad!

FOURTH BEARER: Everybody thought the same thing… that he'd…

MONSIGNOR LELLI: Impossible! Impossible!

FIRST BEARER: The car swerved...

SECOND BEARER: Didn't even go over him...

THIRD BEARER: But it flung him against the wall so violently that he dropped down at once... just like a lump of lead!

MONSIGNOR LELLI: He doesn't seem to show any sign of life!

FOURTH BEARER: Doesn't he? He was breathing up till a moment or so ago.

MONSIGNOR LELLI: He's quite cold!

CICO (*from the head of the steps, intent upon clearing a path through the curious bystanders*): Here's the doctor! Here comes the doctor! Mind out of the way there! Mind out of the way!

The DOCTOR *hurries up the steps and across the stage. He has been summoned in haste from the nearest surgery.*

DOCTOR (*as he hurries over, to* CICO, *who is trying to tell him all about it*): Yes, I know... I'd realized that... run over! Let me through!... Let me have a look at him! (*He bends over* SPINA, *studies his appearance for a moment or so, unbuttons his collar, waistcoat, shirt... Listens to his heart. Meantime there is a low murmur of comment from the bystanders.*)

BYSTANDERS: Looks as if he's dead!

H'm! Yes!

What a terrible thing to happen!

Hush! Ssssh!

DOCTOR (*raising his head*): He's dead.

BYSTANDERS (*in various tones of voice*): Dead?

DOCTOR (*once more he bends down to listen to the injured man's heart. Then he gets up again, and, amidst the bewilderment and anguish, the dismay and the compassion felt by all about him, he repeats*): Dead.

CURTAIN

ACT TWO

The scene is the rustic porch of DIEGO SPINA's *farmhouse in the country. The tiles of the lean-to-style roof, which slopes away towards the back of the stage, are visible from underneath. The roof itself is supported by two pillars which are set in a low outer wall, that is broken into midway along so as to allow access – effected by means of a short flight of steps – to the porch. A stone bench runs along this wall. In the background you can see the farm: a dazzling, exultant expanse of verdure, resplendent in the sunshine – an earthly paradise. In the right-hand wall of the porch there is the opening for the staircase which leads to the upper floor of the villa. On either side of this opening there is a stone seat set against the wall. Towards the back of the stage, and beyond the stage seat, there is a small door let into the wall. In the wall left there is the door which opens into the bailiff's quarters. It is up one step. In the middle of the stage there are an old rustic table, some old chairs and a stool or two.*

When the curtain rises ARCADIPANE *and an old peasant are on stage. The peasant is already laden with one or two bundles, and another bundle is lying on the ground. In addition there's a large saddlebag on the table.* ARCADIPANE *is a tall, powerfully built man, with a curly black beard; his eyes are large, smiling and as innocent as a child's. He is wearing a shaggy black cap which he has made for himself out of goatskin. He's dressed like a peasant, in blue broadcloth and jackboots. Instead of a waistcoat, he's wearing, over his coarse, white linen shirt, another shirt – made from violet flannel, and chequered with red and black squares. The loose, floppy collar of the linen shirt is folded down over that of the flannel shirt. Around his waist he has a leather belt.*

ARCADIPANE (*picking up the bundle from the ground*): See if you can carry this one as well. Then we'll have finished... Everything'll be out. (*Carefully and considerately he loads the bundle onto the peasant's back. Meanwhile another peasant comes in through the door*

447

Left, carrying a chest painted green. SARA *follows him in. The bells of an approaching carriage can be heard in the distance.*)

SARA: Is this chest to go on the cart too?

ARCADIPANE: Yes. (*To the peasant*) But wait till I get there before you put it on the cart. I'll come and do it myself. I'll have to find a place to put it. And make sure everything's strapped down properly. Come on. I'll take the bag. (*He picks it up*)

SARA: The bag goes on the mule.

ARCADIPANE: Oh, there's a carriage coming. It can't be them, surely?

SARA: No. It's too soon.

ARCADIPANE: There's nothing more left upstairs?

SARA: Nothing at all. Go and see who it is, will you? But it can't possibly be them. (*She goes back into the house.* ARCADIPANE *leaves the porch, following the peasants, who have already gone out back and to the left. For a moment the stage remains empty. Then* ARCADIPANE *re-enters back, followed by* DR GIONNI.)

ARCADIPANE: Well, here we are! Do come in, Doctor. If you'd like to go upstairs... I don't know if that's what you want to do... My quarters are over here... and the boy's up there... (*He points to the staircase right*)

GIONNI: No. No. I must be on my way again immediately. I'll come back after I've made my visit. I've got to see a neighbour of yours. Over at Lotti's.

ARCADIPANE: Oh yes, his mother. Yes, I know. Seems she's in a bad way.

GIONNI: Yes, I'm afraid so. *I* just stopped off in passing to let you know that...

ARCADIPANE: Wait a minute. I'll call Sara. (*He goes over to the door left, mounts the step, and calls*) Come down a minute, Sara... The doctor's here. (SARA *comes in through the door left*)

SARA (*apprehensively*): What's happened now?

GIONNI: Nothing. Now don't get agitated. I only want to tell Lucio something... so that he's prepared...

SARA: He must be upstairs. Strange he didn't hear the carriage bells.

GIONNI: He's probably asleep.

SARA: No. Would to God he were! He doesn't sleep a wink. Believe me, I'm so very worried about him. And now, on top of it all, this accident to his father...

GIONNI: Yes, but that's all…

SARA: You can have no idea how his poor head…

ARCADIPANE: He never gives himself a moment's rest…

SARA: Oh, and his eyes… I don't know how to put it… It's as if they were petrified… Yes, that's it!… Petrified with grief!… And yet… they're *blazing* at the same time… as though he were in a raging fever. And what he must be thinking! Last night he told me he felt that the hour of his father's resurrection was at hand.

ARCADIPANE: What did he mean by that? Hasn't he risen already? By means of the miracle… (*A gesture in the direction of* GIONNI)

GIONNI: For pity's sake, don't call it a miracle! Don't you call it a miracle too!

ARCADIPANE: But that's what everybody's calling it! Everybody!

GIONNI: And that's what's so harmful! We must put a stop to it!

ARCADIPANE: Harmful, do you call it? Why, we're all still absolutely flabbergasted by it! There's talk of nothing else in the whole countryside hereabouts.

SARA: And you can just imagine what it's like in town!

GIONNI: Oh, yes, I dare say! But I'm more concerned about the effect it can have on him.

ARCADIPANE: You mean the miracle of his resurrection?

GIONNI: Exactly. He cannot possibly admit that it's true… Believing as he believes, he just cannot admit the possibility of such a miracle as this.

ARCADIPANE: And why can't he?

GIONNI: Because God alone can call the dead back to life.

ARCADIPANE: I still can't see why he can't believe in it. Wasn't this, maybe, the will of God?

GIONNI: Ah, there you have it! Good for you, Arcadipane! So I'm not a devil in *your* eyes?

ARCADIPANE: What on earth are you saying, Doctor?

GIONNI: I see everybody eyeing me, just as if I possessed the diabolical power of bringing the dead back to life…

ARCADIPANE: Well, you know, you have brought *one* back!

GIONNI: Precisely! By means of a miracle! And it's this very man, who ought to be thanking God that I did, who's keeping me on tenterhooks, in case he should get to know what's happened!

SARA: Oh, then perhaps that's why Lucio says…

449

GIONNI: What?

SARA: That his father's true resurrection is at hand?

GIONNI: Does he suppose that in the end his father will admit it himself?

SARA: Perhaps he *hopes* he will.

GIONNI: He'd do well not to build his hopes too high. As a matter of fact I came here on purpose to warn him what attitude to adopt with his father, when he comes. And I'd like to warn you too...

SARA: Oh, there's no need to warn us. We shan't be seeing him, Doctor. We shall be gone before he gets here...

ARCADIPANE: We're just on the point of going now...

GIONNI: Oh, of course, yes. Forgive me...

SARA: I'll go up. I'll just go up and call Lucio. (*She crosses the stage and exits up the stairs right*)

GIONNI: Ah, yes! I know! I've done you a bad turn, Arcadipane. Naturally, when the news of his death reached you...

ARCADIPANE: You mustn't think, Doctor, that Sara and I rejoiced at it...

GIONNI: I don't say you *rejoiced*... but it's quite certain it left you in a position to...

ARCADIPANE: To legalize our union? Ah, yes! We'd have done that at once...

GIONNI (*almost to himself*): That's curious!

ARCADIPANE: What is?

GIONNI: You still could...

ARCADIPANE: *How* could we? With him alive?

GIONNI: There's the death certificate.

ARCADIPANE: It'll be cancelled!

GIONNI: But at the moment it's still valid... All signed, sealed and delivered by the doctor who made the post-mortem examination. *Legally* he's dead.

ARCADIPANE: You don't mean that seriously...

GIONNI: No... but... in the eyes of the law.

ARCADIPANE: The law, Doctor... There's only one law... The law of God.

GIONNI: But your children...

ARCADIPANE: It'll be sufficient for them not to be outside God's law. I've got nothing to leave them, except the example of obedience to that Law. There's only one thing that grieves my heart... that I shall never again hear my own voice under the tiles of this roof. It brings back to me... oh, if you only knew!... the memory of so many nights. Sitting on that step over there. Gazing over at the staircase. You can't possibly imagine the love that I've been able *to put into* these stones... into this earth... into every tree that I've planted here... with her by my side... (*He is alluding to* SARA) She stepped down from being my master's wife and became my companion. Here she comes now... She's coming downstairs with her son. I'll be going. I've never spoken to him in my life. I've never even let him catch sight of me. (*He goes out back, turning to the left.* LUCIO *and* SARA *come down the stairs right.* LUCIO *is twenty-two, slim and very pale, with a face hollowed by the spiritual travail that has kindled a feverish light in his eyes. He has slender, graceful and very sensitive hands. At frequent intervals he wrings them convulsively. He is not at all shy. On the contrary, it's as if he were impelled to speech and action by an anxiety which seems at times to be stimulated by anger. He's rather ill at ease in the clothes he's wearing – a grey, ready-made suit, somewhat clumsy in cut. He looks rather like a schoolboy who's wearing long trousers for the first time. He comes hurrying down the stairs with his mother.*)

LUCIO: No, no, Doctor!...

GIONNI: Good morning, Lucio...

LUCIO: Good morning. I cannot remain silent! I give you fair warning... I cannot remain silent! If he comes here...

GIONNI: All that I meant was... with regard to what's happened.

LUCIO: What is it you want me not to tell him?

GIONNI: ...This thing that everybody's calling a miracle... the help I gave...

LUCIO: And why shouldn't I mention it to him?

GIONNI: Because he doesn't know anything about it yet!

LUCIO: He doesn't know anything about it?...

SARA: He doesn't know that it was you who...

GIONNI: For pity's sake, not a word about *that*! He remembers nothing whatsoever about anything. All he knows is that he was knocked down by a motor car. He thinks that he was concussed and that his memory of everything has been completely blotted out.

SARA: He doesn't even know about the death certificate then?

GIONNI: He knows nothing about anything! Nothing at all! I tell you, he hasn't even the remotest suspicion. He's busy thanking God that, apart from the concussion… oh yes, that might very well have proved fatal!… he suffered no other harm as a result of being knocked down.

LUCIO: And do you really think it's possible that he won't find out what's happened?

GIONNI: The most important thing is that he shouldn't find out about it for the moment… not in the state that he's in just now. You can imagine the effect it would have on his mind, can't you?… His spiritual agony…

LUCIO: You don't think it would do him good to know?

GIONNI: Good Heavens, no! God forbid! You'd better get that idea out of your head as quickly as possible! He damned me as a sacrilegious scoundrel merely for bringing a dead *rabbit* back to life! Just imagine what he'd have to say now, if he found out that!… I give you my solemn oath, Lucio, that if it hadn't been for your little sister… who implored me to do the same thing for him… she was absolutely desperate!… Well, as far as my own predilections are concerned, I'd have thought twice about it… and more than twice… before doing it. Yes, I'd have had serious scruples about doing it… just *because* of what the consequences were likely to be…

LUCIO: And suppose it's… *those consequences*… that I'm relying on now?

GIONNI: No! No! What on earth are you talking about? You're *relying* on the consequences?…

LUCIO: I'm relying on those consequences to call him back to life, and to ensure that God really does accomplish His miracle… not only on my father's body.

GIONNI: You're willing, then, to run the risk of killing him?

LUCIO: Am I?… No, Doctor. *You're* the one that's running *that* risk, not I.

GIONNI: How am I? Why do you say that?

LUCIO: You have made his body walk again… but is it only his body that counts?

GIONNI: No. Your father has his faith!

LUCIO: Precisely. And did you show any respect for that faith of his when you set him on his feet again, using means which he regards as sacrilegious? The moment he finds out the truth, *you* will have killed him!

GIONNI: Nonsense! At this very moment I'm doing all I possibly can to *prevent*…

LUCIO: To prevent his finding out? If he doesn't find out today he'll do so tomorrow.

GIONNI: All I'm asking is that he shouldn't find out at this precise moment. Do remember that, after all, it was on your account...

LUCIO: You mustn't say that it was on my account! Say rather that it was so that this supreme test... the supreme test of life itself... which God has been pleased to visit both upon him and upon me... might be met.

GIONNI (*shrugging his shoulders*): Supreme test... supreme test...

LUCIO: Do you mean you think it's something more important than that? Doctor, you mustn't do anything to hinder him in any way, if he should come up here today in order to face it.

GIONNI: But do you really imagine that he's coming here for *that*?

LUCIO: *Isn't* he coming up here in order to speak to me?

GIONNI: Yes, but I'm quite sure he's not expecting to have to face this supreme test you've been talking about! Not in the least!

LUCIO: What is he expecting then?

GIONNI: *I don't know!* I suppose that... well, that he's expecting you to retract...

LUCIO: To go back on what I've done? And do you mean to say that you expect me not to tell him what my reasons were for doing what I have done?

GIONNI (*getting angry*): Oh, go on! Tell him your reasons! Do whatever you think best! It'll all seem like heresy to him, anyway! You know, when all's said and done, my dear Lucio, mine's a rum fate, and no mistake! Look at me! *Doomed!* Doomed to get everybody's back up! All the time! It must be my face... I don't know... Perhaps it's my voice. I respect other people's faith, and at the same time people get annoyed with me on account of my tolerance! I think like you, I feel like you. And here we both are: you're thoroughly annoyed with me, and I'm thoroughly annoyed with you!...

LUCIO (*smiling*): No. You're wrong there, I'm not the least bit annoyed...

GIONNI: I am, though! And I'm going! I've done my duty as a doctor. I implore you... as a friend... to leave your father in ignorance. Just for the moment. Leave him in ignorance of what's happened to him.

SARA: Yes! Yes! I agree with what you say! You oughtn't to tell him anything. Not just for the present.

LUCIO: If you think that it'll do him the slightest harm, I'll keep silent, even if he forces me to talk about...

GIONNI: That's not what I'm saying!

LUCIO: I shall have to, Doctor! He'll want to talk to me about my loss of faith, and I'll be obliged to tell him it's not true. I've acquired it... If anything – it has been strengthened...

GIONNI: Not as far as he's concerned.

LUCIO: Faith is something everyone acquires for himself.

GIONNI: No... I mean... Well, the way he looks at things...

LUCIO: And do you know how I've acquired it? Simply by denying the reality of that death you're so frightened he'll get to hear about...

GIONNI: *Denying* it? How can you deny *death*?

LUCIO: By ceasing to presume that God, simply because this body of mine... in the natural course of events... will sooner or later fall to the ground, like a withered leaf from a tree...

GIONNI: And isn't that death?

LUCIO: Of course it isn't! *Death!* A handful of dust that returns to dust...

GIONNI: That's what your father says, too!

LUCIO: Yes... But he goes on to assume that...

GIONNI: Yes, quite! That his spirit...

LUCIO: *His* spirit? How is it *his*?... Don't you see that's where he's wrong!

SARA: In saying that it's *his* spirit?

LUCIO: Yes, that's it, Mamma! In admitting that it is eternal... infinite... and yet assuming that it can possibly be mine... something that belongs to a man who dwells within the boundaries of time... a fleeting, momentary form... something that is yesterday's or tomorrow's. You see how it is, don't you? To prevent our little existence coming to an end, we annihilate life. In God's name. And we make God rule over the kingdom that lies beyond this world. No one knows where it is. We make Him rule there too. Over a kingdom of the dead which we have imagined in order that, when we reach it, He may give us our reward or our punishment. We are an insignificant part of the whole existence He has created yet we dare to assume we can decide who is good or evil. We can't bring ourselves to admit that He alone knows what He does and why He does it. Don't you see, Doctor – this wonderful event should be for him – as it is for me – a true resurrection from the dead. He must deny that there is death in God. He must believe in this, which is the only immortality there is. An immortality that is not our own, not something that is in or for ourselves. That is not the hope of reward or the fear of punishment. He must believe in the eternal present of life... which is God... And then indeed will God... after this experience which He has granted my father... then will he... and He alone... accomplish the miracle of his resurrection. I shall say nothing, nothing at all. Nothing, I promise you. I shall let him say just whatever he wishes to say to me. And... don't worry, I'll do everything within my power to avoid sharing your fate, Doctor. I mean, I'll try to say nothing that might irritate him.

GIONNI (*he is lost in wonder and admiration at what* LUCIO *has said so gently, so fervently and so simply*): Exactly! Provided, of course, that by keeping quiet you don't irritate him all the more. That's what you might call *my* fate! Take *now*, for instance... I'm irritated to the point of exasperation with myself for the advice I've been giving you. Oh well, don't let's say any more on that subject. Let's hope that everything turns out well in the end. Goodbye for the moment... signora.

SARA: Goodbye. But you must call me Sara... Will you be coming back?

GIONNI: Oh, yes! Yes! Very soon. Goodbye then. (*Exit back, taking the left turn. Shortly after he disappears we hear the sound of his carriage bells.*)

SARA: And now I'll be going as well...

LUCIO (*hearing the sound*): Can you hear, Mamma?

DIEGO: Hear what?

LUCIO: Those bells.

DIEGO: It'll be the doctor's carriage.

LUCIO: When I was a little boy I used to think that the open country, stretched out there in the morning sunlight, was made especially to spread the sound of the bells.

SARA: The country? But, my dear, when you were a little boy...

LUCIO: I could see it from the courtyard of the seminary, way up there at San Gerlando. I used to look down onto it. During playtime the other boys... used to race about... shouting like mad, and tucking up their cassocks so they could run better. I used to keep in the background. At the end of the yard. Because from there I could enjoy the wide sweeping view of the green valley. With the great wide road that cut through it like a furrow. And I could see the carriages driving out through the countryside... they looked tiny... Three horses harnessed together... And from far away the sound of the bells would come stealing up on me – just as they're doing now. (*His mother is in tears; he turns to her*) Are you crying, Mamma?

SARA: Yes, because of the grief I can hear in your voice...

LUCIO: Yes, I did feel... I did feel a terrible anguish... anguish... regret for life, which might have been so lovely. It seemed to me that I was experiencing all the joys of a drive in the open air... through the countryside... through those green fields... all golden in the sunlight. I sense the atmosphere around me... and the smells of things. I think of how we used to come out of the seminary, two by two, as we went for our walks. And we'd pass by one of those carriages standing on the rank in the square... waiting to be hired. You know, I can still smell the reek of stables. I can even see a wisp of straw between the horses' grey lips. I can hear the ring of iron-shod hooves on the cobbles when they stamped. You see, Mamma, when I was a little boy, up there in the seminary, faith was... it was *smell*... taste... the smell of incense... the smell of wax... the taste of the Consecrated Host... and a terrible dismay at people's footsteps as they echoed inside the empty church...

SARA: You were very tiny... Your face was so very white even then... Oh, how it hurt me, my son, when I saw you come home for the holidays, dressed in your little cassock! *You* used to tuck your cassock up too... So that you could run to me... And then you'd immediately let it drop again... so that the little girls in the street shouldn't laugh at you... and shout after you, "Little priesty! Little priesty!" And it was as if your eyes were filled with terror when you looked at me...

LUCIO (*covering his eyes with his hands*): No, Mamma! No! Don't remind me!

SARA: Why not?

LUCIO: If you only knew the shame of it all! Why there was that look in my eyes. All the filth of life! Child as I was, I had absorbed into myself all the filth of life! It had been put there inside me by one of the boys... one of the big boys. You know the one I mean, don't you? He went mad later on. His name was Spano...

SARA: You were barely six years old...

LUCIO: And I knew everything! And I don't know whether it was more horror I felt, or *terror*. Terror of that evil beast who defiled everything with his foul imagination, and who spared nobody!

SARA: Did he talk to you about me?

LUCIO: You have no idea of how he terrorized me! He did just whatever he liked with me! He simply terrified me!

SARA: Oh my child… I never dreamt that things were as bad as that!

LUCIO: If only you'd known…

SARA: I saw that you were crushed… as a child of your age ought never to be. But I never guessed that that was the reason. It used to tear my heart to shreds to see you two children, you and her, the way you were… dear, tender creatures… wilting away. And it grieved my heart to see your father so hard, so obstinate, so determined not to admit that I was right. He would tell me you were both well…

LUCIO: *Well!*

SARA: Yes, well. And I… I would take your little faces in my hands and make him look at them. "Do you still dare to tell me that they're well?" I couldn't stand life any longer. I felt the tortures that were being inflicted upon you… I felt them as if they were biting into my own flesh.

LUCIO: Yes. And when, in point of fact, poor Lia…

SARA: When I saw them bring her back home to me… a helpless cripple… her life – *finished*… And when I saw that the Sisters… the very Sisters who were to blame for my child's being in that terrible condition… were to help me look after her…

LUCIO: They were?…

SARA: Yes, you understand… *they* were to… I wasn't to be left to look after her myself! They were the ones who were to!… I hurled myself at one of them, just like a wild beast… Oh, I don't know what I did to her! They tore her from my grasp… They thought I was possessed by a devil… (*She breaks off, so that she may curb the frantic onrush of hatred which she feels once more assailing her. She begins again immediately.*) Lucio, they made me go away… they forced me to run away… just as if I'd been a madwoman! I begged them, I implored them to bring my baby up here to me… I was quite sure that I'd have been able to make her well again. But I had to have her up here by herself… without him. I couldn't bear the sight of him any longer… I'd have killed him! He wanted me back again. Yes, because… he posed as a saint... set himself up as a tyrant... And then... Well, what made me furious with him... whenever he came near me... was the feebleness, the softness of the man... (*She breaks off with an exclamation and gesture of disgust*) Oh, God!... And yet, I swear to you, Lucio, I'd have made the sacrifice... I'd have made the sacrifice... I'd have overcome the horror that I felt for him from that time on... provided that some good might have come out of it... for *you*... for you, my children. And I stipulated that you at least should be set free and allowed to come and live up here... you and Lia... up here with me. He refused... he wouldn't hear of it. And so... he refused what I demanded, and I refused his demands! You cannot imagine what I suffered! My agony here... and yours there in the seminary! And even if I'd sacrificed myself I couldn't have brought you one moment's comfort in that agony of yours.

LUCIO: I know that you applied to the courts...

SARA: And I lost.

LUCIO: They decided against you?

SARA: Yes, they decided against me! They said it was my duty to remain with him and my daughter! And that my claim that you ought to be taken away from the seminary was an unjust one. And, to cut a long story short, that it was *I*... I, and not he... who was breaking up the family. I was so furious... after two years of desperate ferocious struggle... that I threw up everything... Everything! What else was I to do? I felt such a loathing! You can see the town from up here. I couldn't bear the sight of it any longer. I turned my face away whenever my eyes... strayed in that direction! I felt such a loathing for those churches... those houses... and the court that... All of them! When they deny a mother the right to look after her own children... when a mother who is trying to provide for the health of her own children is condemned in court... you can't help yourself. Life becomes impossible. They condemn you to act as I acted! I threw away everything I possessed and became a peasant. A peasant! Up here... out in the open air... out in the scorching sun!... I was seized with the need... the overwhelming *need*... to be a savage!... I felt the need to sink down to the ground at nightfall... like a beast that's been worked to death. Hoeing, treading out the grain on the threshing floor with the mules... barefoot in the August sun... tramping round and round, with my legs bleeding... and shouting like a drunkard! I felt the need to be brutal with everyone who asked me to have compassion on myself... You know who I mean! This pure man. He's as pure, Lucio, as a babe newly delivered from the hands of God. This man... who's never been able to endure my setting myself on the same level as himself... and who prevented me from destroying myself... by teaching me all the secrets of the countryside... all the secrets of life... the *true* life that's lived out here... far far away from the cursed town... the true life that is the life of the earth. This life which now I *feel*... because my hands tend it... help it to grow, to flower and to bear fruit. And the joy of the rain that comes just at the right moment. And the calamity of the mist that makes the olives wilt, just as they are about to burst into flower... And... Have you see the grass that grows on the bank at the side of the lane here? So fresh and green at daybreak, when the rime's upon it! And the pleasure... You know, it's something so wonderful!... The sheer pleasure of making bread with the same hands that sowed the corn!...

LUCIO: Yes, Mamma! *Yes!* And, as you see, I've come to you...

SARA: My son, the joy you've given me, God alone... God Who sent you to me... He alone could bestow it on me. And I shouted, I shouted in your father's face that I felt myself once again to be blessed among women... *purified*! You've paid me back in full, my son... for everything... with your coming. And, as you see, I too can speak to you about everything. Without being puffed up with pride or cast down with shame. Because I alone know what I've had to suffer... what price I've had to pay... in order that I might become what I now am... something that perhaps nobody any longer knows the meaning of... something... *natural*.

LUCIO: I do. I understand you completely – looking at you. Listening to you.

SARA: I really *have* set myself free. There's nothing I desire, because there's nothing I lack. I hope for nothing, because what I have is sufficient for my needs. My health is sound, my heart's at peace with the world and my mind is serene.

LUCIO: But, Mamma, you can't, you *mustn't* go away from here.

SARA: I've already gone. All my things are on their way to...

LUCIO: No, no! I'll stop it! Yes, this is something that *I shall* talk to him about! And I shan't mince my words!

SARA: You can't do anything to stop it, Lucio...

LUCIO: Yes, I can, I tell you! *I must!*

SARA: You cannot and you must not! And, what's more, I don't want you to. *I don't want you to.*

LUCIO: But all that you've done up here…

SARA: It wasn't for my own sake that I did it. I should like… yes, it's true – and I said as much to your father… I should like to think that what I'd done, I'd done for your sake, yours and Lia's. Yes, that is something you *can* try to stop him from doing. Stop him letting the farm… all the wealth of this farm… go to rack and ruin. As it most certainly will if there's nobody here who knows how to look after it. You still have the right to stop him doing that with the property. If you can't do it on your own behalf, you can at least do it on behalf of your little sister. But not for my sake… and you *mustn't*. I repeat… *I don't want you to.*

LUCIO: It shall be as you wish. I'll do it for my own and Lia's sake. But… where will you go?

SARA: Don't worry about me. We've made all our arrangements. We know where we're going. Just for the present we're going to stay with one of our friends who's a bailiff on a farm some little way from here – at Le Favare. Then next year we're going to be leasing a farm… It's quite near here. And then there'll be a chance of making a little for ourselves… Because up to now, you know, we've never kept a penny for ourselves. But we shall have to start putting something aside…

LUCIO: Yes, you will, because… Mamma, do forgive me… I've not yet had the courage to talk to you about it… You've got two children…

SARA: Yes, *his* children. You haven't seen them yet, of course. They're two sturdy little peasants… baked brown by the sun.

LUCIO: And he…

SARA: Oh, if you only knew how apprehensive you make him… how you terrify him…

LUCIO: *I* do?…

SARA: Yes… He's afraid, and he's ashamed. He's counting the seconds. He's simply dying to get clear of this place. He knows that I'm talking to you at this moment, and I'm quite sure that he's out there, and behaving just like a bitch with a litter of puppies! When she sees her master pick up one of them to show a friend, and she doesn't dare snarl at him! She just keeps on stealing pitiful glances at them, to see what they're doing to her baby…

LUCIO: Won't you call him in?

SARA: Why? Would you like me to?

LUCIO: Yes. And the children too.

SARA: They're probably just outside… They're waiting for me, so that they can make a start. (*She goes to the back of the stage and calls out towards the right*) Oh, Roro! Come on in, will you? Yes, in here! Come on! And bring the children! Come on! Come on!

LUCIO: You call him Roro?

SARA: Yes, that's *my* name for him. His real name's Rosario, and I call him Roro. The little one was already up on the mule. As soon as he finds himself in the saddle, he's happy as a sandboy!

LUCIO: What are the children's names?

SARA: Tonotto… That's the older one… And the other one's Michele. Here they come now. (ARCADIPANE *enters back, leading the two little boys by the hand*) This is Arcadipane. (*The two boys run to her.* TONOTTO *reaches her first, then* MICHELE.) And this is Tonotto. And this (*she takes the younger boy in her arms*)… is Michele.

LUCIO (*bending down to kiss* TONOTTO, *and then kissing* MICHELE *as he perches there in his mother's arms*): How lovely they are, Mamma! So strong!

SARA: They're healthy. (*To* ARCADIPANE) You don't remember Lucio, do you?

ARCADIPANE: Oh, yes. I remember him as a little chap… no bigger than him. (*Pointing to* TONOTTO)

LUCIO: I've got a memory of those days too… But I don't know whether it's really true or not… It's a memory of you too, Mamma. But perhaps it's not really a memory… Perhaps it's a vision that came to me… I don't know… as though from another life… Like in a dream when you're looking out of a window that's ever so far away… and sunk deep in the world of your dream. But seeing you again now… I don't know… I find myself beginning to doubt whether…

SARA: But of course I'm quite a different woman now, as you know very well!

LUCIO: Oh, yes! Of course! But what I meant was… what I'm beginning to doubt… to wonder whether that picture of you was not just something that I'd dreamt. It showed you as so very different… No, not more beautiful, Mamma, you know… Quite the contrary, in point of fact! You're so lovely now… so very much, so very very much more lovely! And the woman of my vision… she, on the other hand, was so very sad. And the picture of him, too, the one that I carried in my mind… But tell me something, Mamma… don't laugh… don't you remember… when we were at home… when you were still living with us… we had a cat… she was all white?…

SARA: A white cat? When you… (*Suddenly she remembers: she sees the picture…*) Yes! Yes! We did! We did have a… But it wasn't a *she*, it was a *tom*! Yes, we did have one… Yes! Yes! It was white… a lovely big white tomcat: Yes! Yes, I remember!

LUCIO: In that case…

SARA: In that case *what*?

LUCIO: The thing I've been remembering all this time must be a picture of you. Yes. A room… a dining room… very large… with a low ceiling…

SARA: Why, yes! The dining room of the house we used to live in…

ARCADIPANE: At the bottom of the path leading up to San Francesco…

LUCIO: I don't remember it at all clearly… I've only got… well, a vague impression of that room…

SARA: Yes, it had a window looking out onto the vegetable gardens over the road…

LUCIO: There was a square table in the middle of the room… I can see it now… With just one place laid… a table napkin… freshly ironed and with the folds still showing stiffly… a bottle of red wine, with the froth in the neck of the bottle… I could catch it on my fingers… just like this!… that sunbeam which was playing down upon it, through a chink in the closed shutters across the window!… He's sitting there… where that table napkin is… and eating, with his head bowed over his plate… The white cat is sitting there too, perched up on the other side of the table… His front legs are stiff, his head high… His tail is hanging down over the edge of the table, and every now and again it moves… just as if it were moving of its own accord… like a little snake. And, Mamma, you're talking to *him*, and not paying any attention to me… Suddenly you turn round, fall down on your knees and take me in your arms… And… I don't know why… you burst into tears… holding me ever so tightly to your breast. I stick my head over your shoulder… in order to look at him… just as if the suspicion's dawned on me that it was he who'd made you cry. I see him get up from the table… abruptly… and his eyes too are red with tears… He goes over to the corner of the room… and dashes out of the room. I'm terribly afraid, and I'm just going to scream out, when you suddenly let go of me and rush out of the room after him. I'm left there… in a state of suspense and bewildered dismay. And then I see the cat jump across to where the plate is… snatch up the meat in its teeth… and jump down from the table. It's curious how vivid my memory still is of that cat… whilst the pictures I have of you… of him and of you… I can remember very clearly how you were both crying.

SARA: It was on your account, my son. I was crying because of you… and so was he.

ARCADIPANE: She was crying because of what she was suffering…

SARA: I was in such a state that I just had to pour out my heart to anyone that came along…

ARCADIPANE: Everybody was sorry for her!

SARA: Lucio, there's something I'm going to tell you now… here in front of him. I've never said it to anyone before… not even to myself. When, in utter despair, I left the house and came up here… I knew quite well… I'd become aware that, under the compassion that he felt for me, there lay… already… a feeling of affection for me… (*Turning towards* ARCADIPANE) Tell me… wasn't there? It's true, isn't it?

ARCADIPANE (*his bashfulness assails him again: he gives assent more by his nod than by his barely audible*): Yes, its true…

SARA: A woman is very quick to notice such things, even if she pretends not to, and goes on treating the man as I managed then to go on treating *him*…

ARCADIPANE: I was her servant… And I swear that even what I felt then…

SARA: There's no need for you to swear anything of the kind. As you'll remember, I began by telling you that what I'm saying now is something that I'm revealing for the first time to myself… And you didn't want to either… did you?… you didn't want to admit to yourself that you were in love with me?

ARCADIPANE: I was afraid to!…

SARA: Very well then. And now I must confess that it was this very thing, this secret awareness of his love, Lucio, that drew me to the land… that made me want to live the life of a peasant. And I was like Roro – I didn't want to admit it to myself either. Rather as if it were some kind of folly that I was bent on committing. But feeling deep down inside me that this was the only way in which I could keep myself from going mad... yes, the only way!... by acting furiously the part of a peasant woman! And that's why I was always so rude to *him*... when he still wouldn't understand... still tried to prevent me from doing what I wanted to do! And now it's your turn, Lucio, to realize that... having made a clean break in my life... as I was forced to do... I can't find any place for you in my present life. You come back to me out of that life, the life that is no longer *my* life, my son, and I can't find any room for you in my present life. It belongs to him and to these two little children. I must, I *must* go with them.

LUCIO: Yes, Mamma, that's only right. And you mustn't think that I want... or hoped that my coming here...

SARA: I know, Lucio. I'm only saying all this so as to give him the strength to face up to you. (*To* ARCADIPANE) And now we must be going.

LUCIO: I know too that I may not even so much as come with you...

SARA: No, Lucio, you can't...

LUCIO: But I should like at least to...

SARA: To what? Tell me... tell me...

LUCIO: Well... I mean... secretly, if you like, Mamma...

SARA: Secretly?...

LUCIO: Yes, I want you to give me the strength... after I've had my talk with him... to set out on my new path... alone... as I must be... and without any longer having anybody to help me... without even a proper place in society.

SARA: But why?... Of course you won't be... Why should you? Don't you want to stay?...

LUCIO: Stay where? In the same house as my father? Like this? (*He points to his lay attire*) You know what he's like!

SARA: But he can't turn you out!

LUCIO: No, he can't turn me out. But he certainly won't want any longer to give me the money to finish my studies...

SARA: I'll give you the money if he refuses! No matter what it costs me!

LUCIO: No, Mamma, you can't...

SARA: I can... Oh yes, I can! No matter what it costs me, I tell you!

LUCIO: No! What I mean is... you *can't*... for the same reason that I can't come away with you, Mamma.

SARA: But it's not the same thing at all! No! If you were to take the money from him… (*A gesture in the direction of* ARCADIPANE) But you'll get it from me, from what I earn with my work.

LUCIO: You owe everything that you earn by your work to your children. No. And, what's more, perhaps it's all for the best that I should give up studying and make some attempt to free myself… just as you have done…

SARA: No! No!

LUCIO: Yes! So that I too may find my own true nature…

SARA: No!

LUCIO: So that my life too may become simple and easy in the humility of toiling with my hands…

SARA: But you won't be able to!…

LUCIO: Oh yes, I shall! I shall!…

SARA: You won't be strong enough to…

LUCIO: I shall find strength.

SARA: No… No… You must do good in life in another way… oh, my son!… using the light that shines here… here behind your brow…

LUCIO: I shall still be able to do good in that way, even when I'm toiling away as a humble labourer.

SARA: No, you mustn't. In this matter you're not to take me as your example. No. I was able to do what I've done because that was the only way I could find my salvation. But you're different… There are so many paths before you.

LUCIO: At the moment I can't see one single one.

SARA: If you've found yourself unable to follow the path he chose for you when you were a child, it'll be his *duty*… now… to give you both the time and the means to find some other path… one that is worthy of you… one along which you may walk… one that will carry you far!

LUCIO: Yes, you're quite right, Mamma. But I didn't mean just talking about me… I meant, talking about… *everything*. I stand in need of comfort at this moment, and you alone can bring me the comfort I need. I've come to you, defying everybody and everything, simply in order to beg for that comfort.

SARA: …What is this comfort, Lucio?

LUCIO: I want to feel that you're near me – even if you're hidden – when I have my talk with him. Perhaps it's so that I shan't say things which I ought not to say. I need this strength to come to me from you. Don't deny me. Afterwards you can go away. No one will stop you. No one will see you go.

SARA: Very well, Lucio, if that's what you want me to...

ARCADIPANE (*apprehensively*): But hidden... *where*?

SARA: No... not hidden. Why should I hide? I've seen him already, and talked to him face to face. And, if the need arises, I will talk to him again. I'll wait up there... The rooms are all empty. He'll never dream that I'd want to stay here. There's not even a chair left up there. I'll sit on the little ledge under the window, and wait till you've finished your talk.

ARCADIPANE: No, Sara... don't do it!

SARA: What are you afraid of?

LUCIO: I'll answer for her. She'll come away with me. She shall return to her sons and to you. You need have no worries on that score.

ARCADIPANE (*to* SARA): But won't *he* think that Lucio's defending the land for your sake too, if you stay here?

SARA: I've already told him to his face we don't need his farm to keep us alive... for we've never taken anything out of it...

LUCIO: And I shall do nothing to prevent him from disposing of it just as he wishes. Don't worry. I told you, I can't go on living in the same house as him. I shall go away too. Besides, Mamma, it doesn't really matter... You go... you go on your way... with him... I'll find my own strength.

SARA: No! No! I'll stay... I'll go upstairs. (*The sound of carriage bells is heard*) You go on... go on. Wait for me at Lotti's Farm... I'll rejoin you there. If it's not Doctor Gionni on his way back, it'll be them. Go on!... Go on! (ARCADIPANE *and the two little boys exeunt back. The noise of bells comes nearer.* SARA *goes over to the door left, and before she goes off she says to* LUCIO:) I am here, my son. (*Exit, closing the door behind her*)

LUCIO *stands there expectantly. Shortly afterwards the carriage stops outside the house.* CICO'S *voice is heard.*

CICO: Here we are! Here we are! I'll help you down! I'll help you down!

DEODATA: No! Take it easy! No! Let me do it, Cico! I know how to lift her.

CICO: Your wheelchair is all ready! There's a good girl! There she goes... racing along as if it was her own two little legs that were carrying her!

LIA *comes into sight in her wheelchair. She is silhouetted against the sunlight at the back of the stage.* CICO *and* DEODATA *come running in after her.*

LIA: Lucio! Lucio! Where are you?

LUCIO (*running over and embracing her*): Lia!

DEODATA (*her first astonishment is rapidly extinguished by a sense of disillusionment, which is near to contempt*): There he is!

CICO: Oh, look! I didn't even notice…

LIA (*freeing herself from his embrace*): Let me look at you! No-No-o-o-o. You look silly! Oh, goodness! You look as if you've shrunk!

DEODATA: You've got the nerve to show yourself in those clothes?…

CICO: He might be just anybody…

LIA: You don't look like *you* any longer!

DEODATA: If you only knew the effect you have on people who see you again looking like this, after… But where on earth did you buy that suit? Can't you see how badly it fits?

LUCIO: What does that matter? Where's my father? Isn't he coming?

LIA: Yes, he's coming… with Monsignor Lelli… in another carriage. They were waiting for the lawyer.

LUCIO: So that they could settle the transfer of the farm?

DEODATA: Oh, just think of it! The moment he claps eyes on you, looking like that! He won't want to listen to a word you've got to say. And meanwhile, just you take a look at her… (*She takes* LIA'*s face between her hands, and shows it to* LUCIO) It's done her good already… the first breath of fresh air, and it's already done her good. Look at her, she's got quite a colour.

LIA: Oh, it's so lovely up here! So very lovely!

LUCIO: So his mind's still set on it?

DEODATA: Your father's, you mean? More than ever!

LIA: Yes… You'll see… He frightens me… And I felt ever so sorry for him too, Lucio… It hurts me to see him…

LUCIO: But does he still suspect nothing?

LIA: About what?

LUCIO: About what's happened to him?

LIA: Oh, no! He hasn't even the vaguest suspicion.

DEODATA: Not the slightest!

467

There is a prolonged pause.

CICO (*his manner is absorbed, for like all the rest he is thinking of the terrible thing that has happened*): And he was dead! Absolutely stone-cold dead! (*A pause*)

DEODATA: Yes, dead.

LIA: I saw him with my own eyes...

LUCIO (*deliberately, meaningfully*): Dead?

LIA: Yes.

LUCIO: Well, in that case, you must tell him! Dead. You too must tell him that he was dead.

LIA: Dead, yes, dead.

DEODATA: We all saw him!

CICO: Dead.

DEODATA: Monsignor Lelli as well!

CICO: Yes, him as well. Dead. He got a good view of him. And then there were the doctors who examined him and *said* he was dead!

DEODATA: One of them wrote out the death certificate. (*A pause*)

LUCIO (*to* LIA): It *was* you, *wasn't* it?

LIA: Me? What about me?

LUCIO: It was you who got them to send for Doctor Gionni?

LIA: Oh, yes! I started to shout at them! Nobody wanted to at first!

DEODATA: I didn't want to because... Well, because I didn't believe it was possible!

CICO: And Monsignor Lelli didn't want to either! He certainly *didn't* want to! I was the one that ran off to fetch Doctor Gionni! I wanted to see too... I mean, what he'd do... with a corpse stuck there in front of him!

LUCIO: And then?

LIA: You know, it happened immediately! Immediately!

LUCIO: What did?

LIA: His heart started beating again! And his face... instead of being all white... as it had been...

CICO: White as white.

DEODATA: Like wax...

LIA: Came back to life again immediately... Oh, I don't know how to describe it to you!... You could see... You could see that the lifeblood was beginning to flow again in his veins...

DEODATA: And the breath was stirring in his breast...

CICO: His lips opened again...

LIA: Yes! Oh, how wonderful it was! You could just see them moving! Ever so slightly! Oh, the joy I felt then! There he lay... still not conscious of life... but he wasn't dead any longer! Joy... at the same time... something... something *terrifying*!

DEODATA (*there is sombreness in her voice; her words come slowly, emphatically*): It makes me tremble still, just to think of it.

A long pause.

CICO (*softly, to* LUCIO, *as if in confidence – a diabolical note in his voice*): You were quite right, you know, to throw away your cassock.

DEODATA (*instantly, to* CICO, *her voice loud and harsh*): No! Don't say that! You're not to say that!

CICO: It just slipped out! (*And he puts his hand over his mouth*)

DEODATA: You promised me you wouldn't say that.

CICO: Yes, I promised you I wouldn't *say* it! But I go on thinking it all right! With a vengeance! (*To* LUCIO) You do realize, don't you, that... Dead!... And he doesn't know a thing about it! Where's he been? He ought to know... and he doesn't! If he doesn't know he's been dead, that's a sure sign that when we die, there's nothing on the other side... nothing at all.

A pause.

LIA (*gives a strange little laugh – it's almost as if she were laughing secretly to herself*): My funny little wings, Deodata... *Mmm?* Those funny little angel's wings. I was to get them so as to make up for not being able to walk down here in this world. It's goodbye, then, to flying about in heaven!

LUCIO (*moved*): No, Lia...

LIA (*gently*): But if Paradise doesn't exist...

There is a pause. Then CICO's *voice cuts into the silence, the words coming slowly, sombrely.*

CICO: The Lord's other house... the one up there... for all who have suffered in patient resignation down here on earth...

DEODATA (*her voice too is slow and sombre*): And who abstained from pleasure that they might not fall into sin...

CICO (*slowly, sombrely*): Those who are sore distressed and those who have been cast out from their inheritance...

DEODATA (*slowly, sombrely*): The good tidings of Jesus Christ...

CICO (*his voice still sombre, still slow*): Nothing... Nothing left at all.

During these last lines the faint sound of carriage bells has been heard. This sound has now stopped. There is a moment of expectancy, filled with dismay and anguish. DR GIONNI *comes in up back.*

GIONNI: Shh, everybody! Shh! Shh! He's coming. He knows.

LUCIO: He's found out?

GIONNI *gives an affirmative nod of the head. Into the silence that falls onstage – a silence heavy with the weight of all that dismay and anguish – DIEGO SPINA enters. He comes in up back and advances downstage, followed at some distance by MONSIGNOR LELLI and MARRA, the notary. He sees no one. He steps off the raised portion between the two pillars, comes over to the table and falls into a seat beside it. He is white with terror, and his eyes are wide open, gazing into vacancy. Everybody looks at him in an agony of suspense and dismay, continuing to maintain that silence which is, in fact, the utterly terrified silence of life when it is brought face to face with death.*

CURTAIN

ACT THREE

The scene is the same as in Act Two, a few minutes later.

When the curtain rises the audience sees once again the same tableau as that on which the preceding act concluded... That's to say, the same characters are in the same positions and caught in the same attitudes. Only DIEGO SPINA *and* LUCIO *are missing. Shortly after the curtain goes up* LUCIO *comes down the stairs right and everyone turns and looks at him anxiously.*

LUCIO: He's locked himself in.

LIA: Did you call him?

LUCIO: I tried to get him to open the door and let me in.

MONSIGNOR LELLI: Wouldn't he?

LUCIO: No.

DEODATA: Didn't he even answer you?

LUCIO: Well, when I kept on and on calling him he shouted, "Go away!"

Pause.

GIONNI (*apprehension in his voice*): You go up, Monsignore! You go on up and try!

LUCIO: No, Monsignore. From the tone of his voice when he ordered me to go away... Well, I'm quite certain that at this moment he'd refuse to see you, too. Don't go up.

Pause.

MONSIGNOR LELLI: It's terrible.

Pause.

LUCIO: Perhaps it's all for the best that he should be alone while he sounds the abyss into which his faith has plunged. And then God will rise again in him.

MONSIGNOR LELLI (*shocked, severe*): God? What God do you think is ever likely to rise again in him?

471

LUCIO (*simply*): That God who dwells in all of us, Monsignore, and who has set us upon our feet.

MONSIGNOR LELLI (*in his pulpit voice, but sincerely*): Upon our feet? What do you mean, upon our feet? Can't you see? Here we are, our knees trembling with terror! And your little sister here... Look at her!... She is not on her feet. You make the earth fall away beneath us... set a yawning abyss under every one of us... and then you say we are on our feet! Look at that woman! (*A gesture in the direction of* DEODATA) Look at that old man! (*A gesture in the direction of* CICO)

CICO (*trembling all over*): You can leave me out of it, Monsignore! You can leave me out of this! To hell with your God! (*He tears his red cap from off his head and flings it onto the ground*) I've got my own devil inside me! I have, I tell you! And from now on nobody's going to bottle him up... never again! (*He picks up his cap again and replaces it on his head*) There! That settles that! And don't call me *old*! Old, my... foot! (*Suddenly turning towards* DEODATA) D'you want me, Deodata? I'll marry you! (*He runs over and embraces her*) I'll marry you! I'll marry you, Deodata!

DEODATA (*trying to free herself;* MARRA, *all the while, splitting his sides with laughter;* LIA *is laughing too – but hers is a different kind of laugh, almost involuntary*): Take your hands off me! Let me go, you lunatic!

CICO (*still hanging on to her frantically*): I'm going to marry you now! Here and now! We won't bother about the law and the sacraments! We'll get married the way the dogs do! And you'll soon see that there's no sin in having your bit of fun!

MONSIGNOR LELLI (*asserting his authority –* GIONNI *meanwhile has hastened over and, with a thrust of his hand, pushed* CICO *away*): That will be enough of that, Cico!

DEODATA (*freeing herself*): Oh, you're a dog all right! Leave me alone!

GIONNI: Let go of her!

CICO (*rounding on* GIONNI): Who asked you to poke your nose in, anyway?

GIONNI: We're not beasts! We're *men*!

MONSIGNOR LELLI (*to* MARRA, *who's still laughing*): And you too, Marra! Stop laughing! Don't let's all take leave of our senses!

While this has been going on LUCIO *has covered his face with a hand.*

472

GIONNI (*to the notary*): Do remember that everything can be heard up-stairs! And it was you... yes, it was you who...

MARRA: Quite unintentionally... Now, you must grant me that! I was absolutely ignorant of the fact that he didn't know anything about it...

GIONNI (*to* MONSIGNOR LELLI): And to think that I'd come dashing over to warn his son! But how on earth was I to know that... today of all days!... when he was coming over here for the very first time... Well, I imagined that it was to have a talk with him. (*A gesture in the direction of* LUCIO) How was I to know that he'd bring the notary with him?

MARRA: Ah, you see... since he wanted to draw up the deed of gift relating to the farm...

GIONNI: Clear as clear! He'd have to be told! I repeat, I thought that he was coming over to persuade his son not to break his heart by renouncing his...

MARRA: Oh, no! No! What I meant was... well, he was bound to find out what had happened. He has to sign the deed of gift. And how could I ask him to sign it if, according to the registrar, he's legally dead? *I* thought he knew. So *I* laughingly ask him, "Oh, by the way, have you got them to rub your name out in the Register of Deaths?" No sooner have *I* got the words out than *I* see Monsignor Lelli signalling to me... And there *he* is... with his face as white as a sheet... frowning away...

GIONNI (*to* MONSIGNOR LELLI): But didn't you try to?...

MONSIGNOR LELLI: Yes, I tried... But he (*a gesture in the direction of the notary*) without realizing...

MARRA: What you mean is... without having the faintest idea...

MONSIGNOR LELLI: Began to talk about the miracle you'd performed...

MARRA: But I mean to say... well, let me put it bluntly... all this fuss and nonsense!... Oh yes, I realize what it must have been like for him... to hear about it all of a sudden, the way he did! But, when all's said and done... well, if it had happened to me... even if it had been a question of being dead... for... half an hour... How long was it in fact?... Three-quarters of an hour... Why worry? If I can give myself a pinch here and now and say, "I'm *alive*"...

MONSIGNOR LELLI (*drawing himself up, sternly*): So you think that that's all there is to it? *Alive*? (*Spreading the syllables one from another*) What do you mean, "*alive*"?

MARRA: Why... *alive*! You're not trying to deny that, *are* you? Does it matter *in what way*?

MONSIGNOR LELLI: It matters more than anything in the world!

MARRA: Well... the doctor here knows *in what way*... In fact we all know really.

MONSIGNOR LELLI: But we are not put into the world merely to live! No! And the other thing that we must all of us do... *die*... it's the sort of thing that... Well, you've seen for yourselves... to know nothing about it... to be unable to say anything about it... it means... that one feels immediately that life is extinguished... it means that one is annihilated.

Pause.

DEODATA (*breaking the silence*): Utter despair.

Pause.

CICO (*breaking the silence*): His soul, as soon as it had left his body, ought to have appeared before the Seat of Divine Justice. It didn't. So what does it mean? That there isn't any Divine Justice. There's nothing when you get to the other side. (*Pause*) So, Monsignore, it's goodbye, Church! Goodbye, Faith!

Pause.

LIA (*breaking the silence; her voice is light and clear and in it there almost seems to smile – so greatly does it tremble – that anguish which is prompted by a sense of desperate need*): God must... *must*!... exist there too!

LUCIO (*as if transfigured by a sudden tremendous onset of divine emotion*): Yes, Lia, He is there! He is there! Now I feel that He is there... that He *must* be there! *That He must be there!* Yes, Monsignore, He must be there so that He may give back their wings to those who, on earth, lacked the power to walk upon their feet!... He *is* there! He is there!... Now I understand, now I feel, really feel, the meaning of Christ's word, CHARITY! Because men cannot always stand upon their feet... not all of them! God Himself has resolved to build His House here upon earth, so that it shall be promised to man of the true life that lies beyond the grave. His Holy House, where the weary, the wretched and the weak may go down upon their knees... where every kind of sorrow and every kind of pride may kneel down. Yes, Monsignore, like this... (*He kneels*) Just as now I kneel down

474

before you... now that I feel myself worthy once again to put on my habit in the name of the divine sacrifice of Christ and of the faith of my fellow men!

MONSIGNOR LELLI (*stooping and laying his hands on* LUCIO's *head*): My son, blessed are you, for God has stepped down from your mind and once again has entered into your heart!

DEODATA (*in joyous amazement*): He's going to put on his cassock again?

CICO (*almost ferociously*): But what about what happened? What about *that*?

MONSIGNOR LELLI (*still stooping over* LUCIO): What do you mean, "what happened"?

CICO: To him... Him that's up there!... Came back to life, and doesn't know a thing about what's on the other side.

MONSIGNOR LELLI: And who told you that God allows those who return from beyond the grave to *know*? It is your duty to *believe*, not to know!

LUCIO (*getting up*): In God there is no death!

LUCIO *makes his way, radiant, to the stairs right, so as to go up and put his cassock on again.* SARA, *who has remained hidden, listening to all that has just happened, opens the door left at this moment and reveals herself. She is trembling all over with emotion. She calls out to* DR GIONNI.

SARA: Doctor... Doctor... (*They all turn in utter amazement*)

GIONNI (*going over to her*): Oh, it's you, Signora Spina? You were in there?

SARA: Yes. Just as my son wished.

GIONNI: Lucio?

SARA: Yes. So that I might give him strength. But he's found it... he's found it in himself... *for* himself... he's found the strength he needed to carry out the sacrifice...

GIONNI: That had to be made if his father was to be saved. Now perhaps... up there... when he sees him dressed in his cassock again...

SARA: Yes! Yes! I'm trembling all over... Oh, you can see for yourself! Now he no longer has any need of me. So I can go away. Tell him that I bless him for what he's doing. No one can possibly know better than *I* do just what it is that he's doing. He's talked to me about life... about how he *feels* it! How he feels it! How he would *live* it!

He's renouncing it! He is going now to put on his cassock again... Once again he will die.

GIONNI: He himself said that in God there is no death.

SARA: Yes. It's true... in this particular sense... Yes, you see... It's true in this way... There are saints even on earth.

MONSIGNOR LELLI: To rekindle in the darkness of death the divine light of faith... That faith which is charity towards all those to whom every good thing has been denied in life.

DEODATA: He might have kept that light burning in himself, without waiting till he saw his father lying dead... and his father and all the rest of us absolutely out of our wits with despair.

MONSIGNOR LELLI: And then you wouldn't have seen how God recalled him unto Himself. Neither would you have seen how he came to realize how great was his need of faith.

CICO (*utterly fed-up*): Now don't say another word! Not another word! As far as I'm concerned what you said just now is good enough for me... that God can't allow those who come back from beyond the grave to know anything about it... There, you see... That's good enough for me. (*And immediately, in an undertone, just as if there were really someone else speaking from within him*) Although, all the same, He might allow it... He might let us know... seeing that we've got someone here who *has* come back!

MONSIGNOR LELLI: It would be the end of life.

CICO: Why would it be the end of life?

MONSIGNOR LELLI: Because life is given to you on condition that you live it out without *knowing*... simply *believing*. And woe betide the man who believes that he knows! God alone knows everything, and man when he appears before Him must bow his head and bend his knee.

At this moment the deafening report of a gun is heard. The noise comes from upstairs, but it re-echoes and reverberates at the back of the stage left. Everyone is shocked into speechlessness. Their first reaction is to think that DIEGO SPINA *has killed himself. They all turn and look up the stairs.*

DEODATA: Oh, God! What's happened?

CICO: He's killed himself! He's killed himself!

LIA: No! Papa! Papa! Hurry! Hurry!

MONSIGNOR LELLI: Lucio's up there! Can he really have?...

GIONNI (*holding* CICO *back*): No, the sound came from over there! (*He points in the direction of back left*)

And, as a matter of fact, ARCADIPANE *appears upstage left.*

He is in evident distress. He is lightly wounded in the scalp, and he is holding his left temple in his bloodstained hands. As soon as SARA *catches sight of him, she screams and rushes over to him, terrified. Everybody speaks at once.*

SARA: Oh! It's you. Who did it? What have they done to you?

MONSIGNOR LELLI: Did he do it?

ARCADIPANE: He fired at me. From the window. Oh, it's nothing! It's nothing! Look… here… only a scratch!

GIONNI: Let me have a look at it! Let me look at it!

MARRA: Has he gone out of his mind? After all these years?

LIA: What happened? What happened?

DEODATA: Your father! He shot at him from the window!

CICO: He tried to kill him!

SARA (*to* GIONNI, *who is examining the wound*): Is it very bad, Doctor? Is it?

GIONNI: No, as good luck would have it! Nothing at all! Barely scratched him!

At this moment DIEGO SPINA *comes hurtling downstairs like a madman. He is still armed with the gun and is grappling with* LUCIO, *who is trying to hold him back.* LUCIO *is dressed once more in his priest's cassock. At* DIEGO's *appearance there is a burst of simultaneous cries of horror, terror, entreaty, protest.*

ALL: Oh, my God! Here he is!

No! No!

Papa! Papa!

Merciful God!

Hold him, Lucio! Hold him!

Everyone is perplexed, hesitating between courage and fear, wondering whether to fling himself upon SPINA *and disarm him, or to get out of range of his gun. Meanwhile* DIEGO SPINA *points the gun at* ARCADIPANE, *raises it and takes aim, shouting to* LUCIO, *from whom he has managed to free himself.*

DIEGO: Leave me alone! (*And to the others*) Get out of my way! Get out of the way! First of all I'm going to kill him! Then you can arrest me!

SARA (*leaving* ARCADIPANE *and going over to him*): Who are you going to kill? Why should you want to kill him?

LUCIO (*running forwards to shield her*): No, Mamma!

And at the same moment ARCADIPANE, *freeing himself from the restraining hands that are trying to hold him back and out of harm's way, says:*

ARCADIPANE: No! What are you doing, Sara? Let me go!

But when SARA *has uttered her challenge* CICO *has leapt forwards and hurled himself on the gun which is levelled at* ARCADIPANE. *He forces the muzzle down and grabs hold of* DIEGO SPINA *round the waist.* SPINA *struggles to free himself. They all talk at once.*

CICO: Now keep still! Are you out of your mind?

DIEGO: Take your hands off me! (*To* SARA) No, it's not you I want to kill! Get out of the way! He's the one I want to kill!

SARA: You'll have to kill me first!

MONSIGNOR LELLI: Well done, Cico! Hold him! Hold him tight!

GIONNI (*rushing over*): For pity's sake, Signor Spina!

MARRA (*rushing over*): You don't mean that seriously, do you? After all these years?

DEODATA: Your daughter's here! Your *daughter*!

LIA: Papa! Please, Papa!

DIEGO (*just going on with what he was saying, turning to* SARA *and then to the others as he speaks*): He mustn't live one moment longer! *He must not live one moment longer!* Let me go!

SARA (*confronting him*): Yes, let him go! I am here! Let him go, Cico! I want to see what he'll do!

ARCADIPANE: Don't provoke him, Sara!

SARA: You stay where you are!

LUCIO: Mamma!

SARA (*to* LUCIO): And you, don't stand in the way! All of you, let him talk… To *me!* (*To* DIEGO) What is it you want to do?

DIEGO: I don't know! I don't know! I can do anything I like!

SARA: You can do nothing!

DIEGO: I can do anything I want to! *Anything!*

SARA: Because you no longer believe that God sustains and holds you up...

CICO: We're the ones that're holding you now! Holding you *back*!

SARA: Because of this, you've become a beast and *kill*? But not even the beasts kill in this fashion.

DIEGO: I've lost all sense of reason! I see neither rhyme nor reason in anything! There's nothing I can't do! (CICO *hasn't slackened his grip upon him. Now* DIEGO *says to him, in a tremendous outburst of rage and handing him the gun at the same time:*) Take the gun, and let go of me! (CICO *lets go of him, keeping hold of the gun*) There you are... Now I'm disarmed! Go on, arrest me! There he is, over there... wounded. Yes, I tried to kill him... the moment I caught sight of him out of the window... standing down there... on the ground... on this earth that...

SARA: He was waiting for me... We were going away together...

DIEGO: No... I mean... on the ground... this earth... down onto which I've fallen, out of the cloud of falsehood up there... the earth... things... You, you've been living here with him... Oh, but you're not going to live with him any longer, you know! Oh no, not now! Not now! (*And once more he springs forwards, intent upon seizing her, but at once he is caught and held back again, just as at the self-same moment* ARCADIPANE *springs forwards in his turn. Once again everybody is talking at the same time.*)

CICO (*on this side of the stage – he and* MONSIGNOR LELLI *and* MARRA *are grouped around* DIEGO SPINA): Trying it on again, eh? Oh, I shan't let you go again!

MONSIGNOR LELLI: Aren't you satisfied with what you've done already?

MARRA: This is utter madness!

DIEGO: Neither *I* nor he shall have her! I can't bear the sight of him any longer! Neither I nor he shall have her! Yes! Yes! I'm mad!

ARCADIPANE (*who is being held back by* SARA, LUCIO *and* DEODATA): God help you if you so much as try to lay hands on her! Huh, so you'd like to take her back now, would you?

SARA: No! Now be quiet! Stay where you are! This is my affair! And I'm going to deal with it myself!

LUCIO: Let him say what he has to! You must show him some consideration!

DEODATA: He's not himself! No, he's not himself any longer!

479

DIEGO (*carrying on with what he was saying, turning to the three of them who are holding* ARCADIPANE *back*): Yes! Why yes, let him! Let him kill me! Let him kill me! It'd all be all for the best! He's got the right to! I tried to kill him! All the crimes in the world and this as well! Only... There's this, you see... You don't have to pay for what you do... Not a thing!... Not if you pay for everything here! Prison? The whole world's a prison, a prison there's no escaping from! And there's nothing on the other side! *I know!* (*Suddenly addressing himself to* GIONNI) Doctor, did you enjoy yourself? Was it a wonderful joke, sticking a needle into my heart, like a rabbit?

GIONNI: But it was your daughter who... Look at her!

LIA (*in anguish*): Papa... Papa!...

DIEGO (*flinging himself down by* LIA *and embracing her as she sits there in her chair*): Oh, my darling child, why did you do it? Was it because you wanted to make me see the havoc... the havoc I've made of my life? (*Getting up again and turning towards the* DOCTOR) But you, you who knew all the horror that I should find confronting me when I opened my eyes again, how could you possibly bring yourself to do it? Because I was dead... as you know... You all saw me... Dead... Dead... You saw me too, Monsignore!... Dead... And another doctor... Not he... Another doctor examined me and said that I was dead... signed the certificate!... And then he... thrust me back into life again... like a rabbit... And I knew nothing at all about it... *I know* nothing about it! I know nothing about it now, Monsignore! Bankruptcy... If life were a business, I should be bankrupt! I can cry it aloud to the whole world... Bankrupt! I say it and I know! If yours is a faith that is sincere, as mine was, then abandon it! Lose your faith! Lose it!

MONSIGNOR LELLI: But your son... Look at him!... He has regained his faith!

DEODATA: He's put his cassock back on again! Look, he's put his cassock back on again!

MONSIGNOR LELLI: Once more he dwells in the light of God!

DIEGO (*caught in surprise, to* LUCIO): You?

LUCIO: Yes, Father.

SARA: For your sake!

MONSIGNOR LELLI: For all our sakes!

DEODATA: Yes, for all our sakes, for all our sakes, for the sake of his little sister.

DIEGO: But how? Why? Now? Now that I know?...

CICO: No! No! You know nothing at all! God can't allow anybody that comes back from beyond the grave to know anything! So what's happened to you is no proof of anything! No proof of anything at all!

DIEGO: What do you mean, it's "no proof of anything at all"? I was dead, and my soul... My soul!... Where was it during all the time that I was dead?

LUCIO (*simply and gently*): With God, Father. Your soul *is* God, Father. And you call it yours. It is God, don't you see? And what can you possibly know of death, if God now, by means of one of His miracles...

DIEGO: One of *His* miracles?... But it was *he* who did it! (*Pointing to* DR GIONNI)

LUCIO: It was not he! Do you really believe that all the dead can be called back to life by anything that a doctor can do? He himself recognizes that it was a miracle!

DIEGO: Yes, a miracle of his science!

LUCIO: If our soul is God within us, what else would you call his science and a miracle achieved by means of it, if not one of His miracles, wrought when He would have it accomplished? And what can you possibly know of death if there is no death in God? And if He is now once again to be found in you, as He is still to be found in all of us here... eternal, in this moment of our life which only in Him is life without end?

DIEGO: You... You're talking to me like this? Now? You, for whose sake I...

LUCIO: Yes. So that you may rise again from your death, Father. Do you see? You had shut your eyes against life, in the belief that you were bound to see the other life that lay beyond the grave. This has been your punishment. God blinded you to that other life, and now He makes you open your eyes again to this life... which is His life... in order that you may live it... and in order that you may allow other people to live it... toiling and suffering and rejoicing like everyone else.

DIEGO: I? And your sister? And what about you? I tried to... I meant to kill... And all the evil that I've done...

481

LUCIO: I take it upon myself, Father, and I redeem it! If now I take up the burden of all this evil that you have done, and if I feel it... if I feel it to be good... to be a blessing upon me... then that is God! Do you see what I mean? That is God's doing... God who sees you with your own eyes... who sees what you do... what you have done... and what you must do now.

DIEGO: What must I do?

LUCIO: You must live, Father. In God... in the works that you will perform. Arise and walk... walk in the ways of life. And leave to this man (*pointing to* ARCADIPANE), leave to this man the woman that is his. To this mother you must yield her daughter. But you mustn't just sit there waiting, Lia... I feel, my dear little sister... I feel that you mustn't wait for me to go back... You mustn't wait for me to make the organ sing out... in Lia's name... filling the church with all the glory of God's heaven! (*He turns to his mother*) Mamma! Mamma! Call your daughter to you!

SARA (*is transfigured, as if reflecting the divine exaltation of her son; she holds out her hands to* LIA): My daughter! My daughter!

LIA (*she rises from her chair at her mother's call, and runs over to her on her still unsteady legs*): Mamma! Mamma!

LUCIO *appears as if bathed in a divine light.*

CICO: *This is* a miracle! This is the *miracle*! (*And he falls down on his knees*) She's walking... She's walking...

And all the others too, dumbfounded with joy, stand there, their lips shaping the word:

Miracle.

CURTAIN

The Life that I Gave Thee

La vita che ti diedi (1923)

Translated by Robert Rietti

CHARACTERS

DONN'ANNA LUNA
LUCIA MAUBEL
FRANCESCA NORETTI, *her mother*
DONNA FIORINA SEGNI, *Donn'Anna's sister*
PADRE DON GIORGIO MEI
LIDA
FLAVIO
} *Donna Fiorina's children*
ELISABETTA, *Donn'Anna's old nurse*
GIOVANNI, *the old gardener*
MOURNERS

ACT ONE

An isolated house in the Tuscan countryside.

A cold and almost empty room of grey stone in DONN'ANNA LUNA's *home. A bench, a cabinet, a writing table and a few other pieces of antique furniture with a sense of tranquillity banished from the world. Even the light that comes in from an ample window seems to have originated in a very distant life.*

A doorway at the back, and another in the wall on the right, much closer to the back wall than to the proscenium.

As the curtain rises, in front of the doorway on the right, which leads to the room where lies the dying son of DONN'ANNA LUNA, *some local women have gathered, some on their knees and others standing, but all bent in the attitude of prayer, with their hands linked in front of their mouths. One group, almost touching the ground with their foreheads, meekly recite the litanies for the dying; others show distress and dismay as they wait for the moment of death. At a certain moment they indicate to the others that they should interrupt the litany, and after a brief silence, they also kneel and first one, then another offers the supreme invocations for the deceased.*

Some intoning the prayer, others the refrain.

FIRST MOURNER: *– Sancta Maria – Ora pro eo.*

SECOND MOURNER: *– Sancta Virgo Virginum – Ora pro eo.*

THIRD MOURNER: *– Mater Christi – Ora pro eo.*

FOURTH MOURNER: *– Mater Divinæ Gratiæ – Ora pro eo.*

FIFTH MOURNER: *– Mater purissima – Ora pro eo.*

DON GIORGIO *(from within)*: *Proficiscere, anima christiana, de hoc mundo, in nomine Dei Patris omnipotentis, qui te creavit.*

FIRST MOURNER: O saints in heaven, give him your help.

SECOND MOURNER: Angels of the Lord, accept his soul.

THIRD MOURNER: Jesus Christ receives now the soul whom He called to Him.

FOURTH MOURNER: And the blessed spirits lead him from Abraham's bosom to the Almighty.

FIRST MOURNER: Lord, have mercy upon us

SECOND MOURNER: Christ, have mercy upon us.

FIFTH MOURNER: Give him eternal rest, O Lord, and may your perpetual light shine on him.

ALL: Rest in peace.

They remain awhile on their knees, each praying silently, and they then stand, making the sign of the cross. From the room of the dead, DONNA FIORINA SEGNI *and the priest* DON GIORGIO MEI *enter, looking dazed and sorrowful. The former is a quiet lady from the country in her fifties, wearing the latest fashion in an awkward manner because she has lost her shape through the years, but this is the style of those who live in the city, which her children would like to see her wearing. (One knows what it is like when children start taking their parents in hand!)* DON GIORGIO *is an awkward, portly, country priest who speaks with difficulty, and always feels he must add something to what others are saying, or even to what he himself has said, although many times he doesn't really know what. If others give him time to speak in his own way, he will do so pertinently and well, for intrinsically he is literate and by no means a fool.*

DON GIORGIO (*softly, to the women*): Go, my children. Go now – and continue to pray for the soul of the departed.

The women bow first to him and then to DONNA FIORINA *and leave by the door at the back. The two remain in silence, the one as if lost in grief for her sister and the other uncertain between the disapproval that he would like to convey and the comfort he doesn't know how to offer. At one moment* DONNA FIORINA *can no longer bear the sight of her sister's despair. She flings herself onto the bench and covers her face with her hands.* DON GIORGIO *moves closer to her, quietly, and looks at her without saying anything. He shakes his head, then raises his hands in a gesture which seems to signify placing his trust in God. Finally he comes out with what has been on his mind.*

DON GIORGIO: And Donn'Anna did not even kneel down!

FIORINA: She'll go out of her mind, Don Giorgio. Did you notice the look in her eyes and the tone of her voice when she asked us to leave her alone in there?

DON GIORGIO: I did, Donna Fiorina. But we need not fear for her reason. What I'm concerned with is that she will reject the consolation which faith might give her.

FIORINA (*rising, distracted*): But what will become of her now – living here, alone?

DON GIORGIO (*trying to calm her*): No, no – not alone. She has asked Elisabetta to stay with her. Elisabetta is a very sensible woman and…

FIORINA: If you had heard my poor sister this evening… (*She cuts herself short as she sees the old nurse* ELISABETTA *enter from the room of the deceased and make for the door at the back of the room*) Oh, Elisabetta… What is she doing?

ELISABETTA: Nothing. Gazing at him. That's all.

FIORINA: Not crying? Even now?

ELISABETTA: No, just gazing at him.

FIORINA: Oh God!… If she would only cry!

ELISABETTA: …And she keeps on saying that he is "there"!

GIORGIO: He?

ELISABETTA: Yes. There.

GIORGIO: What does she mean by "there", Donna Fiorina?

ELISABETTA: And she keeps wandering about and muttering to herself.

FIORINA: And we can do nothing!

ELISABETTA: She is so sure in what she says. It's uncanny to hear her.

FIORINA: What else does she say?

ELISABETTA: "He's gone," she says, "but he will come back"!

FIORINA: Come back?!

ELISABETTA: Just like that! With such certainty! But as for coming back… he's certainly gone! She stared straight into my eyes and kept repeating, "He will come back." She insists that that body lying there is not his.

DON GIORGIO: Not his?

FIORINA: I heard her say that too… this evening.

ELISABETTA: And she wants the body to be taken away at once.

DONNA FIORINA *buries her face in her hands again.*

487

DON GIORGIO: Does she mean to the church?

ELISABETTA: Away from here, she said. And she doesn't want it clothed.

FIORINA: But...

DONNA FIORINA: Not clothed?!

ELISABETTA: When I said that we really must dress him...

DON GIORGIO: Of course. Before rigor mortis sets in.

ELISABETTA: She seemed quite horrified. My orders are only to see to the washing of the body. She wants him to be washed and taken away wrapped in a sheet – that's all. And I'm going to do what she told me.

She goes out by the door at the back – shutting the door.

FIORINA: She'll go out of her mind! Out of her mind!

DON GIORGIO: I suppose she means it's useless to clothe a person who's already divested of everything.

FIORINA: Perhaps. But truthfully I'm at a loss to understand her motive.

DON GIORGIO: Why can't she behave like other people?

FIORINA: It's not that she's perverse...

DON GIORGIO: No. But it's all very misguided. Behaving, I mean, so unlike other people, flouting all custom, not even allowing others to share her sorrow. You must admit that no normal mother could understand this desire that her son's body should be treated so unceremoniously and left naked like that!

FIORINA: I agree. I'm equally puzzled.

DON GIORGIO: It looks so bad! I mean...

FIORINA: She's always been the same. She seems to listen to what other people are telling her and then, quite suddenly, she'll say the most unexpected things. When you hear what she says – it strikes you as being true, but later... when you think it over... it leaves you hopelessly puzzled, because nobody else would have said such a thing. She frightens me. Honestly, I'm afraid of listening to her. I can't even bear to look her in the face... There's something about her eyes...

DON GIORGIO: Poor unhappy woman.

FIORINA: To see her son die like that... after being ill for only two days!

DON GIORGIO: Her only child, too. And so soon after he came home!

At this moment the old gardener GIOVANNI *appears on the threshold at the back of the room, looking frightened, and makes for the other door on the right. He remains in the open doorway a moment, staring at the corpse inside with amazement and anguish. He kneels down, almost touching the floor with his forehead, and remains in that position while* DONNA FIORINA *and* DON GIORGIO *continue their conversation.*

FIORINA: And after waiting seven years for him to return. He was only a lad when he left.

DON GIORGIO: I remember. He went away to take his engineering course at Liège.

FIORINA (*sadly and disapprovingly*): Liège! That's where...

DON GIORGIO: I know! In fact, I'm only waiting here because there's something I ought to tell her.

The old gardener rises to his feet, crosses himself and makes for the exit at the back.

FIORINA (*waits for the gardener to go, then asks anxiously*): You mean... he told you at the end about...

DON GIORGIO: Exactly!

FIORINA: About that woman? If only they'd got married when they first met – in his student days at Florence!

DON GIORGIO: She's French, isn't she?

FIORINA: By marriage. Italian by birth. They were students together in Florence. Then she married a Frenchman, Monsieur Maubel, and he took her first to Liège and afterwards to Nice.

DON GIORGIO: I see. And I suppose the lad followed her.

FIORINA: It was terrible for his mother. You see, he never came home, never once in all those seven years. Not even to spend a few days with his mother. And at last, when he did return... to die like that... so suddenly... in two days. And he was still writing to that woman – still writing to her. I suppose he must have told you that. Did he – did he make provision for the children?

DON GIORGIO: What children?

FIORINA: Surely you knew? She had two boys.

DON GIORGIO: Ah, you mean *her* children. Yes, he told me. He said they had been the salvation of their mother and of himself.

FIORINA: He said that?

DON GIORGIO: Yes.

FIORINA: Then, they are not – they aren't *his* children?

DON GIORGIO (*immediately*): Oh no, signora. You can't call an adulterous love pure – even if it goes no further than the heart and the

489

mind. And I'm certain that, in this case, nothing of the sort... He even told me so himself.

FIORINA: Actually, my sister was positive too. But, God forgive me, I couldn't believe her. They were so much in love. I couldn't help suspecting that the two children were...

DON GIORGIO (*interrupting*): No, no!

FIORINA (*listening acutely and making a sign to* DON GIORGIO *to be quiet*): Oh God – can you hear her? She's talking to him. (*She quietly goes closer to the doorway, trying to hear what the woman is saying to her dead son*)

DON GIORGIO: She's delirious, poor soul!

FIORINA: No. She understands that we all know about that misfortune. Who knows what she must feel about that!

DON GIORGIO: You must be firm with your sister and insist on her going away from here – at least for a while.

FIORINA: That's out of the question! I wouldn't even try.

DON GIORGIO: At least take her to your own villa. That's quite near.

FIORINA: If she'd come! But she has never left this house for the last twenty years. That's why she's become more and more of a stranger to everybody.

DON GIORGIO: Brooding and solitude are most unhealthy. It's bad for her.

FIORINA: The solitude is within herself. You need only look at her eyes to understand that she could never find any sort of distraction in an ordinary life. But it's unhealthy to shut herself up in this great empty house... I couldn't stand it. These oppressive rooms... all so silent. The sound of the leaves when it's windy... It's frightening. It seems – I don't know – it seems as if time had buried itself here. I can't tell you what I've suffered, thinking of her being all alone here.

The door opens.

(*quietly*) She's here.

DONN'ANNA *enters the room. She is very pale and moves almost as if she were sleepwalking. Her expression and tone of voice give the impression that she is totally remote from everything and everyone around her. This is even more disturbing because of the almost divine simplicity with which they are expressed. She speaks as though she were in a lucid delirium that is almost the tremulous fluttering of interior flames which are devouring her. She goes towards the door at the back without saying*

anything; then on the threshold she pauses when she sees ELISABETTA
*return together with two servants carrying a bowl of steaming water
infused with balsam. She says with mild and pained impatience:*

DONN'ANNA (*whispering*): Quickly, Elisabetta. Do what I told you. Now!

ELISABETTA (*excusing herself*): I have a great deal to do—

DONN'ANNA (*to cut her short*): Of course... go ahead, Elisabetta.

ELISABETTA: And the doctor will be making another visit, just to be
sure that—

DONN'ANNA (*interrupting*): Yes, yes, of course... oh look: there's another
wreath on the floor. One of those women must have dropped it.

ELISABETTA *picks it up and places it on a table, then moves to the door
on the right. Just as she is about to exit,* DONN'ANNA *reminds her:*

Do what I said, please, Elisabetta.

ELISABETTA (*as she goes*): Certainly, signora. I will. (*She goes*)

DONN'ANNA: To pray... to kneel down... yes, one should bend under
the burden of grief. To me, it's not as easy as that. I stood watching
him die, moment by moment in there. I lived through every one of
those terrible moments with the whole of my being. I felt I couldn't
breathe! I prayed to make my knees bend, but they wouldn't. He
wants me to remain on my feet... here... in this house... never to rest.

DON GIORGIO: You know that true life is not here.

DONN'ANNA: I do not believe the being whom God has created is dead
to Him – neither is the being whom I created dead to me. He has
merely been taken to God... to be with Him.

DON GIORGIO (*compassionately*): Yes – that's how it is. Exactly like that.

DONN'ANNA (*with anguish*): But I still remain here, Don Giorgio.

DON GIORGIO: Yes, my poor dear Anna. Yes.

DONN'ANNA: And don't forget that for us God is not distant... out
there... He is still close – within us, and not only us... He continues
to live for all those who have departed this life.

GIORGIO: Yes, the dead exist in our memory.

DONN'ANNA (*stares at him as though wounded by the word "memory",
then lowers her head as if she doesn't want him to see her pain; she
sits down and says almost to herself*): I can't talk about it any more.
I can't listen to anyone else talking about it.

FIORINA: But why, Anna?

DONN'ANNA: Memory – that can be a terrible word.

DON GIORGIO: I mean *in* our memory.

DONN'ANNA: Yes, but you speak of memory as something dead. To me it's a living thing. I have no other life now... none that counts. To me, memory is real and vivid and alive... not just death and shadows.

DON GIORGIO: What would you have me say?

DONN'ANNA: I would have you know that God means my son to go on living – in me! I know that he, as he was, is not eternal, but here, within me, he lives today... tomorrow... and for just as long as I myself endure. My son *must* live... he must live. I do not mean in some other world, but here, among actual living things, and nobody can possibly take him from me.

DON GIORGIO, *as if to recall her from such morbid thoughts, points upwards as if to indicate the Almighty.*

DONN'ANNA (*understanding his gesture*): No! God? God does not destroy life.

DON GIORGIO: I am thinking of the life which he once had.

DONN'ANNA: Yes, you are thinking that in *there* lies a body which can no longer see or hear. And do you really believe that is all that remains of him? Something done with? And you want to clothe him again in one of the suits he brought back with him from France. But I can tell you no clothes will ever bring warmth to that cold body.

DON GIORGIO: But it is customary, signora...

DONN'ANNA: Yes, yes... custom! To recite prayers and burn candles... well, do it, do it, but quickly. I want his room to be just as it was. Alive, alive with the life I gave it... awaiting his return... with everything just as he left it before he went away. My son who went away and never came back. (*She notices the look Don Giorgio exchanges with her sister*) Don't look at Fiorina like that. Her children also went away last year... to go to the city. Flavio and Lida. Do you suppose *they* will return?

This worries FIORINA *and she starts to cry.*

No – don't cry. I too cried my heart out when he left, without knowing why. Just like you who weep without knowing the reason.

FIORINA: No... I'm crying for you, Anna.

DONN'ANNA: He is still away. Not dead. Don't look at Don Giorgio like that, Fiorina. Your children – Flavio and Lida... they will come back soon, won't they?

FIORINA: Yes, Anna. They will come straight here. I want you to see them too.

DONN'ANNA: You don't suppose when they come back, they will be the same? No. The children who went away are as dead to you as my son who came back to me.

FIORINA *sobs bitterly.*

DONN'ANNA: I remember how I wept when he went away. It seemed very foolish, but I know now that I was saying goodbye to my child as I knew him. Why are you crying, Fiorina?

FIORINA: I am crying for you, Anna, not for myself.

DONN'ANNA (*taking her sister's face in her hands and gazing into her eyes with tenderness*): Oh, Fiorina, you no longer exist as you were – neither do I. How can you have changed so much? I see you now as you *were* – like your name: a flower. Wouldn't you rather I thought of you like that?

FIORINA: Yes, Anna, yes.

DONN'ANNA: The body must continually change, and it leaves images that exist only in our mind... shadows, dreams... memories of dreams... that is all!

FIORINA: Yes, memories of dreams.

DONN'ANNA: If we keep our memories *alive*, then the dream to us is a living thing. My son, as I see him, is alive to me. The body, in there, is nothing!

FIORINA (*quietly*): But it *is* in there, all the same.

DONN'ANNA: Try to understand what I mean. Perhaps *you* need to have brooded for seven years over a son who did not come back before you can realize the truth. They never come back. That goes deeper than all sorrow – it is as bitter as death.

FIORINA: My dear, you must try to get some rest.

DONN'ANNA: Not yet. He needs me now more than ever.

DON GIORGIO: What can I say to help you, sister?

DONN'ANNA: I cried when he arrived and I saw how he had changed. I hid my tears from him when I realized that my son – as I knew him – would never come back. What I saw was a stranger... someone quite different.

DON GIORGIO: He was changed. That is what you were saying just now about our sister. We know that life is continually changing us.

DONN'ANNA: I could no longer recognize him as the son who left me. I searched his face for something – anything that I remembered… that smile of his, that sudden lighting up of his face – you remember, Father? But his eyes had grown cold. His face was a mask. His brow was lined… that silky hair, like gold in the sun – was gone. He had grown bald… exactly as he is in there!

DON GIORGIO (*puzzled*): Yes, yes, perhaps…

DONN'ANNA (*continuing with her thoughts*): This was someone whose eyes were so different and I could not even be sure he saw me. When he touched me, the touch was not his. And what do I know about his life? All those seven years he was away from me. How he looked at things, what he felt about them. Don't you see I had only lost something which I never knew and never could know… his life as it was in another place away from me. You expect me to weep for the dead… but what causes the tears?

DON GIORGIO: We weep because something has been taken away from us.

DONN'ANNA: Yes, we mourn our own death in that person.

FIORINA: Oh, Anna, it's not that…

DONN'ANNA: Yes. We weep for ourselves. We weep because the dead person can no longer bring us to life in his mind, no longer see us, no longer touch us. If I were to cry now, I should be crying for myself… When he was far away from me, I used to say, "If he is thinking about me at this moment, I am alive for him," and then I was not lonely. But what can I say to myself now if I acknowledge he is dead? No. He is alive with all the life that I gave him and as long as I live, I shall continue to give him life. Don't you see, life does not depend on a body that may or may not be in front of our eyes. It could be standing right there before us… and be dead in terms of the life we gave. Sometimes his eyes would open wide, as if a joyful thought had made him smile… but he had lost that *joie de vivre* in the course of his life… but not in me! To me he still has that expression of joy that makes his eyes twinkle when he hears me call him. Don't you see, that does not mean that I should prevent him from going away to live his own life… a life which is a wedge between us. No: he will have life here… in my eyes as I see him… on my lips that speak to him. I am not jealous if he wants to live there… with her… whom he loves. Let him give all his love to her, and I will wait here for his return. (*A pause*) Father, you know about his affair with that woman?

DON GIORGIO: Yes. He spoke to me about her. And I must tell you, Donn'Anna (*embarrassed*), he told me he would like her to be informed of his death and that you should write to the woman's mother and break the news gently to her.

DONN'ANNA (*pensive*): His mistress must never lose her love for him.

DON GIORGIO: What do you mean?

DONN'ANNA (*quite naturally*): If her love is strong enough to overcome death and to keep him alive in her heart – as I do now – there is no need of his physical presence. Then... (*she hesitates*)

FIORINA: Anna, you mustn't talk like that.

DON GIORGIO: Do you really believe that we can defeat death in that way?

DONN'ANNA: Is it not the right way? Is it not better than our usual pretence? We put tombstones over our dead so that we can distance ourselves from them. We want our dead to be *really* dead, so that we can live our own lives in peace. Would you have me pass death over in that way?

DON GIORGIO: No, no, signora. We must not forget the dead, that would be wrong, but to think of them alive in the way you speak of...

FIORINA: ...As if we expected them to return...

DON GIORGIO: ...Which is no longer possible.

DONN'ANNA: I see. You mean we should think of my son as a corpse... as he is in there.

DON GIORGIO: What else?

DONN'ANNA: And feel quite certain that he can never return. Cry bitterly, bitterly... and then... soothe ourselves little by little.

DON GIORGIO: Find consolation in some way.

DONN'ANNA: And finally, as though from a long way off, now and again remember something about him... he was like *this*... he used to say *that*... Is that what you would have me do?

FIORINA: As everybody always does, Anna dearest.

DONN'ANNA: How convenient! Make him die in our minds... not suddenly – as he did – but little by little... pushing him from our memory... refusing him that life we once gave him simply because he can no longer return our love. Is that the right thing to do? Never again to reach out to each other – just because there is no hope of any physical contact between us? Simply a tiny remembrance every now and then – like a distant whisper from long ago... Oh yes! That is really and truly death! And you would have his own mother behave in that heartless way?

At this point GIOVANNI *appears on the threshold of the doorway at the back. The old gardener looks stunned. Seeing* DONN'ANNA, *he hesitates to enter and makes a sign to* DONNA FIORINA *about the letter, being careful not to be noticed. But when* DONN'ANNA *sees her sister and* DON GIORGIO *turn, she does too and notices the gardener.*

DONN'ANNA: Yes, Giovanni, what is it?

GIOVANNI (*hiding the letter*): Nothing. I wanted… I wanted to say to the signora…

DON GIORGIO (*who has noticed the letter in the old man's hand, asks anxiously*): Is that the letter he was waiting for?

DONN'ANNA: You have a letter?

GIOVANNI (*hesitantly*): Yes, but…

DONN'ANNA: Give it to me. I know that it is for my son.

GIOVANNI *hands the letter to* DONN'ANNA *and goes out.*

DON GIORGIO: He was waiting for it anxiously.

DONN'ANNA: Yes, for two days. Did he talk about it to you?

DON GIORGIO: Yes, because he wanted me to ask you to open it as soon as it arrived.

DONN'ANNA: Why?

DON GIORGIO: To try to avert the danger of her coming to join him here. He didn't want her to abandon her children – and to make sure of that he told me he had begun to write her a letter to that effect. I was not at liberty to speak about this until the letter from her had arrived.

DONN'ANNA *takes the letter out of the envelope.*

FIORINA: She wrote to him after he had died. How sad.

DONN'ANNA, *as she reads the letter, shows with her eyes, the trembling of her hands and the exclamation that gushes from her heart – the joy of sensing the life of her son in the passion of his far-off lover.*

DON GIORGIO: What does she say?

DONN'ANNA: That she is coming here.

DON GIORGIO: She must not!

DONN'ANNA (*finishes reading the letter*): She is very troubled… very troubled. She writes with so much love… so much. We cannot possibly take from her the help his love has given her now! Her love cries out from the way she writes... Oh God... she even talks of committing suicide. If he were not alive for her it would be terrible!

FIORINA: What do you mean?

DONN'ANNA: The letter he began to write to her... it must be in there. (*She goes to the writing table, opens a drawer and takes out her son's letter*) Ah!

DON GIORGIO: What are you going to do with it?

DONN'ANNA: Here... while he still had breath, he wrote words which were meant to comfort her, to strengthen her.

GIORGIO: You don't mean to send her the letter?!

DONN'ANNA: She must have it. I tell you his life still needs her. Do you want me to kill him at this time by killing her as well?

DON GIORGIO: Come, come, my dear Anna, you really can't.

FIORINA: Think what you're doing, Anna!

DONN'ANNA: I tell you, his life is still necessary to her.

FIORINA: But you must write to her mother.

DONN'ANNA: I will write to her. Now – please go... please.

GIORGIO: His letter is not even finished.

DONN'ANNA: I will finish it. His writing was like mine. I shall finish it.

FIORINA: Anna!

DON GIORGIO: You can't!

DONN'ANNA: Please go. Leave me to what I must do.

As she ushers them out of the room,

THE CURTAIN FALLS

ACT TWO

The same scene as the first act, towards evening – a few days later. Vases brimming with tall flowering plants from the garden stand on both sides of the window on the left. As the curtain rises, GIOVANNI *is holding a third vase, standing at the threshold of the doorway at the back, with* DONN'ANNA *and her sister* FIORINA *near him.*

DONN'ANNA (*indicating that he should place the vase next to the doorway on the right*): There, Giovanni, put it there.

GIOVANNI (*does so*): It looks nice there.

DONN'ANNA: That's right. Now go and get the last one, and place it on the other side of the door. If it's too heavy get someone to help you.

GIOVANNI: Oh no, signora, I can manage.

DONN'ANNA (*smiling*): Dear old Giovanni – you won't *let* it be too heavy, I know. (*Dismissing him*) All right. Can you smell the roses, Fiorina? Beautiful. And aren't those other flowers lovely too.

FIORINA: Surely by doing all this, you will make the explanation more difficult. It seems foolish to me.

DONN'ANNA: Foolish? I like being foolish. You and I were never allowed folly when we were young.

FIORINA: And you are making yourself responsible for *her* folly – in coming here.

DONN'ANNA: No. He attempted to stop her, but she *would* come. Even if I had tried to stop her – it was too late. She had already left.

FIORINA: I do wish you had written to her mother.

DONN'ANNA: I couldn't. I tried to – for three days, but I just couldn't. I was afraid.

FIORINA: Afraid of what?

DONN'ANNA: That she might see it as you do and be left with only a dead memory.

FIORINA: But you should wish that. What is the use of her going on loving him?

DONN'ANNA: You know that she has written to him again.

FIORINA: Again?

DONN'ANNA: Yes. I read her letter. It was even more desperate than the first.

FIORINA: Anna – that's terrible.

DONN'ANNA: Why, Fiorina? Because I read her letter? I read it for him. Or because I am letting her come here? I can help her – and she can help me.

FIORINA: She will only upset you.

DONN'ANNA: Oh, Fiorina, I am longing to see her. Do you remember when your two children were alive only within yourself? You fed your body and fostered them and you satisfied a two-fold hunger... and didn't you feel the joy of it? My son is alive in my heart and I feed my body and foster his memory and so I dull my hunger, and I wish only to go on living if I can keep him alive. Together we shall.

FIORINA: Oh, Anna!

DONN'ANNA: I long to call out his name aloud.

FIORINA: Don't, don't, Anna, don't.

DONN'ANNA: What are you afraid of? Ghosts? I don't need a ghost to tell me he is here. I'm not mad!

FIORINA: But your behaviour, my dear Anna, is so very unusual that anybody might think you were.

DONN'ANNA: My behaviour seems strange to you – but if you knew my life as it has been, as it is, you might not think so. (*Sighing*) Sometimes I am aware – I am aware of the stillness and emptiness of those rooms. Then no memory is strong enough to fill them. That is when I am tired; then I know what you would have me know, and I am filled with terrible desolation. I need the woman who is coming and to whom my son is still alive. In her eyes and her heart I shall see him, feel him, nearer and nearer than ever. All those death thoughts of yours stifle and crush the life that I would give him.

FIORINA: But when she is here, what will you say to her?

DONN'ANNA: You want me to feel now what is going to happen before it happens? That's cruel. Don't you see how restless I am? It is as though I can live only a few minutes and you want to rob me even of those.

FIORINA: She is compromising herself, and uselessly now that it's all over.

DONN'ANNA (*waving the letter*): She says that her husband is in Paris on business and she is taking advantage of his absence.

FIORINA: Suppose he returns unexpectedly and she isn't there – what then?

DONN'ANNA: She had made some excuse for her mother to tell him – to explain her absence for a few days. Her mother still has property in Cortona.

FIORINA: And how could she think of coming to meet your son here... in your house?

DONN'ANNA: I want her to come. I'll meet her at the station.

FIORINA: What will you say to her, and how do you think she will take his not being there too to meet her?

DONN'ANNA: I'll tell her he sent me because he had to go away... but that I'll explain everything when we get here – that I couldn't do so in front all those people at the station. Yes, that's what I'll say.

FIORINA: And when she gets here you *will* tell her everything? Everything?

DONN'ANNA: At the right moment.

FIORINA (*impatiently*): Why have you put out all these flowers?

DONN'ANNA: Because they are beautiful and will give her a welcome. She'll think he filled the room with them – not I. Oh, for goodness' sake don't make me talk now.

The door opens. GIOVANNI *enters with the other large pot of flowers.*

There, Giovanni – where I told you, on the other side of the door. That's good.

GIOVANNI (*putting down the pot*): They're the prettiest of them all.

DONN'ANNA: The loveliest we have in the garden. Is the carriage ready?

GIOVANNI: Yes, signora. It's just coming round. In ten minutes you'll be at the station.

DONN'ANNA: Good, good. Thank you, Giovanni.

GIOVANNI: Good day, signora. (*He exits*)

DONN'ANNA (*calls impatiently*): Elisabetta! Is everything ready for her?

FIORINA: Anna! You're not putting her in... there?

DONN'ANNA: No, no. I'm giving her your favourite room next to mine upstairs.

The door opens and ELISABETTA *enters.*

Oh, Elisabetta… why did you open the window?

ELISABETTA (*excitedly*): The children! The children! Signora Fiorina, they've…

ELISABETTA: Yes, signora. I heard them shouting from the garden. They're running up now.

DONN'ANNA: Your children! Now perhaps you may understand what I mean.

FIORINA: But I thought they were coming tomorrow.

ELISABETTA: Here they are – here they are!

LIDA, *aged eighteen, and* FLAVIO, *aged twenty, burst into the room. Having left the country a year ago in order to pursue their studies in the town, they are now quite changed – in their thoughts and emotions, their appearance, their voices.*

LIDA: Mamma… my beautiful mammina… (*she kisses her*)

FIORINA: My Lida! (*She kisses her*) And you Flavio!

FLAVIO: Dear mother!

FIORINA: But – but I didn't expect you so soon!

LIDA: We managed to get off today, you see.

FLAVIO: Like a rocket. At two hours' notice.

LIDA: A fat lot you did! He didn't even want to!…

FLAVIO: What rot! We dashed all over the place. Tailor, dressmaker, silk stockings! Lida's shopping! What on earth you'll do with them in the country, I can't imagine!

LIDA: You *must* see what lovely things I've brought with me, Mother – some for you.

FIORINA (*has tried to smile, but once having noticed the change in them, she feels as though she were frozen; she looks towards her sister, who has been waiting apart in the shadow which begins to invade the room*) Yes… yes… but… What were you saying, Anna?

Immediately LINDA *and* FLAVIO *remember they are in their aunt's house when they notice their mother glancing at* ANNA, *and they are embarrassed, realizing that they had ignored her recent misfortune when they first came into the room, and they attribute their mother's bewilderment to their forgetfulness. They turn to their aunt, mortified and confused.*

FIORINA: You haven't greeted your Aunt Anna.

FLAVIO: Oh, Aunt Anna… of course… we're terribly sorry about…

LIDA: Do forgive us, Aunt Anna… bursting in like this…

FLAVIO: We haven't seen Mother for a year.

LIDA: Poor Fulvio.

FLAVIO: We're really so terribly sorry.

LIDA: For you, Auntie.

FLAVIO: I was so looking forward to finding him here…

LIDA: And I was hoping to get to know him.

FLAVIO: Why, you must remember Fulvio!

LIDA: I was only nine when he left here.

FLAVIO: Poor Aunt Anna!

LIDA: And you too, Mamma.

DONN'ANNA: No, Flavio. No, Lida – not for me… it's for you two.

LIDA: How do you mean – for us?

DONN'ANNA: Oh, nothing, my dear. Welcome back – both of you. (*Kissing them both*) Welcome back. Well, anyway, Fiorina, they're even better-looking – that's one consolation, even if they have changed. I must be going.

She exits through the door at the back. The others are silent for a moment. The shadows continue slowly to invade the room.

FLAVIO (*a little awed*): We'd quite forgotten…

FIORINA (*as if waking up from a nightmare*): What did she mean, "that's one consolation"?

ELISABETTA: How they have changed.

FIORINA: Oh no, it's not true. Let me look at you, children.

ELISABETTA: It's quite true, signora.

FIORINA: "Even better-looking"!

ELISABETTA (*admiring* LIDA): I'd hardly have known you… why, you're a young lady now. Quite a stranger!

FIORINA (*defensively*): No no, no! Lida, my Lida! Flavio, dear!

FLAVIO: Mother, what is it?

FIORINA: Come here. Let me have a good look at you. Don't worry about anything. Just look at me. (*She takes* LIDA'*s face in her hands*)
I say, what did he die of, Mother? Was it really…

FLAVIO: Because of that woman?

FIORINA (*hurriedly*): No. He fell ill quite suddenly. I'll tell you later how it happened. Talk to me about yourselves.

FLAVIO: There! You see! I told you all *that* was your usual romantic nonsense, Lida. If he was able to break away from her, it shows that dying of a great passion…

FIORINA: Why, what's the matter with you two?

FLAVIO: I warn you, she does nothing but read romantic novels!

FIORINA: You… Lida, darling?

LIDA: Don't believe him, Mammina… it isn't true!

FLAVIO: She's brought at least twenty with her.

LIDA: It's none of your business!

FIORINA: You two – quarrelling?

LIDA: He's hopeless. Don't you mind him, Mammina.

FLAVIO: I wonder which heroine taught you to use that perfume!

FIORINA: What perfume is it?

LIDA: A friend of mine recommended it.

FLAVIO: Who – the Rose girl?

LIDA (*scoffing*): Rose!

FLAVIO: Frances, then!

LIDA: Of course not!

FLAVIO: She changes her friends every day. Just like a weathercock!

ELISABETTA: To think they were like two little cherubs when they left us… And now they're like grand people!

FIORINA (*trying to recover herself*): Of course – that's what living in town does for one. They have grown up and… (*To* LIDA) But you haven't told me what the perfume is?

FLAVIO (*laughs*): Ah! It was very expensive! Ninety lire just for a small bottle!

FIORINA: A child uses perfume?!

LIDA: Mother, I'm eighteen!

FLAVIO: Three small bottles – two hundred and seventy lire!

LIDA: I don't know *how* much you've spent on *yourself* for ties, shirts, gloves – and you've the cheek to haul me over the coals for three tiny phials of perfume!

FIORINA: Please! Please! I can't bear to hear you talk like this. So you've cut your hair. (*She caresses it*) You are grown up, Lida.

ISABETTA: When she left, her hair was down to her shoulders!

504

FIORINA: And you, Flavio – you're taller than I am! I wonder how I must look to you!

LIDA: Lovely, Mother – very, very lovely!

FIORINA: Then why do you look at me like that?

LIDA: Like what?

FIORINA: Never mind… And what are *you* thinking, Flavio?

FLAVIO: Well, naturally, after a year you don't seem quite the same. (*He looks at her and laughs*)

FIORINA: No, don't laugh.

FLAVIO: I know we oughtn't to laugh here, but really, you gave me such a queer look!

FIORINA: Did I? It's so dark in here. I have to peer at you because I can hardly see you.

In fact it has grown even darker in the room, and as a result the light reflected from the room where the dead man is lying seems increasingly strong.

ELISABETTA: Wait. I'll turn on the light.

FIORINA (*uncomfortably*): No. Let's go, children. Let's go. It's late.

LIDA: The light is on in that room. What's there?

FIORINA: Can't you guess?

FLAVIO (*softly*): He died in there?

ELISABETTA: In this house nowadays it's just as if *we* weren't alive any more. As if only *he* was.

FLAVIO: She keeps that light burning?

LIDA (*has moved tentatively closer to the door, wanting to peep in*): And the room… is it… is it just as it was?

FIORINA: Lida! Don't look!

FLAVIO: As though he might come back any minute…

ELISABETTA: More as though he'd never gone away. We must keep on thinking about him – that's what she says – so that he won't go away. (*A short pause*) Because when the children go away, they die – for their mother. They are not the same afterwards.

In the darkness and the silence of a nightmare overcome, FIORINA *suddenly bursts into a subdued cry.*

FLAVIO (*after his mother's cry has shaken the silence of death, mistakes the cause of her grief*): Poor Aunt Anna!

LIDA: Aunt Anna isn't – going out of her mind, is she, Elisabetta?

ELISABETTA: She talks about him so that you almost see him. When I'm alone here, I keep on looking over my shoulder as if he were going from one room to another, or walking to the windows, or into the garden. It makes me all jumpy. She insists on my keeping his room tidy and making the bed. Look – d'you see the sheet is turned down. It's like that every evening… just as if he were going to sleep there.

LIDA: Then she's really trying…

ELISABETTA (*completing the sentence for her*): …To keep him alive!

FIORINA: Lida – my darling – *you* still love me just the same, don't you? Flavio, my darlings… for God's sake, let us go away from here.

ELISABETTA: Just a minute, signora. I'll give you a torch. It's pitch dark outside.

FIORINA: Thank you, Elisabetta. Let's go now. Let's go.

ELISABETTA *is the first to leave, followed by* DONNA FIORINA, LIDA *and* FLAVIO. *The scene remains empty and dark, with only that ghostly light outside the door on the right. After a pause, without any sound, the chair in front of the desk turns slowly as though an invisible hand were moving it. Then the lace curtain in front of the window is lifted on one side, as if moved by an unseen hand, and falls back again. (Who knows what strange things happen – unseen by anyone – in the darkened and deserted room where somebody has died.) After a moment* ELISABETTA *re-enters and immediately turns on the light. Instinctively she moves the chair back to its original position by the desk, then goes to the window, raises the curtain and opens it, looks out into the garden and calls:*

ELISABETTA: Who's there? Giovanni… is that you? Giovanni!

GIOVANNI (*calling from the garden*): Did you see it?

ELISABETTA: See what?

GIOVANNI (*as he enters the room*): On the hill there – between the olives.

ELISABETTA: I see the moon. But why on earth were you staring at the moon?

GIOVANNI: I wanted to see if it's true, what he told me.

ELISABETTA: Who?

GIOVANNI: Why, he who can't see it any more.

ELISABETTA: Oh, him?

GIOVANNI: He was standing there – where you are.

ELISABETTA (*backing a little from the window*): Don't! You give me the creeps!

GIOVANNI (*by the window*): The night he came back, it was.

ELISABETTA: He said something about the moon? What did he say?

GIOVANNI: "The higher it goes," he said, "the less you see of it. Look around you," he said, "and you can see its light on the flowers, in one place and on a hill in another, but if you look at the moon itself, the higher it has gone, the further it seems from the darkness that's around us."

ELISABETTA: What did he mean, "further"?

GIOVANNI: "The darkness of night," he said, "is around ourselves, but the moon doesn't see it because the moon's lost in its own light."

An approaching carriage is heard outside.

Now you know what he thought, looking up at the moon... I can hear the carriage.

ELISABETTA: Quick then, go and open the gate.

She closes the window and goes out of the door at the back. Shortly afterwards, LUCIA MAUBEL *and* DONN'ANNA *enter from the same door.*

DONN'ANNA (*anxiously, leading* LUCIA *into the room*): Come in, do come in. These are his rooms. You see the flowers everywhere which he left yesterday, in front of all your pictures.

LUCIA (*sweetly, yet ironically*): He leaves flowers and then disappears!

DONN'ANNA: He couldn't help that.

LUCIA: I arrive... and he's not here to greet me! I suppose he was being cautious. And don't you think I've a right to be annoyed by this caution? I think it's insulting!

DONN'ANNA: It wasn't caution... no, no!

LUCIA: It's obvious that he's being careful on his own account. He didn't stop my coming, though.

DONN'ANNA: No, but his thoughts were only for you – always for you.

LUCIA: Well, I'm here! I'm not dead yet!

DONN'ANNA: Why do you say that?

LUCIA: I'm sorry, but if I come here and find that he's run away, and has left *flowers* in front of my photographs, what does it mean? Doesn't it mean I'm dead so far as his love is concerned? And to think that I've left the whole of my other life to come to him here! He can't care any more. That's obvious. What *is* his explanation? What is it? Tell me.

DONN'ANNA (*gently*): May I call you Lucia?

LUCIA: Do. I'd like you to.

DONN'ANNA (*lingering over her name, gently*): Lucia… I want you to understand that he didn't mean to hurt you. He had to go, but he left you in my care.

LUCIA: Of course… Don't think… I know he…

DONN'ANNA: He always told me everything – even that you were lovers.

LUCIA: Everything?

DONN'ANNA: He could tell me everything because…

LUCIA: No, no.

DONN'ANNA (*puzzled*): You mean it wasn't everything?

LUCIA: There was something that he didn't know.

DONN'ANNA: Then…

LUCIA: Oh, forgive me, forgive me. I am here because of this *other* thing.

DONN'ANNA: But you sent him away!

LUCIA: Yes – I did. Afterwards, afterwards I felt I couldn't bear it. Our love had been pure for so many years, but in the end it was too strong for us. I couldn't look my children in the face. I forced him to go away. But even after he'd gone, I still couldn't… Can you understand? I'm pregnant.

DONN'ANNA: His?

LUCIA: Yes. That's why I came.

DONN'ANNA (*exultantly*): His? His?

LUCIA: He doesn't know yet. But he must. Where is he? Tell me.

DONN'ANNA: Lucia… oh my little daughter… It's his!…

LUCIA: He *must* know about it at once. Where is he? Tell me – where?… where?

DONN'ANNA: I can't tell you where.

LUCIA: Why? Don't you know?

DONN'ANNA: I can't tell you.

LUCIA: But didn't he say where?

DONN'ANNA: He didn't tell me.

LUCIA: I see now. He thought that only by keeping away we could… (*She breaks off with an exclamation of disgust*) He had no right to think like that about me! How can I break with him *now* and go back to my husband? (*She shudders*) I couldn't possibly!

DONN'ANNA: Of course not.

LUCIA: Won't you really say where he is? Do you truly not know? How can I let him know what's happened?

DONN'ANNA: He will know.

LUCIA: But how – if you don't know where he is? Surely he can't have gone far without telling either you or me?

DONN'ANNA: I'm sure he's not far away.

LUCIA: Oh, why couldn't he trust me? I see now, I ought to have told him the truth when I wrote.

DONN'ANNA (*attempting to calm her*): You did what you thought best.

LUCIA: I felt I couldn't write it in a letter. I had to see him. I suppose he thought me mad to come here, and that if he left me alone with you, you would make me see reason. (*Insistently*) Will he write to you to say where he is?

DONN'ANNA: We shall know. Now come and sit down with me here in his room – and let us feel that you *are* my daughter.

LUCIA: Mother.

DONN'ANNA: My little daughter Lucia!

LUCIA: Mother. Perhaps after all it was best like this – to meet you first.

DONN'ANNA: Yes, you are beautiful. How well I understand it all. Why didn't you both realize when you were free...

LUCIA: And then our love would have been no sin.

DONN'ANNA: Those who sin are not always evil.

LUCIA: I should think of my children at home. Yet I left them and rushed here for something which at present hardly exists. Yet that something has become everything to me. The whole of our love seemed to gather itself up into that one moment... into that one overwhelming moment. And yet, in that moment it became sin. You don't know – you will never be able to imagine what I have suffered. I held on to myself as long as I could, trying to stop my body from ruling me... trying not to give in. And whenever I resisted that terrible physical craving – then I held him in my heart. Only by giving each other up physically could we have carried on and kept what was best in our love. But the torture of it all – can you imagine it? I tried to think of my children. I tried even to pretend that they were not my husband's,

509

but *his*, but I can't pretend that the child within me... created by love... belongs to the man I loathe!

DONN'ANNA: You can't!

LUCIA: You understand that?

DONN'ANNA: Yes.

LUCIA: My loathing for that man is so intense that I can't express it. I bore him two children. I looked after them with my living body but with an agony of soul. I can't tell you, I can't tell you the vileness of it all. Any wrong I've done him is much less than the wrong he has done me. Even during the time I was pregnant his only thought was to get hold of more and more women. And all the time he was so smug and superior. There was nothing good or sacred to him. I couldn't have gone on with it as I have. I couldn't have lived if it hadn't been for your son. He brought something beautiful into all that sordid ugliness. And then to think that that love could become a sin. And I never realized until I found I was going to have a child. Now I am utterly wretched. The beauty of our love is gone. I feel this child also will have been created in sin.

DONN'ANNA: You mustn't say that!

LUCIA: I am saying he must make me see it differently, or it will be the end of me. For three years I did everything to avoid having another child – conceived as it would have been through lust and fear, and now this child conceived in love and which should bring joy with it – I fear it – I am even ashamed for it. What can I do? He *must* help me.

DONN'ANNA: Yes – yes, he will.

LUCIA (*not heeding*): I want him here. I want to see him, to hear his voice, to talk to him. Where is he? Where can he be? How shall I make him know about all this? I can't rest until he *does* know. Surely you *must* know where he's gone!

DONN'ANNA: Do give yourself a little rest.

LUCIA: I can't!

DONN'ANNA: You're trembling all over, you're tired out. That long journey...

LUCIA: There's a buzzing in my ears. I'm dizzy.

DONN'ANNA: All the more reason to...

LUCIA: All this worry, this worry!

DONN'ANNA: Rest, rest.

LUCIA: And then not to find him here...

DONN'ANNA: Try to rest... And tomorrow...

LUCIA: Oh I can't stand another night of it!

DONN'ANNA: Lucia, listen. I will tell you what to do. I did it so often when he was away from me. I felt him to be with me because I drew him close to my heart – more than close – he was within my heart. Try to do that. Draw him close to your heart. Say to yourself: "He is here."

LUCIA (*turning her head*): Is that where he sleeps? In that room?

DONN'ANNA: Yes. And here is the table at which he wrote to you.

LUCIA: Wrote to stop my coming...

DONN'ANNA: And this is the chair where he sat and talked to me so much about you.

LUCIA: Yet when I come, he rushes away!

DONN'ANNA: He didn't know everything then, did he?

LUCIA: No. But now – will he come back to me now?

DONN'ANNA: Yes. He will come back to you. But now come – come upstairs with me. I've put you in the room next to mine. It's quite ready.

LUCIA: I would like to see *his* room.

DONN'ANNA: Yes. Go in.

LUCIA: I suppose you would not let me rest in there?

DONN'ANNA: Why not?

LUCIA: I could – in his room. I should feel nearer to him.

DONN'ANNA: You feel that already, do you?

LUCIA: Yes, I could... what was it you said? Draw him closer to me.

DONN'ANNA: In your heart.

They enter the room. After a pause we hear confused voices from within the room – not sad, but joyous. LUCIA *even laughs.* DONN'ANNA *returns and talks through the doorway.*

DONN'ANNA: I'll have your things sent to his bedroom and bring you something to eat.

LUCIA: No, no, please don't bother. I want only to sleep – sleep as long as I can. I don't care about anything else.

DONN'ANNA: Very well, I'll see you are not disturbed. If you want anything you have only to ring. Shall I shut the door?

LUCIA: Yes, please. I'll sleep now.

DONN'ANNA *closes the door and leans against it for a moment with her eyes closed, as if exhausted, but then a cheerful, divine smile shines on her face and she says… more with her eyes than with her lips:*

DONN'ANNA: HE LIVES!

THE CURTAIN FALLS

ACT THREE

The same room early the following morning.

Shortly after the curtain rises GIOVANNI *appears in the doorway at the back, ushering in* SIGNORA FRANCESCA NORETTI, *who has just arrived from the station and is greatly perturbed.*

GIOVANNI: This way, signora. Please come in.

FRANCESCA: Is my daughter still asleep?

GIOVANNI: She was that tired after her journey yesterday evening, you see, signora, and it's only just gone seven.

FRANCESCA: Which is her room? Do you know?

GIOVANNI: Yesterday Elisabetta got the room ready for her on the next floor.

FRANCESCA: Will you take me there?

GIOVANNI: I don't work upstairs, signora. But I'll tell Elisabetta. Mistress is up already. I saw her just as dawn came, opening her window.

FRANCESCA: You say my daughter arrived last night?

GIOVANNI: Yes, last night. Mistress went to pick her up at the station.

FRANCESCA: Did you see her when she got here? Was she crying?

GIOVANNIA: No, signora. Not as far I could see.

FRANCESCA: Then she doesn't know yet?

GIOVANNI: Well, signora, you see – look at these flowers. I put them here yesterday evening… It's just as though he weren't dead… so far as mistress is concerned. She's not even wearing black.

FRANCESCA: And he has been dead eleven days, you say?

GIOVANNI: Come today.

FRANCESCA: How is it possible that my daughter hasn't heard? I knew it as soon as I arrived at the station.

Anna opens the door.

513

GIOVANNI: Here's the mistress. I'll be getting along. (*He exits*)

DONN'ANNA (*approaching* FRANCESCA): You are her mother? Lucia is still sleeping. We must talk quietly.

FRANCESCA: Signora, you can't imagine how upset I am. I was simply distracted all through the journey. Where is my daughter? Does she still not know your son is dead?

DONN'ANNA: Hush. Please. She does not know.

FRANCESCA: Let me see her. I must tell her.

DONN'ANNA: Please don't.

FRANCESCA: Why didn't you let us know? It would have prevented her from committing this madness.

DONN'ANNA: Please don't worry. Won't you sit down?

FRANCESCA: I shall be worried till I have got her home again. I left the moment I read the letter she left asking me to look after the children. Perhaps you don't know she has two children. It's really terrible!

DONN'ANNA: Please talk quietly. She is sleeping in there.

FRANCESCA: In there? I'll go in at once. (*She moves quickly towards the door*)

DONN'ANNA (*intercepting her*): No, no. You don't know what harm you may do. (*Her tone is so compelling that* FRANCESCA *stops*)

FRANCESCA (*apprehensive*): Harm?

DONN'ANNA: She didn't come for his sake only.

FRANCESCA: What do you mean?

DONN'ANNA: Perhaps you do not know all that I know.

FRANCESCA (*looks in dismay at* DONN'ANNA): You mean that she told you that she had been his...

DONN'ANNA: Yes, and that he is not dead as you think.

FRANCESCA: What do you mean?

DONN'ANNA: He is alive – in her now. Do you understand?

FRANCESCA: A child? Oh, my God! Is that why she came rushing here?

DONN'ANNA: When she came here she was distracted, I could not possibly tell her. So I said he had gone away. Then she felt that he no longer cared for her and that thought was such torture to her, how could I tell her then that he was dead?

FRANCESCA (*testily*): You ought to have let us know, then she wouldn't have compromised herself by coming here.

DONN'ANNA: I can't say how glad I am that I did not. At one time I even believed I should, but instead I sent your daughter the unfinished letter he was writing when… I finished it myself.

FRANCESCA (*horrified*): You wrote it when he was dead?

DONN'ANNA: He is not dead to me, nor to her. And I will not kill him for her.

FRANCESCA: Oh God! Then you mean to keep her tied to a dead body!

DONN'ANNA: The man to whom *you* have tied her – *he* is the corpse for her.

FRANCESCA: But she can't leave her children.

DONN'ANNA: She told me about them, and she told me things that made me shudder.

FRANCESCA: About the children?

DONN'ANNA: Yes. They were not born of love!

FRANCESCA (*after a pause*): And when she knows that your son is gone… what is going to happen then?

DONN'ANNA: He can still be alive for her if she will keep him so.

FRANCESCA (*dazed*): You are going to let her think that she will see him again?

DONN'ANNA: When she goes back home he will go with her.

FRANCESCA (*rather frightened, with a horror that gradually changes into a deep compassion*): Oh God! You're… you're mad!

The door opens and LUCIA *appears.*

LUCIA: Mother… You! (*She goes closer to her mother and looks from one to the other*) What has happened? I had an awful dream! I know something terrible has happened. What have you been saying to each other?

DONN'ANNA: Your mother came to look for you.

LUCIA: That's not true! Mother, why don't you answer me? What is it? Oh, tell me.

FRANCESCA: Some days ago, darling… (*She hesitates*)

LUCIA: Is he dead? Is he? No! How can he be? It's not possible. Oh God! My dream! Dead? Tell me, TELL ME!

FRANCESCA: Some days ago, darling.

LUCIA: Days? (*She turns to* DONN'ANNA) But you – why didn't you tell me? How did he die? Where? Oh God – in there, where I was sleeping? You could let me sleep there? I know I asked to, but you… how *could* you? "The flowers" you said, and "He has gone away" and "that's his room" and "I don't know where he has gone…" And I dreamt that he could not come back because he had gone so far away. In my dream I saw him, and there was death in his face. Oh, God! (*She breaks into a fit of uncontrollable tears*) And to let me go on thinking about his not being here to meet me, as he should have been – of course that could only have happened if he were dead. And I didn't understand because you… you… (*Astonishment takes the place of weeping*) Oh, what have you done? How could you do it? For my sake? But he is dead for you too – I can hardly believe it! You talked to me as though he were alive. And all the time he was dead!

DONN'ANNA: I can see him.

LUCIA: When he is dead? Did you see him die?

DONN'ANNA: Not then, but now!

LUCIA: How?

DONN'ANNA: I am watching him die now.

LUCIA: What do you mean? I knew it. I knew that he would die. I wanted not to believe it. He said to me himself, when he went away, that he was coming here to die.

DONN'ANNA (*uncovering her face*): And I didn't understand!

LUCIA: He was dying for years. He had changed so much. His eyes had no light in them. So pale, he looked, so pale and wretched. I knew then that he was dying!

DONN'ANNA: You're killing him for me. I could not cry because I did not see it… now I see.

LUCIA: What are you saying? What are you saying?

DONN'ANNA: My son. The dear body of my son – had it come to this – you do not exist now and can never exist any more for me. I tried to keep you alive, to embalm you within myself as you were when you left me. I wanted to give you that life that had long ceased for you. Poor flesh of my flesh that I can no longer see and shall never see again. Where are you? Where are you? Don't go. Don't go. (*With a cry*) Don't take him away from me!

LUCIA: I won't leave you, "mother". (*With determination*) I shan't!

FRANCESCA: But you must. You must come away with me at once.

DONN'ANNA (*to* FRANCESCA): This is her home now, signora.

FRANCESCA: This is madness. And her children! (*Vehemently, to* LUCIA) You have two children, Lucia. Are you going to leave them for the sake of staying here with someone who is half-mad?

DONN'ANNA: His child belongs here.

FRANCESCA: You don't know what you're saying.

LUCIA (*to her mother*): And you don't know what you are trying to do, Mother.

DONN'ANNA (*suddenly collapsing*): No. No. Your mother is right. She sees that I have been thinking only of myself – not of him. For a time you will bear within yourself his child and then... when the child is born, you will have him again... my son, my little son – he will be yours, yours, he will not come back to me. You are his mother now, not I any more. It *is* so. It *is*. (*She weeps as though she had never wept before. By degrees she controls her grief.*) I could not cry for him, but I can cry for myself. Go, my dear. Live your life even though it burns you to ashes, and death when it comes is only another change... There is no more to say. Now we must think of your mother. She must be tired.

FRANCESCA: Signora, when is the next train to Pisa? We must be getting home.

DONN'ANNA: You will have to wait awhile. The train is not due yet. You have plenty of time to rest. And you, dear daughter...

LUCIA: I shall stay here with you.

FRANCESCA: You must come with me. She said so herself.

DONN'ANNA: There is nothing to keep you here now.

FRANCESCA: Your children will be waiting for you.

LUCIA: You know that I'll never go back there! I couldn't. It's not possible. I can't. I can't and I won't. What is there for me to do there now?

DONN'ANNA: Or I – here? This is the real death... that we must go on doing and saying things whether we wish to or not. Now we are going to look up the trains, and then there will be the carriage to the station, and then your journey. What "restless" ghosts we are! We torment ourselves, and sometimes find consolation, and then we become quiet. That is the true death.

THE CURTAIN FALLS

Limes from Sicily

Lumie di Sicilia (1910)

Translated by Robert Rietti

CHARACTERS

MICUCCIO BONAVINO
TERESINA (SINA MARNIS)
AUNT MARTA
FERDINANDO
DORINA
THE COOK
GUESTS (*heard offstage*)

A room in a hotel in Sicily. A few articles of furniture. A screen in the left-hand corner. Doors to the centre, left and right. The centre double doors are of glass and lead to another room which is in the dark, and beyond this can be seen a brightly lit dining salon with a well-laid table. It is night and the room is at present in the dark. Snoring is heard from behind the screen.

FERDINANDO *enters from the right and turns on the light. He is in his shirtsleeves, but has only to put on his jacket to be ready to serve at table. He is followed by* MICUCCIO BONAVINO, *carrying an old travelling bag in either hand, a straw basket of fruit under one arm and the case of a musical instrument under the other. He is struggling under the weight and the cold and is very tired. Once the light is turned on, the snoring ceases and* DORINA *asks from behind the screen:*

DORINA: Who is it?

FERDINANDO: Get up, Dorina. Signor Bonvicino's here.

MICUCCIO (*shaking his head to get rid of a drop of rain on the tip of his nose, he corrects him*): Bonavino... not Bonvicino.

FERDINANDO: Oh. Bonavino!

DORINA (*yawning behind the screen*): Who is he?

FERDINANDO: He's related to the signora. Did you say she was your cousin?

MICUCCIO (*embarrassed, hesitating*): N... o... we're not exactly related. I am – I am – Micuccio Bonavino. She knows who I am!

DORINA (*her curiosity is now aroused and she appears from behind the screen*): Her cousin, did you say, Ferdinando?

FERDINANDO (*cross*): No, no. (*To* MICUCCIO) Then why did you ask for "Aunt Marta"? (*To* DORINA) I thought he was a nephew or something. Sorry, in that case I can't let you stay.

MICUCCIO: What do you mean? I've come all the way from our village to see her.

FERDINANDO: Well, she's not in. Anyway, you can't come to a posh hotel dressed like that and ask to see people at this hour.

MICUCCIO: Is it my fault if the train only just got in? Could I tell it to run faster? (*Persuasively*) It's only a train; it can't get here before it's due. I've been travelling for two days...

DORINA: That's not difficult to tell.

MICUCCIO: What?... (*Glancing at his clothes*) Oh, you mean the way I look.

DORINA: Not a pretty sight, dear boy!

MICUCCIO: Am I very dirty?

DORINA: Well – you could put it like that.

FERDINANDO: Look, you can't stay here. Come back tomorrow and you'll be able to see her. The signora is still at the opera now.

MICUCCIO: What d'you mean – "come back"! Where d'you expect me to go at this time of night? If she's not here, I'll wait for her. The cheek! Can't I wait for her here? (*He puts down his cases*)

FERDINANDO: Without her permission I can't...

MICUCCIO (*sitting down and taking off his shoe to remove a stone*): Permission? But you don't know who I am!

FERDINANDO: For that very reason. I'm not going to risk losing my job on your account.

MICUCCIO (*smiling, with a knowing air*): Don't worry. I'll see that doesn't happen. (*He removes the other shoe*)

FERDINANDO: What d'you think you're doing, taking your shoes off?

MICUCCIO (*shaking it*): I've given a home to these stones long enough.

DORINA: Look, Signor Bonvino...

MICUCCIO: Bonavino.

DORINA: Bonavino. There's going to be a party here tonight.

MICUCCIO: Oh?

DORINA: Yes. In her honour.

FERDINANDO: And we won't be done with it till morning – and that's only if we're lucky!

MICUCCIO (*removing his coat and shaking the rain and dust off it*): All the better. I'm sure that the moment Teresina sees me...

FERDINANDO: Do you hear that? He calls her Teresina. He comes to the hotel suite of the greatest singer in Italy and just asks if "the singer Teresina" lives here!

MICUCCIO: Well, isn't she a singer? And isn't that her name? Are you trying to teach *me* what to call her?

DORINA: Do you really know her so well?

MICUCCIO: Know her? We grew up together.

FERDINANDO: What shall we do, Dorina?

DORINA: Oh, let him wait!

MICUCCIO: Of course I'm going to wait! You don't imagine I came all the way here just to...

FERDINANDO: Oh sit down! I wash my hands of it. I must get things ready. (*He goes out towards the lit room at the rear*)

MICUCCIO: That's a fine way to treat me! As if I were just a... oh, perhaps it's because of the way I look... all dusty from the train and still in my working clothes... But if I were to tell Teresina when she comes back from the opera... (*He has a sudden doubt and looks around the room*) Er... excuse me, signorina – who does this house belong to?

DORINA: House? It's a hotel, silly. And we have *the* most expensive suite of rooms... for as long as we stay here.

MICUCCIO: Carrumba! (*He moves towards the double doors leading to the brightly lit room*) Is it a big house... I mean... suite?

DORINA: So-so.

MICUCCIO: Is that somebody else's suite through that door?

DORINA (*laughing*): No... that's the reception room. She's holding a banquet tonight.

MICUCCIO: What bright lights! And what a lot of food!

DORINA: Makes your mouth water, does it?

MICUCCIO: So then it's true.

DORINA: What?

MICUCCIO: You can see it. She's doing well now.

DORINA: Doing well? Don't you know who Sina Marnis is?!

MICUCCIO: Sina? Oh yes, of course! That's what she calls herself now. Aunt Marta wrote to me about it.

DORINA: Just a minute – now that I think of it, you must be... (*She calls to* FERDINANDO) I say... Ferdinando... come here. I've found out who he is! The one her mother's always writing to.

FERDINANDO'S VOICE: Really?

MICUCCIO: Teresina never learnt how to write, poor thing.

DORINA: Yes, of course... Bonavino. And your first name's Domenico, isn't it?

MICUCCIO: Yes, but back home they call me Micuccio. It's all the same.

DORINA: You were very ill, weren't you... just recently?

MICUCCIO: Ill... I should say so. Dead – very nearly. They'd already lit the candles.

DORINA: And Signora Marta sent you a money order. Yes, I remember. I went with her to the post office to get it.

MICUCCIO: That's one of the reasons why I came. I have the money with me.

DORINA: You're going to give the money back to her?

MICUCCIO (*worried*): Money? No… no, I don't want to talk about it. Tell me, will it be long before they get back?

DORINA: Oh – quite a while yet, I'm afraid. Especially tonight. It's a gala performance. She's singing *La Traviata*.

MICUCCIO (*smiling*): She's got a wonderful voice, hasn't she?

DORINA: Mm… not bad.

MICUCCIO: I don't want to boast, but it was my doing.

DORINA: What was?

MICUCCIO: I discovered her voice!

DORINA: Really? (*Calling*) Ferdinando, come here.

FERDINANDO (*off*): Coming. (*He enters*) What is it now?

DORINA: What do you think, Ferdinando; he discovered her voice!

MICUCCIO: I'm a musician.

FERDINANDO: Oho! A musician! Bravo. And what do you play? The trombone?

MICUCCIO: No, no. Me… the trombone! I play the piccolo! I'm in the band – in our village band, where I live.

DORINA: What's the name of your village?… No, don't tell me… See if I can remember.

MICUCCIO: Palma Montechiaro of course. Where she comes from.

DORINA: Oh yes! Palma, that's it!

FERDINANDO: So it was you who discovered her voice!

DORINA: Tell us how it happened. (*She winks at Ferdinando*)

MICUCCIO (*shrugging his shoulders*): There's nothing to tell. She used to sing…

DORINA: …And hey presto, you – being a musician—

MICUCCIO: Oh no, not immediately. It wasn't like that at all.

FERDINANDO: When did you discover her then?

MICUCCIO: Well, she was always singing. She said it was to take her mind off her troubles.

DORINA: Troubles?

MICUCCIO: Yes, she was going through hard times then, poor thing. You see, her father had died. I helped her – and her mother, Aunt Marta. My mother was against it, though, so… (*He shrugs his shoulders*)

DORINA: Were you in love with her?

MICUCCIO (*another shrug*): My mother wanted me to give her up because she was so poor after her father died; whereas I… well, I had my job as a shepherd as well as playing in the band.

FERDINANDO: But were you actually betrothed?

MICUCCIO: My parents wouldn't let us then. So Teresina used to sing spiteful songs… her "hymns of hate" she used to call them.

DORINA: Well I never! What did *you* do?

MICUCCIO (*thoughtfully*): It must have been Heaven. I can honestly say it was an inspiration from Heaven. You see, no one had ever taken any special notice of her singing, not even me. Then suddenly – one morning…

FERDINANDO: She lost her voice!

DORINA: Shut up, Ferdinando!

MICUCCIO: Oh no… not at all! It was one morning in April, I remember. She was singing at her window, up in the attic… (*Apologetically*) They… they lived in an attic then!

FERDINANDO: D'you hear that, Dorina?

DORINA: Sh…

MICUCCIO: There's no disgrace in that! That's where they discover great talents sometimes!

DORINA: Of course. Well? She was singing, you say?…

MICUCCIO: Yes, I had heard her sing that little song a hundred thousand times if I'd heard it once…

FERDINANDO: A little song? Not the – "hymn of hate" did you call it?

MICUCCIO: Oh no… not that… just a little folk song we sing in our village. I had never listened to it particularly before, but that morning, it was as though an angel were singing. I didn't say a word to her or to her mother, but that evening, I took the maestro – our band leader – to their attic. Saro Malaviti… he's a friend of mine – oh, a great friend in fact – and a good man, poor soul! Well, he listened to her… and he knows what he's talking about, when it comes to music, and as for conducting a band, well, everyone thinks the world of him in Palma… and he said: "But this a voice from God"! You can imagine how I felt. I'd never been so excited in my life. I hired a piano – oh what a job it was to get it up all those stairs... and I bought some music... and the maestro started to give her lessons. He was so good, he wouldn't charge anything. He just let me give him a little present from time to time. After all, how could I manage more than that? What was I? Just what I am now... just a shepherd.

DORINA: Never mind. What happened?

MICUCCIO: The piano cost money: the – music cost money... and then, Teresina had to eat well.

FERDINANDO (*winking at* DORINA): And can she eat!!

DORINA: She had to be strong to sing, of course.

MICUCCIO: Meat every day! You know what that costs!

FERDINANDO: I should say so!

DORINA: And then?...

MICUCCIO: She began to study. And even that early you could tell how far she'd go. When she sang from her attic – almost in the sky, you might say – you could hear her all over the village. And everybody used to stand under her window – packed like sardines! She was all on fire... and when she finished singing, she used to grasp me by my arms... like this... (*he grabs* FERDINANDO) and shake me!

FERDINANDO: Take it easy. Take it easy.

MICUCCIO: She was mad with joy, poor thing. Because she already knew... she could see that she was going to do big things. And she didn't know how to thank me. Aunt Marta, on the other hand, poor soul...

DORINA: Was she against it?

MICUCCIO: It wasn't that she was against it; she just didn't believe it. She'd had so many disappointments in her life, poor soul, and she didn't want Teresina to get grand ideas, to aim too high. Besides, she knew what it was costing me, and that my parents... but I broke with them; my father, my mother... that was when an important conductor – a man who used to give big concerts – came to Palma... I've forgotten his name, although he's pretty well-known...

DORINA: Never mind, go on.

MICUCCIO: Anyway, when he heard her voice, he said it would be a shame, a terrible shame, not to let her continue studying in a big music school. That settled it. I sold the farm which an uncle of mine (he was a priest) had left me when he died, and I sent Teresina to Naples, to the Conservatoire.

FERDINANDO: *You* did?

MICUCCIO: Me, me. Who else!

DORINA: He means he paid for her.

MICUCCIO: For four years I paid for her lessons there. Four years – and I haven't seen her since.

DORINA: Never?

MICUCCIO: Never.

DORINA: Well!

MICUCCIO: That's because... well, afterwards she began to sing in opera, you see. All over the place. From Naples to Rome, Rome to Milan, then to Spain – to Russia... then back here again.

FERDINANDO: She certainly made a hit!

MICUCCIO: Oh I know. I kept all the newspaper cuttings. I've got them with me, there in my case. And I've got her letters too. (*He takes a bundle out of his breast pocket*) From her and her mother. Here they are. Listen, this is what she wrote me when she sent me that money.

FERDINANDO: Money?

MICUCCIO: Money – yes. When I was nearly dying.

FERDINANDO (*whispers incredulously to Dorina*): She sent him money?

DORINA: Her mother did.

FERDINANDO: Oh! I was going to say...

MICUCCIO (*reading*): "Micuccio dear, I haven't time to write, but mother's given you all the news. Get well soon – and always think of me. Teresina." (*He is moved*)

FERDINANDO: Did she send you a lot of money?

DORINA: A thousand lire, wasn't it?

MICUCCIO: A thousand, yes.

FERDINANDO: And – forgive my asking – but your farm... the one you said you sold... how much was that worth?

MICUCCIO: How much could it be worth? Not much. A tiny piece of land like that.

FERDINANDO: Ah – of course, I thought as much.

MICUCCIO: But I've got the money with me. I don't want it. The little I did, I did for her. We agreed to wait for two or three years, till she began to get on... Aunt Marta always kept reminding me of that in her letters. (*Thoughtfully*) I certainly wasn't expecting money, but if Teresina sent it, it's a sign that she's doing well now... that she's made her way...

FERDINANDO: She's made her way all right!

MICUCCIO: And so it's time...

DORINA: To get married?

MICUCCIO (*smiling, half-embarrassed*): So – I've come.

FERDINANDO (*laughing*): You've come to marry Sina Marnis?

DORINA: Of course he's come to marry her. Didn't you hear him say they were betrothed?

MICUCCIO: I dropped everything back there in the village; my family, the band, everything. I had a row with my parents over that thousand lire. It came without my knowing, when I was more dead than alive. Mother wanted to keep it. I had to tear it from her. Money? No, signore! I can manage all right as I am. I shan't starve. I'm a good shepherd. Besides, I have my art...

FERDINANDO: His art?

MICUCCIO: I have my piccolo and...

DORINA: You brought your piccolo with you?

MICUCCIO: Of course. I always carry it with me. I'd never be without.

FERDINANDO: She sings – and he plays, you see? (*He laughs*)

MICUCCIO: You imagine I couldn't play with the orchestra?

FERDINANDO: Of course you could. Why not?

DORINA: I expect you play well.

MICUCCIO: So-so. I've only been playing for ten years.

FERDINANDO: Well – what about a little tune? (*He picks up the instrument case*)

DORINA: Wonderful idea. Play something for us.

MICUCCIO: At this time of night?

DORINA: Any little tune. Please do.

FERDINANDO: Just a short one.

MICUCCIO: Oh no – really, I'd rather not.

FERDINANDO: Do we have to beg you? (*He takes the piccolo out of its case*) There.

DORINA: Come on... just to show us how well you play.

MICUCCIO: But how can I – like this – on my own.

DORINA: Never mind, we'll imagine the rest of the orchestra. Come. Try.

FERDINANDO: You'd better. If you don't – I will!

MICUCCIO: Oh no! Give it to me. (*He takes the piccolo from* FERDINAN-DO) Very well then, if you insist. I'll play you the little song Teresina sang that day from her attic.

FERDINANDO: When you discovered her?

MICUCCIO: Yes. Will that do?

FERDINANDO: Bravo. ⎫

DORINA: That'll do fine. ⎬

MICUCCIO sits down and prepares himself very seriously. He holds the piccolo to his lips as though about to start, then stops and asks:

MICUCCIO: Ready?

DORINA: Yes, of course.

FERDINANDO: Carry on.

MICUCCIO blows a false note. The others laugh.

MICUCCIO: Sorry. A little dust… must have got in… from the train. (*He shakes the piccolo*) I'll start again.

MICUCCIO plays very sweetly. The COOK *enters from the other room to see what is going on. The other two indicate to him to keep quiet and not to laugh. Suddenly* MICUCCIO's *tune is interrupted by a loud ringing of the doorbell.* FERDINANDO *and* DORINA *are galvanized into action.*

FERDINANDO: They're here.

DORINA (*to the* COOK): You get a move on. She said she wanted dinner served the moment she got in. (*The* COOK *nods and disappears*)

FERDINANDO (*in a panic*): Where's my jacket? Where did I put my jacket?

DORINA: Over there, stupid. (*She indicates behind the screen. The bell rings again.*) Oh – I'll go.

She goes off to let the others in. FERDINANDO *hurriedly dons his jacket.* MICUCCIO *is about to follow* DORINA *when* FERDINANDO *stops him.*

FERDINANDO: You stay here. I must let the signora know first. (*He goes.* MICUCCIO *remains standing there, confused and troubled.*)

AUNT MARTA (*off*): Take them straight through to the reception room, Dorina. Straight through.

DORINA (*off*): Very good, signora.

AUNT MARTA (*off*): And you can serve dinner right away, Ferdinando.

FERDINANDO (*off*): Certainly, signora.

DORINA *and* FERDINANDO *and another waiter enter right and cross towards the other room, carrying expensive-looking baskets of flowers, bouquets etc.* MICUCCIO *tries to look into the room and glimpses men in dinner jackets, talking and moving about.* FERDINANDO *enters again hurriedly and crosses to the door, right.*

MICUCCIO (*catching his arm*): Who are they all?

FERDINANDO (*without stopping*): The guests. Let me go – I must be in there to receive them. (*He goes off right*)

MICUCCIO (*trying to follow him*): Did you tell her I was h—

But FERDINANDO *has gone.* MICUCCIO *looks again. He is dazzled. He is not conscious that his eyes are blurred with tears. He shuts them behind one hand and strives to pull himself together, as if to master the anxiety, the stab of pain, that a burst of shrill laughter gives him. It is* TERESINA's *laugh. She is in the reception room with the others.* DORINA *returns with two more bouquets of flowers.*

DORINA: Oh dear – what a rush! I've never seen so many flowers. What's the matter? Crying?

MICUCCIO: Me? No… but all those people!… Did you tell her I was…

DORINA: Sorry, I haven't time! (*She goes*)

AUNT MARTA *enters, right. She is wearing a large hat and is lost in the splendid velvet cloak she has on. Seeing* MICUCCIO, *she utters a cry, which she smothers at once.*

MARTA: Micuccio! You – here?

MICUCCIO: Aunt Marta… you… dressed like that!

MARTA: How? Like what?

MICUCCIO: With that velvet cloak – and that hat!!

MARTA: Oh dear. But what are you doing here? Without letting us know… what has happened?

MICUCCIO: I… I have come…

MARTA: But tonight of all nights! Oh dear… what shall we do? What shall we… You see, all those people in there are guests… it's a party for Teresina.

MICUCCIO: I know.

MARTA: Her gala performance, you see – a party… in her honour. Wait: you wait here a moment.

MICUCCIO: If you... if you think I ought to go...

MARTA: No. Wait here a moment for me. (*She goes towards the reception room*)

MICUCCIO: But I wouldn't know where to go... in this strange city.

MARTA *signs to him with her gloved hand to wait. She goes into the reception room, where, suddenly, there is silence. We hear* SINA MARNIS *say distinctly: "One moment, boys!"* MICUCCIO *realizes that he is still holding his piccolo – and in a dazed manner, puts it back in its case. There is a burst of laughter offstage and a moment later,* AUNT MARTA *returns without her hat, gloves and cloak, and much more at ease.*

MARTA: Well, here I am, Micuccio.

MICUCCIO: And... and Teresina?

MARTA: I told her you were here, and as soon as she can, she'll come out. She'll only be a moment or two. Meantime, we'll have a little chat together – just you and I. What do you say?

MICUCCIO: I don't mind waiting by myself now that she knows I'm here...

MARTA: No, I'll stay with you.

MICUCCIO: No, Aunt Marta... if you... if you feel you ought to be in there with the others...

MARTA: No, no... they're having their dinner now. Her manager, her agent, you understand... it's necessary for her career. We'll eat here all by ourselves.

DORINA *enters with a tablecloth and things for setting the table.*

DORINA: In here, signora?

MARTA: Yes, yes... that's good, Dorina. You set this little table for us straight away.

DORINA: Very well, signora.

MARTA: And we'll have dinner together, just us two. We can talk about the good old days. Dear Micuccio... Micucciolino... it doesn't seem real to me to be here with you.

DORINA: Shall I serve it now, signora?

MARTA: Yes, yes, Dorina... go and fetch it. (DORINA *exits*) Come, Micuccio, let's sit down.

MICUCCIO: Thank you.

MARTA: That's right. There are so many people in the other room... she's forced to entertain them all. What can she do? It's her career! Have you seen the newspapers? (MICUCCIO *nods*) Wonderful notices she gets. Wonderful. But I can't get used to it – I feel completely at sea. Dear, dear Micuccio… it doesn't seem real to see you again after all this while!

MICUCCIO: But – she will come, she said! I mean… I mean… at least to see her.

MARTA: Of course she'll come. The moment she finds a second to breathe. Didn't I tell you? She'd much prefer to be here with us – especially with you – after all these years. How many is it? (*She gives him no time to answer*) Oh so many… so many… Ah, my son, it seems only yesterday – and yet it feels like an eternity. And the things I've seen, Micuccio… I still can't believe they're true. If anyone at home had ever told me what to expect in the big cities, I'd have said they were mad! You remember how you used to visit us up in the attic – with the swallow's nests in the rafters… you remember? They used to fly all around the room – sometimes right into our faces. And my beautiful pots of basil on the windowsill… and Donna Annuzza?… Donna Annuzza, the little old woman next door… how is she?

MICUCCIO: Eh! (*He makes the sign of the cross*)

MARTA: Dead? I was afraid she might be. She was much older than me – even then! Poor Donna Annuzza; with her "just a pinch of garlic", you remember? She was always turning up with that excuse – to borrow "just a pinch of garlic" – just when we were sitting down to eat. Poor Donna Annuzza! And who knows how many more have died, there in Palma, eh? But at least the dead can lie in peace in our churchyard, with their own relations. Whilst I… who knows where I'll leave these old bones of mine! But come now, that's enough of sad thoughts. Ah, Dorina.

DORINA *has entered with the first course and stands by* MICUCCIO, *waiting for him to serve himself.* MICUCCIO *looks at* DORINA, *then at* AUNT MARTA, *confused and shy. He is about to help himself when he notices that his hands are dirty from the journey. He drops them, more embarrassed than ever.*

MARTA: Here, Dorina. Bring it here. I'll serve him. There. Is that enough, Micuccio?

MICUCCIO: Oh yes… thank you.

MARTA: And now myself.

MICUCCIO: Mm… it smells wonderful.

MARTA: Something special for the party tonight. Come, let's eat. Oh but first I must… (*She crosses herself and quickly mutters grace.* MICUCCIO *follows suit – but not so hurriedly.*) You too? dear Micuccio… you haven't changed. I'm so glad. Would you believe me… when I have to eat in there… without being able to say grace first, I feel as though the food just won't go down. Come, eat! Eat!

Now and then waiters pass through the room, carrying courses to and from the reception. Whenever they open the inner glass door, the merry-making can be heard.

MICUCCIO: You don't know how hungry I am. I haven't had a bite for two days now.

MARTA: What d'you mean? Didn't you eat on the way?

MICUCCIO: I took something with me – it's there in my case, but…

MARTA: But?

MICUCCIO: Well, I… there were so many people in the train, Aunt Marta. I tried to eat, but I felt as though everyone were watching me… and I felt ashamed.

MARTA: So you didn't eat at all! For two whole days? Silly boy! You must be starving. Come, eat up. And taste some of this wine. (*She pours out a glass*)

MICUCCIO: Thank you. Enough… that's enough. (*He raises his glass but is prevented from drinking by a burst of laughter from the other room. He looks at the doorway. There is the sound of guests toasting* "SINA" *followed by applause.* MICUCCIO *looks into the sad, pitying eyes of* AUNT MARTA, *searching for an explanation of the noise.*) They're laughing.

MARTA: Yes, but drink… drink up. Oh – what rubbish this is next to our good wine back home. You remember the wonderful wine Michela used to make… the woman who lived on the floor below us? What's happened to Michela?

MICUCCIO (*between mouthfuls*): Michela? Oh she's all right, she's all right.

MARTA: And her daughter Luzza?

MICUCCIO: Married… she's got two children.

MARTA: Already? She used to come up to see us often, d'you remember? Always laughing, dear Luzza. Who'd have thought it – married already. Who did she marry?

MICUCCIO: Toto Licasi – the man at the custom's house.

MARTA: Ah yes. So Donna Mariangela's a grandmother already: lucky woman! Two children, did you say.

MICUCCIO: Yes, two.

Another burst of laughter from the other room. He looks up, disturbed.

MARTA: You're not drinking.

MICUCCIO: Yes, I was just...

MARTA: Don't pay any attention to them; they're noisy people. And there are so many of them. What can you do? It's life, my boy. She has to – for her career. Her manager's there too. (DORINA *enters with the second course*) Ah, Dorina... that's good. Give me your plate, Micuccio. You'll like some of this too.

MICUCCIO: No, thank you. I couldn't eat any more.

MARTA: Oh, very well then, Dorina. (DORINA *goes*)

MICUCCIO: What a lot you've learnt. I just can't believe my eyes.

MARTA: You have to learn, my son.

MICUCCIO: When I saw you with that velvet cloak – and with your hair dyed this funny colour – and *that hat*! If they saw you back home in Palma...

MARTA: Santa Maria, don't make me think of it, Micuccio. I feel so ashamed. Sometimes I look at myself in the mirror and I say: "Is this really me?" And it seems to me I'm dressed up for a carnival. But what can you do? You have to!

MICUCCIO (*rising*): In that case – it means she really has got somewhere. (*Indicating the richness of the room*) You can see it. They pay her well, I suppose.

MARTA: Oh yes, of course.

MICUCCIO: How much a concert?

MARTA: That depends. That depends on the... season, the... theatres... you understand? But you know my son, it costs so much... this life. Jewels, evening dresses – the bills...

There is a loud burst of noise from the other room. Shouts of: "Where are you going?" "Come back, Sina." "Let's see him." "We want to see what he looks like!" and Teresina's voice, topping them: "One moment, boys... one moment!"

MARTA: That's her. She's coming, I think. I told you she would.

SINA *appears in the doorway. As she enters, the room appears to get brighter. She is a little the worse for champagne. She laughs stupidly, waving her shoe in her hand.* MICUCCIO *stands staring. He stammers:*

MICUCCIO: Teresina.

SINA: Oh there you are, Micuccio. How are you? Well again now? So sad you were ill. Listen, I'll be out again a bit later. Mother'll keep you company meantime. All right? See you presently... (*She blows a meaningless kiss and disappears again through the doors. Loud clamour greets her reappearance.* MICUCCIO *remains standing as though transfixed. After a long moment,* MARTA *timidly tries to break his trance.*)

MARTA: Aren't you... aren't you going to finish your meal? (MICUCCIO *stares at her uncomprehendingly*) Micuccio – your dinner – it's getting cold.

MICUCCIO: Dinner? No... no... (*For a moment he is silent, humiliated*) How she has changed. I wouldn't have known her. Her voice – her eyes – it isn't her. It isn't her any more. Teresina. (*A pause, then more to himself*) No, of course not. It's no use... no use thinking about it any more. All over.

MARTA: What d'you mean?

MICUCCIO: What a fool I've been. What a fool! They warned me back home... but I didn't believe them. I broke my neck to get here. Thirty-six hours on the train – only just to... (*A sudden realization*) So that's why they laughed at me. But how could I have known, Aunt Marta? I came because Teresina had promised to... to... but perhaps – yes, of course! How could she have known then that one day she'd be famous, while I stayed back there at home, playing my piccolo in the village square...

MARTA: Believe me, Micuccio...

MICUCCIO (*turns to her brusquely*): Listen Aunt Marta, if I ever did anything for her, nobody here now must think I came here to... to sponge on her!

MARTA: But Micuccio dear...

MICUCCIO: Oh – I almost forgot. I came to bring this too. (*He takes his wallet from his pocket*) The money.

MARTA: What money?

MICUCCIO: I know you meant to try and pay me back for what I spent on her – to put her where she is... But what's that to me now? I can

535

see that Teresina has become a... a queen! I see that... never mind! But money? NO. I didn't deserve that from her. What's it for? A polite way to break off our betrothal? There, take it. I'm only sorry it's not all there.

MARTA: What are you saying, my son? What are you saying?

MICUCCIO: I didn't spend it myself; my people did while I was ill. But we can set that against what I spent for her before, you remember? It's not worth talking about. The rest is here... and now I'm going.

Offstage, a guitar strikes up the opening bars of a vulgar French song. SINA *sings. The company joins in boisterously, punctuating it with bursts of laughter.*

MARTA: So soon? At least wait till I'll go and tell her.

MICUCCIO (*preventing her*): No – it's no use. Listen: it's Teresina. She's singing.

MARTA: But...

MICUCCIO: Hush! (*He listens in silence to a few bars, then begins to speak very quietly*) How different from the way she used to sing – back there in our valley. I used to listen to her from afar, coming over the hill every evening, carrying the baskets of fruit she'd been gathering. Her hair was wild – like snakes writhing in the wind. Her eyes sparkled like stars at night... and her voice echoed through the valley. I used to rush out to help her carry the baskets of fruit and when she saw me, she'd laugh! Her laugh was like the gurgle of the stream running down the hill and her voice wandered through my heart like the murmur of the leaves rustling in the wind. Teresina... Teresina... (*The song ends in the other room. There is loud applause and shouts of "Encore".*) Listen! Do you hear that? Let her stay there. That's where she belongs. And you too, Aunt Marta – you'd better go and join her. Do you hear them laughing? I don't want them to laugh at me. I'm going! (*He takes up his cases*)

MARTA: No... no... Micuccio, please! You don't understand. She's so different now... I – I can't control her any longer. She's... she's bad, Micuccio!

MICUCCIO (*turning*): What did you say? Why is she bad? Why?

MARTA (*sobbing*): She's always surrounded by those awful men. She never listens to me – never has time for me. The things she does! The men she goes with! Micuccio... if you'd only listened to me back home.

She... she isn't fit for you any longer! (MICUCCIO *places his hand over her mouth to stop her*)

Offstage the guitar strikes up again. MICUCCIO *stands still for a few moments, his eyes closed, biting his lip, his hand still over* MARTA's *mouth. Then he turns to her, takes her head in his hands, turns it up towards him and gazes deeply into her eyes, then rests her head on his chest, stroking her hair.*

MICUCCIO: So... that's what she's become! (*He moves slowly towards the other room, his hand taking a belt knife from his jacket.* MARTA *clutches him.*)

MARTA: No... Micuccio... please... please. For my sake, Micuccio!

MICUCCIO (*calmly and with sincere sorrow*): All right, Aunt Marta – for your sake. (*He puts away the knife*)

MARTA (*heartbroken and with such sincere, simple sorrow that his anger cools*): It would be better if you went, Micuccio. Please go.

MICUCCIO: I am going, Aunt Marta. All the more reason now.

SINA *reappears, her hair and dress a little disordered.*

SINA: Hello, you two. Having a good time?

MICUCCIO *catches her by the arm and draws her close.*

MICUCCIO: So that's what you've become, is it? That's why you're dressed like this – with your arms bare, your shoulders bare... everything!

SINA: Micuccio... you're hurting my wrist!

MARTA (*frightened*): Micuccio – please!

MICUCCIO (*throwing her to the floor*): Don't be afraid – I'm not going to harm her. What a fool I was, Aunt Marta, not to have understood before. I'm going. Goodbye. (*He takes his things and makes for the door, then remembers something*) Oh – I almost forgot. Look, Aunt Marta – look at these limes. I carried them all the way from Palma. Fresh limes. I picked them myself.

The guitar strikes up again in the next room. MICUCCIO *empties the straw basket of limes onto the table. They roll over, some onto the floor.* SINA *tries to gather them.*

SINA: Oh – limes... limes from Palma.

MICUCCIO (*grabbing her wrist*): Don't you touch them! You're not fit to look at them now – even from a distance. (*He holds one under her nose*) There... smell, smell the scent of our valley at home. I've a good mind to take them one by one and throw them at the heads of your boyfriends in there!

MARTA: Oh no, Micuccio!

MICUCCIO: And as for you, Teresina...

SINA *gives a slight scream.*

MARTA: Micuccio, please!

SINA *begins to whimper.*

MICUCCIO: Don't be afraid. I told you I wouldn't hurt her. But don't you dare touch those limes, Teresina. I brought them for you. I even paid duty on them! But now you're not to touch them. They're only for Aunt Marta – you understand? (*He looks at the money on the table, picks it up and thrusts it into* SINA's *low-cut dress*) Here's something for you – the money your mother sent me... all that dirty, filthy paper. Take it... there! Plenty of it! And here's some more! What are you crying for, Sina Marnis? You've got what you wanted from life, haven't you? Goodbye, Aunt Marta. Good luck to you! (*He picks up his things and goes out*)

MARTA: Micuccio... Micuccio... (*She turns to look at* TERESINA, *who is in hysterics at her feet and lets her arms drop limply by her side*)

The music swells up as

THE CURTAIN FALLS

The Man with the Flower in His Mouth

L'uomo dal fiore in bocca (1923)

Translated by Gigi Gatti and Terry Doyle

CHARACTERS

THE MAN WITH THE FLOWER IN HIS MOUTH
A CAREFREE TRAVELLER

Towards the end of the play there occasionally appears around the corner the shadow of a woman, dressed in black, in an old hat with weeping feathers.

NOTE ON THE TEXT

"Un pacifico avventore": *We have translated* avventore *as "traveller" rather than "customer" or "client". Otherwise* THE MAN WITH THE FLOWER IN HIS MOUTH *could be taken for the proprietor of the café, which is confusing: perhaps Pirandello really meant it to be ambiguous?*

We have translated pacifico *as "carefree", even though the traveller is not by circumstance or character "carefree". He is only "carefree" in relation to* THE MAN WITH THE FLOWER IN HIS MOUTH, *who is dying. We assume this to be Pirandello's meaning.*

In the background an avenue; street lights glimmering through the leaves of the trees. On both sides, the end houses of a street leading into the avenue. Among the houses a dingy all-night café; tables and chairs out on the pavement. In front of the houses, on the right, a street lamp, shining. On the corner of the last house, on the left, at right angles to the avenue, another street light shining. It's just gone midnight. From afar, the occasional haunting strum of a mandolin.

As the curtain rises, THE MAN WITH THE FLOWER IN HIS MOUTH *is sitting at one of the tables, slowly, silently, observing* THE TRAVELLER *at the next table who is calmly sucking a crème de menthe through a straw.*

THE MAN WITH THE FLOWER: Well, you're quite a cool customer, I must say. So you missed the last train?

THE TRAVELLER: Missed it by a minute. I arrived at the station and saw it vanish right in front of my nose.

THE MAN WITH THE FLOWER: You could've run after it!

THE TRAVELLER: Yes, I suppose it is a bit of a joke. If only I hadn't had all those damned parcels, packets and packages with me... for Christ's sake, more loaded up than a mule I was! Women! Shopping here... shopping there... There's no end to it. Do you know, it took me three whole minutes after I got out of the taxi, just to arrange all those loops around my fingers. Two packets for every finger.

THE MAN WITH THE FLOWER: Must've been a fine sight! You know what I'd have done in your place? I'd have left the whole lot in the taxi.

THE TRAVELLER: Oh, yes! And what about my wife? And daughters? And all their friends?

THE MAN WITH THE FLOWER: Screams and shouts, eh! I'd have really enjoyed that.

THE TRAVELLER: Maybe you don't know what women are like once they're on holiday!

THE MAN WITH THE FLOWER: Of course I do. Precisely because I do know. (*Pause*) They all say they won't be needing a thing.

THE TRAVELLER: As if that was all. They're even capable of claiming they go on holiday to save. Then, the moment they set foot in one of these little villages round here – the uglier it is, the more plain and simple – the more pains they take to tart it up with all their frippery. Women! But then that's the way they are... "If only you'd pop into town for me, dear! I could do with a thing or two... And

541

while you're there, couldn't you just get me this as well… and that? And if you don't mind too much" (I like the "if you don't mind") "seeing you'll be going that way anyhow…" – But my dear, how on earth am I to do all that in three hours? – "Oh, come on, if you took a taxi…" The trouble is that, thinking I'd be away only for three hours, I came out without my keys.

THE MAN WITH THE FLOWER: Nice one. What next?

THE TRAVELLER: I dropped the pile of packets and parcels in the left-luggage at the station and went to eat at a trattoria. Then, to let off steam, I went to the theatre. The heat in there was enough to finish me off. When I came out I asked myself: what next? It's already midnight; I'll be catching the four o'clock train. It's not worth spending the money just to get three hours' sleep. So here I am. This café stays open all night, doesn't it?

THE MAN WITH THE FLOWER: Never closes, no, sir. (*Pause*) So, you dropped all your parcels in the left-luggage, at the station?

THE TRAVELLER: Why do you ask? Aren't they safe there? They were all wrapped up…

THE MAN WITH THE FLOWER: No, no, I didn't meant that! (*Pause*) Well wrapped up… yes, I'm sure: with that special flair shop assistants have for gift wrapping… (*Pause*) What hands they have! A large double sheet of red, smooth paper, so beautiful in itself… so smooth it makes you want to press your face against it. Cool as a caress… They spread it out on the counter, and then, with such casual elegance, position the fine, well-folded cloth right in the middle. First they lift up a flap from underneath with the back of one hand; then, with the other hand, fold over the other flap, and then they tuck in the corners with such graceful ease – a little extra touch just for the sake of art. After that they fold the end flaps into triangles and tuck the points away; they reach out for the roll of string, give a tug to unravel just the right length, and tie up the parcel with such speed that you've hardly time to admire their skill, before you're presented with the package, complete with the loop for you to put your finger through.

THE TRAVELLER: I can see you've spent a lot of time observing shop assistants at work.

THE MAN WITH THE FLOWER: Me? My dear sir, I spend entire days watching them. I can stand in one place for a whole hour, watching them through the shop window. I forget myself while I'm there. I feel as though I were… I'd like to be that roll of silk… that piece of cloth… that red or blue ribbon the young girls from haberdashery measure out by the metre – have you ever noticed how they do it? They gather it into a figure of eight between thumb and little finger, before wrapping it up. (*Pause*) I watch the customers coming out of the shop with the parcel looped round their finger, or in their hand, or under their arm… I gaze after them, until I lose sight of them… imagining… ah, so many things! You have no idea. (*Pause. Then darkly as though to himself:*) But that's what I need. Just what I need.

THE TRAVELLER: Just what you need? I'm sorry… what exactly?

THE MAN WITH THE FLOWER: To attach myself to life like that – I mean, with my imagination. Like a creeper round the railings of a gate. (*Pause*) I can't let my imagination rest, not even for a moment. I must use it to cling, cling to other people's lives… but not to people I know. No, no, that I couldn't do! The mere thought of it disgusts me – if only you knew – sickens me… No, I cling to the lives of strangers, where my imagination may work freely. Not capriciously though: on the contrary, I take note of every little mannerism of one person or another. If only you knew how my imagination works, and how hard! How deeply I can penetrate their lives! I see people's homes; I live there; I see myself right inside them, until I even become aware of… do you know that particular odour that nests in every home? Yours, mine… But in our own home we're no longer aware of it, because it's the very odour of our lives. Are you with me? Yes, I can see you're nodding…

THE TRAVELLER: Yes, because… I mean to say, you must get great pleasure from imagining all those things…

THE MAN WITH THE FLOWER (*irritated, after having given it some thought*): Pleasure? Me?

THE TRAVELLER: Yes… I mean…

THE MAN WITH THE FLOWER: Tell me. Have you ever been able to see a good doctor?

THE TRAVELLER: Me? No, why, I'm not ill!

THE MAN WITH THE FLOWER: Don't be alarmed! I was only wondering if you've ever had a look at one of those good doctor's waiting rooms where the patients sit, waiting their turn.

THE TRAVELLER: Ah, yes, once, when I had to take my daughter, who was suffering from nerves.

THE MAN WITH THE FLOWER: Good. I didn't want to pry. I mean, waiting rooms... (*Pause*) Did you have a good look? Dark-covered, old-fashioned sofas... odd, upholstered chairs... Furniture picked up here and there in some second-hand shop and dumped there for the patients. None of it really belongs in the house. For himself and for entertaining his wife's friends, the dear doctor has quite a different reception room. Elegant, tastefully furnished. How out of place they would be, those nice chairs and armchairs, if they were brought out into the waiting room, where the patients have to make do with decent, sober furniture. I'd like to know if, when you took your daughter there, you observed carefully the chair or armchair on which you sat, waiting.

THE TRAVELLER: No, not really...

THE MAN WITH THE FLOWER: Of course not. Because you were not ill yourself... (*Pause*) But even those who are ill don't always notice these things, wrapped up as they are in their own suffering. (*Pause*) And yet, how often you see people sitting there, staring at their own finger, tracing vague patterns on the polished arm of the chair! Lost in their thoughts, not seeing a thing! (*Pause*) But then what an impression it makes on you, when the doctor's finished with you, and you come out and see, there, in the waiting room, the chair where not so long ago you sat, in ignorance, awaiting the verdict! Now you find it occupied by some other patient, he too with his own secret illness. Or you may find the chair empty, impassive, waiting for someone else to come and sit on it. (*Pause*) But what were we saying? Ah, yes... The pleasures of the imagination – I wonder how I came to think of a chair in one of those doctor's waiting rooms where patients are waiting to be seen?

THE TRAVELLER: Yes... actually...

THE MAN WITH THE FLOWER: You don't see the connection? Neither do I. (*Pause*) The thing is this: we all have our own private, apparently unconnected, images and memories; images created by such deeply personal experiences, that if we allowed ourselves to expose them in everyday conversation, we just wouldn't understand one another. There's nothing more illogical, often, than analogies based on such private images. (*Pause*) But perhaps the connection here is this, look: do you think those chairs get any pleasure fantasizing about the patients sitting on them in the waiting room? About what illnesses they may be hatching, where they'll go, what they'll get up to after the consultation? No pleasure at all. It's the same with me: none at all. So many patients come and go, and the chairs, poor things, just stay there waiting to be sat upon. And that's exactly the way I spend my life. One moment I'm taken up by this, another by that. At this moment I'm taken up by you, and believe you me, I get no pleasure from the fact that you missed your train, from your family waiting for you on holiday, from all the worries I suppose you must have too.

THE TRAVELLER: If only you knew!

THE MAN WITH THE FLOWER: Thank God, if they're only worries. (*Pause*) There're those who are worse off, my dear sir. (*Pause*) I was saying how I need to use my imagination to cling to other people's lives, but that's all it is, there's no pleasure in it, it's not because I'm interested, on the contrary... It's that I need to share everyone else's problems, so I can judge life as futile and vain, so much so that nobody should really mind if it comes to an end. (*With dark rage*) But you have to go on proving it to yourself, you know, on and on, without mercy. Because, my dear sir, we all feel this unquenchable thirst for life, we feel it here, like an ache in our throat, but we don't know what it's made of, we can never satisfy it. Because in the very act of living, life is always so full of itself, we can never taste it to the full. All we can really savour is the past, which remains alive inside us. That's where the thirst for life comes from, from the memories that bind us. But bind us to what? Why, to all this nonsense here... to these petty worries... to so many stupid illusions... fatuous oc-cupations... yes, yes, what now seems nonsense to us... what now seems a bore – and I'd go as far as to say, what now seems to us a misfortune, a real misfortune – yes, sir, I wonder what flavour all that will acquire in four, five years' time. What taste these tears will have... And life, by God, the mere thought of losing it... especially when you know it's a matter of days... (*At this point the head of a* WOMAN *dressed in black peers around the right-hand corner of the street*) There you are... Can you see? There, look, on that corner... Can you see the shadow of a woman? There, she's hiding herself!

THE TRAVELLER: What? Who... who was that?

THE MAN WITH THE FLOWER: Didn't you see her? She's hiding.

THE TRAVELLER: A woman?

THE MAN WITH THE FLOWER: Yes, my wife.

THE TRAVELLER: Ah! your wife?

THE MAN WITH THE FLOWER (*after a pause*): Keeps an eye on me from a distance. Sometimes I feel like going over and kicking her, believe you me. But what's the point? She's like one of those stray, obstinate bitches: the more you kick them, the closer they stick to your heels. (*Pause*) You have no idea how that woman is suffering on my account. Doesn't eat, doesn't sleep. Follows me around day and night. Like that, from a distance. If only she took the trouble to dust that slipper of a hat she wears on her head, those rags… She doesn't even look like a woman any more, more like an old rag. Even her hair has turned dusty for ever, here, at the temples. And she's barely thirty-four years old. (*Pause*) You can't imagine how angry she makes me sometimes. I jump at her, and scream in her face – Idiot! – shaking her at the same time. She takes it all. Stands there, looking at me with such eyes… eyes that make me feel, I swear to you, here, in my fingers, a wild urge to strangle her. But it's no good. She just waits for me to move away, and starts following me again, from a distance. (*At this point* THE WOMAN *peers around the corner again*) There, look… that's her peering round the corner again.

THE TRAVELLER: Poor woman!

THE MAN WITH THE FLOWER: Poor woman my foot! You know what she'd like? She'd like me to stay at home! Calmly, quietly, so she can cuddle me with all her most ardent love and care. So that I could wallow in the perfect order of all the rooms, in the cleanliness of all the furniture, in that mirrored silence which there used to be in my home, measured out by the tick-tock of the dining-room clock. That's what she'd like! Now I ask you, so that you may understand the absurdity – but no, what do I mean, absurdity, the macabre ferocity of this pretence… I ask you, whether you think it possible that the houses of Avezzano, the houses of Messina, knowing that an earthquake was about to shatter them, would have been quite happy to stay there calmly in the moonlight, standing in an orderly line along the streets and squares, obeying the planning orders of the town council. No, by God, those houses of stone and beams would've run for their lives! Imagine the citizens of Avezzano, the citizens of Messina, calmly undressing themselves to go to bed, folding up their clothes, placing their shoes outside the door, and tucking themselves underneath the bedclothes, to enjoy the freshly laundered sheets in the full knowledge that in a few hours they would be dead. Does it seem feasible to you?

THE TRAVELLER: But perhaps your wife...

THE MAN WITH THE FLOWER: Let me finish! If only, my dear sir, death were like one of those strange, disgusting insects which someone unexpectedly finds on you... You're walking down the street; suddenly some passer-by stops you and, extending two fingers of one hand, cautiously says to you: "Excuse me, may I? You, my dear sir, have death on you." Wouldn't it be wonderful? But death isn't like one of those disgusting insects. I wonder how many people walking around, casually, unawares, have it on them? No one sees it. They go around making quiet plans for tomorrow, and the day after. Now I... (*Gets up*) Look my dear sir... Come over here... (*Makes* THE TRAVELLER *get up, and leads him over to the street lamp*) Here, under the light... Come on... I want to show you something... Look here, under the moustache, here, you see that pretty, violet nodule? You know what it's called? Ah, such a sweet name, sweeter than a caramel: epithelioma, it's called. Say it, hear the sweetness: epithelioma... Death, you understand? passed by, stuck this flower in my mouth and said to me: "Keep it, my friend: I'll be back in eight or ten months!" (*Pause*) How can you tell me: with the flower in my mouth, could I possible stay at home, calmly and quietly, as that poor wretch would like me to? (*Pause*) I scream at her: "Oh yes, you want me to kiss you?" – "Yes, kiss me!" – Do you know what she did? The other week, with a pin. She scratched herself here, on the lip and took hold of my head and tried to kiss me... Kiss me on the mouth. Because she says she wants to die with me. (*Pause*) She's crazy... (*Pause*) I will not stay at home. At the shop window is where I need to be, so I can admire the skills of the shop assistants. Because, you see, if I found myself faced for one moment by the void inside me... well, you understand, I could easily take the life of a perfect stranger just like that... take out a gun and kill someone, someone like you, who just happens to have missed his train... (*Laughs*) No, no, have no fear, my dear sir, I was only joking! (*Pause*) I'm going now. (*Pause*) I'd kill myself if ever... (*Pause*) But there's such beautiful apricots in season just now... How do you eat them? With the skin on, I bet, is that right? You break them in two, you squeeze them open with your fingers, like two succulent lips... Ah, how delicious! (*Laughs. Pauses.*) My best wishes to your dear wife and daughters on holiday. (*Pause*) I can just picture them all dressed in white and blue, in a beautiful green meadow in the shade... (*Pause*) Please, do me a favour, in the morning, when you arrive. I imagine the village is some little way from the station. At dawn, you might easily feel like walking there. The first little tuft of grass you see by the roadside, count the blades for me. However many blades there are, that's how many days I have left to live. (*Pause*) Make sure you pick a nice thick one. (*Laughs, then:*) Goodnight, my dear sir.

He strolls off, humming to the sound of the distant mandolin, in the direction of the right-hand corner, but at a certain point, thinking his wife might be waiting for him, he turns and scurries off, in the opposite direction, followed by the stupefied gaze of the carefree traveller.

CURTAIN

The Vice

La morsa (1910)

Translated by Carlo Ardito

CHARACTERS

ANDREA FABBRI
GIULIA, *his wife*
ANTONIO SERRA, *a lawyer*
ANNA, *a servant*

The action takes place in a small provincial town.

A room in the Fabbri household. Upstage, the main entrance. A side door to the left; two side windows to the right.

Shortly after the curtain rises, GIULIA, *who has been looking out of the window, her back to the audience, starts in surprise. She puts her crochet work down on a small table and, quickly but warily, shuts the door on the left, then waits by the main entrance.*

ANTONIO SERRA *enters.*

GIULIA (*hugs him, happy though quietly*): Here already?

ANTONIO (*fends her off nervously*): No. Please.

GIULIA: Are you alone? Did you leave Andrea?

ANTONIO (*his thoughts elsewhere*): I came back first. Last night.

GIULIA: Why?

ANTONIO (*irritated by her question*): I made up an excuse. Actually, it wasn't really an excuse. I had to be back here this morning. On business.

GIULIA: Why not tell me? You could have warned me.

ANTONIO *looks at her silently.*

GIULIA: What's happened?

ANTONIO (*in an undertone, tensely, almost angrily*): What's happened? I think Andrea suspects us.

GIULIA (*startled with fear in her voice*): Andrea? How do you know? Did you give us away?

ANTONIO: No. Maybe we both did.

GIULIA: When? Where?

ANTONIO: Here. When we were coming downstairs. Andrea was in front of me, remember? Carrying a suitcase. You were by the door, holding a candle. And as I walked past... God, how stupid one can be!

GIULIA: He noticed?

ANTONIO: I thought he turned round, as he walked downstairs.

GIULIA: Oh my God! So you've come to tell me... Go on...

ANTONIO: You didn't notice anything?

GIULIA: Not a thing. But where is Andrea? Where?

ANTONIO: Tell me, was I already coming down the stairs when he called you?

551

GIULIA: And said goodbye to me! Was that when he turned on the landing?

ANTONIO: No, it must have been before that.

GIULIA: But if he saw us...

ANTONIO: Caught a glimpse of us, at most. A matter of a second.

GIULIA: He let you come on ahead? Is this possible? Are you sure he didn't leave as well?

ANTONIO: Quite sure. There's no train from town before eleven. (*Consults his watch*) It's just about due. Meanwhile we're not sure... the suspense is intolerable. You understand?

GIULIA: Let's calm down. Tell me everything. What did he do? I must be told everything.

ANTONIO: What can I tell you? In this kind of situation the most casual remark seems charged with significance: every look or gesture, or tone of voice...

GIULIA: As I said: let's keep calm.

ANTONIO: That's easy to say. (*After a brief pause, and more relaxed*) It was here, do you remember? Before we left we were discussing the case we had to take care of in town. He was getting all worked up...

GIULIA: Well?

ANTONIO: The moment we were in the street, Andrea went quiet and walked with his head down. I looked at him: he seemed uneasy about something. He was frowning. "He's found out!" I thought. I was shaking. Then all of a sudden he said, quite simply and naturally: "Isn't it sad," he said, "travelling at night... leaving home of an evening..."

GIULIA: Just like that?

ANTONIO: Yes. He thought it was sad for those left behind, too. Then he said something that really put me in a cold sweat: "To have to say goodbye, on a staircase, by the light of a candle..."

GIULIA: He said that? *How* did he say it?

ANTONIO: Perfectly naturally. In the same tone. I don't know, maybe he did it on purpose. He mentioned the children, he said he'd left them in bed, asleep, but not in his usual loving, reassuring tone. He mentioned you.

GIULIA: Me?

ANTONIO: Yes. But he was looking at me.

GIULIA: What did he say?

ANTONIO: That he loved your children so much.

GIULIA: Nothing else?

ANTONIO: On the train, he returned to the subject of our legal business. He asked me about Gorri, the lawyer, whether I knew him. Oh yes, he wanted to know among other things whether he was married, and laughed. This, you see, had nothing to do with the matter in hand. Or was it I who—

GIULIA (*quickly*): Be quiet!

ANNA (*from the threshold of the main door*): Excuse me, madam. Shall I go and pick up the children?

GIULIA: Yes. But wait a little.

ANNA: Isn't Mr Fabbri coming home today? The carriages are already on their way to the station.

ANTONIO (*looking at his watch*): It's nearly eleven.

GIULIA: Already? (*To* ANNA) Wait a few more minutes. I'll tell you when to set out.

ANNA: Very good, madam. I'll finish setting the table while I wait. (*Leaves*)

ANTONIO: He'll be here presently.

GIULIA: You've nothing to tell me? You couldn't find out anything?

ANTONIO: Yes: that he's good at pretending, if he really does suspect anything.

GIULIA: Andrea, who is so bad at controlling his feelings?

ANTONIO: And yet… could it be I'm so nervous I'm blind to the obvious? Is that possible? Once or twice I thought I saw through his words. But then I reassured myself by thinking I was just plain afraid. I studied him, observed his every move and gesture, the way he looked at me, the way he talked. As a rule he's a man of few words, and yet over the three days we were together you should have heard him! But often he'd relapse into a disquieting silence, only to break it by bringing up the legal business. Could this be why he seems so worried? I asked myself. Or is it due to something else? Maybe he is talking just now merely to allay any suspicions on my part. On another occasion I had the impression he avoided shaking hands with me. And mind you, he was aware I had put out my hand first. He pretended not to notice. The day after we left he was decidedly odd. He started walking away, then he called me back, as if he'd regretted his lack of civility. He's going to apologize, I thought. In fact he said: "Sorry – I forgot to say goodbye. Never mind!" On other occasions he'd talk about you, the house, but it was just small talk. It occurred to me he was avoiding looking me in the eye. At times he'd repeat a sentence three, four times, for no reason at all, as if he was thinking of something else. And when he changed the subject he somehow managed to change tack suddenly and start talking about you and the children. He threw questions at me – was he trying to trick me into an admission? He was laughing, but with an ugly look in his eyes.

GIULIA: And you?

ANTONIO: Oh, I was always on my guard.

GIULIA: He must have noticed you were nervous.

ANTONIO: Did he already have suspicions? Maybe he did.

GIULIA: In that case you confirmed his mistrust. Anything else?

ANTONIO: Yes... The first night, at the hotel – he insisted on taking one room with twin beds – we'd been in bed for some time and he noticed I wasn't asleep, that is... he couldn't have noticed since it was pitch dark! He must have assumed it. Bear in mind that I lay still, in the middle of the night, in the same room with him and afraid he'd find out... can you imagine it? I lay there staring into space... you know... ready to defend myself. All of a sudden he broke the silence and said, and I quote: "You're not asleep."

GIULIA: How did you react?

ANTONIO: I said nothing. I didn't answer. I pretended to be asleep. A little later, he repeated: "You're not asleep." Then I called out: "Did you say something?" And he said: "Yes, I wanted to know whether you were asleep." But he had not been asking me a question, he'd said quite plainly: "You are not asleep" in the sense that I couldn't sleep. At least, that's how it struck me.

GIULIA: Nothing else?

ANTONIO: No. I couldn't sleep for two nights after that.

GIULIA: Afterwards, how was he with you?

ANTONIO: The same as always. No change.

GIULIA: Andrea? Putting on an act? If he'd really seen us...

ANTONIO: And yet he turned round, as we were coming down...

GIULIA: I doubt whether he noticed anything. Could he?

ANTONIO: He may not be completely sure...

GIULIA: You don't know Andrea. Control himself like that, without giving anything away? What do you know? Nothing! Even supposing he'd seen us as you passed by and leant towards me... If he'd had the least suspicion... that you'd kissed me... he'd have walked back upstairs... yes! Just think how we'd both have felt! Listen – no: it just isn't possible. You panicked, that's all. Andrea has no reason to suspect us. You've always been pretty friendly towards me in front of him.

ANTONIO: I grant you that, but suspicion can arise from one minute to the next. Don't you see? A thousand other things acquire a particular significance. The slightest hunch becomes proof positive, doubts turn into certainty: that's what I'm afraid of.

GIULIA: We'll have to be careful.

ANTONIO: Now you tell me. That's what I've always urged.

GIULIA: Are you blaming me now?

ANTONIO: I'm not blaming you. Haven't I asked you a thousand times to be careful?

GIULIA: Yes. You have.

ANTONIO: Why did we have to flaunt ourselves so stupidly... giving ourselves away, just for the sake of a whim... like the other night. You were the one—

GIULIA: That's right, blame me.

ANTONIO: If you hadn't—

GIULIA: Yes... You're afraid, is that it?

ANTONIO: Do you think we've reason to be merry and carefree, you and I? You in particular! (*Pause. He paces up and down.*) Yes, it is fear. Don't you think I worry for you as well? You think I'm afraid, do you? (*Another pause. He resumes walking up and down.*) We were too sure of ourselves, that's it! And now all the stupid risks we took are staring me in the face. I ask myself how could he have failed to suspect us both up till now. How could he? We were making love right here... under his very eyes, you could say. We took advantage of every situation, the least opportunity that offered, whether he left us alone or even when he didn't. We were giving ourselves away with every gesture, with the look in our eyes... It was madness!

GIULIA (*after a long pause*): You blame me now. It's only natural. I have betrayed a man who trusted me even more than he trusted himself. Yes, it is my fault. I am mostly to blame.

555

ANTONIO (*stopping to stare at her, then resuming his pacing, curtly*): That's not at all what I meant.

GIULIA: Of course you did! I know you did. Look, you may as well add that it was I who decided to run away from home with him. It was I who pushed him into eloping with me, because I loved him – then betrayed him with you. You're right in blaming me now, absolutely right! (*Goes right up to him, and speaks feverishly*) But I, listen, I ran away with him because I loved him, not in order to settle down to a dull, quiet life… to all this luxury in a new home. I had all that before. I wouldn't have gone off with him… But he, as you know, felt he had to apologize for what he'd done. Andrea: a paragon of respectability! The damage was done. Now it had to be patched up somehow. Quickly. And how? He gave himself up to his work, provided us with a luxurious home and plenty of leisure for me to enjoy it. He worked like a slave, work and nothing but work was all he thought about. All he expected from me was a little praise for his hard work and integrity… and maybe a little gratitude, too! I might have fared worse. He was a good man, he'd have made me rich all over again if need be. Richer, in fact. All this was meant for me. Every night I waited for him impatiently, happy at his return. He'd come back exhausted, satisfied with the day's work, planning tomorrow's tasks. Frankly, in the end, I got tired, too, of having to force this man to love me, and reciprocate my love for him. A husband's esteem, trust and friendship can seem like insults to a wife at times! And you took advantage of the situation, though you now blame me for having loved you and betrayed my husband: now that we're in danger you are afraid, I can see you're afraid! What have *you* got to lose? Nothing. While I… (*She buries her face in her hands*)

ANTONIO (*after a short pause*): You ask me to keep calm. If I'm afraid at all it's for you… for your children.

GIULIA (*with disdain, hardly stifling a shout*): Don't you dare even mention them! (*Breaks into tears*) Those poor innocent creatures!

ANTONIO: Tears, now. I'm going.

GIULIA: That's right: go! There's nothing left to detain you!

ANTONIO (*quickly, and in earnest*): That's not fair! I have loved you, just as you have loved me. You know it's true. I warned you to be careful. Was that wrong? More for your sake than for mine. You've said it yourself: if it came to the worst, I'd nothing to lose. (*After a short pause*) I've never blamed you or reproached you. I had no right to.

(*Passes a hand over his eyes, then changes his tone of voice*) Come on, get hold of yourself! Andrea probably doesn't suspect a thing. That's what you think, isn't it? He didn't notice a thing. So... come on, nothing is finished. We can—

GIULIA: No. No. It's impossible. How could you even think of it? No, we'd better end it now.

ANTONIO: As you wish.

GIULIA: So much for your love.

ANTONIO: You're driving me mad!

GIULIA: No, we'd better end it now, this minute, no matter what happens. It's definitely over between us. What's more I think it would be better for Andrea to know everything.

ANTONIO: Are you mad?

GIULIA: Far, far better. What kind of a life am I leading? Think about it! I've no longer the right to love anyone. Not even my own children. When I kiss them I feel that the shadow of my guilt falls across their faces! No. No. Would he kill me? I'd do it myself if he didn't!

ANTONIO: You're talking nonsense!

GIULIA: Am I? I've always said it: it's too much for me. There's nothing left for me now. (*Attempts to control herself*) You must leave now. He'd better not find you here.

ANTONIO: You want me to leave? Leave you alone? I came specially... Wouldn't it be better if I...

GIULIA: No. He mustn't find you here. But come back once he's here. That's important. Come back soon, but try to control yourself. Be relaxed, at your ease, not as you are now. Talk to me normally, in front of him. I'll help you.

ANTONIO: Very well.

GIULIA: Yes. Soon. If anything...

ANTONIO: If anything... what?

GIULIA: Nothing. Anyway...

ANTONIO: What is it?

GIULIA: Never mind, I'll say goodbye.

ANTONIO: Giulia!

GIULIA: Go!

ANTONIO: I'll see you later. (*Leaves*)

GIULIA (*stands still in the middle of the room, her eyes staring into space, lost in gloomy thoughts. She lifts her head with a desolate, weary sigh and presses her hands to her face. But she does not succeed in ridding herself of her obsession. She paces up and down the room, stops in front of a cheval mirror, next to the main door, and is briefly distracted by her own reflection in the mirror. She walks away, and eventually sits by the small table on the right. She buries her head in her arms and, after sustaining this attitude for a little while, lifts her head, deep in thought.*): Might he not have gone back up the stairs? Made an excuse… He'd have found me there, behind the window, looking out… (*Pause*) If only Antonio weren't so afraid! (*She shakes her head, in an attitude of contempt and disgust. A pause, then she gets up, paces up and down for a while and returns to the coffee table, undecided. She rings the bell twice.*)

ANNA (*enters*): You rang?

GIULIA (*still deep in thought*): Yes, everything must be ready. You'll make sure, won't you Anna?

ANNA: Everything is ready, madam.

GIULIA: The table is set?

ANNA: It is.

GIULIA: The master's room?

ANNA: It's ready.

GIULIA: Go and get the children.

ANNA: Immediately. (*Begins to leave*)

GIULIA: Anna!

ANNA: Madam?

GIULIA (*still undecided after some thought*): Let them be a while longer. You can pick them up when my husband is back.

ANNA: That'll be better. He should be here any moment. In fact, if you'd like me to wait downstairs for the carriage to come back from the station I could help with the luggage.

GIULIA: No. Wait. Not yet.

ANNA: The children are so happy their daddy's coming back today. He promised them presents, you know: a horse this high for Carluccio… Ninetto would like one as well. They were squabbling this morning, in front of their granny: "Daddy loves me better than you!" said Carluccio. And Ninetto said to him: "Yes, but Mummy loves me better. So there!"

GIULIA: The darling!

ANNA: And he can barely talk!

GIULIA: Go and fetch them!

ANNA (*listening*): Wait – I can hear the carriage… (*She leans out of the window*) It's back. Shall I go down and help?

GIULIA: Yes. Do.

ANNA *leaves.*

GIULIA (*extremely nervous now, she resumes pacing the room; she stops, listens, goes back to the small table and mechanically picks up her crochet work*): I'll know straight away. (*She listens again, then starts crocheting with feverish movements, unaware of what she's doing. Suddenly she stops and listens again.*)

ANNA (*off*): The master is here! (*She enters, carrying a suitcase which she places on a chair near the entrance*)

GIULIA *rises with her crocheting things, affecting indifference, and walks towards the entrance.* ANDREA *enters.*

GIULIA (*holds out her hand*): I've been expecting you. (*To* ANNA) Go and get the children.

ANNA (*hesitatingly*): The master said…

ANDREA: They're at my mother's? Let them stay awhile. I'll unpack first. Then they'll find their presents when they get back.

GIULIA: As you wish.

ANNA *leaves.*

ANDREA: I'm exhausted. And I've a splitting headache.

GIULIA: Did you open the windows on the train?

ANDREA: No. I kept them shut. But the noise… I couldn't sleep a wink.

GIULIA: Was the train full?

ANDREA: Yes it was.

GIULIA: And my little feather pillow?

ANDREA: Bother! Isn't it here? I must have left it on the train. No doubt about it. Pity. Still… You're well? The children?

GIULIA: Everybody's fine.

ANDREA: You said you were expecting me? Serra must have told you.

GIULIA: Yes. He dropped in a little while ago. You didn't write to me. Not even once.

ANDREA: True, but I was only away three days. Serra came back last night…

GIULIA: He mentioned it. Said he'd call later.

ANDREA: Good. I'm glad you sent the children to my mother. She dotes on them. Did you go and see her?

GIULIA: No. You know I only go there with you.

ANDREA: I know, but by now, surely…

GIULIA (*changing the subject*): How did your case work out?

ANDREA: Didn't Serra tell you?

GIULIA: Hardly… briefly, at any rate. He didn't stay long.

ANDREA: We're making good progress. Though Antonio left me in the lurch… By the way, Gorri, the lawyer, praised him to the skies! Yes – a clever chap, your partner! He handled the case very well. As far as that goes… (*He breaks off and changes his tone of voice*) If everything works out as I hope it does, guess what? I'll wind everything up here – and wham! Off we go. No more headaches for me, no more work! We'll up and move into town! What do you say to that?

GIULIA: Live in town?

ANDREA: Look at you – aren't you keen?

GIULIA: It isn't that.

ANDREA: Ah! The city! The city! I'd like to live it up, now! Enjoy myself!

GIULIA: What made you decide?

ANDREA: I haven't quite decided yet. But if it's at all possible… Listen: I'm not going to rot away in this place. I've had it up to here! After all they've done to me! And in any case it's for your sake too.

GIULIA: As far as I'm concerned, anywhere would do…

ANDREA: Come on, come on! In town you'd have diversions you couldn't possibly dream of in the country. You need a change too. If only to breathe in the atmosphere of a city, the hustle and bustle of it all. Then again, here, there's my mother, and you and she—

GIULIA: I hope it isn't because of her that you want to move.

ANDREA: No. That wouldn't be the main reason.

GIULIA: You know only too well that it's your mother who doesn't like me…

ANDREA: I know, I know, and this would be an additional reason. But there are others. (*A short pause*) You know, in town I bumped twice into your brothers, and every time—

GIULIA: What did they do?

ANDREA: Do? Nothing. What could they do? I'd like to see them try. Nothing. As usual, they pretended not to have seen me. Oh yes! (*Hums a tune*) It's no use – they just can't get over it! What pride! And anger, too, now. You see, I'm no longer the nonentity I used to be! That robbed them of the satisfaction of seeing you suffer, sorry you'd left their roof to join me. They can't get over it! And I – that's it – am determined to settle down in town just to spite them. I bet they'll enjoy it! Even Serra would come along with us, I believe. What's to keep him here?

GIULIA: His practice?

ANDREA: Oh yes: big deal! Business proper is dealt with in town. What's here? A herd of sheep, once we've left. Incidentally, we'll have to think of some way to reward him. Of course I've done him a number of good turns, but this doesn't really count.

GIULIA: He might think otherwise.

ANDREA: Nonsense. Business is business, and good turns don't come into it. Friendships are bought in business. He deserves something, anyway. If only you knew how well he backed up my claims! With perfect fairness, of course. Sometimes they even try to deny I've done this place some good. Not so much gratitude as – never mind! I'm not saying I've enriched the place – and I could easily say I have – but they could acknowledge, if nothing else, that I've managed to get rid of malaria and a few other things. Why deny me that much credit?

GIULIA: They don't understand.

ANDREA: Quite so. When it's a question of showing gratitude, no one ever understands. It was a swamp they turned over to me; you remember what it was like, when we came here. You remember, don't you, we'd run away from town. All that land produced was weeds which even the sheep wouldn't graze on. I risked all my capital, that is... yours, to drain it, fertilize it, cultivate it. I turned that land into the richest in the area. Very well. My lease comes up for renewal and what happens? Not only do they try to dispossess me but they even deny I've given the place a new lease of life! "You made money out of it!" Thank you very much! Who was it that took risks? Risked everything? Come on! Besides, it was your money.

GIULIA: What's that got to do with it?

ANDREA: It was your money. And if I'm a rich man now, it's due to you.

GIULIA: I didn't do the work.

ANDREA: I did the work. I'll grant you that. And I took my chances. I looked around me on the train. They were all full of admiration for the work I've done. But in the old days they all thought I was mad. A swamp! Yes, that's what they thought it was. To me it was the land of plenty! I'd been obsessed with the idea ever since I was a lad. Think about it: people used to die like flies from malaria. Old Mantegna was in my compartment; you know him, don't you? Two of his daughters died of it. He told us about it with tears in his eyes. His wife also died of it.

GIULIA (*has resumed her crocheting*): They didn't live together by then.

ANDREA: I should think not! Especially after what... (*Laughs*) But he missed her more than his daughters. We all had a good laugh over that. Poor man, he's gone gaga. They poke fun at him now. Did you know they beat him up?

GIULIA: Really?

ANDREA: Yes. A long time ago. His wife's lover beat him up – Mantegna himself told us all about it, in great detail, on the train. Can you imagine how we laughed? "Put yourself in my shoes," he said. Then he turned to Sportini (he was there too, sitting next to me, the customs officer, you know?) "Ah Sportini," he said, "You of all people should feel sorry for me!" Pandemonium followed. Luckily a young fellow was with us, you know, a worldly young chap... full of modern ideas. Are you listening?

GIULIA: Yes, I wanted to ask you...

ANDREA: To go in to dinner? Is it ready? Let's go then. Now listen: this young chap started to talk. "You wanted to catch them at it?" he said. "Good Lord, that's prehistoric stuff. What's the point? The gentleman here got beaten up. The usual sudden trip... the wrong train... silly stunts employed by elderly husbands who pretend they've lost their railway timetable, when in fact they've lost their wits. There's no psy-cho-lo-gy to it! Let me explain. You have your suspicions, and you want proof? Why on earth should you want to catch them at it? What a ridiculous idea! Why bother two people who are having a perfectly agreeable time together?" – Witty young fellow, don't you think? – "If I," he said, "had a wife, and – God forbid! – and I suspected her" (I thought he was pulling old Mantegna's leg at this point) "I'd pretend not to have noticed anything at all. I wouldn't look for proof, I wouldn't upset her prematurely. I'd see to it – and here's the test – that she herself, and I mean all of her, should give herself away to me, that she herself became the living, shining proof of her own misdeeds!" Interesting, don't you think? (*He pulls the chair closer to her*) Listen to what he went on to say. "At the psychologically right moment I'd turn to my wife, ask her to sit down and then, casually, I'd tell her a story about these fashionable affairs which nevertheless touched on her guilt, and gradually I'd screw the vice even tighter until…" (*He takes a small mirror from* GIULIA's *work basket and puts it in front of her face*) Presto! You place a hand mirror under her nose and ask her, quite politely: "But my dear, why have you gone so pale?" (*Laughs a trifle strangely*) Ha ha ha! Isn't it perfect? "As you can see… I know everything!"

GIULIA (*pushes the mirror away with her hand, forces herself to smile and rises, pretending to be unaffected by his words*): Nonsense!

ANDREA: Have I upset you? Tell me the truth. Weren't you interested?

GIULIA: Why should I be interested… in Mantegna's wife? (*Begins to leave for the dining room*)

ANDREA: Well then, Serra…

GIULIA *turns slightly, very pale, to look at him over her shoulder.*

ANDREA (*controlling himself, changing his tone of voice*): Yes, I'll say to him: listen, chum, I don't quite know what to do about you. Let's not stand on ceremony, we are friends. Tell me what I should give you and I'll give it to you. What do you think?

GIULIA: Do as you think best.

ANDREA: The thing is, I'm afraid, if I put it to him like that…

GIULIA: He'll refuse?

ANDREA (*rising with a sigh*): Conscience, my dear, spawns strange scruples! Having seduced my wife, he'll refuse my money.

GIULIA: What are you saying?

ANDREA (*frowning, but still in control of himself, as if on the verge of laughter*): Isn't it the truth?

GIULIA: Are you quite mad?

ANDREA: You're telling me it isn't true? Well well! She denies it!

GIULIA: You are mad.

ANDREA: Me? Mad? So it isn't true?

GIULIA: You think you can frighten me? How can you say such a thing? What right have you to insult me like this?

ANDREA (*grabs hold of her*): Me... insult you? You're trembling!

GIULIA: It isn't true! What proof—

ANDREA: Proof? Right? Do you think I'm an idiot? A madman? And you... an innocent victim? I saw it with my own eyes. I did, I did, do you understand? I saw it all.

GIULIA: It isn't true. You're imagining things.

ANDREA: Really? You think I'm stupid into the bargain? I saw it all with my own eyes, and you dare deny it? You have no shame. You started shaking the moment you heard me... like him... like him... over there... I tortured him for three days! He ran away in the end... he couldn't stand it any more. He came to tell you, didn't he? He came to tell you. I let him come ahead of me. Why didn't you go off with him? Deny it, deny if you dare!

GIULIA: Andrea... Andrea...

ANDREA: You're coming clean, now...

GIULIA: Have pity!

ANDREA: Pity?

GIULIA: Kill me. Do what you like with me.

ANDREA (*grabs her again, in a towering rage*): You'd deserve to die, you wretch! That's what you deserve. Yes, yes, I don't know what's stopping me. No, no – look – (*releases her*) I don't want to soil my hands... for my children's sake. Did you give them any thought? Of course you didn't, you coward! (*Seizes her again and pushes her violently towards the door*) Go! Get out of my house! This instant! Get out!

GIULIA (*desperate*): Where do you want me to go?

ANDREA: You dare ask me? Go to your lover! You even betrayed your brothers to come with me, to run away with me! It'd serve you right if they shut the door in your face! Go to your lover... I'll give you everything, everything... Take your money with you... Do you think I want to hang on to your money? It'd soil my hands now! I'll start all over again, for the sake of my children! Get out!

GIULIA: Andrea, please! Kill me, rather! Don't talk to me like that. I ask you to forgive me, for their sake. I promise you I'll never look you in the face again. For their sake...

ANDREA: No.

GIULIA: Let me stay, for them...

ANDREA: No!

GIULIA: I'll do anything. I beg you!

ANDREA: No!

GIULIA: Please, Andrea!

ANDREA: No, no, no! You'll never see them again.

GIULIA: Do anything you want with me...

ANDREA: No!

GIULIA: They're my children, too!

ANDREA: Now you think about that? Now?

GIULIA: I wasn't myself. I was insane...

ANDREA: And so was I!

GIULIA: I wasn't myself! It was my fault, I've no excuses, I know. I accuse myself and no one else. It was a moment of madness, believe me. I loved you, yes! I felt you were neglecting me... But I'm not blaming anybody. I'm the only guilty one. I know, I know, I'd run away with you... But, don't you see... I loved you?

ANDREA: Loved me? So you could betray me? Was I the first man in your life? You'd have done the same with anyone.

GIULIA: Never! But I'm not trying to find excuses...

ANDREA: Get out then!

GIULIA: Wait! I don't know what I can say any more... I'm to blame, I know... as far as the children are concerned... yes, yes it's true... But if there's no way you'll put up with me, allow me to make amends for them... You can't deny that! Don't take them away from me!

ANDREA: So I'm taking them away from you? Come, come! I can't listen to that rubbish! You'll never see them again!

GIULIA: No! No! Andrea! I'm asking you for the last time, I beg you, on my knees, look... (*Kneels before him*)

ANDREA (*violently*): No! I say no! That's all! I don't want to hear your voice or see you any more! The children are mine and stay with me. Get out!

GIULIA: If that's the case, then kill me!

ANDREA (*shrugs his shoulders, unconcerned*): You do that. (*Goes up to the window and gazes out*)

GIULIA, *as if crushed by circumstance, slowly bows her head, her eyes fill with tears and then she sobs convulsively.* ANDREA *turns to look at her, then looks out of the window again motionless.*

GIULIA (*gradually stops sobbing, and after a short interval rises, pale and sobbing intermittently; she approaches her husband*): Now... listen...

ANDREA *turns to look at her again.* GIULIA *bursts into tears again.*

ANDREA (*his back turned*): You're just pretending again!

GIULIA: No. Listen. If I'm never to see them again... not even for the last time... Now... I beg you! Please!

ANDREA: No. I've said no!

GIULIA: For the last time... just time to kiss them... to hold them in my arms... and... nothing more!

ANDREA: No!

GIULIA: You are very cruel. Very well. At least... promise me that... when they come home... later... you'll never... speak badly of me... promise me! They're not to know, ever! And when...

ANDREA (*in a strange tone of voice, turns to* GIULIA *and beckons her with a gesture*): Come... come... here...

GIULIA (*hesitating, terrified*): Why? (*Then, with a start*) Ah! They're here!

ANDREA (*grabs her and pushes her towards the window*): No, no... look... look... over there... do you see him?

GIULIA (*clutching him*): Andrea! Andrea! Have pity!

ANDREA (*pushes her in the direction of the door on the left*): Go in there. What are you afraid of?

GIULIA: Please, Andrea! Don't!

ANDREA: In there, I said! Are you afraid for him?

GIULIA: No! No! He's a coward.

ANDREA: Wait for him in there. You're two of a kind.

GIULIA (*her back against the door*): No! No! Goodbye, Andrea! Goodbye! (*Kisses him quickly and rushes into the next room, slamming the door*)

ANDREA, *stunned, surprised, facing the closed door, puts his hands to his face.* ANTONIO SERRA *enters. On noticing* ANDREA *he lingers on the threshold. A shot is heard from the next room.* ANTONIO *cries out.*

ANDREA (*turns suddenly towards* ANTONIO): Murderer!

THE CURTAIN FALLS

A Dream – or Is It?

Sogno (ma forse no) (1929)

Translated by Carlo Ardito

CHARACTERS

THE YOUNG WOMAN
THE MAN IN EVENING CLOTHES
A WAITER

A room – or is it? A sitting room perhaps. There is certainly a young woman lying on a bed: or is there? Maybe it isn't a bed, but a sofa, the back of which has been lowered.

In any case to begin with nothing much is clearly visible, since the room is barely lit by an unnatural light which issues from a lamp placed on the lawn-green rug in front of the sofa. The light seems likely to disappear from one moment to the next at the slightest stirring of the sleeping woman.

The lamp is in fact part of the young woman's dream, just as the dream has turned the sitting room into a bedroom, and the couch into a bed.

Upstage is a closed door. On the right wall is a large mirror on a small console artistically worked to resemble a gilt casket. The console just now is not visible, and for the time being the mirror looks like a window.

The reason for this deception is simple: the mirror reflects the window opposite, on the left wall, and naturally, in the young woman's dream, the window is where the mirror reflects it. The dream window will, in fact, be opened later by the man, who has yet to appear.

Below the mirror a drape is drawn across the shelf of the console. The drape is of the same material as the wall coverings, and cannot therefore be picked out from the rest. Thus lowered, it serves to conceal down to ground level the void into which the dream has made the console vanish. It will reappear, with the drape on it, the moment the dream is over, and the mirror has once more become a mirror. From the ceiling hangs a chandelier, now unlit, with three rose-coloured globes of frosted glass.

At a given point, in the semi-darkness of the room barely lit by the dream lamp, there emerges from under the couch now acting as a bed a hand – an enormous hand – which gradually lifts the hitherto lowered side of the sofa. And as the back of the sofa gradually lifts into place, so does a man's head, outsized also, behind it. Its expression is troubled, the hair tousled, the forehead wrinkled into a frown, the eyes frozen into a hard stare laden with menace.

It is a spectral mask out of a nightmare.

It continues to rise until the trunk is revealed of a man in a dinner jacket under a black cape and a white silk scarf. He hovers over the young woman who has opened her eyes and is now protecting her face with her hands in fear, shrinking away from the apparition.

The lamp over the rug on the ground dims, and the head disappears behind the back of the couch. It is the matter of an instant. The three globes of the chandelier are now lit and from them there issues a soft roseate light: we now see standing upright by the sofa the man in evening clothes, no longer a spectral figure out of a nightmare but of normal proportions. This does not mean that he appears as real, but as someone out of a dream, with the same menacing expression, though altogether more normal than a little earlier.

The ensuing scene, changeable and as it were suspended within the inconsistency of a dream, will be continuously punctuated by pauses of varying length, and also with sudden interruption in the action. The man will from time to time abruptly stop moving and become completely expressionless, like a puppet at rest. He will recover from these sudden stoppages and each time will assume attitudes in marked contrast with previous ones, in accordance with whatever new impressions the young woman forms of him in the erratic imagery of her dream.

THE YOUNG WOMAN: You here? How did you get in?

THE MAN IN EVENING CLOTHES *stands still at first: then barely turns to look at her. He takes a shiny door key out of his waistcoat pocket and shows it to her, then replaces it in the pocket.*

THE WOMAN: Ah, you found it again. Just as I suspected. Remember when I asked you to give it back, after your last indiscretion?

THE MAN *smiles.*

THE WOMAN: Why are you smiling?

THE MAN *stops smiling and looks at her darkly, as if to convey to her that it is useless to lie to him or to expect him to believe that the key had been taken from him owing "to his last indiscretion".*

THE WOMAN (*attempting to control the fear caused by his gaze*): That's the only reason I asked you for it. I wasn't that concerned about having it back. I just slipped it into my pocket and forgot about it. It must have dropped to the carpet when I rose to go into the other room.

The moment she turns her head to indicate the other room, with all the speed of a pickpocket THE MAN *performs the deed she imagined: he bends down as if to pick up a key from the floor and slips it into his waistcoat pocket. As he performs this action, his eyes light up with malice and his lips twist into a malevolent grin. But the moment he stands up again he resumes his former posture, as if he had never moved.*

THE WOMAN (*after waiting for him to say something*): What's the matter with you? Why are you looking at me like that?

THE MAN: Nothing's the matter. How am I supposed to be looking at you? (*As he is speaking these words he approaches her, bends over her, placing one knee on the edge of the sofa, one hand on the back of it and the other, with great delicacy, on her forearm*) I can't keep away from you. I don't feel I'm alive, as I am now, unless you're next to me, just like this – unless I'm inhaling the perfume of your hair – the ecstasy of it! – the smoothness of your skin... the scent of your flawless being. You're my whole life.

THE WOMAN *jumps to her feet and moves away, brushing past him as she does so. She is showing him that she finds it intolerable to hear him repeating his usual endearments. It was her, in fact, who made him repeat those words, by remembering for a moment that he – in love with her – has appeared to her so often with that same disquieting expression which now, in her dream, is filling her with fear. She at once regrets her sudden gesture, which might give him the impression she no longer loves him: will he now pretend he's spoken those words merely to taunt her? Consequently she turns towards him with some unease.*

THE MAN *having lingered in suspense, like an automaton, in his amorous attitude, bent over her or rather the place where she had been lying, the moment she turns towards him collapses unceremoniously onto the sofa, his legs and arms spread out, throws back his head and bursts into a long scornful laugh. As he laughs, the back of the sofa gives way under pressure until it is level with the seat. At the same time the chandelier gradually dims until he lies flat on the bed, still laughing. During the fleeting period of darkness between the extinction of the chandelier and the relighting of the lamp on the floor, he will have turned on his side on the sofa which has again turned into a bed, leaning on an elbow, his head supported by his hand. It is as if he had been lying there for some time, talking quietly, a sad smile on his lips, addressing the young woman who is now sitting on the bed at his feet.*

THE MAN: Naturally a woman can't force a man, or a man a woman, to return a love he no longer feels. But then one should have the honesty to come straight out with it: "I don't love you any more."

THE WOMAN: One often doesn't say it out of pity, not because one's not sufficiently honest. It's often convenient to be honest.

THE MAN: Just as it's convenient for a woman to convince herself she's keeping quiet out of pity. When a woman says her silence is due to pity she's already deceived the man.

THE WOMAN: Not true!

THE MAN: Yes it is. And she's deceiving herself. Concealed within this pity of hers you'll always find some other reason.

THE WOMAN (*rising*): Thank you for making your opinion of women so clear.

THE MAN: But even if there were no concealed reasons, don't you see that the pity would be a sham?

THE WOMAN: I've always known that deception can be tempered with pity.

THE MAN: How so? By making someone believe you still love him when you no longer do? A futile deception. Anyone who's really in love immediately notices the absence of love in a partner. And Heaven help him if he pretends not to notice: that'd signal an invitation to betrayal. True pity, devoid of ulterior motive, can only be just that to those who feel it – pity, no longer love. To pretend otherwise is a corruption of pity. And this will give way to contempt, which in turn will lead to and induce betrayal. In any case the original betrayal was caused by neglecting to admit the deception.

THE WOMAN (*sits down again as before*): You think one should admit it?

THE MAN (*unruffled*): Yes. With frankness.

THE WOMAN: You think deception, even when tempered with pity, amounts to betrayal?

THE MAN: Yes. When it is accepted, as a beggar accepts alms. (*Pause*) I'd like to know how you'd deal with a beggar who kisses you full on the mouth to show gratitude at your charity.

THE WOMAN (*with a vague smile*): If the charity handed out to him in the first place was love, a kiss is the least the beggar could ask for.

THE MAN (*rises suddenly and angrily pulls up the back of the couch*): I was forgetting I was talking to a woman. (*He walks excitedly up and down the room*) Loyalty – now loyalty is a debt, the most sacred debt we owe to ourselves. Betrayal is horrible. Horrible.

THE WOMAN: I can't make out why you're talking to me like this tonight. Or why you're getting so excited into the bargain.

THE MAN: It's not so much what *I* said: it's what *you* said. I'm speaking in the abstract.

THE WOMAN: And so am I, my dear. How can you possibly doubt me?

THE MAN: You know perfectly well I'm always doubting you and have every reason to do so. (*He moves deliberately and opens the dream window, letting in an outsized moonbeam and a soft sea murmur*) Don't you remember? (*He stands by the open dream window, looking out*)

THE WOMAN (*gazing straight ahead, sitting down, searching her memory*): Yes, it's true. Last summer… by the sea…

THE MAN (*still by the window, as if lost in contemplation of the sea*): …Shimmering in the moonlight…

THE WOMAN: Yes, yes; it was sheer madness…

THE MAN: I said to you: we are challenging the sea by feeling so safe and snug in this frail dinghy. A wave could sink us from one moment to the next.

THE WOMAN: …And you tried to frighten me by rocking the boat…

THE MAN: Do you remember what else I said?

THE WOMAN: Yes. Something unpleasant.

THE MAN: I wanted you to feel the fear I experienced by entrusting myself to your love. You took it amiss. Then I tried to make you understand that just as we were both trying, that night, to challenge the sea by feeling so safe in that little boat which the merest wave could sink, so was I challenging you by placing my entire trust in your love, however slight it might have been.

THE WOMAN: You dared to think it slight? Even then?

THE MAN: But of course! From the start, my dear! Necessarily so. Not so much because you wanted it. In fact you thought you'd given me every assurance. But it didn't amount to much, since you yourself, my dear, could never be sure that tomorrow, or the day after, you'd still love me. There was even a time when you felt you loved me, as you did not earlier. There will come a time when you'll feel you no longer love me. Perhaps that time has come… Look at me!… Are you afraid to look at me?

THE WOMAN: I am not afraid. I know you're a reasonable man. You said yourself just now that no one can force anyone to return a love he no longer feels.

THE MAN: I dare say I was being reasonable. But Heaven help you, Heaven help you if you should stop loving me while I'm still in love with you, with every fibre of my being!

THE WOMAN: You simply must be reasonable.

THE MAN: Oh yes, yes, I'm going to try to be reasonable. I'll be as reasonable as you like, just to please you. And so that you won't feel afraid any more, shall I show you how reasonable I can be? Here goes: I shall be very understanding as long as the flame burns bright only up here – (*he touches his forehead*) I understand full well, as you know, that your love, which began quite suddenly, can die just as suddenly for any reason at all, due to something unforeseen, unforeseeable. What more can I say? I'll say this: at the crossroads, through a chance meeting, a sudden blinding combination of circumstances, an unexpected, irresistible stimulation of the senses...

THE WOMAN: Oh, come to that...

THE MAN: Well, it could happen... Why not?

THE WOMAN: Because we are reasonable beings. Reason pulls us back.

THE MAN: Back? Back to what? Duty?

THE WOMAN: It stops us being overwhelmed...

THE MAN: But that's just what life does to us. It overwhelms us, it always has done! Why should I be the one to tell you, as if you didn't know it? God help us if the flame should burn here... (*touches his breast*) and you turn your heart to ashes! You've no idea what ghastly smoke can rise from a burning heart, from blood... bubbling blood... what a dreadful night the smoke causes in your brain – a veritable tempest that darkens and blots out your reason! Do you think you're up to preventing this storm from hurling lightning... setting fire to your house and killing you? (*As he speaks these words his countenance undergoes a terrible change: no sooner has he mentioned a storm than the growing distant rumble of thunder is heard beyond the open window, and the ray of moonlight turns into a sinister flash of lightning*)

THE WOMAN, *terrified, hides her face in her hands.*

THE MAN, *immediately when she hides her face, stops in mid-gesture, his face expressionless, like a robot. The sound of thunder and flashes of lightning also cease suddenly, replaced by a soft moonbeam as before. Everything is now mysteriously still and will remain so as long as the young woman hides her face in her hands.*

THE WOMAN, *her hands still hiding her face, rises and moves a few steps towards the window as if to shut it.*

THE MAN, *though remaining still as if in suspended animation, barely turns his head and arms in her direction, as though moving towards the window she had caused his slight movement.*

THE WOMAN *takes her hands from her face and gazes out of the window, amazed by the stillness and serenity of the moonlight. In her astonishment she smiles, remembering "the moment" when she fell in love with the man – it happened in fact in a living room, by a window through which the moonlight was flooding in. She turns to him, smiling.*

THE MAN (*immediately assumes the expression of that "moment", that is of a man in a living room who has noticed from the corner of his eye the woman he is in love with move towards a window; pretending he needs a breath of fresh air, he shows surprise at finding her by the window*): Oh, excuse me. You here? It's unbearably hot, isn't it? Far too hot to dance. Perhaps we should all go into the garden – look at that moon! We could leave the orchestra behind, indoors. They could go on playing... think how nice it would be to listen to the music from a distance, in the coolness of the garden, dancing in the clearing by that fountain! (*From a distance, muffled, as if from above, the sound of a piano*)

THE WOMAN: I thought the sight of the garden and the moonlight wouldn't encourage you to go out there with a crowd... but only with that beautiful lady in the pink dress... the one you've been dancing with all evening.

THE MAN: How can you say that? It was you who—

THE WOMAN (*cutting in*): Quiet! They can hear you.

THE MAN (*lowers his voice*): ...It was you who said I shouldn't dance with you too often, so as not to make it obvious... now you reproach me...

THE WOMAN (*in hushed tones, after signalling him to be quiet*): Go into the garden, but don't let anyone see you. I'll join you in a little while, the moment I can.

THE MAN (*delighted, after a quick look around to make sure no one is looking, furtively takes her hand and kisses it*): I'm going. I'll wait for you. Hurry! (*He leaves the window, and moves cautiously through the living room in the direction of the closed door. Once there, he turns round for a final look before opening the door. He opens the door and leaves.)*

THE WOMAN *stands, as if in hiding, by the window, bathed in moonlight. Gradually the moonbeam fades, as well as the light from the lamp on the floor, and the sound of the piano music grows fainter and more distant, since the vision of that "moment" is fading within her. When it has faded completely, all the lights are extinguished and the piano music has ceased, in the instant of darkness which will precede the relighting of the three pink globes, the window will be closed, and the young woman will again be sitting on the sofa.*

THE MAN *stands by the sofa, scowling as before.*

THE WOMAN (*after waiting for him to say something, stamps her foot*): Come on, are you or are you not going to say something? Don't tell me you're going to stand there in front of me all night looking like that! (*In an attempt to control her mounting rage she is on the verge of tears*)

THE MAN: The way I'm looking is not my fault: you've put that frown on my face. You know I'm still in love with you, that if I were to turn and look at myself in the mirror, with this expression on my face, I wouldn't recognize myself. The mirror would be telling the truth, showing an image of myself unknown to me, an image you've imposed on me. For that very reason you've made the mirror vanish and made me open it as though it were a window.

THE WOMAN (*almost shouting*): No, no, it is a window. It's a window! I swear it's a window! Don't even bother to turn and look!

THE MAN: Don't worry, I won't look. Yes, it's a window all right. Of course it's a window, since I've gone and opened it! And is there not a garden over there, where our mouths met for the first time in an endless kiss? And in front of the garden is the sea, which we challenged together one moonlit night this summer? Nothing frightens an uneasy conscience more than a mirror. And you know that for other reasons, all due to you, when I think of what I've done for you and am actually doing – why I daren't look in a mirror. Now, at this very moment, looking as I am, standing here, you know full well where I am – you came there once – in that yellow gambling room at my club – and I'm cheating, cheating for your sake – nobody luckily caught me in the act – but I'm cheating, I'm cheating all right, in order to make you a present of that pearl necklace…

THE WOMAN: No, no, I don't want it any more! I don't want it! I know I told you once I'd like to have it, but just to—

THE MAN: …To humiliate me.

THE WOMAN: No. To make you realize that I expected too much from you.

THE MAN: You're lying still! You weren't trying to convince me your demands were excessive – no. You wanted me to realize you were made for a rich lover, someone who could easily satisfy your expensive tastes.

THE WOMAN: Oh my God, you should have worked that out right from the beginning, knowing who I was, the kind of life I was used to leading!

THE MAN: You too knew who I was when we started off. I've never had much money. I did my best to find the means to keep up with your lifestyle, so you wouldn't miss much or make too many sacrifices. And if you were honest about it, you'd guess that everything I've done—

THE WOMAN (*cutting in*): I did guess.

THE MAN: I got up to all sorts of tricks…

THE WOMAN: I guessed… and admired the way you managed to hide any embarrassment you might have experienced…

THE MAN: Because it was nothing to me… it was the least I could do to reward you for allowing me to love you.

THE WOMAN: But you did expect me to—

THE MAN: …To what?

THE WOMAN: Need you ask? You've appealed to my honesty! You expected me to take into account what it was costing you…

THE MAN: I told you: it cost me nothing. Just as I hoped it would cost you nothing to give up your most expensive tastes.

THE WOMAN: And I did! So as not to force you to spend money I knew you couldn't afford. Oh yes, I did give up a lot, an awful lot. You can't imagine how much!

THE MAN: On the contrary. I can well imagine it.

THE WOMAN: And you call that natural?

THE MAN: Yes… if you loved me, that is.

THE WOMAN: It made me furious!

THE MAN: That I thought it natural?

THE WOMAN: Yes. That simply because I loved you I should stop wanting things! That's why that evening, on purpose, as I walked past the jeweller's window – on purpose I tell you, I did it on purpose just to be cruel!

THE MAN: You believe I didn't realize it?

THE WOMAN: Did you think me cruel?

THE MAN: No. Just a woman.

THE WOMAN (*striking her fist on her knees, then rising*): That again! Can't you understand it's your fault, you men, if women behave as we do, because of the idiotic idea you have of us? It's your fault if we're cruel. It's your fault if we deceive you. It's your fault if we betray you.

THE MAN: Gently, gently now… Why are you getting so worked up? Do you think I'm not aware of the fact you're trying to justify yourself?

THE WOMAN (*turns to him, astonished*): Me?

THE MAN (*steadily*): Yes – you. What's so surprising about that?

THE WOMAN (*embarrassed*): Justify myself? What for?

THE MAN: You know perfectly well what for – I said "just a woman" to balance your word "cruel". I thought it fair, not cruel, that on that particular night as you walked past the jeweller's window you should, in jest and yet seriously make a mouth-watering grimace… (*Imitates a child in the act of eyeing a favourite sweetmeat, at the same time rubbing his hand over his chest*) "Ooh, how I'd love to have that pearl necklace!"

She laughs and, suddenly as she laughs, the set is plunged into darkness. A shaft of light picks out the panels of the gilt casket or cabinet beside the upstage door, which slide open to reveal a lavish jeweller's shop window, displaying many unnatural-looking pieces. Among them, eye-catchingly in the centre and beautifully laid-out on a bed of velvet, is the pearl necklace, which also looks somewhat unnatural. At the very moment the shop window is lit up, like a sudden mirage, the woman will stop laughing. The vision will last for some time and utter silence will prevail. The spotlight on the shop window will render the actors invisible, just as the rest of the room will be plunged in darkness. In any case, the two have turned their backs to the casket. The vision of the jeweller's shop window is intended for the audience only. At a given point two male hands, slender and very white, will be seen parting the curtains within the shop window and then picking up the necklace with great care. Without causing the vision of the jeweller's shop window to disappear, the three pink globes of the chandelier will fade up slowly, revealing the man in evening clothes and the young woman, standing still, entranced by the vision behind them, which causes them to speak stiffly, in an undertone, staring straight ahead.

THE MAN: Would you like me to steal them?

THE WOMAN: No. No. It was just a passing thought on my part. I don't want them, not from you! I've already told you that I said I asked for them out of cruelty! You couldn't possibly give them to me unless you stole them!

THE MAN: Or by stealing from others so I could buy them for you! Which is what I am doing! While – didn't you notice? – hands other than mine removed the pearls from the window – for you – and you know it – you know it – (*at this point he relinquishes his rigid manner and turns on her menacingly*) – and you dare tell me you don't want them from me any more? Of course you don't want them from me! Someone else will give them to you! You've already betrayed me, you wretch! (*He grabs her by the arms, since she has got up in a fright trying to get away from him*) And I know who it is! Bitch! (*He shakes her*) You've gone back to your first lover, haven't you? He's just come back from Java! I saw him! I saw him! He's trying to hide, but I've seen him!

THE WOMAN (*has been struggling with him and now succeeds in breaking free*): It's not true! It's not true! Let me go!

THE MAN (*seizes her again, throws her onto the sofa and puts his hands round her throat, as if to strangle her*): Not true? I tell you I've seen him, the loathsome creature! You're expecting him to give you those pearls, while I'm soiling my hands cheating my friends at the club! You're only happy when you can satisfy your cruelty!

He is on her and about to strangle her. She is already yielding under his savage attack. The lights flicker, then suddenly go out, since she is dreaming she is being strangled by him. Absolute darkness, which is to last only a moment or two. During the period of darkness, loud, heavy, surreal knocks on the door are heard, as though they were reverberating within the dream. Meanwhile the panels on the console shaped like a casket will slide shut, and a drape will again cover it; the mirror will again become a mirror proper, no longer reflecting the window which, on the left wall, is now open, admitting the light of the setting sun. The man in evening clothes has vanished, and the room is lit by soft, clear daylight. As this light comes up, the hitherto heavy and loud knocking at the door turns into normal, discreet knocks – three in fact. At the same time the young woman will wake up from her dream and raises her hands towards her throat, a reminder that she had recently been choking. She takes several deep breaths, which clearly cause her discomfort, and express the fear she experienced in her dream. She is still surprised by the nature of her dream, and looks around like someone unsure of the reality of her present surroundings. She attempts to rise from the couch, but falls back, her legs too weak to support her. She hides her face in her hands and sustains this posture for some time. Again we hear three discreet knocks at the door.

THE WOMAN (*stands up and listens for a while before answering*): Come in. (*She steps towards the open window, straightening her hair. A waiter enters, carrying a salver bearing a jewel case wrapped in the finest tissue paper and tied with a silver ribbon. He begins to approach her but she stops him.*) Leave it over there. (*She points to the console. The waiter leaves the packet as instructed, bows and exits, shutting the door. She stands still, as if uncertain. In the jewel case is the precious gift she was expecting. But her joy at receiving it is countered by the recent nightmare and the menace of its message. What if the lover she has just seen in her dream in the act of strangling her should suspect her betrayal, proof of which is staring at her on the console? She furtively goes up to the console, intending to hide the jewel case. She picks it up and looks suspiciously for some time at the entrance door. However, unable to resist the temptation to take a peep, she nervously unwraps the packet, then opens the jewel case. She first takes out a visiting card and reads the words written below the name. Finally, she takes out the pearl necklace, looks at it, admires it and smiles. She clutches it with both hands to her breast and closes her eyes. She tries it on in front of the mirror, but without securing the clasp on the nape of her neck. More knocking at the door. She quickly removes the necklace, picks up the visiting card from the console, opens the small drawer below it, stuffs everything in it and shuts it. She turns to the door.*) Who is it? – Come in. (*The waiter enters and hands her a visiting card*) Show him in. (*Ushered in by the waiter, the man who in the dream was in evening clothes enters. He is now wearing a lounge suit, and is to all appearances calm and collected.*) Darling! Come in, come in. (*The waiter bows and exits, shutting the door*)

THE MAN (*after kissing her hand at some length*): Am I late?

THE WOMAN (*affecting the utmost indifference*): No, no... (*She sits on the sofa*) Can you tell I've been asleep?

THE MAN (*looks at her carefully*): Not really. (*In an undertone*) Just a nap? (*He sits down on a chair*)

THE WOMAN: Yes. Just now. I suddenly felt very sleepy. Strange...

THE MAN: Any dreams?

THE WOMAN: No. No. The proverbial forty winks, that was all. I don't know... I must have been lying in a cramped position. (*She strokes her neck with her hand*) I... I suddenly felt I couldn't breathe. (*She smiles*) Ring the bell, please. Let's have some tea.

He rises and presses the bell button by the mirror. He sits down again.

THE MAN: I was afraid I was late. I had a disappointing experience. I'll tell you about it later. (*The waiter knocks at the door and enters*)

THE WOMAN: We'll have tea now, please. (*The waiter bows and leaves*) A disappointing experience?

THE MAN: I was planning to surprise you.

THE WOMAN: You? Wanted to surprise me? (*Laughs*)

THE MAN (*crestfallen*): Why are you laughing?

THE WOMAN: Surprise me? You?

THE MAN: You don't think I can surprise you any more?

THE WOMAN: Of course you can, darling. Anything is possible. But you know how it is. If you've known someone too long, surprises... well – anyway, you sounded so depressed – (*imitating him*) "I wanted to surprise you..." (*Laughs again*)

THE MAN: I sounded depressed because I was genuinely disappointed.

THE WOMAN: I bet I can guess why.

THE MAN: Guess? What?

THE WOMAN: Wait a moment. Were you disappointed on my behalf, or sorry for yourself?

THE MAN: For you, of course, and me too since I couldn't surprise you.

THE WOMAN: Then I've guessed. And I'll show you you can't surprise me any more. (*Goes behind the chair he is sitting on, puts her arms on his shoulders, without embracing him, but locking her hands*

581

together in front, and leans her face on his cheek) You really wanted to give me that pearl necklace?

THE MAN: I went into the jewellers to buy it. (*In sudden astonishment*) Then you knew it had been sold?

THE WOMAN: Yes, darling. That's how I guessed.

THE MAN: How did you know it was sold?

THE WOMAN: Simple! How, you ask? Last night I went past the shop and noticed it was gone.

THE MAN: It was there till four in the afternoon. I saw it myself.

THE WOMAN: Impossible. I was there at about seven: it wasn't there.

THE MAN: That's odd. They told me they sold it this morning.

THE WOMAN: You went and asked?

THE MAN: I went in to buy it. And they said it was sold this morning.

THE WOMAN (*feigning indifference*): Who did they sell it to? Did they say?

THE MAN (*without a trace of suspicion, thus not attaching any importance to her question*): Yes. They sold it to some man. (*Pulls her round in front of him*) Forgive me, but – since you knew of my disappointment – and guessed immediately it had to do with the necklace – surely that's a sign you'd given it some thought.

THE WOMAN: Not at all.

THE MAN: What do you mean… no? It shows you were expecting me to give you the necklace.

THE WOMAN: Well, I knew you'd been gambling heavily every night at the club, and were on a winning streak…

THE MAN: Quite so. And do you know why? I'm sure of it in fact: because I was so obsessed with your desire to own that necklace – and that obsession somehow helped my game: as a result I kept winning.

THE WOMAN: Have you won a great deal?

THE MAN: Yes. (*With spontaneous warmth*) And now you'll help me pick some other beautiful pieces for you. Something you really want!

THE WOMAN: No! No!

THE MAN: Please say yes! If only to do away with my disappointment for failing to give you what you coveted!

THE WOMAN: No, darling. I never seriously wanted that pearl necklace, or that you should be the one to provide it. It was all due to a sudden whim, that evening, walking past the shop window… No. I'm going to be good from now on.

THE MAN: I know. I know you're good – so good... to me. All my winnings of the past few nights are yours... all yours. I can assure you of that. I owe it all to you.

THE WOMAN: So much the better! I'm even happier now – that I've brought you luck... and even that you couldn't find the pearls. Let's not talk about it any more, please. (*A knock at the door, and the waiter enters with a groaning tea tray*) Here's our tea. (*The waiter puts down the tray on a lacquered table by the console and moves it next to the sofa. Just as he starts serving, the woman stops him.*) That's all right, leave it. I'll do it. (*The waiter bows and leaves*)

THE MAN (*with forced indifference, for the sake of saying something*): Incidentally, I meant to tell you... Guess who is back from Java?

THE WOMAN (*pouring tea*): Yes, yes, I know...

THE MAN: Oh, somebody told you?

THE WOMAN: Yes, the other night... I forget who it was.

THE MAN: They say he's made heaps of money.

THE WOMAN: Milk or lemon?

THE MAN: Milk – thank you.

CURTAIN

A Note on the Translators

Carlo Ardito is a playwright and translator whose works have been performed on the stage and on radio. His English translations of Italo Svevo, Goldoni and other Italian writers have been much lauded, and his translation of De Filippo's *Three Plays* was shortlisted for the Florio Prize.

Susan Bassnett is Professor of Comparative Literature at the University of Warwick. She has written extensively on theatre history, English poetry, Pirandello, comparative literature and translation. She is also a poet and translator.

Diane Cilento became famous as a stage and film actress, and won an Oscar nomination for her performance in the film *Tom Jones*. She has also gained recognition for a number of successful novels and is Director of the Karnak Playhouse in Queensland, Australia.

Terry Doyle ran a BBC Television programme on teaching Italian, and is the author of several books on learning Italian, Russian and other languages. His wife Gigi Gatti was an actress who worked as Robert Rietti's assistant for several years and also published work on language-learning and psychotherapy.

Felicity Firth has spent her working life lecturing on Italian literature, and has published extensively on Italian theatre, particularly the work and thought of Pirandello. She founded the Society for Pirandello Studies in 1980.

David L. Hirst was a freelance director and Lecturer in the Department of Drama and Theatre Arts at the University of Birmingham. He also published a number of books on Dario Fo, Giorgio Strehler, Edward Bond and tragicomedy.

Frederick May was a senior lecturer and head of the Department of Italian at the University of Leeds, and later Professor of Italian at the University of Sydney, 1964–1976. He is best known for his work on Pirandello, many of whose plays he both translated and directed.

Victor and Robert Rietti have worked together on translations of many Italian and French playwrights for theatre, radio and television, including works by Octave Mirbeau, Jules Renard, Dario Niccodemi and Roberto Bracco. Victor won the Critics Award for the best play of the year on BBC Television for his adaptation of Forzano's *To Live in Peace*. Robert has also written three books of Holocaust stories and a recently commissioned autobiography entitled *A Forehead Pressed against a Window*. Both he and his father were honoured by the Italian government with the title of Cavaliere al Merito (Knighthood of Merit) for their services to the Italian theatre and films, and Robert's honour was recently upgraded to Officer Knighthood of Merit. Victor was also a noted actor, violinist, conductor and composer.

Donald Watson was one of the best-known translators of twentieth-century French literature and Special Lecturer in French Drama at Bristol University. His translations of Ionesco in the Fifties – in addition to notable translations from Italian and German – brought him a great deal of critical acclaim.

www.oneworldclassics.com

LUIGI PIRANDELLO

PLAYS • VOL. 1

This is the first of three volumes collecting the complete plays of Luigi Pirandello, one of the foremost playwrights and fiction writers of the twentieth century. This volume contains ＿＿＿＿＿＿ dello's most famous plays, ＿＿＿＿＿＿＿＿＿＿＿ *arch of an Author*, *Henry* ＿＿＿＿＿＿＿＿ *Gave Thee*, as well as several of his lesser-known works for the stage, some of which are translated into English for the first time.

Preoccupied with the nature of truth and delusion, Pirandello's plays are a daring exploration of human actions and the dark motives lying behind them, and the culmination of the school of theatre inaugurated by authors such as Ibsen and Chekhov.

"Something close to classical tragedy
that evokes our primal fears..."
– *The Guardian*

Luigi Pirandello (1867–1936) was an acclaimed writer of drama and fiction. One of the most influential and innovative playwrights of the last century, he won the Nobel Prize for Literature in 1934.

www.oneworldclassics.com

ISBN 978-1-84749-144-2

9 781847 491442

Classics • £12.99